MAGILL'S LITERARY ANNUAL 1978

Essay-Reviews of 200 Outstanding Books
Published in the United States during 1977

With an Annotated Categories Index
and a Listing of 990 Review Sources

Volume One
A-Jac

Edited by

FRANK N. MAGILL

SALEM PRESS
Englewood Cliffs

LIBRARY OF CONGRESS CATALOG CARD NO. 77-99209

ISBN 0-89356-278-5

First Printing

PRINTED IN THE UNITED STATES OF AMERICA

PREFACE

HERE, in essay-review form, is a survey of the literary year of 1977 comprising a study of two hundred outstanding books published during the year. Represented in this volume are 47 works of fiction, 26 volumes of poetry, 5 dramas, 11 collections of essays, 33 biographies, 18 works dealing with autobiography, memoirs, diaries, and letters, 47 historical studies, 4 books concerning current affairs, 6 volumes of literary criticism, and 3 works which fall into special categories.

Fantasy and folklore enriched the fiction of 1977, contributing a special enchantment to the field of imaginative writing. THE BOOK OF MERLYN, bringing T. H. White's THE ONCE AND FUTURE KING to a close, appeared during the year. In this work the animals that guided the education of Arthur in his youth return to join with Merlyn in an effort to persuade the aging Arthur to forego his battle with Modred. Their arguments come to naught and Arthur goes out to meet his fate. Tolkien's THE SILMARILLION again demonstrates the breadth of the author's imagination and the power of his words to make us see what he shows us and believe what he tells us. In ANPAO, Jamake Highwater presents a fascinating collection of traditional tales based on American Indian culture, the stories held together by the boy Anpao and heightened by the author's insights through his own Indian tribal heritage.

Another work dealing with the American Indian is Douglas C. Jones's fine novel ARREST SITTING BULL, which depicts the winding down of Indian/ white confrontation at the end of the nineteenth century. Out of Australia comes THE THORN BIRDS, set on a huge ranch in the romantic vein, a novel alive with all the ingredients of the popular best seller. With THE THIN MOUNTAIN AIR, Paul Horgan brings to maturity, and to a highly civilized view toward life, the young protagonist of two earlier novels. Other titles of outstanding merit published during the year include John Hersey's THE WALNUT DOOR, John Fowles's DANIEL MARTIN, Jerzy Kosinski's BLIND DATE, Joan Didion's A BOOK OF COMMON PRAYER, Toni Morrison's SONG OF SOLOMON, THE DARK LADY by Louis Auchincloss, HOW TO SAVE YOUR OWN LIFE by Erica Jong, John Cheever's FALCONER—a metaphorical story of a "solid citizen" who goes to prison for fratricide—MADDER MUSIC by Peter De Vries, and THEY BURN THE THISTLES by the Turkish writer Yashar Kemal, which continues the story begun in MEMED, MY HAWK, published in 1961. Also not to be overlooked are YUKIKO by MacDonald Harris, and the amusing WHO IS TEDDY VILLANOVA? by Thomas Berger.

Short story collections were plentiful in 1977, some of the best being THE BOOK OF SAND by Jorge Luis Borges, THE STREET OF CROCODILES by the Polish writer Bruno Schulz, SILKEN EYES by Françoise Sagan, eighteen stories by Joyce Carol Oates collected under the title of NIGHT-SIDE, and collections by Donald Barthelme and the late Isak Dinesen.

Of the numerous volumes of poetry published in 1977, among the best were THE COLLECTED POEMS OF HOWARD NEMEROV, winner of the 1978

National Book Award for Poetry; DAY BY DAY, Robert Lowell's last collection before his death; SELECTED POEMS: 1923-1975 by Robert Penn Warren, an impressive array; William Stafford's STORIES THAT COULD BE TRUE, a definitive collection to date; and COLLECTED POEMS, 1919-1976 by Allen Tate, which presents Tate's poetic artistry over a period of fifty-seven years. Other excellent volumes that appeared during the year include John Berryman's HENRY'S FATE & OTHER POEMS, 1967-1972, John Ashbery's HOUSEBOAT DAYS, and LUCKY LIFE by Gerald Stern.

Few dramas of note saw print in 1977, but AMERICAN BUFFALO by David Mamet, which won the Drama Critics Circle Award for the 1977 season, is one that is worthy of consideration by those concerned with serious dramatic experiences. In a lighter vein are two examples of Tom Stoppard's dramatic vision published under the title of DIRTY LINEN and NEW-FOUND-LAND. Martin Duberman's VISIONS OF KEROUAC is a drama based on a cultural phenomenon of unique proportions; and Harold Pinter's THE PROUST SCREENPLAY is an even more arresting attempt to stretch the dramatic format beyond its normal limits.

Three excellent studies in literary criticism add to the enjoyment of those who relish in-depth analyses of the works of established literary figures: A. Dwight Culler's THE POETRY OF TENNYSON; Richard Poirier's examination of Robert Frost and his canon; and A FEAST OF WORDS, Cynthia Wolff's analysis of Edith Wharton as woman and artist.

Several collections of essays deserve mention, including ESSAYS OF E. B. WHITE; THE HUMAN SITUATION, Aldous Huxley's 1959 Santa Barbara Lectures; LIFE/SITUATIONS by Jean-Paul Sartre; MISSING PERSONS AND OTHER ESSAYS by Heinrich Böll; and Edward Butscher's collection of essays about Sylvia Plath and her work.

Many fine biographies were published in 1977, studies ranging in time from the fifteenth century (William Caxton, Joan of Arc) to 1977 (Simone de Beauvoir and Jean-Paul Sartre). Literary figures under study include J. R. R. Tolkien, Delmore Schwartz, Vladimir Nabokov, Jack London, Samuel Johnson, and Ivan Turgenev, the latter treated in an excellent work by V. S. Pritchett under the title of THE GENTLE BARBARIAN. Political leaders dealt with include Winston S. Churchill; Harry Hopkins; political philosopher Edmund Burke; Jefferson Davis; Adlai E. Stevenson; Charles Stewart Parnell, leader of the Irish National League; and Catherine the Great. Military leaders are represented by Robert V. Remini's scholarly study of Andrew Jackson, the first of two volumes planned; by Frank E. Vandiver's BLACK JACK, examining the life of General John J. Pershing and stressing his military career; and by David Irving's fine study of Field Marshal Erwin Rommel. Biographies of inventors Thomas A. Edison and Robert Fulton also appeared during the year.

Autobiographies or memoirs, by Will and Ariel Durant, Earl Warren, Milovan Djilas, Anthony Eden, Anthony Powell, and N. Scott Momaday, appeared in 1977 as well as the ninth volume of the Yale Edition of James Boswell's journals, with the subtitle "Laird of Auchinleck, 1778-1782." Also published during the year were Volume I (1915-1919) of THE DIARY OF

VIRGINIA WOOLF, THE DIARIES OF EVELYN WAUGH, and volumes of letters of Franz Kafka, Anne Sexton, H. L. Mencken, and Edmund Wilson.

Interesting works in history are extremely popular in these times and the year 1977 provided its share. Readers who enjoy ancient history will probably be intrigued with THE CELTS by Gerhard Herm. Nearer to our own time is David McCullough's engrossing story of the creation of the Panama Canal in THE PATH BETWEEN THE SEAS. Fritz Stern's GOLD AND IRON is an excellent study of Bismarck's shaping of the German Empire with the financial aid of Gerson von Bleichröder. In THE RIVER CONGO, Peter Forbath provides a fascinating history of this fifth largest river in the world from the time of Prince Henry the Navigator to the twentieth century. MAO'S CHINA and THE CHINESE COMMUNIST PARTY IN POWER, 1949-1976 delineate the progress of Communist China from 1949 to 1976 and offer new insights to Western readers. THE GULAG ARCHIPELAGO: THREE (Parts V-VII) concludes Alexander I. Solzhenitsyn's monumental report depicting the harsh, inhuman conditions in Soviet Corrective Labor Camps, a work that has moved the conscience of the Western world. All the other history works represented here are recommended reading. They cover a wide spectrum and invite those with special interests to examine the insights their favorite authors have provided.

Several works which do not readily lend themselves to classification appear under the heading of miscellaneous. Of these, Annie Dillard's HOLY THE FIRM is perhaps the most intriguing. Those who admired PILGRIM AT TINKER CREEK will be equally rewarded by Dillard's latest work.

Acknowledged as highly selective because of space limitations, this group of essay-reviews is presented as representative of the year's output of fiction and nonfiction. Some of the books entertain, some instruct, some may serve as links with our almost-forgotten past. Whatever the author's purpose, whatever the reader's response, we should all be grateful that no one in our corner of the world has been told what he must write, and no one has been told that he must read what has been written.

FRANK N. MAGILL

LIST OF TITLES

LIST OF TITLES

LIST OF TITLES

LIST OF TITLES

TITLES BY CATEGORY

ANNOTATED

FICTION

POETRY
DRAMA

LITERARY CRITICISM
LITERARY HISTORY

ESSAYS

BIOGRAPHY

AUTOBIOGRAPHY
MEMOIRS
DIARIES
LETTERS

CURRENT AFFAIRS

MISCELLANEOUS

CONTRIBUTING REVIEWERS FOR 1978 ANNUAL

Vernon Allsup

William D. Anderson

Anthony Arthur

Carolyn Wilkerson Bell

Mae Woods Bell

Meredith William Berg

Gordon N. Bergquist

Gary B. Blank

Marcel L. Bolduc

Carol B. Borowski

William Boswell

Peter A. Brier

John C. Carlisle

Frederick B. Chary

James W. Clark, Jr.

Gordon W. Clarke

Lois A. Dahlin

Paul M. Deblinger

E. Gene DeFelice

Phyllis C. Deleo

R. H. W. Dillard

Leon V. Driskell

Rand Edwards

Charles Elkabas

John W. Evans

Barry Faye

Kathryn Flaris

George J. Fleming

Jonathan M. Furdek

Betty Gawthrop

Roger A. Geimer

Leslie E. Gerber

Leonard H. D. Gordon

William E. Grant

Alan G. Gross

Gloria Sybil Gross

Max Halperen

Stephen L. Hanson

Jutta A. Helm

Janet H. Hobbs

Charles Ingrao

Willis Knapp Jones

Harold J. Joseph

Edward P. Keleher

John R. Kelly

Paul B. Kern

Henderson Kincheloe

Thomas R. Koenig

Anthony Lamb

Richard L. Langill

Saul Lerner

Elizabeth Johnston Lipscomb

Margaret McFadden-Gerber

David Madden

Robert E. May

Walter E. Meyers

Leslie B. Mittleman

Sheldon A. Mossberg

Keith Neilson

James E. Newman

Robert E. Nichols, Jr.

Guy Owen

Mary Paschal

Doris F. Pierce

James W. Pringle

David L. Ransel

John D. Raymer

Bruce D. Reeves

Ann E. Reynolds

Michael S. Reynolds

Lance Roepe

Karl A. Roider, Jr.

Alfred D. Sander

Steven C. Schaber

Margaret S. Schoon

R. Keith Schoppa

Kathryn L. Seidel

Robert L. Selig

Don W. Sieker

Sofus E. Simonsen

Gilbert Smith

Gregory S. Sojka

James D. Startt

Shirley F. Staton

Leon Stein

Joan Hinde Stewart

Linda Klieger Stillman

James T. Sullivan

Carol Whyte Talabay

Henry Taylor

William Tillson

Donald R. Tracey

Lance Trusty

Harry Tucker, Jr.

Stuart Van Dyke, Jr.

James R. Van Laan

Richard A. Van Orman

John N. Wall, Jr.

Thomas N. Walters

Robert B. White, Jr.

Dara Wier

Mary C. Williams

Mary Ann Witt

Leonora Woodman

R. V. Young

Edward A. Zivich

ABBA EBAN: AN AUTOBIOGRAPHY

Author: Abba Eban (1915–   )
Publisher: Random House (New York). 610 pp. $15.00
Type of work: Autobiography
Time: 1915–1976
Locale: England, the United States, Israel

A recounting of the major assignments of Israel's foremost diplomat and former foreign minister

Principal personages:
ABBA EBAN, Foreign Minister of Israel, 1966–1974
CHAIM WEIZMANN, first President of Israel
DAVID BEN GURION, first Prime Minister of Israel
DAG HAMMARSKJÖLD, Secretary-General of the United Nations
HARRY TRUMAN, President of the United States, 1945–1953
JOHN FOSTER DULLES, American Secretary of State, 1953–1959
HENRY KISSINGER, American Secretary of State, 1973–1977

Abba Eban's autobiography is evidence that the post-World War II era has produced leaders of the same caliber as the giants who dominated the tumultuous thirty years' war which raged in Europe from 1914 to 1945. Of all the major political events since 1945, only the Chinese Revolution has captured the imagination and will stand out as much as the establishment of the state of Israel. While Eban's story is familiar to historians, his lucid style, sense of humor, and personal involvement make his book a valuable document and an excellent introduction to the drama from an Israeli point of view.

Not least of this work's assets is the opportunity it provides of getting to know Eban himself. By the end, the reader is left dazzled by the achievements of the man. A tireless worker with very high standards, Eban, as the most important Israeli diplomat, can justly claim much of the credit for the enviable position of international security which Israel has reached. With tongue in cheek, he writes at one point that as foreign minister he never received a dispatch from an Israeli ambassador reporting on a conversation in which he was bested. One might add that Eban himself rarely recalls a diplomatic duel in which he was touched. Nevertheless, the reader finishes this autobiography with the impression that Eban is a modest, sensible, and humane man. It might be said, however, that he would have done as well to have omitted the all too frequent quotations from newspapers describing his speeches as "Churchillian," for his accomplishments stand on their own. Basically, Israeli diplomacy has triumphed over its Arab counterpart through unrelenting effort and unsurpassed mastery of material and argument. If Eban needed a vote at the United Nations or support at the State Department or in Congress, he called as often as he decently could, courted his object and finally won it over with his impressive reasoning and his sympathetic personality. His dedication and his willingness to try and try again, combined with his finesse and personal appeal, made him an extremely successful diplomat in an often hostile environment.

1

His dedication stems from the religious and cultural heritage he received from his grandfather. The rest of his childhood upbringing, though, is an example of the impressive pluralism of Jewish society as a whole and Israel in particular. Eban's maternal grandfather was a Lithuanian Jew who emigrated to South Africa and then to London. His father was also a Lithuanian Jew in South Africa who died of cancer in 1916, having taken his family to London in search of a cure. There his mother married Isaac Eban, an English Jew who had a medical practice in the English capital. Here, young Eban, known as Aubrey, divided his time between weekdays at an English public school run by a classics-minded Cambridge scholar, and weekends spent learning Hebrew and poring over Jewish scriptures with his grandfather. It is difficult to imagine two more contrary influences than that of a practical and socially competitive English public school and a mystical and intellectually demanding Old World Jewish grandfather. In his public life, though, Eban has been able to synthesize these two currents by putting the social and verbal skills so well inculcated by an English education to use for the creation and survival of a Jewish state.

Upon graduation, he went to Cambridge, where he won a triple-first—an extremely rare accomplishment. It probably was not quite good form for most Cambridge students to do so well or work so hard at academic subjects. He also became more and more involved in Zionist activity, which was headquartered in London and dominated by the venerated Chaim Weizmann. Eban was appointed to the faculty at Cambridge and continued to divide his time between his research and his political work for the Zionists until the outbreak of World War II. He does not appear to have seriously considered leaving England at this point, but when he describes his loyalties, not one is to Britain. "I was a Jew, a Zionist, a democratic socialist, an advocate of resistance to Fascism, a supporter of the Spanish Loyalists against Franco and an adherent of the League of Nations concept." There was no necessity to be loyal to England, but he should not have been surprised when during the war, the British army, of which he was an officer, seemed to question how far he could be trusted. It took the war and the desperate situation of European Jews finally to convince Eban to abandon an academic career at Cambridge and devote himself completely to Israel.

In this service, he rose meteorically, becoming at the same time the youngest ambassador to the United Nations and to the United States. He served in this dual role from 1950 to 1959, then returned to Israel, where he was first appointed Minister of Education, then Deputy Prime Minister, and finally Foreign Minister in 1966, a position he held until 1974.

One of the most interesting aspects of Eban's career was his intimacy with American political life, and his vignettes of American presidents and secretaries of state are authentic and honest. For Eban, Truman was a typical Midwesterner, neither sophisticated nor erudite, who supported Israel instinctively. John Foster Dulles was a hypocritical moralist suspicious of Israel, but who finally learned to respect her power in the United States and the skill of her leaders. As for Lyndon

Johnson, Eban recounts a poignant scene with him when Israel was preparing to fight Egypt in 1967. Johnson, the born power broker, had been shorn of his international influence by the domestic turmoil over his Vietnam policy. With Eban in front of him, and with Israel and Egypt on the verge of war, the American President was incapable of initiating any forceful policy. It is Henry Kissinger, though, entertaining, dynamic, purposeful, and friendly to Israel, who is most sincerely admired by the author. One of Eban's major concerns has been the American commitment to Israel, and its increasing strength ·is chronicled in this book. In 1948, the United States recognized Israel's right to exist; and in 1957, guaranteed its rights; in 1967, it accepted Israel's expansion, and in 1973, supplied the arms necessary to defend the new borders.

The bulk of Eban's memoirs concern the four great crises of the state of Israel; its founding in 1947–1948, the Suez invasion of 1956, the Six Days War in 1967, and the Yom Kippur War of 1973. In the struggle for Israel's creation, the young Eban was completely convinced of the justice of his cause. Rather noticeably, especially for an Israeli moderate, Eban makes no mention whatsoever of Palestinian rights, and from his account one would imagine that the problem was simply that of an indigenous Jewish population yearning for its right to nationhood and oppressed by an Imperial England. Unfortunately, too, he skirts the complex issue of Jewish terrorism which was primarily responsible for evicting the English; terrorism which today, of course, is used by the Palestinians to evict the Jews, much to their outrage. When one has finished Eban's book, one's distinct impression is that Israeli policy has been to dominate its neighbors militarily without serious thought of conciliation. He would argue that this policy has been necessary for survival, and he may be right, but he would have done well to present the situation as completely as possible.

Given the dramatic position of the Jews in postwar Europe, it is difficult to know what else could have been done in 1947 other than acceding to Israeli demands for a state, despite the obvious infringement on the Palestinian Arabs. Once founded, with the sanction of the Great Powers and the United Nations, it was difficult for these groups to take a position contrary to this decision. Mere survival was not easy for Israel, however. The Arabs were resentful of Israel's presence and were worried that the new nation would expand further, which, in fact, strategic concerns and their inclinations to power caused the Israelis to do. With the accession of Gamal Abdel Nasser to power, the departure of British troops from Egypt in 1954, and the step-up of Arab raids into Israel, the two countries moved closer to confrontation. When Britain and France decided to take over the Suez Canal by force after Nasser's nationalization, Israel, in a decision made by David Ben Gurion, agreed to join them. Without United States or Soviet approval, however, Eban was caught in Washington trying to salvage what he could from the military gains. Menacing notes from the Soviet Union and anxiety on the part of the United States made the Ben Gurion government accept Eban's advice that the Israelis withdraw after "satisfactory arrangements" had been made at the United Nations. In months of hard-fought diplomatic encounters, Eban and the Israeli government won the right to defend their shipping through the Straits of Tiran, laying the legal basis for Israel's attack on Egypt in 1967. In 1957, Israel withdrew from her occupied territory, because the United States was adamantly opposed to her aggression and powerful enough to make life very miserable for the Israelis if they did not comply. Circumstances in 1967 were quite different.

Eban was by this time foreign minister and in an important decision-making position. As a result of Arab guerrilla raids and Israeli retaliation, Soviet agitation and Egyptian pride, Israel and the Arab states were again confronted with a very serious situation which had developed very rapidly in the spring of 1967. When U Thant agreed to withdraw the United Nations peacekeeping force from Egypt, and Nasser announced that he would prevent shipping through the Straits of Tiran, the Israelis felt they were extremely close to war. This time, though, the Israelis had the 1957 agreement guaranteeing freedom of passage into the Gulf of Aqaba, so that Washington was committed to her. Remembering the forced withdrawal of 1957, however, this commitment had to be confirmed, and Eban flew to Washington to confer with President Johnson and Secretary of State Dean Rusk. To Eban's relief, the Americans recognized Israel's rights, but were not able to enforce them. By giving the United States a week to demonstrate its weakness, the Israelis made certain that when they acted themselves, they would be supported by Washington. After the lightning Israeli victory in the Six Day War, the Americans did back Israel diplomatically, especially in the well-known Security Council Resolution 242, which avoided setting either a timetable or a territorial schedule for Israeli withdrawal. The contrast between American policy in 1956 and 1967 is startling, and by the latter date, the U.S. was in the position of fundamentally accepting the decisions of the small Jewish state. Eban feels justly proud of his contribution to this development.

The Arab surprise attack of October 6, 1973, confirmed and strengthened this alignment. Stunned and suffering heavy casualties, Israel received a massive American arms shipment which helped turn the Arab incursions into the fourth Israeli victory. From Eban's account, however, the Yom Kippur War did change public opinion in his country. Losing three times as many lives percentage-wise in three weeks as the United States did in ten years of fighting in Indochina, the self-confidence of Israel was shaken, and more serious attention was paid to the problem of reaching a permanent settlement. Eban supports significant territorial withdrawal, but as with his United Nations resolutions, he leaves his formulation vague.

Eban's book makes clear the dual nature of Israeli foreign policy, a strong and resolute military posture and Great Power backing, in particular by the United States. As a product of both English and Jewish culture, Abba Eban is especially well suited to form the bridge between Washington and Tel Aviv. The increasingly cordial relationship between these two capitals is testimony to his diplomatic success, although in 1978 a more evenhanded attitude toward Israel and the Arab countries has been growing in the United States.

Stuart Van Dyke, Jr.

Sources for Further Study

Book World. December 18, 1977, p. E1.

Booklist. LXXIV, September 15, 1977, p. 134.

Christian Science Monitor. LXX, January 5, 1978, p. 21.

Guardian Weekly. January 15, 1978, p. 18.

New York Times Book Review. December 18, 1977, p. 1.

Newsweek. XCI, January 16, 1978, p. 78.

Saturday Review. V, December 10, 1977, p. 56.

ADLAI STEVENSON AND THE WORLD

Author: John Bartlow Martin (1915–   )
Publisher: Doubleday and Company (New York). 946 pp. $15.00
Type of work: Biography
Time: 1952–1965
Locale: Illinois, New York, and locations on several world tours

   This second volume in Martin's biography covers the years 1952 through 1965 and focuses on Adlai Stevenson's presidential candidacy of 1956, the effects of his party leadership throughout 1952–1960, and his Ambassadorship to the United Nations from 1961–1965

   Principal personages:
   ADLAI EWING STEVENSON, II, politician and statesman
   ARTHUR M. SCHLESINGER, Jr., his adviser
   JOHN F. KENNEDY, 35th President of the United States
   HUBERT H. HUMPHREY, U.S. Senator, and Vice-President of the United States
   LYNDON B. JOHNSON, 36th President of the United States

   John Bartlow Martin, the author of this two-volume biography, is eminently qualified as an award-winning journalist, having written many articles on social and political issues since the decade of the 1940's. He is qualified as a statesman, having served as presidential envoy twice and having been Ambassador to the Dominican Republic and most especially qualified as a close associate of Adlai Stevenson, having worked as his adviser and writer for many years, most notably from 1952 onward. Martin brings all of these faculties to bear and, with the help of voluminous written data gathered from personal records and many public papers, has produced a highly detailed, nearly day-by-day account of Adlai Stevenson's hectic public and social life.

   This second volume is divided into two phases of Stevenson's public commitment, titled simply "The Nation" and "The World," by which author Martin indicates that during the decade of the 1950's, Stevenson's major impact was in national politics, while after 1960, his achievements were in the field of international diplomacy. Hence, *Adlai Stevenson and the World* recounts the years of most prestige, most popularity, most challenge, and most fulfillment for this important American who became a world leader.

   During the thirteen years covered in the second volume, Adlai Stevenson enjoyed ever-increasing world renown. He was always traveling, meeting with associates and friends, giving speeches—an informed, delightful, articulate, and inspiring spokesman for his political party and for his nation. His trips abroad were numerous, lengthy, and wide-ranging, during which he visited with most of the dignitaries on every continent. The quality and quantity of honorary degrees he began receiving became noteworthy. And yet, his career was paradoxical.

   Despite having been twice defeated for the Presidency in 1952 and 1956, and not winning his party's nomination as candidate in 1960, Stevenson seems never to have been regarded as a loser, but rather as a shining paragon of high-mindedness in public service, one of the most noble figures on the political scene, here and abroad, the like of whom, incidentally, we have not seen since. Reasons for this good opinion of him, according to biographer Martin's suggestion, include the probable fact that Eisenhower's popularity was unbeatable anyway and so to lose to him was no disgrace, and more specifically, the fact that Stevenson's courage and determination were indomitable in the face of his upsets, becoming a sort of trademark of his, as he smilingly, gallantly, and eloquently continued the pursuit of important national and international goals.

Even though Stevenson was not in public office during 1952–1960, he affected public policy. Beginning shortly after the 1952 elections, in the spring of 1953, the political advisers of his first presidential campaign set about immediately after the defeat to remain in his service, and that of their party, by continuing to study major issues of the day and to draft position papers for Stevenson to present in speeches as the spokesman for the Democratic party, now that they were out of office and ex-President Truman had officially retired from active politics. These advisers included Kenneth Galbraith, Arthur M. Schlesinger, Jr., George Ball, Averell Harriman, Chester Bowles, and Tom Finletter, among many other experts in several fields. They became known as the Finletter Group, met periodically for four years or more, and served their party and the nation well by researching and speaking out on important issues. Martin indicates that such assemblages of political adivsers as the Finletter Group, and other groups who continued during the entire eight years of the Eisenhower Administration, actually established critical attitudes in the nation and were responsible for many of the policies which later became enacted, especially under the following Democratic presidents, John F. Kennedy and Lyndon B. Johnson. Therefore, as a figure about whom others gathered, Stevenson was both a catalyst and a prime mover himself, whose party leadership engendered many beneficial effects, even though he held no policymaking office in the federal government during these years.

A great part of Adlai Stevenson's later life was taken up with campaigning, a facet of his endeavors which Martin knew intimately, and which is therefore reported here in the presidential election years of 1956, 1960, and to a lesser degree 1964, when one reads of the exhaustive travel and speechmaking schedule which national campaigning required. Stevenson not only accomplished these taxing assignments but seems to have thrived on that kind of public exposure, because even in off-year elections he was always ready to stump for the party candidates throughout the country; and he did so with verve, resilience, and, generally, widespread success. And yet, paradoxically again, although a fully committed national politician, his scope was never limited to this nation alone.

Frequent trips abroad to all parts of the world, coupled with a lifelong interest in world affairs, made Stevenson ever aware of international politics. It is the international scope of his endeavors which he seems always to have cherished.

Foreign affairs were the aspect of the presidency of this country in which he was apparently most interested, as can be quickly corroborated by noticing the internationalistic tone of all of his speechmaking. At the advent of President Kennedy's election, the cabinet post of Secretary of State was Stevenson's prime desire; and his disappointment at not getting that post was only partially mitigated by his acceptance of President Kennedy's appointment of him as the U.S. Ambassador to the United Nations, taken only after assurances that he would be allowed to help make policy and not merely be a spokesman. During the years 1961–1965, Adlai Stevenson was a firm, patient, successful negotiator, working together brilliantly with two United Nations Secretaries-General, Dag Hammarskjöld and U Thant, and achieving much in prestige and good will for his country and the free world during very difficult and varied world crises. They now read like a recital of horrors: strife in the Congo, Angolan independence, the Berlin Wall, Formosa, Red China's admission, the Bay of Pigs, Cuban missiles, Khrushchev's attacks, NATO, constant disarmament talks, Dominican Republic intervention, Vietnam. During all of this extreme international tension, we had a most respected and capable world diplomat as our representative. His record in the UN is enviable; his counsel to two presidents on international diplomacy was consistently wise. Even though Martin indicates in the subtitle of the first chapter of this volume that the period of 1952–1955 was his "finest hour," that may be hyperbole and a Churchillian echo for dramatic effect, because a very strong case can most assuredly be made for the position that his UN years were the culmination of a lifetime of internationalist tendencies and that Stevenson's most important contributions were his positive effect on the rest of the world.

Nowhere are paradoxes more evident than in the social aspect of Stevenson's life. Martin provides us with an objective recounting of social events and some of the man's personal habits. We appreciate, for example, that although generally considered an intellectual, Stevenson very rarely read; instead, he gathered information by association with many intelligent colleagues and friends who discussed issues with him, thereby becoming more of a "broker of ideas" than a creator of them. His speeches, as an indication of this, were generally prepared by others; he would then edit and re-edit them up to the last minute before delivery.

In a similar fashion, one is surprised to realize that despite nearly continuous movement, constant traveling, and extremely intermittent interaction with people, Stevenson nevertheless inspired great loyalty and admiration from many gifted and dedicated persons. His admirers reacted emotionally to him as well as intellectually, in that they felt affection for him as well as respect. It is stated that he almost never terminated a friendship but continued them until, in only one or two instances, the friends reluctantly separated from him. Such constancy occurred either in spite of his lifestyle or because of it.

Many of his closest friends were women who fit into a discernible pattern:

they all were quite intelligent, very sensitive, openly and unashamedly flattering to him, usually married, many older than he, some quite wealthy and influential. He carried on enduring associations with Alicia Patterson (Mrs. Harry Guggenheim), Jane Dick (Mrs. Edison Dick), Agnes Meyer (Mrs. Eugene Meyer), Barbara Ward, (Lady Jackson, wife of Sir Robert Jackson), and Marietta Tree (Mrs. Ronald Tree), the latter of whom was out briskly walking with him in Grosvenor Square, London, the morning in July, 1965, when he died suddenly of a heart attack. Mrs. Eleanor Roosevelt was a close and venerated friend continually until her death in 1963. All gave Stevenson valuable assistance, support, and advice, and campaigned for him. It could be said, therefore, that he held the deep affection of several women. It might also be said that he had no lasting intimacy with any one woman, inasmuch as divorce followed a shattering marriage that ended with the mental deterioration of his wife, Ellen Borden Stevenson, so that he was never again willing to remarry.

Throughout this biography, we read, predominantly, excerpts from Stevenson's speeches, his correspondence, daily appointment calendar, and travel notebooks, including the realistic touches of his abbreviations and occasional misspellings. Martin explains in the biography's "Source Notes" at the end of the volume that he has spent the past twelve years culling over speeches, press conference transcripts, public statements, program papers, lectures, law-firm records, and the private effects which he himself helped catalog. Therefore his method has been to set down the chronological series of events with such excerpts. Actual conversations with others are paraphrased rather than re-enacted. He states, "I have let the material speak for itself." But while such techniques are not only defensible but desirable as the journalist's stock in trade (apparent objectivity being the means to promote complete believability), in any creative literary endeavor, such fact-gathering and reporting seems singularly one-dimensional, and in a biography can be unnervingly superficial and unsatisfying.

Some critics of this work have said that it contains too much detail and that its style is ponderous. Closer scrutiny discloses that the rub comes from the fact that its length does not seem to reward the reader with fresh insight about this public figure. An objective compilation of source data with interpolation of narrative is a worthwhile technique, but readers require help in being able to decipher the public and social pose in order to get to the man within. After insisting, in the "Acknowledgements" section at the end of this second volume, that Stevenson was complex and sometimes ambiguous, Martin states: "But I think that the important questions have been answered." Not only have they not been answered, they have not even been asked in these volumes.

One thoroughly respects Martin's disinclination to delve into psychological and moral dimensions which he may feel inadequate to discuss; such may be, after all, completely out of his domain. But what is a biography if it is not an appraisal of the protagonist's substance and essence? One reviewer praised

Martin's stringent lack of sentimentality in this work. It is true that one is supposed to be convinced of Martin's impartiality toward his subject by recognizing his meticulous avoidance of anything resembling prejudice favoring Stevenson, but the sheer physical evidence, the years of study, of patient sifting of data, of careful elaboration of two long volumes, all combine to overwhelm us in exactly the opposite direction: this biography has to have been a labor of devotion. And that being so, it hardly seems worth the effort for Martin to have denied the obvious and to have composed a concatenation of outward activities with little or no depth into the character he knew very well.

Martin states in the "Acknowledgements" that the interpretation of Adlai Stevenson in these volumes is his, yet that is precisely what is lacking—his unique interpretation of one of this century's most interesting public figures. The facts of his life are masterfully given, but no interpretation of them is offered, and the facts do not always speak for themselves. Stevenson was anything but obvious; he was never deceitful, with himself or with others, but he *was* multifaceted, variegated, ambiguous whenever the situation defied resolution, a dynamic criss-cross of influences and ambitions, inspiring yet needing inspiration, courageous and yet vulnerable, disappointed on occasion but not daunted for long. So, while this two-volume work can well be pointed to as an outstanding example of a political biography, it is not a personal one.

Adlai Stevenson and the World is nevertheless a very valuable and penetrating examination of recent political history in this country with many informative and enlightening passages concerning the interworkings of the federal government and the international diplomacy at the United Nations. Perspectives are given which show how policy becomes determined under the pressures of state, and many revealing glimpses of famous people are intertwined in the narrative.

Anthony Lamb

Sources for Further Study

Christian Century. XCIV, November 16, 1977, p. 1078.
New York Times Book Review. October 2, 1977, p. 1.
Newsweek. XC, October 24, 1977, p. 117.
Publisher's Weekly. CCXII, July 25, 1977, p. 63.
Saturday Review. V, October 15, 1977, p. 34.
Wall Street Journal. CXC, October 26, 1977, p. 22.

THE ADVANTAGE OF LYRIC
Essays on Feeling in Poetry

Author: Barbara Hardy
Publisher: Indiana University Press (Bloomington, Ind.). 142 pp. $10.95
Type of work: Literary criticism

An attempt to restore "feeling" to a central place in literary criticism

Barbara Hardy's *The Advantage of Lyric* is a commendable attempt to call our attention once more to the importance of "feeling" in lyric poetry, and to find an alternative to the, by now, mechanical aspects of formalist and American "New" criticism. She provides us with subtle analyses of particular poems and, more significantly, she discovers some structural principles that may become central in the criticism of the lyric in the decades to come. However, there are three immediate problems that must be taken into consideration before we look at the particulars of the book. These are the origin of the book as separate lectures and articles, the inadequacy of the theoretical framework for the study, and the failure of the introductory essay to provide a clear description of what is later developed in the separate essays.

The structure of the book is, to an extent, faulty. All of the nine essays were previously given as lectures and then published as separate essays before they were collected here. The essays have been only "slightly revised." Thus, the promise of a theory worked out and exemplified is seriously weakened by parts that do not always connect. This is especially apparent in the essay on Clough which is taken from a book that reconsiders the Victorian poets. Clough's major works were long narrative poems, not lyrics, and they do not seem to belong to this book, even if the narratives have "feeling" within their structure. The selection of poets to be discussed also seems arbitrary. We move from Donne to Dylan Thomas and Sylvia Plath with no mention of the place of the lyric in particular periods or movements.

The theoretical justification for the "isolation of feeling" also seems rather limited. The definition of a lyric, which should control the approach to the work, is casually tossed off:

> Lyric poetry isolates feeling in small compasses and so renders it at its most intense. To say more about the form is to raise doubts and exceptions.

Such a definition limits, for the most part, analysis to the stages, shifts, and patterns of feeling. This is a welcome addition after so many years of New Criticism, but is it a sufficient alternative to imagery, tone, metaphor, paradox, tension, irony? Later in the book we see the "pattern of feeling" give way to the merely personal element in poetry, an obvious diminishment of the promise of the introductory essay.

A more important difficulty in the book is that the first essay promises to focus exclusively on "feeling," a promise that it cannot and does not keep.

> The advantage of lyric poetry comes from its undiluted attention to feeling and feeling alone,
> and its articulateness in clarifying that feeling, in attesting conviction or what may somewhat
> misleadingly be called sincerity, and transferring this from privacy to publicity.

In fact, we seldom find "undiluted feeling" in the poetry that Hardy analyzes.
She includes tone, imagery, generalization, and thought as elements that
connect or compete with feeling in the structure of the poem. Indeed, she is at
her best when she discovers patterns that show feeling and other elements
working together. However, the expectation of "undiluted feeling" and the
failure to provide it is frustrating to the reader. The book is too good to be
marred by such difficulties, and the introductory essay should be revised for a
future edition.

The eight remaining essays can be divided into three groups. The essays on
Donne, Hopkins, and Yeats all work out a structural unity that is derived from
various elements; the essay on Clough is interesting but does not belong; the last
four essays are on three modern poets: Auden, Thomas, and Plath. In the last
group, there seems to be an evaluative as well as a descriptive focus; the modern
poets are tested by the touchstone of feeling and then praised or dismissed.

The chapter on Donne's "Songs and Sonnets" fails to break away from Eliot's
famous definition of the "unified sensibility," a union of thought and feeling.
Hardy talks of the way "the passions grow, move, shift, combine, and relate to
intelligence and sensation." And she quotes Donne's marvelous phrase, "A
naked thinking heart." But she does little to modify the terminology or the
approach to Donne's poetry. She does not succeed in making the poems new for
us. Her analysis of "Love's Growth" is thorough and subtle, but the various
shifts from cynical to sincere might be described just as well, if not better, by
using "tone" instead of the "stages of feeling." Her description of "Love's
Growth" as a series of "lifts" is more cumbersome than illuminating. Her later
attempts to find opposition in Donne's poetry are more successful. There is,
however, a puzzling ending to the chapter. Hardy makes a teasing reference to
the biographical nature of Donne's poetry.

> I am very far from wishing to smuggle in an argument about the biographical origins of
> Donne's poetry. What this range and variety of passionate lyric tells us, if we need to be told,
> is that the imagination, passion and intelligence which belong to poetry, and which are both
> displayed and discussed in Donne, do not belong only to poetry.

She seems intent on having it both ways, and her dismissal of the subject in a
footnote does not help to clarify the problem. The question of the relationship
between feeling and actual experience is hinted at many times in the book, but it
is never fully discussed.

Hardy is better on Hopkins' poems of religious doubts than on those that
celebrate nature and God. She describes "Pied Beauty" as: "the process of
expansion, in which we move from one stage of feeling to another, usually from
the sensuous and phenomenal to the larger spiritual adventure. In such poems
the emotional stages of feeling are transcended but not obliterated." This seems

to be a laborious and tedious working out of a pattern that could be better described in terms of descriptive imagery which is followed by a command to "Praise" the author who is both unchanging and the source of variety. The "stages of feeling" are misleading and inadequate here. Hardy's analysis of "The Caged Skylark" is competent if a bit dull for such a splendid poem. She really does not come into her own until she discusses "My Own Heart Let Me Have Pity On." She fully exemplifies in her analysis of this poem her own theory and an idea of Lawrence that it is inadequate to give "names" to feeling. The description of the structure of feeling is revealing and exciting:

> Between the initial statement, in itself both a generalisation and a kind action, and the final comforting address and performance of love in the second part of the sonnet, is an intricate movement of feeling: the passional action between the two movements has been frustrating, frustrated, advancing a little, slightly relieved, fatigued, opening and relaxing with effort.

The style is difficult but the analysis has taken on some of the qualities of the poem to render the movement and structure. This type of criticism may appeal to students who are tired of categories and feel the poem is often lost in the analysis.

The essay on "Yeats's Love Poetry" does not have to extract feeling from conceptual structures or narrative. The poems are filled with the immediacy of feeling. Hardy does show how Yeats "excludes" all other elements from "The Lover Tells of the Rose in His Heart." The worldly elements are "wronging" the image Yeats has of his love, and they must be discarded. However, Hardy then shows that "every discarded item here is to recur as an essential aspect of love, defiantly or shockingly acclaimed, in the later love poetry." The book is at its best when it discovers mixtures of feeling and some other element rather than pure feeling. We can see the lesser interest in the poetry of pure feeling in her clear but unexciting analysis of "The Lover Mourns the Loss of Love ("not so complex as to be able to make a space for both a victory and a loss") and that of "Against Unworth Praise" where the passion is "generalised." Obviously, complexity is needed as well as feeling in a great lyric. Later, in speaking about "An Image from a Past Life," Hardy describes the poem as a "drama of imagery, and the imagery is punished" which once again suggests the importance of impurity, complexity. Finally, Hardy is excellent on the erotic poems; she shows how Sheba "seizes on the abstract excuse to return with the philosopher to bed and bedrock." If feeling has a place in criticism, it must surely be in dealing with erotic literature.

The essay on Clough is impressive, although it does not further her thesis on lyric poetry. Basically, it is an attack on those who see Clough as an "intellectual" poet. Hardy wishes, of course, to place him in the pantheon of the poets who express feeling. She does successfully link the method of Clough to that of Donne and Hopkins, the union of thought and feeling. She then goes on to more fully define the nature of poetry that has a lyric quality within a narrative. She places Clough in Joyce's "epical" mode where "the artist prolongs and broods upon himself as the center of an epical event and this form progresses till the centre of emotional gravity is equidistant from the artist himself and from others." This seems to be an impressive working out of a difficult problem. It is, once more, an attack on the purity, exclusiveness of literary forms. It is also similar to Pound's sudden move to a startling image in *The Cantos,* or the sudden exclamation in Eliot's *The Waste Land.* It is curious that in the essay that is least involved with feeling we find the most productive insight.

W. H. Auden is dealt with in two essays, one on "reticence" and the other on the poetry of the 1930's. Both essays are attempts to rescue Auden from critics who ignore feeling in his poetry. She feels that Auden "*is* interested in personal experience and that he writes the kind of poetry which engages us, in every sense of the word, by the recognizable voice of personal feeling." This feeling is achieved, according to Hardy, by withholding information from the reader. The structural principle is the "lack of history and character and causality which throws full weight upon the feeling," "the minimal anecdote." Once more, Hardy has discovered a technique that gives a voice to what was silent and makes it possible for future scholars and students to fill in what is incomplete or elliptical.

Hardy has less luck with Auden's 1930's poems. She claims that in "1929" abstraction is attained in an "act of feeling" when it seems clear that the abstract "man" blots out the facile emotion of the speaker. She also seems to feel that a plea for "Union" which "Needs death, death of the grain, our death,/Death of the old gang" is somehow "personal address." It is not clear why Auden needs to be forced into the camp of feeling; it will hardly affect his deservedly high reputation, and his poems seem to resist the method of analysis, especially those from the political 1930's. There is, however, one poem that the author cites from this period that does unite thought and feeling:

> And since our desire cannot take that route which is the straightest
> Let us choose the crooked, so implicating these acres,
> These millions in whom already the wish to be one
>   Like a burglar is stealthily moving,
>   That these, on the new facade of a bank
>   Employed, or conferring at a health resort,
>   May, by circumstance linked,
>   More clearly act our thought.

Hardy describes the poem as a "joy both secret and abounding," a description sufficient to the poem.

The chapter on Dylan Thomas is really an evaluation, a test that he fails. Hardy finds an "imbalance of narrative and feeling" in three of Thomas' major poems, "After the Funeral," "A Refusal to Mourn the Death, by Fire, of a Child in London," and "Over Sir John's Hill." Her analysis and judgment of Thomas is, perhaps, the best yet published. Many were swept away by Thomas' personality, tragic life, voice, and the sound of his poetry rather than the content. The author gets right into the structures that are so hard to penetrate. She does grant that "Fern Hill" and "Poem in October" are successful in working out the structure that was deficient in the earlier poems, and she gives "The Hunchback in the Park" the close attention it deserves. She claims that "The Hunchback in the Park" is an example of an "abstraction" that is arrived at in a "personal" way. Perhaps an analysis of the contrasting images and tones, along with some archetypal idea of the wounded poet, would be more successful than her insistence on the personal.

The last essay is primarily a defense of Sylvia Plath. Hardy cites the attacks of David Holbrook and Robert Lowell on poetry they consider to be filled with excessive emotion. Hardy uses what most critics would consider a lesser poem of Plath, "Nick and the Candlestick," as an example not only of appropriate feeling but also of maternal feeling, a rare subject for poetry in this century. Hardy praises Plath's "sensuous precision" in the poem, a quality she finds lacking in Thomas. She dwells on the use of one word, "Ruby," which is used to describe the child. Above all, she discovers a structural principle in Plath's use of "enlargement" in her poetry. The principle, in this case, comes directly from the poet. Plath stated, "I think personal experience shouldn't be a kind of shut box and mirror-looking narcissistic experience. I believe it should be generally relevant, to such things as Hiroshima and Dachau, and so on." The "enlargement" is clear in the terrible poems, "Daddy," "Lady Lazarus," and "The Applicant." In these and other poems, Plath has successfully connected her personal condition to historical sufferers, especially the Jews in the Holocaust. Hardy has added to the concept of enlargement that of a "derangement of structure," a dislocation of time, logic, and movement that allows Plath to do what most of the other confessional poets could not do, fuse the public and the private.

The Advantage of Lyric is an important book. It is likely to generate other books, articles, perhaps even textbooks that trace the structure of feeling, thought, and various other elements. There are some faults, but these are forgivable in the light of what is achieved. Hardy has written a number of books on the novel, and this is her first attempt at poetry. If she does write on this form again, it is to be hoped that she provides her readers with a better introduction, a more fully explained critical theory, and a less rich and opaque style.

James T. Sullivan

Sources for Further Study

Choice. XIV, July, 1977, p. 674.
Encounter. XLVIII, July, 1977, p. 82.

THE AFTERLIFE

Author: Larry Levis (1946–   )
Publisher: The University of Iowa Press (Iowa City). 61 pp. $7.95; paperback $4.95
Type of work: Poetry

Levis explores themes of death and disillusionment using a surrealistic technique which he has fashioned from his readings of Lorca, Neruda, and other South American poets

The Afterlife, Levis' second volume of poetry (*Wrecking Crew* was his first), won the 1976 Lamont Poetry Prize of The Academy of American Poets. All of the poems in *The Afterlife* are finely crafted; there is not an image, word, syllable, or comma which seems unnecessary or out of place. The images are clear and crisp although they are unusually new, esoteric, erotic, and frequently—if not pervasively—surrealistic.

The tone of these poems resembles quite often certain poems of Wallace Stevens such as "Domination of Black" and "The Snow Man" in which images are grouped together in such a way as to create a fantasy world, a world which is ultimately an unanswerable, paradoxical riddle.

The words Levis uses are not difficult, rather typical; the reader is not burdened with vague connotative meanings. However, like Stevens, Levis is a master craftsman because he fashions the ordinary words in such a way as to evoke strange, haunting, and sometimes terrifyingly beautiful images. For example, in "Rhododendrons," from which the title of the book is taken, the *persona* ("I") realizes that the end of Winter, which ought to be a time of rebirth and hope, has left him inarticulate, "afraid to speak"

> as if I lived in a house
> wallpapered with the cries of birds
> I cannot identify.

Then, in a dreamlike image, the *persona* sees that

> Beneath the trees
> a young couple sits talking
> about the afterlife,
> where no one, I think, is
> whittling toys for the stillborn.

The afterlife is a metaphor for love as well as death, and also a place from which to view all the events of life and death. In the afterlife no one creates useless toys. They create poetry.

At the beginning of stanza five of "Rhododendrons" the *persona* says that as he writes "this" (the poem), he wishes to be like the flowers in the Spring, tossed and blown by the breezes. To be like them, natural and innocent without thought or memory, seems to be an idealistic state for which the *persona* hopes. In another image, to be like smoke circling in the air is to be free from mortality and, therefore, free from death.

In the final stanza, the *persona* wishes for a return to the past where he can confront himself at age twenty on a street in Fresno, give himself five dollars for a place to sleep, and then disappear forever in the crowd "that strolls down Fulton Street." He wishes to meet his past self as a stranger would bump into someone on a crowded street. Self-confrontation juxtaposed with the desire to be anonymous gives "Rhododendrons" a haunting mood and tone.

All of Levis' poems are highly personal, with a very private mythos and a symbolic elegance. The image of the afterlife itself seems to be symbolic of that place which is as private as the place reserved for the creation of poetry; for example, the writer of the unfinished letter in "The Witness" comments:

> I stared at the words
> no one could have
> fathered, until they
> grew still and took on
> the depth of woods, . . .

There appears to be an intentional ambiguity in the antecedent for "they." It refers to both "words" and "no one." The words as well as the writer of words involve a private ritual; whether it is a letter or poem or letter within a poem, the act of creation—like the rituals of loving, remembering, and dying—is sacred and as unexplainably and terrifyingly beautiful as "the depth of the woods,/ the patience of ponds/ blackening under/ the flat shadows,/ all the hearses/ of shadows that ride/ quietly as glass/ placed over the eyelids/ of the dead."

The images in Levis' poetry are various and are created by the juxtaposition of the natural world and the private world of memory, fear, and the instinct to survive. Because of this welding together of the real world of nature and the surreal world of dreams, most of Levis' poems are not grounded in a specific time and place. The dream life, like the afterlife, clearly dominates his poems. Consequently, the images float free of concrete settings.

For instance, "The Witness" opens with the image of a carp frozen in ice; the fish's eyes do not blink but his gills work: "His gills open and close,/ thoughtless./ He's an eye only. . . ." Suddenly the scene shifts to some hotel lobby in Missouri where the *persona* has been sitting all night with "still lips/ slightly parted,/ listening." Like the fish frozen staring thoughtlessly at his world, the witness of the disjointed events of his personal world is dumbfounded. After asking three metaphysical questions concerning birth, the *persona* concludes by answering: "I don't know./ Ask the heel/ of your mother's shoe,/ ask the rain/ whose one syllable/ becomes the voice/ of your father/ who stares up/ from the couch." The witness can explain nothing; only the things around him have the means to relate answers. "No one knows anything" he says in the last line of the first part of this poem.

The witness is an isolato for whom answers about birth and death are as mysterious as the fish frozen in the first ice of Winter. There are no answers. The natural world continues for man to witness, to ask questions about, and to juxtapose events of the world and of dreams in order to give meaning to a universe which keeps the answers to itself. The *persona* of "The Witness," however, survives the hostility of a dream-rain which he imagines "is eating its way,/ finally, into/ every stranger I know"; he walks out into the real rain to see death:

> . . . the thrift shop
> where someone goes on
> quietly polishing,
> shining the shoes
> of the dead
> until they look
> almost new.

Although the images and events recorded in Levis' poetry do not have particular and concrete settings, the unifying core of the poems in this volume is the narrator-*persona*. Through disaster, despair, and disillusionment—the night-marish tension produced by the emerging of the real and the psychic world—the *persona*, the "I," survives. Not only does he survive, but he narrates the events which are the poetry itself. The image of the poet as the creator and survivor unifies the vision presented in *The Afterlife*.

This self-reflexive technique, when the image of the poet himself is central to the overall unity of his work, reflects the long legacy in American letters handed down by Emerson, Thoreau, and especially Whitman whose *persona*—the self—becomes the narrator-hero in *Leaves of Grass*.

So there is the image of the poet as the creator of his own world, a survivor, and a prophet of hope over despair in a world where there are no definite answers, where, as Levis states in "In Captivity," he can explain nothing. The only explanation is in the poet's ability to see what is around him and to communicate that experience. Levis' vision is similar in this respect to Williams' poetic philosophy, "no idea but in things." However, where Williams is more concerned with delineating the concrete historical facts of Paterson in a poetic form, Levis sharply focuses the sometimes misty dream-world of the unconscious by relating it to the ideas of things in the real world.

In the real world as well as the surreal and subconscious one, however, the poet is the fashioner, the maker, the creator and controller of his vision. Poetry becomes the mirror of the poet's self and his creative energy. This is apparent in "The Double" where the *persona* states:

> This poem so like me
> it could be my double.
>
> I have stood for a long time
> in its shadow

Levis' perception of the world is like a concrete image of his own conscious and unconscious thoughts. He looks through the world as through a one-way mirror into a room where events happen and are reflected by a mirror on the opposite wall which in turn reflects the one-way mirror Levis looks through. He stands in the dark part of the world, behind its images and events, in the unconscious afterlife where nothing can be explained and where poetry is the only way to bridge the gap into the real world beyond the mirror.

In some poems like "Inventing the Toucan," Levis uses the second person "you." The reader is uncertain to whom the poem is addressed, only that in this particular poem it is a girl sailing "placidly down the Orinoco in a white dress." Mysteriously, from one side of the river, her parents drag a dead mule "out of the shade" and call to her. The toucan observes the scene from a tree branch above where the girl and her parents kneel over the dead mule. The *persona* addresses the girl: "It seems you too are clutching a limb with huge claws,/ As the skin over each knuckle hardens." In the following stanza the girl thinks of her life elsewhere, and in the final four-line stanza she suspects that "The mule's lips are becoming a little too intimate," and that the two people who called her to the riverbank are not her real parents. The poem is ambiguous, especially from the *persona*'s point of view. He seems to be only reporting particular facts, grotesque as they are, about the death of innocence. The last several lines are hideous in their sexual implications. However, the tone of this poem is ambiguous; we do not know what the *persona*'s feelings are toward the bizarre events both he and the toucan witness. The mood of the poem is of impending danger; perhaps the only salvation is the *persona*'s hint that the girl could be magically transformed into a toucan as the last two lines of the third stanza seem to imply.

The fall from innocence is again shown in a prose poem entitled "In a Country," which follows "Inventing the Toucan." "In a Country" has a more clearly delineated theme and tone. It begins, "My love and I are inventing a country. . . ." The country they are inventing will have certain imperfections, like the river which will flood, the sky which will have clouds or smoke, and birds whose eyes fill the trees and "what they see we can never erase." Inventing and dreaming appear to be simultaneous activities, and the invention has as many flaws in it as the dream. Whether it is the invention of a toucan or a country—or even a poem—the world is a flawed place from which there is no escape. After the lovers of "In a Country" invent the rivers, sky, and birds, the second stanza finds them attempting to enter that country which they have dreamed. The narrator says the new country looked like the land they left, but he is not sure. The final lines indicate that the poem is a variation on the myth of Adam and Eve's fall from Eden: "And as we entered that country, it felt as if someone was touching our bare shoulders, lightly, for the last time." We are unsure what country the lovers are entering, whether it is the real world or the one they have been dreaming. However, it is clear that whichever world it may be, flaws are inevitable. Because the world is an invention, the product of dreaming, it is as flawed as the dream itself. In Levis' universe there is no such thing as perfection or pure innocence; there are no ultimate places and no definite answers.

In "The Crimes of the Shade Trees" and "The Morning After My Death" the themes of despair and disillusionment are combined with the personal voice and point of view of the poet who concludes in the first poem that ". . . it is possible I am not Levis./ I smoke and think possibly I am the smoke—/ Drifting through Omaha as smoke does,/ Past the new sofas on sale." The major symbol, the smoke which pervades everywhere and everything, is a metaphor of the poet's self, which, like the smoke, seeks release, escape, and freedom in the movement of air. The hope is expressed in the word "possible"; the possibility of not being himself, of being other than real, of being ethereal substance like smoke is a more comfortable state in which to be because the material world can no longer be disillusioning. One can float above it, or escape quickly on currents of air.

In "The Morning After My Death" the theme of selflessness is again expressed. This time, however, the *persona*-narrator despairs: "How little I have to say;/ How little desire I have/ To say it." The need to get away from self, especially the physical embodiment of self in the material world, is a recurring theme in Levis' work. To survive in the real world is not enough; to survive in the real world as something other than flesh and blood, to be able to function with all the senses and yet remain apart from the despair which infiltrates them from the material world is the poet's ultimate wish. "And so," Levis concludes, "I think of the darkness inside the horn." Music flows through the horn; the darkness remains, like death—no one can blow it out. Music flows through the poet who remains hidden in the darkness of the afterlife where no one can remove, blow out, that eternal muse: "like a note so high no one/ Can play it. . . ."

In the long narrative poem entitled "The Rain's Witness" which concludes the volume, Levis explores further the themes of guilt, destruction, death, and escape. He is also concerned with how one can create beauty in a world of grotesque and misshapened forms.

"The Rain's Witness" has twelve parts. The story concerns the *persona* whose brother has shot "what he said was a linnet." Because of his crime, his brother becomes a salesman who wears "loud ties and two tone shoes." The *persona* assumes, unwillingly at first, the guilt of his brother's actions. However, he is condemned to be pulled by his brother through the streets on a cart. During this trial, he tries to create a linnet, restoring that thing his brother has killed. Many attempts fail; there are no materials in the real world suitable for fashioning a linnet. Perhaps, Levis implies, there is hardly much of anything in the real world by which to create poetry, but the attempt is what counts; and the survivor of despair is ultimately the poet who tries to create beauty in an ugly world. The conclusion of the poem is the *persona*'s hope for anonymity, for an escape from the agony which comes with bringing an idea, a linnet, a poem into the world: "I will not have written these words,/ I will be that silence slipping around the bend/ in the river, where it curves out of sight among the weeds. . . ."

The Afterlife is an important book of poetry because it combines the techniques of surrealism, as expressed in the best South American poetry, with the characteristically American theme of discovery of self—or nonself—through the use of a highly articulate and sensitive *persona* who, like the poet himself, struggles against forces of despair and destruction to create a new way of seeing the real and the hidden world.

Lance Roepe

Sources for Further Study

Choice. XIV, February, 1978, p. 1645.

THE AGE OF UNCERTAINTY

Author: John Kenneth Galbraith (1908–   )
Publisher: Houghton Mifflin Company (Boston). Illustrated. 365 pp. $17.50
Type of work: Current affairs

A historical and philosophical analysis of changing political and economic institutions throughout the world, focusing on the problems and changes in American capitalism

Those who are familiar with John Kenneth Galbraith and his works think of him as the economist who attacked the large producers, large buyers, and large unions which exert substantial economic power. Others think of him as a radical in his profession who attacks traditional economic theory and prefers the development of a large and active public or government sector in America to solve its problems. Galbraith is a Professor of Economics at Harvard University and former chairman of the Americans for Democratic Action. However, it is frequently overlooked that Galbraith is an exceptionally talented literary artist as well as a contemporary political philosopher and historian who would probably much prefer to be compared to John Locke or Karl Marx than to Paul Samuelson or Simon Kuznets.

Galbraith has published a series of books, several of which have gained popular acclaim. He is probably best known for two books that have generated considerable controversy: *The Affluent Society* (1958), in which he argues for a strong public sector, and *The New Industrial State* (1967), in which he argues .that the traditional businessman has been replaced by a technostructure of specialists in the modern corporate world. Whether or not one accepts Galbraith's views, there is no question that he raises provocative issues and provides insights as well as informative material in an interesting and understandable style. It is this particular quality that makes his books so popular and pleasurable to read. *The Age of Uncertainty* is no disappointment in this sense.

As a matter of background, *The Age of Uncertainty* is a consequence of the effort to develop the film series of the same title, which was produced by the BBC and shown throughout the United States on the Public Broadcasting System. For his pilot attempt with the new media, Galbraith proceeded to write a series of concise essays that focused on a single contention: that there is worldwide tension which results from the "shaking up" of traditional political and economic doctrines. In other words, Galbraith examines the contrasts between the certainties of the past century with the uncertainties of our time. Capitalism, with its well-defined theory of markets and profits, was certain of its success, yet now we are witness to the uncertainty of its future. Socialism was certain of the rightness of its views; now it is haunted by uncertainty. Imperialists, certain that colonialism was the proper way to deal with underdeveloped societies, are now being toppled in many places throughout the world. These are the issues that Galbraith approaches in his typical evolutionary style. As would be expected, much of his material is derived from his earlier works. Indeed, parts of this book are taken directly from earlier publications. But for those who are familiar with Galbraith, *The Age of Uncertainty* will not be a disappointment. Galbraith pursues his challenge to the powers of the marketplace and questions the assumed dangers of the State. He also takes a position that appears to have substantial public sympathy, in favor of increased government involvement in economic affairs.

Galbraith's approach is methodical and thorough. First he examines the political-economic philosophers in a detailed, comprehensive way and discusses their impact on the political-economic systems. From the viewpoint of an economist, he outlines the evolution of economic thought and history. Galbraith is able to present his information in a way that is generally appealing and fascinating, by blending details with interesting anecdotes and major historical events to provide pointed insights and reflections into the evolution of historical episodes over the past two hundred years.

Purely by coincidence, 1776, the year of the American Declaration of Independence, is also the year that Adam Smith published *The Wealth of Nations,* a treatise that has come to be accepted by economists as the origin of modern economic thinking. Smith concluded that the wealth of a nation results from the independent pursuit of each of its citizens to seek his own interest; Galbraith takes the reader through the more familiar episodes and examples in Smith's classic work in order to set the scene for the events of that era and to contrast the view of Adam Smith with our current economic structure, with its conglomerates, multinational corporations, and international labor unions. He pursues what he calls the "tyranny of circumstance," contrasting the historical situation with the theoretical interpretations. He explores such events as the New Lanark experiment near Glasgow, Scotland, where David Dale, a Scottish capitalist and philanthropist, attempted a new social order where children were taken from orphanages to go to school and to work in his cotton mill. He then looks at the New Harmony experiment in Indiana operated by Robert Owen, Dale's son-in-law, as an attempt at a new social and economic order.

In exploring the influences of Thomas Malthus, best-known for his essays on population and his doctrine that it is generally possible to have an overproduction of goods, and the arguments of David Ricardo, who argued against that possibility, Galbraith recalls the famines that have plagued the world. He includes an impressive pictorial supplement interspersed in the narrative. This section is masterful in its ability to focus on persistent problems and relate these problems to our present age of uncertainty. Another particularly interesting essay deals with the lifestyle and morals of the rich, focusing on Herbert Spencer, an English philosopher and pioneer sociologist who applied the phrase "survival of the fittest" to account for the position of the successful and the wealthy. Galbraith analyzes the rich in America and argues for the important role of the railroads in maintaining a wealthy class. Recalling the struggle for the railroads and their control, he weaves a net of events while highlighting important problems and concepts; he includes the Church in his explanation of the power wielded by the rich. A particular example is Galbraith's treatment of Thorstein Veblen, the son of poor Norwegian immigrants, born in Wisconsin, and known to economists for his depiction and analysis of what is called "conspicuous consumption." Galbraith not only explores Veblen's background but also illustrates the theory of conspicuous consumption with a pictorial barrage depicting the parties of the rich, the Riviera, gambling, and other exhorbitances familiarized to moviegoers in *The Great Gatsby.*

Probably the most fascinating section in *The Age of Uncertainty* deals with Karl Marx. Having laid an adequate background, Galbraith characterizes Marx as a social scientist, brilliant journalist, and historian, but not as a revolutionary. A startling reminder to the Capitalist world are some of the demands of *The Communist Manifesto,* such as progressive income tax, abolition of inheritance, a national bank with a monopoly of banking operations, public ownership of transportation and communication, extension of public ownership into industry and the cultivation of idle lands, better soil management, work by all, free education, and abolition of child labor. Galbraith points out how many of these demands have been and are being met, but not without some conflict and opposition. Again, the author supplements his treatment of Marx with pictorial images of the revolutions and analyzes the rationale for opposition to these social reforms, evidenced by our own prejudices to social changes when identified as "Communist." Galbraith discusses these issues calmly and rationally, defining the basic ingredients for a successful revolution as determined leadership with a vision and a specific plan, dedicated followers, and a weak opposition; he also identifics the nemesis of revolution as reform and nationalism.

Galbraith then examines one last "certainty" of the past: Imperialism. He examines the Spanish empire in some detail to demonstrate fully the implications of colonialism, and discusses changing attitudes toward attempts to govern indirectly and to shape the political development of distant lands. He points out that what were once the colonial powers are now identified as "developed nations," while what were once the colonies are now referred to as the poor "developing nations." In order to appreciate fully recent developments, Galbraith next elaborates on the major events of Lenin's career. He focuses on such concepts as the territorial imperative; what he calls the "stupidity problem," typified by leadership stemming from tradition or social rank rather than ability; and the "rogue reaction"—those actions such as general strikes which lack direction and predictable results. The author points out Lenin's need for a highly disciplined, loyal, and committed group which does not involve the general population in the revolution. His detailed treatment of and anecdotes about Lenin are an especially interesting aspect of the book.

Galbraith also attacks another less obvious "uncertainty" of our age: the role of money. In exploring the origins and role of money, Galbraith focuses on the historical importance and prosperity of Amsterdam. Pointing out both the prosperity and the abuses that arise from banking, he cites the familiar fate of the Dutch East Indian Company and the ensuing "panics" in the Western world. By examining the revolution of paper money and centralized banking, and detailing the conflicts of Andrew Jackson and Nicholas Biddle, the author centers focus on the uncertainty implicit in paper exchange in a very enlightening fashion. He also offers an interesting interpretation of the contemporary economics figure, Sir John Maynard Keynes, and looks at the weaknesses of the Keynesian theory and the chronic problem that arises from its practice: deficit spending can be a cure for unemployment under *certain* circumstances, but the theory does not explain what to do under a variety of *other* circumstances.

Using his own experiences in Germany before World War II, Galbraith next deals with the Cold War. Depicting the Cold War as a moral crusade with a focus on liberation and a rolling back of the iron curtain, he addresses some of the consequences of its tactics, including the behavior of the CIA, the American episode with Cuba, and the Vietnam War with the unprecedented demands which it placed on our economic resources.

Finally, no work by Galbraith would seem complete without an analysis of the large corporations and the technostructure he has often written about. The corporation is typified as a purely economic entity and is rationalized on economic grounds as an amoral entity with no higher purpose; but Galbraith illustrates the falsity of this picture by showing us examples of fights for extended power by corporate heads with self-aggrandizing motives. He presents his near-classic case of the James B. Glow Company, a seemingly insignificant competitive butcher shop on the south side of Chicago that had a weak reputation in the industry for quality and business ethics, yet which grew to become Unified Global Enterprises, a large conglomerate with extensive overseas operations and earnings, now centered in New York. Galbraith emphasizes that the capitalist "uncertainty" is epitomized by UGE, which he argues is neither a powerless and passive instrument of market forces nor the passive servant of the stockholders.

It is important to recognize Galbraith as a social philosopher and literary artist in order to place his work in honest perspective. *The Age of Uncertainty* is not light reading—the subject matter does not lend itself to simplicity—but it is more correct to consider *The Age of Uncertainty* as a learned book, written in a style both interesting and readable, and buttressed by a strong central theme and purpose.

Jonathan M. Furdek

Sources for Further Study

Critic. XXXVI, Summer, 1977, p. 84.

Journal of Economic Literature. XV, September, 1977, p. 932.

New York Times. March 28, 1977, p. 27.

New York Times Book Review. April 3, 1977, p. 12.

Saturday Review. IV, April 16, 1977, p. 43.

Time. CIX, April 4, 1977, p. 85.

ALFRED HUGENBERG
The Radical Nationalist Campaign Against the Weimar Republic

Author: John A. Leopold (1937–   )
Publisher: Yale University Press (New Haven and London). 298 pp. $17.50
Type of work: Political biography
Time: 1861–1951
Locale: Germany

An account of the political career of the leader of the influential German Nationalist People's Party in the Weimar Republic

One can easily understand why this work was given the International History Honor Society's manuscript award in 1975. It is a key study of a major figure in modern German history who helped pave the way for the National Socialist victory of 1933.

Along with Papen and Schleicher, Alfred Hugenberg (1861–1951) was one of the principal gravediggers of the Weimar Republic. But he was much more than even that: he was a political, economic, and ideological link between the older, conservative Wilhelmian period and World War I, and the new radical Weimar Republic and the Nazis. Hugenberg's intermediate position between traditional and radical German conservatism was a source of both his early strength and his ultimate failure.

John Leopold's excellent political biography illuminates and traces the crucial aspects of Hugenberg's role in modern German history. The book rests on a foundation of exhaustive, meticulous research. Leopold had complete access to the Hugenberg papers at the Rohbracken Estate in addition to the Federal Archives, the files of the Pan-German League in Potsdam, and the Westarp Papers. Though availability of Industrial Archives was limited and only a portion of the correspondence between Hugenberg and Hitler has been preserved, every possible avenue of documentation has been pursued in this study.

Part of the success of the book is also due to the lucid, skillful style and organization by which Leopold guides us through the complex labyrinth of German right-wing politics of the first third of the twentieth century. Subsidiary factual material is reserved for the footnotes that occupy one-third of the length of the book. This system works well for primarily political biography. We appreciate the detailed documentation, but do not lose our train of thought or necessary perspective.

As a radical nationalist, Alfred Hugenberg linked the old and the new German conservative traditions of the first third of the twentieth century. From the late nineteenth and early twentieth century Wilhelmian era he took his beliefs in the supremacy of a governing and managerial elite of industrialists, landlords, and bureaucrats—a "cartel of the producing classes." He believed that the dynamism of the upper middle classes and the rootedness of the peasantry should constitute the basis for the *Volk*. The masses were to be manipulated and guided toward nationalism and imperialism, and away from Marxism and democracy. By 1914 Hugenberg had developed into a ponderous combination of manager and ideologue. His administrative and managerial talents led to his directorship of Krupp enterprises, wartime propaganda efforts, and later to the chairmanship of newspaper syndicates and film companies. As an ideologue, he was one of the founders of the Pan-German Society of the early twentieth century. His views featured beliefs in crude social Darwinism, imperialist expansion, militarism, economic autocracy, and anti-Marxism. He clearly belonged to the group of radical annexationists and reactionaries during World War I.

The elements of Hugenberg's even more radical conservatism appeared in the Weimar Republic. Like the Nazis, he wanted to have his political cake and eat it too. He foreswore all compromise with the hated "unGerman" democracy and parliamentary system of Weimar, yet helped to found the DNVP *(Deutschnationale Volkspartei)*, the German National People's Party. The founding of this group precipitated a crucial division in German conservatism, for it sought to sabotage moderate conservative groups (such as Stresemann's German People's Party) that were willing to support the Weimar Republic.

Hugenberg was not an effective political leader, and Leopold does well to point out his subject's numerous personality defects. Though he was a self-made middle-class man, Hugenberg was insignificant in appearance, a poor orator devoid of any charisma, and ineffective in developing strong interpersonal relationships. These qualities probably led to overcompensation that took the form of stubbornness and self-righteousness. There was also the problem of his age. When Hitler became chancellor at the young age of forty-three, Hugenberg was already sixty-five. Moreover, his managerial training in economics and propaganda, as well as his personality, led him to aspire to control things behind the scenes, to become the indispensable man of the conservative opposition to the Weimar Republic.

Hugenberg was by no means disposed to a totalitarian solution in the manner of a Mussolini or to a terroristic putschist regime to solve the problems of Germany. His anti-Marxism was probably stronger than his racism. But like members of other conservative circles he began to collaborate with the Nazis as early as 1923. Leopold asserts that the immediate origins and mechanisms of this cooperation are not clear. Given the importance of this problem, Leopold should have pointed out the source of the difficulty of pinpointing the beginnings of the collusion between the old and new conservatives. In any case, Hugenberg appreciated Hitler's oratorical talents and abilities. Like his fellow elitists, he believed that the conservative right could manipulate the masses by using Hitler as a sort of Nazi "pied piper." Hugenberg's growing radicalism was also revealed in his wish for a crisis to topple the Weimar Republic.

One of Leopold's most important contributions to the study of the German right is the way in which he underscores how the conservative party became more and more divided over aims and tactics. From 1925–1928 under the leadership of the moderate conservative Kuno Westarp, the DNVP collaborated in two coalition governments and exhibited some willingness to compromise with other moderate parties. But Hugenberg bitterly opposed Westarp's support of national and international stabilization. He even opposed the election of Hindenberg in 1925, for he felt it would strengthen the Republic.

As early as 1926 the remnants of the Pan-German League were willing to support Hugenberg to head a right-wing dictatorship. But Hugenberg, with his power over the press and his influence with some industrialists, shrewdly decided to await a crisis. By 1928 the crisis was approaching: with the election of a Socialist government the Nationalists were at the crossroads. Either they had to live up to their nationalistic program or cooperate with the Socialists. With the support of radical veterans organizations, Hugenberg was elected party chairman by a slim majority. He advocated that the German Nationalists lead all the conservative groups to create an authoritarian elitist government to replace the decadent Republic and to restore Germany's rightful position in the world.

But like all elitist conservatives, Hugenberg was unable to build a mass party. To compensate for this serious political defect he turned to the Nazis. By the Depression of 1929 Hugenberg was willing to "drive out the devil with Beelzebub," that is, to take what he thought was the lesser risk of allying with the Nazis against the greater risk of letting the hated Republic survive, or even of ending up in revolution. To this end Hugenberg was prepared to fight such fellow conservatives as President Hindenberg and Chancellor Brüning. Leopold shrewdly points out that Hugenberg was hampered by his lack of control over the very elites he claimed to represent—industrialists, big landowners, and conservative ideologues. For this reason Hugenberg also solicited Nazi support.

But in the critical election of 1930 the German Nationalists were outbid by the even more radical Nazis. By avoiding the moderate conservatism of Westarp and the ultraradical conservatism of Hitler, Hugenberg gained the advantage of neither approach. In desperation, he instigated the "Harzburg Front" of radical conservative opposition groups in 1931, hoping to achieve his coveted *"Sammlung"* (unification), a conservative condominium to topple the hated Republic. This was a turning point for Hugenberg and the entire German right. First, this conservative front actually created a model for Hindenberg's coalition cabinet of 1933. Second, Hugenberg sought to "frame in" the Nazis and failed. Most historians of the period assume that the Harzburg Front was a unified movement of reactionary forces. Leopold emphatically disagrees, and he is right to do so. He argues convincingly that the Harzburg Front led to an intensified struggle between the Nationalists and the Nazis. Hitler was far more brutal, cynical, dynamic, and charismatic than Hugenberg. The Nazi leader sought direct political control rather than a preeminence behind the scenes. And unlike Hugenberg, Hitler was able to make himself indispensable to both the desperate elites and the radicalized masses. By 1932 the Nazis became vital to those conservative groups jockeying for power. Leopold illustrates this point by producing the interesting evidence that it was Hugenberg who was instrumental in obtaining German citizenship for Hitler in that year.

By 1933 Hugenberg had alienated both the National Socialists and many traditional conservatives. He played no role in the authoritarian Papen and Schleicher governments from 1932 to 1933. He also did not figure in the key negotiations between Papen and Hitler for a new coalition government in January of 1933. The bedeviled Hugenberg was now finally wary of joining a Nazi-dominated cabinet in a parliamentary context of legality. Leopold presents an irony of history to his readers when he says that Hugenberg preferred the conservative mayor Goerdeler of Leipzig as chancellor in 1933. This was the same Goerdeler who was selected to lead a new post-Nazi government after the planned overthrow of Hitler in 1944. It was indirectly because of Hugenberg that this never came to pass.

Though he had his reservations regarding the Nazis, the stubborn Hugenberg gave way and joined the cabinet of January 30, 1933. The illusion of *Sammlung* and the temptation of control over industry and agriculture won him over.

Hugenberg did not oppose the Third Reich as he had the hated Weimar Republic. For the revolutionary totalitarianism of the Nazis destroyed his radical conservatism even as it promised to preserve it. His wish for an elitist authoritarianism turned to dictatorship, his hope for living space and social Darwinism to racial extermination and a new war, his party and projected economic empire to ruins. Such was the price that the German right wing ultimately paid for its radical conservatism. But to the end, Hugenberg refused to admit that he was ideologically and politically responsible for the rise of Nazism. He would only own up to the tactical error of allying with the "worst demagogue in history."

Leopold's political biography is sure to stand the test of the foreseeable future. His research is prodigious and his judgments sound and balanced. Though Hugenberg's family cooperated completely in providing Leopold with personal documents, the author saw virtually no redeeming features in his subject. For Leopold, Hugenberg catered to "selfish and unenlightened tendencies of men." Above all, he must bear a large portion of responsibility for the triumph of German National Socialism. This judgment is based on objectivity and integrity. Still, a lesser historian might have overestimated Hugenberg's role; but Leopold avoids that temptation, and does not see his subject as sole, decisive cause in the triumph of National Socialism. One must agree with this judgment too, for there were individuals and forces that overshadowed even the powerful Hugenberg, among them Hitler and the Depression.

Despite the excellence of the book, some primarily ideological aspects of Hugenberg's career remain unresolved. One weakness of Leopold's study (and an understandable one) is his failure to explore the question of the relationship of the ideas and attitudes of the Nationalists and the Nazis. Was Nazi ideology a continuation or merely a perversion of Hugenberg's ultranationalist and Pan-German ideas? Moreover, the author could have been more detailed on the essentials of Hugenberg's ideology. Though he effectively summarizes the major elements in his introduction and conclusion, he does not amplify or analyze these ideas in the body of the book. And he is vague on some issues: What were Hugenberg's real attitudes toward the Jews, despite his Jewish supporters in the DNVP? What were his views of the monarchy and the churches? Though Leopold strongly documents Hugenberg's connections with heavy industry, very little is said about his connections with big agriculture. Finally, how can Hugenberg's "social Darwinism," his views of a "Third Reich," and his idea of the *"Volk"* be defined as compared with the moderate conservatives in his party and the Nazis? Though these questions are not fully answered, the author manages in the course of his study to highlight Hugenberg's ideological, rhetorical, and tactical dilemmas, which in itself is no mean achievement. As political biography Leopold's *Alfred Hugenberg* is a thought-provoking study and a major contribution to its field.

Leon Stein

Sources for Further Study

Library Journal. CII, November 1, 1977, p. 2259.

ALL THE YEARS OF AMERICAN POPULAR MUSIC

Author: David Ewen (1907–   )
Publisher: Prentice-Hall (Englewood Cliffs, N.J.). 850 pp. $19.95
Type of work: Music history
Time: Colonial times to the present
Locale: The United States

*A comprehensive chronological survey of American popular music from Colonial days,
with a much-needed emphasis on the new musical trends of the last two decades*

All the Years of American Popular Music is rumored by at least one source to
be David Ewen's eightieth book. Whether or not the figure is actually that high,
there is absolutely no doubt that Ewen is the most prolific writer on music in
history. This latest work in many respects caps a career that has spanned most of
the twentieth century. It might be better named "All the Years of David Ewen,"
for it is very much a product of the author's earlier works as well as a lifetime of
experience.

Born in 1907 in Lemburg, Austria, Ewen was introduced to music through
private instruction in piano, harmony, and music theory. He completed his
education in New York City at C.C.N.Y. and Columbia University. His first
book, *Unfinished Symphony: A Story-Life of Franz Shubert* was published in
1931 and was praised by the *New York Times* as a product of "earnest and
painstaking work." After that the books kept coming. His second book, *Hebrew
Music,* came out the same year, and 1933 saw the publication of *Wine, Women
and Waltz; A Romantic Biography of Johann Strauss, Son and Father* and *From
Bach to Stravinsky: The History of Music by Its Foremost Critics. Composers of
Today* followed in 1934 and a second edition appeared in 1936. 1936 also
witnessed Ewen's marriage to Hannah Weinstein, a New York teacher.

Although still publishing books, Ewen expanded his horizons in 1937 to
become music editor of *Cue,* a New York music magazine. In 1938 he became
record editor of *Stage* and in 1940 editor of *Musical Facts.* The author took time
out for service in the United States Army in 1944–1945, and in a radical
departure from his prior literary subject matter, he wrote the authorized history
of paratroopers. After the war, he became director of Allen, Towne and Heath
Publishing Company—a position he held until 1950 when he published his
thirtieth title, *The Story of Irving Berlin.*

Now, thirty or forty titles later, Ewen's career reaches its pinnacle with *All the
Years of American Popular Music.* This massive 850-page volume is a stunning
work of research and writing. With almost fifty years of music study behind it,
this volume is in some respects a rehashing and collating of previous Ewen
books, but its major strength is that its one-volume format convincingly and
dramatically demonstrates how American popular music has developed out of
the experience, tragedy, soul, and passions of the people of all races who came to
this country. It has become an accepted fact that American music even at its
poorest is reflective of the manners, customs, and habits of common people to a

degree of precision unmatched by more scholarly music. Thus, Ewen makes no apologies for his serious treatment of popular music, but treats it as a form of folk music that is, in his mind, much broader than the traditional rural material that has been long viewed as forming the basis of such music. *All the Years of American Popular Music* is a comprehensive, well-documented sourcebook on every kind of popular music written, played, danced to, or sung by Americans from the Puritans and their hymns to the rock phenomena and the currently frenetic pop music scene.

Ewen's vast chronological narrative contains a tremendous array of names, facts, titles, stories, anecdotes, and critical assessments. The book effectively revives songs, singers, and composers long forgotten. When our country was young, our popular music consisted of the patriotic and political type; such songs had a national rather than an individual orientation. Among our early songs were many borrowed from England, including "Yankee Doodle" and the "Star Spangled Banner."

As the country expanded, Ewen notes that songs relating to pioneering became popular, particularly nostalgic tunes of home and family. Songwriters like Stephen Foster and James A. Bland were popular during this period. Songs of transportation, still popular today, also got their start at this time with writers addressing horse and buggys, railroads, steamships, and the bicycle.

American music became more leisurely in the "Gay Nineties" and represented life in an innocent and unhurried stage with major emphasis on a somewhat artificial sentimentality. The waltz was the predominant form of musical expression, and popular songs told a story usually of frustrated love. The advent of ragtime, however, in the early years of the twentieth century expressed a gradual protest against such leisurely living and music and popular arrangements developed some excitement culminating in the elaborate embellishments of jazz.

Following World War I, music became unrestrained, and very few aspects of American life evaded the attention of musicians and songwriters. Our clothing, our games, our slang, and our dances were celebrated in music. Even national events inspired songs. It has been estimated that Lindbergh's flight alone encouraged the publication of over one hundred now forgotten (except by Ewen) songs. For the most part, though, the author attempts to deal with musical pieces that were the "standards" of their period. A "standard" is defined by Ewen as being the popular music equivalent of a "classic" in serious music. For the music of the twentieth century, Ewen is able to detail fully names of composers, lyricists, circumstances surrounding the composition of a piece, its performance history, major productions of the tune on the stage or in motion pictures, and all relevant additional historical information.

About a third of the book deals with people and events occurring after 1960. Ewen treats "Rock 'n' Roll" with a certain respect, even while a certain pessimism regarding its survival seems to come across in some of his comments.

He concedes that this form is now the dominant mode of musical expression and thus cannot be ignored. The result is that Rock and its practitioners are treated in a more objective and meticulous vein than in many works by so-called historians of that music.

While *All the Years of American Popular Music* is, on one level, a history of American popular music, its major value in the long term will be as a source book. Ewen has generously strewn his history with thousands of names and dates which are made accessible through a seventy-one-page index in which the reader can discover, for example, who composed "A Summer Place." He can also learn that John Denver was once Henry Deutschendorf, Jr. But this points up a weakness of the book: there is little, if any, cross-indexing. One cannot look up Henry Deutschendorf, and find out that he grew up to be John Denver. Cross-indexing would have made more of the minutia contained in the book accessible to readers.

Although Ewen shows genuine enthusiasm for the progress of American popular music and has compiled much interesting material, his book may well be of little interest to serious music scholars. *All the Years of American Popular Music,* like Ewen's earlier efforts, is plainly written for popular consumption and, as such, is less concerned with being a specialized and scholarly piece of work. Its size, while lengthy, is still too small to permit in-depth discussion of all the important phases of our musical history. The catchy title is a snap judgment that proves untrue for a scholar desiring the final word on a musical topic. The serious student will also be disappointed by the lack of treatment given to some major but peripheral areas of popular music in the United States. American scholars and critics of popular music, for example, are given no systematic discussion, and some important ones are neglected entirely. Additionally, there is little discussion of the progress of musical education in addressing the many issues involved in the appreciation of popular music. In a volume which attempts to be as extensive as this one does, there will naturally be some omission of this kind, and some topics will be treated in a more superficial manner than others.

One major area where Ewen's book is impressively strong is that of music biography. The author is well known for his biographical treatments of musical artists, and he maintains his reputation in his latest work. He presents clear and interesting pictures of the men and women who have made a permanent contribution to our nation's musical life through their compositions, orchestrations, and performances. He also does not hesitate to mention artistic defects where they are relevant to the discussion of an individual's musical development.

The biographical materials in the book are not devoted exclusively to the musicians and composers of yesterday. A significant portion of the book contains biographical material treating those artists who still have significant meaning to music lovers. The younger musicians, particularly those involved in

Rock whose music is new and vibrant and vital, are given serious and objective treatment as well.

As a reference work, this book has some limitations and is not as all-encompassing as the title would have us believe. The arrangement is of necessity historical and designed for popular appeal, but it also collects and makes available to the more serious reader much valuable material. If it is accepted for what it is, it will prove more stimulating and useful as time goes on. *All the Years of American Popular Music* succeeds admirably in its attempt to trace the growth and interest in musical activity in America from the beginning to the present. Unexpected but greatly appreciated is the attention the work pays to the phenomenal developments in the music of the last two decades. While in the final analysis the book does not claim to be the counterpart for popular music of *Grove's Dictionary of Music and Musicians,* it is one of the few books which attempts to deal with the whole spectrum of American popular music.

Stephen L. Hanson

Sources for Further Study

Kirkus Reviews. XLV, August 1, 1977, p. 824.
New York Times. VII, December 4, 1977, p. 13.
Publisher's Weekly. CCXII, August 1, 1977.

AMATEURS

Author: Donald Barthelme (1931–   )
Publisher: Farrar, Straus and Giroux (New York). 184 pp. $7.95
Type of work: Short stories
Time: The present
Locale: New York City, where specified, though largely in the mind of the author

Twenty-one whimsical sketches, notable for the author's facility with language and his comic inventiveness, which depend for their effect upon paradox and wit rather than on insight into character and ideas

Proteus, the Greek god, would give anyone who could catch him directions on how to reach a desired destination. But Proteus did not like to answer questions, and he had the unique ability to change himself into fire, water, tiny sea-creatures, or giant monsters—whatever he chose to be. His questioner was usually frustrated, sure that valuable knowledge and understanding of mysteries beyond his grasp were there before him, tantalizingly out of reach.

Donald Barthelme, in this collection of twenty-one short stories, some of them no more than a few thousand words long, has something of the quality of Proteus. He has a daring imagination; he may know much more than he is telling; and he is maddeningly elusive.

If imagination and verbal facility are considered alone, Barthelme is surely one of our best writers. Unlike most authors, though, his work seems to come not from observation of real life but almost entirely from his own wildly inventive imagination, because hardly anything in it has any resemblance to "fact." Consider, for example, "Our Friend Colby," which begins: "Some of us had been threatening our friend Colby for a long time, because of the way he had been behaving. And now he'd gone too far, so we decided to hang him." The rest of the story, building from the absurd premise, is rigorously logical in the same way that Lewis Carroll's *Alice's Adventures in Wonderland* is logical and yet insane. Colby's musical preference for the occasion is regretfully refused; he wants Ives's Fourth Symphony, obviously a delaying tactic because it would take weeks of rehearsals. Besides, the large orchestra and chorus required would put the hanging committee well over their budget. Other considerations include the possibility of importing a hangman from South America, since there are so few in this country; the relative merits of using a gibbet and scaffold or a tree, in a bucolic setting; and whether or not to use wire instead of rope (wire is rejected, much to Colby's relief, because it might scar the oak branch they have decided to use, and is thus environmentally unacceptable). Ingenious Tomás, the architect, hits upon a method of hanging Colby that will do away with both the potentially unreliable hangman and the alternative, having Colby jump off a chair, which would be "tacky." He will instead be placed atop a ten-foot rubber ball, painted green to harmonize with the landscape, and the ball will simply be rolled out from under him. Everything goes splendidly: "It didn't rain, the event was well attended, and we didn't run out of Scotch, or anything." We never do find out what Colby's offense was.

Several conclusions may be drawn from a consideration of this story. First, Barthelme is one of the few writers for whose plots summaries are funny. Second, his method depends upon a juxtaposition of the possible and the impossible, which places his work in the fictional subgenre of fantasy; third, he is intrigued by death and attitudes toward it; fourth, he deliberately short-circuits attempts at finding clear central meanings to his stories; and fifth, the reader may be amazed or amused by Barthelme, but he is seldom moved: the appeal of his work is to the mind, not the heart.

Concerning the matter of plot, it may be noted that relatively few of the stories have so clear, though crazy, a plotline as "Colby." Most of them are vignettes that can be described in one sentence. "Our Work and Why We Do It" describes the routine in a print shop; "The Wound" is about a torero who watches himself in slow motion TV re-runs being gored in the heel as he flees from a bull; "The School" is narrated by a teacher who wonders why everything connected with the school dies, including gerbils, goldfish, children, and parents; in "I Bought a Little City" the narrator buys Galveston, Texas, and shoots six thousand dogs; "Porcupines at the University" describes the last great porcupine drive to New York. These are only a few examples of an incredibly varied collection of whimsies. Barthelme is the kind of writer who can take an idea—say, for example, where do all of the tons of fat that people lose every year *go?*—and weave it into a narrative. But except for one or two pieces, there are no people in these stories, only figures. It is when Barthelme deals with people, as in "110 West Sixty-first Street," about a couple whose son has died, that he is least satisfactory; the relatively straightforward realism of the grief which Eugenie and Paul are said to feel turns into satire at the end—Paul has been promoted from dealing with bus company bankruptcies to railway company bankruptcies, and now has the Cincinnati and West Virginia line ("the whole thing") for his very own. The couple then go to bed and masturbate. John Cheever or John Updike could take these characters and make them live, but in Barthelme they are merely cartoon figures, and repulsive ones at that.

Barthelme's true metier is allegory, in which he can freely associate ideas and emotions without having to show directly how they influence real people. "The Great Hug" is a totally successful and delightful allegory, with echoes of E. E. Cummings and James Thurber; it describes the conflict of illusion and reality in the form of the Balloon Man and the Pin Lady. The Balloon Man sells balloons only to adults; children are not eligible. The balloons are named Not Yet and Sometimes, the Sir Isaiah Berlin Balloon, the Wish Balloon, the Not-Nice Balloon. He is predestined to meet the Pin Lady; it was "in the cards, in the stars, in the entrails of sacred animals." They embrace and roll down the hill together; but as is the case with illusions even when punctured, they are indestructible, and the Balloon Man returns with his finest product: "The Balloon of Perhaps."

The opposition of reality and illusion provides the narrative framework for a number of Barthelme's stories. Quite often the frame or the setting is mundane, even banal; an army camp, a board room, a schoolroom, a museum. Within these institutions, each of them dedicated to the preserving of order, Barthelme introduces elements of fantasy and comic nightmare. Two stories in particular are significant examples: "The Sergeant" and "The New Member."

"The Sergeant" is a story which allows Barthelme to demonstrate his good ear for speech patterns—the emphasis on the first syllable, for example, in the words "economic" and "recruit" that is part of Southern dialect in military camps; he is also familiar with the jargon of the military: "You want me to cut some orders for you, sarge? You want a nice TDY to Havana?" The real meaning of this story, however, will only be apparent to a reader who has been in the military some years ago and who still has bad dreams that for some reason he is back in the service and no one will listen to him explain why, at forty-two, he shouldn't be there at all. The power of an institution which lost its formal hold on one half a lifetime ago, but which still persists in one's dreams, is very effectively rendered here—right down to the conclusion, when the sergeant is given a choice between shooting someone or stuffing the general's martini olives with onions: "eight hundred thousand gallon cans of olives and four hundred thousand cans of little onions." Because this is Barthelme writing a comic fantasy, and not Roald Dahl or Alfred Hitchcock or Rod Serling, the sergeant chooses to stuff the olives.

The second story which depicts institutions in an oddly interesting way is "The New Member." A perfectly ordinary group of men and women is holding a meeting; as the meeting begins they notice a man standing at the window looking in. "Mr. Macksey moved that the record take note of the fact. Mr. O'Donoghue seconded. The motion passed." The meeting continues, and it becomes apparent that the group is a modern pantheon of gods deciding the fate of ordinary mortals, in particular a young woman named Worth. Some of these pedestrian gods are of a kindly disposition, like Ellen West, who suggests that the Worth girl has been doing nicely and should be allowed to fall in love—perhaps with the man outside the window. Some are jealous, like Mrs. Birnbaum, and some, like O'Donoghue, are vindictive. He suggests "that the Worth girl be run over by a snowmobile." His motion is tabled so that the group can invite the man at the window to explain what he is doing there. The man says he just wanted to "be with somebody," so they invite him in to join in their deliberations. He accepts, takes his seat, and announces a new regime, effective immediately, of prayers, grey overalls, and the prohibition of boutonnieres and nose rings.

Absurd though the details of the story are, anyone who has endured certain kinds of meetings will recognize the principle at its heart: the most outlandish things can be accepted if they appear to be offered seriously. On another level, of course, Barthelme is doing what an earlier humorist, Mark Twain, did in *The Mysterious Stranger.* In that story Twain argued that our fates are determined, that free will is an illusion, and that there is no guarantee that the good will be rewarded or the evil punished—the opposite is just as likely.

The difference between Mark Twain and Donald Barthelme is that Barthelme seldom seems interested in pursuing an idea far enough for it to be developed into any kind of philosophical system or statement, whereas Twain went perhaps too far in this direction. Rather, Barthelme is content to play with his notions, so that a consideration of his stories, in which character and idea are both relatively unimportant, will finally come down to a consideration of his style.

The most significant part of Barthelme's style is his love of words for their own sake. In the first story, "Our Work and Why We Do It" (which could be taken as cryptic autobiography) there is a list of typefaces which by itself assumes a kind of beauty; it is a kind of "found poetry," accidental but not the less delightful for that: "Annonce Grotesque/Compacta/Copper Black/ Helvetica Light/Melior Microgramma Bold Profil/Ringlet." Like Joyce, whom he greatly resembles in this way, Barthelme likes to coin words for their sounds as well as for satirical purposes: "aprickledee" being an example of the first, and "semiantire-prophetical" of the second. Sometimes the words are merely playful: "Stock options" becomes "ox stoptions." And sometimes they are exquisitely appropriate: a pathway where muggers lie in wait becomes a "lurkway."

As might be expected, Barthelme also has a perfect ear for clichés, which are sprinkled throughout his stories like so many lumps of coal: "vast underground parking garage," "many great Nashville personnel," a character who went "right through the middle of the line and never failed to gain yardage . . . he had a lust for life." In another writer, such as Sinclair Lewis or Evelyn Waugh, this kind of ear is used for satiric purposes, but Barthelme is not usually interested in satire, which is a corrective attack; he is satisfied simply to entertain, often by shockingly funny aberrations from the norm of language and human behavior.

There are many examples of shocking anomaly. To "Our Friend Colby" we may add "Rebecca," which begins "Rebecca Lizard was trying to change her ugly, reptilian, thoroughly unacceptable last name," and "You Are as Brave as Vincent Van Gogh," which concludes: "You should not have left the baby on the lawn. In a snowstorm. When we brought him inside, he was covered with dime-size bruises."

Paradox is also common: "Tiger (in "110 West Sixty-first Street") was a black artist who hated white people so much he made love only to white women"; the narrator in "The Captured Woman" notes that his violation of his captive "enables her to regard me very kindly." Sometimes the paradox is a simple matter of substituting conjunctions: "They were pleased *and* suspicious" where "but" makes syntactical sense. And sometimes the paradox is a matter of simple reversal: something flies through the window in the first story—"It is a note with a brick wrapped around it."

Ultimately, of course, Barthelme's stories constitute a denial of meaning. The title is "Amateurs," but it could just as easily have been "Philodendron" or "Yard Furniture" for all the relation it seems to have to the stories it heads. Most of the narrators are crazy, the stories are spun from moonbeams, and the language itself is frequently senseless. If these selections can be said to have any meaning, it may be the same sort of meaning that nonsense verse holds, with the same sort of appeal. By twisting the real into distorted, often comical shapes, Barthelme forces us to redefine what is in fact real—to realize that the "truth" which the philosopher Bergson is represented in one of the stories as having perceived is indeed "a hard apple, whether one is throwing it or catching it."

Anthony Arthur

Sources for Further Study

Hudson Review. XXX, Summer, 1977, p. 304.
New Statesman. XCIV, October 28, 1977, p. 591.
Observer. November 20, 1977, p. 29.
Publisher's Weekly. CCXII, October 24, 1977, p. 75.

AMEN

Author: Yehuda Amichai (1924–   )
Translated from the Hebrew by the author and Ted Hughes
Publisher: Harper & Row Publishers (New York). 110 pp. $7.95; paperback $4.95
Type of work: Poetry

A translation of Amichai's poetry which reflects his personal reaction to the state of war in Israel as well as his reactions to sex, Israel, people, religion, and life

Amen is a private yet universal prayer which the reader is privileged to overhear. It continues Amichai's sensitive response to love, war, and loss begun in *Poems,* his first collection translated into English by Assia Gutman in 1969. Another volume, *Songs of Jerusalem and Myself,* published in 1973 and translated by Harold Schimmel, contained selections from three volumes of Amichai's Hebrew poems. Finally, in 1977, the poet himself has translated his work, with the aid of Ted Hughes, so that his own voice, tone, and cadence come through. However, at times there are problems of phrasing which cause some awkwardness or ambiguity and problems of sound or rhythm. Despite these problems, however, *Amen* successfully echoes the restless soul of Yehuda Amichai.

Born in Würzburg, Germany, in 1924, Amichai emigrated with his family to Palestine in 1936. Since 1948 he has published poems, novels, and plays in Hebrew. He is highly respected and successful to the point of being often published in newspapers and read over the radio in Israel. Today he is Israel's leading contemporary poet and had also earned his place among contemporary world poets.

Amen is lyric poetry at its best. The restless soul of Amichai drives him to record the external, pathetic, and dark pictures of people in wartorn Jerusalem and the internal reactions of himself and others to being killed or torn apart by the war and its uncertainties. He is not full of anger or frustration, but three emotions do dominate his poetry: despair, love, and hope. In addition, the Jewish cultural heritage and religious background underlie each poem.

Poems like No. 34 of the cycle of "Patriotic Songs" and "The Candles Went Out" suggest that Amichai yearns for a rest or quiet time, but that his remembering will not allow this; he is possessed by the memories to record in poetry his very personal pain, loss, despair, love, and hope. Therefore, he writes intimately about sex, war, love, politics, and religion. In other autobiographical poems we get insights into the poet's relationship with his father, mother, grandfather, and grandmother: "The Song of My Father's Cheeks," "Letter of Recommendation," "My Father's Memorial Day," and "My Mother and Me." Yet, these are also insights into what it means to be a Jewish boy and man.

Many different kinds of love abound in *Amen*. Love of country, of self, of people, of war dead, of ancestors, of religious history, of women, and of sex is woven throughout the poems. The book begins with "Seven Laments for the Fallen in the War," and continues with "Patriotic Songs" and numerous love songs involving or describing women. Feelings of a lost love are interspersed with affectionate descriptions of Jerusalem, his home, war holidays, the Israeli landscape, or tourists. One of his most powerful poems is " 'Memorial Day for the War Dead,' " which, through poignant similes and metaphors, presents the image of Memorial Day as "bitter salt" as dressed up as "a little girl with flowers." The irony is that everything is "in three languages:/ Hebrew, Arabic, and Death." Amichai's strong metaphors in common, everyday language convey his message powerfully. In another poem, he says, "Sorrow is a heavy wooden board./ Tears are nails." The simplicity of diction heightens the comparisons and enables emotions to be explicitly stated. Furthermore, these are comparisons to which many people can relate whether they are in Israel or in another part of the world, and whether they are under war conditions or other stressful situations.

Another love, love for his father, is revealed in "Letter of Recommendation." In this poem his sense of humor is reflected; he can laugh at the constant threats of danger and disaster:

> On summer nights I sleep naked
> in Jerusalem on my bed,
> which stands on the brink
> of a deep valley
> without rolling down into it.

The humor here heightens the seriousness of the scar on his chest which is his letter of recommendation. However, he only wants to be recommended to his dead father whom he highly respected. The poem is a serious prayer asking God to wake his father gently on the Day of Resurrection because his father was a gentle man.

Flowing through the collection, sometimes in just a line of reference, sometimes in a simile or metaphor, and often in entire poems, is another form of love—erotic love. Sexual images continually appear in a wide range of encounters which are never completed or which have occurred but are terminated so that the separation causes longings to return. Even when the *persona* knows the loved one cannot be united again, the sexual longing is an arousal. For example, "Love Poem in California" is about longings the writer has for Diane, whom he is forbidden to love. It is one of the gentle, tender love poems, and it ends on the sensitive thought that "We shall be beautiful, each one separate." On the other hand, Amichai's love lost can also cause a violent reaction in him. In "A Dog After Love" the writer sends a dog after his lost love's present lover to "tear the/ Testicles of your lover and bite off his penis. . . ." Even humorous poems of sexual love appear. "Ideal Love," for example, in which the blowing of the ram's horn calls souls, eyes, navel, and emotions to a military line up, readying them for combat, comes under this category.

A second emotion which pervades much of the private thoughts of Amichai is despair; if he is not careful, the reader might think that it dominates the poetry.

For Amichai, Jerusalem is "an old, tired man . . . in which people move and wriggle like worms . . . because heavens are empty above." For him, Israel exists in a "sweet world soaked, like bread,/ in sweet milk for the terrible toothless God." Again, because of the effects of the war the solar system is out of kilter:

> The sun is circling round the earth. Yes.
> The earth is flat, like a lost, floating board. Yes.
> God is in Heaven. Yes.

So God is above, watching, but not doing anything to eliminate the losses and sufferings of Israel:

> Into God's closed book
> we shall be put, and there we shall rest
> to mark for him the page where he stopped reading.

Amichai does not leave the reader without an answer to this depressed state or without hope. Even though his poems are full of the human nature to become depressed in a world which never fulfills his longings for love and which brings death and destruction, Amichai admits in No. 6 of "Seven Laments for the Fallen Dead":

> Yes, all this is sorrow. But leave
> a little love burning, always,
> as in a sleeping baby's room a little bulb,
> without it knowing what the light is
> and where it comes from. Yet it gives
> a little feeling of security and silent love.

For Amichai, the Jewish belief that man is good and that something good will come from distress is dominant over his despair. The two tones go hand in hand throughout his poetry. Love and caring for others enables people to carry on their lives in a country where even the monument of the unknown soldier stands in enemy territory, where a man is buried in the sand in which he played as a child, and where a son looks older than his father. In "Quiet Joy" the "world is made beautifully and built/ For a good rest, like a bench in a park." Furthermore, even in his powerful description of Memorial Day, Amichai repeats that "Behind all this some great happiness is hiding." Even the title of the collection, *Amen*, reflects his resignation and hope rather than despair. Finally, the collection ends with a humorous description, "A Tall Girl and Very Precise" in order to leave the reader in high spirits.

In addition to being gifted at conveying the internal ravages of war on the people, Amichai is gifted with a keen eye for describing the external effects on the landscape and the people. Jerusalem is a dead city in which people move and wriggle like worms. "Jerusalem is a place where all remember/ that they have forgotten something/ but they don't remember what." But the worse destruction is of the people. "Mr. Beringer, whose son fell by the Canal, . . . has become very thin; has lost/ his son's weight." And in the Memorial Day parade a man whose son is dead "walks in the street like a woman with a dead embryo in her womb." Even the young girls wear "the coat of a soldier, discharged/ Or dead— by victory or defeat—/ In some worn-out war." In many of the poems the destruction of the people and the land combine. They are inseparable, for one affects the other. To be able to grasp the external and internal ravages of a wartorn country is an accomplishment indeed.

The poems are often short, but their messages are compact and powerful, the images vivid. However, often there are leaps from one association in the poet's mind to another which the reader must follow to comprehend. Sometimes these leaps are difficult, and the outcome is confusion for the reader who then misses the poignant conclusion. When one can follow these leaps, however, the outcome is dynamic. For example, "Letter of Recommendation" starts out laughing at constant, daily danger; leaps to the immediate present with a shout to the woman next to him; moves backward in time to thoughts about his gentle relationship with his father; and finally, requests God to

> let him be woken up
> gently and with love
> on the Day of Resurrection.

Yehuda Amichai's poetic voice is not only the voice of one man, but also the representative of the Jewish voice which speaks a universal message of despair and hope sealed together by love. Truly, *Amen* is a mine to which one returns to find new insights and treasures with each reading. Amichai has earned his international stature.

Carol B. Borowski

Sources for Further Study

Booklist. LXXIII, July 15, 1977, p. 1698.

Choice. XIV, October, 1977, p. 1068.

Library Journal. CII, July, 1977, p. 1508.

AMERICAN BUFFALO

Author: David Mamet (1947–   )
Publisher: Grove Press (New York). 106 pp. $2.95 (paperback)
Type of work: Drama
Time: The present
Locale: Chicago

A tense, provocative drama about three men planning the robbery of a valuable coin collection

Principal characters:
> DON DUBROW, a man in his late forties, the owner of "Don's Resale Shop"
> BOB, his young friend
> WALTER ("TEACH") COLE, a petty crook, Don's friend and associate

Ever since Samuel Beckett demonstrated with *Waiting for Godot* in 1954 that an intense exploration of a static situation, replacing the conventional causal plot, could not only be philosophically provocative, but dramatically exciting as well, the modern theater has been glutted with such "situational" or "metaphorical" plays, ranging in quality from unquestioned excellence to thorough mediocrity. Thus, the basic situation in *American Buffalo* has been exploited by a score of contemporary dramatists to the point that it has almost become a cliché.

Two or three men wait somewhere for something or to *do* something. While waiting, they fill the time with apparently aimless dialogue, act out their idiosyncrasies, and play "games" with themselves and their surroundings. Their concealed and not so concealed prejudices, dislikes, and perversities surface and clash with those of their associates; tension mounts as whatever they are waiting for fails to arrive or whatever they are to do becomes increasingly delayed, difficult, or unlikely. Eventually the conflicts either erupt into violence or near-violence (Harold Pinter's *The Dumb Waiter* or *The Caretaker*) or they simply unwind and dissipate (as in Beckett's *Waiting for Godot* or *Endgame*).

To present such a play in 1977, twenty-five years after *Waiting for Godot*, required audacity leavened with folly. Not only to succeed, but to do so with originality in a form that would seem to be dried up, requires an exceptional talent indeed. Echoes of the contemporary masters—especially Pinter—are present, of course, but Mamet's vision and vocabulary are his own and *American Buffalo* is as fresh and unique a product as any on the recent American stage.

The primary reason for Mamet's success is probably that, while Absurdist ideas and techniques have been in the dramatic atmosphere for more than two decades, attempts to harness it to the American experience have been largely unsuccessful, Edward Albee's periodic forays into the area notwithstanding. David Mamet is really the first dramatist to weld the force of the situational play to the American environment with a characteristically American rhythm and diction (although two other fine young playwrights, David Rabe and Sam

Shepard, have utilized absurdist materials quite effectively. Rabe's plays are, however, more conventionally experimental and essentially realistic, while Shepard's are wildly powerful in language and image, but generally lack the focus needed for a coherent theatrical experience).

As in all effective examples of the situational approach, the setting of *American Buffalo* is crucial. Mamet's three would-be felons wait and plan in Don's Resale Shop, a crowded, messy junk shop that becomes a metaphor for the lives of those characters that inhabit it. Its claustrophobic density suggests their narrow, trapped lives. The various objects that are piled and jammed aimlessly together are all bits and pieces of the American culture turned to worthless scrap. These "things" (the word takes on ominous connotations during the play) have little present value, but retain the dangerous capacity to stimulate the thoughts, false expectations, and absurd dreams of these three sad men who sit amidst the clutter.

It is not stretching the metaphor too far to see the characters themselves as "junk objects," as individuals outside society, whose only connection to it lies in those distorted expectations and fantasies it induces. Perhaps such vague hopes and unlikely dreams can even have a positive value in such lives as they blunt the dismal reality of the bleak present and negative future. But, given the stimulus that opens up a glimmer of real possibility—however far-fetched—to these longings, they can potentially provoke violence and destruction. This is the simple dynamic that animates *American Buffalo*.

Don Dubrow, middle-aged owner of the salvage shop, discovers a gem in his trash, or, rather, has it discovered for him. A well-dressed stranger walks into his shop, spots a buffalo-head nickel and, after a short negotiation, buys it for ninety dollars. This sudden, amazing profit awakens Dubrow to the possibilities of coins. With his young friend and helper Bob, an addict painfully trying to stay clean, Dubrow develops a crude plan to rob the dealer of his entire collection. Uneasy about his dangerous project, he mentions it to another friend and "business associate," Walter "Teach" Cole, a petty crook and second-rate gambler. Teach quickly convinces Dubrow that the job is too complex and risky for Bob and so replaces him as the would-be thief.

Thus, the play in many ways resembles Pinter's *The Caretaker,* but with an emphasis and twist that makes it distinctly American. As in the Pinter play, an ambiguous, subtle relationship between two men is threatened by the intrusion of a third male figure, a volatile, manipulative character who would use and then sacrifice the others to his own needs and desires. The pending crime, however, makes the conflict more than simple manipulation; it becomes a test of all the individuals concerned. It also establishes a social and psychological context for the play that is distinctly American (as Pinter's work is distinctively British).

The relationship between Dubrow and Bob is undefined, but strong. Dubrow clearly enjoys his dominance over the younger man, and Bob expresses no resentment as a dutiful, subservient "gofer." He has a real need, both practical and emotional, for the older man, although the precise nature of the need is not clear: father and son? Lovers? Both? It is hard to say, but, whatever it is, Mamet is able to suggest a real emotional bond between them with a minimum of verbiage.

Teach is the dynamic center of the play (as is Davies in *The Caretaker*), a volatile, self-pitying, grandiose paranoic, whose mounting frustrations and desperate manipulations increasingly threaten to explode into violence. He is also a catalog of American clichés, prejudices, anxieties, dreams, and hates. A small-time sneak thief and chiseler, Teach sees himself as the epitome of the American system and defender of free enterprise, which he defines as the freedom to do whatever one wants in order to make a quick profit. He refers to his petty thefts as "business enterprises," and sees the coin collection as his one shot for success. Thus, the play becomes a kind of parody of the American Dream story, the Horatio Alger tale of success which goes to those daring enough to recognize and seize that sudden opportunity when it appears. But all three characters are comically inept as thieves; they are clowns, but desperate clowns. The real driving force behind their potential crime is not greed, but fear and hatred; fear that they are indeed thorough failures, and hatred toward the coin dealer for his success, the apparent ease with which he makes money, his snobbishness, his lifestyle, the sexiness of his girl friend.

As Teach's bragging becomes more extreme, his fears, cruelty, and suppressed violence become more overt and dangerous. His hostility, especially toward the mild and inoffensive Bob, intensifies; his paranoic fears become more open—he quakes whenever a police car passes by; and his ridiculous incapacities, as well as his own awareness of them, become more blatant and desperate. His irritation sharpens when Dubrow decides to bring in another crook, a slightly more skillful thief-gambler named Fletcher, actually to steal the collection. Teach's desperation and paranoia are made concrete when he produces a gun, and after the whole project is aborted (when Fletcher is mugged and hospitalized), his rage strikes out at Bob. He gets the sudden delusion that the mugging is fake and that Bob and Fletcher have somehow managed to steal the coin collection out from under him.

Teach's violence is, of course, a product of his frantic attempt to preserve his ludicrous self-image as a skillful, respectable "businessman" whose lack of material success can be attributed only to bad luck. This one job is vital to both Teach and Don because it will prove that they are not the mediocre failures that, inside themselves, they know they are. Put to the final test it is obvious that they lack both the intelligence and the nerve to carry out the robbery; they can turn their hostility only towards each other. Don is actually relieved by Fletcher's mishap, which both aborts their plans and gives them an excuse for it. But Teach, forced to a final acceptance of his failure, cracks completely. After hitting Bob he goes on a rampage, shouting and raging around the junkshop.

But if Teach is thoroughly broken, Don and Bob are somewhat restored and their relationship is repaired. Of the three, only Bob was never actually absorbed into the "dream." His willingness to attempt the crime, as well as his disappointment at being replaced by Teach, was a product of his devotion to Don, not his greed. On several occasions he attempts to borrow money from both Don and Teach. Knowing of his drug problem, we assume he wants it for dope. But in the end he produces a buffalo-head nickel for Don which, we learn, he has purchased. Seeing how the previous coin has become a symbol for Don, he tries to replace it. This final act of love forces Don to see how distorted his perceptions and values had become and enables him to come to terms with his failure. Thus, a modicum of meaning and dignity is salvaged from the fiasco.

All of which may not sound like the sort of tragic insight that great drama is made of. Admittedly the three characters in this play are neither admirable nor likable, although both Don and Bob have redeeming qualities. But—and this may be the special power of such a play—the audience identifies not so much with the characters as with their situations. The world of Don's Resale Shop is not an especially pleasant one, but, as Mamet presents it, a very real one. We feel the frustrations and fears of the characters and we can understand their inarticulate and even foolish dreams. By reducing the conflict between them to the most basic primal urges (fear, greed, frustration), reinforced by powerful cultural myths, underscored by a vivid setting and reinforced by a potent, almost incantory speech (liberally sprinkled with four-letter words) that sounds like "authentic" Chicago dialect, but has a simplicity, repetitiveness, and rhythm that is closer to dramatic verse, Mamet is able to draw us into this barren, squalid, primitive world for an impressive and lasting dramatic experience.

American Buffalo won the Drama Critics Circle Award as the best American play of the 1977 season.

Keith Neilson

Sources for Further Study

Hudson Review. XXX, Summer, 1977, pp. 259–260.
Plays and Players. XXIV, June, 1977, p. 37.

ANDREW JACKSON AND THE COURSE OF AMERICAN EMPIRE, 1767–1821

Author: Robert V. Remini (1921–   )
Publisher: Harper & Row Publishers (New York). 502 pp. $15.00
Type of work: Biography
Time: 1767–1821
Locale: The United States

The first volume of a scholarly two-volume biography of one of the most important early American presidents

> *Principal personages:*
> ANDREW JACKSON, lawyer, judge, Tennessee politician, general
> RACHEL JACKSON, his wife
> WILLIAM BLOUNT, his early political friend
> JOHN COFFEE, his friend, business partner, and military associate
> AARON BURR, former Vice-President who led a conspiracy against the
>   United States government
> JOHN SEVIER, his early political rival
> JAMES MONROE, President of the United States, 1816–1824
> JOHN QUINCY ADAMS, U.S. Secretary of State during the Florida
>   conquest

Robert V. Remini is a Professor of History and Distinguished Professor of the Humanities at the University of Illinois, Chicago Circle. He is best known within the historical profession as a leading scholar of the Jacksonian Era. He has chronicled various aspects of Andrew Jackson's America, both as author and editor, in seven previous books. *Andrew Jackson and the Course of American Empire, 1767–1821* is the first volume of a two-volume biography of Jackson. With this work, Remini begins the first full-length scholarly biography of Jackson to appear in recent decades. The book is a signal work by a significant historian.

Andrew Jackson was born on March 15, 1767, the son of Scotch-Irish immigrant parents who had settled in the Waxhaw Settlement, South Carolina. He received his small amount of youthful education during the late 1770's. In 1780–1781 he served in the American Revolution, an experience marked by extreme difficulty; he was wounded, captured, and imprisoned. When released in an exchange of prisoners, his health had so deteriorated that he came down with the fearful smallpox, a disease that almost claimed his life. The tragedy was compounded by the 1781 death of his mother.

Yet, from these harried aspects of Jackson's youth emerged a man who would indeed be a towering figure in early United States history. After a brief career as a schoolteacher, Jackson studied law, and eventually became a licensed attorney. The legal profession gained for him entry into the world of the frontier courts, both as attorney and judge. More importantly, the law provided Jackson with significant opportunities to fulfill his single-minded ambition. He moved to Tennessee, where newer settlements meant opportunity for advancement, and became a gentleman in Tennessee society. He engaged (sometimes disastrously) in the massive land speculation that played such a key role in the Western territories, and he served Tennessee as representative and senator to the federal government. Like many other prominent Westerners, he was drawn into the famous Burr conspiracy, but he learned a valuable lesson when Burr's plot was unmasked—that Western interests could only be served with the backing of the United States.

To further those Western interests, which centered on elimination of the Spanish and Indian barriers to white American settlers, Jackson became an officer first in the Tennessee militia, later in the U.S. Army. He finally gained national prominence during the War of 1812. He conducted successful campaigns against the Creeks, and led American forces at the Battle of New Orleans. His victory at New Orleans assured him of a heroic place in American history. General Jackson was the winner in a climactic, epic battle during the war that fused American nationalism. National acclaim and gratitude were his. Jackson capped his military career during the years covered in this volume by "removing" major Indian groups from the old Southwest, and by securing Florida for the United States by invading that Spanish possession. Western interests had indeed been fulfilled, using the legitimate power of the Army.

Remini proves to be a historical traditionalist when constructing his description of Jackson's personality. He chooses not to employ any shaky theorizing from the recently developed field of psychohistory, although Jackson certainly is an inviting case to study. While acknowledging psychohistorical approaches in a footnote, Remini maintains the traditional approach to historical biography, by drawing his information from the extant primary sources. Readers will find little innovation in his study of Andrew Jackson's character. Remini describes—he does not theorize.

And Remini's descriptions of the Jackson personality are overly restrained to the point of distortion. The obvious profanity of Jackson's language is indicated, but Remini discreetly eliminates even low-key examples. In addition, Jackson's whiskey drinking is relegated to a footnote, except for vague references in the text. The author has stripped Jackson of a coarseness that was an essential part of the general's character.

Remini is more successful in presenting Jackson's boundless ambition, which was such a driving force in his early career. Remini also clearly shows Jackson's deliberate use of anger and rage (expletives deleted) to obtain the results he wanted. Feigned anger worked well in most situations, but real Jacksonian anger was not to be countered—nobody crossed Jackson when he had " 'shoot' blazing in his eyes." Yet, Jackson the firebrand had a strikingly different side to his personality, a side marked by genuine tenderness, warmth, and generosity. Remini reveals this aspect of the future president's makeup by quoting his letters to his wife and family, documents that show Jackson could be a truly gentle man. Remini also includes the story of an incident during the Creek War. While fighting what was clearly a war of extermination against his Indian foes, Jackson encountered an Indian infant in the arms of his dead mother on the battle site, and the destroyer of the Creeks adopted the baby boy. Remini satisfactorily presents the two sides of a personality which was complex, paradoxical, and contradictory.

Remini's volume is rich in the military history of the period. The battles of the Creek campaign, including the famous Battle of Horseshoe Bend, are reconstructed in vivid detail. The monumental Battle of New Orleans is given a properly expansive account, as is the campaign against Spanish Florida. In this respect, Remini contributes a significant, exciting book to the literature of military history through his study of a military man.

The author also unravels the evidence surrounding Rachel's date of divorce from a prior husband. Jackson and Rachel did begin a life together before she was legally divorced. Yet, the evidence suffered from the controversy about the divorce raised by Jackson's opponents during his presidential campaigns. Remini presents a reasoned account, outlines several alternative theories, and resolves this often-muddled question.

The biographer also includes useful geneological tables in the book, as well as maps which enhance the military accounts of the volume. The section of illustrations is well chosen.

The most significant contribution that Remini makes in this book lies in the realm of historical interpretation. He finds that the fortunes of Andrew Jackson and the early United States were clearly linked—that Jackson influenced for all time the direction and course of U.S. expansion on the North American continent. He demonstrates that Jackson was involved in the expansionist sentiments and politics that surged through the early American frontier areas. Indeed, Jackson's personal ambition placed him at the head of that movement. The War of 1812 proved to be crucial. Attempted expansion into the northern part of the continent—British Canada—never materialized, despite the fervor of "War Hawk" congressmen. Campaign after campaign was bungled by less-than-competent generals. After the Treaty of Ghent, which ended the war, the Canadian-United States border was finalized with the sole exception of "Oregon" in the extreme Pacific northwest. In effect, the War of 1812 and its aftermath barred United States territorial expansion to the north.

But the situation was very different in the old Southwest during the war. With Jackson at the head, the Army smashed organized Indian resistance to white American penetration and conquest. The Battle of New Orleans gave the United States its most important victory of the war. Jackson's postwar drive against Spanish Florida gained support in Washington. What Remini argues is that these Jacksonian triumphs set the course of future U.S. territorial expansion. While Canada was closed to American expansionism, the old Southwest was definitely open to U.S. advances. Jackson not only crushed the Indians, but broke the weak Spanish hold on Florida. Later, from his position of military strength, he negotiated huge cessions of Indian land to white American land speculators and settlers. After ending effective Indian resistance, Jackson "removed" the remnants of Indian settlements to territory west of the Mississippi River. United States territorial expansion would subsequently follow a westward rather than a northward path. The westward direction of American conquest was assured because victory against the "hated dons" and the "savages" had been demonstrated clearly and forcefully. Andrew Jackson had seen to that.

Edward A. Zivich

Sources for Further Study

Booklist. LXXIV, December 1, 1977, p. 596.
Christian Science Monitor. LXX, December 21, 1977, p. 19.
Kirkus Reviews. XLV, September 15, 1977, p. 1029.
Library Journal. CII, November 15, 1977, p. 2342.
New York Times Book Review. January 8, 1978, p. 9.
Publisher's Weekly. CXII, October 24, 1977, p. 70.

ANNE SEXTON
A Self-Portrait in Letters

Author: Anne Sexton (1928–1974)
Edited by Linda Gray Sexton and Lois Ames
Publisher: Houghton Mifflin Company (Boston). Illustrated. 433 pp. $15.00
Type of work: Letters
Time: 1928–1974
Locale: Newton Lower Falls and Weston, Massachusetts

A collection of the confessional poet's letters from 1948 to 1974 with editorial comment by her elder daughter and her close friend

> *Principal personages:*
> ANNE GRAY HARVEY SEXTON
> ALFRED MULLER SEXTON II, her husband
> LINDA GRAY SEXTON, her elder daughter
> JOYCE LADD SEXTON, her younger daughter
> ROBERT LOWELL, a poet, critic, teacher, and friend
> GEORGE STARBUCK, a poet, critic, and associate at Boston University
> W. D. SNODGRASS, a poet, critic, and friend
> STANLEY KUNITZ, a poet, critic, and friend
> JAMES DICKEY, a poet and critic
> C. K. WILLIAMS, a poet and friend
> MAXINE KUMIN, a poet, collaborator, and confidant

The hand that stilled the heart could not stifle the voice. Since Anne Sexton's suicide in 1974, the literary world has received a legacy in three posthumously published works. *The Awful Rowing Toward God* (1975) and *45 Mercy Street* (1976) complete her volumes of confessional poetry. But nothing has augmented her poetical gifts more than *Anne Sexton: A Self-Portrait in Letters* (1977) edited by Linda Gray Sexton, her elder daughter, and Lois Ames, her biographer. The letters themselves show the richness of Sexton's life as poet, critic, philosopher, friend, lover, wife, and mother. They show the complexities and difficulties of Sexton's playing all these roles in one brief lifetime of forty-six years.

Linda Gray Sexton, perhaps more than anyone else, knew her mother and shared her most intimate thoughts for twenty-one years. Linda was sometimes a mentor, sometimes a sounding board, often a cause for concern, but always an understander of "the language." This perception not only has made Linda Gray Sexton a poet in her own right, but it has made her a highly qualified editor of this collection.

Lois Ames, too, knew Anne Sexton well before her suicide. First introduced to her as Ames was searching for biographical information on Sylvia Plath, Ames became a correspondent, traveling companion, and confidante to Sexton, sharing the last nine years of her life. While Lois Ames and Linda Sexton's compiling this collection was obviously a "labor of love," it was more accurately an attempt to share with the literary world this very special woman with whom they were on such intimate terms.

The paradox of Anne Sexton's being so special is that in so many ways, she was so ordinary—a daughter anxious for parental approval, a mother delighted with and sometimes depressed by two daughters, a true wife (although she "loved" many people), a suburban housewife who pecked out the moments of her existence with two toddlers running in circles around her.

And yet, Sexton was far from ordinary. Her accomplishments include nine published volumes of poetry, a collection of letters, several children's books; the Pulitzer Prize in Poetry in 1967 for *Live or Die,* an honorary doctorate from Tufts University, Fairfield University, and Regis College; an honorary Phi Beta Kappa from Harvard and Radcliffe; a guest professorship at Colgate University; and a professorship at Boston University.

Sexton's friends and acquaintances are as extraordinary as her list of credits: Robert Lowell, George Starbuck, Maxine Kumin, Elizabeth Bishop, W. D. Snodgrass, Tillie Olsen, Anthony Hecht, Sylvia Plath, Ted Hughes, Louis Simpson, Kurt Vonnegut, Stanley Kunitz, and James Dickey. These people were among her best friends as well as her most severe critics. Vast numbers of letters attest to the special camaraderie Sexton shared with some, the special antipathy she had for others.

The attraction of Sexton is this unique blend of special and ordinary. She was the self-made woman who, with little "formal" education, was a professor at Boston University. She was simply a mother who found time to pour her soul into numerous volumes of poetry with children underfoot. She was a sharer of fragmentary thoughts and joys with those she loved and respected. She was open, very honest, and sometimes silly. Sexton was casual, conversational, and yet sometimes censorious simultaneously. This blend of so many polarities was the Sexton intrigue.

A large part of the Sexton mystique stems from her suicide itself, the constant wondering of "when" and "how," the desire to see precisely what went wrong and where. The mystique is the search through the letters and poems for clues to the tragedy of October of 1974. The end of *A Self-Portrait in Letters* is itself the answer. The suicide was deliberate, planned, a composite of many years of deciding on the tools. "But suicides have a special language./ Like carpenters they want to know *which tools.* They never ask *why build.*" ("Wanting to Die" from *Live or Die*).

And yet so much of Sexton's work is filled with life, a celebration of her own existence and the existence of others. Her letters are a testament to this. To a stranger in need of encouragement, a mental patient, Sexton writes, "So I say live, because of the sun, the dream, the excitable gift" ("Live" from *Live or Die*). Sexton observes life and blooming all around her and participates in that growth as in "Little Girl, My Stringbean, My Lovely Woman." "My daughter at eleven/ (almost twelve) is like a garden./ . . . where apples are beginning to swell./ . . . But what I want to say, darling,/ is that women are born twice." Not only is Sexton's love affair with death part of the intrigue, but so is her exuberant celebration of life.

These major themes of life and death are prevalent in her letters. While she rejoices at the rebirth of Linda and Joy at adolescence, the birth of eight Dalmatian puppies, the births of new collections of poems of W. D. Snodgrass *(Heart's Needle)* and C. K. Williams *(I Am the Bitter Name),* Sexton spends considerable time dwelling on the death of her mother ("The Division of Parts" from *To Bedlam and Part Way Back*), her father, Sylvia Plath, Joan Sexton, and herself.

Another major, related theme is illness, especially her own. Sexton gives detailed accounts of her hospitalizations for mental as well as physical problems: her dilation and curettage and her broken hip. She discusses her medication, Thorazine, which stifles her creativity and makes her sensitive to the sun she loves so much; her psychiatrists, Martin, Deitz, and Chase; and her close encounters with death. Many letters, especially those to closer friends such as Anne Clarke, a California psychiatrist introduced by Tillie Olsen, and W. D. Snodgrass, in early years, portray her deep depression and fears. Letters to Kayo Sexton written from Europe dwell on fears of being away from him, of not knowing what he is doing, of being in an unfamiliar environment. As Anne Sexton fluctuates between states of normalcy and illness, so her letters reflect it.

Many letters requesting love, encouragement, and help are inextricably bound to these mental states and represent another major motif in Sexton's correspondence. She begs for letters from her family to ease her loneliness as she tours Europe on a grant from the American Academy of Arts and Letters. She corresponds with James Dickey, hoping to learn the cause of his repudiation of her poetry. As books of poetry are about to be published, she writes to her poet-friends expressing anxiety, almost begging for reassurance that she is indeed a good writer. To unknown and known writers, she sends fan mail, the probable by-product of which is a complimentary letter in return. This is not to imply that she was ungenuine: she was totally honest, but also insecure.

Sexton was anxious about money, and her protests about her poverty become yet another prominent thread running through her correspondence. To George Starbuck she complains that she should be a full professor and not simply a lecturer at Boston University. To Thomas Alexander of Cape Cod Community College she comments that James Dickey received $900 for a poetry reading while she was offered $775. Sexton mentions that Houghton Mifflin pays her smaller advances than other poets and worries about a daughter ready to enter college. She argues with her psychiatrist, Dr. Chase, about a fee increase. This anxiety, too, contributes to her insecurity.

An additional major idea reappearing throughout Sexton's letters is that of faith. Her initial doubts are discussed with Brother Dennis Farrell, a fan from a California monastery with whom she developed a long relationship via letter. To Anne Clarke she writes "God? spend half time wooing R. Catholics who will pray *for* you in case it's true. Spend other half knowing there is certainly no

God." Sexton's ambivalence is evident as she expresses to Erica Jong the thought that no poem is written by any writer, no poem is singular, all is part of one vast poem written by God.

Sometimes Sexton is not so philosophical. Her thoughts are not of God, but of her swimming pool, her girls and summer camp, and her vacations with Kayo. She is just plain Mom. A significant amount of correspondence shows her in this role. She loves Linda, Joy, and Kayo. Letters are filled with the girls' antics and their importance to her. She advises them at camp by letter on every subject from birth control to psychiatric help. But always, Sexton's pet names, "Bobolink," "Linda Pie," "Joy Ball" hint at the extreme closeness of their relationships. Kayo, too, is "Boots" and she is his "Princess" and "Button." Theirs is a language of love and caring.

Life and death; her own illnesses; her need for love, encouragement, and help; her need for financial security; her reflections on God; and love of family are all major thrusts throughout Sexton's letters. Over and over again, through years of correspondence, these themes resound, reflecting her current mental, physical, emotional, and intellectual states. The abundance of major themes is suggestive of the variety of letters present in the collection.

The style of Sexton's correspondence, too, is varied. Letters are composed often of fragmentary sentences, sometimes incomplete in meaning. Ellipses follow many sentences, allowing the letter's recipient to supply the remainder. While this is sometimes difficult for the Sexton reader, it is not difficult for the Sexton friend who can predict her intimate thoughts. Letters to close friends rarely stay on a single subject or maintain an even tone. Their intent is to suggest Anne-sitting-at-her-typewriter-right-at-the-moment-talking-person-to-person, and they accomplish this goal. These familiar letters are filled with myriad misspellings and typographical errors, a Sexton stock-in-trade. Only after hiring a "girl Thursday" with money received from a grant do the letters become more readable to the outsider. Nevertheless, even dictated, the letters are still delightful.

To people with whom she has not yet established a correspondence, Sexton writes letters that are more complete and even in tone. She stays on a single train of thought more readily, but like in her letters to close friends she still reveals a significant portion of humor, love, respect, and craft. While these are the easier type of letter to read, they are not the more revealing.

The principal strength of this volume is that the correspondence does reflect Sexton's life intimately; the letters offer a look at her soul. Because they are chronologically arranged, one can see the progression of mental states, creativity, honors, love, and friendship. While the letters have been selected, they are in every sense complete, not even omitting details that are deprecatory or personal because these details are Anne Sexton. The goal of the editors is an objective presentation of Sexton's life and in this goal, they succeed. In addition, the reader is treated to a collection of photographs that spans Sexton's life, and can associate faces, names, and letters—the outcome of which is more personal interest and involvement in the volume.

An additional strength of *A Self-Portrait in Letters* is its inclusion of individual poems which greatly augment the text or serve to foreshadow a stage in the poet's life. For one who is not a Sexton reader, the poems are still sufficient to grasp the greatness of the poet. For one who is already familiar with her work, the poems recall the best of the best. The poetry is reprinted chronologically throughout the book of letters, and, juxtaposed with the letters, it becomes more meaningful.

Also accompanying the letters is thorough and excellent explanatory material that prefaces the major divisions of the book as well as some individual letters. When letters themselves do not reveal enough, Linda Sexton and Lois Ames supply the details, adding continuity to the volume. Hence, the reader does not get fragments, but a whole.

A further editing bonus is that Linda Sexton and Lois Ames have included in brackets within individual letters the titles of books in which specific poems being discussed are printed. This aids the Sexton researcher, as does the index, which is significant, comprehensive, and complete. It allows this collection to be a major text for students of confessional poets of the last three decades.

Linda Gray Sexton and Lois Ames have taken their craft seriously, a legacy they inherited from Anne Sexton.

> Writing a poem is a lonely thing, each word
> ripped out of us . . . and you know . . . and then
> later on the wrong things start to happen;
> you get to be fashionable or 'a new kind of
> orthodoxy' and the only way to prevent your-
> self from going sour or becoming an art climber
> is to go back to your desk.

Anne Sexton: A Self-Portrait in Letters has been back to the desk.

Carol Whyte Talabay

Sources for Further Study

Book World. November 20, 1977, p. E3.

Christian Science Monitor. LXX, January 12, 1978, p. 19.

National Review. XXX, January 20, 1978, p. 109.

New York Times. December 14, 1977, p. 57.

New Yorker. LIII, December 12, 1977, p. 206.

Time. CX, November 28, 1977, p. 124.

ANOTHER WORLD: 1897-1917

Author: Anthony Eden (1897-1977)
Publisher: Doubleday and Company (New York). Illustrated. 175 pp. $7.95
Type of work: Memoir
Time: 1897-1917
Locale: England, the Western Front

An account of Anthony Eden's childhood and experiences in World War I, as well as a tribute to the generation which suffered in the trenches of the Great War

Before his death in January, 1977, Anthony Eden composed a charming memoir of his earliest years and joined to it a sober rendition of his experiences as a young officer in World War I. The result, published posthumously as *Another World: 1897-1917*, offers an intimate glance at both the personal life of one of England's leading twentieth century politicians and an aristocratic way of life which is now as far in the past as the *Ancien Régime* of France. Eden's description of that life reminds one so much of Talleyrand's observation on eighteenth century France that it could be paraphrased to read, "No one who was not a member of the English upper class in pre-1914 Britain knows how sweet life can be." It was the catastrophe of World War I, along with more prosaic economic changes, which destroyed this world, and Eden is an example of how one of its most illustrious members faced the destruction of his civilization.

It is rare for a world leader to write with the tenderness and insight about his childhood which Eden does. When it happens, it is revealing about both the man and his country. In Eden's case it unveils a sense of humor, modesty, enthusiasm, innocence, discipline, and generosity. In fact, he comes across as an extremely sympathetic person. Those with an inclination to view life cynically might regard him as a bit of a do-gooder, while his stiff upper lip in the face of enormous personal and national loss appears almost inhuman, but all in all Sir Anthony Eden was one of the most natural and sensitive men ever to achieve supreme political leadership. The fact that a man with such qualities could be rewarded with the highest office of his country attests to the continuing English tradition of emphasizing human values as much as sheer power.

Eden's political career was not uniformly successful, and to his permanent disgrace, he left office in the wake of the humiliation of the forced retreat from Suez in 1956. The triumphs, though, outnumbered the defeats. Entering Parliament in 1923, he made a mark with his speeches on foreign policy and was soon rewarded with sub-Cabinet governmental positions. From this vantage point, he was able to participate in European diplomacy in the 1930's, building up a formidable expertise and firsthand contact. When Stanley Baldwin appointed him Foreign Secretary in 1935, he became the youngest man to hold that office since the eighteenth century.

Diplomacy in the 1930's was extremely contentious business, with unsavory Fascist dictators strutting on the stage, small East European states bickering about their borders, an uncertain and threatening Communist regime in Russia, and civil war in Spain. Eden's constant exposure to this mixture convinced him that England must stand firm and deal from strength, although he was not opposed to all negotiation. When Neville Chamberlain became Prime Minister and began acceding to the demands that Mussolini and Hitler were making without receiving any *quid pro quo,* his Foreign Secretary disagreed vehemently and resigned in protest in February, 1938. This was Eden's finest hour, and Winston Churchill later wrote, "he seemed to me at this moment to embody the life-hope of the British nation."

Eighteen months later, after war had broken out, Eden rejoined the cabinet. With Churchill's appointment as Prime Minister, he was elevated to Minister of War and then Foreign Secretary again. In this position, he worked extremely closely with the often irascible Churchill, and for six long years devoted himself heroically to the defense of his country. He fully supported the Prime Minister's emphasis on the American alliance, smoothed the path to wartime cooperation with the Soviet Union, and then tempered Churchill's enthusiasm for his Eastern ally as its postwar ambitions became more apparent. He was also instrumental in bringing France back into the war as a full-fledged member of the alliance. By all accounts, Sir Anthony was a gifted diplomat, and even figures as difficult to deal with as Charles de Gaulle paid him tribute.

The elections of July, 1945, brought the Labor party to power, and Eden stayed in opposition until the Conservatives came back in 1951. With Churchill still in command, Eden returned to the Foreign Office. From 1951 to 1955, he showed a deft hand by outwaiting the anti-British Mossadegh in Iran, re-negotiating with the Egyptians, and helping to terminate the French war in Indochina. In April, 1955, he became Prime Minister after Churchill turned the government over to him.

The complex Middle East situation grew more tangled in 1955 when the newly emergent Nasser signed an arms deal with Czechoslovakia. To retaliate, the United States and Great Britain withdrew their offer to fund the Aswan Dam project and Nasser in turn struck back by nationalizing the Suez canal in July, 1956. The canal was a vital link for British oil supplies and trade with India and the Far East; it was as sensitive an issue for Britain as the Panama Canal has been for the United States. In addition, drawing on his experience from the 1930's, Eden equated Nasser with Hitler and believed that a refusal to act would lead to a collapse of Britain's position in the world. As a result, he joined France and Israel in an attack on the Canal in October, 1956, but the hostility of the Superpowers forced all three to withdraw their forces. Faced with a recurrent intestinal illness, Eden resigned in January, 1957. In this way, the distinguished career of a statesman known for his morality and contributions to peace ended unhappily.

In *Another World: 1897-1917,* Sir Anthony Eden, Earl of Avon, returns to his childhood and young manhood and provides the background which places his years of political activity in perspective. His heritage was uncommon. On his father's side, the Edens had been landowners in County Durham for four centuries, a remarkable achievement which made Anthony feel the responsibility of upholding a tradition which would be tested during his lifetime more severely than at any point since the Napoleonic Wars. The Edens were no ordinary landowners, and their manor, Windlestone, was an enormous nineteenth century mansion situated in a beautiful park. Having the run of such a place was a delight to a young boy, and he describes in detail its world. Sir William Eden, Anthony's father, genuinely headed a small kingdom, with its numerous tenant farmers, laborers, woodsmen, craftsmen, blacksmiths, gardeners, and keepers of the stables and hounds. The agent who took care of financial matters was himself the brother of an Admiral, and there was an intimidating second-in-command who directed the foxhunts among other duties. The household staff, too, was quite an affair, with valets, cooks, butlers, chauffeurs, maids, nannies, and the governess "Doodles." His mother's side had the political connections. She was a Grey; her father had been Governor of Bengal; his uncle was the celebrated Lord Grey who had passed the Great Reform Bill of 1832, while Edward Grey, Foreign Secretary at the outbreak of World War I, was his mother's cousin. Reared in this environment, there could have been no doubt in Anthony Eden's mind about what the future might hold for him.

Yet, somehow, it did not go to his head. For one thing, his father was an unusual and apparently difficult man. He was an artist who spent much of his time buying paintings, and he frequented a set including the novelist George Moore and the painter Walter Sickert. He paid very little attention to his four sons and made Anthony feel that he was "a plodder of conventional ability and tolerable good looks, taking after my mother's family and not very exciting." Lady Eden, a beauty, also had trouble relating to her children. She was a believer in duty, founding a local hospital, visiting the tenants, and supporting old soldiers with generous gifts. Educated at Eton, Anthony Eden certainly enjoyed the best England could offer—wealth, connections, culture, and a moral sense of purpose. While he may not have received all the love he could have wanted, he was a happy child, close to his younger brother Nicholas and entranced by the world.

In the summer of 1914, though, war swept across Europe, and Eden, along with millions of other Englishmen, responded to the challenge with exemplary courage. His eldest brother, Jack, was killed in October, 1914, and Nicholas, only sixteen, went down with his destroyer at the Battle of Jutland. Anthony's third brother, Timothy, was interned in Germany the length of the war and his only uncle, Robin Grey, was shot down and put into solitary confinement because he was the cousin of the foreign secretary. To add to the family's bereavement, Sir William Eden died in 1915. (Anthony Eden's oldest son died in action in World War II.)

Such tragic loss is overwhelming, and one can only admire the stoic determination which animated men such as Eden. The second half of his short volume depicts the war as he knew it. World War I remains the pivotal historical experience of twentieth century Europe, and *Another World: 1897-1917* may be one of the last firsthand accounts of it which will be written. Although Eden's description does not have the demonic force of Robert Graves's *Goodbye to All That,* it does not minimize the brutality, confusion, and slaughter which were the hallmarks of the conflict. As befits a statesman, however, Eden brings some order to the telling of the experience.

The author left Eton a year early in the summer of 1915 to become an officer. in a regiment. The following spring his platoon was sent to Flanders, where it was decimated in the battle of the Somme. Re-formed by new recruits, it spent a year in the trenches, where Eden participated in the Messines attack under General Plumer. He received the Military Cross for the rescue of a wounded comrade in no-man's-land, and in May, 1917, he was promoted to the staff at Second Army headquarters. For the most part, life at the front was a tedious routine, with the constant threat of death from snipers and shells, and combat restricted to risky patrols at night into no-man's-land. Once every six months or so the great offensives would be organized with hundreds of thousands of troops attacking the enemy lines. These were the periods of complete hell, when in a matter of days, if not hours, the strength of a company might be halved or worse. Like most in his generation, Eden felt the comradeship of arms strongly, calling it "the finest form of friendship." The war taught him the irrelevance of class distinctions; it tempered him, but left his illusions intact.

Eden's background, with its artistic as well as political influences, plus its infusion of duty, helped produce the morally upright, sensitive, and self-assured statesman who directed British foreign policy for two decades. It was the strength of his own character, though, which enabled him to withstand the shocks of World War I and emerge from it with a continued belief in the value of civilization and a readiness to lead the fight for it twenty years later.

Stuart Van Dyke, Jr.

Sources for Further Study

Booklist. LXXIV, November 1, 1977, p. 456.
Kirkus Reviews. XLV, September 15, 1977, p. 1021.
Library Journal. CII, November 15, 1977, p. 2337.
New Republic. CLXXVII, December 17, 1977, p. 28.
New York Times Book Review. November 27, 1977, p. 18.
Publisher's Weekly. CXII, October 3, 1977, p. 87.

ANPAO
An American Indian Odyssey

Author: Jamake Highwater
Publisher: J. B. Lippincott Company (Philadelphia). Illustrated. 256 pp. $8.95
Type of work: Folklore
Time: From the beginning to the present
Locale: North America

The story of Anpao, who wanders in search of his heritage so that he may attain wisdom and marry the maiden he loves

> *Principal characters:*
> WASICONG, a holy man who tells the story
> ANPAO, an Indian boy who cannot remember his origins
> KO-KO-MIK-E-IS, the girl he wishes to marry
> OAPNA, Anpao's twin brother and mirror image; the other half of himself
> THE MOON, estranged wife of the Sun
> THE SUN, who loves beautiful women and has spoken for Ko-ko-mik-e-is
> OLD MAN, creator of the visible universe
> GRANDMOTHER SPIDER, who raised Anpao and Oapna
> AMANA, a girl who saves Anpao's life
> RAVEN, from whose people came the deer and buffalo
> MORNING STAR, child of the Sun and the Moon
> SMALLPOX, a missionary who brings death to the people
> THE BIG KNIVES, who come from the east

Western civilization has long since lost its most basic heritage. Several thousand years ago the precursors of that civilization still lived in harmony with their universe and were as much an integral part of it as the stars or the grass. As millennium succeeded millennium and Western culture became more and more urbanized, giving greater attention to technological advancement, the links with origin were gradually severed. The universe required more interpreters and its interpreters became of necessity more sophisticated; in time it assumed an adversary role and was no longer a mystery to contemplate but a puzzle to be solved—and an entity to conquer as well. Mere acceptance of it was no longer possible.

Western man continues to invent tools of astonishing complexity in his search for final answers, but the universe tends to ignore him. Each solution has to be discarded in its turn and ultimate understanding remains elusive. That cheerfully iconoclastic observer of scientific achievement, Charles Fort, once observed that looking for a final answer to anything is like searching for a needle that was never lost in a haystack that isn't there. The essential truth of his remark is becoming more obvious to us. Although our endless research has brought about a vast increase in knowledge and material benefits, its dividends in terms of wisdom and human happiness are relatively obscure. Each fresh discovery carries with it the dual potential of technical advancement and widespread disaster; these dilemmas have proliferated until Western man finds himself living in a world of perpetual crisis, with his survival resting in precarious balance on a razor's edge of human frailty. It is a vicious circle from which he cannot escape.

This position is rendered more intolerable by long alienation from the need to live in harmony with a surrounding universe, and modern man now finds himself without an anchor. Religion, undermined by various discoveries, no longer affords the authority and support he once depended upon; and in many cases the replacements he has devised have closed the door to that refuge with grim finality. Modern man has become a stranger in his own universe, and he is homeless in the truest sense of the word. It is no wonder that loneliness and isolation are the demons that torment him.

Until quite recently, Western man has described those cultures which developed along lines other than his own as primitive. This is a misnomer, for all cultures are complex and highly developed, regardless of the course their development may have taken. While it is true that the effect of Western civilization upon cultures it considered primitive was often calamitous, verifying an obvious technological advantage, it has become evident to us that they were not inferior in any other way. It has also become increasingly clear that inheritors of Western culture are not as happy, or perhaps as fortunate in the human sense, as those of the cultures it has destroyed or assimilated. These vanishing peoples were consciously an integral part of a sentient and harmonious universe: they belonged to one another and to everything around them. Western man belongs only to himself or to his sociopolitical group and suffers from feelings of inadequacy; he has rejected the ancient concepts so long ago that he can no longer understand the nature of such cultures, though he envies them even as he destroys them.

In spite of the extent to which they have suffered at the hands of those who gradually conquered them, the Indians of what is now the continental United States were fortunate in many ways. They never found it necessary to concentrate themselves in urban developments or to organize themselves on a large scale; their technology was adequate for survival and for their social requirements; their warfare was limited and was a game that never proliferated into wholesale slaughter as we know it today. Their social organization had its catalog of restraints, codes, binding traditions, and customs, but they enjoyed a high level of personal freedom. Of greatest importance was their close relationship to the world around them. This link with the infinite has never been broken, although the destructive pressures of a civilization that has overrun their own are making inroads more and more difficult to resist.

Although the culture of the American Indian has had many recorders and interpreters among non-Indians during the past five centuries, such efforts have been in many ways inadequate. The author of a recent book on Frederic Remington states that the artist was a bigot, principally because Remington remarked that the white man would never understand the Indian. This is the sort of gratuitous accusation currently fashionable in intellectual circles, and it reveals an ignorance of both artist and subject. Remington's conclusion was both perceptive and honest, and any Indian would have agreed with him. He admired and respected the Indian for qualities of strength, intelligence, competence, and courage; that attitude is reflected in his work, for his portrayals of Indian warfare are graphic and impersonal, and when he shows us the Indian in defeat, he does so with implied compassion or regret. The same author goes on to mention other white artists who have studied Indian culture exhaustively and to equate their work with genuine understanding, but this is erroneous. Appreciation, admiration, and respect it is and should be; understanding, it is not.

It is never really possible for the inheritors of one culture to understand those of another. The effort to do so is of necessity superficial, however intensive or dedicated it may be. Hearn so steeped himself in Japanese culture that he considered himself to all intents and purposes a Samurai, but no authentic Samurai would have been deceived for a moment. The accumulated nuances of millennia are not assimilated in a decade or two. Eliot and James, endeavoring to be more British than the British, had the advantage of a partially shared heritage but even so were not entirely successful. Such assumed identities are at best an illusion. White men who lived with the Indians, intermarried with them and were adopted into the tribes, were accepted but never made any pretense that they were really a part of the culture. They enjoyed and appreciated the lifestyle and they learned a certain wisdom from it, but that was all.

If true understanding of the American Indian and his world is not entirely possible for outsiders, the reasonable approximation afforded through enjoyment and appreciation is well within our capabilities; and the best approach to any culture, if our goal is at least a partial understanding of the people themselves, is through its literature. This is the key to an entire heritage, and if the literary tradition is an oral one, it contains little that may be regarded as insignificant. The American Indians never found it necessary to develop a true written language, and the art of storytelling was an important part of their education. Although each gifted storyteller developed an individual style, the stories themselves remained essentially intact from one generation to the next; as in the case of Icelandic saga, everyone in the audience knew each tale by heart, and the teller was corrected if he strayed from accepted fact. Oral traditions of this kind often produce a people notable for the beauty and eloquence of their formal speech, and many white men have paid tribute to the oratorical and poetic powers of the Indian.

Ideally, one who interprets a literature should belong to those who produced it and should also be educated in the culture of those for whom it is being interpreted. Jamake Highwater is eminently qualified for such a task. His own tribal heritage is Blackfeet and Cherokee, and his degrees in cultural anthropology and comparative literature provide him with a broad basis for intercultural communication. An added bonus is the fact that he is a superb storyteller in his own right.

Anpao is a good collection of the traditional tales, retold by Highwater and arranged in roughly chronological order from ancient to modern. They are linked by the character Anpao, whose pilgrimage serves as a narrative thread which ties the stories together. Anpao is Highwater's own creation, but is so skillfully employed that he is not perceived by the reader as a superimposition. The tales themselves include samples of various literary categories, ranging from theology to history to humor; they are told with freshness and enthusiasm, and to read them is a delightful experience.

Highwater has provided a brief essay in the form of an appendix, entitled "The Storyteller's Farewell," which should be read first as an introduction to the tales. Although not necessary for enjoyment, it is essential to full appreciation of their significance and forms a very necessary bridge. In addition to discussion of sources and some evaluation of earlier collections, Highwater explains a number of elements that would otherwise be puzzling to the general reader. He also points out the impropriety of describing traditional literature as myth, a term that connotes lack of authenticity or presupposes an inferior spiritual concept.

The reader of *Anpao* will immediately recognize that sense of oneness with the total environment which has already been noted. To the Indian, the universe and all things in it are alive and sentient; all are closely related and there is communication between them. Most of the people Anpao meets during his journey are personalities who wear the forms of various animals, although some appear as natural forces. These entities provide him with knowledge, assistance, entertainment, and wisdom: through their guidance he traces the heritage of his people and, in the end, achieves his destiny and wins his heart's desire.

Most memorable of all the tales, perhaps, is that of the Creation. Old Man, who builds the visible universe, is not quite the great spirit who pervades all things but rather its focal point. He is motivated by curiosity and delighted with the things he invents, being both artist and experimenter, and he is not immortal. He ages as he continues to create, and many of his discoveries are accidental— among them death. His love for all creatures could not be better exemplified than in the special honor he confers upon that humblest of waterfowl, the coot.

Some of the stock characters in Indian literature have their counterparts in the folklore of other cultures, as might be expected. The most notable and amusing of these is Coyote, the wily and clever rogue who shares obvious affinities with Reynard the Fox. Coyote does not always fool the other person but he always makes the attempt; and even when the joke is on himself, Coyote remains optimistic and irrepressible.

Literature of the American Indian is an important part of our national heritage and deserves to be much more widely known and studied than it is. The work of Jamake Highwater will do much to correct that deficiency. He has already provided important bridges to other aspects of Indian culture: his first widely acclaimed book, *Song from the Earth,* explored contemporary Indian art and artists; a second major contribution, *Ritual of the Wind,* surveyed Indian music, ceremony, and dance. He has also published articles in various magazines. *Anpao* is an equally important introduction to the rich treasury of Indian literature and will, it is to be hoped, constitute the first volume of a series. In addition to its other merits, the book is handsomely and appropriately illustrated by the well-known Luiseno artist Fritz Scholder; however, the reader will wish that more of Scholder's artwork had been included.

It is not surprising that interest in American Indian culture is growing steadily among non-Indians, particularly the younger generation. Many, reacting to the pressures of a civilization that is increasingly less human, search for simpler and more natural ways to live. That they should investigate Indian crafts and lifestyles, and find them compatible, is not surprising. Perhaps in time they will even regain an approximation of that intimacy with the universe their culture enjoyed in the beginning, but abandoned so long ago.

Although understanding may never be complete, it can be much closer than it has been in the past. If Jamake Highwater continues his efforts and others take up the challenge he has provided, a much closer bond between the two peoples, red and white, may not be far away. The bridges are being built; if all are as revealing and as rewarding as this one, the traffic over them can only increase.

John W. Evans

Sources for Further Study

Catholic Literary World. XLIX, December, 1977, p. 235.
Booklist. LXXIV, November 15, 1977, p. 542.
Kirkus Reviews. XLV, October 1, 1977, p. 1053.
School Library Journal. XXIV, October, 1977, p. 124.

ANTONIN ARTAUD

Author: Martin Esslin (1918–   )
Publisher: Penguin Books (New York). 148 pp. $2.95
Type of work: Biographical and critical study
Time: 1896–1948
Locale: France

An examination of the life and works of Antonin Artaud, the French actor and theatrical theorist, best known for his essays on The Theater and Its Double

This slim but engaging volume on Antonin Artaud is the most recent addition to Martin Esslin's essays on modern theater, which include his well-known treatise on *The Theatre of the Absurd,* as well as studies of Bertolt Brecht, Samuel Beckett, and Harold Pinter. In his approach to Artaud, Esslin leans heavily toward biography because of his stated intention of placing Artaud's theatrical theories and activities "within the wider framework of his importance as a cult figure, a revolutionary force, and a unique psychological case history." Generally, Esslin effectively relates Artaud's life to his work and almost manages to convince the reader that this man, whose life was marked by failure and madness, was uniquely important precisely because of his ability to exploit his madness and turn his suffering and failure into a form of art.

Artaud's enterprises, encompassing a broad range of activities and fields, leave a detailed picture of his life, mind, and soul. Esslin repeatedly speaks of the two most poignant visual images we have of Artaud: first, the young actor's face as the sensitive monk in the film *La Passion de Jeanne d'Arc,* and then the much later self-portrait which shows the ravaged face of an aging and suffering Artaud. Having been largely dependent on acting for his means of support, Artaud played many minor roles in films which leave visual images of him for posterity. Besides these images, there are tape recordings, Artaud's own play scripts, theoretical writings on theater and language, poetical texts, and voluminous correspondence; all combine to provide such a striking portrait and such an abundance of information about the man, that Artaud has become the perfect subject for various cults to adopt as their central theme or symbol. Esslin indicates that Artaud's personality, more than his writings (which, moreover, tend to be contradictory), has been seized upon by diverse groups and movements, anxious to find a saint or hero-figure. Yet, whether his image is borrowed by Catholics or left-wing rebellious students, Artaud apparently strove consciously to develop his image, an incarnation of suffering. As he said to a fellow actor in 1948, "Tragedy on the stage is not enough for me, I am going to carry it over into my life."

The longest and seemingly most important chapter of Esslin's study is entitled "The Road to Rodez" because it traces the major outlines of Artaud's troubled career and progressively weakening mental health up to his stay in the asylum at Rodez, the last of several asylums where he had been confined. The detailed accounts of Artaud's more bizarre hallucinations, found in both this chapter and the chapter "Master or Madman," paint a far more impressive picture of Artaud the madman than Artaud the genius. One tends to be so thoroughly convinced of Artaud's insanity that certain of Esslin's statements become difficult to accept. One of the most notable claims is:

> Seen in retrospect Artaud's life falls into a pattern and becomes, as he himself so often proclaimed, his supreme work of art. There is an inner logic and consistency in his creation of his youthful image in films like *La Passion de Jeanne d'Arc* to provide a stunning and heart-rending contrast with that of the wizened martyr of society's rejection and contempt which became the image of his final epiphany.

One might wonder if a man like Artaud, who at times believed he was being poisoned by the sperm and excrement of the entire world (or who claimed to strike lightning from St. Patrick's cane outside of the *NRF* offices in Paris) was capable of lucidly ordering his life in the logical fashion Esslin suggests. It seems a bit exaggerated to intimate that Artaud had the foresight to project an image in his youth that would contrast so nicely with his image in middle-age.

More likely, Artaud's public image and notoriety were partially shaped by accident and the historical moment in which he lived. Because he was an artist and a troubled genius, his particular case became a *cause célèbre* and provoked much discussion about the relationship of society and madness, as well as a reevaluation of psychiatric care. Yet it seems doubtful that Artaud had any control over, for instance, his electric shock treatment; simply, he was subjected to it because such treatment was a fairly common psychiatric practice at that moment in history. Chance and history had as significant a role in the formation of Artaud's fate as the man himself.

Indeed, one of the most exciting aspects of this book is the vivid impression it conveys of the historical era which Artaud's life spanned. One often senses that Artaud was placed at the crossroads of French art and thought during the first half of the twentieth century. His first success as a writer grew out of his correspondence with Jacques Rivière, an important figure in the lives of many modern French writers since he edited the *Nouvelle Revue Française,* France's major literary organ. (What Rivière eventually published was not the poems Artaud had originally sent him but the letters in which Artaud explains his difficulties in capturing his thought in language.) Many other famous names which are woven into the tapestry of Artaud's story come from diverse areas of French life—such as the feminist writer, Anaïs Nin (with whom Artaud fell in love), or Jean-Louis Barrault, one of the major French actors of this century, who put many of Artaud's theatrical theories into practice. While officially a member of the surrealist movement and contributing to its various publications, Artaud was in close contact with the major surrealist writers, such as André Breton and Paul Eluard. Finally, the list of those who worked for Artaud's release from the asylum at Rodez reads like a French *Who's Who* of twentieth century artists and writers: Arthur Adamov, Pablo Picasso, Alberto Giacometti, Georges Braque, André Gide, and Jean-Paul Sartre, to mention a few.

The two chapters in which Esslin treats the more positive and impressive aspects of Artaud consider two of his major contributions: his thoughts on language and, most importantly, his theories on the theater. While some of Artaud's ideas about language have been developed by several French poets since Stéphane Mallarmé (a point which Esslin omits discussing), Artaud exemplifies modern man's painful awareness of the limits of language, his fears of verbal inadequacy, and his basic mistrust of language. This mistrust of the articulate forms of expression led Artaud to seek out new languages for the theater (languages based on body movement, breathing, costume, music, and inarticulate cries) to transmit human emotions and provoke emotional responses within the spectator.

Artaud sought to invent a "theater of cruelty" whereby the audience would undergo a profoundly moving experience which would release the hidden, subconscious, as yet unverbalized emotions that centuries of rationalism have taught man to repress. Theater would return to its origins in religious ritual and would perform acts of "magic" upon the human psyche. (It is surprising that Esslin makes no reference to Aristotle's theory of the cathartic function of theater since he goes to great lengths to indicate other influences from Artaud's Greek background.) In the long run, Artaud believed that new forms of theater held a revolutionizing potential for transforming mankind and the world. It would have been interesting if Esslin had elaborated on this point in greater detail.

Although Artaud himself was generally unsuccessful at implementing his theories, his influence on the theater has been widely felt: for example, in American *avant-garde* theater (such as Julian Beck's Living Theater) and in memorable productions such as Peter Brook's interpretation of Peter Weiss' *Marat/Sade*. The few pages that Esslin devotes to noting Artaud's influence on the theater and cinema are useful in understanding his importance as an innovative thinker. Particularly insightful is Esslin's observation that Artaud may have instituted the modern-day phenomenon known as the "happening."

But perhaps Artaud's greatest contribution is his recognition that, as Esslin formulates it:

> . . . the spirit of rationalism, analytic and discursive thought, formal logic, and linguistic pedantry [has] desiccated the fullness of Man's emotional life and cut him off from the profound sources of his vital being. . . .

This constitutes the one constant in Artaud's life and work, the direction of his revolutionary impetus, and the possible explanation of how a madman can also be called a "master."

One might wish that Esslin had further elaborated the reasons behind Artaud's reputation as an artist or thinker and concentrated more on his works and real achievements in theatrical innovation. Too many pages deal with Artaud's weaknesses, and much time is spent exposing and apologizing for his failures. Esslin's primary goal appears to be a portrayal of the martyred Artaud who, during the French student rebellion of 1968 (twenty years after his death), became a symbol of the nonconforming individual misunderstood by society and crushed by it. Apparently the reader is supposed to identify Artaud with Vincent Van Gogh, the troubled nineteenth century painter whom Artaud so staunchly defended. Yet it is not the bouts of madness which made Van Gogh famous, but his artistic accomplishments. Therefore it is unfortunate that this extremely readable book on Artaud, which serves as a fine introduction to his life and thought, is less concerned with proving his positive contributions than describing his life and depicting his personality. Whether it is because of his intent to explain Artaud's importance as a cult figure or because of a certain disorganization in the telling of his story, Esslin assigns to the reader much of the task of searching out and recovering those elements which actually manifest Artaud's genius. Surely it is not enough to say that Artaud's final achievement was that his own life embodies his concept of "Theater as the double of Life and Life as the double of Theater" or that his dramatic and tragic story resembles an artistic creation.

Lois A. Dahlin

Sources for Further Study

Booklist. LXXIV, November 1, 1977, p. 459.
Library Journal. CII, April 15, 1977, p. 924.
New York Times Book Review. July 17, 1977, p. 20.

ARREST SITTING BULL

Author: Douglas C. Jones (1924–   )
Publisher: Charles Scribner's Sons (New York). 249 pp. $8.95
Type of work: Novel
Time: December, 1890
Locale: Standing Rock Indian reservation, North Dakota

A novel which explores the nature of nineteenth century Indian and white violence, and the catalysts that incited it

> *Principal characters:*
> SITTING BULL, medicine chief of the Hunkpapa Sioux and veteran of
>   Little Bighorn
> JAMES MCLAUGHLIN, career Indian agent in charge of Standing Rock
> WILLA MAE FAVORY, schoolteacher at Standing Rock day school
> STANDING ELK, a bright young agency policeman

Douglas C. Jones is the author of two earlier books, a factual work, *The Treaty of Medicine Lodge,* and a historical fantasy, *The Court-Martial of George Armstrong Custer.* In his current work he combines the meticulous research of the historian displayed in his first book with the literary flair and pace of his fantasy, to create the best kind of historical novel. Jones is a professional artist and journalist; these disciplines serve him well as he reconstructs each ambience with the eye of the artist and the ear and voice of the journalist—a happy amalgamation of talents.

Jones builds a flawless novel around the nucleus of the arrest of the recalcitrant Sitting Bull, the Sioux leader in the last days of the white man's war with the Indian. He molds, polishes, and defines characters who spin around the central act of the arrest, each personality a clear, believable part of the whole, each adding his bit of energy to the relentless vortex that is pulling a people toward disaster. The incidents fit neatly into the total story; each is a carefully measured and complete statement, adding to the plot as closely as stones mesh in a flagstone walk. The themes of displacement, alienation, ambition, frustration, rebellion, acculturation, and loyalty are dealt with realistically and with remarkable insight.

Billed on the dust jacket as a "spine-chilling novel of death and deception, of misunderstanding and bureaucratic bungling, of attempts at conciliation and of burning hatred—all of which combine to sow the seeds of disaster," it is certainly more than that; it is a study of the motives behind a conquered people's last desperate attempt to resist change, of white men and women unsuccessfully attempting to penetrate the mystique of the Indian by using the Anglo-Saxon measuring stick, of the Sioux' naïve attempt at blending their old beliefs with those promulgated by the Christian missionaries, of old enmities and loyalties, of the inner ideological struggle of the Indians serving as the white man's police force.

The time of the novel is December, 1890. There is unrest on the Indian reservations in the Dakotas. Seasons of drought have depleted the grain and cattle on the land to which the Indians have been assigned. The supplementary rations provided by the government have been drastically cut by a penny-pinching Congress in a classic case of bad timing. Anarchy rules on some reservations, and wily old Sitting Bull takes advantage of the situation to foster as much dissension and resentment as he can. He encourages the spread of the ghost dance, a virtual religion promising an Indian Messiah who will free them from the white oppressor. The old warrior has no faith in the cult, but he uses it as a convenient device to harass those in authority. He knows, too, that his stirring up of the ghost dancers may lead to his arrest, an action that he hopes will instigate violence on the part of his followers.

James McLaughlin, Indian agent at Standing Rock reservation, does all in his power and wisdom to head off an uprising, but he knows an explosion is inevitable. He plans to delay it by arresting Sitting Bull, for he knows only too well that the canker of rebellion is nourished by the old man's vitriol. Hastening the urgency of the arrest is General Nelson Miles, an Army officer insensitive to the wishes of the agent and the mood of the times. Miles wants to make the arrest his way, inviting unnecessary violence in so doing. McLaughlin must act summarily to prevent Army intervention; the arrest ends tragically in a way neither McLaughlin nor Sitting Bull had anticipated.

On one level this book is a fast-moving western with all the prerequisites, even an understated romance. On the more significant level, Jones makes the important statement that despite their overt differences, both Indian and white man share a common humanity—one of accomplishment and frustration, love and hate, heroism and weakness. He makes it clear that both are diminished by their condition; the white man is robbed of his morality as he robs the Indian of his identity.

Sitting Bull symbolizes man's violent response to loss of self-esteem through loss of dignity. His resistance to change, and the manifestation of that resistance, is treated with understanding—Old Bull's wily manipulation of his followers, his realistic assessment of conditions but refusal to accept them, have earned the grudging respect of the author. Jones sees both sides of issues and does not lose his perspective. While Sitting Bull does loom large in the narrative, it is those around him who are more memorable.

Agent James McLaughlin typifies the ideal government employee, a bureaucrat in the better sense of the word. Called "Whitehair" by the Indians who respect age and wisdom, he is recognized as firm but fair, and even loved by some. McLaughlin knows that he is more than the voice and hand of the Bureau of Indian Affairs; in his own eyes, and those of the people, he has proved himself a friend. A career employee of the Department of the Interior, he has been with the Bureau most of his adult life, surviving changes of administration because he is good at his job. Like anyone involved with topheavy management, he is frequently frustrated by the workings of bureaucracy. One of his keenest annoyances is the tendency of top level politicians in the Bureau to play it safe, and let the Army solve militarily what the Indian Bureau should be doing for itself. Jones has McLaughlin rant, "These gutless bureaucrats . . . . Pass the buck . . . . The Army, the Army, the Army, at the first sign of discontent on the reservations." He always points out that, "You have to keep soldiers and warrior societies apart. When they rub together, you must expect a little disaster now and again."

McLaughlin feels that the ghost dance will run its course, and the Indians will cause no problem, if there is no intervention. It is to the south, where political appointees have caused things to get out of hand, that there is trouble, not at Standing Rock. Jones sums up McLaughlin's attitude: "Even as President Benjamin Harrison sends troops into the reservations to the south and the newspapermen flock there and the politicians wring their hands, Standing Rock remains the domain of Whitehair. His Indians know it and so does the Fort Yates commander, Colonel Drum." Unfortunately General Miles does not see it that way. The character of McLaughlin rings true. He is not Solomon, but he is wise; he is human enough to grit his teeth in annoyance when his Indian policemen refer to Sitting Bull as "Old Uncle," despite the fact he is aware that is what they call most older men in the tribe; he rails at bureaucrats even though he is one himself; he enjoys making pompous Buffalo Bill Cody look silly, and foiling General Miles.

Willa Mae Favory, agency schoolteacher, is depicted as finding her solace in religion, but not fanatically so; she is aware of an undefined lack in her life; she has never had the reassurance and support of family ties. Her father, a widower and a career sergeant in the Tenth Cavalry, had taken her with him from post to post—the only real warmth she remembers is a period in her childhood when the troopers under her father's command played with her, made toys for her, and generally spoiled her, as soldiers away from home have always done. At age twenty-nine she applied for a teaching position with the Indian Bureau and was assigned to the Standing Rock day school. The reservation was the home of the Hunkpapa Sioux and of their chief, Sitting Bull. Soon after her arrival in the summer of 1890, she realized she had moved into a gathering storm of rebellion. Willa Mae does not really understand the Indians, although she has lived among them as long as she can remember; she cannot measure their actions and motives by any but her own standards and background. Jones makes clear her inability to assess the essential truth of her relationship with them—she fails to understand that people so savage in war can at the same time be so considerate of another's feelings, that their apparent deception may be a desire to avoid offending. Willa Mae is puzzled by her reaction to young Standing Elk, an agency policeman who comes to her to learn to read and write; she does not recognize love, for she has never experienced it. Willa Mae and Standing Elk provide the tentative, barely suggested romantic interest—a welcome softening of the edges of what is, by design, a lean, hard, spare narrative.

Standing Elk himself comes through as an essentially tragic figure, a symbol of innocence and human dignity trying to accept the restrictive forces about him without denying his heritage. He recognizes the greatness in Sitting Bull, yet he realizes that some of the greatness has been created in the minds of the Sioux by the old man himself. He recalls the songs and stories of his childhood that soothed him and made him feel secure. Now they come to trouble him, no longer pointing the way, for they have become riddles. He recalls the legend of the pipe woman who came from the sky, warning the warriors that no one could smoke the pipe if he had murdered another Sioux, yet he knows many who have murdered their brothers and still smoke the pipe. Even as the stories of the old ones confuse him and make him feel alienated, he wonders at the white man's religion; it does not show much evidence of consistency, either. Standing Elk senses that his contentment is increasingly threatened by his exposure to the white man's mores and the reading lessons, lessons that tell him about things he must think out, somehow. He does not know how to deal with his own frustrations; Standing Elk, white man's policeman, attracted to a white woman, finds himself still emotionally tied to the old way of life, afraid to go near the ghost dance for fear of being affected by it, afraid to be in the presence of Sitting Bull, for fear the old man's magnetism may cause him to be drawn away from Whitehair. He agonizes, "I do not think my spirit is ready yet to become a white man." Ironically, when he dies, it is carrying out a white man's orders and at the hands of one of his own people.

Standing Elk's death presents a moral problem for another Sioux. Old Gall, a convert and an Episcopalian to the best of his understanding, secretly buries Standing Elk with traditional Sioux ritual, his love for the young warrior winning out over his newfound religion and his loyalty to Whitehair. The personality of Gall, who fought at Little Bighorn along with Sitting Bull, is the antithesis of that of the old dissident; through these two aging warriors, Jones clearly defines the extremes of response by the Indian to the encroachment of the white man.

Gall's burial of Standing Elk gives an excellent detailed picture of traditional Plains Indian rites; the chapter dealing with the burial is one of the most moving sections of the book. There is detail and symbolism in the account—the use of the old doeskin jacket, brittle old moccasins, fringed leggings, all treasured things from Gall's past, placed on the body along with a loincloth of trader's blanket and the elaborate headdress given to Gall by the agent; he no longer has need for these things. The old man pulls the hide from the cabin door. "It is the only thing left of the buffalo," he says, as he and his wife wrap Standing Elk's ceremonially garbed body in the robe. Young Standing Elk, whose spirit was not ready to be a white man, is laid to rest as he would have wanted to be.

Despite earlier qualms, once the burial is completed Gall is at peace with himself; he is glad of the evidence of Standing Elk's courage—the pistol in the dead man's hand had been empty, the wounds in his body were in front. Jones develops the poignancy of such an experience. With a vestige of the old warrior still apparent, Gall thinks, "That is a good way to die. Dying with one's face toward one's enemies." Gall soliloquizes:

> What I have done is good, as well. Whitehair will have to know. What is important has already been done . . . the funeral conducted as it would have been in the old days. . . . And now I stand before the white man's God. He will forgive me. . . . But even without that there is a goodness within me. . . . As if my fathers were smiling down on me. . . . There is a feeling like the old days, when we ate buffalo tongues and fought the Crow and killed Custer at Greasy Grass. It is hard to come completely away from those times.

There are subordinate characters who exemplify types that shaped the history of the period; standing out among them are General Nelson Miles and Sergeant McSweeney. Miles typifies the rigid military mind, a man in the position of authority who yields to a sense of power and forces his methods on others. He wants action, and he will get it if he has to go to the top to procure it; arrogantly contemptuous of politicians, he uses them, nonetheless, to gain his ends. Foiled in the first attempt to force his will on McLaughlin, he plans to strike again, totally unable to understand the possible consequences of his arbitrary decision. Miles is unable to relate to Sitting Bull's refusal to relinquish his code under pressure, not able to understand that the motivation behind the old warrior's stance is one of maintaining his dignity—living by that code, or dying by it, if need be. In his own way, Miles is as unyielding as Sitting Bull; the two are more alike than either would believe. A more sympathetic treatment of the military is presented in the vignette of Sergeant Major McSweeney. A tough, earthy, responsible man with pride in his cavalry outfit, he is everywhere; shaping up the troops, settling their brawls, cursing or encouraging the men as the need arises.

This book is as instructive as it is entertaining. The author's sense of drama makes history live, breathe, and speak. The past becomes as clear and vital, and sometimes more credible, than the present, in this highly successful view of a complex period in our nation's history.

Mae Woods Bell

Sources for Further Study

Atlantic. CCXL, November, 1977, p. 104.

Booklist. LXXIV, October 1, 1977, p. 268.

Kirkus Reviews. XLV, July 1, 1977, p. 682.

Library Journal. CII, August, 1977, p. 1678.

Publisher's Weekly. CXII, August 1, 1977, p. 104.

ATTACHMENTS

Author: Judith Rossner
Publisher: Simon and Schuster (New York). 392 pp. $9.95
Type of work: Novel
Time: 1950 to the early 1970's
Locale: Southern California and Dixonville, New Hampshire

An unconventional novel, narrated by one of two women who marry Siamese twins, in which the narrator attempts to understand why people are attracted to each other and why they drift apart

Principal characters:
> NADINE TUMULTY SMITH, the narrator, whose fascination with the Siamese twins leads to her marriage to Amos
> DIANNE SHAPIRO SMITH, Nadine's best friend and sister-in-law; married to Eddie
> AMOS SMITH, Siamese twin and Nadine's husband
> EDDIE SMITH, Siamese twin and Dianne's husband
> CAROTTA (CARLY) SMITH, daughter of Dianne and Eddie
> PHILIP SMITH, son of Nadine and Amos
> DAISY SMITH, daughter of Nadine and Amos
> DR. MARIANNA STORY, Nadine's college mentor
> KEN MCDOUGALL, filmmaker and neighbor of the Smiths' in Dixonville

Attachments, Judith Rossner's most recent novel, could as easily be entitled "Disentanglements," since as the title implies, the novel attempts to describe and explore not only the ties that bind people together but also the reasons they break apart. To fulfill her purpose, Rossner creates two female characters and two male so that she can depict the whole range of relationships of pairs of lovers and pairs of friends: the friendship of the women, of the men, of one man and one woman, and the intimate pairing of male and female lovers. Certainly her premise, stated so succinctly in the title, is not unusual in the novel, and she has dutifully created appropriate characters to act out her purpose. Yet it is Rossner's deliberation that seems to have resulted in the central core and the central problem of the book: the two men are Siamese twins, joined by a twenty-inch piece of flesh on their abdomens.

It is as if Rossner asked herself, What emblem could I use to provide a tangible, objective correlative for human attachment? What better emblem than an actual bridge of flesh? Perhaps her premise is that one can talk about normal human relationships in relief, as it were, by depicting those that are grotesque. An interesting, even bizarre premise, but does it mean Rossner fulfills her purpose? She does, but only in part, because of the limits that the selection of the situation of the twins, a first-person narrator, and certain characterizations impose on the novel from the onset.

Think about it. What sort of plot is the only plot possible if two characters are Siamese twins? Amos and Eddie Smith (is there some reference here to Amos and Andy of television fame?) meet two women, Nadine Tumulty (whose life, as her name implies, is a chaotic, random series of events), and Dianne Shapiro, her friend. The girls marry the twins, and the reader is permitted to view at length their marital relations. Friction results, children result, the twins have a successful operation to separate them, more problems occur, and finally the couples divorce. The inevitability of these events slows the pace of the novel since one already knows the outcome of any given segment of the book. Indeed, perhaps because of this plot, Rossner chooses to tell the story from the point of view of one character, Nadine, so that the unpredictableness of personality can mitigate the predictability of the plot itself.

Nadine is the instigator of the plot. Fascinated from an early age with the idea of Siamese twins because of her loneliness, her "empty space" inside, she has wished to be a twin. She has always been, she tells the reader, seeking an "other," a self to fill up this space. Hence to her, the twins, Amos and Eddie, are "beautiful," not freakish at all. The first part of the novel is a *bildüngsroman*-like account of Nadine's Hollywood upbringing and subsequent education from which the reader can discern her motivations for feeling so alone. She gets good grades, we find, because of her "attachments" to teachers, she loses a mentor to breast cancer and feels alone; she finds virginity a burden and sets out to lose it; her parents are electrocuted in a freak (yes) accident. It is no wonder, the reader is to conclude, that she wishes to marry Amos and convince her best friend, Dianne, to marry Eddie. When the two couples move from Los Angeles to the more quiet and curiously tolerant town of Dixonville, New Hampshire, Nadine becomes the housewife, cook, and mother, while Dianne goes off to work to support the "family." Nadine, however, never is quite believable as a housewife since as she herself points out, she has been the "life manager" of both herself and Dianne.

Nevertheless, Nadine's motivations are at least accounted for. When she realizes that the twins' physical attachment of flesh is preventing her from loving her husband, her best friend, and herself, she yearns for the operation, no longer seeing the arrangement as "cozy." The motives of the other characters, however, are more sketchily presented. Amos and Eddie understandably seem indistinguishable in the early sections of the novel—true, one is sullen, one is cheerful, but no reasons for these differences are given. Dianne's feelings are only somewhat more fleshed out. A lawyer from a seemingly happy Jewish home, Dianne's disinterest in mothering her child, Carly, her affair with Ken, a filmmaker, and even her friendship with Nadine, are never adequately accounted for. The other characters who are important insofar as they help the reader understand Nadine are also neglected. When Dr. Story, Nadine's college mentor, dies of cancer, the reader has not learned enough about her to care and therefore cannot assess Nadine's loss.

Despite these problems, it must be said that Rossner's imagination is rich and consistent within the frame her very difficult premise provides for her. In one fine segment, Dianne's daughter Carly realizes that her "fathers" as she calls them are physically joined. With the chilling logic of childhood, she decides that she too wishes to have such a secure, intimate, permanent attachment to another self. On Carly's insistence, Nadine ties a rope between Carly and a Raggedy Ann so that she too can have a " 'tachment."

Rossner's perception into the workings of human relationships is also quite probing and insightful. On the eve of their marriages, Nadine reports that she, Dianne, and the twins did not discuss who was to earn the money, or what "form" and what "content" their marriages were to take—a typical omission in many relationships. Also, after their marriage, as Nadine begins to see her friendship with Dianne disappearing, Dianne disliking Amos, Amos disliking Eddie, Nadine sees that what was once a "cozy" bond represented by the men's joining becomes a chain that enslaves them all. Rossner thus uses her emblem of this piece of flesh as variously as possible.

The novel is ultimately about the distinction between self and other, and the need within us all for an other. Amos's affection for Nadine after the operation results from his loss of Eddie and the need therefore for an other. In our society, his wife, Nadine, is the acceptable choice. Even Carly's desire for her doll suggests this need. Overwhelmingly, Nadine's longing to be attached to an other as a prerequisite to establishing her own identity as a self permeates the novel and carries forth this theme.

Rossner's craft as a writer is to be commended as well. While the book seems to move slowly because of the predictableness of the plot, such a pace is consistent with the first-person narration she has selected. The brusque, chopped, juxtaposed short sentences work well to convey that sometimes grotesque content. A reference at one point to Nathanael West, whose *The Day of the Locust* and *Miss Lonelyhearts* depict the freakish world of Southern California, indicates Rossner has studied her predecessors and, indeed, writes aware of a tradition. As West's novels read like screenplays where one scene fades into another, the early parts of *Attachments* seem like a slide-show of juxtaposed scenes whose paradoxical quality, witness, and speed convey forcibly the chaotic, disconnected quality of Nadine's youth. The scenes in New Hampshire have a slower pace, that of a home movie in fact, as if Rossner creates a screenplay, even a documentary on paper, of the lives of the two couples.

If the ending of the novel, a dual divorce, seems inevitable, and Nadine's comment that she needs to find out who she is predictable, still, upon closing the book, the reader is left with a feeling that Rossner has made a valiant effort, that she has talent and insight, but that her choice of a bizarre initial premise forced her to make decisions that interfered with her own gifts as a novelist. She can create excellent characters and intriguing, suspenseful plots, as *Looking for Mr. Goodbar* evidenced. Moreover, her control of style in *Attachments* is never in doubt. One can only hope that this novel is a steppingstone to the next, in which style and content can be more congenially attached.

Kathryn L. Seidel

Sources for Further Study

Best Sellers. XXXVII, November, 1977, p. 232.
Ms. VI, October, 1977, p. 36.
New York Times. September 12, 1977, p. 31.
New Yorker. LIII, October 3, 1977, p. 160.
Newsweek. XC, September 19, 1977, p. 115.
Observer. November 6, 1977, p. 30.
Saturday Review. V, October 1, 1977, p. 30.
Times Literary Supplement. November 4, 1977, p. 1285.

BAD MOUTH
Fugitive Papers on the Dark Side

Author: Robert M. Adams (1915–   )
Publisher: University of California Press, Quantum Books Series (Berkeley).138 pp. $7.95
Type of work: Essays
Time: The last fifty years
Locale: Chiefly America

Adams argues that the "bad mouthing," invective, insult, lying, obscenity, ugliness, and filth that dominate contemporary vocabulary reflect an exhaustion of the modern imagination

Bad Mouth by Robert M. Adams is a slim little volume in the Quantum Books Series which publishes short studies distinguished by the authors' ability to offer a "richness of detail and insight" in about one-hundred pages. This collection of six essays discusses the gradual debilitation of the English language, especially vocabulary, into modes of malice, obscenity, and ugliness; it is a lively work short enough to be read at one sitting. Unfortunately, the informal nature of Adams' discussions severely limits his effectiveness as well as the overall value of his book for future research in this area.

Adams' discussions group into three pairs of essays: "counterlanguage," lying/obscenity, and the "ugly" with its metaphoric expression in American life. Although the individual chapters proceed from many areas—linguistics, sociology, literary criticism, and psychology, to name a few—their central thesis entails the slowly evolving "offensive mode" in art and literature which now predominates. Unfortunately, the author assumes the role of a "cultural commentator" who is *not* concerned with the causes or consequences of this change. Thus, he provides mere random samplings of examples to illustrate theories and observations. Adams readily admits that his all-encompassing inquiry involves a self-questioning mode which may distress readers who expect to be told clearly defined observations and opinions concerning our corroded vocabulary. Indeed, his speculations do prove to be provocative and provoking. But, effective trailblazing cannot be useful unless it leaves well-defined paths for later pioneers to follow and extend. A disregard for scholarly methods and academic modes leaves the reader with neither primary or secondary bibliography nor footnotes and index to serve as sources for further study. Stimulating reading is no excuse for the total lack of professional scholarship; a professor of English at a major academic institution should know better than to deprive his readers of his resources.

"Bad Mouth and Other Second Games" and "Invective and Insult" focus upon "counterlanguage" that hinders and hurts people in a variety of symbolic and practical ways. "Bad mouthing" denotes a vocal hostility, an "evil verbal sign," directed toward an enemy. Muhammad Ali and former UCLA basketball player Tommy Curtis provide excellent examples of athletes who frequently employ this "psyching" technique in order to goad their opponents into errors.

Other variations upon these "putdown" games include "bait-and-switch," "private-key," and "undervoice": catchy terms which lack clear definition, explanation, and illustration.

The types of invective and insult are more clearly defined by familiar examples. The warriors' boasts in the *Iliad* serve as extensions of their egos, while curses in Shakespeare's plays are uttered in defiance of the cosmos. Today's stand-up comedian, a Lenny Bruce type, trades insults with customers who laugh at his skill and massage their own egos by giving and taking verbal abuse. Deep insults consist mainly of sexual expressions; "bastard" and "son-of-a-bitch" have found their way firmly into American conversation. The "insult vociferous" depends upon an unbroken stream of invective, while a succinct insult, like Doctor Johnson's "Sir, your mother, under pretext of keeping a bawdy house, was a receiver of stolen goods," gathers its force from implication rather than from abundant verbiage. Indirect insults and buried insults receive less immediate attention than direct insults, but illustrate more clearly their speaker's cleverness. Adams' observation that today people use insults more frequently to prevent conflicts rather than to provoke them, closes this chapter with one of the few optimistic statements in a predominantly misanthropic volume.

"The New Arts of Political Lying" contains the most relevant material of the entire volume. For today's society mass-produces political lying, like many other entities verbal and otherwise, with less skill and more abundance than in the past. Free-form lying features an "indistinctness" that invites readers to project "personal particulars into abstractions": the sublimal suggestion of getting that pretty girl with the purchase of that overpriced automobile. "Tying things together," the association of a political candidate like George McGovern with the omnipresent "red menace," for example, becomes a strategy frequently used by politicians. The idealized lie, although equally as malicious as other lies, involves more creativity in its execution. The systematic or schematic lie and the "myth of consistency" (lying under pressure) are other examples of free form prevarication. This specific analysis of lying evolves into a general critique of contemporary politicians who corrupt society and themselves (Nixon and his cabinet) by their deeds. A topic all too encompassing to pursue at great length within the narrow scope of one chapter, the "art" of political lying stands as Adams' most self-contained discussion.

Originally appearing in the *Columbia Forum,* "Dirty Stuff" includes the "obscene" where polite codes regarding sex and excretion are knowingly violated in our society. These codes differ from society to society; for example, South Americans emphasize food and not sex or excretion. Two variants of obscenity involve the blasphemer who directs outrage against the diety and his laws and the foul insulter who attacks specific individuals or groups. While inviting hatred, obscenity also releases pent-up emotions in a therapeutic function. The pain of a hammered thumb necessitates the release of an emotional curse. Since an obscenity is only as strong as the taboo which it attacks, the naked women on today's stages represent an emblem of honesty, frankness, and steady reproach to a hypocritical audience. The difficulty in distinguishing between the decent and the obscene in order to define "pornography" points to the present chaotic state of moral values. The Supreme Court's decision to favor local censorship can only provoke additional confusion and ineffectual enforcement of obscenity laws.

"Ideas of Ugly" presents the theory that "ugly" and "beautiful" share a dialectic; they merely represent loose clusters of aesthetic, social, religious, and utilitarian qualities. Therefore, enlarged lips and fat wives gain admiration in societies much different from our own. Conversely, our society often appreciates music and art which hurts or offends our inherited tastes for the "beautiful." Penderecki's faithful audiences evolve from those listeners who booed Stravinsky's "Rites of Spring." The "morbidly fascinating," which evolved as a major theme of romanticism, exists today in a number of forms. The Byronic heroes of the past, those suffering, suicidal victims of insensitive societies, become the sado-masochists, vampires, and devil-worshipers that populate film, fiction, and television. Popular rock music performers like "Kiss," "The Sex Pistols," and "Alice Cooper" flagellate, urinate, and masturbate their way into their paying customers' hearts. Adams' assertion that the world is becoming uglier as it commercializes, pollutes, and generally compromises the standards of truth and principals of beauty is well-taken. This chapter raises questions, but not answers, to problems for metaphysical aestheticians to answer in the future.

In his concluding chapter, "Rags, Garbage, and Fantasy," Adams defines the former items as "materials exhausted of their value by human wear or consumption," while he never mentions "fantasy." History is currently in a "rubbish-phase" for the first time since the eighteenth century when Swift and Gay used rags as powerful images. Young people wear old clothes as a social protest, and "found" works of art, whether off the street or from the gutter, form an intellectual bond between artist and viewer as "co-creators." The work of Eliot, Pound, and especially Joyce utilizes secondhand materials to suggest the "seamless garment of total history." Garbage and carrion raise more sensitive feelings since they attack deeper taboos. Beckett's emphasis on disintegration and decay implies the very decomposition of civilization. The author recognizes, enumerates, and classifies ugliness, but cannot verbalize the psychic strategies involved. In conclusion, Adams suggests that writing exclusively about the hateful and negative side of the imagination has affected his own perceptions and style—an intuitive suggestion that he has not really succeeded.

Reprinted essays under one cover without enough thematic coherence to connect them produce structural weaknesses in *Bad Mouth*. For instance, what connection exists between political lying and the many obscenities uttered on the Watergate tapes? Adams raises many interesting questions without answering them—an effective pedagogical technique utilized by the best teachers.

However, his total lack of acknowledgment concerning what research is currently being performed in the areas he discusses is inexcusable. Any discussion of political lying written in the post-Watergate era should include some discussion of political ethics, morals, psychology, and sociology. Machiavelli's *The Prince* could provide needed illustration as could the works of Hobbes, Spinoza, Godwin, and Marx. Myles L. Cowers' *Understanding American Politics Through Fiction* and *Political Language and Oratory in Traditional Society* edited by Maurice Bloch provide fertile areas for future work. Linguistics research, particularly the relationship of language and behavior and psycholinguistics, provides many answers to the questions raised in *Bad Mouth*. Noam Chomsky's career and work present a wonderful place to initiate a discussion of contemporary politics and linguistics. *Lady Chatterley's Lover, Tropic of Cancer*, and *Fanny Hill*, and all obscenity law victims bear witness to changing concepts of censorship. Slang, particularly the work of Eric Partridge—his dictionaries of clichés, Armed Forces' slang, historical slang, vulgarisms, and underworld entomologies—could provide much needed reinforcement to Adams' chapters on "counterlanguage."

    Bad Mouth fulfills Quantum Books's policy of being short enough to be read in an evening. However, if the result of that reading is only eight hours of sound sleep, then the reader cannot help but "bad mouth" this volume.

Gregory S. Sojka

Sources for Further Study

Kirkus Reviews. XLV, October 15, 1977, p. 1120.
Library Journal. CII, October 15, 1977, p. 2162.
New York Times. December 12, 1977, p. 33.
New York Times Book Review. December 11, 1977, p. 12.

BARGAINING FOR SUPREMACY
Anglo-American Naval Collaboration, 1937–1941

Author: James R. Leutze (1935-   )
Publisher: The University of North Carolina Press (Chapel Hill, N.C.). 328 pp. $17.95
Type of work: History
Time: 1937–1941
Locale: Washington, D.C., and London

A monograph which examines Anglo-American naval relations in the years immediately prior to the United States' entry into World War II

Naval relations comprise a particularly vexed chapter in the history of Anglo-American diplomacy between 1919 and 1941. Until recently the nature of this troubled relationship has not been subject to close examination. There are several reasons that explain this neglect. Among these is the fact that the issues that divided Great Britain and the United States on the development, maintenance, and deployment of their war fleets were overshadowed by the larger and more ominous conflict between the Fascist powers and the Western democracies. In addition, the achievement of a high level of Anglo-American cooperation during World War II has detracted from a proper appreciation of the discord that preceded that achievement. And, perhaps most important, until the early 1970's crucial official British documents relating to the late interwar period were closed to scholars. These factors combined to stifle important inquiry into the subject as a whole.

Captain Stephen Roskill did much to set the record straight in his two-volume work, *Naval Policy Between the Wars.* However, for all of Captain Roskill's contribution to a better understanding of Anglo-American naval relations, which is considerable, there are deficiencies in his interpretation. Perhaps chief among these is his contention that the 1930's witnessed a steady improvement in Anglo-American naval relations. James R. Leutze convincingly argues otherwise. American and British civilian and naval authorities, he contends, continued to regard one another with suspicion and even hostility until at least 1941. War and the prospect of war finally created the necessary imperative for military cooperation between the two countries. Many of the old antagonisms, however, continued to rankle; they were, for the most part, only shoved into the background.

Leutze begins his account in 1937. The year is well chosen. The system of naval limitation by treaty, which was central to the peace-keeping efforts of the interwar period, had just broken down. As a result, all of the major naval powers were free to build warships to levels imposed by the limits of national will and resources. Japan, in a deliberate attempt to upset the delicate balance of naval power established by the Washington and London treaties, launched a new program of naval construction that included a novel class of superbattleships. More threatening still was the calculated Japanese escalation of the China

Incident of July into a full-scale invasion of that country. These actions posed a real danger to traditional British and American interests in the western Pacific. Since the turn of the century the United States had emerged as the most consistent champion of Chinese sovereignty. Moreover, even though the Philippines were ticketed for eventual independence, the American military still assumed that the islands would be defended if attacked. The British had even more at stake: principally Australia, New Zealand, India, and Malaya. A common fear of Japanese aggression thus provided the first important stimulus to the closer coordination of Anglo-American naval policy.

The Ingersoll Mission was the initial fruit of this fear-induced cooperation. Captain Royal E. Ingersoll, director of plans for the United States Navy, had seen previous service as technical adviser at the London Naval Conference of 1935–1936. He was personally chosen by President Roosevelt to represent the United States in informal talks with British naval personnel concerning the possibility of imposing a blockade against Japan. The British had indicated interest in discussions of this nature, and Roosevelt desired to strike while the iron was hot. Ingersoll was informed of the nature of his mission on December 23, and three days later he boarded a ship for London.

In view of the haste with which Ingersoll was prepared and then sent to England, it is not surprising that the results of his mission were general and tentative. The main accomplishment of these conversations was the establishment of guidelines for a joint blockade. If and when such action were taken, the British agreed to interdict Japanese trade south of the Philippines, while Ingersoll agreed that the United States would do the same from the Philippines to North America. Unfortunately, this nascent *rapprochement* was neutralized by other developments. In the midst of Ingersoll's discussions, Roosevelt sent word requesting British acquiescence in international negotiations devoted to arms reduction, international law, and unspecified economic issues. The British were not interested and the suggestion went for nought, much to Roosevelt's displeasure. British suspicion that, despite the President's willingness to send an impressive contingent of warships to Hawaii and Singapore, the United States might well leave Britain in the lurch should a crisis with Japan occur further clouded the atmosphere. Finally, on February 20, 1938, three weeks after Ingersoll returned home, Anthony Eden, British Foreign Secretary and a good friend of the United States, resigned. As a result of these factors, Ingersoll's mission failed to invite immediate new initiatives from either side for closer naval cooperation.

In 1938 and 1939 a pattern began to emerge in the naval relations between Britain and the United States. On the one hand, each country was resistant to conceding advantages to the other without full compensation. Thus the United States was refused a request for detailed information about the Singapore naval base because it offered nothing in return. Similarly, Roosevelt continued to withhold specifications of the Norden bombsight from the British on the ground that London possessed no technical information of equal value. On the other hand, the deepening crises in Europe and the Far East created a mandate for Anglo-American cooperation that could not easily be denied. Acting on a proposal made by Roosevelt in early 1939, the British in August-September of the same year granted the United States restricted rights to their bases in the western Atlantic. The mutual advantages conferred by such an arrangement were evident. The agreement enabled the United States to extend the range of its hemispheric defense while, at the same time, the neutralization of the western Atlantic by United States forces not only helped to insure the integrity of British possessions in North America, but also enhanced the safety of British trade in that area.

Germany's blitzkrieg into western Europe in the spring of 1940 touched off a new flurry of diplomatic activity between Britain and the United States. The previous September Roosevelt had initiated a private correspondence with Winston Churchill, then First Lord of the Admiralty. Although London questioned the propriety of such a relationship, it was calculated that the advantages of having a clear line of communication to the White House outweighed this disadvantage. The wisdom of this decision became evident in May, 1940, when Churchill replaced Neville Chamberlain as prime minister. Within a matter of days after assuming his new post, Churchill put his relationship with Roosevelt to the test. The Prime Minister requested a variety of war materials from the United States, including forty to fifty overage destroyers.

The "destroyer deal" is a familiar episode in the history of Anglo-American relations prior to World War II and need not be recounted in detail here. Leutze demonstrates rather persuasively that this unquestionably important event is more complex than previously believed. Roosevelt, who could on occasion be impetuous, now played the more familiar role of cautious politician. Churchill's request for military aid from a neutral was a political red flag. The year 1940 was an election year and Roosevelt was seeking an unprecedented third term. Any congressional involvement in the requested transfer of equipment was certain to touch off an acrimonious debate which could only damage the President's prospect of reelection. While sorting out the many factors that would have to be weighed before a decision could be reached, Roosevelt dispatched Colonel William J. Donovan, an old friend, to England to assess that country's prospect of surviving a full-scale German attack.

Just as Roosevelt was resolved to act with deliberation, so Churchill was determined to obtain the equipment that Britain desperately needed and, at the same time, to inch the United States away from its stance of neutrality. His trump card in these negotiations was the deployment of the British fleet in the event that England should be overrun. The role of the disposition of the British fleet is a point that has been largely overlooked by previous writers. In the end, Churchill gave written assurance that in the unlikely event that Hitler's Operation Sea Lion succeeded, the fleet would continue to fight from bases dispersed throughout the empire. This pledge was guarded with great secrecy for fear of its demoralizing effect on the English people.

Churchill's guarantee that the British fleet would neither be scuttled nor transferred to Germany, no matter what happened, was important to Roosevelt. But that concession, since it was not publicly disclosed, did not affect his political problems. A gift of warships by a neutral to a government at war was political dynamite which would doubtless be exploited by Republicans. Leutze credits Secretary of War Henry Stimson and Secretary of the Navy Frank Knox with major responsibility for resolving this difficulty. First, the two proposed that Roosevelt bypass the Senate by incorporating the transfer of destroyers in an executive agreement rather than a treaty. Later, Secretary Knox further suggested that the destroyers be given to Britain as part of an exchange that would include extended American rights to British bases in the western Atlantic. Such an exchange, which became crucial to the agreement, would allow the administration to argue that it received more than it surrendered. Thus the "destroyer deal" was rationalized to the American public not on the ground that Britain's defense was vital to our own, but rather on the basis that it enhanced America's hemispheric defense. In political terms the distinction between these explanations is significant. When assurances were sought and received from Wendell Willkie, the Republican presidential candidate, that he would not make a campaign issue of the destroyer transfer, the last important obstacle to an executive agreement was removed. The end result was, as Leutze points out, a "destroyer-bases-fleet deal" rather than simply a "destroyer-bases deal."

The "destroyer-bases-fleet deal" constitutes a milestone in the history of American neutrality before Pearl Harbor. Not the least significant implication of this agreement was a strong pressure for closer Anglo-American coordination of military strategy. As early as May, 1940, London had inquired into American interest in joint military staff conversations. Three months later secret preliminary negotiations for such a conference began in London. The increasingly desperate plight of British defense and the growing intransigence of Japan lent urgency to a staff conference. Safely past the election, Roosevelt in late November consented to American participation in staff discussions which would be held in Washington among military representatives of Britain, Canada and the United States.

The ABC Conference of January-March 1941 without question represents the high-water mark of Anglo-American military cooperation between World War I and World War II. The key to the success of this conference was British acceptance of a redefined role for the American fleet in the event that the United States became involved in the war. By late 1940 the United States Navy, with Roosevelt's approval, had abandoned its primary commitment to the protection of American interests in the western Pacific in future wars that included both Asian and European foes. This change of basic strategy was the result of several considerations. Most important of these was the calculation that hemispheric concerns were more likely to be threatened by a European power than by an Asiatic power. A strong reinforcing consideration in this redirection of strategy was a reluctance to concede British dominance in the Northeast Atlantic, which was now recognized as more crucial to America's postwar welfare than was the western Pacific. Finally, there was great reluctance among naval officials to take major responsibility for the defense of British interests in the Pacific.

The British would have much preferred a United States policy that left the Royal Fleet ascendent in the Northeast Atlantic. In defending this position, however, the British had no high cards to play. The United States, after all, was free to come into the war on whatever terms it chose. And, as Churchill persistently pointed out to Foreign Office and Navy personnel, the important objective was to get the United States into the war. The conditions of that participation were secondary. In conceding to the United States a senior partnership in all theaters of the naval conflict, the British abandoned the last pretense to *de facto* Anglo-American naval equality, a principle that had been scrupulously defended throughout the interwar period.

While *Bargaining for Supremacy* advances no significant new thesis about Anglo-American naval relations prior to World War II, readers might be surprised by the tenacity of the bargaining that preceded the "destroyer-bases-fleet deal" and the ABC Conference agreements. The British were desperate for American aid. Churchill was relentless in his effort to move the United States from a position of neutrality to one of belligerency. It was not an easy task. He needed to convince Roosevelt that American aid was vital to England's survival in the war while avoiding any appearance of defeatism. The large American commitment to the material support of the British war effort and the close military collaboration between the two governments that was achieved by early 1941 is a great tribute to Churchill's skill and persistence.

Roosevelt did not exert an equivalent leadership in American policymaking. For all of his self-proclaimed interest in naval affairs, Roosevelt's attention to the details of Anglo-American negotiations on naval matters was at best sporadic. His most original contribution to these negotiations was the proposal for a joint blockade of Japanese trade, a proposal that was rife with serious implications which he clearly did not appreciate. The positions that Roosevelt ultimately took with regard to the "destroyer-bases-fleet deal" and the strategic deployment of the fleet were influenced in large measure by representatives of the Navy.

Bargaining for Supremacy is well researched in both American and British sources. Its principal flaw, which is shared by many monographs in diplomatic history, is an occasionally cluttered narrative. The chapters devoted to the preparation for the ABC Conference are the worst in this respect. All the same, Leutze has made a solid contribution to an improved understanding of Anglo-American naval relations in the critical period that preceded United States involvement in World War II.

Meredith William Berg

Sources for Further Study

Library Journal. CII, November 1, 1977, p. 2260.

BEGINNING WITH O

Author: Olga Broumas (1949–   )
Publisher: Yale University Press (New Haven). 74 pp. $2.95
Type of work: Poetry

A collection of poems of salient and sensual proportions in sequences unified by a bold narrative stance

Olga Broumas begins her first book of poems in Greece, her homeplace, in a poem which describes a dive into the Greek sea, or any dive into any body of water, any descent into any receptive medium, "so startled/it held the shape of your plunge." Broumas takes water as matrix, as that womb from which all originates; she turns water into die, that which holds a shape for casting; she implies a juxtaposition of the two—of the presence and absence of source, of the now-you-see-it-now-you-don't nature of the meditations poets make of the questions which ask where have I come from, where am I going? She is journeying after essence, after center, after force, "the mineral-bright pith." Early and swiftly she introduces the ancient, exemplified by the Greek sea, and the modern, represented by Oregon. Broumas links aspects of the living and of the dead in complex textural patterns which issue from her interest in word derivations, that series of little bridges which metaphorically, if not literally, epitomizes the horizontal appreciation of our perpetual human condition. Perpendicularly, her concern for puns, connotation, paradox, irony, and ambiguity offers a context in which the finite, the beginning and the end, the alpha and the omega, accomplishes the neat trick of suggesting the infinite, "something immaculate, a chance/crucial junction: time, light, water/had occurred, you feel your bones."

Onomastics is at the heart of her poetic method; her specialized field is alphabet; her substratum, the poet's ritual of naming. In "Artemis" the narrator says, "significance stirs in me/like a curviform alphabet/that defies/decoding, appears/to consist of vowels, beginning with O, the O-/mega, horseshoe, the cave of sound." It is a large cave, and perhaps am ambiguously promising one, for tradition has it that unless the horseshoe be turned so that its shape suggests a cup, all its luck is in jeopardy of spilling away. According to all of the signs, without luck we will never be able to "cross into each other's language," to that place "where braille/is a tongue for lovers, where tongue/fingers, lips/share a lidless eye."

Follow for a moment the kind of lesson Broumas affords. She gives us *O*. Quickly we know to think of oval, ovum, oculos, other; we may begin to play with omega or omicron, osmosis or orifice. The Sanskrit *mandala* is circle, o. The mandala, the Hindu or Buddhist symbol of the universe. The universe, O! The ecstatic, O! The registration, O. The disappointment, O. The moon. Robert Graves's invented word, *mandalot,* from the Greek *mandalós,* the bolt you put in the socket, the tongue-kiss, something to be reserved for those you truly love.

Where Broumas can guide us by means of this kind of process is everywhere, but if we refuse to participate, it gets us nowhere. She is mindful of the possibility of failed communication, or of failure's root in saying too much or too little, saying it right or wrong. Words have such powers. In "Rumplestiltskin" she writes, "The words we need are extinct." So, in order to save us, in order to save her poems, in order to save herself, the narrator becomes an archaeologist, a trader in relics, remains, and signs. Clues from the past are evident as gods and goddesses and events of the narrator's past life which appear "like fossils: *something/that did exist.*"

Often these poems look back, turn to see what part of their journey they've passed, return to survey their source, turn about to celebrate or reprimand their cause. The narrator's reflection proceeds from this rearview mirror and serves a meditation which is finally fixed on the future, though a future of measurable uncertainty:

> I am a woman commited to
> a politics
> of transliteration, the methodology
>
> of a mind
> stunned at the suddenly
> possible shifts of meaning—for which
> like amnesiacs
>
> in a ward on fire, we must
> find words
> or burn.

Duality of vision is central to this book: mean and end, process and product, matter and spirit, love and hate, satisfaction and discontent, are all evident everywhere. Even while this narrator frequently complains and contests, the language in which she addresses the reader is replete with delight in its own antics.

One useful way to read this book is to engage yourself in its own gamey techniques. Broumas means for us to play and to partake of her witticisms and wisdom piecemeal. The poems perform a variety of poetic devices—pun, synesthesia, rhyme, enjambment, allusion, simile, metaphor; all of these abound, alone and in combination:

> we are partners in this bee
> partners
> & spell each other against the wall of fame
>
> you will know what I mean, words
> are supposed to claw you with
> beauty, tear at you
> spirant by sonorant
> tongue by tongue
>
> some weird mutation of orgasm
> a spasm

Ordinarily the poet's punning goes as punning goes: we get the stereoscopic picture, we cheer or we boo, the defining lines converge at the point of poetic promise or they disintegrate at the crossroads of silly collision. In "Amazon Twins" the narrator claims, "you gave/me food from your plate, alert/to my blood-sweet hungers/double-edged." This poem has asked that the reader watch as the speaker and another character compare bodily details point by point. The comparison itself reveals a pun, an instance in which two which are superficially alike, two women, are momentarily understood to be essentially different. As in all comparisons which grow of a desire to generate love, the differences, the qualities of complimentarity, appear to be essential. Broumas intrigues the reader with her puns, her offering in this book of probable and improbable meetings, one more insight into the intersections of those things which we ordinarily think of as opposites or unlikely. The ancient Greeks used poetry not only as a means of expression but also of instruction, the pun long defined as a particularly deft instrument of persuasion.

Offering her reader an incredible amount of information, Broumas instructs us in geography, mythology, fairytale, folklore, literature, physics, linguistics, photography, physiology, physiognomy, pop culture, occultism, biology, matrimony, lesbianism, and eroticism. Should we fail to find enough in the poems and in what we know of what we find in them, we are offered more information in an addendum of notes which explains particular details pertinent to their appearances in the poems. One of the notes makes it plain that Broumas will not be accused of disarming herself of reason, even while she wholeheartedly embraces a belief in what she knows to be of mystical origin. She writes of being unable to identify authorship of the epigraph, "She who loves roses must be patient/and not cry out when she is pierced by thorns." In the poem "Bitterness" Broumas attributes this epigraph to Sappho, although her note tells us that it is possible that Broumas herself wrote it under Sappho's influence, or that it might be part of a lyric from the *Greek Anthology*. She concludes this particular excavation, "At the risk of mysticism, I feel the couplet to be hers, regardless of its actual provenance." She makes it a gift outright and strikes one more note for the sake of unification, unification growing out of the illustration of paradox and irony.

Orbiting about this book's centrally earthbound, reason-designed imagery are all manner of extraordinary and extrasensory means to understanding. A list of words will do: *mantra, abnegation, liturgies, cast, inspiration, charm, talisman, tarot, mystified, mandala, constellation, spell, eidetic, spellbound, transform, labyrinth, epiphany, dreams, secret, priest, gods, miraculous, anathemas, gift.* Apprehension and recognition of poetic truths will be got by means immanent and transcendent, as well as linear and rational, "our harvest continuous/as a moan, the tilled bed luminous/with the future/yield." We reap what has been sown, seaming process and product, partners in a dizzy dance which defies the critics who pick up their sticks and cry "mixed metaphor, mixed metaphor." Mixing, commingling, fusing, is what all good poetry teaches. Compounding goes on in many ways; hyphenization is one of them. Broumas has a penchant for using such things as these: *infinite-clad, oil-whipped, breath-sharp, mineral-bright.* To vary the formation of simile she chooses: *crustacean-like, tongue-like, gazebo-like, mandala-like.* The interlacing tissue of her vision is gently emphasized in instances of synesthesia such as "perspiration of light," and "hand/precise as an eyelid, a hand with a sense/of smell."

O, in another guise of its suggestive force, is the connective vowel which joins word elements of Greek origin, and is now used to join word elements of Latin and other origins. We have our drunkometers, speedometers, and odometers, measuring what we've consumed, how quickly we've consumed it, and how far from where we began we have come. Broumas drops many little o's among the stanzas of her poems in a process which chainlinks her entire book:

> when the latch slips its lock this time
> past our linked fingers
> more doors than this
> one are closing
>
> o
>
> o

She has constructed a fence of voice, image, detail, and technique which functions to include or exclude as she sees fit. In one more example of paradox she writes, "i hold/my tongue, what i keep from you/keeps/me from you."

Olga Broumas has not written a book which is easy or which proposes simple solutions to the puzzles of our existence. Her poems will not heal their readers of doubt or uncertainty; they will not cure us of our inabilities to be objective, to be everywhere at once; they will not make us omniscient, or even tease us with the possibility of that vain wish. They say this very plainly:

> here we are, a curve
> on a piece of paper, a line of ink
> the improbable in high contrast, a contact
> sheet, black & white
>
> here we are, fixed.

And for once, for having partaken of what of the world one woman has assembled, we can know that this is an immensely ecletic and eccentric universe, and be glad of it. The poet has elegantly gathered and composed her signs; it is up to the reader to do as well with her poems.

Dara Wier

Sources for Further Study

Atlantic. CCXL, October, 1977, p. 102.
Book Forum. III, Spring, 1977, p. 322.
Booklist. LXXIII, July 15, 1977, p. 1698.
Choice. XIV, October, 1977, p. 1045.
Hudson Review. XXX, Summer, 1977, p. 459.
Village Voice. XXII, August 29, 1977, p. 41.
Yale Review. LXVII, October, 1977, p. 72.

BLACK JACK
The Life and Times of John J. Pershing

Author: Frank E. Vandiver (1925–   )
Publisher: Texas A&M University Press (College Station). 2 vols. Illustrated. 1,178 pp.
   $35.00
Type of work: Biography
Time: 1860–1948
Locale: The United States, the Philippines, Japan, Manchuria, Mexico, and France

Although considerable attention is given to Pershing's relationships with family and friends, the focus of this minutely detailed biography is on his military exploits

> *Principal personages:*
> JOHN J. PERSHING, Commander-in-Chief, American Expeditionary Forces, 1917–1919
> FRANCES WARREN PERSHING, his wife
> FRANCIS EMORY WARREN, his father-in-law and United States Senator from Wyoming, 1890–1893 and 1895–1929

By any quantitative measurement *Black Jack: The Life and Times of John J. Pershing* is a monumental biography. Eleven hundred pages of text describe a life that spanned eighty-eight years, almost half of which were devoted to active service in the United States Army. Frank E. Vandiver spent eighteen years in research and writing about his subject. His bibliography, which runs to twenty-four pages, includes an impressive list of unpublished sources. Vandiver acknowledges by name over one hundred and eighty people who at various stages of the project lent assistance. It is hard to imagine that any scholar will soon attempt to duplicate this effort.

Despite these impressive credentials, *Black Jack* is on balance a disappointment. It tries too hard to be magisterial. The attempt fails because there is insufficient grist in Pershing's life to merit a multivolume study. Longevity notwithstanding, Pershing's fame is anchored almost entirely in two events: the Punitive Expedition against Pancho Villa in 1916–1917 and the United States participation in World War I. The Punitive Expedition, while interesting, was a military failure. It is generally considered today as one of those bizarre episodes that marked American imperialism in the twilight of the Monroe Doctrine. As for World War I, it must be kept in mind that the direct American military contribution to the Allied war effort was slight. American troops were present in force only during the last half year of the fighting. Thus it seems fair to conclude that the basis of Pershing's fame is highly confined. That Black Jack became a hero to his age reflects more on the needs of that age than it does on Pershing.

All of which is not to say that Pershing is undeserving of serious investigation. The essential point is that the substance of his life does not warrant Vandiver's extended treatment. It hardly seems necessary to devote the first third of this biography to a career that appeared to be dead-ended in the rank of captain. Yet it is not until page 402 that the reader is told that Pershing's jump promotion to brigadier general has been confirmed by the Senate. One of the unfortunate results of this expansiveness is that much of the writing is excessive. One suspects that Vandiver has employed conspicuous language to compensate for a lack of inherent significance in Pershing's early career. In any event, words such as "thrilled," "zestful," and "throbbed" abound. "Glee" and "gleeful," the worst offenders, appear dozens of times. This tendency toward overwriting is most evident in descriptions of Pershing's private life. One example will suffice to illustrate the problem. The setting is Zamboanga, the Philippines. Pershing's wife, Frankie, has just surveyed the family's residence on the military base. Her reaction is described as follows:

> An obvious advantage teased Frankie's femininity. The house shrieked for renovation. As her eye swept the maze of rooms, Frankie's fancies soared—endless changes beckoned. Clearly care had been lavished in creating this dowdy edifice, but additions and remodelings had spoiled an old simplicity. The place now brooded in slovenly pretension.

In addition to a distracting wordiness, the narrative also suffers from misleading generalization. Vandiver writes, for example, that prior to the outbreak of the Spanish-American War Spanish officials were puzzled by the hostility of the United States. Since Spain had conceded autonomy to Cuba in November, 1897, these officials could only conclude that the United States "simply spoiled for a fight." This observation neglects the very important fact that "autonomy" was a sham, known to be so by the Spanish as well as the Cubans and Americans. The Spanish concession excluded control over all matters relating to the military, foreign affairs, and the administration of justice. Thus the conflict between Spain and her colony (and ultimately the United States) after November, 1897, was substantial rather than casual and largely emotional, as Vandiver implies. His treatment of Woodrow Wilson is equally defective. Any serious student of Wilson will wince at the following assessment: "With a zealot's simplistic eye, he saw government as moral trust, denied the need for political maneuver." Later on, and less justifiable still, Vandiver compares Wilson's optimism with that of Candide. The suggestion of such similarity is, at the very least, gratuitous. What is particularly disturbing about the foregoing examples is that they suggest a greater concern for verve than for accuracy.

If one is willing to take the time and effort, important information about Pershing can be gleaned from the detail provided by the author. A particularly decisive moment in Black Jack's career came in 1901. After moving laterally through a variety of assignments since his graduation from West Point, he was sent to the Philippines where he demonstrated considerable perception in volunteering to lead a pacification mission in Mindanao, home of the wild Moros. Mindanao was far from the amenities of Manila and thus considered by most an unattractive assignment. Pershing, however, shrewdly calculated that Mindanao offered a likely prospect of military action, action that promised visibility. His technique in pacifying the Moros displayed solid common sense. Less truculent natives were separated from the "hostiles" by offers of protection and even-handed justice. The intransigents that remained were then sought out and subdued. Pershing's efforts were made easier by the Moro habit of making last-ditch stands from primitive forts where their swords and rifles were no match for the army's artillery. Hand-to-hand combat was mainly avoided, with the result that few Americans were seriously wounded or killed.

Pershing's initial exploits in Mindanao (he subsequently returned as commander of the Department of Mindanao and governor of Moro Province) were instrumental in his dramatic promotion to brigadier general. In the absence of more exciting action elsewhere, Pershing's successful forays against a barely civilized people in an exotic part of the world attracted attention. Even President Roosevelt took note. This fame, combined with the influence of Senator Francis Warren, Pershing's father-in-law and chairman of the Senate Military Affairs Committee, was sufficient to obtain a much sought-after promotion from captain to brigadier general. Such leapfrogging, while not unprecedented, was unusual. Raised eyebrows and jealous recriminations notwithstanding, the promotion was confirmed by the Senate. Without this stroke of good fortune it is doubtful that Pershing would have received the command position that he needed to demonstrate his ability.

The second volume of the biography is dominated by Pershing in the role of Commander-in-Chief of American Expeditionary Forces in Europe. The period from the spring of 1917 to the spring of 1919 witnessed the apogee of Pershing's long career in the military. Vandiver writes this section with a surer hand than elsewhere. The quiet strengths of Pershing's character are revealed by the pressures of fighting a determined foe and cooperating with headstrong allies. In order to prepare American recruits for a combat role as quickly as possible, Pershing shuffled personnel, conducted on-site inspections, and listened without prejudice to criticism. Meanwhile he struggled with the French and British on issues of strategy. Generals Foch, Pétain, and Haig worked tirelessly to persuade Pershing to permit the assimilation of American units into their armies. He resisted all of their blandishments, and, when sufficient numbers of doughboys were ready for battle, they joined the conflict as a separate force. While Belleau Wood, Château-Thierry and Saint Mihiel came late in the war, the results of those engagements removed any doubt about the quality of American soldiers.

Vandiver's coverage of the remainder of Pershing's life is mercifully brief. After the signing of the Armistice, ceremonial duties increased enormously. There were celebrations to be attended and monuments to be dedicated. Although Pershing became Chief of Staff, a position that he coveted, in 1921, the glory days passed with the war. In subsequent years he devoted much time to the American Battle Monuments Commission. But by the late 1930's he had become chronically ill and infirm. After lingering through another war—one which he was powerless to affect—Pershing died in 1948.

Upon reaching page 1,097 of *Black Jack,* this critic was convinced that a biography half that length could have been much more successful. By including too much material, some of which is extraneous and distracting, Vandiver fails to delineate a three-dimensional personality. With the possible exception of the period of World War I, Pershing seems to pass through his life leaving only surface impressions behind. In the final analysis, *Black Jack* demonstrates the proposition that in biography detail is an inadequate substitute for definition.

Meredith William Berg

Sources for Further Study

Choice. XIV, November, 1977, p. 1275.
Library Journal. CII, October 1, 1977, p. 2056.
National Review. XXIX, June 10, 1977, p. 673.
New Republic. CLXXVII, July 9, 1977, p. 36.
Publisher's Weekly. CCXI, April 18, 1977, p. 53.
Southwest Review. LXII, Summer, 1977, p. 422.

BLACK ORCHID

Authors: Nicholas Meyer and Barry Jay Kaplan
Publisher: The Dial Press (New York). 310 pp. $8.95
Type of work: Novel
Time: The late 1800's
Locale: Manaus, Brazil, along the Amazon River

An adventure novel centering around Harry Kincaid's attempt singlehandedly to break the Brazilian monopoly on rubber by smuggling out some seeds

Principal characters:
HARRY KINCAID, a cynical adventurer
PROFESSOR LONGFORD, his companion, a botanist disguised as his valet
PIERRE COUTARD, the foppish, dissipated heir to a rubber fortune rivaling that of the Mendonças
MERCEDES COUTARD, Pierre's sister, the cold, ruthless power behind the throne
COLONEL ARMANDO MENDONÇA, a dying rubber magnate trying to keep his empire together
DOLORES MENDONÇA, his headstrong daughter, bethrothed to Pierre Coutard but in love with Harry Kincaid
IQUITOS, an Indian reared by Colonel Mendonça

Nicholas Meyer and his co-author Barry Jay Kaplan are popular novelists. Nicholas Meyer is the better-known, having recently written *The Seven-Per-Cent Solution* and *The West End Horror.* Before coauthoring *The Black Orchid,* Barry Jay Kaplan had written and published numerous romances and gothic novels under various pen names. Both authors are thus well equipped for this present task—the creation of a historical potboiler which presents itself firmly as light reading and looks fondly toward film sale.

The *donnée* of this adventure story is its Brazilian setting—the city of Manaus, the center of the late nineteenth century rubber monopoly, and the adjoining Amazon River. Manaus is truly extraordinary—the result of the attempt of suddenly rich rubber magnates to create a European city and culture on the sweltering banks of the Amazon. Electric trains, copies of European architecture, an opera house, and cobblestone streets are part of the physical imitation; fashionable clothing, French food, and the latest dances are part of the cultural. Everything—the marble, the food, the cobblestones—must be imported. And the effort is a gigantic failure, a case of substance without spirit.

The phenomenon of Manaus is by no means treated seriously. In fact, the details seem conveniently woven into the novel from note cards gathered specifically for the purpose: "The Hobby Horse Quadrille (the latest New York rage) was succeeded by the Alice Wonderland Quadrille, which was in turn supplanted by the first waltz of the evening, regarded as slightly daring in Manaus." This short passage taken from the costume ball scene is one of many examples of pointless attention to detail. It is bad enough that it is unconnected with plot or character; it is worse that it makes little sense to call a waltz "slightly daring" in a society as dissipated as that of Manaus. The authors know the names of some popular dances; they know that the initiation of the waltz created a mild sensation in Europe. Mindlessly, they combine these facts into a pointless and inappropriate sentence. It is this continual name-dropping which is, in fact, the novel's chief means of suggesting historicity.

The defender of light adventure fiction might well answer that such name-dropping is a harmless, painless method of education: a bit of history has been woven into an exciting format. One may be permitted some doubts. The authors have not attempted to give history life, but have used history for their own melodramatic purposes by making "free with events and dates, telescoping time willy-nilly." And one wonders too whether the details are really accurate, or just seem so. When we are asked to eat in a "formal *salle à manager*" or to heed to the views of "*grandes homens,*" we may well be taken aback. If the other details of the novel are as uneven as the authors' French, perhaps none are reliable.

The City of Manaus is the centerpiece of the novel, but the Amazon River dominates the opening scene as well as the exciting close of the story. In their use of the river, the authors are far more successful in integrating setting and plot. The size and menace of the Amazon are effectively conveyed. One can feel the stifling heat, the constant annoyance of insects, and the incredible width of the river. The menace of the Amazon is also very clear: alligators, piranhas, killer ants, and the thick jungle that reaches to the water. The climax of the book—a chase down the river—weaves all of these elements into an exciting, suspenseful series of episodes. Of course, even in this, the novel's climax, some may entertain skepticism concerning the authors' true inventiveness. They trot out a piranha episode, an attack by killer ants, and so on, in faithful sequence, almost as if they were following a list entitled "useful melodramatic dangers."

If the novel's setting is largely original, the characters are largely stereotyped and threadbare. At the center of the novel is Harry Kincaid, an American adventurer in his mid-forties starting out on what he hopes will be a profitable last adventure—breaking the Brazilian rubber monopoly by the smuggling of rubber seeds for germination in English hothouses and later transplantation in Malaya. He is entirely cynical; when offered a better price, he is quite willing to betray his original employers. In one of the novel's few attempts at wit, Harry, attending a costume party in evening dress, is twitted about being out of costume. "Oh, but I am," Kincaid countered . . . . "I'm here disguised as a gentleman." Near the novel's end Harry decides to bury his companion-in-adventure, Longford, killed in a horrible accident. High motives are ascribed to him, but Harry knows better: "he had insisted on the burial not because his feelings for Longford were so great, but because they were so little." Finally, in a blinding flash of synthetic insight, he realizes that he is "imitating a human being . . . his entire existence (is) nothing more than a sustained attempt to flee from his own absence."

Nothing of this fashionable cynicism prevents Kincaid from being an adventurer who earns the admiration of friends and enemies for his skill at his chosen trade. He thinks of every eventuality. For example, when he realizes that a hydrogen balloon has the ability to track the vessel in which he plans to escape, he cuts it from its moorings on the fateful night. When he rows back alone to send an encoded cable, he immediately afterwards cuts the cable line, but in two places—one visible, the other hard to find. Moreover, his prowess is not limited to adventure, but also includes romance. An otherwise unapproachable dancer yields to him with few preliminaries. Both of the novel's heroines seduce him.

To some extent, the novel is built on fantasies of seduction. Partly these fantasies are male-oriented. Harry is irresistible; women, despite their better instincts, throw themselves at him. Of these fantasies Harry's relationship with Dolores Mendonça is the apotheosis. She develops a schoolgirl crush on him that disappears when she realizes his true purpose in Manaus. Nevertheless, ultimately her knowledge of his true character awakens in her a passion far deeper and far less eradicable than the first. But the novel's fantasies are not entirely male-oriented. Dolores and her sister-heroine, Mercedes Coutard, are not the wispy, receding heroines of romantic fiction. Mercedes is ruthless and aggressive; Dolores becomes ruthless and aggressive as the novel progresses. Thus we have fantasies created to please not only male readers but female readers who like to think of themselves as assertive but not unfeminine.

Male-female relationships, however, are only peripheral to the plot of *Black Orchid;* central to it is the fantasy of a single adventurer pitted against the collective power of the rubber barons: Colonel Mendonça and Mercedes Coutard. Mercedes, realizing that Colonel Mendonça is old and dying, anxiously plans to gather all power for herself. In pursuit of this end, she organizes a civil war to destroy the Colonel's rubber plantation. The Colonel, equally ruthless, but obviously in the old style, proposes a marriage between the Coutard and the Mendonça families as a way of bringing a final and lasting peace. Both of these schemers—Miss Coutard and Mendonça—are equally reprehensible because their power rests entirely on the virtual enslavement of the Indian population on whose misery the splendor of Manaus depends. But if the reader thinks that this novel is going to offer him a special insight into the workings of power, the injustices it perpetrates, and the means of dealing with it, he is mistaken. Social injustice and corporate power are introduced only to foster melodramatic encounters between the lone adventurer and the forces bent on destroying him.

In the end, *Black Orchid* is not a novel of character or of atmosphere but of plot. On reflection, this plot may seem mechanical; much of it can be anticipated. However, there is no denying the sheer ingenuity with which the authors arrange the novel's incidents. Let one example suffice. An aerial balloon is introduced quite naturally as a tourist attraction at the rubber convention. Surely, the reader thinks, the balloon must be an important prop in the plot. This impression is confirmed when Harry Kincaid takes a well-planned and thoughtful ride in the device. However, the reader's expectations are defeated. During the costume ball, the balloon is noticed, rising, freed from its moorings. This is Harry Kincaid's doing, but the balloon is not a direct part of his escape plan. Harry, forever ingenious, has realized that the vehicle could be used to track the steam yacht in which he escapes. We are suitably impressed by Harry's skill and by the authors' also; they have surprised us in any ingenious way.

One would like to feel that *Black Orchid* could stand by itself as an interesting light fiction on the strength of its exotic setting and its mechanical and exciting plot. It should then make no difference that the book is little more than a motion picture scenario, slightly fleshed out. Why should we ask more of it than of the film it yearns to be? Precisely because it is a novel, and, in the nature of things, we expect more of a novel than of a motion picture. Adventure films can be enjoyably watched in a state of diminished attention, while *Black Orchid* demands our full attention. Nevertheless it gives us little in return because it is not so much written as manufactured. It insults the cultivated reader and provides strong evidence to those concerned about a general debasement of taste.

Alan G. Gross

Sources for Further Study

Booklist. LXXIV, December 1, 1977, p. 602.
Kirkus Reviews. XLV, September 15, 1977, p. 1007.
Library Journal. CII, November 1, 1977, p. 2278.
New York Times Book Review. October 23, 1977, p. 23.
Publisher's Weekly. CCXII, August 29, 1977, p. 353.
West Coast Review of Books. IV, January, 1978, p. 34.

BLIND DATE

Author: Jerzy Kosinski (1933–   )
Publisher: Houghton Mifflin Company (Boston). 236 pp. $8.95
Type of work: Novel
Time: The present
Locale: International

The chronicle of the adventures of George Levanter, a modern picaro who uses disinterested, diabolical cleverness to outwit his antagonists

Principal characters:
GEORGE LEVANTER, a private investor who travels in search of business, adventure, and romance
PAULINE, his last lover, a famous concert pianist
JACQUES MONOD, his friend, a dying scientist
ROMARKIN, his friend from school days in Russia
SERENA, his lover, a high-priced prostitute
FOXY LADY, another lover, a transsexual
MARY-JANE KIRKLAND, his short-lived wife, a rich heiress
OSCAR, a young rapist

Readers of Kosinski's *Blind Date* will not be surprised to discover the same heights of stylistic achievement as well as the familiar depths of sexual perversion that critics have praised and damned since the appearance of his first work, *The Painted Bird* (1965). *Steps* (1968), *Being There* (1971), *The Devil Tree* (1973), and *Cockpit* (1975) all portray a terrifying vision of a world dominated by barbarism, sadomasochism, and violence; Kosinski's art reveals itself not in his endless chapters of scenic cruelty but, in the manner in which he arranges, conveys, and describes these experiences to the reader to achieve maximum dramatic impact.

George Levanter, *Blind Date*'s protagonist, is a private investor whose business ventures take him from Russia to New York, from the Alps to Los Angeles; however, his East European heritage, especially the trauma of being a Russian Jew in Nazi Germany, constantly surfaces into his consciousness. Levanter has clearly descended from the ten-year-old boy of *The Painted Bird* (a victim of World War II Nazi atrocities), "Chance," the main character of *Being There,* and Tarden, *Cockpit*'s antihero. All these heroes are individuals who learn quickly to survive in a world devoid of justice and morality. As a result, Levanter lives as a picaresque con-man whose good and evil acts are purely serendipitous. Early in the novel, he blackmails a despicable corporate chairman; shortly thereafter, he becomes victimized by the prosecutor of a divorce case. Chance, not justice, prevails.

Levanter is a picaro in both the traditional and modern sense. Like Gil Blas, he is a rogue, but unlike Le Sage's protagonist, he does not come from a low social level. He deals with people from all classes and different locations and quickly learns their foibles and frailties. Kosinski's picaro also bypasses the line between petty rascal and criminal which places him in the distinct American picaresque tradition initiated by Herman Melville's *The Confidence Man.* Like Melville's work, *Blind Date* often surpasses the satiric humor of the traditional picaresque rascal and progresses into pure vitriol and pessimism; the laughing is replaced by horror.

The picaresque hero defines the book's structure: a loosely connected series of adventures, many quite impossible to conceive as happening in one man's life, with a cumulative effect rather than a resolving conclusion. Levanter's journeys have no goal. Yet, the novel's episodes consist overwhelmingly of scenes of manipulation. As the dust cover (a man controlling a number of individuals as so many puppets bound by strings, yet his own movements are also controlled by attached strings) suggests, free will and dignity are rare commodities in a world shaped by whimsey. The central metaphor for the entire novel, the "blind date," is what Oscar, a youthful rapist, calls his attacks upon helpless young women; since the victims never see their assailant who attacks them from behind with scientific proficiency, the brutal impersonality of the acts remains intact. When young Levanter finally brutalizes a young girl he calls "Nameless," Oscar is jailed for the one crime he did not commit; the irony of injustice increases.

This metaphor of impersonality is reinforced by the numerous disguises and masquerades which Levanter perpetrates in the novel; at various times he charades as a Russian government official, a secret agent from the American Council for Global Security, and an Eskimo. He gains personal satisfaction or revenge through each of these ploys. For example, he double-crosses a Communist agent by posing as an agent; thus, he avenges the death of his friend, a fencing champion, by impaling the treacherous agent on a sabre. He also kills the Deputy Minister of Internal Affairs from a kingdom which tortures intellectual dissidents. Afterward, Levanter feels elevated by executing such seldom-seen justice. Another attempt at mercy backfires, however, as his release of other political prisoners results in the death of an innocent translator. Such are the brutal ironies of Kosinski's fictional universe.

Sexual identities also become merged in this fictional universe which confuses illusion with reality. Levanter becomes enamored of "Foxy Lady," whose sexuality seems satisfying but ambiguous to him. She, unlike other women, seems to understand "everything he wanted." He feels cheated upon discovering that Foxy Lady did not have a tumor but a penis removed in recent surgery. Later Levanter marries Mary-Jane Kirkland, a rich widow whom he meets on a legitimate blind date. Her death by cancer is clearly foreshadowed by the appearance of Levanter's article in *Investor's Quarterly* concerning the "role of chance in creative investment." The hero's one true attempt at emotional investment with love extending beyond mere sexual gratification ends in emotional bankruptcy. This metaphor of life as a game where victory is sweet, but where defeat is inevitable, accounts for the death of Kosinski's protagonist. The last skier with a chance of a solo run on his favorite range which he could ski "blindfolded," he becomes lost in an icy fog and succumbs to the indomitable will of nature despite an admirable struggle.

Levanter's demise answers the death wish of the novel's epigraph from Jonathan Swift, who asks: "Remove me from this land of slaves,/Where all are fools, and all are knaves,/Where every knave and fool is bought,/Yet kindly sells himself for naught;—" Through this struggle to assert his individual will upon the people and circumstances that surround him, George Levanter becomes the first Kosinski character to approach heroic stature. His triumphs and defeats illustrate the author's conception of life as a "blind date" where chance prevails.

Blind Date is not, however, entirely free from those gratuitous parables which dull Kosinski's other works. For example, Levanter becomes enamored of a woman who has no body; a bone disease has withered all her limbs into vestigial stumps so that she must be wheeled in a baby carriage or carried from place to place. Levanter desires this woman since "she had incorporated her deformity into the totality of her life." Luckily, she rebuffs his advances to prevent the description of a truly bizarre seduction.

Kosinski wisely offsets such solipsistic parables by skillfully weaving true historical characters and incidents into the fabric of his fictional narrative. While teaching an investment course at Princeton University, Levanter rents a home next door to Svetlana Alliluyeva, Stalin's daughter. The shock of this situation—a Russian refugee living next to the daughter of the former Russian dictator—stops Levanter from speaking to her in their native Russian tongue. His friend Romarkin shakes his head at this coincidence and observes that "anything can happen." "Anything" can and does occur in the novel to verify Levanter's father's claim that "civilization is the result of sheer chance plus a thousand or two exceptional men of ideas and action." Levanter meets one of these famous "investors"—people who utilize personal energy and means to aid civilization—Charles Lindbergh. When they meet, Levanter mentions the aviator's citation from Hitler and participation in keeping the United States out of World War II as great blows to his faith in human wisdom. Lindbergh defends his interest in Germany as a model technocratic society; he overlooks its racial hatred as merely a temporary aberration. The mass atrocities, of course, prove him wrong.

The most effectively utilized historical incident, and perhaps the best executed section of the novel, involves the Manson murders. Kosinski introduces the re-creation of this brutal act through a Russian woman whom Levanter encounters in Cannes; she was the lover of "Woytek" (Wojiciech Voityck Frykowski), a man whom Levanter brings to America against her wishes. Levanter enlists "Gibby" (Abigail Folger), a rich American heiress, to look after the Russian immigrant. They move to California and stay in Beverly Hills with their pregnant friend, "Sharon" (Sharon Tate, wife of director Roman Polanski). Levanter plans to join them, but a baggage mixup delays his Los Angeles arrival and, ultimately, saves his life. As news reports of the tragedy flood his consciousness, Levanter reimagines the crime from Woytek's point of view; the result is the best descriptive writing in the entire novel. These scenes read cinematically faithful to the facts presented by Vincent Bugliosi's *Helter Skelter,* and their emotional impact parallels scenes in Truman Capote's *In Cold Blood* for terror and veracity. These murders also restate Kosinski's chief thematic thrusts: the role of sheer chance upon men's lives, the brutality of human nature, and the defeat of rational man by blind nature.

Other scenes dramatize science's attempt to influence life's outcome. Levanter visits a famous immunology research laboratory, where thousands of mice are caged and diligently monitored to prevent contamination. When he tries to convince his guide that a mouse runs loose in the room despite reliable, responsible scientists, the man will not believe his claim. Upon seeing the mouse, the scientist reports its existence to a young research assistant who also denies its existence. Only when all have witnessed the mouse scampering across the floor will they admit a "human error" has occurred. In another instance, when Levanter learns that Jacques Monod, an esteemed French biologist who discovers how the living cell manufactures the substance of life, is actually being deprived of this very substance, he is stunned into silence at life's cruel ironies. Monod tells him that "blind chance" determines each random event of life. An orderly predetermined life scheme "bypasses the drama of each unique instance of man's own existence." Monod, the author of the appropriately titled work *Chance and Necessity,* accepts his fate, but Levanter leaves him "mute and dispirited" at life's injustices.

In the novel's other epigraph Jacques Monod asks who can "define crime" and distinguish "good" and "evil" when the "traditional systems" place ethics and values "beyond man's reach?" George Levanter lives in this world of moral ambiguity: his life is a succession of "blind dates" which rarely gain profits for their investor. He lives by his wits and dies knowing that he has done his best. His death is not a surrender to the blizzard which freezes him, but merely an "acknowledgment of its might." He "scores quite well in the games he plays"; even if "few others . . . would ever want to learn to play his game."

Gregory S. Sojka

Sources for Further Study

Atlantic. CCXL, December, 1977, p. 108.
Book World. August 28, 1977, p. F2.
Kirkus Reviews. XLV, September 1, 1977, p. 949.
New York Times Book Review. November 6, 1977, p. 14.
Publisher's Weekly. CII, September 19, 1977, p. 140.
Time. CX, October 31, 1977, p. 104.

BLOCKADE BUSTERS

Author: Ralph Barker (1917–   )
Publisher: W. W. Norton and Company (New York). 224 pp. $8.95
Type of work: History
Time: 1939–1945
Locale: England, Sweden, the North Sea and the Skagerrak

A detailed account of British attempts to run the German blockade of the North Sea and the Skagerrak during World War II

Blockade Busters is an adventure story with a special purpose. Author Ralph Barker is not only concerned that an important, but little known, episode relating to the British war effort against Nazi Germany be brought to light; he is equally determined that the organizing genius of that effort, Sir George Binney, be properly celebrated. That Binney has been neglected by historians of World War II seems evident. Volumes I and II of *The War at Sea, 1939-1945,* the official history of British naval operations during the war, fail even to mention him by name. Yet, Binney not only conceived the idea of running the German blockade of the Baltic Sea and masterminded its execution, he also shared the fate of his crews on four separate voyages between Sweden and England.

When war broke out in Europe in September, 1939, George Binney was employed as a steel executive. His career to that point was rich and varied. It included two Arctic expeditions while still a student, as well as a period of employment with Hudson's Bay Company in London and Canada. The existence of a state of war, combined with Binney's interests and experience— and, one should add, a high sense of adventure—soon drew him into the vortex of the life-and-death struggle between his country and the Axis powers. In December, 1939, Binney was sent to Stockholm in order to superintend British steel interests in Norway and Sweden.

From the very outset, Binney's mission to Scandinavia transcended the private concerns of British steel. Officially he represented British Iron and Steel Control in Sweden and Norway, but unofficially he was also to report to Military Intelligence on matters of interest. Sweden was especially crucial to the British war effort because of its high-grade steel. Virtually all phases of essential war-related production were dependent upon Swedish-produced hollow tubes, steel strip, wire rods, special alloys, and bearings. By the terms of the Anglo-Swedish War Trade Agreement of October, 1939, Britain was entitled to the same share of Swedish exports that it had enjoyed in 1938. It was Binney's responsibility to facilitate the export of these products to Britain.

During the first six months of the war, Swedish steel exports to Britain continued from the Arctic port of Narvik. In May, 1940, however, Germany occupied Norway and that vital lifeline was closed down. Sweden became an island of neutrality in a sea of German-controlled territory. Even though Britain enjoyed the legal right to a percentage of Swedish exports, it appeared increasingly doubtful that she would be able to act on that privilege. In time,

Germany believed, the Anglo-Swedish War Trade Agreement would in effect be voided, with the result that increasingly larger percentages of Swedish produc-tion would be channeled to Germany. In order to deprive Germany of access to these goods, Binney requested and received permission from the Ministry of Supply to continue purchases of Swedish products for storage. Binney was already showing signs of the independence and resourcefulness that would become the hallmark of his wartime career.

Purchase and storage were, of course, only temporary expedients. Binney's ultimate task was to facilitate the shipment of Swedish products to Britain. Aside from air transport, which was costly and inadequate in the best of circumstances, the only alternative was to challenge the German blockade of the Baltic. The ports on the west coast of Sweden were separated from the North Sea by the Skagerrak, a narrow channel between Norway and Denmark some one hundred and fifty miles long and sixty to ninety miles wide. The Skagerrak was not only heavily mined by both Britain and Germany, it was also intensively patroled by German planes and ships. Despite these hazards, Binney was confident that a breakout could be successful. Winter conditions of fog and snow were powerful allies in neutralizing the effect of German air and sea patrols.

The availability of merchant shipping was perhaps the most intriguing feature of Binney's bold proposal. Just before going into exile in London, the Norwegian government had requisitioned all Norwegian ships outside of Norway whose owners were resident in Norway or German occupied territory. These ships were placed under the authority of Nortraship (Norwegian Trading and Shipping Mission), a newly created marine directorate that operated out of London. Since the Swedish government recognized the authority of Nortra-ship—over German protests—and Nortraship was willing to place Norwegian ships anchored in Swedish waters at Britain's disposal, Binney had no problem procuring the necessary merchant tonnage. Several of these Norwegian ships were oil-burners which had sufficient fuel on board for the one-way voyage to Britain. The pieces of Binney's scheme were beginning to fit into place.

As Barker repeatedly demonstrates, Binney was one of those rare persons who seem to thrive on adversity. And, from the spring of 1940 until the winter of the following year, he encountered a maddening succession of obstacles to the launching of Operation Rubble, the code name for the enterprise. At home, the Admiralty doubted that the proposed expedition stood much chance of success, while the Foreign Office, innately cautious, feared that any attempt to run the blockade might cause Germany to occupy Sweden. These misgivings notwith-standing, the law of necessity ultimately prevailed; the importance of Swedish steel to English production offset all risks. Once the die was cast, the opposition within both ministries melted away. In Sweden, the recruitment of crews to man the five ships selected for the first expedition was a frustrating and time-consuming process. A large number of the original crews of the Norwegian ships, including all of the captains, declined to participate in the venture because of the dangers involved. The fact that many of the Norwegians had been joined in Sweden by their families tended to increase their caution. The gaps left by these defections were bridged mainly by British seamen stranded in Norway at the time of the German occupation who subsequently had been forced marched to internment in Sweden. The few positions that remained were filled by Swedes, who were usually persuaded to join the venture only after receiving assurances of substantial cash bonuses.

The matter of secrecy, which was essential to the successful launching of the Nortraship fleet, was largely dependent upon the good will of the Swedish government. Barker fails to appreciate the considerable courage displayed by the Swedish government in the cooperation that it gave to Operation Rubble. Swedish officials incurred much German displeasure in their determination to dispense evenhanded justice to British interests. And Binney was not the least bit reluctant to press his advantage at every turn. Utilizing the Swedish sense of fair play, he resolved to transfer his loaded ships from Gothenburg, where German agents could easily monitor their every move, to Brofjord, an isolated fjord some fifty miles north of Gothenburg. Swedish ships escorted the convoy the entire distance between Gothenburg and Brofjord. Once the transfer was completed, Swedish officials cleared all known Nazi agents from the area. Thus, while the Germans knew the location and objective of the Rubble fleet, they remained ignorant of the timing of the breakout. Under cover of darkness and bad weather, precious hours might be gained before the disappearance of the ships was noted by German reconnaissance.

Barker is at his best when he describes the passage of the blockade runners through the German gauntlet to the North Sea. On January 23, 1941, after waiting weeks for suitable weather, the fleet struck out into the Skagerrak under cover of light snow. Each vessel was to sail independently, and in no circumstance would any of them come to the aid of a sister ship in distress. Radio silence would be maintained at all times. Every ship was equipped with a special explosive device that would insure quick scuttling in case of capture. The focus of the mission was clear: the valuable cargoes must reach Britain. The vessels, and even the safety of the crews, were secondary.

By early morning of the next day the snow had stopped and the remainder of the night was clear. Daybreak found all of the ships critically exposed to German air patrols. By that time the three speedier ships were into the North Sea and streaking toward a prearranged rendezvous with British air and naval units. The two slower ships, however, did not reach the mouth of the Skagerrak until seven hours after dawn. Miraculously, none of the Rubble ships encountered important German opposition until it was within range of British protection. Binney's faith in Operation Rubble was completely vindicated. All of the cargoes aboard the five ships arrived in Britain intact. Their total value, estimated at one million pounds sterling, is more accurately expressed in other terms. The 25,000 tons of steel products represented one year's quota of Swedish exports under the terms of the War Trade Agreement. Binney was the man of the hour. Former critics rushed forward to offer simultaneous apologies and congratulations. He was even knighted by a grateful government.

For the remainder of the war Binney continued to challenge the German blockade with mixed results. Increased German vigilance and a more stringent Swedish interpretation of neutral rights combined to devastate a second attempted breakout in March, 1942. Of the ten ships that comprised Operation Performance, only two reached Britain. In human terms, the expedition was equally costly. Approximately 150 crew members were captured by the Germans and incarcerated in slave labor camps. Undaunted by these losses, Binney continued to penetrate the blockade with fast motor gunboats that were converted to haul cargo. These ships, although plagued by mechanical difficulties, were fairly successful in achieving their objectives, especially in the waning stages of the war when German enforcement of the blockade began to break down.

Blockade Busters is intended for a general audience. While the military significance of the daring voyages between Sweden and Britain can scarcely be denied, the focus throughout Barker's narrative is upon the heroism of individuals caught up in one small corner of a great war. The author is a good storyteller. By the skillful use of unpublished manuscripts of key participants in the various breakouts, including Binney himself, in addition to many interviews with surviving crew members, Barker has been able to re-create in a vivid and personal way the experiences that these people shared.

In terms of its broader importance to the military and diplomatic history of World War II, *Blockade Busters* has relatively little to offer aside from the oft-repeated impact of Swedish steel exports on British war industry. Despite the fact that the publisher's advertising of the book emphasizes the use of recently declassified materials, there are few indications that Barker spent long hours in archival research. Since there are no footnotes, it is impossible to determine which sources the author relied upon most heavily. Internal evidence, however, suggests that official British records were utilized mainly to provide background for Binney's exploits.

Still, as a self-contained adventure story, *Blockade Busters* succeeds admirably. And that, perhaps, is justification enough.

Meredith William Berg

Sources for Further Study

Kirkus Reviews. XLV, March 1, 1977, p. 251.
Publisher's Weekly. CXI, March 21, 1977, p. 81.
Yachting. CXLII, July, 1977, p. 92.

BLOOD, HOOK & EYE

Author: Dara Wier (1949–   )
Publisher: University of Texas Press (Austin). 70 pp. $7.95; paperback $3.95
Type of work: Poetry

A first collection of poems filled with the voices of people telling their stories, inner and outer, by a new and very gifted young poet with an original and distinctive voice all her own

We are, I hope, now permanently past the era of the "poetess," that too recent time when all women poets seemed to have three names and to write with a delicacy appropriate to those rhythmic names, or, if they wrote with a vigor and original skill, were required to wear the tricornered hats of eccentricity or to brood over a private poetry not really meant for others to read. We are finally reading Gertrude Stein instead of talking about her or, worse, making her into cheap jokes; we are finally discovering the genuine in the poetry of Marianne Moore as well as the charm.

The danger for a young woman poet today is not that she will be forced back to the authoress section of our attention, but that she will be taken too seriously for the wrong reasons, that she will be studied and admired as a woman poet rather than just as a poet, that she will be praised for raising a woman's voice rather than for extending and exploring the ground where only the imagination, the poetic imagination, may ever dare venture.

The fault is, of course, Sylvia Plath's or Anne Sexton's; or—and this is much closer to the truth—the fault lies with those readers and critics who love to probe the personal anguish and sharp confession of their poems and who insist that a woman's place in the writing of poems is the back fence of gossip where she may confess her own fears and failings, her own hungers and cravings, her own emotional and very human nature, where we may eavesdrop and sit back smugly, saying that women's lives are led on such a different level, on such an intensely emotional level, on such an excoriatingly honest level, that it is no wonder the poor things do themselves in so frequently. Perhaps we haven't come so far after all.

All this is by way of saying that Dara Wier's poems require that they be read and admired and discussed not as a woman's poems, but as poems; not as a bid for poetic identity through gossip and confession, but as an expression of poetic entity by means of a poetry that is as fresh as its language is vigorous, a language honed to clean edges that cut to the bone and marrow of its subjects. Her language is personal and uniquely hers, with a diction and syntax that are startling and daring but which come to sound inevitable and undeniably right as you see them operate poem by poem. But her language is also an accumulation of voices, varied and vital—the voices of people caught in the eddies and floods of the blood's turmoil, telling their stories, not so much confessing their secrets as confessing for us all.

The first poem in the book, set apart from the others as introduction, professes to be a poem told by someone "just / before she committed suicide," and from that startling claim it moves on to play upon the commingling of lies and truth in art, in poems. The poem is spoken by listeners at a poetry reading (already a fair sample of how Dara Wier turns things inside out to make their double natures clean and clear). The poet's parents are in the audience, not looking a bit like the poet, while the poet tells of "your brother who shot / himself, a likely story."

> Your mother rubs sleep from her eye,
> we think she is crying. Your father
> yanks on his tie.
> We are worried that what you say
> is true.

That small poem, with all its doublings and double-dealings, its doubts and downright lies, teaches the reader who will listen how to read these poems, or any real poems: how we should not look for fact or the poet's face or the poet's family and past, how we should instead worry about the truth of the poems, the dark fact at the very marrow of our own bones or the bright vision that makes us leap up from our chairs ruffling our hair.

These poems, for all their linguistic wit and mental double vision, are filled with the sensuous details of living, the astonishing discoveries of all the senses caught in these words; the reader enters these scenes, sees them, hears them, touches them, even smells and tastes them, shares them in a way that only the best poems ever allow, physically and fully. A poem like "When the Skins Fall Apart" must surely be one of the most sensuous poems in the language:

> The fertilizer plant grinds fish into stink.
> In the icebox a dove carcass cools while Momma
> boils pumpkin in a castiron pot.
>
> The house upfront is full of drying garlic
> where you wait for the boy from Buras.
> River sand's as soft as any barnbed.
>
> You two roll in the garlic bulbs shaking the skin to pieces.
> Momma stuffs shirts in starch clabber, twists them
> into clubs and puts them aside for ironing.

The poem goes on to describe the smell of sperm, the starch drying under the mother's nails, the daughter's slicing the skin from the blister her school shoes give her heels, her pitching the skin in the river. This poem is not a pretty thing, but it has the truth in it about which we should worry, the truth of first love, of sex, of first loss and early despair, blood's truth that traces back to that initial fall from Edenic grace, lasting sin in the blood's original and terribly familiar demands.

As this poem's sensuous details develop into a complex imaginative exploration of the spirit's travail in the world of flesh, so the entire book has an integrity and movement beyond its accumulation of sharp details and particular experi-

ences. It is, as its title indicates, constructed in three sections: "Blood," which
concerns blood ties and the ties of blood, both within the family and beyond in
the larger family of humankind; "Hook," which presents the ironies and desperate comedies of sexual need and our dealings sex to sex, the mysteries and
surprises of life in this flesh; and "Eye," which draws the themes and words and
scenes and people of the earlier sections together in a moving field of energy
and life. It moves from the slightly bewildered character in the first poem, "Toad
Suck Ferry," who doesn't know for sure just where he's at, to the closing image of
the last poem of the book, "To Become a Field," where everything is presence,
unified and whole, even "the mountainless space, / the mountain holding
mountain / in place."

The first section, "Blood," is a movement of surfaces, of people and things
moving and touching, skin to skin. Flesh, wood, bone and oil, even a mobile of
fish fins, these skins cry out the names of what they cover, of what they strive to
define. Even the roof of a shed, its skin, sings out in the moving air, performs its
own way, "wind holding off wood. / Wood and tin, what instrument of wind."
We move like a river through this world of surfaces, and we find in its sensuous
vitality recurring patterns of death, nightmares in a day of ordinary things made
intensely strange. A mother, her husband gone off to a job out of state, her baby
still unweaned, feels buried inside her house, where even the goblet on the
sideboard looks like a greedy mouth. She feels eaten alive, feels buried inside
herself; on a day when the child won't stop crying, she decides there's "nothing
to do / but scald it with milk until it stops." A woman keeps her severed arm in
an antique clarinet case, or the phantom arm as she remembers it, dreams it,
denying in her care harsh fact. A woman makes a mobile of fish fins and twirls
them by, each one with her name engraved with a pinhead. Men and women act
like strangers; a man runs over his brother's head with his Studebaker's tire; a
man calls over the river to his drowned sons. Do we laugh or do we cry? The loss
fills these poems to the brim, everyone squirming in the fresh blood catch.

The section ends with the long and important poem, "Complaints," in which
memory moves through the skins of the world like a slow river, accepting its
terrible patterns, discovering its connections, redeeming it with the clear-eyed
honesty of love. The poet, apparently speaking for once directly in her own
voice, remembers her family house below New Orleans and her grandmother,
Mère. The Mississippi river, the house and the grandmother, all flow in the mind,
gather substance and form. Death appears, but only as a dance with the fish.
Violence and blood hover in the poem, the cancer that eats away a breast, the
chicken that bursts away from its severed head like a balloon. The roots may pull
loose like the chicken's feathers, but the fact of connection remains, the love, the
prophecy that repeats and comes true: *"you will swim on the dew."* All the major
strengths of the volume are represented in this poem; it is a powerful and wise
work, one that lingers in the mind like a memory, that flows on like a river to stay.

The second section, "Hook," carries us on beneath the skin, where the hooks and snares of living bite and tear. It is a section in which the bodies of its characters speak for themselves, the self hooked into flesh, into flesh's terrible dreams and caught desires. These poems, for all their irony and the distance that the imagination's cool eye can give, are a texture of sex and opposition, snakes and tongues like snakes, a pounding of fists and hips and bones. A character, one woman (or is she more than one woman?), lets us share her needs, her wishes, her ventures to the outer confines of her cage of bone and flesh. Doctors probe her and offer her astounding advice; she tries on dresses, looks at all the lotions in the drugstore, takes exercise and lies in the sun—always dreaming of the man who is watching or will be watching or should be watching, the man of her dreams that she somehow must make incarnate in her own flesh. These poems are comic but sad at the heart; they would do those women poets caught in the cage of confession a world of good if they would read them with a careful eye. But the body's dreams are often sweetened, given light in all their darkness with laughter, with the grace of surprises, the awakening of love. The last poem in the section, "Baiting a Line with Darkness," tells us what to do with our own darkness, allows the fish with whom we shall all someday dance to fill the air as rain, lets us know the presence of the light we cannot see, the sun that shines even as we watch the night with its weak light, what Jeremy Taylor called "inflamed jelly, the shining rot of stars."

In the last section, "Eye," vision asserts itself. Death continues to make its unrelenting demand, but these poems do not allow it the last word; they put things in motion, see the world not as set and solid fact, but as a tension of energies, spending and spent, never lost, never saved like a relic or a dog's buried bone. Madness is in the world, there's no denying, and death is no lie, but the dying become liars, and the eye does find the lie of death. In the last poem, "To Become a Field," mountains are moved by an act of imaginative faith, and the poem's speaker becomes a field of clear energy in a way that reason cannot comprehend, no matter how many books of directions are read, no matter how many material explanations are offered. The mountain interrupts all space, and space holds the mountain in place. As Mach's principle asserts, the whole universe matters locally, and it does.

Dara Wier uses everything with the frugal economy of a pioneer, things of the day, faint light of the night, and she is a pioneer, leading us with grace to the new lands that stretch before us every day. *Blood, Hook & Eye* is an extraordinary book, a young poet's close look at life. She has seen more than she tells us, but she tells us more than enough.

R. H. W. Dillard

Sources for Further Study

Booklist. LXXIV, September 15, 1977, p. 133.
Hudson Review. XXX, Winter, 1977–1978, p. 576.
Times Literary Supplement. November 18, 1977, p. 1354.

BLOOD MOUNTAIN

Author: John Engels (1931–   )
Publisher: University of Pittsburgh Press (Pittsburgh, Pa.). 54 pp. $6.95
Type of work: Poetry

A third collection of poems by John Engels, a book of unusual vision whose center is the yearning to see and to name

The rhythms of nature and the rhythms of language struggle in *Blood Mountain,* John Engel's third collection of poems. Engels was not afraid to use dark visions as the center of his two previous collections, *The Homer Mitchell Place* and *Signals from the Safety Coffin,* just as he is not afraid to use bold rhythms that resound deeply and echo off the face of Blood Mountain.

Echoes and after-images are important in this work. It is not what one man actually sees but what a blind man thinks he sees that is crucial, as seen in "Dawn on Blood Mountain":

> I am blind.
> I know you by touching
> your face. You are blind.
> My fingers cover
> where your eyes might be.
> Your hair is bright
> to my hand. Try nòt to see.
> What is there to see?
> I turn to go
> down? I am
> a contriver.
> You know.

Blindness, dreams, and remembrances make up the subjects of the twenty-one poems in *Blood Mountain.* Six poems are "Blood Mountain" poems by name; the others are not linked to Blood Mountain by geography but by a similarity of voice and rhythm. All the poems carry out the idea presented in the epigraph:

> *It is how I try to tell you*
> *There are no imbalances: we stand*
> *At whatever center most*
> *employs us.*

"At the Top of Blood Mountain," the central poem in the book both physically and spiritually, employs the senses as a means of describing a trip to the top of a mountain; seeing, hearing, tasting, smelling, and touching, are linked to the concept of thinking in the organization of the poem. This parallel rhetoric, a dangerous device in a poem, is used smoothly and effectively by Engels. The ascent of the mountain takes place in the physical world of linear time, but as the narrator depicts the center of the mountain, time begins to flow in erratic patterns similar to the unusual rhythms of the poem, whose line lengths break the natural rhythm of the poem just as the narrator breaks the natural rhythm of Blood Mountain's peak by trying to describe it. The narrator finally understands that language is a contrivance, but a necessary contrivance if one is not only to find the exact center of the mountain, but also to discover the center within himself.

There is an unnamed "you" in the "Blood Mountain" poems to whom the descriptions and the account of the search for the center of the mountain, are directed. This unnamed character, a woman, is a casual link in the narrator's life. In the poem "Falling on Blood Mountain," where she slips and falls ("the shock of your fall/unfolding into the root/of Blood Mountain . . .") she becomes the center of the narrator's consciousness, the recipient of his romantic contriving, the focus of his dreams. Sometimes the woman is addressed directly in the second person, the main character of a particular poem; sometimes she is alluded to as merely a force in the narrator's life. She is able to manipulate the narrator's physical world in the same fashion that the mountain manipulates his relationship to the natural world.

In the second poem in the book, "A May Snowstorm" a dream becomes a way of extending the length of mortal life, a means of moving toward immortality. Engels employs dreams in the poems as a director of a film would employ stylistic devices to achieve an artificiality that affirms the imaginative process of his art. Imagination is the key to many of these poems, the key that enriches them and elevates them to a new plane of reality. Changes in the weather, symbols of man's short existence, are used in a visual sense by Engels. The snowstorm changes the light of the spring day, blinding the narrator and his companion. They block the light, another reminder: "It ought to remind us/how between one breath and the warm next/the great silence lengthens." Even the presence of the woman he loves dejects him by reminding him that when she leaves,

> departure a darkness. And I
> shall be eternally
> dejected with it.

In "Vertigo on Blood Mountain" the narrator imagines staring into the red sun and falling off the mountain. As he pictures gliding off the mountain like a kite, his link with the physical nature of the mountain becomes tenuous. The higher he gets on the mountain the more he is reminded of his mortality, as if the mountain, bathed in close sunlight, is some type of burning prophecy.

In "Bad Weather on Blood Mountain," another poem directed to the narrator's unnamed love, the lover is caught in a storm on the mountain and for an instant feels the surge of a real mountain, Mt. Everest, within her. The weather clears, a sign that Blood Mountain's climate is suited for this type of climb: "You tell yourself/this is a hard climate, but not relentless." The woman is trapped between the hard world of the mountain and the imaginative world of the narrator. He wants her to choose between worlds, but it is clear that the choice is unnecessary because both worlds can exist simultaneously—something the narrator cannot see. Engels blinds the narrator of the poems in the same fashion a director uses the camera: the reader is confined to the singularity of one vision, but is reminded that there are other visions outside the realm of this particular world. Unfortunately, the narrator cannot see this; his blindness, though not total, does not allow for peripheral vision.

In "Toutes les lumieres" the same type of cinematic vision is used to separate the two worlds of physical and imaginative reality. The poem reads like a screenplay or a set of stage directions. Engels manipulates light to form shadows, which are the connection to the imaginative world. The narrator and his unnamed woman are standing on a lamplit street in a world of black and white. As in a black and white film the characters are caught in a world of shadows—they become shadows themselves. The vision becomes dreamlike as the narrator grows confused, unable to distinguish between the shadow of his friend and the physical bulk that causes the shadow:

> . . .She
> is standing in a circle
>
> of white light, she wears
> a white gown, and she is
> holding out her hand to
>
> someone I cannot see.

The woman who gestures is gesturing to the narrator, but he has become a mere shadow and cannot see into her world. The woman wears the light; the gown becomes the woman. Engels' craft thus establishes the imaginative world, a world of twins.

In "Photograph When You Are Not Looking," the narrator is a secret photographer who catches his subject offguard. When the woman walks out of range, his world diminishes:

> And there is nothing you can do
> but turn and walk away and even then
> this is what the last photograph
> will show: the street empty before you
> and the light gone bad.

When the narrator stares through the lens into the sun, he is blinded again, and in the final poem in the book, "Letter," he tries to come to terms with his blindness. This epistolary poem calls up the artificiality of his world, and brings the elements of the previous poems into focus: the weather clears, sounds crispen, the mountain becomes a world of motion. Blindness gives way as the narrator discovers the sounds and movements of the natural world. The poem begins optimistically: "I have been able to see Blood Mountain/for over a week." Later Blood Mountain darkens, but the narrator seems to understand that it is not night darkening the mountain but his own blindness.

The book closes with the narrator finally being able to achieve a distance from the woman he loves. When he understands the space between them, a space and separateness not governed by time or physical laws, he can more fully understand the world he has not been able to see. He can describe the world by feeling and hearing it though he is still not able to see it. The approximation of reality is an achievement he can appreciate.

Unlike his first two books, which have a single solitary vision of darkness, Engels here has been able to build on the subject of darkness and blindness by creating an imaginative world as depicted by a narrator blinded by the lack of a vision. Imagination is the key, as the narrator finally understands that he can only approximate the world around him and can never really enter it.

Like the blind narrator trying desperately to see, Engels strives for uniqueness of diction and voice and achieves both. The mountain climber, when asked why he climbs the mountain, responds: because it's there. Engels similarly creates and then climbs a mountain of imagination. Imagination is the rocky surface of the poet's language, and John Engels manages to traverse it with bold forthrightness and energy. It is not easy to create an imagined universe and sustain it through twenty-one poems without losing the energy of the invention, but Engels manages. *Blood Mountain* is a rich book that deserves to be read over and over again.

Paul M. Deblinger

Sources for Further Study

Booklist. LXXIV, September 15, 1977, p. 130.
Hudson Review. XXX, Winter, 1977–1978, p. 581.

A BOOK OF COMMON PRAYER

Author: Joan Didion (1935–   )
Publisher: Simon and Schuster (New York). 272 pp. $8.95
Type of work: Novel
Time: The present
Locale: The fictitious Central American country of Boca Grande with flashbacks to San Francisco and various cities of the American South

A realistic narrative of what it is like to live in the contemporary world, which is teetering absurdly on the edge of spiritual collapse

> *Principal characters:*
> GRACE STRASSER-MENDANA, the narrator, a sixty-year-old American woman
> CHARLOTTE DOUGLAS, an American woman in her early forties
> WARREN BOGART, her first husband
> LEONARD DOUGLAS, her second husband
> MARIN, their eighteen-year-old daughter
> VICTOR, Grace's brother-in-law, the Defense Minister of Boca Grande, one of Charlotte's temporary lovers
> GERARDO, Grace's son, a young international playboy and supporter of Victor's overthrow, another of Charlotte's lovers
> ANTONIO, Grace's other brother-in-law, a "sociopath"

In the preface to her well-regarded essay collection entitled *Slouching Toward Bethlehem* (1968), Joan Didion recounts that the title essay about the subculture of the Haight-Ashbury district of San Francisco was the first time she "had dealt directly and flatly with the evidence of atomization, the proof that things fall apart." She continues to investigate this contemporary phenomenon in *A Book of Common Prayer*, her third and best novel. In this clarification exercise on the contemporary milieu—a world of shorn values, smashed hopes, and harsh realities—Didion through her setting, her central character, and her narrator informs the reader of the desperate state of contemporary life, of the desperate attempts of those who try to live decently on the edge of the yawning void.

Ironically, Didion's representations of the great cosmic chill usually are set in subtropical climates—Los Angeles, Las Vegas, New Orleans—and the setting for *A Book of Common Prayer* is perhaps the most fitting of any for her themes. Boca Grande squats on the equator, its humid days and nights passing in a monotonous, forgettable succession of seeming changelessness. But change of one sort or another is always occurring—bacteria flourish, reproduce, and die; the natural cycles of innumerable insects continue; rust destroys automobiles and tin roofs; vegetation grows over the $34 million road built into the interior. Much is growing, but much more is rotting, from the vegetation and the cars to the people and their institutions. The country's history, like its landscape, is utterly forgettable. Governments are overthrown so frequently and with so little meaning that only the disintegrating ruins of the monuments of previous administrations and the memories of a few people attest to their existence. Throughout all the cycles, one senses no evolution, no progressive pattern, no purpose or design to the growth and the rot, a sameness of prodigality and waste. With Boca Grande, then, Didion creates an effective metaphor of the modern environment—a world characterized by great growth and great disintegration but by no design.

To such a country comes Charlotte Douglas in search of asylum, peace, and purpose, in search of a retreat from her history. What better refuge from flux than a world that seems not to change? What better haven from a past than a country that seems to lack one? Charlotte is on the run from emotional involvements—from her former husband, Warren Bogart, a profligate parasite who, unknown to Charlotte, is near death; from her present husband, Leonard, a lawyer who seems too busy with Third World countries and leftist clients to have much time for her; from the newspapers and F.B.I. men who have constantly been hounding her for information concerning her daughter, Marin, a Berkeley dropout turned inchoate bomb-thrower; and from the baby that Charlotte had to replace Marin, a baby who was born prematurely, hydrocephalic, and who died in the parking lot of a Coca-Cola bottling plant in Mérida, Mexico. From all of this, Charlotte retreats into a dream of life, a life of delusions which ironically lead her into an accidental entanglement in a political overthrow and her purposeless death. She had not expected this; she had not really anticipated any of the nightmares that afflict her; she had been unprepared for almost everything, especially the equatorial nothingness and absurdity of Boca Grande.

True, "as a child of comfortable family in the temperate zone she had been as a matter of course provided with clean sheets, orthodontia, . . . one brother named Dickie, ballet lessons, and casual timely information about menstruation and the care of flat silver"; but she never developed much clearsightedness. So naïve does Charlotte seem that her typical response to any personal, political, or historical difficulty is that everything will turn out all right in the end. "Immaculate of history, innocent of politics," possessing instead of knowledge a great faith in the inevitability of progress and "the generally upward spiral of history," Charlotte Douglas typifies the *norteamericana*. And her reaction to her own past is typical also. Instead of developing a realistic outlook, Charlotte decides instead to manipulate her history to eliminate thinking of the horrible events of her life; to stay sane, she erases rather than reconciles the pain of her betrayal of her husbands, their betrayal of her, Marin's disownment of her, and the loss of her baby. Those that she cannot erase, she revises into delusions, myths built from fragments of reality, dreams, lies, and wishes.

Her reaction to Boca Grande is rather typical of her reactions to her past. She refuses to see it as it really is—an absurd, rotting, purposeless world—and attempts to revitalize it: first through letters she tries to sell to *The New Yorker* about Boca Grande as a " 'land of contrasts,' " as the " 'economic fulcrum of the Americas,' " as one marked by "the 'spirit of hope' "; then through her ideas of establishing an annual international film festival in the country, of opening up a fashionable boutique there, of caring for the sick, and of providing birth control information to the natives. These notions and actions came to nothing.

Her letters are rejected; no film festival is ever seriously considered; her boutique, a shabby hole-in-the-wall, becomes a meeting place for political plotters; her attempts to immunize the populace from cholera are stopped by the government; no one bothers to come to her clinic; and she is finally killed during a political upheaval called the October Violence after refusing to leave when she had the chance. One could assume from all of this that Charlotte is only a naïve contemporary American, foolishly optimistic, that she is only a rich, deluded do-gooder. But if one investigates her more carefully, a more pitiable and somewhat heroic person emerges.

Charlotte is on the run from her history. To prevent it from impinging on her and ultimately destroying her, she has sought escape into another country, literally and metaphorically. In Boca Grande, she immerses herself in projects, routines, and affairs that offer some distraction, some escape from the Eumenides of memory. That she is partially successful is reflected in a scene in which the narrator says of Charlotte's stay in the Hotel del Caribe, "You're at the mercy of the maids." Charlotte responds, "They're very nice here" and "Actually I'm never depressed." But throughout the novel, she also reveals that her attempts at forgetting, erasing, and revising are futile. Her desires to re-create a life, to establish order, and to forget seem halfhearted, tentative, their actor detached, separated, an outsider. From spending hours reading and rereading newspapers and books written in Spanish and not understanding a word of them to having affairs both with Victor, the Defense Minister, and with Gerardo, Charlotte seems inattentive to the realities of her situation and surroundings. Her actions, then, some of which appear vacuous, overly idealistic, or childish—those of "an outsider of romantic sensibility"—reflect detachment from the present and the impossibility of complete divorce from the past.

Not seeing clearly her present reality, covering up the anguish of memory, Charlotte must create fictions of both. Boca Grande would be famous for its film festival; the people would use IUD's and diaphragms to ease the population increase; she would one day at the Boca Grande airport see Marin returning to her. Delusions coupled with a country that "seemed not to demand attentiveness" produce such a seeming obliviousness in Charlotte that she appears to walk unknowingly to her death by AR-15 submachine gunfire during the October Violence. She is, however, perhaps a stronger, more perceptive character than one would like to believe. She shows some remarkable toughness in spots— at one point killing a chicken by breaking its neck cleanly with her bare hands, at another saving a man's life by performing an emergency tracheotomy with a boning knife—and there is evidence that she purposely stayed in Boca Grande and incited the guerrillas to shoot her, in short planned her own death rather than pulling the trigger herself. Her character, then, is complex, ambiguous: she is not just a deluded American fool, but a woman trying to forget the past through an unrealistic clouding of both memory and reality, a person who has finally confronted the realities of nothingness, of rot, of the past and has taken the option of death, the only exit.

The ambiguity of Charlotte's fascinating character is made possible by the point of view Didion employs. A *persona,* Grace Strasser-Mendana, is Charlotte's witness. Interestingly enough, Grace, while attempting to narrate with the precision of a research chemist, actually creates uncertainty about Charlotte's ultimate nature. A year after her death, Grace now feels that she has gathered enough evidence to tell accurately Charlotte's story. Trained as an anthropologist and then switching to biochemistry because the former did not yield conclusive enough evidence, Grace establishes very early in the novel her objectivity. Applying the scientific methods of biochemistry, a "discipline in which demonstrable answers are commonplace and 'personality' absent," the narrator observes acutely and reports flatly, the product being rather brutal but accurate treatises about Boca Grande, its people, its history (or lack of it), and the past and present life of Charlotte, the narrator's chief concern.

From her initial view, the reader perceives Charlotte to be a rather deluded, driven woman, one who dreams her life away. As Grace is detached from any illusions about life, so too is the audience detached from Charlotte, seeing her through the vital data found in passports, entry visas, and the contents of her handbag. The narrator also relies on much hearsay evidence and her own personal observation to construct Charlotte's history, one which initially appears silly but pathetic. As the novel proceeds, however, Grace realizes that her scientific method does not seem to be producing conclusive results about the main character's nature; tempted once to use the word "unstable" to describe her, Grace pauses and then comments that she is "less and less convinced that the word . . . has any useful meaning except insofar as it describes a chemical compound." At the end of the work, Grace finally admits, "I also recognize the equivocal nature of even the most empirical evidence" and that "I am less and less certain that this story has been one of delusion. Unless the delusion was mine." As the narrator loses faith in her method, the reader's perception and understanding of Charlotte's character become simultaneously and paradoxically clearer and more ambiguous. Charlotte Douglas appears not as silly and pathetic, but as a confused mixture of strength and vulnerability, passion and detachment, delusion and realism.

As Grace fails in the final analysis to understand unequivocally Charlotte's nature and motivations, the reader ironically is presented a portrait that in its complexity and ambiguity seems closer to the realities of human existence, Didion's technique moving the novel one step closer to the accurate portrayal of life. One cannot know through objective analysis the essence of a total person. Even one small aspect, fear of the dark, is remarkably complex, consisting, as Grace says, of "an arrangement of fifteen amino acids." No human, then, can ultimately be charted, diagrammed, and absolutely known, as the narrator has attempted in the novel. What appears instead is only a somewhat confusing re-creation of a personality, but as close to the essence of Charlotte Douglas as one may come, as close to one who lives on the edge of despair and oblivion as one can get.

The style through which the author communicates her vision is somewhat loose, quite pure and simple, the unadorned reportorial voice of the author of *Slouching Toward Bethlehem* mixed with the *persona*'s Flaubertian and somewhat cynical habit of recording simultaneously the grotesque and the romantic in the same sentence. When asked whether she had a technical intention for the novel, Didion remarked, "Yes, I wrote it down on the map of Central America. 'Surface like rainbow slick, shifting, fall, thrown away, iridescent.' I wanted to do a deceptive surface that appeared to be one thing and turned color as you looked through it." So, too, with the reader's perception of Charlotte, the narrator, and the country. Through them, Didion in *A Book of Common Prayer* creates simultaneously both a vision of and a prayer for all caught in the age of dysfunction, of disintegration, of the cosmic chill. One understands a bit better our fragmented world after reading this fine novel.

Harold J. Joseph

Sources for Further Study

America. CXXXVII, September 10, 1977, p. 135.

Choice. XIV, July, 1977, p. 680.

Critic. XXXVI, Summer, 1977, p. 680.

Hudson Review. XXX, Summer, 1977, p. 311.

Listener. XCVIII, July 14, 1977, p. 62.

New Statesman. XCIV, July 15, 1977, p. 91.

Observer. July 10, 1977, p. 24.

Sewanee Review. LXXXV, October, 1977, p. 687.

THE BOOK OF MERLYN

The Unpublished Conclusion to *The Once and Future King*

Author: T. H. White (1906–1964)
Publisher: University of Texas Press (Austin, Texas). Illustrated. 158 pp. $9.95
Type of work: Fantasy
Time: The legendary past, on the eve of the battle between Arthur and Mordred
Locale: Salisbury Plain and Cornwall

The concluding book of White's treatment of the Arthurian legend, in which he brings Merlyn back to his former pupil

> *Principal characters:*
> ARTHUR, the once and future king
> MERLYN, his magician-tutor
> T. NATRIX, a snake,
> CAVALL, a hound,
> BALIN, a falcon,
> ARCHIMEDES, an owl,
> GOAT,
> HEDGEHOG, and
> BADGER, members of the Committee on Might in Man

T. H. White's *The Once and Future King,* published in 1958, has the distinction of being a work from which not one but two movies have been made. Walt Disney adapted the animated cartoon *The Sword in the Stone* from the first book of White's tetralogy, and Alan Jay Lerner and Frederick Lowe freely selected material from it for their musical success, *Camelot.* But despite the popularity of *The Once and Future King,* it was not until 1975 that the extent of White's plan for the work was rediscovered: *The Once and Future King,* as White wrote it, was composed not of four parts, but of five. *The Book of Merlyn* is the fifth part, the conclusion to that work.

A prologue by the British novelist Sylvia Townsend Warner outlines the ironic history of *The Book of Merlyn* and its thirty-three-year disappearance. Apparently White had no ending firmly in mind when he began his retelling of the Arthurian legend, yet historical forces were already in action that would lead him to a conclusion. He completed the first book of the story, *The Sword in the Stone,* in 1938. The book was immediately successful both in England and America, but White's enjoyment was diminished because his mind, like those of most Englishmen, was fixed on Hitler's threat to the peace of Europe. Although Prime Minister Neville Chamberlain's appeasement bought a temporary respite from war fears, it was clear to many, including White, that a conflict of monstrous proportions was inevitable.

In January 1939, while working on *The Witch in the Wood,* the second book in the series, White accepted an invitation to spend some time in Ireland. His diary reveals the turmoil in which he found himself in 1939: at one moment he planned to become a conscientious objector, at another to enlist in the armed forces, at still another to seek some kind of defense work. In a revealing comment to a friend he wrote of his hatred for war and his judgment that he would find being a coward more endurable than being a hero.

The fighting had already begun when White started work on the third part of his theme, *The Ill-Made Knight,* which he finished quickly. By November of 1940, he was well into the fourth part, *The Candle in the Wind,* and out of his fear of war and his fervent pacifism an idea for the conclusion of the whole series was beginning to take shape. The end of *The Candle in the Wind* depicts Arthur on the night before the battle with Mordred, his nephew and son. The old king has seen the failure of all his plans to civilize his people and bring peace to the realm; his life has been spent in vain. But with this picture of Arthur in mind, White devised a new ending for his story, one that seemed appropriate not only for Arthur's times but also for his own.

White came to see the whole Arthurian legend as a search for a means of preventing war, and decided to organize his five-part work around that theme. In the fifth and concluding book, he would have Merlyn return to Arthur on the eve of the last battle, and bring the despondent king to the committee of animals who had helped guide his education as a youth. Placing the main part of the final book in a badger's den had two advantages for White: first, the book would end as it had begun, emphasizing man as a part of nature, not as something above and separate from it. Second, and more important, the badger's den provided White with an apt setting for an examination of man as a political animal.

Any discussion of the nature of man, given what was occurring in Europe at that time, was bound to be profoundly pessimistic, and White's discussion is no exception. We must make allowances for the sincerity of the author's pacifism; it seems heartfelt and profound. But after that allowance is made, there remains the nagging thought that *The Book of Merlyn* is in part self-justification for White's departure from England. This thought arises from the air of unreality that hangs over White's endeavors in 1940–1941. No Englishman needed to have the horrors of war preached to him while the Battle of Britain was raging in the skies over his head. Anyone in the streets of London was much more keenly aware of and involved in man's brutality to man than was White, sheltered in the safety of Ireland. What could the author realistically hope to accomplish with an antiwar novel when a German invasion was expected at any time? The answers to questions like this will have to await a complete biography of T. H. White.

If we do not now have that biography, at least we have all of *The Once and Future King* as White intended it to be, and no future discussions of the story will be complete without taking *The Book of Merlyn* into account.

If *The Book of Merlyn* would not bring peace to England, and White could not reasonably expect that, at least its arguments could bring peace to his mind. Having decided on the theme of the story as a whole, White realized that some early parts would need to be rewritten. The revisions, together with the manuscripts for *The Candle in the Wind* and *The Book of Merlyn,* went to the publisher in November of 1941. It hardly need be stressed that antiwar tracts did not find a congenial reception in England in 1941. Yet White insisted that *The Once and Future King* should be published as a five-book whole, or not at all. Unsurprisingly, the decision was made not to publish it at all.

Sylvia Warner's brief preface to *The Book of Merlyn* does not answer an interesting question: in 1958, *The Once and Future King* was published, but only in four parts—*The Book of Merlyn* was omitted, although some of its material appeared in earlier books. But to what degree was White involved in this truncated version? Why had he relaxed his earlier objection to partial publication? Once again, we do not know. In any case, the manuscript for *The Book of Merlyn* was sent, with the bulk of White's papers, to the archives of the Humanities Research Center at the University of Texas at Austin. There it was discovered in 1975, and, after being prepared for publication, saw print in 1977.

In the context of the preceding volumes, *The Book of Merlyn* comes as an abrupt change in tempo. Every version of the legend of Arthur is filled with incident and action. That was surely the case with White's primary source, Thomas Malory's *Morte d'Arthur,* and it is likewise the case with those parts of *The Once and Future King* that faithfully follow Malory. Even those parts of his work which are White's original inventions make their points primarily through what the characters do, not through what they say. In the first two books, Merlyn is a good teacher not because he lectures Arthur wisely but because he places the boy in situations from which he can gain a surer and more lasting lesson. But White's method changes in *The Book of Merlyn;* what we have is, for the most part, a monologue. Merlyn has many words to say, and the animals join in from time to time, but the voice is always that of White, heaping condemnation on the human race, whose only defender is a rather slow-witted Arthur.

White himself may have felt that the change in method was too abrupt. Perhaps in an effort to enliven the static situation of the book, he brought to it two episodes from earlier parts. In these, Arthur is changed by Merlyn into first an ant, and then a wild goose. As an ant he learns what life is like in a totalitarian state, where everything not forbidden is compulsory. As a wild goose, he learns the arbitrary and artificial nature of human boundaries, the natural aristocracy of the capable, and, surprisingly, the sanctity of private property. The two parts contain some of the most vivid scenes and powerful arguments of the whole work, but they are only parts. The rest of the book depends entirely on ideas for whatever liveliness it may possess.

When the debate begins, the Committee (Merlyn and the animals) has been debating the proper adjective to describe human beings. The members reject the term *homo sapiens* since *sapiens* means wise and is therefore unsuitable in the light of human history. The first suggestion is *homo ferox; ferox,* ferocious, seems appropriate since man is unique among animals, they argue, in killing for pleasure. Merlyn describes every animal fleeing in terror at the approach of a human being. At this point it may occur to the reader that we do not *know* that other animals do not take pleasure in killing, nor do domesticated animals flee from man. But the only defender of the human race present is Arthur, and the deck is stacked against him. Effective counterarguments do not occur to Arthur, here or elsewhere.

After a short discussion of the applicability of *stultus,* foolish, to the human race, Merlyn changes Arthur into an ant, and at the end of the lesson, supplies the moral for him. In reducing every member of the species to absolute equality, the ants have made themselves slaves. Any society that denies the uniqueness of the individual (here he names fascism and communism) approaches the society of the ant. And the magician further argues that any society with aspirations toward democracy will inevitably follow down that path. Merlyn reads "Liberty, Equality, Fraternity" as "Liberty, Brutality, and Obscenity."

In its disgruntled view of human nature, the book may at this point remind the reader of nothing so much as the fourth book of *Gulliver's Travels.* Swift is in White's mind, to be sure: at this low ebb in Arthur's spirits, White has the king refer to humans as yahoos. With the king almost despairing, Merlyn changes him into a wild goose. His sojourn with the geese does not have the expected result. Rather than desiring to return to human society full of insight, the king wants only to stay with the geese. Merlyn has to bring him back forcibly in order to continue the lecture. The cause of war, the magician tells him, is nationalism. The cause of war is the desire of groups of humans to lay claim to some part of the earth as their communal property.

White has the easiest of tasks—arguing for a proposition that most people already agree with. Yet he makes Merlyn sound curiously inept in his discussion of nationalism, since his examples come as a shock: "The petty and driveling advocates of Irish or Polish nationalism: these are the enemies of man." More than anything else, White seems out of touch. If his examples lack force in 1977, how ludicrous might they have seemed shortly after Russia and Germany had torn Poland in half for no other crime than existing? And the inclusion of the Irish is at best ungrateful, coming from a man who, at the time he wrote those words, was spared the fury of air bombardment only by the Irish nationalism of which he complains.

In the last analysis, White's argument is overwhelmed by the particular. It is easy to argue against war in the abstract, to argue against the idea of war. But in the midst of a specific war, those arguments may or may not have a purpose. Arthur, after all the wrangling, returns to the battlefield out of duty and there meets his fate. It is cold comfort for him and the reader to be told that ten thousand years may breed the desire for war out of the race, but that is the only consolation and hope that White extends. And if the far future is not a comfort, neither is it a guide to present action. If one agreed entirely with White, what was he to do at that time, when British nationalism, which the author despised, stood in opposition to antlike fascism, which he also despised? In short, what does one do when there is no Ireland to run to? Clearly, White preferred Britain to Hitler's Germany, if only as the lesser of two evils, and the book closes with a request for prayers for the soul of Thomas Malory and T. H. White, his humble disciple, who, he says, "now voluntarily lays aside his books to fight for his kind." But he did not. White remained in Ireland and returned to England only after the war was over.

Walter E. Meyers

Sources for Further Study

America. CXXXVII, October 8, 1977, p. 224.
Atlantic. CCXL, September, 1977, p. 96.
Book World. October 16, 1977, p. E8.
New York Review of Books. XXIV, November 24, 1977, p. 3.
New York Times Book Review. August 28, 1977, p. 31.
Progressive. XLI, December, 1977, p. 60.
Wilson Library Bulletin. LII, November, 1977, p. 211.

THE BOOK OF SAND

Author: Jorge Luis Borges (1899–   )
Translated from the Spanish by Norman Thomas di Giovanni
Publisher: E. P. Dutton (New York). 125 pp. $7.95
Type of work: Short stories

A collection of thirteen stories by the Argentine master recalls the Borges of the intricate, ironic stories of Ficciones *and* The Aleph

Jorge Luis Borges, who will turn eighty next year, has been writing and publishing for fifty-six years of his life. Because of the widely held belief of many readers in the United States that nothing of any literary consequence has been written in Spanish since *Don Quixote,* Borges was not "discovered" until the 1960's by the English speaking world. Some tardy discoverers refuse to recognize the South American origin of Borges and continue to place him in anthologies and works of criticism dealing with modern European fiction and literature, but both Borges' life and literature remain very much Latin American. Just as the Nicaraguan Ruben Dario revitalized Spanish poetry in the nineteenth century, so Borges renovated the prose idiom of the Spanish language.

Borges is the chronological father of modern Latin American writing as well, a paternity readily admitted to by such progeny as Gabriel García Márquez *(One Hundred Years of Solitude),* Carlos Fuentes *(The Death of Artemio Cruz, A Change of Skin, Aura),* Julio Cortázar *(Hopscotch, Blow-up),* and still others less famous or less translated. His late appearance made him anachronistically a contemporary contributor to that explosion of novels, short stories, and poetry starting in the mid-1960's in Latin America known as the "boom." Ironically, most of Borges' influence and fame rests upon a corpus of essays *(Inquisiciones,* 1925; *Evaristo Carriego,* 1930; *Discusión,* 1932; *Other Inquisitions,* 1952) and short stories *(A Universal History of Infamy,* 1935; *Ficciones,* 1935–1944; *The Aleph,* 1949) that generally appeared between 1925 and 1952. As with any writer as productive as Borges there have been ups and downs of critical success. In fact, after the publication of *Doctor Brodie's Report* (1970—Spanish, 1972—English), a new style and somewhat new subjects emerged, indicating an unexpected and regrettable change toward narrative simplicity. Fortunately, Borges has forsaken his flirtation with Rudyard Kipling and has returned to his stock of doubles, Platonic archetypes, mirrors, dreams, repeating patterns across time, and literary works-within-works in *The Book of Sand.* The same economical style and the same thematic preoccupations here echo those of the 1930's and 1940's.

The Book of Sand's thirteen stories explicitly and implicitly avoid, even disclaim novelty. In "The Congress" the aging narrator states that "novelties—maybe because I feel that they hold nothing essentially new and are really no more than timid variations—neither interest nor distract me." Borges' specific usage of the adverb "essentially" underscores his point that attempts at originality and newness are only pale reflections of eternal essences. With the possible exceptions of "The Bribe," by his own admission a psychological story, and "There Are More Things" (also the title in the original), a tribute to and pastiche of the horror fiction of H. P. Lovecraft, these compact narratives constantly stir up memories of plots, themes, and lines of earlier stories and essays and further heighten the Platonic effect so dear to Borges that "to know is to know again."

Among the themes that Borges has used in the past those of the double, time, pantheism, and the existence of a magic word that expresses everything reappear singly or in combination in these stories. "The Other" employs the double. This initial story resembles "The Circular Ruins" of *Ficciones* and the poem, "Borges and I." "Ulrike" uses cyclical time as the characters perform fundamental timeless acts. In "Ulrike" life imitates literature as it did in *Ficciones'* "Theme of the Traitor and Hero" where the narrator suspects the "existence of a secret form of time, a pattern of repeated lines." In this instance, however, the Colombian narrator imperceptibly becomes Sigurd and Ulrike, Brynhild, characters of the Volsungs Saga. Apparently casual allusions to De Quincey and his Ann of Oxford Street, the Niebelungen, Henrik Ibsen, and William Morris, both of whom wrote versions of the Volsungs Saga, enrich the structure of this work and make it typically Borgesian. In this and in other stories of the collection the characters tend to disintegrate, one character blending with another, or often they remain nameless like their fictitious narrator.

Personal time, the important theme in "Avelino Arredondo," contrasts Arredondo's personal experience with a rigorous, unrelenting, external chronology. "Utopia of a Tired Man" uses the voyage in time to take the narrator out of the present and set him down into the distant future. This situation provides Borges with a vehicle for satirizing the ephemera of the present with the nightmarish reduction and simplification of the future. The narrator returns to the present with proof of his journey, a very small painting which "represented, or suggested, a sunset and which encompassed something infinite." It is no accident that his painting reminds us of Coleridge's dream flower or H. G. Wells's wilted flower of the future. The old narrator of "The Night of the Gifts" remembers and relives in the retelling two fundamental eternal acts, love and death, which he experienced in his youth. The two most ambitious stories of the book deal also with forms of time. "The Congress," which bears no small resemblance to *Other Inquisitions'* "A New Refutation of Time," attempts to relate how a given moment, an imminence of eternity was experienced and how imperfectly words describe it because the successive nature of language contradicts the concept of the eternal or the intemporal. "The Book of Sand," the closing story, postulates the existence of a monstrous book that contains nothing less than infinity between its covers. Borges' peculiar irony, making it both the last story and the title of the collection, should not be overlooked.

Language becomes the theme of "Undr" and "The Mirror and the Mask," although language's inability to express adequately man's thoughts and feelings figures as a leitmotiv in several other stories. In "The Mirror and the Mask," the poet in three successive attempts refines his poetry from his initial lengthy panegyric, to an ode, and finally to a single line of spoken verse. The poem devastates two men: "not venturing to repeat it aloud, the poet and his king savored it as if it were a secret prayer or a blasphemy." His one verse, much like the book of sand or the painting from the distant future, encompasses all experience. The bard admits to the origin of the poem in a dream (remember Coleridge and Caedmon, who also received their poems in dreams) and, in a Borgesian sense, he becomes the vocal instrument of something quite beyond him and the confines of this world of substance. The poet kills himself; the king wanders his kingdom as a beggar never daring to repeat the poem.

"Undr" shares in the same search for the poem that contains all experience. Set in the eleventh century, Ulf, a poet of the race of the skalds, seeks the Urns, a race whose poetry consists of a single word. The skalds, as any knowledgeable reader of Borges' *Literaturas germánicas medievales* (1966) or of Scandinavian literature would know, were poets who multiplied and combined lengthy recondite metaphors known as *kenning* in their verses. Ulf witnesses the death of the Urn king who hears the Word from his court poet, but the Word eludes him. The Urn poet, forbidden to reveal this word, urges Ulf to search for it. After many adventures and years, Ulf returns to the Urns' village only to find his poet friend dying. Ulf, after retelling "in exact order and with a great many details" what he experienced, hears the waning voice of the Urn sing one word, "undr," meaning wonder. That one word reveals to Ulf everything that he is and has done. Signaling his understanding, Ulf picks up the harp and sings to a different word which, of course, is not disclosed to the reader. There is in this concept of the single word or in the picture or in the book composed of infinite pages the pantheistic theme which finds repetitions scattered throughout the pages of this collection. In "Undr" the dying bard reveals how "life gives everything to everyone, but most men are unaware of it." Poetry and the poet do make men aware. This same expression reoccurs in "The Night of the Gifts" where "all things are revealed to all men—or, any way, all those things it's granted a man to know." And again in "The Sect of the Thirty" a fragment of an anonymous ancient manuscript reveals that at the Crucifixion of Christ there were intentional and unintentional participants: the two intentional ones were Christ and Judas, and all of the rest of mankind were the unintentional. The nameless author relates that members of the abominable, heretical sect worship Christ and Judas equally and forgive all the others, since "there is no one culprit. Everyone, unwitting or not, is an agent in the scheme laid down by Divine Wisdom. All of them now share the Glory." This pantheistic reduction helps to explain Borges' lack of strong individual characters and the consequential difficulty of remembering them since they all fuse together.

These themes encountered in *The Book of Sand*, of course, are not unique to Borges, but the mode in which they find expression is. Borges is very much a stylist. Even in translation the special quality of his prose emerges. The very fact that writers and critics now speak of plots, phrases, and so on as distinctively Borgesian indicates how remarkable is his style. The allusion, the dream entering the real world, irony, the juxtaposition of opposites ("secret prayer or a blasphemy"), the voyage in time, the story-within-a-story narrated by receding first-person narrators, the disturbing mixture of reality with fiction, all are his stock-in-trade.

Borges' essays resemble fiction or certainly allow the welcome incursions of the fictional world to intrude upon the real one; his fictions acquire a veneer of reality by imitating the objective essay, the book review, or the scholarly commentary. For example, "Undr" and "The Sect of the Thirty" appear to represent fragments of ancient manuscripts glossed by an anonymous neutral researcher. In the latter story, however, the authenticity of the nonexistent manuscript is provided by a deceptively casual reference to its being mentioned in one of the footnotes of Gibbon's fifteenth chapter of *The Decline and Fall of the Roman Empire.* The fifteenth chapter, indeed, deals with the early Christian heretical sects, but there is no such footnote. Borges uses the apocryphal reference to legitimize his fictional world.

Fully ten of the thirteen stories are first-person narratives, told generally by anonymous men, or nearly so, and quite advanced in age. Often one narrator cedes his function to another and he in turn to still another. "The Night of the Gifts" provides a good illustration. Embedded within the story are no less than three different narrators, each retelling an episode from many years before. This concatenation of time and events draws the reader into Borges' fictional world, making him lose his own sense of time and reality. The distant memories and dreams of the telescoping narrators create similar effects in the other stories.

It would not be difficult to detail at some considerable length the delightful ironies, the clever allusions to other literatures, the sources, and the metaphors so patent in Borges, but it would defeat one of the avowed intentions of the author, who, in his Afterword, hopes that "these hasty notes . . . do not exhaust this book and that its dreams go on branching out in the hospitable imagination of those who now close it." Indeed this volume, like the book of the title story and like the sand, has no beginning and no end. In a very genuine sense *The Book of Sand,* borrowing from Borges' own lexicon, vindicates his reputation as one of the most important and influential writers of the century.

John R. Kelly

Sources for Further Study

Book World. October 23, 1977, p. E8.
Booklist. LXXIV, October 1, 1977, p. 266.
Kirkus Reviews. XLV, August 15, 1977, p. 863.
New York Times Book Review. October 16, 1977, p. 14.
Saturday Review. V, October 15, 1977, p. 30.
Time. CX, November 14, 1977, p. 110.

THE BOOK OF THE BODY

Author: Frank Bidart
Publisher: Farrar, Straus and Giroux (New York). 44 pp. $7.95
Type of work: Poetry

A confident, coherent volume dealing with existential themes, which appears to be "confessional," although it is actually more controlled and objective than work belonging to the school of Sexton

The Book of the Body is a confident, coherent volume of five poems in which Frank Bidart takes risks a younger poet would not have attempted. Structurally, he has built this volume on variations of a single theme, which, if it were to fail, would destroy the book. Technically, Bidart mixes open and formal verse with prose—sometimes within the same poem—which, again, might have been disastrous. Moreover, the male poet risks creating female *personae* at a time when feminists deny that such is possible. These risks were worth the taking. A female reviewer in *New Republic* has said that the book "is a wonderful refutation of the theory that a man can't successfully write in the *persona* of a woman. In fact Bidart seems able to write with power and ease in any *persona* he chooses." *The Book of the Body* is a tightwire act that succeeds; its success is even more impressive when the reader realizes that Bidart is performing without a net.

In terms of style, Bidart at first glance appears to be writing the open, naked poetry that so many confessional poets have used and reused. But when the poems are read out loud, the reader hears the difference. Lines break because they must break just at that point. Consider:

> —She is saying: "If the cancer
> pops out somewhere else, I won't let them operate.
> I'd rather die.
>   They just
> butcher you . . . Besides, it never works."

This is not free verse. There is an irregular iambic meter at work here, which does not control the lines so much as it catches the natural rhythms of American speech. This is what William Carlos Williams said the American poet had to learn; but instead poets gradually turned breath-control lines into a kind of formalism that became as restrictive as the old iambic pentameter. Two generations back, Ezra Pound and the Imagists demanded that poetry learn to create its lines as if they were music. Bidart has developed a mixture of natural speech and formal rhythm that allows him freedom without absolutely sacrificing form. He has eclectically combined the maxims of Williams, Pound, and Olson. The resulting poetic line responds to the natural speaking voice as well as the breath. Bidart belongs to the third generation of American modern poets, who have, at last, begun to develop a recognizable American line unselfconsciously.

Bidart's tone of voice also appears confessional: in other words, the I-speaker revealing to the listener personal problems of the sort not usually spoken about. The long opening poem, "The Arc," lends itself to this categorization:

> When I wake up,
>   I try to convince myself that my arm
> isn't there—
>   to retain my sanity.
> Then I try to convince myself it is.

What follows is a tense exposé by a man who has lost one of his arms at the elbow. After finishing the book, the reader understands that Bidart creates characters in monologues and dialogues with the skill of a dramatist. Although the poems look confessional, it is not the poet himself speaking. This skill allows Bidart the distance between himself and his art which is so necessary for objective control. One need only compare these poems with the hysterical intenisty of Plath or Sexton to realize that this is not the confessional poetry that has inundated us of late. If one were looking for Bidart's roots, a comparison with Lowell's *Life Studies* would be profitable. Lowell opened new ground in that volume, mixing poetry and prose, which has only been partially explored by the confessional poets. Bidart seems to be developing another aspect of that seminal volume.

Thematically, *The Book of the Body* is built around cripples: physical (amputation, mastectomy, anorexia nervosa), sexual (divorce, homosexuality, abortion), and spiritual (isolation, nausea, suicide). The speaker in "The Arc" has lost an arm and must live with the knowledge "I was no longer whole; proportioned; inviolate." "Happy Birthday" remembers athletes no longer young, their bodies having betrayed them. In "Elegy," a mother laments her mastectomy:

> "I'd rather die than let them
> take off a breast. I'd rather die
> than go through cobalt again."

Ellen West, in the final poem of that title, is a woman starving herself to thinness inside a body that yearns to be fat. The world, Bidart is telling us, eventually cripples us all. Late or soon our bodies betray us. We only experience this world through the flesh, but ultimately the pleasures of the body lead to revulsion when the flesh fails.

This revulsion is the feeling of nausea, which one comes to understand, via Sartre and Camus, as the proper sense of alienation. Bidart is, finally, an existentialist. The waves of nausea that sweep over *personae* and reader are exactly that existential awareness of self. Camus has said that the first question is suicide. Once the mind has rejected that exit, it must accept its alienation, in fact take joy in it. Bidart lists what he calls the seven deadly sins: "Sex. Identity. History. Family. Affection. Obsession. Chance." Each of these "sins" leads one *persona* after another to the point of alienation. In a world of chance, "insanity is the insistence on meaning." True freedom for Bidart's characters is the denial of self: "But I don't want an identity! This way I'm free." The one-armed man tries desperately to imagine that he never had that arm. It works for a while, but the world turns to "cardboard." To deny his past experience is to deny meaning to the world. In what might have been a terribly suicidal poem, the speaker finally comes to an existential acceptance of his condition via an illumination in Paris:

> Paris is still the city of Louis XVI and
> Robespierre, how blood, amputation, and rubble
> give her dimension, resonance, and grace.

This final recognition allows the speaker's loss to give meaning to his existence. In the process he has retained his sanity.

Another recurring theme is the crippling effect of an ego-centered mother on the fatherless boy. In "Elegy," a sequence of poems, we see a boy whose greatest love is his dog, that has died from poison. The mother reminds the boy that he and the dog were alter-egos; she got the dog to take his place when he left. "We used to laugh at the comparison." As the sequence progresses, we gradually understand how badly the mother has crippled the boy by raising doubts about his own sexual identity, which finally result in homosexuality. Family cripples us. Sex cripples us. No one comes through the experience whole. However, annihilation of the body is not an answer, merely another kind of failure. Bidart, in his own painful way, is facing the ancient problem of the dualism of mind and body. As much as some of the characters want to deny the body, Bidart ultimately affirms it. It is only through the body that the mind has anything to know.

"Ellen West," the longest poem of the book, is based on the English prose translation of a German book, *Der Fall Ellen West*. The resulting distance between the poet and the experience allows Bidart to create his most impressive piece. It is a poem in two voices: Ellen West's monologues and final suicide note alternate with the prose entries from her doctor's case book describing the progress of her illness.

Ellen suffers from a twentieth century disease: *anorexia nervosa*. Unable to accept her natural corpulence, she consciously starves herself to thinness. She tells us, "my true self/is thin, all profile/ and effortless gestures, the sort of blond/ elegant girl whose body is the image of her soul." This inability to match the ideal with the real drives Ellen to alternate stages of starvation and gluttony. Not only alienated from her body, she is also alienated from Nature: "I loathed Nature." She is faced with a paradox: identity begins with the flesh, but "the ideal of being thin/ conceals the ideal/ *not* to have a body . . . without a body, who can/ know himself at all?" Finally, Ellen West becomes so ashamed of the embarrassment and disappointment she causes her husband, she kills herself with poison. In her suicide note, she explains that she could not match her ideals with this world. Each compromise left her sterile and unreal:

> I am crippled. I disappoint you.
> Will you greet with anger, or
> happiness,
> the news which might well reach you
> before this letter?
>
> Your *Ellen*

These are the last words of *The Book of the Body.*

Bidart's world is not a pleasant one. It is filled with small-time losers whose painful experiences mirror our own. The characters he has created are people trapped in a deterministic universe. Some of them rise above their circumstances to an existential acceptance which leads to bleak joy. Others give in, like Ellen West. Suicide and insanity, the double edge of our time, are continual threats in Bidart's world, or perhaps escapes, for both lead out of the body. Although this is painful poetry, it is very well done. Bidart has found his voice and his style without egotistically reminding the reader that he is reading a poet. The subject matter of this volume is a stage Bidart must pass through. To stop with these themes would probably be self-destructive in spite of the distance Bidart is able to maintain between himself and his subjects.

Michael S. Reynolds

Sources for Further Study

Atlantic. CCXL, October, 1977, p. 102.

Booklist. LXXIII, July 15, 1977, p. 1698.

Library Journal. CII, August, 1977, p. 1653.

New Republic. CLXXVII, October 22, 1977, p. 35.

Yale Review. LXVII, October, 1977, p. 72.

BOSWELL
Laird of Auchinleck, 1778–1782

Author: James Boswell (1740–1795)
Edited by Joseph W. Reed and Frederick A. Pottle
Publisher: McGraw-Hill Book Company (New York). 570 pp. $19.95
Type of work: Journals
Time: 1778–1782
Locale: Edinburgh and Scotland; occasionally London and England

The ninth and most recent volume in the Yale Edition of The Private Papers of James Boswell, *this book covers the period when Boswell had settled in Edinburgh with his family, was attempting to establish and extend his law practice, and finally came into his inheritance as Laird of Auchinleck*

> Principal personages:
> JAMES BOSWELL
> MRS. BOSWELL, his wife
> LORD AUCHINLECK, his father
> LADY AUCHINLECK, his stepmother
> SAMUEL JOHNSON

James Boswell was a constant embarrassment to his family, and, when he died in 1795, so the story went, the family burned all of his papers so that he could cast no further disgrace on the family honor. The early twentieth century view of Boswell was essentially that of his family, reinforced by the sneering Victorian estimation of Macauley: that James Boswell had been a vain, loose, superficial, foolish social climber who had, by some process not well understood, ingratiated himself with the great Dr. Samuel Johnson and had stumbled onto the writing of the world's greatest biography, *The Life of Samuel Johnson.* Then in the third decade of the present century, through a series of remarkable accidents, discoveries, and manipulations, the fact that the Boswell papers had not been burned came to light. Then the papers themselves were acquired from the Boswell descendants through some devious financial operations, and, by the combined efforts of Yale University and McGraw-Hill publishers, these papers began to appear in well-edited and annotated form to an eager audience. The present volume is the ninth in a series presenting Boswell's private diaries and journals for our examination.

Boswell was just twenty-two when, in 1762, he left his native Edinburgh behind and set out to see the world, especially that great and wonderful center of British civilization, London. As his journey began he made several resolutions. He was, he thought, going to meet people, important people. James Boswell of Scotland was going to be known among the salons of Europe and to all the important members of those select groups, for most of all, except perhaps for wine and pretty women, Boswell craved fame with an intensity that bordered on obsession. Furthermore, Boswell was convinced his adventures would be of such significance that he should keep a journal from day to day in which he would record his actions, feelings, intentions, and impressions. This habit of maintaining a daily journal, begun in his youth, prevailed throughout almost the entirety of Boswell's life. With amazing candor he entered everything, leaving himself utterly exposed to a curious world when these papers began to be published a few years ago. Everything is here: the excessive drinking bouts and the hangovers and remorse that followed in their wake; evenings spent with Samuel Johnson, Sir Joshua Reynolds, Oliver Goldsmith, and other famous men of the time; intrusions into the privacy of anyone of sufficient importance that Boswell would wish at a later time to drop their names in casual conversation; the sights, sounds, and smells of the bustling metropolis of eighteenth century London; and, of course, escapades with various ladies of various degrees of virtue, escapades followed not only by remorse but occasionally by attacks of venereal disease as well.

And yet the reader of the early volumes in this series is entertained with a lively sense of narrative and with a vivid sense of background: the eighteenth century comes alive under Boswell's touch. We meet Dr. Johnson face to face, informally and unbuttoned. And the brash young man did have something apparently; he was, after all, admitted, and at times welcomed, into the company of writers, artists, philosophers, and statesmen with impeccable credentials. And so the image of Boswell was revised, and he began to be seen as urbane, witty, sophisticated, and in every way the superior of the character who had emerged from Macauley's critical observations. He had his foibles, of course, but then so has everyone; and to be sure one can find redeeming qualities in anyone welcomed by the great Samuel Johnson. And, too, out of these accounts of his conversations with Johnson came the revisions that passed through a series of metamorphoses to become the *The Life of Samuel Johnson,* one of the world's great books.

Through the efforts of modern editors, Boswell's private journal covering a period of more than twenty years has now appeared. He may be seen as a gawking young man from the provinces just entering London, and then learning his way thoroughly around that great town. His visit to Holland in 1763–1764 followed next; he then took the Grand Tour through Europe, intruding on Voltaire, visiting the Corsican patriot General Paoli, conversing with Frederick the Great. This journey took him three years and into Germany, Switzerland, Italy, Corsica, and France. The well-traveled Boswell, now twenty-six years old, returned to search for a wife and to attempt to establish himself in his chosen profession, the practice of law. He was not a highly successful lawyer; indeed, he experienced several years of growing family and financial distress. And so he is to be found in 1778, at the beginning of the present volume, anxious concerning his meager legal activities and troubled with a host of other problems.

The text of the present volume is quite a different thing from the text of the first volume. Boswell, obviously, is older now and is beset with all the problems that growing old involves. His family is growing, and with it his expenses and worries. He no longer has the leisure for maintaining his journal that he had earlier; many of his entries, therefore, are highly abbreviated reminders to himself, presumably for future expansion which never took place. Many entries are made several days after their nominal date when Boswell had forgotten many of the details of a particular day's events. Thus the lively narrative character of the earlier volumes is quite lost here, and the reader is given, instead, a series of discrete moments, some quite vivid and others without color and detail. Many entries are cryptic, and the reader can but guess at the meaning with the editor's assistance. There are numerous gaps of days or even weeks in this manuscript which the editor often attempts to fill out with interpolated quotations from *The Life of Samuel Johnson,* if an allusion to the missing events should be found there, or with passages from other journalists who were present at the same events. In some instances there are no alternative accounts, and the gaps simply stand with no clarification. As in the earlier volumes the reader is given a view of a vast panorama of places and personages, but the landscape of Edinburgh pales beside that of London and Europe; and there is no Dr. Johnson, or Oliver Goldsmith, or Voltaire, or Rousseau in Edinburgh, though some of the Englishmen who enlightened the pages of earlier volumes do recur here during Boswell's occasional short trips to London. But by and large the narrative and the colorful backgrounds of the earlier volumes are no longer noticeable.

If this book lacks narrative structure and the interesting anecdotal material of fascinating persons, besides Boswell himself, of course, it does have several threads of thematic material running through it that tend to give it structure and unity of a quite different order. Perhaps the most prominent, as well as the most interesting, of these unifying and ordering themes is that of Boswell's relationship with other members of his family. There are distinct gradations, including his attitude toward his wife and children, toward his aging father and his father's second wife, toward his brothers, and toward a host of distant relatives. A second pervasive theme running through the volume is that of Boswell *vis-à-vis* his chosen profession, the bar. This theme is inextricably bound up with the conflict in Boswell's own heart between his affections for his Scottish homeland and his conviction that everything worthwhile lies south in London. A third theme involves Boswell's relationship with himself and his aspirations to be "a considerable figure" in the literary world. And finally, there is the kaleidoscopic view of Boswell in his many manifestations as man of the world, rake, socialite, traveler; graceful, charming, witty, or debauched, with debauchery always followed by black remorse and vows to leave off this aspect of his life.

Despite his avowed belief in concubinage and his almost obsessive trips to the stews, one cannot doubt the sincerity or the depth of Boswell's affection for his wife and children. By August, 1778, when this volume begins, Boswell's wife was obviously consumptive; she suffered from fits of violent, racking coughing spasms and spitting up blood alternating with periods when, in Boswell's words, "she never looked better." Boswell's own spirits vacillated wildly between hope and despair with the cycles of his wife's health, but tragedy always lurked in the background. Death, or the threat of it, runs throughout this book. Boswell's wife and father were both very ill, Dr. Johnson was growing old, and the deaths of at least a dozen friends and relatives found their ways into these pages. Boswell is very fond and proud of his children, chronicling each new word which enters the vocabulary of the youngest. The older ones often read scripture in the evening, and their father is always pleased with the performance.

Boswell's relationship to his father has been a constant theme in the journals, and now he is old and agonizingly ill. Boswell loved his father and desperately wished to be loved by him. But the old Laird of Auchinleck regarded his eldest son as a profligate wastrel; yet Boswell was the heir of entail. He had to inherit the family estate by law, and the old man seemed to resent this fact. He has kept his son on a very meager allowance for many years, even against the advice of his friends. He considered, with no evidence whatever to support such an opinion, that Boswell's wife encouraged Boswell in his spendthrift ways, and his treatment of his daughter-in-law and his grandchildren, to Boswell's great distress, was often cold and almost cruel. Boswell was anxious to succeed as Laird of Auchinleck and was concerned that his wife "might perhaps die before my coming to the estate . . . which would place her in a situation which she so well deserves." He was even driven at one point to confide in his journal that he "could not help viewing his [his father's] death as a desirable event." Yet when the old man did die, near the end of this volume, and Boswell became in fact the Laird of Auchinleck, the difficulties he had encountered on the way rendered the event of very little satisfaction. Lord Auchinleck was agonizingly ill; Dr. Gillespie had to empty his bladder three times each day by catheter. The old man, in his frugal Scots way, had settled an annuity on the doctor in order to guarantee his services, and Boswell saw this as an erosion of his future estate and wondered if he could modify the bequest when he became Laird.

Lord Auchinleck's second wife, Boswell's stepmother, was another source of difficulty. She tenderly cared for the old man, seeing her role as one who would protect him from a son who would ruin him; Boswell, on the other hand, considered her to be an obstinate obstacle to the establishment of a better relationship between him and his father. Fortunately, however, these two later came to understand each other better and to share a genuine mutual fondness.

Boswell's law practice had never been extensive, but its decline during the period covered here was cause for anxiety not only because of the resulting financial problems, but also because he was forced to admit the connection between his declining law practice and his father's less and less frequent appearance on the bench in the Court of Session. He longed to transfer his practice to London, "yet feared I should not be able to rise to any eminence there." Yet, if he did leave Scotland, he would forfeit all his income except for the parsimonious one hundred pounds a year his father allowed him. But in his fantasies London remained always a possibility, and he begged his friend Edmund Burke to seek an appointment for him. He was constantly torn in two directions: he wanted very much to assume his inheritance as Laird of Auchinleck, but he also yearned to go to London, hopefully to sit in Parliament. The invitation from Burke never came, and Boswell never resolved the conflicting desires in his own heart and mind.

Of more importance for readers today than Boswell's legal career was his literary life. By now, he had a substantial reputation; "I am," he observed quite accurately, "better known in the world than most of my countrymen." We see him at work on his *Hypochondriack* essays, searching Edinburgh libraries for apt mottoes and quotations. His anonymous pamphlet to Lord Braxfield was very well received, and Boswell never tired of asking various persons who had not pierced the cloak of anonymity what they thought of the pamphlet, just to hear himself praised. He had a series of letters in the *Public Advertiser;* his editorials were printed in the *Caledonian Mercury;* and he wrote rather mediocre occasional verse. Several years earlier he had toured the Hebrides with Dr. Johnson, and during the period covered in this volume, he was revising his notes on that adventure into what would become a very well-known travel account. He was also planning his *The Life of Samuel Johnson,* which would become his greatest work and, in the estimation of many, the greatest biography in the world. "I told Erskine," he recorded, "I was to write Dr. Johnson's life in scenes. He approved."

And so the Boswell who emerges from these pages is a continuation of the Boswell of the earlier volumes. He is older now; he has troubles as well as responsibilities. He still has his foibles, but they have become less youthful amusements and more flaws of character. Yet his perception of life is maturer and his intellectual grasp is strengthened. If he is no longer as amusing and entertaining as he once had been, he is nevertheless more human and more genuine.

Robert B. White, Jr.

Sources for Further Study

Library Journal. CII, November 1, 1977, p. 2262.
New York Times Book Review. September 25, 1977, p. 11.

THE BRITISH REVOLUTION
1880-1939

Author: Robert Rhodes James (1933-   )
Publisher: Alfred A. Knopf (New York). 653 pp. $17.95
Type of work: History
Time: 1880-1939
Locale: Great Britain

A narrative account of British politics from the time of Gladstone and Disraeli to the outbreak of World War II, interpreted as a series of revolutions which democratized political life and ended the separation of Britain into two nations, the rich and the poor

Principal personages:
> STANLEY BALDWIN, Conservative Prime Minister, 1923-1924, 1924-1929, 1935-1937
> A. J. BALFOUR, Conservative Prime Minister, 1902-1905; served in wartime Coalition cabinet at Admiralty and Foreign Office
> ANDREW BONAR LAW, Conservative Leader of Opposition, 1911-1915; served in wartime Coalition cabinet; Prime Minister, 1922-1923
> JOSEPH CHAMBERLAIN, Birmingham manufacturer; leader of Radical wing of Liberal Party until split with Gladstone over Home Rule in 1886; eventually leading figure among the Conservatives
> NEVILLE CHAMBERLAIN, Conservative, son of Joseph Chamberlain, Prime Minister, 1936-1940
> BENJAMIN DISRAELI, Conservative Prime Minister, 1868, 1874-1880
> WILLIAM GLADSTONE, Liberal Prime Minister, 1868-1874, 1880-1885, 1886, 1892-1894
> J. RAMSAY MACDONALD, first Labour Prime Minister; Prime Minister, 1924, 1929-1935

In 1880, Great Britain was the richest and most powerful nation in the world, proud of her ancient liberties and tradition of limited government, ruler of an extensive empire of which India was the centerpiece. Although her government was limited, she was not a democracy: the franchise had been extended in 1867, but the right to vote was still limited and government was in the hands of an elite group of aristocratic and wealthy middle-class politicians. Out of the confusion of the 1850's and 1860's, two parties had emerged—Conservative and Liberal— and the apparatus of modern party organization was beginning to take shape. By 1939, Robert Rhodes James tells us, a revolution, or rather several revolutions, had taken place. Great Britain's position in the world had diminished. Her industry had lost its lead to the United States and Germany and her status as a world power was challenged by Nazi Germany. India was well on its way to self-government, and the Liberal Party had little political importance, having lost its place to Labour. Political democracy had been achieved little by little, the final step coming in 1928 when the franchise was extended to all adult women (limited suffrage for women having been adopted in 1918). In 1880, there were still two Britains—that of the rich and that of the poor. In 1939, there were still great social problems, but Britain was essentially one nation, more fair, more united than it had been in 1880.

The British Revolution: 1880–1939 is a highly readable, thought-provoking account of how these changes came about. Robert Rhodes James's stated purpose is to bring the individuals and struggles of the past to life again, to convey to the reader some element of the human dramas, the achievements and failures of these important years of British history. He succeeds very well. The emphasis is on political history: not the dry recital of voting patterns in the constituencies and contents of bills but the personal side of politics. The scene is almost always the House of Commons and the play of personality and issues there. As each leading personage is introduced into the narrative, James pauses to analyze his personal history and character, his motivations, his mannerisms, his reception by his colleagues. These sketches have the authority of long acquaintanceship; it is as if an elder statesman of unusual psychological insight and literary ability were summing up his observations of colleagues formed over many years. It is hard to believe that James, born in 1933, could have had no personal experience with any of the men or events he discusses. He has, however, had direct experience of the life he describes: he was clerk of the House of Commons from 1954 to 1964 and is currently a Conservative Member of Parliament for Cambridge. He knows and loves the parliamentary scene and is well qualified to convey its special flavor to the reader.

James believes that the character of British politics changed at the time of World War I. Until 1914, a small group of men centered in Westminster made political decisions for Britain, but with the very active interest and involvement of a large audience of the British public. After 1914, the electorate was widened greatly, problems became more ominous, and new methods of communication brought the mass of people more directly into the political process. James's perspective widens then to include the scene beyond London. But the House of Commons is too fascinating to leave for long; there may be flying trips out to the constituencies, but he and the reader are happy to return as quickly as possible to Westminster.

When the narrative begins in 1880, the Liberal Party under Gladstone's leadership had just won a great electoral victory. The widening of the franchise in 1867 had worked in their favor, and with a still further extension in 1884, it appeared that the Liberals would rule Britain for years to come. All this was turned upside down by Gladstone's espousal of Home Rule for Ireland in 1886 and the breakup of the Liberal Party over that issue. As it turned out, it was the Conservatives who became the dominant party, in power from 1886 to 1939 with the major exception of the Liberal Government of 1906–1916 and three minor exceptions (the Liberal Government of 1892–1895, and the Labour Governments of 1924 and of 1929–1931). The author rightly considers the coalition of 1916–1922 and the National Government of 1931–1939 as essentially Conservative, although led by a Liberal in one case and a Labourite for at least a portion of the other. The major responsibility for guiding Britain through its revolution was then that of the Conservative Party.

If the Conservatives had been inflexible in their defense of the *status quo,* the course of modern British history might have been very different. In fact that party proved to be rather flexible, for most of the time at least. The credit belongs to Benjamin Disraeli. As the right to vote was gradually extended, the dominant question for the wealthier classes was whether social reform could be achieved without upsetting their own social and political control. Disraeli persuaded his party that change was inevitable and that if the Conservatives themselves took up the cause of reform, they could carry out change in ways compatible with the privileges and traditions of the upper classes. "Controlled reform" was the key concept, and to carry it out, the Conservatives had to be in office. As James concludes, "Power was henceforth the ideology of their party—Power to preserve power, to control movements which, if ignored or alienated, could sweep them away." From this it was but a further step to the conclusion that if the Conservatives were to lose power, there would be a national catastrophe.

Viewing themselves as the saviors of the nation led the Conservatives to the one major departure from Disraelian principles in this period: the vetoing of Liberal legislation by the House of Lords in the period 1906–1911. The result was, of course, disastrous for the Lords. Their power was permanently curtailed in 1911, and party politics on the verge of the Great War were charged with a hostility and venom rarely seen in British history. James lays the blame for this on A. J. Balfour, briefly Prime Minister in succession to his uncle Lord Salisbury and then Leader of the Opposition from 1906 on. When the Liberals took over in 1906 with a large majority, Balfour chose to use the permanent Conservative majority in the House of Lords to defeat one major Liberal measure after another. He encouraged the Conservatives in the belief that theirs was the natural right to rule and in the assumption that since this was true, no weapon or tactic was too low to be used against the Liberals. After five years of frustration, the Liberals were moved in 1910 to propose successfully the limitation of the Lords' veto power to a delaying power through three sessions. Thus, in a negative way, the Conservatives were responsible for this major aspect of the British Revolution. The brutalization of political life by Conservatives under Balfour was a notable feature of the years before World War I, brought to an end only by the outbreak of hostilities in 1914.

World War I brought about a long interlude in normal party politics, broken decisively by the fall of the Coalition Government in 1922. Then the Conservatives returned to power, which they held, with brief interludes in 1924 and 1929–1931, until the outbreak of World War II in 1939. During this time, the government was faced with a number of crucial issues. In the 1920's, the ever-present threat of a confrontation with the Trade Unions finally came to a head in the General Strike of 1926. In the same decade, the Labour Party achieved its maturity and twice undertook responsibility for governing Britain. Many

Conservatives were prepared to oppose the Trade Unions and the Labour Party to the bitter end. But Stanley Baldwin, who became the Conservative leader in 1923, led his party in rejection of extreme policies. In general, the Conservatives moved gently to the left between 1919 and 1929, not so far left as younger members would have liked, but still far enough to continue the tradition of gradual reform recommended by Disraeli.

In regard to another great issue of the age, Dominion status for India, the Conservatives were also willing to be flexible. The Labour Government of 1929–1931 had begun negotiations with the Indian nationalist leaders. This was supported by Baldwin against vigorous opposition from the right wing of his party, who found a spokesman in Winston Churchill. Passage of the India Bill of 1936 by the National Government (but with Conservative votes) was another victory for the spirit of moderate reform. James concludes, "The overwhelming rejection of extreme policies, both in Dominion and home affairs, was of real historical significance in heralding the final decline of the 'two nations.' " That Britain entered World War II as a united nation, less troubled by divisions between the classes than at any time in her history, was a matter of great importance. Credit for this development is given by James to Stanley Baldwin, in many ways the real hero of the book. For Baldwin to emerge as a hero of this dimension and a statesman of major importance is rather surprising since he has often been regarded as, at worst, a superior Calvin Coolidge, and at best an enigmatic and essentially unknowable figure. All would agree that he was a courteous and compassionate gentleman who was adept at cooling tempers and avoiding extreme solutions. He was notably kind and helpful to members of the Labour Party as they learned to be comfortable in the House of Commons and in governing the country. He also managed to relate to trade union leaders and Indian nationalists in ways that made them trust him. He was a kindly and lovable person, popular with all parties and all segments of the population. Often these virtues of character and manner of conducting politics have been considered secondary to his policies in assessing Baldwin as a political leader, but James elevates them into the highest position and claims that they were in fact what counted most in bringing Britain peacefully and progressively through the conflicts of the 1920's and 1930's. The author's case is persuasive.

Just as James stresses the influence of Stanley Baldwin in the interwar years, he also correspondingly diminishes that of Winston Churchill. He claims that historians have been too willing to view the 1930's through Churchill's own eyes, using his account of these years, *The Gathering Storm,* as a guide and thus exaggerating Churchill's importance. James's account of the 1930's appears in fact to be an effort to de-Churchillize those years. Essentially, he claims that Baldwin and other governmental leaders were more correct than Churchill in assessing the extent of German rearmament, that they were actually moving ahead in rearming Britain when Churchill was accusing them of slothfulness, and that they were developing such superior technology as the Spitfire fighter and radar while Churchill and his scientific adviser, Professor Lindemann, were causing confusion on the Air Defense Research Committee. It is now clear that the government was moving ahead more competently with rearmament than was at one time believed. But to write an account of the 1930's in which Churchill appears for the most part as a noisy nuisance is carrying revisionism too far. And it is interesting that when, in the narrative, Stanley Baldwin retires from politics in 1936 and no longer needs defending, Churchill emerges in a more favorable light than before, playing much more the responsible, important role that we have seen him in before.

One should not close without paying tribute to James's sixteen pages of plates containing sketches and photographs of the leading political figures of these sixty years. They have been extremely well selected, each a gem in itself, and collectively they form a portrait gallery which adds greatly to this fascinating book.

James E. Newman

Sources for Further Study

Booklist. LXXIV, October 1, 1977, p. 263.
Kirkus Reviews. XLV, September 15, 1977, p. 1030.
Library Journal. CII, October 1, 1977, p. 2061.
Publisher's Weekly. CCXII, August 29, 1977, p. 360.

CARNIVAL
Entertainments and Posthumous Tales

Author: Isak Dinesen (1885–1962)
Publisher: University of Chicago Press (Chicago). 338 pp. $10.00
Type of work: Short stories
Time: The twentieth century
Locale: England, Scandinavia, Italy

A collection of eleven short stories which covers the entire span of the author's career

Isak Dinesen is the pen name of the Baroness Karen Blixen of Rungstedlund, born in 1885. Her first published work is included here, "The de Cats Family," dating from 1909, and "Second Meeting," the last story in this collection, is an unfinished fragment planned for a larger collection in 1961, a year before the author's death. Whereas most of Dinesen's work was in the form of short stories carefully grouped in collections, this edition, while striving to present only work representative of her best quality, has been prepared posthumously to make available tales not previously readily accessible. Three of these tales, "The de Cats Family," "Uncle Theodore," and "The Bear and the Kiss," have been translated from the Danish for this volume by P. M. Mitchell and W. D. Paden. Most of Dinesen's work was written in English, and she has enjoyed great popularity in this country. Four of her books have been Book-of-the-Month Club selections, and her stories have appeared in *The Ladies Home Journal* and *The Saturday Evening Post.* The present collection, while not as cohesive as the carefully constructed *Seven Gothic Tales* or *Winter's Tales,* does provide an overview of the development of Dinesen's style as well as an insight into her process of creation, since several of the works are really only preliminary drafts, still in need of the final polish. The diversity of theme also gives a good idea of the range of Dinesen's work, though one should not forget that beyond her mastery of the story form she also wrote the autobiographical *Out of Africa,* resulting from her years in British East Africa where she and her husband established a coffee plantation. The story "Carnival" is also a product of that period.

The stories are presented in a roughly chronological order, beginning with "The de Cats Family," a simply structured and dryly narrated satire of subdued, rather tongue-in-cheek humor, which becomes a basic element of Dinesen's style. But this early work lacks the depth of her mature style, being elegant and mannered in its presentation of a bourgeois family that has become synonymous with the highest probity and virtue, though always at the cost of containing one member who, scapegoatlike, exemplifies the very opposite qualities. The irony is created when one of these ne'er-do-wells reforms, and as a consequence the family's virtue begins to crumble, until after long plotting and finally at great expense, he is persuaded to return to his life of vice, and the virtuous members return instinctively to upholding the family honor. This elegant structure is presented in a clear and straightforward prose that makes easy reading, yet already in this earliest work one can see Dinesen's predilection for whimsical inversions of order, the creation of patterns of symmetry, and an artificially ordered world in which characters are more like figures in a dance, revealing by their relative positions and motions an underlying structure. These underlying structures may impart a philosophical idea, a social critique, or a psychological truth, but because they are entirely aesthetic the reader faces them from the standpoint of amused delight, and only in a few of the mature works is one gripped by a profounder sense of insight. The concept "entertainments" is applied specifically to those works conceived for American magazine publication, but this quality applies to the majority of the works in this collection.

"Uncle Theodore," another of the very early works, shares this lucid style which takes delight in elegant twists of plot. Like "The de Cats Family," it was written in Danish and appears here in translation; thus one cannot be entirely certain of the actual qualities of tone and phrase that may have been lost in translation. It is clear, however, that this work is also superficial, in the sense that it is the surface of the tale that holds our interest, and the pattern of the plot which contains the substance of the story. There is very little to think about when one is done, and yet the strange permutations of reality that occur as coincidence follows coincidence open up this simple, humorous tale and create a world in which illusion and reality mirror each other, and fantasy proves a more valid tool for identifying the true nature of things than reason—while in a final ironic twist, no sooner is the reality of the fantasy confirmed than a counter movement sets in to bring all elements back to the opposite swing of the pendulum. All ends happily and serenely, antagonism proves ephemeral, and the artfully constructed dance leaves both the element of fantasy and its corrective intact. Here perhaps we begin to see the possibilities inherent in Dinesen's style, which she will later exploit precisely through the development of this romantic element of fantasy, as well as through mythic and magical elements.

"Carnival," the title piece of the collection, is in fact the unrevised version of a piece originally part of the work that later coalesced into *Seven Gothic Tales*. It was written in the late 1920's, after the author's departure for Africa. While still rough in quality, it shows a deepening of perspective perhaps implicit in the theme of masks and masquerades. Again we find the fascination with illusion and reality, in this case creating some confusion, as the eight guests at a carnival supper party are all costumed, sometimes as the opposite sex, and the interplay of the masquerade *personas* with the real characters develops a multifaceted world of fantasy. In the expected twist, reality breaks in in the form of a robber, also costumed, whose costume again relates thematically to his situation in the plot. He is, however, seduced into joining the game which the eight are playing, thus submerging his level of reality in their more compelling illusion. The fatuous world of these self-indulgent and spoiled aesthetes is doubtless depicted ironically, and there is an obvious element of social criticism, but this, too, is submerged beneath the primary concern for the manneristic convolutions of the narrative, in which the refractions of the various elements cast strange lights upon what seems at first to be a straightforward depiction.

Whereas "Carnival" is rambling and diffuse in its unpolished state, the next tale, "The Last Day," though also unfinished, shows the mature state of the author's craft. It was intended for *Winter's Tales* in 1942, but was put away and only taken up again a year before the author's death. We find in it a far more complex structure, with several themes skillfully interwoven. The device of a narration within the tale, which is a favorite technique in her later works, is used to great effect, as the subject of the first half of the tale becomes the object of the tale told to him in the second half, while both halves remain knit together through the thematic relationships established. That the story is set on Pentecost gives a clue to the increasingly metaphysical dimensions of Dinesen's work. The irony and the play with levels of reality take on greater significance here; they are not merely formal elements, or humorous in their effect, but the potential latent in her very first works is here released, and, though the central character, Johannes, is not aware of it, a kind of epiphany occurs in the inset narrative, only intensified by the irony that Johannes, a student of theology, receives a sermon from a ship's officer, and that in accord with the prayer of a whore. Once again the conventional order of things is inverted, and while there is still a humorous tone to the tale, the elements of coincidence, inversion, irony, and illusion are used here to create a sense of mystery and to hint at a level of understanding which passes beyond the surface of the story. In these later works, one comes away with food for thought, with new insights and an awareness of the impenetrable mystery underlying the simplest of events. Each work creates its own world, and from the clever but unindividual concoctions of the skilled beginner, Dinesen progresses to a mastery of her art.

In "The Fat Man," for example, we find a convincing depiction of psychological obsession, as a young man irrationally fastens on a certain fat man as the man who was seen walking off with a young girl who was later found murdered. He sees the man every day, and becomes possessed by his intuitive perception. The familiar element of the play-within-a-play is used here, with direct reference to *Hamlet,* with the ironic twist, the precise opposite of that in *Hamlet,* that the man shows his guilt not by an emotional reaction to the "play," but by his failure to react—for he, too, is obsessed, and the crime and its victim are so present to him that he is not at all shocked to see them; the girl is the only thing he sees everywhere he goes. Again the ironic twist is used to convey an insight, and the story is no mere formal arabesque, but a compelling work.

While "Anna," a splendidly constructed romance in twenty-five brief chapters, is a breathtaking series of coincidences and ironies told in an almost mocking vein of arch bemusement, the elements of magic and mystery again combine to create a mood in which the events of the tale take on a heightened significance. The images of the saintly dancer, the deaf-mute, the decay and potential regeneration of the family, and the allusions to the fairy-tale world of Cinderella, are all combined to create a miniature fairy-tale epic with much the same power to fascinate and charm.

Toward the end of this collection, each story presents this quality, and one can observe how Dinesen develops the technique of allusion to myth and fairy tale, as well as to established literary works, such as *Hamlet,* or Schiller's ballad "The Glove." These allusions become a kind of prefiguration, and again expand the resonance of the work, as the events of the plot are seen to fit into archetypal patterns of experience, and take on mythical proportions. In works like "The Ghost Horses" or "The Bear and the Kiss," the ironic, humorous element almost disappears, and the techniques developed earlier are used to create the experience of a semimagical world where the boundaries between fantasy and reality are obscured. In "The Ghost Horses," a young child lies ill, and can only be drawn back into life when a man enters into her fantasy world, previously shared with a now dead boy. In the old stable room of an estate, he had found a secret cache of jewelry. To him they are not jewels, but horses and guards in a royal procession, and the man reenacts this with the sick girl. In this world, the jewels are actually more glorious in their fantasy role than they are as mere jewels—again we see Dinesen's inversion of fantasy and reality. In "The Bear and the Kiss," the combination creates a powerful mysterious constellation of intimations and mythical reminiscences. There is the sea voyage into the primitive world of the Arctic, legends of a heroic figure, Joshua, and his witch wife, Lahula, a quest for an elusive bear, an initiation through the confrontation of death and eros. The tale is told in a lucid, realistic style, but the figures of the story are richly suggestive, and the work builds to more than a mere ironic turn; Dinesen brings the reader into this fantasy world, and the climax, in itself elusive, is nonetheless powerful.

This collection is at times disappointing; it is, after all, not uniform in respect to the maturity or finish of the pieces, and one must inevitably turn to the author's own composed collections for an adequate judgment of her work. But as a document of the growth of a style from gifted promise to mature fruition, and indeed for a collection of diverse tales ranging from the amusing to the magical, this sampling of the work of Isak Dinesen, the literary mask of Karen Blixen, can be appreciated by any who respond to the artful creations of a master of the storyteller's craft.

Steven C. Schaber

Sources for Further Study

Atlantic. CCXL, October, 1977, p. 107.

Best Sellers. XXXVII, December, 1977, p. 263.

Nation. CCXXV, November 5, 1977, p. 474.

New York Times Book Review. October 16, 1977, p. 10.

New Yorker. LIII, December 5, 1977, p. 231.

Progressive. XLI, November, 1977, p. 58.

Publisher's Weekly. CCXII, July 25, 1977, p. 65.

CATHERINE THE GREAT

Author: Joan Haslip (1911–　)
Publisher: G. P. Putnam's Sons (New York). 382 pp. $12.95
Type of work: Biography
Time: The eighteenth century
Locale: Russia

The story of one of Russia's most colorful, ambitious, and accomplished rulers

> Principal personages:
> CATHERINE II, Empress of Russia, 1762–1796
> CATHERINE DASHKOVA, her friend, co-conspirator, and director of the
>   Academy of Sciences
> GREGORY ORLOV, her lover during the first decade of her reign
> STANISLAUS PONIATOWSKI, another lover and later King of Poland
> GREGORY POTEMKIN, another lover, administrator of New Russia
> PETER ULRICH (PETER III), Emperor of Russia (for six months) and
>   Catherine's husband

The life of Catherine II of Russia is fascinating enough to command a regular and secure place in the book trade, and every four or five years a new popular biography appears. Joan Haslip's volume is the latest offering, and it meets all the requirements of the popular genre. Haslip faithfully recounts Catherine's string of romances and sexual encounters, her correspondence with great literary and royal personages, and her major foreign policy triumphs. However, the author builds the story on the often repeated and long outdated secondary accounts of Brückner, Soloveytchik, and Walezewski, plus some gossipy diplomatic dispatches. As a result, we get no new information or interpretation.

It is unfortunate that Haslip took this easy route, when, with a little extra effort, she could have produced something fresh and valuable. In the past fifteen years American, British, and French scholars have published a number of original monographs and shorter studies opening whole new lines of inquiry and discovery, and they have substantially modified the previously accepted knowledge about Catherine's reign. Haslip gives us none of this. The professional historian will certainly be dismayed to find how little of hardwon scholarly research gets translated into popular history. To her credit, Haslip writes with flair, and readers with no previous knowledge of the topic or period will profit from this entertaining introduction. They may, however, miss entirely the true reasons for Catherine's greatness.

The focus throughout this book remains on Catherine the woman of insatiable sexual appetite, Catherine the witty correspondent of philosophers and kings, Catherine the imperial conqueror of Turks and Poles. To judge from this account, about the only serious work she did on her own was identifying and buying major collections of Western art. This treatment trivializes Catherine both as a person and a ruler. One can scarcely come away from this book without feeling that Catherine was a nymphomaniac. Time and again we hear of lovers staggering out of her bedroom in complete exhaustion, pumping themselves up on aphrodisiacs, and seeking escape from her constant need for genital stimulation (we are at least spared the story of the horse). In reality, Catherine's love life was prosaic. She worked hard at the job of reigning and ruling, often twelve to fourteen hours a day, and sex was merely her way to relax and let off tension. But a woman ruler who scorned the expected prudish standards and who was clever and powerful enough to thwart the designs of foreign representatives and their masters could scarcely avoid being a target of slander. The stories of Catherine's sex life were largely the fantasies of frustrated men. Such tales were naturally picked up and peddled by popular book sellers. They sold well then, and apparently there is still a market for them today.

Haslip writes history in the grand manner. In her pages the "great person" theory is alive and well with an almost made-for-television baldness. Nothing of importance happens without the personal intervention of a heroic character. A typical case is the description of the 1771 bubonic plague epidemic in Moscow. The favorite Gregory Orlov was sent to deal with it, and, according to Haslip, his "boldness and decisiveness . . . cleared the city of the pestilence." As simple as that. Of course, no one then knew anything about the etiology and treatment of plague; its abatement was a function of changes in the weather and the rat-flea vector. Orlov just happened to arrive at the right time to take credit for it.

The book assigns too much power and influence to the Orlov brothers generally. They provided the muscle for Catherine's *coup d'état* in 1762, and in the early years she was indebted to them and dependent enough not to want to alienate them. But there were three loci of power in eighteenth century Russia: the imperial guards (where the Orlov strength lay), the Senate (seat of the leading families), and the court parties. Haslip gives the impression that Catherine did not believe she could rule without the support of the Orlovs, which falsely diminishes her stature. While no ruler could act effectively without the cooperation of these three institutions (as Peter III learned too late), Catherine was an astute politician who well understood how to manipulate this political configuration and keep its various elements in check.

Perhaps the biggest problem with popular history is its uncritical acceptance of any good story. Haslip's first chapters rely heavily on Catherine's famous memoirs, a source written with an obvious political purpose and reworked several times. Haslip simply accepts it as a true account, not merely repeating Catherine's self-serving portrayal of her husband as a dangerous madman, but even elaborating on it with a little popular psychology of her own. Yet there is no evidence that Peter was deranged. He was a drunkard, and his boorish and occasionally even silly behavior is fully explained as the actions of a drunken man. Catherine's effort to convince us otherwise by recounting each incident in lurid detail does not succeed, even if we can sympathize with her need to justify an act of usurpation and regicide.

At one point, however, Haslip declares her independence of Catherine's interpretation. This is on the issue of the paternity of her son Grand Duke Paul. Despite Catherine's hints that the real father was not Peter Ulrich but Sergei Saltykov (her first extramarital lover), Haslip grants the honor to Peter on grounds of supposedly similar physiological and personality traits. She adds the interesting suggestion that Catherine denied Peter's paternity in order to exonerate herself before her grandchildren for having condoned her husband's murder. Haslip may be right about Catherine's conscious bending of the truth here, but the empress' motives were no doubt different. One of the chief elements in Catherine's justification of her power seizure was the need to protect her son Paul, whom, she argued, Peter intended to get rid of. Raising doubts about Peter's fatherhood made the threats to Paul more credible. As for the question of paternity, it is far from clear that Catherine herself knew who the real father was.

The superficial treatment of most events described in this work leads to some serious misrepresentations of the workings of Russian politics. An obvious example, and one that scarcely requires any special analytical ability, is the cliché about Alexis Orlov acting for Catherine in killing Peter III, the implication being that Catherine had all but ordered the killing. In fact, Catherine had no need to do or say anything about Peter's fate. His continued existence posed a greater threat to the Orlovs and other conspirators than it did to Catherine, since his return would certainly have brought them to the scaffold and probably only landed Catherine in a convent. Peter's end would therefore have come soon enough without any complicity on Catherine's part.

Most distressing, on any issue of real importance to the social and political development of Russia, Haslip falters, if indeed she tells us anything at all. In regard to the secularization of church property, a major reform begun by Peter III, she speaks of a "storm of protest from all classes of people," when in fact what was most striking about this reform was the virtual absence of any protest. By the late eighteenth century the church stood in such abject dependence on the state that protest from within was unthinkable. Nor could an institution that provided little by way of social, intellectual, or even spiritual refuge expect the defense of its interest by other classes. About the only reaction to the reform came from the enserfed peasantry, which saw the "liberation" of ecclesiastical peasants (as well as the freeing of the nobility from obligatory state service, which occurred in the same year) as a harbinger of their own emancipation from bondage to the landed nobility. When this promise failed to materialize, the serfs interpreted the overthrow of Peter III as a plot by the "evil boyars" to suppress the manifesto granting their freedom, and, not surprisingly, they soon discovered Peter III's (twenty-three of them, in fact) living in the villages and ready to lead the serfs to victory over the usurpers.

The most successful Peter III was Emelyan Pugachev, whose peasant war of 1773–1774 engulfed vast areas of central-eastern Russia and threatened to ignite rebellion in Moscow itself. This last great social upheaval of the early modern era—Haslip inexplicably calls it the first—destroyed the walls protecting Catherine's compulsive personality. It is a tribute to the quality of Catherine's public relations that Haslip could be led to assert that during the crisis "only the empress kept her head." In reality, she came altogether unglued, babbled about leading the gentry on the battlefield, and then sank into a period of prolonged despondency.

Much to Catherine's credit, after recovering she quickly polished up and began implementation of a major reform of the provincial administration, a measure she had been perfecting for more than a decade. The reform was her crowning achievement as a ruler. With it she did what Peter the Great had long struggled in vain to accomplish: create a domestic administration separate from the armed forces. This meant that the next time Russia went to war its provincial administration did not evaporate and with it the government's capacity to collect taxes, muster recruits, and, not least, to contain peasant insurgencies and thus forestall another Pugachev rebellion. Catherine's government reforms established the basic framework of Russian administration until the emancipation of the serfs in 1861.

These reforms were not Catherine's only claim to greatness. Her tolerance and encouragement of public discussion, even to the point of subsidizing independent journalism, gave impetus to a budding intellectual life and provided Russia with the greatest freedom of expression it was to enjoy at any time prior to 1905. She also granted to the nobility and towns corporate rights, which, however fragile and circumscribed, were the first recognition in modern Russia of the notion that citizens could exercise rights against the state. Finally, there was Catherine's remarkable ability to select the ablest field commanders (P. Panin, Suvorov, Rumiantsev, Repnin, Kutuzov) and some of the most skilled government ministers (N. Panin, Viazemskii, Teplov, Bezborodko) of modern Russia. These were the true sources of Catherine's greatness and her legitimate claim to that title. Any history that neglects these aspects of her work and dwells on her supposed need to be physically subjugated by men, her insatiable sexual demands, her art collecting and monumental building projects greatly diminishes its subject and misses much of the point of studying the life of Catherine II.

David L. Ransel

Sources for Further Study

Best Sellers. XXXVII, May, 1977, p. 50.
Booklist. LXXIII, April 1, 1977, p. 1138.
Economist. CCLXIII, April 23, 1977, p. 130.
New Statesman. XCIII, March 18, 1977, p. 361.
New York Times Book Review. March 27, 1977, p. 4.
Observer. March 13, 1977, p. 28.

CAUGHT IN THE WEB OF WORDS
James A. H. Murray and the *Oxford English Dictionary*

Author: K. M. Elisabeth Murray
Publisher: Yale University Press (New Haven, Connecticut). 386 pp. $15.00
Type of work: Biography
Time: 1837–1915
Locale: The Scottish border and England, chiefly London and Oxford

The story of the chief editor of the Oxford English Dictionary, *a delightful and readable biography which gives a strong sense of the enormous effort and personal cost that went into the making of the premier dictionary of the English language*

Literary scholarship is rarely considered a noble and heroic undertaking; such terms are usually reserved for mountain-climbing, or other equally dangerous activity. But the *Oxford English Dictionary* is justly termed the greatest dictionary in the language, and the model for other national dictionaries. In over sixteen thousand pages, it chronicles the definitions and first appearances of practically every word in the English language, illustrated with copious quotations from original sources, both literary and subliterary. That it was ever done is miracle enough; that it was done by chiefly voluntary labor in an age before computers and typewriters makes of it a truly monumental achievement. *Caught in the Web of Words* is the story of the making of that dictionary, told from the perspective of the man chiefly responsible for its appearance.

James A. H. Murray's labors were truly herculean, carried out at great personal cost and sacrifice. Without his special learning and special determination, the work would never have been done. All who care about the English language are forever in his debt. This is, therefore, the story of a noble and heroic undertaking, the story of a noble and heroic man. It really consists of two parts, an account of Murray's life in preparation for his work on what is known everywhere as the *OED,* and a description of the work on the dictionary itself. As his biographer, who is also his granddaughter, makes clear, Murray had no real inkling until it was too late that his great life's work would be the *OED,* but even if he had, he could not have gone about preparing for it in any better way. Murray was, in some ways, an unlikely candidate for the job. He lacked formal university training, a situation which made entry into the scholarly life difficult in the class-conscious world of Victorian England. But precisely because he was largely self-taught, precisely because he had to seek out opportunities for learning in his relatively isolated early years on the Scottish border, Murray developed qualities of determination and high standards of excellence which were invaluable when the chance to do the dictionary actually came his way.

That the dictionary was done at all, Elisabeth Murray points out, resulted from the unique coming together of several disparate circumstances. Even late in the nineteenth century, English university education was dominated by the study of the classics; study of English language and literature was left, for the most part, to learned and devoted amateurs who gave to it the time they could spare from their other careers. They therefore had the sort of ambition and drive that only the amateur can have. Willing to take on projects simply to prove the value of their interests to all the world, the founders of the Philological Society and the Early English Text Society, and especially their leader, Frederick Furnivall, came to believe that the production of a grand dictionary of the English language would prove their point about the value of vernacular literary study and support their other work in the editing and study of early English literature. At the same time, since no one had ever undertaken a project of such magnitude, the task seemed manageable; in fact, Murray, when he became editor, projected the work would be done in a mere ten years. Nevertheless, the tools were at hand, since the prior work of the Early English Text Society had made generally available a large number of heretofore rare and unusual sources for much of the historical evidence used in the dictionary.

In 1879, two further elements fell into place, and the project was duly launched. The first was the publisher; the Oxford University Press agreed to provide salaries and expense money in advance for a dictionary, to be seven thousand pages long and completed in ten years. The second was the editor; James Murray, formerly a schoolteacher and bank clerk and now a Master at Mill Hill School, agreed to take charge of the dictionary project. That the final product was not complete until fifty-four years later, and that it ran to over sixteen thousand pages, is some indication of how greatly its originators underestimated the magnitude of their task.

Three elements of this biography support its special and highly memorable retelling of the story of the *OED*. The first is the detailed portrait of James Murray himself, from his childhood and early education through his years of young adulthood through the early years of labor to support his growing family and the great sweep of years at work on the dictionary itself. The second is the description of the process which produced the dictionary, and the third is the account of the swirling array of personalities who had their roles, great and small, to play in the grand undertaking.

In the portrait of Murray, several themes stand out. The first is the quality of his mind. A man of enormous brilliance, Murray found that he learned languages with great facility, so that he soon mastered the classical and modern European languages and proceeded to the ancient languages of Europe and the languages of the Orient. Coupled with this special linguistic skill was a rapacious curiosity, especially about things ancient and unusual. From early in his life, Murray helped found an Antiquarian society in his native region and contributed greatly to the local understanding of history, as well as to the knowledge of local geography and natural history. It was this passion for knowledge that drove Murray to a lifelong pursuit of learning in all its forms. It also enabled him to transcend the limitations of his provincial background, to enter the life of learned London, and to make his unique contribution to the study of English letters. But Murray was not a man of a single passion; in spite of the long hours he devoted to scholarly pursuits in addition to his regular jobs, he was able to father a large family and to support and encourage the kind of rich and loving family life that all his children looked back on with fondness and deep affection.

Such talents and drive made him uniquely suited to take on the task of the *OED,* a task that was never easy or simple. The miraculous thing about the great dictionary was that much of the labor was done by volunteer work. Murray's method, initiated by Furnivall before him, was to recruit volunteers to provide him with samples of word-usage drawn from ancient and more recent literary and subliterary sources. People from all over the English-speaking world, but especially from England and the United States, spent much of their spare time reading and noting unusual and not-so-unusual word usage. Each example they noted on slips of paper and sent them on to Murray at Mill Hill and, later, at Oxford. Murray, with the aid of paid helpers and the voluntary support of his ever-growing family, would compile the samples and from them work up the actual dictionary entries. All the work was done in a special building, made of iron for fear of fire, called the Scriptorium. The size of the task called for literally millions of slips, all of which had to be carefully sorted, and then preserved in some semblance of order. In our age of professionalism, the use of amateur volunteers seems a haphazard method of working, but the glory of what resulted is proof of the effectiveness of the process.

Murray's biographer is careful to make the point that the *OED* project became for many of its workers a major outlet for their talents. Especially, she finds, for women whose able minds were not challenged by the routines of Victorian housekeeping, their voluntary work on the dictionary gave them a sense of purpose in life, and a sense of personal value, which redeemed some of the drudgery of everyday existence. And Americans can take pride in the fact that many of Murray's ablest and most dedicated volunteers came from that side of the Atlantic.

At this point, the retelling of an anecdote may suggest how the *OED* project came to have a life of its own as a cultural institution during the long years of its execution. Once Murray needed to account for the etymology of a word derived from the Greek and used as a technical term in botany. He wrote to a learned botanist for help, and was told in reply that the botanist had consulted a Greek scholar. Soon Murray received a letter from a friend telling him that another friend, a Greek scholar, had asked him to write to Murray to find out the etymology of a Greek word, now used as a botanical term. A botanist had asked him, wrote the scholar, and he hated to admit his ignorance, so if Murray, who was the only man in the realm who was sure to know, would only supply the information, everyone would be pleased. Thus, the inquiry had come full circle, and only the growing importance of the *OED* was proved.

In this, and in many other ways, the task was to become increasingly difficult. As Elisabeth Murray demonstrates abundantly, the very lack of understanding of the magnitude of the project, which perhaps contributed to the readiness with which Murray took it on and the Oxford Press agreed to publish it, became itself a stumbling block to the work's completion. The Philological Society and the Press both thought the dictionary would be done in short order, and that it would prove a great money-maker for all concerned. Such was not to be the case; the project quickly fell hopelessly behind schedule and began to cost more and more money. As a result, Murray was constantly under great pressure to speed up the process, or to compromise his standards, or both. In addition, the conflicting personalities within the Society and the University, coupled with their lack of sensitivity to the man engaged in sorting all the slips in his Scriptorium, united to threaten the very existence of the project time and time again. In 1978, one cannot imagine the world without the *OED:* all the conflicts and pressures that swirled about its inception and creation can only make us value even more highly the fact that we have the work, and that Murray was able to resist all pressures to give us less than he in fact did. But the cost was high, in personal terms. One point on which Murray was willing to give was financial; as a result, he was never paid what he deserved, and his family suffered the consequences with him.

But go forward the project did, and although Murray died before the task was done, he had seen the bulk of it through the press. Those who had come to work with him brought it to its final completion, a tribute to a man who had the personal resources of mind and will to take on a project of enormous dimensions, struggle to continue it against great odds, and take it to a point from which there could be no going back. We are in his debt, and we are also in debt to his granddaughter, who has given us a delightful and stirring account of his life, his work, and his character, a noble and heroic story, a tribute to the human spirit.

John N. Wall, Jr.

Sources for Further Study

Economist. CCLXIV, September 24, 1977, p. 140.

New Republic. CLXXVII, November 12, 1977, p. 33.

New York Times. October 19, 1977, p. 29.

New York Times Book Review. October 30, 1977, p. 13.

New Yorker. LIII, November 21, 1977, p. 222.

Newsweek. XC, November 7, 1977, p. 98.

Saturday Review. V, November 12, 1977, p. 30.

THE CELTS
The People Who Came Out of the Darkness

Author: Gerhard Herm (1931–   )
Publisher: St. Martin's Press (New York). Illustrated. 312 pp. $10.95
Type of work: Archaeology and history
Time: c. 2500 B.C.–A.D. 1000
Locale: Western Asia, Central and Western Europe, and the British islands

A survey of the Celtic peoples from their presumed origins, through the height of their civilization, to their eclipse in the early medieval period in Western Europe

Principal personages:
BRENNUS THE ELDER,
BRENNUS THE YOUNGER,
DUMNORIX,
VERCINGETORIX,
CASSIVELLAUNS,
KING ARTHUR,
QUEEN MAEVE,
CÚ CHULAINN,
ST. COLUMBA, and
CONOR MAC NESSA, Celts
DIODORUS SICULUS,
POLYBIUS,
POSIDONIUS, and
STRABO, Greeks
CAIUS JULIUS CAESAR,
TACITUS, and
LIVY, Romans

Most of our conceptions and misconceptions about the early Celts, until quite recently, have been based on a few scattered reports of ancient Greek and Roman writers, and on the myths and legends of the Celts themselves. All of these sources mixed fact and fancy to varying degrees. Not until the late nineteenth century did serious efforts to sort out the truths about the Celts begin. Scholars in several disciplines—archaeology, history, linguistics, and the physical sciences—have conducted extensive and intensive research into what the Celts were truly like. Many of the old notions have been revised and today we probably have a better understanding of the ancient Celts than their contemporaries did. There is much that is still puzzling, but the curtain of mystery has been somewhat lifted; the Celts have partially come out of the darkness.

Gerhard Herm is not himself a trained archaeologist or historian; he is a professional writer with an interest in ancient history. One of his previous books, a popularized study of the Phoenicians, has been translated into twenty-four languages and seems to have been widely read. To gather materials for *The Celts,* Herm traveled through Europe studying the sites of Celtic settlements, and he has also drawn substantially upon the writings of such authorities in the field of Celtic studies as Nora Chadwick, Jean-Jacques Hatt, and Kenneth

Jackson.

Always intriguing are the researches of scholars into the possible origins of various human societies. As to the origins of the Celts, Herm finds plausible a current theory which suggests that the Celts—and all Indo-Europeans—emerged from certain tribes living in the steppe lands of the lower Volga River around 3000 B.C. One archaeologist has called those particular tribes the Kurgan (mound) people, and has found that they were taller, more long-headed and possibly more graceful than the squat, round-headed, Ukrainian tribesmen who inhabited the same general area. Some linguists consider it possible that the Kurgan tribes spoke what is known as the "Ur-language," the supposed ancestor of the later Indo-European tongues. By c.2400–2300 B.C., the theory continues, the Kurgan people had domesticated horses and, hitching those animals to their carts, the tribes began migrating eastward and westward, probably impelled by population pressures. Those who migrated eastward came into contact with the Sumerian and Akkadian civilizations of the Fertile Crescent, adopted elements of civilized life from those more advanced societies, and then migrated on further to Iran and India.

The tribes which traveled to the west settled in the plains and mountains of Bohemia and central Germany where they found copper and tin which they used to make bronze. The Bohemian bronzemakers established the Unětice culture which, at its greatest extent around 1500 B.C., included much of central Europe. Two subsequent Indo European cultures probably emerged from the Unětice: the Urnfield in northern Europe and, later, the Hallstatt in Western Europe, differing from the Unětice in the kind of burial for the dead they used, and probably in the languages they spoke. The Urnfield and Hallstatt cultures by c.1000 B.C. resembled what is known to be the Celtic way of life at a later date: ironmaking had appeared, people resided on solitary farms rather than enclosed villages, had more interest in raising animals than in the cultivation of the soil, included a warrior class which used two- or four-wheeled chariots and fought with battle axes, and priests who sacrificed to sun gods.

It seems likely that Celts or Proto-Celts shared in and learned these cultural features, and that sometime between 1300 and 600 B.C. a distinctive, identifiable culture which can be called Celtic evolved. However, scholars will surely never be able to say "suddenly the Celts arrived" because no people come out of the darkness into history with a full panoply of the national customs, language, and culture already intact. As Herm puts it, rather picturesquely, the Celts appeared when the first man said "good morning" to his wife in Celtic, but no one will ever know just when that happened.

In the mid-nineteenth century, at a site in Switzerland called La Tène, archaeologists uncovered a rich store of various artifacts dating from the fifth century B.C.—swords, spears, tools—many of them decorated in almost naturalistic patterns which came to be known as the La Tène style, which is now regarded as uniquely Celtic. The Celtic artists were eclectic, taking motifs from the arts of the Mediterranean and from the splendid artwork of the Scythians who lived to the east. Over several centuries following the early La Tène artifacts, Celtic artists and craftsmen produced numerous practical and decorative objects, many of which were brilliantly executed and technically perfect.

From Bulgaria and Rumania in eastern Europe, to France and the British islands in the west, investigators have found many other indications of Celtic culture since the first finds at La Tène. These later discoveries show that from the fifth to the first centuries B.C. the Celts acquired a wide variety of civilized skills. They learned to inlay metals, and could cast soft iron. They knew how to enamel and to make ornamental glass. The weaving and dyeing techniques they used produced excellent wearing apparel.

In the same period (450–50 B.C.), Celtic towns sprang up; some ninety Celtic *oppida* have been located in ancient Gaul alone. Trade routes joined these to other Celtic towns from the Atlantic to the Carpathians. One of the most impressive archaeological finds of recent years is the discovery of a large Celtic community on the Danube River in Bavaria near the village of Manching. Excavations at Manching began in 1955 and are not yet completed, but enough has been revealed to show that the Celts had a good-sized community there, and that it was a major trade and industrial center for much of Celtic Europe. The town covered some four hundred hectares contained within a four-mile-long defensive wall. Within the town were hundreds of mud-faced stone dwellings, numerous shops and workplaces including iron and glass works, potteries, goldsmiths, and bronze foundries. Herm, upon visiting the Manching town site, finds it astonishing that some Celtic prince, whose name we do not know, was able to organize, discipline, and direct his barbarian tribesmen to erect such an establishment as Manching town. The town was conquered by the Romans about A.D. 15, and its end was violent as attested by many split skulls found among the ruins. Still, the fact that it did exist, and flourished for many years, is evidence of considerable cultural advances by some of the Celts since the pre-La Tène era.

One of the more interesting chapters of *The Celts* deals with the Druids, "the authentic and most important representatives of the Celtic people." It was in respect to the Druids and their functions that the contemporary Greek and Roman writings about the Celts were often most in error. That the Druids were priests (called "miraculix") who performed ceremonies in oak groves using golden sickles, branches of mistletoe, and white cloths, and that sometimes those ceremonies involved human sacrifices, was known to the Romans. But the Druids were more than priests; they were seers who knew the past and the future, medical healers who, over generations, had acquired an extensive and efficacious pharmacopeia, and they were students of nature and the seasons; "they were university, church and court of the realm all in one." Some Celtic scholars find parallels between the Druids of Western Europe and the Brahmin ruling caste of Aryan India, both groups having roots in the "shaman" of the early Indo European tribes. Like the Brahmins, the Druids were poets who sang the songs and told the legends of their people, and they were students and teachers of the law. No class or group had more influence among the Celts than the Druids, not even the tribal kings. It is not surprising, therefore, that when the Romans conquered the Celtic tribes, the Druids and their practices were banned for political and moral reasons.

The Romans first met the Celts around 400 B.C. when the Gauls, as the Romans called them, migrated into the Po River valley. Diodorus Siculus gives a description of the striking and terrifying appearance of the Celts at this time: "like wood-demons . . . hair long and shaggy and bleached white . . . those of high rank shave their cheeks but wear a moustache . . . the way they dress is astonishing." They wore brightly colored shirts and trousers, and striped or checkered cloaks. Some of the warriors wore bronze helmets with horns to make themselves taller and more ferocious, and covered themselves with chain armor, but "most of them went naked into battle."

Around 390 B.C. hosts of these blond giants led by Brennus the elder with wild singing and horrible yells advanced on Rome. They overwhelmed the defenders and captured the city. After months of negotiation, Brennus agreed to accept a tribute of one thousand pounds of gold and declaring "woe to the defeated," returned north with his army. The Romans rebuilt their city, but the scars of fear and hatred for the Celts never healed.

Not until three and a half centuries had passed did Romans repay their enemy with the conquest and subjugation of Gaul by Julius Caesar. A substantial portion of *The Celts* is devoted to Caesar's Gallic Wars. Those wars culminated in the battle at Alesia in central Gaul where the Celtic chief, Vercingetorix, had assembled some eighty thousand warriors of several tribes for what proved to be the last defense of their homeland. After resisting the Roman siege for several months, the starving Celtic warriors surrendered. Vercingetorix was taken to Rome to adorn Caesar's triumph and then executed. All Gaul became a Roman province. The Gallic Celts merged and blended with Romans in the generations after Caesar's conquests, and lost much of their special way of life.

Across the Channel in Britain, however, the Celtic tribal kingdoms kept their independence and identity for a longer time. It was not until a century after Caesar that the emperor Claudius undertook the invasion of Celtic Britain and began the "campaigns at the world's end." Those took many years and were never fully completed, for the Celtic Scots and Irish could not be brought under Roman sway. In Scotland and Ireland, the Celts and their culture survived on the fringes of the Roman empire.

For many readers the final chapters of *The Celts* may be most interesting. There, Herm delves into the lost world of Celtic Ireland and Britain, retelling the stories of the fabulous Irish hero Cú Chulainn, of the fascinating Queen Maeve, and of the great King of Ulster, Conor Mac Nessa. And he tells of the British war chief who fought the invading Saxons and defeated them many times before he was slain; and then of the mythic transformation of that chief into the most remembered of all the Celtic heroes, King Arthur.

More significant historically than these legends, however, was the conversion of the Irish Celts to Christianity in the fifth century A.D. After that conversion, there emerged in Ireland a remarkable period of learning, literature, and art, and out of the Irish monasteries then went missionaries to bring the gospel of Christ to Celts and non-Celts in Britain and all over Europe.

The Celts is a competent work of historical popularization. Herm's intention was to provide an introduction for the general reader to the history of the Celtic people; seemingly he has succeeded, since the book is said to be a bestseller in Germany, where it was originally published. The English translation has produced an occasional odd sentence structure and clumsy syntax, but many portions are clearly, even lyrically, expressive. The photographic illustrations are few and not particularly illuminating, and some of the maps are not well juxtaposed with the text. The organization of the book is rather confusing with some of the early chapters out of chronological sequence; to help clarify matters, Herm has wisely provided a list of dates and events in an appendix.

James W. Pringle

Sources for Further Study

Booklist. LXXIII, May 1, 1977, p. 1318.
Books and Bookmen. XXII, February, 1977, p. 31.
Christian Century. XCIV, August 31, 1977, p. 763.
Library Journal. CII, April 15, 1977, p. 917.
New Yorker. LIII, August 1, 1977, p. 71.
Times Literary Supplement. April 29, 1977, p. 535.

CHARLES STEWART PARNELL

Author: F. S. L. Lyons (1923–   )
Publisher: Oxford University Press (New York). Illustrated. 704 pp. $20.00
Type of work: Biography
Time: 1846–1891
Locale: Ireland and England

A biography of Parnell which traces one of Ireland's most controversial political figures from his early childhood to his position as leader of the Irish National League

Principal personages:
CHARLES STEWART PARNELL
JOHN HENRY PARNELL, his father
DELIA TUDOR STEWART PARNELL, his mother
ISAAC BUTT, leader of the Home Rule League
MICHAEL DAVITT, founder of the Land League
JAMES STEPHENS AND JOHN O'MAHONEY, founders of the Irish
    Republican Brotherhood (Fenians)
WILLIAM EWART GLADSTONE, British Prime Minister, leader of the
    Liberal ministry
KATHARINE O'SHEA, Parnell's mistress, later his wife
CAPTAIN WILLIAM HENRY O'SHEA, one of Parnell's followers and
    husband to Katharine O'Shea
JOHN DILLON, leader of the Irish National Federation after Parnell's
    death

F. S. L. Lyons has written an excellent biography on the life of one of Ireland's most controversial political figures. *Charles Stewart Parnell* is a comprehensive investigation into Parnell's rise to power during the final decades of nineteenth century Ireland. There are no new theories introduced about Parnell's accomplishments; there are, however, a number of misconceptions corrected regarding his political motives and achievements, as well as the man's legacy to Ireland. Lyons carefully traces the course of Parnell's rise to power, and with equal attention he studies the forces which ended his career in public affairs. It is a clearly written and well-organized book, with conclusions amply supported by sound scholarship. The author has to his credit a number of other books treating Irish political figures and historical events. *Charles Stewart Parnell* is, perhaps, the most complete biography of Parnell and Irish political activity in the 1870's and 1880's currently available to the general reader.

The political issues Parnell encountered as a parliamentarian were firmly rooted in Ireland's troubled past. Few of them had been resolved during centuries of British occupation and rule. For example, it was only twenty years before Parnell's birth that Irish leaders managed to obtain Catholic emancipation. And 1845, the year before Parnell's birth, ushered in another crisis: the Potato Famine (1845–1850), a catastrophe of such magnitude that it temporarily eclipsed all of Ireland's other pressing problems. In the late 1840's, the English attempted to combat the disaster by initiating a land reform scheme that was designed to sell estates with vast holdings to investors in England. The plan called for a large influx of foreign capital to revive Ireland's depressed agrarian economy. The measure failed when speculators purchased the estates and remained absent from their new holdings. Neither the money nor the landlords arrived in Ireland to confront the problem. By 1850, three million people were being fed at public expense, a million had starved to death, and hundreds of thousands had emigrated to Canada and America.

Because the British had proved so ineffectual in successfully resolving any of Ireland's crucial problems, a new impetus was given to the cause of Irish nationalism. Radical groups sprang up committed to the idea that Ireland should be free to grapple with her own problems without British interference. The Irish Republican Brotherhood (Fenians) was established, their manifesto demanding the violent overthrow of British control. And other groups, less radical, were formed to pressure the British into legislating land reforms and home rule. Complicating the political landscape were the interests of the Protestant minority, the Unionists and anti-Unionists, the Catholic majority, and the Anglo-Irish ruling classes. This was Parnell's inheritance once he decided to enter the political arena: a confused, demoralized, and leaderless movement in opposition to British rule in Ireland. And according to Lyons, he appeared at first the least likely candidate to organize a movement which would bring the various factions together in a concerted effort to win for Ireland the right to determine her own destiny.

Charles Stewart Parnell was born on June 27, 1846, at Avondale, County Wicklow, into an Anglo-Irish landlord family. His forebears had emigrated to Ireland in the 1660's, immediately after the Restoration, and had prospered in their adopted home. Charles' mother was an American and the daughter of Commodore Charles Stewart, captain of the *U.S. Constitution,* America's flagship during the War of 1812. She was staunchly anti-English, and it is possible that Charles inherited from her his distrust of British colonial policies. Young Charles received the customary education afforded gentlemen of his class, including studies at English boarding schools and three and one half years at Magdalene College, Cambridge (he left a semester before taking his degree). When he returned to Ireland in 1869, it was to manage the family estate in a responsible manner, not unlike the one practiced by his father, and his father's father. There were no outward signs that Parnell differed in any appreciable way from other Anglo-Irish landholders: he was educated abroad, a Protestant who spoke the language with an English accent, and who was only mildly curious about politics. In addition, as Lyons points out, he was not a gifted public speaker; also, he possessed, among other superstitions, a morbid dislike for funerals and a fear of the color green. These were hardly credentials which would endear him to the Irish, least of all the Catholic majority. Yet Parnell became one of Ireland's great patriots, a champion of Irish liberties who dominated Irish politics for nearly fifteen years. Given his Anglo-Irish background, the concessions he obtained from the British during his leadership are impressive.

It is Lyons' contention that Parnell overcame many of his inherited handicaps with qualities not immediately visible to the eye. He did display remarkable leadership abilities, possessed enormous physical energies, and was shrewd enough to conciliate the differences which separated the various political attitudes. In 1875, when he was elected to represent County Meath in Parliament, his only qualification was an illustrious family name. But as early as 1877, Parnell began to sense his aptitude for politics. He joined the movement for Home Rule and aligned himself with those demanding major land reforms. In moving closer toward the leadership of his party, be began to exhibit a genius for synthesizing divergent views. He was able, for example, to appease the impatient Liberals who wanted immediate concessions from the British. And when the more conservative factions became alarmed, he would attack the radical views of the Fenians. The English were also a major force with which to contend, and he had to plot a course of action which would allow them, without losing face, to make compromises. And there were the Irish-Americans to please. They provided money and support and were keenly interested in his political strategies. Added to this was the lack of unanimity within his own party. Parnell's ability to keep all interested parties reasonably content was achieved, observes Lyons, by his playing one faction against the other in order to win temporary compromises and regain support. It was a continuing process, performed by a man without political training or oratorical eloquence—and it was handled very well.

In 1881, when Parnell appeared to be hedging on the critical issue of landlords versus tenants, he delivered his famous speech in which he declared that "England's mission in Ireland has been a failure. . . . Irishmen have established their right to govern Ireland by laws made by themselves on Irish soil." The speech invited tenants to withhold their rents until the Land Act was properly reformed. It was politically well-timed and it achieved a number of desired effects. Because Parnell had advised the tenants to break the law, he was immediately arrested and imprisoned in Kilmainham jail. This satisfied the liberal faction, convincing its members that Parnell was prepared to defy the British openly. His example also served to inspire the Irish tenants. An unexpected benefit came from England, where many citizens sympathized with Parnell's nonviolent approach to political change and became increasingly critical of their own government's management of Ireland.

Parnell addressed many other problems confronting Ireland in his remaining years as a political leader, the most important dealing with the question of Home Rule. But before he could do more than make this matter a public issue, he was to become embroiled in a private matter that cost him his political leadership. Named as correspondent in a divorce suit prepared by Captain William O'Shea, Parnell refused to defend himself in open court (he had been Mrs. O'Shea's lover for many years). The case went against him, and with it his credibility. His party saw him as a political liability and his followers, acting on the advice of

Gladstone and fearful that Home Rule was unobtainable with Parnell as party leader, forced him to withdraw. If heeded, the advice sent by Cecil Rhodes from Africa—"Resign-marry-return"—might have saved him. But at the end of 1890, his political career was in ruins, and the support he had labored so hard to win was all but gone.

This reversal in Parnell's political fortunes did not, however, deter him from planning a return to politics in the interests of Irish affairs. Indeed, as Lyons clearly illustrates, Parnell was convinced he could regain the confidence of the people if allowed sufficient time to organize a new campaign. But time did not cooperate; a year after the disastrous O'Shea affair, Parnell was dead. Ironically, Ireland's "uncrowned king" died in England, a relatively young man whose great promise was never fully tested.

What Lyons' biography does so well in presenting Parnell is to separate the man from the myth which has pursued him to this day. According to Lyons, Parnell's fall from grace put an end to Ireland's hope for Home Rule. This was not, in Lyons' view, a disastrous turn of events. On the contrary, the Home Rule bill Parnell might have achieved could conceivably have delayed Ireland's eventual independence. The men who followed Parnell, notably Patrick Pearse and James Connolly, were a different breed of political activist, operating under far different circumstances and in another time. They were quick to seize on Parnell's memory, but they went about achieving their political aims in an altogether different manner. This is not to deny Parnell his contributions to Ireland and Irish interests, nor to suggest his followers learned little from his political examples. Parnell did manage reforms in the Land Act, and he was instrumental in getting Ireland included in the Reform Act of 1884. In addition, he built the first highly disciplined parliamentarian party and brought to Westminster issues of grave importance to Ireland. But Lyons believes Parnell's most important achievement was to give back to the Irish their self-respect. In accomplishing this goal, he bequeathed to his followers a people better prepared for the momentous events which were to follow—in particular, Irish independence after seven hundred years of British rule.

Lyons' intentions in this biography are not to minimize Parnell's achievements, but to study them with critical objectivity. His conclusions about Parnell might irritate some staunch Parnellites; they are reached, however, by a careful interpretation of the facts. The outcome is that Parnell emerges from this study as a large and impressive figure, but one capable of making political errors, and one who was, to a large extent, responsible for his own undoing. Lyons' study is fair and well balanced and it makes its subject understandable and human. And this virtue helps to explain better Parnell's true place in Irish history. Parnell may not have fully succeeded politically during his tenure, but he unquestionably raised the Irish spirit and made it possible for others to carry on the fight. And in Lyons' view, Parnell's most precious gift to his people was the powerful force of his memory, called upon again and again by the political leaders who were to form the Irish Free State.

Don W. Sieker

Sources for Further Study

America. CXXXVII, November 19, 1977, p. 366.

Booklist. LXXIV, October 15, 1977, p. 353.

Economist. CCLXIII, June 4, 1977, p. 137.

Guardian Weekly. CXVII, August 14, 1977, p. 23.

New York Review of Books. XXIV, November 24, 1977, p. 19.

New York Times Book Review. August 21, 1977, p. 11.

New Yorker. LIII, August 15, 1977, p. 89.

THE CHINESE COMMUNIST PARTY
IN POWER, 1949-1976

Author: Jacques Guillermaz
Translated from the French by Anne Destenay
Publisher: Westview Press (Boulder, Colorado). 614 pp. $24.75
Type of work: History
Time: 1949-1976
Locale: The People's Republic of China

A narrative account of Chinese history since 1949 which emphasizes the role of Mao Tse-tung in directing the Communist Party and establishing the policies of the People's Republic

For the first time in the memory of Chinese living in the early 1950's, China had begun to experience a period of unification, peace, adequate food, economic growth, and international respectability. A century and a half of decline and disorder had abruptly come to an end with the emergence of a formidable Communist movement that came out of the fields and paddies of China's agrarian society. The challenges at the time were enormous. War with Japan and civil war with Chiang Kai-shek's nationalists had left China devastated. Public works were destroyed, fields were left unattended, and starvation was rampant. China's deprivation, however, brought on the anguish and despair among its people that facilitated the Communist Party in setting up a new government and a new society.

In viewing the events that followed "liberation," Guillermaz narrates, in great detail, the Communist Party's policies and methods of implementation. He is particularly interested in identifying the problems that beset the Communist leadership and the role of Mao Tse-tung in seeking solutions within the context of Marxism-Leninism. Obviously focused in the author's mind is an answer to the question: How has the Communist Party been able to maintain effective control over such a large nation under the trying conditions that beset China in 1949?

The problems were widespread. China's population, Guillermaz considers, is the most important. Without an accurate tally, no effective means to check population growth, and inadequate agricultural technology, a substantial shift in the country's food-people ratio could result in disaster. A second problem given the Party's attention is economic development. In this area, the Communist government has sought to devise policies which would expand both agriculture and industry, interrelating their expansion. Third, to bring about extensive political and economic change in China, the Party has experimented considerably with policies that would create an egalitarian society to break class distinctions and "elitism." Guillermaz, however, detects residual strength in family and clan ties, as well as the prevalence of materialism and individualism of Chinese tradition that impedes the development of a "new society." A fourth problem is to overcome factionalism which has historically plagued Chinese politics. Power struggles have continued to play a role in the casting of

Communist directions, especially in the shifting between moderate and radical leaders. Guillermaz, however, could not unwrangle Mao's last days. When the book was completed in 1976, Mao was still alive and the "Gang of Four" leftists had not yet been incarcerated; and the unsettled political scene at this juncture did not allow the author to assess accurately China's future political course.

The assertive hand of Mao Tse-tung in China's socialist transformation is evident throughout the upheavals of the Communist experiment. The "Hundred Flowers" campaign (1956), seeking the adulation of China's intellectuals; the "Great Leap Forward" campaign (1957–1958), China's fanatical drive for instant communalization and industrialization; and the "Cultural Revolution" (1966–1969), Mao's effort to make his revolution and "Maoism" permanently ingrained in the mind of every Chinese, were all part of Mao's strategy. The fact that they failed to achieve their objectives is not important. What is significant is that the movements were part of the Maoist brand of Communism that differed from the Soviets' and brought Maoism to an equal footing (at least in Chinese eyes) with Marxism and Leninism.

Guillermaz envisions Mao as "compliant and inflexible" and yet as one who contributed seriously to Communist doctrine and who had an influence on the international movement. Nevertheless, the author regards Mao as a leader who outlived his usefulness as a nation-builder and confused the past with the future. The watershed was the Cultural Revolution, according to Guillermaz, as the cyclic phenomenon of revolution was too disturbing to peace, order, and planning; and he questions the "seriousness of [the] Maoist vision." More credit should be given to Mao. While his tactic might have been overdrawn, his vision was not. He knew the difficulty of erasing old traditions in China, and he was fully aware of the "capitalist tendencies" that forged an emphasis on consumer production in the Soviet Union. He earlier expressed his concern to visiting American journalist, Edgar Snow, that China's youth might some day lose their revolutionary zeal. Mao was looking beyond Mao and *his* revolution.

In his analysis of the success of China's Communist Party to maintain effective control, despite periodic convulsions that threatened stability, Guillermaz generally presents balanced and well-reasoned views. Despite his recognition of the continuity of tradition in China's Communist state, he sees the necessity of the new institutions created by Mao and the Party's control of the media and the educational system to mold new thoughts and practices among the people. The task, he believes, was not difficult. Facilitating rapid changes in Chinese thinking was the small middle class, the lack of China's experience in political democracy, limited religious sentiment, the subordination of the individual to clan and family requiring only a transfer of loyalty to Party and state, and the search for new values by China's youth. The intensity of the Communists' psychological techniques used to accomplish "ideological remolding" does not figure in Guillermaz's analysis. This is unfortunate, because an account of oppressive tactics and China's legal system that places a defendant at the mercy of the state would render a more accurate view of the human cost of Mao's revolution.

The key to understanding Mao's success in establishing a viable government out of the ashes of chaos lies in the highly centralized administration of the People's Republic. Supported by most writers of the Communist period, Guillermaz believes that China's leadership of dedicated adherents to the Communist creed who could effectively command a loyal and disciplined cadres were most responsible for the new government's success.

China's yearning for a decent livelihood in 1949 commanded the attention of Mao and the Communist Party. While all aspects of economic improvement were sought, the communalization of the Chinese countryside was a prime target for Mao's Communist experiment. Despite Guillermaz's critical view of the Great Leap failure and the chaos it caused, he regards the Communist economic programs, both in food production and industrial development, generally successful. Considering the odds—diverse and difficult topography, uneven distribution of resources, the lack of a modern scientific tradition, and poor transportation—China's achievement has been great. Placing this economic gain in its proper perspective, Guillermaz observes that China has really "not yet emerged from its backward condition." While optimistic about China's future, the author believes that the nation can no longer experiment with risky shortcuts to bring about rapid modernization.

An important observation made by Guillermaz is that when China experienced periods of political stability and economic progress, it appeared strong internally and influential in its foreign affairs. Periods of rapid communization, however, disturbed the equilibrium and led to disaster. Despite the turmoil, the Communist experiment did not collapse. Rather, it hastened the decentralization process which Guillermaz regards as necessary and advantageous.

Ever since its inception, China's Communist government made changes in Chinese society. Western observers have speculated on how much has actually changed. Recognizing the thoroughness of certain institutional changes, Guillermaz sees many remnants of the past and does not feel that the Chinese spirit and lifestyle has been undermined. The Chinese reasoning by means of analogy, the coexistence of opposites, and ways of doing things are familiar. The Chinese remain industrious and frugal. The homes in which they live, the food they eat, the transportation they ride, and the tools with which they farm would easily be recognized by a returning Old China Hand. This is an observation reported by many Americans who have been to China in recent years.

Guillermaz substantiates his positions very well and presents a rational analysis, but a few of his contentions can be questioned. For example, he sees the Korean War in political terms for its value as a "mass campaign" to unite the people more firmly behind the new Communist government in China. He regards the war as an "unfortunate mistake" because it led to the strengthening of Western defenses in the Pacific, delayed China's entrance into the United

Nations, and encouraged China's doctrinal intransigence. While the war may have indeed been a mistake for North Korea and its Soviet backers, the China involvement was essential for its own security. In its consolidation phase, China's Communist government was too preoccupied with internal affairs to prepare schemes of foreign ventures for its propaganda benefits. The security needs of China that require friendly states on its borders have always been a primary concern of that nation's foreign policy.

In his discussion of Soviet relations, Guillermaz explains that China could not accept *détente* as it would seriously weaken her position in the socialist camp and in the world generally. China, he believes, also feared *détente* because it would "lead to a progressive liberalization within the socialist camp as a whole." He points out that China was undergoing "a hard period, a phase of great internal tension" and that a relaxation of its hard line was unacceptable. China's opposition to *détente*, however, is complex, involving historic, ideological, and territorial disagreements. Consequently, the severity of China's disdain for its northern neighbor has been consistent since 1956 regardless of whether its internal policies have been "hard" or "soft."

During the pragmatic years of Liu Shao-ch'i in the early 1960's, Chinese enmity toward the Soviet Union intensified to the point of including racial overtones. The resumption of moderate policies under the leadership of Hua Kuo-feng, Teng Hsiao-p'ing, and Li Hsien-nien (which Guillermaz had not witnessed when he completed his book) brings no change to Chinese fears and suspicions about Soviet intentions. Whether China's leadership is moderate or radical, the depth of the Sino-Soviet schism is likely to prevent *détente* from becoming a viable alternative to public denunciation, armed borders, and military clashes.

Guillermaz pays little attention to cultural developments, especially painting, in China under Communism; and when he does, he discards its value as a serious creative contribution to art. He regards painting as having come to an end with Hsü Pei-hung, who died in 1953. The rest is mediocre, socialist realism portraying base and insignificant subjects. This is too simple an explanation, however, as it overlooks other fine talents. In general, Chinese artists painted in the socialist mold during periods of harsh political policies such as the Great Leap and Cultural Revolution eras; but when moderate leadership relaxed the hard line, they took advantage of the situation and exhibited their creative talents. Sometimes they felt compelled to include a subtle political overtone in their predominantly traditional painting, while on other occasions only the native tradition is evident. Ch'i Pai-shih and Fu Pao-shih receive a mere mention, but they deserve more. They painted in ink (rather than Western oils) and used such traditional themes as Fu's "Poets of the T'ang." In addition, how can we overlook Yu Fei-an ("Pigeons and Plum Blossoms,") and Wu Tso-jen ("Thundering Yaks")? And how can we find anything political in Lin Feng-mien's "Cormorant in Flight"? In addition to painting, porcelain, lacquerware, and embroidery were produced—admittedly, with an eye on the Hong Kong tourist market.

This excellent, detailed account of the history of the Chinese Communist Party in power is a worthy reference for any interested reader. What few flaws the book has are not so serious as to mar its value; they merely provoke new considerations about China's myriad faces. The narration ends just before Mao's death in October, 1976, but the history of Chinese Communism continues to be written.

Leonard H. D. Gordon

Sources for Further Study

America. CXXXVI, June 4, 1977, p. 509.
Booklist. LXXIII, April 15, 1977, p. 1223.
Choice. XIV, July, 1977, p. 732.
Nation. CCXXV, July 2, 1977, p. 21.

CIRCLES
A Washington Story

Author: Abigail McCarthy (1915–   )
Publisher: Doubleday & Company (New York). 251 pp. $7.95
Type of work: Novel
Time: 1976
Locale: Washington, D.C., and campaign sites across America

A novel based on an incident which occurred in the 1972 presidential campaign, which follows the brief but intense presidential aspirations of Senator Sam Nordahl and his supporters

> *Principal characters:*
> SAM NORDAHL, United States Senator
> ALICE ANN NORDAHL, his wife
> JEFF STREATOR, a television documentary producer
> SARAH STREATOR, his wife
> TIANA BRIGGS, a political columnist
> LAURA TALBERT, a widow living in Washington, D.C.

The political novel, a once respected genre produced with sophistication and style by such writers as Bulwer-Lytton and Anthony Trollope, has in recent decades become almost exclusively the province of the hacks, who churn out massive volumes in which potential disasters and personality guessing games take precedence over any feeble attempts to explore the real nature of power or the consequences of power on the human personality. Perhaps because she came to fiction-writing late in life, and perhaps because she is a wise and gifted individual, Abigail McCarthy has written one of the finest political novels to appear in many years. As the wife of a former United States senator and presidential candidate, Mrs. McCarthy had the opportunity to observe the national political scene in a way few authors outside of politics can hope to. (This may also be why so many political novels are written by reporters, rather than by experienced novelists.) But what she made of this material can only be the product of her own special sensibility and talent. In *Circles: A Washington Story,* McCarthy is first a novelist and secondly a social commentator.

Many readers will, no doubt, enjoy *Circles: A Washington Story* because of its insider's point of view and its shrewd observations and comments about the most minute aspects of political and social life in Washington, but the book offers greater rewards than that. Although the author is brilliant when dealing with the desperation inherent in Washington social circles, she is equally sharp when writing of the changes which have taken place in Washington over the years, from decade to decade, administration to administration, election to election, crisis to crisis. The changing styles of social form and political ambition are all clearly delineated with the economy of words of a skilled craftsman. McCarthy's observations—or those of her characters—about the factors which make or break politicians ring true. This is not a book of scandalous revelations, but it is one which only a person who has spent years on the scene could have written. One feels certain that this picture presents Washington as it is.

But, more than merely satisfying the reader's curiosity about the workings of national government and the secrets of power-trading, *Circles* offers an intelligent woman's concern with moral issues that go beyond political games to the profound concerns of all human beings. McCarthy probes old suppositions, stereotyped opinions, and irrational but stubborn myths. In the pages of *Circles,* the values and moral righteousness of Western materialism are confronted by a shrewd mind and unjaded moral sense.

The narrative is refracted through the points of view of several characters. Although the story is of Senator Sam Nordahl's attempt to win the presidential nomination, he actually is not the central character, except in that his personality acts as both a catalyst and a mirror for the other characters who revolve around him. The men and women surrounding Nordahl see what they want to see—what they *must* see—in his handsome, bland features. The press representatives, the other politicians, and his wife, all find themselves confronting new visions of themselves, as well as of their candidate. This gradual stripping of layers is what this fine novel is all about.

The story is framed by the reflections of Laura Talbert, a genteel lady of the old school, a woman who has spent most of her life in Washington, part of the inner circle for decades, but now gradually receding into the background. Rather wistfully, Mrs. Talbert ponders her fate, the fate of many a Washington widow. She is not bitter about the outcome of her life, but she wonders just what it all has meant. There have been undeniable satisfactions, but at times she is inclined to wonder what her destiny might have been if she had chosen a different, more aggressive, pattern for her life, one not so much in the shadow of her husband. For it is a fact that any small influence that she had, any brief power or long-lasting respect that she achieved, was due to her primarily as the wife of a man who possessed power and commanded respect. The situation of Laura Talbert reflects but one aspect of the position of women in Washington circles. Gradually, with infinite subtlety, McCarthy exposes additional layers of the lives of women in Washington, both directly involved in government and on the sidelines. But her interest is chiefly with the wives, with the women who are expected to be always attractive and on duty, to serve and wait until needed to serve again, but who hold no official offices and receive no pay. Laura Talbert represents but one facet of this complicated and fascinating picture.

Laura Talbert's personality is sharply and subtly revealed in the opening chapter as she begins telling her own story. The reader comes to understand gradually what makes this woman as she is, and to pick up bit by bit the various aspects of her life. Her need for discretion is fundamental, yet she has lived a life not without its secrets. She is not ashamed of having had an affair many years before, and she is rather proud of the discreet way in which she carried it off, hurting no one. She is somewhat shocked when she looks around her at the world of the 1970's, when people are more blatant about their lifestyles. She sympathizes with the needs of younger women to express their own personalities, but only up to a certain point.

Alice Ann Nordahl is the perfect candidate's wife, attractive, intelligent, charming, and poised, yet she too is not immune to the new trends and alterations in the roles of men and women. Why can't a woman be affirmative in her choice of marriage and homemaking as a way of life, she asks? Yes, she admits that there are injustices, that women should receive equal pay for equal work and should have economic equality on all levels, as well as opportunity when they desire it. But what will all of these changes bring, she asks? The fact is that life is a matter of choices and chance, and there is no point in making choices on the basis of what ought to be, rather than what is. Here, we come close to the heart of the novel, for the narrative, with its many threads, is really about choices, and about the incidents which compel those choices, right or wrong, to be made.

But perhaps the novel is most biting and poignant when dealing with the character of Tiana Briggs, a political columnist whose struggle for professional success has led her to the inner circle, but at a cost that only she knows. A vividly conceived, brilliantly drawn character, Tiana represents the career woman of the past thirty years who was forced to make sacrifices if she chose to compete in a "man's world." The women who have come after her and built on her success cannot imagine the difficulties and pains that she has had to overcome to reach her level of power and respect. The contrast between her life and that of young Sarah Streator and the other women belonging to later generations is startling.

However, McCarthy may hit closest to home when dealing with the political wives and the condescension with which they are viewed by both the press and male Washington. There can be a very positive role for a political wife to play, as Alice Ann Nordahl explains, if she enjoys a variety of people and is good at campaigning, but that only works if the husband can accept her help and her sharing; some men cannot. Some women feel exploited when forced into that role, others relish it. The family is supposed to be the center of life in America, and the political wife is supposed to represent the best features of this vision; it is an unfair position for anybody to be placed in, and one almost impossible to live up to.

As Sarah Streator reflects when she has tried to rebuild her own career, after giving it up for marriage and family, one must have one's own identity. One is what one does. She sees, among the faces at the farewell luncheon for Laura Talbert, the faces of women who never woke up to their full potential, the faces of women whose lives ended before they really had begun. The thought is intolerable to her, yet many of those women do not even realize what they have missed. They never learned to recognize themselves as separate, responsible individuals; they always were the lesser part of a team. The subtle variations between the conditions of these different women are skillfully pinpointed and analyzed by McCarthy; it is here that her artistry reaches its peak.

Older women are seldom seen sympathetically in fiction and are not supposed to be noticed in an America which worships youth. Yet the older women portrayed in this novel are rich and rewarding characters, among the best in the book. They are drawn with affection and understanding and more than a little compassion, in all of their complexity and diversity. They make clear the great loss that we all suffer by the current preoccupation in our society and literature with the concerns of youth.

With this book, McCarthy has confirmed her position as a writer of skill and distinction. First in her well-crafted autobiography, *Private Faces/Public Places,* and now in *Circles,* she shows both insight and precision in detailing the insecurities and ambiguities that gnaw at the women whose lives are sacrificed to the pursuit of power—usually a power which they can only share in the most minute way. She has shown in both books the subtle techniques of these women who alternately follow behind and deftly lead their political husbands. *Circles* portrays more accurately than any male-authored Washington novel the social life by which the politicians, journalists, lobbyists, and bureaucrats seek to manipulate one another and the fate of the country. For it is a fact that the cocktail and dinner parties, the luncheons and teas, the carefully prepared social functions and apparently accidental encounters all affect the country's political course.

Circles is quiet in tone, but it is all the more effective for that. Abigail McCarthy may lack a flair for the emotional, but her clear, lucid style and sharp intellect make vivid the dilemma of the contemporary political woman. Everyone, even the political male, who reads this novel should understand the conflicts and recognize the frequently devastating results of these conflicts on human lives. For all of its quiet tone, this is, at last, a deeply moving novel.

Bruce D. Reeves

Sources for Further Study

America. CXXXVII, September 10, 1977, p. 132.
Best Sellers. XXXVII, September, 1977, p. 168.
Booklist. LXXIII, July 1, 1977, p. 1634.
Commonweal. CIV, November 25, 1977, p. 759.
Time. CX, July 11, 1977, p. 78.

THE CLOUD OF DANGER
Current Realities of American Foreign Policy

Author: George F. Kennan (1904–   )
Publisher: Little, Brown and Company (Boston). 234 pp. $8.95
Type of work: Current affairs

An analysis of current American foreign policy and suggested necessary changes

George F. Kennan has had a distinguished career as an American diplomat, serving as Ambassador to the Soviet Union and to Yugoslavia. After retiring from the Foreign Service in 1953, he became a member of the Institute for Advanced Studies in Princeton, New Jersey. He taught at Princeton University and the University of Chicago and was visiting professor at Oxford University. His books about foreign policy and international relations include *American Diplomacy, 1900–1950; Soviet-American Relations, 1917–1920; Russia and the West Under Lenin and Stalin; Soviet Foreign Policy, 1917–1941; Memoirs, 1925–1950;* and *Memoirs, 1950–1963.*

In his latest book, *The Cloud of Danger,* Kennan reviews United States foreign policy and suggests changes that need to be made. Basically, he urges that we restrict our involvement to those areas that are important to our national interest and turn our attention to our great domestic needs. He is unusually sensitive to our domestic problems such as the decline of urban areas, high unemployment, inflation, and energy. He is correct in calling our attention to the fact that we do not have unlimited resources and cannot do everything. Furthermore, we cannot remake the world in our own image because of the concept of the sovereignty of nations. Although we claim we are not the "policeman of the world," we often act as if we were. We have not restricted our involvement to those areas that by Kennan's definition are within our national interest.

However, we face a more fundamental dilemma than Kennan acknowledges. On the one hand, our commitment to freedom and individual rights makes it difficult for us to avoid involvement wherever these principles are being violated. Yet the concept of national sovereignty prevents our intervening in the affairs of other nations even if we are motivated by our concern for freedom and human rights. Kennan does not address this ethical dilemma, but restricts himself instead to a pragmatic assessment of our national interest.

Discussing at length the effect of our system of government on foreign policy, the author stresses the loss of flexibility that may result from the extensive involvement of the Congress and the consequent involvement of domestic interest groups. He regrets that more discretion is not left to the "highly competent persons" in the executive branch who are not distracted by interest groups but have only the national interest in mind as they make decisions. His willingness to rely on experts leads him to make a special plea for more professionals in the American embassy in Moscow and for greater reliance upon the embassy as a source of information and day-to-day advice for high-level policymaking. This thinking is consistent with the author's aversion to summitry. Yet he does not seriously consider the technological advances in travel and communications that have changed the ways nations communicate with one another. Instead of looking backward with the hope that the traditional ways will return, what is called for are bold new ideas in exploiting technology to enhance communications.

Yet the widespread feeling that too much "secrecy" and not enough involvement by the Congress and the public in foreign policy matters have contributed to serious errors in our foreign policy will not allow us to be satisfied with his easy solution. We must strike a balance; ultimately, the President is responsible for the direction and consequences of our foreign policy, but there must be more extensive involvement in the policymaking process. It cannot be left to the experts.

Since this demand for greater involvement in the policymaking process cannot be denied, the public must become more sophisticated regarding foreign policy. This requires greatly improved reporting and more thorough education of the public by the elected representatives. Kennan correctly says the press tends to stress the sensational and the trivial and often dramatizes events or people, leading to a misunderstanding of the real situation. Perhaps the best example of this was the handling of the agreements and events which came to be labeled *détente* by the press and led to unrealistic expectations by the American public. Thus, fundamental changes are needed in the sense of responsibility of the press, in access to information by the press, and in explanations to the people by elected officials.

Despite the insight Kennan shows in the interlacing of domestic and foreign affairs, his lack of emphasis on economic and financial affairs is striking and can perhaps be explained by the era in which he received his training and completed his foreign service career. While acknowledging the economic interdependence of countries today, he rather wishfully deplores it. He states that most of the exchanges between the United States and Western Europe relate to economic and financial matters, then dismisses the entire subject in an almost cavalier manner. He suggests that the important decisions become neglected because they are specialized matters that need to be handled by specialists. His failure to understand the economic problems of the world today and his dismissal of the matter are the greatest shortcomings of the book.

Kennan does, however, have a clear vision of some of the complications which result from the new economic interdependence and some of the subtle yet fundamental differences it will make in foreign policy decisions. He recognizes that domestic interest groups will be much more intimately involved with foreign affairs and that their involvement will limit the options of the decision-makers. He calls upon the President of the United States to assume a greater role in educating the public by warning against the dangers of a policy that is excessively protectionist.

But there are other parts of the book which show an insensitivity to the economic interdependence of the nations of the world and the effect of actions by the large developed nations on the developing nations. In pursuing his valid position that we should not and cannot presume to solve the problems of the developing nations, Kennan draws a comparison with the experience of his ancestors who arrived in Wisconsin and through diligence overcame the hardships and created a good life for themselves. The differences between the situation of the people in the developing countries in a world containing huge industrial nations involved in world trade and the settlers in Wisconsin are too numerous to mention; in fact, they are so numerous that the analogy does not hold.

However valid Kennan's arguments may be for reducing our involvement in the developing nations, they are central to his basic idea that we should limit our world commitments and concentrate our resources in those areas that are vital to our national interest. In Kennan's judgment our national interests are in our relations to the Soviet Union, Western Europe, China, Japan, and the Near East (his term).

The greatest danger is in our relations with the Soviet Union, but it is not from a military attack by the Soviets. The danger is that the weapons race will get out of hand and will, through proliferation or by accident, carry us all to destruction. This is the "cloud of danger" of the title. The author sees no hope for substantial progress in the reduction of armaments until each side is willing to give up the idea that it will win when it has forced the other side to give up a bit more than it has. Kennan thinks there must be some measure of unilateral restraint in weapons development on the part of each side. At the very least, this would require some change in our attitude toward the Soviets and our relationship with them.

Therefore, Kennan tries to lead us to a more accurate assessment of the Soviet Union. He lists some of the major influences on their foreign policy and then coaxes us to see ourselves through their eyes. As he describes the deployment of our bases and the huge arms sales we make to Iran, for example, it does become clear that we are asking a great deal of the Soviet leaders to accept our repeated avowal that we have no aggressive intent. We become greatly alarmed when the Soviets assist factions in various parts of the world, but see nothing amiss when we do it ourselves.

An additional barrier to our objective evaluation of the Soviet Union is the rhetoric of world revolution and domination. But as Kennan explains, the Soviets themselves are bound up by this rhetoric since it requires them to take actions which can legitimatize their claim to leadership in the Communist world. This may lead the Soviet Union to intervene in the internal affairs of other nations by supplying arms or other support to one or another faction.

Thus, Kennan views reducing the military rivalry between the United States and the Soviet Union as the most important item on our international agenda, but other than encouraging us to look at the relationship of our two countries from their point of view, he does not have many suggestions on how to improve relations. He does suggest that we divest ourselves of the idea that military strength must be the final arbitrator of our relationship. This obviously would require a fundamental change of attitude in the United States, and many of the perspectives in this book would lead us in that direction. For this reason, *The Cloud of Danger* is valuable and should be read; nevertheless, more thought about ways to reduce the mutual distrust and to dispel suspicion is needed.

Reduction of our arms sales would help to lessen mutual distrust, but there are many obstacles to be overcome. In discussing our great role in arming the world, Kennan sees domestic interest groups and inflation as among the factors which make it so difficult to modify our practice, but he gives little attention to one factor which is now so important in the Near East. As we enter an area and sell arms to one nation, we upset the military balance. Surrounding nations demand arms so they will not feel threatened. Currently, the various Arab countries request arms to counterbalance the sales to Israel. We are whiplashed between the two sides.

In keeping with his general proposal to reduce our military rivalry and involvement, Kennan would support the gradual removal of our military forces from Korea. The withdrawal would need to be done carefully and in consultation with Japan.

In the case of Africa, the author follows the same principle in urging that we scale down our involvement. He has several reasons for this. He questions whether there is any real feeling in Angola for the Soviet Union in spite of the fact that the faction the Soviets supported is now in control. Thus, even though the faction that won in Angola received aid from the Soviet Union and Cuba, there is no indication that the relationship created means that Angola would support the Soviet Union in other intervention or involvement in Africa. He urges a position of neutrality for Rhodesia for two major reasons besides his determination that it is not in our national interest. First, it is questionable whether the guerrillas fighting from outside the country do represent the blacks within the country. In the second place it is questionable whether the blacks in Rhodesia would in the long run be any better off under majority rule than they are now. The obvious weakness of the latter position is that it is restricted to a consideration of material wealth without due attention to the significance of the freedom and dignity of the individual in which we profess to believe.

It is good to have this long perspective of American policy, but there is a lingering feeling that we are hearing a voice from another age when there were fewer nations, less economic interdependence, and less complexity in the world. Nevertheless, George Kennan is accurate in focusing on the nuclear arms race as the "cloud of danger."

Doris F. Pierce

Sources for Further Study

Choice. XIV, November, 1977, p. 1279.
Commentary. LXIV, November, 1977, p. 30.
Economist. CCLXIV, September 24, 1977, p. 135.
New York Review of Books. XXIV, July 14, 1977, p. 19.
New York Times Book Review. July 17, 1977, p. 11.
New Yorker. LIII, August 8, 1977, p. 70.

COLLECTED POEMS: 1919-1976

Author: Allen Tate (1899–   )
Publisher: Farrar, Straus and Giroux (New York). 218 pp. $12.50
Type of work: Poetry

The volume which sums up the life's work of one of America's foremost poets and men of letters

Allen Tate, American man of letters, critic, commentator on the literary and social scene, is first and foremost a poet. Associated from the beginning of his career with the movement that created a truly modern American literature, he is one of the few still with us from that exciting time in the 1920's and 1930's when Hemingway and Faulkner in prose and Eliot, Ransom, Tate, and Warren in poetry broke new ground in the handling of language in imaginative literature. He has also been connected with two other movements which have, in greater or lesser ways, shaped our sense of ourselves and our society. The first was the New Criticism, which taught us to read our literature with great care and precision, and which taught us to discover in that literature the great riches of the English language. The second was the Southern Agrarian movement, which called to our attention the cost in social and personal terms of the technological revolution. Now, at the end of a long and distinguished career, during which he has received most of the honors which America can bestow on its men of literature, he has been given the opportunity to sum things up, to bring together his past achievements and indicate those things which he wishes to be remembered for. The most notable of these summary volumes is his recent *Essays of Four Decades* (1968), a compilation of those essays in literary criticism which he feels are worthy of preservation. His *Memoirs and Opinions* (1975) is a more relaxed volume, a collection of informal essays and memoirs, which gives us more of the reflective Tate, the great writer who is also a gentleman.

The present volume, however, is the central one, the one which informs the others, which makes clear the source and power of Tate's reputation, his place in twentieth century American literature. For it is his poetry, after all, that has built Tate's reputation, that has given his opinions on other matters their value and authenticity. And it is a tribute to Tate's faith in the quality of his work, and in the perceptiveness of generations of readers to come, that for *this* volume, uniquely among his summary volumes, he has chosen to avoid the route of selectivity. Instead, he has taken the risk of giving us everything, a collected poems rather than a selected poems. All the familiar great works are here—"Ode to the Confederate Dead," "Cold Pastoral," "The Swimmers," "Seasons of the Soul"— but there are all the minor poems and very early poems as well. In fact, the poems in this volume range in date from 1919 to 1976; to read them in order of their composition, which one can easily do since each poem is carefully dated, is to trace the development of one major poet in his sureness and confidence in handling his language, forms, and themes. Tate's corpus is not large—in all about one hundred and twenty poems—but what strikes the reader is the high quality of so much of this work, a richness and a complexity of language and vision which we can ill afford to be without in our day.

If there is a central quality to all Tate's work, it is what we might expect from a close student of T. S. Eliot and an associate of the New Critics Cleanth Brooks and Robert Penn Warren—a pervasive sense of irony. The New Critics taught us that irony is at the heart of poetic language, an irony which derives initially from a sense of the distance between the ideal and the real, and which usually expresses itself in Tate's poetry in a juxtaposition of unlikely elements. In his "Mr. Pope," the central figure strikes fear because his "tight back was rather a goat's than man's." On broader, and more thematic level, Tate's poems generate an irony of perspective by juxtaposing again and again the present with the past. In his most famous poem, "Ode to the Confederate Dead," the sacrifices of the past, and the agonies of defeat, are presented to challenge us to see ourselves in their light. In other poems, the past to be juxtaposed with the present is specifically the classical past, as Aeneas is conjured up to pay a visit to Washington and New York. In other poems, the classical appears only as an allusion, a brief of passing reference, but still generates a perspective from which to see, and judge, our present situation.

What the poet gives us is precisely, therefore, a way of looking at ourselves and our present, a perspective which calls us to depths of seeing, to a range of vision, which is often rare in our age. When Tate first joined with the other agrarians in questioning a naïve faith in progress and in future hope, his voice seemed bitter, acerbic, cynical. In the face of what we now know about the costs of "progress," we may hear him again as a more familiar voice, one which sees the hollowness at the center of so much that we may hold dear, and yet does not despair. What may seem obscure in Tate, his range of learning and his depth of classical allusion, can now seem a reminder of the riches we still have access to. His sense of the value of community and tradition may call us to rediscover them for ourselves. His confidence in the value of poetic language may be seen as an act of faith in man the poetic maker, who may use his skills both to show us painful realities and to cure us of holding on to false hopes.

There is development in Tate's poems, a movement which this volume makes accessible. The early "Elegy" conjures up dark images of the "dry hollows of the mind," an image close to Eliot's "Hollow Men," which will recur in more subtle form in Tate's later poetry. In the imagery, more generally considered, there is also movement, from what is little more than ordered prose to a richness of expression that often seems remote and obscure, but turns into powerfully moving and evocative language on closer examination. Tate's early work shows a tendency to create a poetic world remote from the realities of his existence; locales of Greece and the Orient seem far from Nashville, Tennessee. The later poems, however, and his best, fuse poetic vision with a deep sense of place, of real places—the Confederate graveyard, the subway, Christmas Day—to create a moving and profound sense of the heights and depths of reality.

But there is wit here, too, wit and an ability to laugh at human pretension, as in his "Two Conceits," which builds on the nursery rhyme "Sing a Song of Sixpence": "Sing a song of London/Paris and Berlin/Washington and Moscow/ Where the Ids are in/When the I's were opened/They saw ne'er a thing/But Phoenix in the Turtle/The Turtle on the Wing." Such moments give Tate's work a delightful variety to complement its overall richness.

That Tate's poetry has been so much in the mainstream of modern literature in America, and his politics and social views so much of the minority, suggests something telling about the role of art in our culture. So much of our attitude toward the present and the future is bound up in a naïve optimism about the value of progress, an approach to life that crumbles quickly before any sensitive man's reflection. As a result, much of our art has been an act of dissent, whether a naturalistic call to see life as it is really lived, a revolutionary plea for rapid social change, or an impassioned cry for what is being lost. Whether the criticism is launched from the left of the political spectrum or from the right, it has the quality of dissent in common with other acts of artistic expression. The response of Tate and many of his fellow Southerners to the coming of industrialization in the South was the creation of a world of value in art, especially in poetry. In this way, if not politically, Tate and the other agrarians, such as John Crowe Ransom and Robert Penn Warren, have reshaped American thought in significant ways. In so doing, they are linked with that other American so ill at ease in our technological society, T. S. Eliot. Tate the Southerner and Eliot the expatriot Midwesterner shared their sense of dissent from the mainstream of twentieth century American life; both men sought in tradition and in hierarchically organized society a sense of order and stability, a richer sense of humanity, to serve as an antidote for the rootlessness and restlessness of much of American society. It is Eliot's shadow that stands just behind so much of Tate's poetry, but to say that is to take nothing from the younger man, just to locate him in a realm of common voices. Tate's sense of history, his sense of time, of the realities of human life, of loss, of tragedy, of the value of community and tradition—these are the distinctive marks of his poetic vision. It is a vision for which we must be deeply grateful. In the midst of our own second thoughts about the nature of progress, the cost in personal and global terms of our technological society, Tate's poetic voice seems no longer reactionary, if it ever did, but prophetic. In an uncertain future, we will be grateful to him for it.

John N. Wall, Jr.

Sources for Further Study

Kirkus Reviews. XLV, October 1, 1977, p. 1088.

Library Journal. CII, December 1, 1977, p. 2436.

New Leader. LX, December 5, 1977, p. 15.

New York Times Book Review. December 11, 1977, p. 13, and January 8, 1978, p. 3.

COLLECTED POEMS: 1948-1976

Author: Dannie Abse (1923–   )
Publisher: University of Pittsburgh Press (Pittsburgh, Pennsylvania). 204 pp. $9.95
Type of work: Poetry

Primarily lyrical, these poems celebrate the human imagination, affirm human possibility, explore the dangers of the analytical mind, and insist on individual autonomy

In a brief introductory note to this volume, Dannie Abse writes that his wish for some time has been "to look upon the world with the eyes of a perpetual convalescent." The observation is apt, not only because Abse is a poet who happens to be a medical doctor—he has himself suggested the order of his professions—but because it suggests his capacity to confront the abyss yet refuse its call to inertia and resignation. If Abse's despair is real, occasioned as much by self-doubt as by the obscenities of the Holocaust and Vietnam, it is never mortal. The will is to recovery, never achieved, always precarious, yet never abandoned. "Any man may gather images of despair," he writes in the aptly titled "Poem of celebration," but Abse refuses such fashionable cynicism, affirming instead the power of the imagination: "I'll say 'I will' and 'I can'/and like an accident breathe in space and air."

Solace is fleeting yet abiding in a poetic career that spans some thirty years and six volumes of poetry. If, as a post-romantic, Abse lacks the certainty of a transcendental order, he nevertheless retains the spirit of natural piety, his will to believe balanced precariously against a skepticism that can "by doubting first,/ believe; believing, doubt" ("The water diviner"). At times piety resides in the wide-awake senses, in the innocent eye that can perceive the quotidian with unabashed wonder. Like William Carlos Williams, Abse finds the miraculous in the common. "Surprise! Surprise!" counsels pristine vision, the capacity to peer at the world with "greenhorn observation," to discover in a toenail, a tree, a foot, the mystery in the seemingly charted, the strange in the familiar. In the late poem "Mysteries," acknowledging the impossibility of certainty, either of self or of the divine, he can nevertheless affirm that "I start with the visible/and am startled by the visible."

Reciprocity between self and world does not, however, always suffice. Several poems from *Poems, Golders Green* more insistently hunger for spiritual transport, but always with a wry self-deprecation, more puzzled than certain. If, as in "The grand view," the poet would "flow/into One invisible and still," it is with the acknowledgment that his spiritual yearning lacks both dogma and icon. "I do not know who/it is that I love," he concedes, yet withal he will hearken to psychic promptings whispering "visions, visions." "Watching a cloud" similarly considers the numinous character of life, questioning whether revelations of the divine reside in the poet's tropes. Answers prove elusive, yet the will to believe persists, as Abse yearns "to be theological, stare through/raw white angel-fabric at holy bits of blue."

The note of nostalgia that persists in Abse's work appears to be linked to this need for some intimation of the divine. Like Wallace Stevens, whom he so often resembles in theme, if not always in idiom, Abse seems haunted by a sense of loss and exile, as if in some unspecified past he had possessed a wholeness, now absent, which he yearns to recover. Only the vestigial memory of this wholeness remains, but it is enough to occasion the hope of retrieval. Thus, the odor of the poet's hand in "Olfactory pursuits," a poem reminiscent of Stevens' "The Weeping Burgher," inspires the search for "old foundations,/buried mosaics, tomb tablets crumbled." Similarly, the elegiac tone of "Forgotten" suggests a sense of estrangement, as the poet yearns to revisit the "old country" whose name he seems to have forgotten.

Despite his hunger for spiritual transcendence, Abse remains firmly attached to things of this world, especially to the miracle of life, which he continues to celebrate despite his unflinching appraisal of the demonic and the irrational in human life. Occasionally, candor compels a Hobbesian view: the mordant political parable "Emperors of the island" counterpoints the stylistic innocence of its nursery jingles against its theme of human savagery, chronicling how the will to power of five souls marooned on a deserted island results in systematic annihilation, until only five ghosts remain. Or Abse can, in a poem like "No more Mozart," confront the horror of the Holocaust from the perspective of its six million victims, their vacant eyes fixed on a German landscape "soaped in moonlight," its streets "clean/like the hands of Lady Macbeth."

To acknowledge the dark night of the soul is not, however, to deny human possibility. Daringly, Abse can title a poem "The second coming," but in place of a Yeatsian great beast that "slouches towards Bethlehem to be born," Abse proposes the birth of a chthonic god-man, his "noble head" and "ivory forehead" straining to emerge from the darkness, "lightward pushing." Birth remains incomplete, for human assistance is required, but clearly man can choose. The will to confront and to master human imperfection remains a possibility, as the poet instructs us to "Dig, I say dig, you'll find arms, loins, white legs, to prove my story-/and one red poppy in the corn."

Nowhere is the theme of moral strenuousness linked to a faith in the sanctity of life more clearly defined than in the moving lyric "The smile was." Set in a delivery room, the poem records the push and strain of birth, juxtaposing the certainty of pain and death that attends all life to the radiance of fecundity. Creation is both mystery and miracle: the smile of the mother who "hears the child crying the world/ for the first time" is ineffable, unique, resistant both to man and to art. Human history may be soiled, the poet muses, but the moment of birth remains untainted, alive with promise, with the possibility of "an uncaging/a freedom."

Allegiance to the protean self is the bedrock of Abse's affirmation of human possibility. Beneath the hardwon faith lies a deep distrust of systems and conventions that would eliminate human vagaries and subordinate every individual impulse to preconceived pattern and mechanical orthodoxy. The positivist mind, the formulaic, unreflective faith, the institutional force that demands obedience at the cost of personal identity, self-forged and self-directed—all are scrutinized and resisted; "curse those clever scientists/who dissect away the wings and haggard heart from the dove," Abse adjures in the much-anthologized "Letter to Alex Comfort," but the condemnation is not wholesale. To the methodical and plodding "German thoroughness" of a Koch and an Ehrlich, Abse contrasts the fortuitous insights of Newton and Archimedes, also men of science, but men whose creative act parallels the intuitive vision of the poet or any man of imagination. Similarly, in "Moon object" Abse counsels the "blue-eyed scientist" seeking to understand the origin of life in the samples of dust and rock brought back from the moon to exchange his "white coat" for a "purple cloak"—the dress of the imagination—for it is only so garbed that he can discover life's meaning, a nobler goal than mere sterile description.

The political mind bent on power and self-aggrandizement also threatens the inviolable self. In "New Babylons" Abse adroitly draws on biblical lore to suggest that the clash between self and authority is venerable, as is the refusal to capitulate. The tale of Shadrach, Meshach, and Abed-nego, three martyrs cast into the fire because they refused to adore the golden image of Nebuchadnezzar, can still nourish the defiance of the modern Daniel, a "maverick such as I" who would "oppose, oppose orthodoxies." But, the poem darkly concludes, it may be that all mankind participates in the tyrant's crime. If in contemporary life "police bring truncheons down" to compel obedience, it may be that the ordinary citizen tacitly endorses such coercion, not from fear but from xenophobic passions intolerant of the aberrant: "When Nebuchadnezzars rage/ no maverick is immune/for it's we, ourselves, who cry:/ 'Conform, conform and die.' "

Abse's experience as a Jew born and raised in Cardiff, Wales, and now living in London, accounts in part for his sensitivity to the marginal and aberrant in human life. Occasionally, Jewish themes appear explicitly, as in the eloquent "After the release of Ezra Pound," where Abse refuses to excuse Pound's apostasy, or in "Tales of Shatz," which explores the question of Jewish assimilation. More often, however, Jewish notes enter obliquely, more as a mode of perception, feeling, and attitude suggesting alienation or oddity than as direct statement. A poem like "Tree," for example, has as its ostensible poetic subject a maimed tree deformed by lightning, a "buffoon" among stately oaks. Such a grotesquerie excites derision and contempt, its oddity a persistent invitation to insult. Yet, withal, "this caliban tree" that refuses to conform and is not "properly dressed" survives to "soar/ unanchored, free, in prosperous moonlight and amaze." Clearly, the outsider suffers, but that very suffering, Abse suggests, can become a source of strength.

The theme of the two selves, especially prominent in *Tenants of the House,* is another variation of Abse's allegiance to the idiosyncratic and unmediated in human life, but here the conflict centers on psychic division, often with strong Freudian overtones. The poem "Duality," as its title suggests, proposes the double nature of man embodied in two faces worn beneath a single profile. The one—protean, black, and nourished by wine—responds to the promptings of the id; the other—rigid, white, and nourished by bread—hearkens to the demands of culture. Though "each would go their separate ways," they are, the poem concludes, destined for perpetual internecine conflict until "they die on his doublecrossed head."

If "Duality" strikes an uneasy balance between accommodation and dissent, "The trial," a powerful narrative poem written in strongly accented couplets, proposes defiance, even in the face of certain retribution. Again, Abse uses the motif of the mask, but here the narrator, on trial for discarding his conferred identity imposed by fiat, is determined to "seek [his] own face, find [his] own grave." The quest takes him underground, where, upon discovering the "invisible wealth" of his unique soul, he unscrews his acquired face. Culture, however, does not lightly abide such independence: swiftly, the Judge advises the jury that "the man who can choose is dangerous," to be hanged on the gallows tree as an example to those who would challenge the fixed arrangements of institutional life.

Abse appropriately concludes his work with the fine lyric "The stethoscope." Written in the easy colloquial rhythms characteristic of his finest work, the poem brilliantly captures Abse's abiding themes: his fierce attachment to the mundane; his profound commitment to human possibility; his disdain for ritualized response; his celebration of the human imagination; and his will to believe. Characteristically, the poem proceeds through self-questioning, as the poet inquires whether the medical instrument that can record the throb and rhythm of new life, as well as the silence of death—two mysteries traditionally associated with the religious quest—deserves to be apotheosized and codified with Church, prayer, and priest. Refusal is predictable: the instrument is merely a tool, useless and meaningless until manipulated by its human maker and auditor. Thus, the poet concludes that he will "celebrate [his] own ears"; only the self, as it thinks, loves, creates, feels tenderness, compassion and joy, is the proper object of spiritual wonder. No more stirring hosanna to the humane in man exists.

Leonora Woodman

Sources for Further Study

Books and Bookmen. XXII, July, 1977, p. 35.

Contemporary Review. CCXXXI, July, 1977, p. 54.

Encounter. XLIX, August, 1977, p. 53.

Listener. XCVIII, August 11, 1977, p. 189.

Observer. August 21, 1977, p. 29.

COLLECTED POEMS 1956-1976

Author: David Wagoner (1926–   )
Publisher: Indiana University Press (Bloomington, Indiana). 301 pp. $12.50
Type of work: Poetry

A collection in which Wagoner extends nature poems to the mythic, narrative to dramatic, and lyric to formal song

David Wagoner's collection is an update of selected poems of a decade ago, a kind of progress report. It does not contain poems from his first volume, published—as are most of his poems—by Indiana University Press; but it does have forty-two new poems. After a twenty-five-year academic career as Professor of English as the University of Washington and at DePauw and Penn State, and after a tour of duty in the Navy, David Wagoner brings a varied experience into this compendium of a life lived. His novels are adventure stories, folksy, and in his poetry he has as he says, "an affinity for the dramatic lyric, in tones ranging from the loud and satiric through the quiet and conversational."

Wagoner is essentially a poet, although he has written eight novels. He no longer writes in the vein of his mentor and colleague, Theodore Roethke, perhaps having exorcised this spirit through an excellent editing of the notebooks. Nor does he emulate the *Poetry Northwest* writers, being farther above prose. He has established an idiom, a clear line of development that is varied in theme, eclectic in method. The idiom derives from a vision of man at ease in nature, at home, among friends.

A thread of continuity is provided by epigraphs—news items, notes, quotations, recollections, even directions. These furnish themes ranging from frivolous to profound. Wagoner's metaphors are always original and exact; verses are based on a calculus problem, a profile form, a social note, and such quotations as "nobody can enlarge upon an odor," or "Everyman, stand still." Often the titles evoke the theme, as in a series of etiological myths retold as "How" poems or the "Song" sequences, which, if not the most successful pieces in the collection, are bold and experimental. Another series of poems extends the dedication to Patt; these are oblique love poems to a marriage that lasts, of an anniversary, a picnic, a gift wrapping, a gesture, or a series of observations of the beloved at ease with, say, a jealous parrot who quotes Yeats, or a refractory burro ("one arm around his neck, she whispers/ Into his unpromising, uncompromising ear . . ."). The *persona* of the poet, here and in all the character sketches, is the wondering, if often inept, observer.

An open, varied form combined with carefully cadenced lines best suits the poet's strengths. The few poems with exactness of rhyme and meter, such as "The Boy of the House," seem forced, copied, while those with accidental, internal, or repeated rhymes and varied stanzas best fit Wagoner's themes. Wagoner is at his best in Dungeness Bay, in the rain forests, among the things he catalogues in nature, though often he neglects the image for the simple delight in a name: tern, whelk, coot, moon snail, limpet, maidenhair, coltsfoot. Some critics see these evocations as timeless and extended, the presentation of a macrocosm; yet such cataloging techniques are not as effective as the close and local scrutiny for which Wagoner is known, in which he pinpoints the patch of blue, the grain of sand, "eternity in an hour"—the presentation of a microcosm. An early poem which balances these two approaches is "The Death and Resurrection of the Birds":

> Falling asleep, the birds are falling
> Down through the last light's thatchwork farther than rain,
> Their grace notes dwindling
> Into the downy pit where the first bird
> Waits to become them in the nest of the night.
>
> Silent and featherless,
> Now they are one dark bird in darkness.
>
> Beginning again, the birds are breaking
> Upward, new-fledged at daybreak, their clapping wingbeats
> Striking the sides of the sun, the singing brilliant
> Dust spun loose on the wind from the end to the beginning.

Wagoner's occasional verse—to friend, teacher, Hemingway, a special day, "Note to a Literary Club"—is sometimes pedestrian, and often too limited or obligatory for his free-ranging spirit. But there is mischief in his rhapsodies, and he harangues often against established values and practices, even against his geometric concretionist friends who build double acrostics and jigsaw patterns. "Song to Accompany the Bearer of Bad News" is a three-way sketch that tears such a poem to tatters. Both indoor and outdoor fooling are apparent in "Plainsong for Everyone Who Was Killed Yesterday," which comforts since nothing much happens, nothing is missed, everything goes on, the news, the weather, the lamentations, and "next week or next year/ Is soon enough to consider/ Those brief occasions you might rather/ Not have lost. . . ." Here is no existential anguish, though there is often regret for the diminutions of faith, of values; here no crabby confessional, though there is a self revealed within a larger context of joy.

One poem in particular reveals the poet's method of offering the challenge to the reader to complete his meaning. It begins, "This is a Wonderful Poem," and warns in the second line, "Come at it carefully, don't trust it. . . ." After a series of tests it asks, "Now, what do you want to do about it?" Wagoner cares about readership, wants response, it seems, beyond the academic or the slick. He escapes the schools, remains independent, responds individually. Poets of surer status could go to school here among these dithyrambs, elegies, odes, ballads, and songs, among these owls, fields, and dreams.

William Tillson

Sources for Further Study

Carleton Miscellany. XVI, Summer, 1976–1977, p. 184.

Poetry. CXXX, June, 1977, p. 162.

THE COLLECTED POEMS OF HOWARD NEMEROV

Author: Howard Nemerov (1920–   )
Publisher: The University of Chicago Press (Chicago). 510 pp. $20.00
Type of work: Poetry

The Collected Poems, *winner of the 1978 National Book Award for Poetry, testifies to Nemerov's depth of insight and breadth of experience, as well as to his ability to write both rarefied poetry and a more accessible variety*

Howard Nemerov's poetic achievements, it is quite safe to say, are fully insured against a future loss of immediacy and damage done by hostile critics. Though very much the poet of twentieth century America, he addresses age-old problems and concerns with rigor and notable insight. His subjects and themes are drawn from the many ages of man, his audience is universal, his imagery, Daedalian, and his capacity for satirical comment, memorable—at times, Swiftian. This volume of verse, his *Collected Poems,* is a compilation of distinguished Nemerov collections beginning with *The Image and the Law* (1947), proceeding through *Guide to the Ruins* (1950), *The Salt Garden* (1955), *Mirrors & Windows* (1958), *New and Selected Poems* (1960), *The Next Room of the Dream* (1962), *The Blue Swallows* (1967), *Gnomes & Occasions* (1973), and ending with his latest volume, *The Western Approaches: Poems 1973–75* (1975).

To examine critically Nemerov's success as a poet, it is instructive to look toward the major themes, then toward Nemerov the intellectual poet and satirist.

Three themes recur in *The Collected Poems:* time's mysterious passing, war, and the natural world. Returning to childhood for clues to his meaning and for emotional sustenance, the poet faces the harsh truth expounded in "An Old Photograph" that "No one escapes the perjury of time." After all, it is time itself (rather than any mere reexperiencing of childhood moments) that the poet is after. It is time, variously described and decried as a thief and liar, that tricks all of us and steals from us our most valuable, painfully earned lessons—even our fondest memories. Time conquers. As the poet, surveying the New Jersey boardwalk in "Elegy of Last Resort" finds, "We enter again November, and the last/ Steep fall of time into the deep of time,/ Atlantic and defeated. . . ." Together with time, we experience the descent into the void from which there is no escape and no awakening.

Many Nemerov poems have to do with the mystery involved in time's passing. As an American living in the Northeastern states, this poet knows well his seasons; yet the one season he writes about more than others is that quiet, ominous period between fall and winter when the bite of time is felt most acutely by the perceptive observer. Like the "cinnamon moths" of the poem "The Rent in the Screen," who, upon being awakened from cocoons by the treacherously "sweet mildness of the late December day," fly "Across the gulf of night and nothingness" into "The falling snow, the fall, the fallen snow," we too make our yearly and all-too-brief flight into hopes and dreams, lulled by the summer's heat, only to fly into the sad and puissant arriving winter. Like the *persona* in "Observation of October," human beings have that "old desperation of the flesh" when confronted by the annual drying up of the easy and free times of spring and summer.

Time, that implacable enemy against which there is no weapon to employ, is, to the poet, an "angry wheel" that "might burn away in air," giving the thoughtful individual very few quiet meditative moments of genuine insight before forcing him on to do battle with the encroaching tide of everyday duties. In "A Harvest Home," the *persona* is able, if only for the briefest time, to bask in the august stillness of "the long field in fall," reflecting upon the sun's silent bending of earth toward afternoon. This momentary blessing is, however, nothing more than one of time's confidence tricks, "a snare/ For time to pull from and be torn/ Screaming against the rusty brake." Or time may be cast in the image of an ocean voyage from which there is no return and it may be found in the painting, "Triumph of Time," by Pieter Brueghel, wherein time is depicted as a great elephant bearing a trumpeting angel which tramples the books and crowns and kings to dust.

Nemerov is much like certain anonymous artists of the Middle Ages whose paintings portray the victory of the grave over worldly ambitions and hopes and yet, unlike them, he is unable to paint the companion scene: that of the uncorrupted body rising to the New Jerusalem.

Poetry is the poet's chief bulwark against the aggressor, time, who must in the end conquer all. And yet, the poet questions the efficacy and enduring value of what he writes, knowing full well that he cannot hope to compete with the ancients, the old masters like Homer whose poetry had a sufficient, sustained vision of life and a wholeness destined to survive the centuries.

In addition to time, Nemerov is obsessed by another destroyer: modern warfare. Having participated in World War II, the poet knows well what that conflict said about us and our technological world, what it elucidated for us, what ambiguity of response it and other wars manifest within us.

Modern warfare cannot be sung in the manner of Homer or Virgil: it is more cruel than ancient warfare because it is more mechanical, more difficult to conjure up because it is too awesome a phenomenon. And yet, Nemerov, working with isolated memories of conflict, makes the attempt to tell what war is really like without saying too much in the process. In one of his earlier poems, "For W___, Who Commanded Well," the poet speaks of the ironies inherent in being an officer in charge of men in an era when the individual soldier or officer no longer matters—an era when technology decides outcomes of battles and big money interests control wars. This theme is vividly reiterated in other creations such as "September Shooting" (ostensibly about bird hunting, but actually dealing with modern warfare) in which the poet finds that "death comes quickly/ And is not famous nor ever identified. . . ." It is a time when, "The anonymous bullet flies out of/ An irrelevant necessity, and knows no evil."

But it is the smaller things that say as much about Nemerov's view of war as anything possibly could: those mummified blue eyeballs ripped from a dead enemy soldier that his killer keeps in his pocket as rattling souvenirs. Without God and without any great faith in the motivations of fellow men who always have in them the capacity to rip out the eyeballs of others for a joke, Nemerov frequently finds some measure of solace in the one place poets have traditionally sought comfort: nature. Although his finest collection of nature poems is found in *The Salt Garden* volume, poems honoring nature's moods are scattered freely throughout *The Collected Poems*.

As has been previously noted, nature is both a mirror and an agent of time. Those seasonal changes mirrored in meadows, woodlands, and beach areas seem to push the poet relentlessly toward his death. And even spring, portrayed as a "powerful bear,/ Drunken with deathlessness" in the poem, "Zalmoxis," instructs the poet in the vagaries of human fortunes and gives him powerful intimations of his mortality. In the lyrical "Dandelions," for instance, spring brings those small yellow flowers that delight everyone but the most hardened lawn enthusiast. But dandelions, like everything that lives, change, becoming the "Stricken and old, ghosts in the field . . ." that the poet depicts withering away in the most merry of seasons. Like the dandelions, it is inferred, we too will become, with horrifying rapidity, like those ". . . ruined spinsters," who sway in the field parading "ghostly hair."

Destruction is a part of Nemerov's summer as well as his spring. For summer is the time when the sun beats hardest upon creation, drying flowers and plants, while encouraging the rankest and ugliest weeds to grow. In "Midsummer's Day," the poet surveys an abandoned farm that bakes in midsummer heat, noting, "that fate runs/ Wild as the summer—Babylon and Rome,/ As ruin remains brought in a sense home."

Autumn is, as has been noted, a time for people to reflect upon the fleeting pleasures they experienced in the summer (whether such pleasures are real or imagined, the poet does not say). It is, as always, the melancholy season when even a falling leaf offers an intricate lesson to the perceptive onlooker, who sees in its slide to earth, "An old story;/ How youth may go from glory to glory/ Changing his green for a stiff robe of dry/ Magnificence. . . ." And it is a time to store sheaves of wisdom and memory for the coming of the dark, ancient ceremonies of winter when visual inspiration will be all but gone until spring's return.

"The Pond," one of Nemerov's most anthologized, most important poems, speaks of winter's taking of a young boy's life. The boy (named Christopher) is an unwitting victim of thin ice on the pond, and his death's dignity and significance is almost erased by the winter's apathy: its blank ice sheet's stare, the dead woods, and the silent, uncaring surrounding terrain. Winter is eternal (or so it first appears): cold, dark, static, unknowing, a perfect void. But juxtaposed against the implacable, deadly face of winter are the awakening cries of spring's first birds, summoning life from the apparent grave and bringing hopes to a once hopeless world. Nature—more specifically, nature as she is found in the Northern United States—is a creation whose seasons serve as reminders to man of his fate and yet are also providers of hope and joy.

Nemerov has been saddled with the appellation "academic poet," the implication being that his is a pedantic poetry, a stale product of the "academy." Nothing could be further from the truth. His lifeblood is, admittedly, the world of ideas, for he is essentially an intellectual poet (as opposed to a poet whose horizons are established by an amorphous and mythical "academy"). He is familiar with the world's greatest movers and shakers—those artists and thinkers who have pointed the way: Homer, Virgil, Dante, Lu Chi, Brueghel, Shakespeare, the English metaphysicals, Vermeer, Valery, and Rimbaud, to name but a few. To understand Nemerov, one must have more than a surface acquaintance with the literary, religious, and artistic traditions of both East and West, for Nemerov is one of this century's "difficult" poets, in a league with poets such as Pound, Yeats, and Breton who write for the tiny minority of poetry readers. Yet, this is not to say that he cannot be earthy and concrete, because one of his strengths lies in his ability to be both abstract and concrete in the same poem.

Nemerov writes about all sorts of things, both private and public, earthy and ethereal. He can, for instance, illuminate Mafia "cement-overcoat" killings and Sunday papers strewn across a floor, the horrors associated with suburban lawnmowers and suburban social functions, the meaning of a rotten-in-the-grill Cadillac prowling American city streets, as well as discuss Plotinus or the *ars poetica*. His far-searching poetic vision is often reminiscent of the later Yeats: "And man, geometer, construes his arcs/ And angles to cathedral poise, of which/ Sunday's massive reserve composes still/ Continuous limits of the possible." Increasingly, however, his poetry turns from abstraction to concreteness; his language becomes more "common" and his images more accessible as one moves from his earlier poems to his later ones. Of football on a television screen, he makes vivid what he sees, speaking of "a spaghetti of arms and legs/ Waving above a clump of trunks and rumps" and of ginkgo trees, he notes, "fallen yellow fruit" that "mimics the scent/ Of human vomit. . . ."

Nemerov's poetic voice very often is spoken of as something detached and lordly, somehow quietly ironic—and, for the most part, this is true. Nonetheless, his measured, calm language increasingly gives way to the more colloquial language of his later volumes in which lines like the following turn up (this passage is taken from his "Ozymandias II"):

> I met a guy I used to know, who said:
> 'You take your '57 Karnak, now,
> The model that they called their Coop de Veal
> That had the pointy rubber boobs for bumpers.'

Yet, at his most characteristic, Nemerov remains the poet assuming a traditionally aloof narrative tone that keeps his verse impersonal and authoritative:

"You will remember, Theseus, that you were/ The Minotaur, the Labyrinth and the thread/ Yourself; even you were that ingener/ That fled the maze and flew— so long ago—/ Over the sunlit sea to Sicily."

Known for his lyrical evocations of time's passing and nature, Nemerov also has a reputation of being a satirist of the first rank, who, with the usual moralistic undergirding of the true satirist, judges his own society and finds it lacking in many crucial ways. His satirical poems evince a sensitivity toward destruction, hatred, bigotry, war, and the human suffering they create.

In "A Negro Cemetery Next to a White One," the poet expresses profound indignation over the plight of black people in this country by speaking of black ghosts turned away from heaven by a blond angel; or a university museum exhibit in which a decorated pottery skull serves as the very emblem of the artist's own vanity and essential emptiness and preciousity; or of the platitudes recalled after a commencement ceremony wherein a new generation of young people was stuffed with clichés and lies.

In all, Nemerov's satire has become more powerful and less enigmatic in the last three volumes of his poems than it was previously. He has mastered the most demanding of satirical devices: the epigram (or, as he might call it, the "gnome"). Worthy of Swift or Wilde is the gem called "The God of This World" in which God "smiles to see His children, born to sin,/ Digging those foxholes there are no atheists in." His wit, particularly when presented in so compact a vehicle, is devastating.

As a portrayer of the ironies and ambiguities of our time, Howard Nemerov has few—if any—equals. His line of vision, hitched as it is to his proper, poised, and classical tone, is an expansive and encompassing one. Sufficiently humble to take lessons from past and present masters and sufficiently outspoken and self-assured to denounce present-day mediocrity, cruelty, and waste, this poet has achieved something few poets ever do. His achievement resides in the fact that for over thirty years, he has exhibited a capacity for intellectual growth as well as an unruffled—even majestic—ability to say important things crisply, nobly, memorably. His is a unique and forceful American voice.

John D. Raymer

Sources for Further Study

Christian Science Monitor. LXIX, November 16, 1977, p. 23.
Kirkus Reviews. LV, August 15, 1977, p. 923.
Library Journal. CII, July, 1977, p. 1502.
Saturday Review. V, November 12, 1977, p. 34.

THE COMPASS FLOWER

Author: W. S. Merwin (1927–   )
Publisher: Atheneum (New York). 94 pp. $4.95 (paperback)
Type of work: Poetry

A volume by a well-known and experienced modern poet which attempts to suggest the possibility of new directions

With the publication of this, his ninth separate volume of poetry since 1952, W. S. Merwin is close to becoming a man of letters: He has reached the watershed age of fifty; he has a considerable (and deserved) reputation as a translator of some dozen volumes; he has published miscellaneous prose and poetry in a wide variety of places; he has received awards and fellowships; he is a favorite author of *The New Yorker;* and most indicative perhaps, his poetry has begun to be collected *(The First Four Books of Poems,* 1975).

That Merwin himself recognizes the dangers of becoming institutionalized is perhaps indicated by the title of his present volume. The compass flower is a plant whose leaves, it is alleged, tend to align themselves so as to indicate the cardinal points of the compass. To reinforce this idea of directions, the volume itself is divided into four sections; each section is self-contained, but it would probably be a mistake to attempt to read the poems within any one section as any sort of official sequence. The title does not seem to be intended to refer to physical direction, but whether it is meant to imply new directions for the poet or simply the possibility of a variety of directions is not clear. It should be said at the outset that though there are a number of good things in this collection, there is not a great deal that is really new.

The poems of the first section spring from the experience of the lonely countryside, while the second presents common city scenes. The third section is more mixed, combining some poems of the countryside with a group of love poems. The final section ranges more widely, presenting poems drawn from life and travel in foreign lands.

But no matter what the subject or source, all the poems of the book are private. The outside world rarely intrudes, and there is an air of distance and remoteness. As one slight example, there is not a single place-name—real or imagined—in the whole book except in the poem "St. Vincent's." Again, there are few persons (and no names) mentioned except in the love poems and in some of the city and travel poems. These are only externals, of course, but they do indicate a quality that runs through Merwin's work; most of the poems, though not internally vague or fuzzy, seem rather to float suspended in air.

If one common image of a modern poet is that of a man raging passionately against any or all of the evils which beset humankind and can be seen daily catalogued in the newspaper, in the manner of a Ginsberg or a Ferlinghetti, then Merwin is an uncommon modern poet in at least two respects: a deliberate avoidance of passion (though not necessarily intensity) and an almost inhuman unconcern with the outside world. Merwin is not of the school which mistakes emotion ripped raw from the soul for poetry. He does not deal with the big, the eventful, or the publicly important; he seeks rather what revelations and insights he can muster in the small, the private, and the isolated. Like Housman, he seems to have set himself limits beyond which he will not go, and he returns again and again to meditations on the varying combinations of his favorite images of mountain, stone, cloud, rain, the coming on of night, and certain slants of light. As a result, the dominant tone of this poetry is low-key, understated; there is a deliberate and conscious restraint and neutrality which inevitably brings with it a coldness. Merwin is not a master of a variety of poetic styles or subjects; he has chosen to speak mainly in a single voice, which often becomes a monotone. Emotion never overcomes syntax; images rarely surprise or startle, though they often creep insidiously into the reader's consciousness by their polish and fitness.

In the polishing and fitting of simple word and image, Merwin reminds one not only of Housman but perhaps also of some of the more cultivated minor Latin poets. Merwin can describe apparently simple objects and scenes in apparently simple language and yet achieve a fixity and a definition not allowed to the more florid or stunning. When he describes a "bell rope moving like a breath" ("The Heart"), or "the dew brushed from the pine needles onto my fingers" ("The Wine"), or "the green wooden doors thrown away" on a mountainside ("The Arrival"), one has that feeling that comes with all good poetry, that the word is here exactly right, that it could be said no other way at that moment, that the word is *inevitable.* It is a deliberate part of Merwin's poetic strategy that his poems are unplaced and floating, that his language is unadorned, that he strives for restraint and understatement. This allows him to see what he wishes more clearly; the inessentials are stripped away. The result is a sense of timelessness and hopeful permanence which Merwin clearly seeks.

But Merwin can do more than simply write a precise line or a restrained line. He can use those simple-appearing words and images to expand the thought and resonance of a passage, as in a poem on death ("The Snow") in which he describes "the cataract forming on the green wheated hill/ ice on sundial and steps and calendar." The leap from the physical to the conceptual at the word *calendar* is done so smoothly and so easily that we are perhaps unaware of just how the poet has, at this point, begun to open up the poem to the resonances available beyond the mere physical description. Or again, in "An Encampment at Morning," when he sees a group of spider webs as "spread tents at dusk in the rye stubble," he goes beyond simply a "pretty" image to suggest the oppositions of light and dark, of man and nature, of permanence and transition, of past and present.

Merwin seeks the meaning of things most often in the simple, even lonely and barren, scenes of the countryside. But more to the point, it is not simply the seeing of these things that attracts the poet but the experiencing of them. In

poem after poem, he makes the speaker (and the reader) feel the harsh rocks
under his feet on the mountainside, the damp as the mist bedews the hair, the
chill breath on the cheek as the wind cuts through the pine trees. The great
majority of poets are primarily visualizers; Merwin is one of the most tactile of
poets. It is in the experiencing that there comes the moment of insight, the
revelation, for which the poet waits so collectedly and so patiently. Commonly,
this moment is suggested by the last two or three lines of a poem, following upon
a relatively straightforward description of scene or experience. After rendering
the experience of a morning mountain wind ("On the Mountain"), the poet says
that the wind "carries deep reflections of birds/ and of sunrise clouds/ thoughts
into the sea of day." After imaginatively reentering the childhood fantasy of
feeling a fish hit a taut line, he says "bright color in darkness through half a life/
beating suddenly toward me" ("Fishing"). Or, in one of the travel poems
("Remembering a Boatman"), after describing a boatman rowing slowly across
the water in front of him, the poet comments: "A few times the wake turns up
light/ then I forget him for years." And in one of the city poems ("The
Estuary"), after establishing his metaphor of an apartment house as a stone
boat, his final lines are "and at the bow of the stone boat/ the wave from the ends
of the earth keeps breaking."

Each one of these sets of final lines attempts to take a step beyond the
immediate world of the poem, to suggest something of the insight that the poem
and its experience has gained for the poet. It is clear in such lines that the poet
has been moved or affected; we can see that something has happened—the shift
in the imagery makes that clear. But it is rarely clear at all just what has been
revealed; the poet cannot tell us. There is a mystery here which is beyond the
literal scope of words. There is an ambiguity and a hesitancy in such conclusions
which spring both from the poet's own restraint, from his reluctance to claim too
much, and from the probable fact that such insights are not quite clear to the
poet himself. Merwin is objective and honest, willing to admit, through his
imagery, that all things are not clear and definite, that the poet does not have all
the answers, that there is the possibility of misreading the experiences. It is
refreshing in modern writing to find a writer who does not know it all, who is
honest with himself and the reader. Merwin admits that he sees only momentarily and in fragments, but it is these fragmented moments that he has shored
against his ruins.

The image of the cold, stony mountain looms over all of Merwin's poems
here, even the city poems and the love poems. It is a mountain which must be
climbed, but progress is impeded and obscured by the clouds, the mist, the rain,
and the dark. It is a lonely climb and the top is never reached; never does the
speaker attain to a clear, unclouded vision and rest. Many poets tell you about
their loneliness, often at great length; Merwin *is* lonely. Perhaps no other
modern poet is so alone.

But despite the rocks and the darkness, there is in Merwin a simple but restrained joy in being alive, being able to touch occasionally the mystery within existence. In "The Wine," for example, the speaker, carrying a case of wine up a mountain, after noting how cold his hands are and how awkward the wine is to carry on his shoulders, concludes "that's part of the joy." And in "A Contemporary" he considers the benfits of living as a blade of grass which would

> feel worms touch my feet as a bounty
> have no name and no fear
> turn naturally to the light
> know how to spend the day and night
> climbing out of myself
> all my life

Though this is far from being a Whitmanesque reveling in sensation, and though what comes before and after may be darkness, life nevertheless holds the possibility of penetrating the mystery.

Because of the recurring images and diction, the countryside poems tend to blur together. But the city poems, though fewer in number, seem more individualized, more memorable. In these, Merwin deals again with the commonplace: the checkout line at the supermarket, the lighted windows of great apartment houses, the hospital opposite his apartment window, the rubber bands which stretch like bands of memory. Though there is much in these poems of the coldness and impersonality of the city, they are sharply realized and derive their own benefit from the restraint and polish of the poet. In one poem, "The Helmsmen," the poet even presents his own version of the old ships-that-pass-in-the-night theme. As a group, the city poems are the most striking in the book, partly because they are not run-of-the-mill Merwin, and partly because the audience is simply more familiar with the things of the city, the rural experience having largely faded in modern America.

The single most striking poem in the book is the longest, a love poem, "Kore" (Greek for *young maiden),* in twenty-four lyric sections of between six and twelve lines each. Though many of the individual lyrics are set against the familiar background of cold, stone, dark, and rain, there is more of a warmth and a going out of oneself. Love has, for the time at least, pushed back the dark and some of the loneliness. It is perhaps easier for a poet to go wrong in writing love poetry than in anything else; it is dishearteningly easy to fall into the clinical or the sentimental or the mawkish—or to pretend to an emotion that is expected. In a single lyric from "Kore" one can see the riches which come with restraint:

> I found you the bracelets of plaited straw
> you found me the old tools
> that I had been looking for
> you knew where they were
> in my garden
> few are the words for finding
> as I told you under the beating flights

of autumn
and will tell you again
as I find them

If W. S. Merwin has become, or is about to become, a man of letters, then, in view of his output and quality over a quarter of a century, perhaps it is time for him to be, not collected or reprinted, but edited. The repetitious, the prosaic, and the awkward could be removed and the best presented. Such a volume would be of substantial size and would certainly include a number of poems from the present collection.

Gordon N. Bergquist

Sources for Further Study

Book World. July 17, 1977, p. K4.
Hudson Review. XXX, Summer, 1977, p. 282.
Kliatt Paperback Book Guide. XI, Summer, 1977, p. 15.
Times Literary Supplement. July 29, 1977, p. 936.

CONFLICT AND CRISIS
The Presidency of Harry S Truman, 1945-1948

Author: Robert J. Donovan (1912-   )
Publisher: W. W. Norton & Company (New York). 473 pp. $12.95
Type of work: History
Time: 1945-1948
Locale: The United States

A history of the first administration of Harry S Truman, which saw the origins of the Truman Doctrine and the Marshall Plan as outgrowths of the developing Cold War with the Soviet Union

Principal personages:
    HARRY S TRUMAN, President of the United States, 1945-1953
    DEAN ACHESON, Under Secretary of State, 1945-1947
    JAMES F. BYRNES, Secretary of State, 1945-1947
    CLARK M. CLIFFORD, Special Counsel to the President, 1946-1950
    JAMES V. FORRESTAL, Secretary of Defense, 1947-1949
    GEORGE C. MARSHALL, Secretary of State, 1947-1949
    JOHN W. SNYDER, Secretary of the Treasury, 1946-1953

Harry Truman has become something of a folk hero in recent years. A factor in forming this popular image of Truman has been a tendency to compare his bluntness and lack of pretense to the manipulation and deception characteristic of Nixon's "imperial presidency." This view of the man has been reinforced on the stage and in the media by presentations based on Truman's self-serving recollections as recounted in Merle Miller's *Plain Speaking*. This is not the Harry Truman who emerges from Donovan's well-researched and ably written account of the postwar President's first administration.

Robert Donovan was particularly well equipped to write this book. The Truman period is ripe for serious historical analysis because of the availability of source material. The death of Truman resulted in the opening of many of his private papers which had been closed to researchers, and coincided with the opening of State Department files and even some of the records of the National Security Council. In addition to these advantages which are available to all Truman scholars, Donovan had the opportunity to observe the events he describes as a White House correspondent during the Truman years. In addition, for this book he has recently interviewed many of the men he knew then to fill out the written record.

Truman was one of our least prepared Presidents, yet the problems he faced were probably greater than those encountered by any modern president with the exception of Franklin Roosevelt. He was a small-town politician who had grown somewhat during eight years in the Senate, but he had not gone to college, had no training in policymaking or management, and had no diplomatic experience. He liked to say that being President was not much different from running Jackson County, Missouri, but this was more of a rationalization for his meager background than his honest perception of the presidential office. Truman had only conferred with Roosevelt twice while he was Vice President, and these were political or social discussions rather than policy sessions. As a result, Truman knew virtually nothing of the current concerns or plans of the Administration. He did not even know of the work being done on the atomic bomb.

Being new to executive work and having little background on which to draw, it is little wonder that he stumbled badly. Because of his lack of preparation he was forced to rely on his advisers, but most were Roosevelt's appointees and few of these could imagine anyone else being President, particularly Harry Truman. Most soon quit or were fired. As a result he had virtually a new cabinet within a year. He tried to learn. Conscientiously he read everything given to him, but he had so few people on his staff who were experienced enough to sort things out for him that this task became an excessive burden. Though blessed with extraordinary physical stamina, some feared he would break under the strain of trying to do too much himself.

Through his many years of experience in Washington, Roosevelt had acquired a knowledge of the federal government which was as great as any of his subordinates'. By drawing on this knowledge and developing a network of contacts throughout the federal bureaucracy, he was able to preside over and control the tremendously expanded executive branch which developed during the New Deal and World War II. With none of these advantages Truman had to rely on an enlarged White House staff to manage the bureaucracy he had inherited. Though he eventually developed a competent corps of aides by the time he left office, it was a slow process. Eventually Clark Clifford, John Steelman, and Charles Murphy provided the kind of White House staff that succeeding Presidents have found essential.

In many ways the immediate postwar period has been a watershed for our own times. It was then that the Cold War with the Soviet Union began and that tension is still one of the most significant influences on our lives. The reconversion of the industrial system from war production to consumer items has served as the basis of the country's postwar economy and foreign trade. The essence of Donovan's book is an analysis of Truman's impact on these developments.

In the process of facing and attempting to dispose of these monumental problems, Truman drew on inherent traits of courage, humor, and capacity to learn. He was never able to overcome entirely, however, his basic provincialism, ineptness, impetuosity, and crudeness. In making his decisions he was ever conscious of maintaining the power of the presidency intact as well as keeping a personal political advantage.

Truman has been more severely criticized by historians for his part in the origin of the Cold War than any other single development during his presidency. While most of his contemporaries applauded his leadership in foreign policy, the historical record has brought many of these decisions into question. In his treatment of these controversial decisions, Donovan typically provides the available evidence for the reader and then gives his own, usually judicious, explanation of Truman's actions.

Many revisionist historians have pointed to Truman's hard-line attitude toward Soviet actions in Poland in April, 1945, as a significant milestone in establishing a climate of tense relations with Russia. They usually attribute what appears to be a radical shift from Roosevelt's policy to Truman's inexperience, his provincial anti-Communist attitude, and a desire to show that he was tough and capable of being President in his own right. Donovan does not think Truman was trying to establish a new policy because there had not yet been time to even consider such a change. Rather he believes that Truman was simply trying to adhere to Roosevelt's policy as interpreted for him by his diplomatic advisers. Donovan does not seem to consider seriously the possibility that these advisers had not agreed with Roosevelt's policy and took advantage of Truman's ignorance to establish a more uncompromising attitude toward the Soviets. In advancing this interpretation, Donovan demonstrates that his views have not been much influenced by the revisionist writings of the 1960's and 1970's.

Similarly, Donovan explains Truman's decision to use the atomic bomb as a continuation of what he believed Roosevelt's attitude to have been. Some revisionists have seen the dropping of the bomb in Cold War terms, and concluded its main purpose was to impress the Russians with our new weapon rather than to force Japan to surrender. Donovan sees it in essentially a political context. Truman, as a new accidental President, could not hope to challenge the unconditional surrender doctrine handed down by Roosevelt even if he was inclined to do so. Also it appeared that the Japanese would not surrender unconditionally without an invasion of the home islands. The atomic bomb represented an alternative to the huge loss of American lives anticipated in such an invasion. Needless loss of American life would be a heavy burden for any politician to carry. On the evidence he submits, Donovan concludes that the "simple" reason Truman dropped the bomb was to save lives by ending the war quickly. He admits, however, that Truman's advisers were "sophisticated enough" to realize that a demonstration of the bomb's potential would increase American leverage in postwar negotiations.

Revisionist historians have also pointed to the announcement of the Truman Doctrine—and the accompanying exaggeration of the Soviet threat which was used to get Congress to accept it—as the American declaration of a Cold War on the Soviet Union. It was this announcement which established the American policy of intervening in any country that was perceived as being threatened by Communism as a device for containing the Soviets. Donovan's account of this development follows the orthodox view and does not add anything to our understanding of it. Nor does he ever deal with the question of Truman's role in the origin of the policy. This gap must be considered a major flaw in the book.

Donovan does break new ground in his analysis of Truman's attitude toward, and his role in, the establishment of the new state of Israel. It is a tangled web of

State and Defense Departments' opposition to the Zionists for strategic reasons, the efforts of Truman's old haberdashery partner Eddie Jacobson to serve as a conduit into the White House for Israeli views, and the significance of the Jewish vote to a Democratic president in a particularly difficult election year. Donovan skillfully blends the documentary evidence with information obtained through interviews with some of the principals in telling his story. He concludes that in spite of all the unique factors in Truman's situation, after "the full disclosures about the gas furnaces it is inconceivable that any president of the United States in office in May 1948 would have done essentially other than that which Truman did."

It is in his treatment of domestic politics and problems that the author is most effective and original. Yet even in this area, Donovan is much more descriptive than he is analytical and the reader must search for his interpretations. For example, he describes Truman's close friend, Secretary of the Treasury John Synder, as having a typical banker's view of the economy. He adds that Truman's economic instincts were very similar to Snyder's. This would imply that Truman did not really believe in the Fair Deal that he proposed and presumably advocated it for political reasons alone, but Donovan does not explore this theme further.

Truman's twenty-one point message delivered to Congress on September 6, 1945, laid the basis for the Fair Deal. It was written primarily by Roosevelt's old speechwriter Sam Rosenman, who was anxious to commit the new President to a liberal course. Rosenman had gone to Potsdam with Truman and was able to take advantage of the voyage home to counteract some of the President's conservative instincts and commit him to a continuance of the New Deal. Rosenman later believed it was the most important thing that he did during his work with Truman. When Rosenman began to prepare the message for Congress, the President's conservative advisers tried to dissuade him from delivering it. Curiously, in view of the significance of this first statement of domestic policy of the new Administration, Donovan drops the story at this point. Perhaps this is where the historical trail ends, but the reader is entitled to the author's view of why Truman stood firm in his support of the message.

In a sense the twenty-one point message was characteristic of the basic political strategy that Truman used during most of his first term and the election of 1948. In this message and many others he asked for much more than Congress could deliver even if they had been sympathetic with the proposals called for. It was a way of making a political record without worrying about the consequences or the costs. It might win elections, but it produced little in the way of concrete legislation. When the Republicans gained control of the Eightieth Congress, Truman pursued this strategy with a vengeance. He was thus able to gain the initiative and blame Congress for all the country's problems because they would not accept his recommendations.

Donovan feels that the election of 1948 with its whistle-stop campaign changed Truman's public personality and established the "Give 'em hell" image which he sought to live up to ever after. Egged on by desperation, Dewey's unaggressive campaigning, and the enthusiasm of the audience, Truman went into his act and threw out any charge that came into his head. Prominent among his targets were the "do-nothing" Republican-controlled Congress and Herbert Hoover. When told that Hoover had been hurt by his irresponsible charges, Truman admitted privately that he had not meant a word of it.

Realizing that he was behind Dewey, Truman desperately searched for some dramatic gesture to give his campaign a shot in the arm. Some of his political advisers suggested a peace mission to Stalin. Truman accepted the idea and pressured Chief Justice Fred Vinson into undertaking the task. Such a move would have undercut our allies and circumvented the United Nations at a critical time. It was only when Marshall put his foot down that Truman reluctantly dropped this very risky injection of politics into diplomacy.

Conflict and Crisis is a book which is rich in personal detail and perceptive character sketches which reflect the author's intimate observation of the times he describes. While probably not the definitive history it strives to be, it is the best so far on the early Truman years and will become the new standard. One hopes that Donovan is now at work on a second volume which will complete the story. It will be eagerly awaited.

Alfred D. Sander

Sources for Further Study

Book World. October 30, 1977, p. E1.
Guardian Weekly. CXVII, November 20, 1977, p. 18.
New York Times Book Review. October 16, 1977, p. 1.
New Yorker. LIII, November 7, 1977, p. 223.
Publisher's Weekly. CCXII, August 22, 1977, p. 56.

THE CONSUL'S FILE

Author: Paul Theroux (1941–   )
Publisher: Houghton Mifflin Company (Boston). 209 pp. $8.95
Type of work: Short stories
Time: The immediate past
Locale: Ayer Hitam in Malaysia

Stories of post-colonial Malaysia which, although uneven, present a colorful and often bizarre picture of a small group of expatriots stranded in the midst of a jungle world in which they are neither respected nor wanted

There are as many kinds of short stories as there are short story writers. From the half-glimpsed incident, the obliquely revealed scene, to the fully-plotted, well-constructed tale, the story can be made to do almost anything. Paul Theroux is a gifted writer, but perhaps he never quite made up his mind what he intended to do in this collection of connected stories dealing with the observations of a young American diplomat in Malaysia. Often the stories contain shrewd insights and bits of stylistic bravura, but just as often they fall flat and seem pointless. The general effect is of a work that does not quite come off, but which might have been brilliant if it had been better focused. Nevertheless, there are numerous pleasures to be found in *The Consul's File.*

Stories can be created from the stimulus of dreams, emotions, reality, impressions, memories either false or true, and from the act of creation itself, but whatever the inspiration, the author must heed Ezra Pound's advice to "make it new." For all of the charm of Paul Theroux's stories in *The Consul's File,* they all sound familiar. Here the plot reminds one of a story read long ago, or there the tone is familiar, and yet again the characters are reminiscent of the characters of another, earlier writer. The stories are too derivative to stand on their own, although they do possess definite merits. Perhaps the basic problem with the collection is that the shadow of Somerset Maugham lurks behind it.

Paul Theroux is quite open about the fact that he is working a vein long ago opened and mined by Maugham. English and American expatriots at the "Club" in a dreary, hot Malaysian town, English snobbery and American callowness and the secretive deviousness of the natives: we've read about it all before. We already know the down-at-the-heels club and the seedy cafes and bars; we even have spent time at the no longer elegant Raffles hotel in Singapore. The difference, perhaps, is that Theroux likes his characters less than Maugham did. In the last story, called "Dear William," which takes the form of a letter to someone whose life he saved in an early story, the consul takes on Somerset Maugham. What tedious eccentricity Maugham was responsible for, he claims, by making heroes of the men and women stuck in the tropics for whatever reasons. The Consul (and apparently Theroux) seems to feel that Maugham glorified these expatriots by being selective and leaving out their essential flaws. But did Maugham create a romantic lie around his characters? Anyone who is really familiar with Maugham's short stories would have to deny that he glorified his characters. He wrote honestly and often brutally about the men and women he encountered on trips around the world. He could show compassion for a Sadie Thompson or a Reverend Davidson, but he did not hesitate to lay bare their flaws, and he could be devastating when dealing with the likes of a Leslie Crosbie. If any later men and women came to look upon Maugham's characters as role models and tried to fit themselves into a "glamorous" conception of the expatriot as inspired by Maugham's writing, that was not the fault of Maugham or his frequently acidic stories.

The important difference between the tales of Maugham and the brief pieces in this book is not the romantic treatment of character by Maugham as opposed to the "realistic" treatment of Theroux; rather, it is the fact that Maugham would have made real stories out of the material. Many of the stories are little more than sketches, often nicely observed, but without point or resonance. Maugham would not have let them slip through his fingers in this condition.

Here, too, Theroux seems to have tried to cover his bases by announcing in his "letter" to his friend "William" in the last story that stories have no beginning or end; they are "continuous and· ragged." He seems to be apologizing for the incomplete quality of many of the tales in the volume.

Theroux has managed to control much of the sensationalism that marred his previous fiction; strains of perversion and vice still run through many of the stories and some of the incidents are more bizarre than believable, but the tone of most of the stories is more controlled and restrained than in the earlier books. Here, too, the influence of Maugham is discernible; the style has become dry and elegant and less florid, more like that of Maugham than like the Theroux of *Saint Jack* and *The Family Arsenal.* The focus now is on how the uprooted individuals fail to connect with each other, despite their pathetic attempts. The result often is strange, and usually disastrous. Occasionally, the stories turn into social comedy, but just as often they seem to be attempting to rise toward tragedy, although they seldom succeed in achieving it. Theroux is better with his comic routines and his essays with the supernatural than with his "serious" stories. Individually, some of the stories seem thin, but taken together they reinforce one another; the sum of the parts is greater than any of them alone would suggest.

Perhaps the main problem with the book is that Theroux never thought out his point of view: his focus is blurred, his attitude toward his characters unclear. He seems to be attempting to write knowledgeably and sympathetically about the locals and their customs on the one hand and yet to show his superiority on the other. The Consul, Theroux's narrator, is *in* Malaysia, but not part of it. He is too much the disinterested observer. Only in the rare stories in which he loses his objective distance can he draw in the reader enough to sustain an emotional reaction. These tend to be the tales which deal with supernatural events. Some of the best of these stories suggest the rich, mystical world of dreams; in dreams anything is permitted to happen without censure and without explanation.

In stories such as "The Tiger's Suit" and "Dengué Fever," Theroux is playing with the nature of reality. In these tales his writing achieves an intensity that it lacks in the others, and approaches a genuine immediacy and emotional truth. In some stories, such as "White Christmas" and "Autumn Dog" he writes with an irony and sense of social comedy which are sure and acute, but the stories are not as satisfying as the others in which he has more emotional involvement. "The Tiger's Suit" blends superstition and fact in a spine-tingling manner which displays Theroux at his best; he performs a literary juggling act, combining the surreal and the plausible, the bizarre and the ordinary, the impossible and the possible.

In these stories, Theroux seems purposely to have clipped his stylistic wings, to have made an effort to write plainly, without the tricks and fireworks of his early books. If anyone was too influenced by Maugham it was not his characters but he, himself. Maugham wrote plainly because he knew his own limitations and made the best of them. Theroux, as we know from his previous novels and his fine nonfiction book, *The Great Railway Bazaar,* does not possess these limitations and should not have imposed them on himself.

At times, however, Theroux manages to rouse himself to a kind of rough and ready compassion for his expatriot characters. They are people trapped in desolate jungle places, talking of a culture and traditions they feel they should respect and admire, whether they do or not. They are like children with old, inaccurate memories, preparing for something which never will occur. Life for them is reduced to habit in a pseudoexotic setting. Their lives are eternally set in 1938. They do not realize that times have changed, that the missionaries and teachers have done their work and, for the most part, moved on. Now the question that they never asked—what happens when a half-starved world mumbles in heavily accented English, "I want . . ."—is about to find a answer, whether they like it or not.

Many of the stories deal with aspects of freedom—personal, national, mental, physical, and emotional. The story titled "Conspirators," for example, deals with the return of a political prisoner to life in his village. But, after seven years in prison, Rao does not comprehend the nature of freedom. He not only is incapable of acting as a free agent and thinking on his own, he does not even desire freedom of thought anymore. He was released, the narrator gradually comes to realize, only when he no longer was able to make use of his freedom. He possesses no desires, no hopes, no aspirations, and might as well have remained in prison. The fact is, of course, that he now carries his prison with him, and never will be able to escape it, this side of the grave. The story in this sense is reminiscent of George Orwell's *1984,* yet with a subtle, perverse twist. It is a less devastating story than Orwell's, but it leaves the reader with an almost equal sense of futility.

The stories follow one another, like exotic flowers in a hot house, diverting, sometimes strangely beautiful, occasionally perversely gaudy, and, in a few instances, small masterpieces of perfection. The individual scenes are what one remembers mostly, scenes such as the final humiliation of Margaret Harbottle, writer of travelogues and a chronic freeloader, in the story "Pretend I'm Not Here," and the scene of the epic tennis match between the Japanese salesman and the bar boy at the Ayer Hitam Club. The humor often carries even the weakest stories, but occasionally, as in the story called "Loser Wins," about a woman who loses everything, including her husband, the joke is stretched too thinly to succeed. *The Consul's File* can be placed on the shelf with Paul Theroux's other works and glanced at now and again for the rewards it does offer, but probably it would be just as well to look forward to Theroux's next piece of fiction. Almost anything else that he writes is bound to be more representative of his substantial talent.

Bruce D. Reeves

Sources for Further Study

Christian Science Monitor. LXIX, September 2, 1977, p. 30.

Harper's Magazine. CCLV, September, 1977, p. 90.

New York Review of Books. XXIV, November 10, 1977, p. 28.

New York Times Book Review. August 21, 1977, p. 1.

Newsweek. XC, August 15, 1977, p. 72.

Saturday Review. IV, September 3, 1977, p. 30.

CROMWELL

Author: Roger Howell, Jr.
Publisher: Little, Brown and Company (Boston). 269 pp. $8.95
Type of work: History
Time: 1599–1658
Locale: England, Scotland, and Ireland

A biography of Oliver Cromwell, the Puritan squire and army general who became Lord Protector of the Commonwealth

> Principal personages:
> OLIVER CROMWELL
> SIR THOMAS FAIRFAX, commander of the New Model army
> MAJOR THOMAS HARRISON, left-wing opponent of Cromwell
> HENRY IRETON, Cromwell's son-in-law and close associate
> JOHN PYM, early leader of the Parliament against the Crown
> JOHN THURLOE, secretary of the Council of State in the Protectorate

The story is told that when Oliver Cromwell sat for an official portrait as Lord Protector, he directed the artist to "paint me as I am, wart and all," without idealizing or distorting. In the three centuries since Cromwell sat for that portrait, many artists, biographers, even dramatists have tried to show the great Puritan as he truly was, "wart and all." A most recent attempt to understand and explain Cromwell is this biography by Roger Howell, professor of history and President of Bowdoin College. Howell has written several worthwhile books and numerous articles on English history and is currently the editor of British Studies Monitor. This biography is a conventional, nearly chronological, tracing of the life of Cromwell from birth to death, concentrating almost exclusively on Cromwell's military and political accomplishments.

In the first chapters, Cromwell's early years are sketched. Born into a family of country gentry of Huntingdonshire, Oliver was sent to the school of Dr. Thomas Beard, where he seems to have learned "small Latin and less Greek," but received heavy indoctrination in the theology of puritan Christianity. Young Cromwell was then accepted as a Fellow Commoner at Sidney Sussex College, Cambridge. That college was a hotbed of Puritan piety at the time, and the young man's religious bent must have been further fortified by his associations there. He had to leave after only one year's attendance when his father died; as the only son in the family, Oliver returned to manage the family lands.

Information of Cromwell's life between 1617 and 1628 is sparse. His enemies later circulated talk that, in this period, Cromwell had been a dissolute person who did excessive drinking, gambling, and wenching. If those charges are true—and Cromwell's own assertion some years later that he had once been a great sinner lends some credence—the wild life did not last long. In 1620, he married Elizabeth Bourchier, daughter of a wealthy London merchant, and together they settled down to a life of quiet respectability.

The Cromwell family were related by blood or marriage to many of the leading gentry of the region: the Hampdens, Whalleys, St. Johns, and others were his "cousinry." Men from those families would, in time, be among the leaders of parliamentary opposition to the Stuart monarchy. Through his connection with those cousins, Cromwell's political attitudes were being formed.

His own respected status and the ties of his relatives enabled Cromwell to be elected to the Parliament in 1628 as a burgess from Huntingdon. Little notice was taken of the unsophisticated young squire. One observer noted that Cromwell made an "impetuous" speech in support of the Petition of Right, one of the early efforts by the parliamentarians to curb the powers of the Crown. Cromwell was not among the parliamentary leadership, but he was marked as a man with strong feelings about the rights and liberties of Englishmen.

In 1636, Cromwell inherited properties around Ely in East Anglia and went to live there. About that time, he also underwent a religious conversion, a rebirth of his Christian faith: "I lived in and loved darkness," he wrote to a cousin, "yet God had mercy on me. Blessed be His name for shining upon a heart so dark as mine." By the grace of God, Cromwell believed that he had joined the Company of Saints, "the congregation of the first-born" who had been chosen to lead an upright life dedicated to Christian piety and the propagation of the faith. Religion, more than ever, became the central influence on his thoughts and conduct.

His devotion to the Puritan faith and to English liberties were thus fixed and well known when Cromwell was elected again to sit in the Parliament of 1640. His activities in this so-called Short Parliament were not of sufficient importance to be mentioned in the records, and, indeed, the Short Parliament itself accomplished nothing of note except to further exacerbate the differences between itself and the king; it was soon dissolved. New elections were held that same year (1640), and Cromwell was again returned. This new assembly eventually would be called the Long Parliament because it sat for thirteen years, being dissolved by Cromwell himself in 1653. It was the Long Parliament that broke with the king and made civil war against the Crown.

Opposition to the Crown in the first months of the Long Parliament coalesced around John Pym, whose intention was to bind the king "hand and foot" by establishing parliamentary control over royal finances, ministerial responsibility, and the command of the armies. Cromwell supported those limitations on the royal prerogative, but the chief issue—as he said himself—was religious freedom; to end the authority of the Anglican hierarchy over "tender consciences" like his own. Accordingly, he supported and worked for the passage of the Root and Branch Bill to abolish the Anglican bishops and their coercive powers, and to end the required usage of the Book of Common Prayer in English churches.

Cromwell was still not in the front rank of parliamentary leadership during 1641, but when Pym and other leaders drew up a lengthy summary of all the grievances that the Parliament held against state and Church governance, called the Grand Remonstrance, Cromwell worked to have it passed and printed, declaring that if the Grand Remonstrance had not passed he would have sold all that he had "and not seen England more." He had considered emigrating to New England as other Saints of the time were doing.

He did not emigrate, of course, but stayed to work for some accommodation between the prerogative claims of King Charles and the demands of the Parliament for reform. As Howell points out, Cromwell was no republican intending to destroy the monarchy at this time. Rather, he hoped and worked for some amicable agreements between the Parliament and the Crown.

Finally, however, no satisfactory agreements could be reached, and in the summer of 1642, Parliament declared war on the King. Although not an extreme antimonarchist, Cromwell inevitably sided with the Parliament.

Now forty-three years old and lacking in formal military training, Cromwell was nevertheless appointed a colonel of horse. He returned to East Anglia to recruit a "godly troop . . . of honest, sober Christians" to oppose the royal forces. He insisted that his men conduct themselves in an exemplary fashion, and he imposed a firm discipline on their behavior. He also insisted that they tolerate one another's differences in questions of religion: "take heed of being sharp against those not with you . . . in every matter concerning matters of religion." Now and later, Cromwell, although deeply convinced of the rightness of his own religious beliefs, showed himself to be more tolerant about religious conformity than his enemies and subsequent historians have asserted. He believed himself a humble instrument selected by God to carry out His will; he did not see that insistence on rigid conformity to a particular set of Christian teachings would further God's "providences."

By 1644, Cromwell's "godly company" had increased to fourteen troops of horse, and were participating in the campaigns against the royalists in eastern England. In that year, he was elevated to Lieutenant-General of Horse under the command of the Earl of Manchester. The culminating military event of 1644 was the battle of Marston Moor in which Cromwell and his men took a prominent part. "God made them as stubble to our swords" he wrote with cruel delight in describing the great victory over the Royalists. Marston Moor brought the whole of northern England under the authority of the Parliament, but it did not end the war.

At that point, the parliamentarians themselves divided; the Earl of Manchester, and the moderate faction in the Parliament known as the Presbyterians, now wanted to suspend further fighting and make some settlement with the king. Cromwell and the other faction, the Independents, held that King Charles could not be trusted to honor any treaty and that the Royalists must be decisively beaten so that terms could be imposed on the Crown. Cromwell, with great heat, criticized the reluctance of his commander, Manchester, to pursue the war vigorously. And it was proposed that a Self-Denying Ordinance be passed by the Parliament whereby all members of both Houses would resign their military commands. The Ordinance did pass. Manchester had to relinquish his command, while Cromwell, through some rather dubious maneuvering, was able to keep both his seat in the Long Parliament and gain appointment to the New Model parliamentary army led by Sir Thomas Fairfax.

The crucial battle of the first Civil War came at Naseby in 1645. Cromwell commanded the right wing of the New Model armies. "This happy victory is none other than the hand of God," he piously asserted as the Royalists were scattered at Naseby. After Naseby, Fairfax and Cromwell carried out mopping-up operations in the west of England. Basing House, a last Royalist stronghold, was taken after a lengthy siege, after which Cromwell permitted his troops to ransack and kill; he no longer insisted on exemplary behavior by his men. Shortly after, the first Civil War came to an end with the taking of the King's headquarters at Oxford in June, 1646.

For his part in defeating the Royalists, Cromwell was granted the lands of one of the King's wealthiest supporters, the Marquess of Worcester. Those estates brought in a large income; Oliver could now live quite splendidly. At the same time, his enemies charged that Cromwell was an ambitious Grandee who rose to wealth on the dead bodies of others.

Howell finds Cromwell's motives and actions in the period 1646–1649 hard to fathom but presumes that his consistent aim was to achieve a settlement "that would preserve a maximum degree of unity among the previously contending forces." And, as always, Cromwell devoutly believed that the will of God would point the way to answers and solutions. Cromwell's chief aim was to reconcile the differences between the Presbyterians in Parliament and the left-wingers of the New Model army. For that, he was damned and attacked by both sides. By 1648, his attempts at reconciling the two elements had failed, and Cromwell threw in with the army against the Presbyterians. He did not, however, share the views of that portion of the New Model called the Levellers who were advocating political and social equality for all Englishmen. When he chaired the famous army debates at Putney in which questions of the future political settlement of the kingdom were aired, Cromwell declared that, while he was not "wedded and glued to forms in government," he would not support the doctrine of universal manhood suffrage being advanced by the Levellers.

At the end of 1648, multiple negotiations were being held with the king, the army, the Parliament, and the Scots, all trying to reach some kind of arrangement. Again, as in 1642, negotiations broke down, and a second Civil War commenced in December, 1648. This was a most confused struggle involving the English army against the Parliament, the Scots joining the king against the Parliament and the English army, and therefore initiating a war between England and Scotland. Cromwell took command of the New Model forces when Fairfax resigned. He moved against the Scots who had invaded the northern counties of England. At the battle of Preston, the Scots were beaten and the second Civil War was quickly ended.

Charles I, "that man of blood," then was tried for crimes against the English people and found guilty by a high court of Parliament. Cromwell signed the death warrant, apparently now convinced of the need to remove the man who had brought about the second Civil War, and who could be expected to make more trouble if he were allowed to live. With the execution of Charles I in January, 1649, a republican government for England came into being, called the Commonwealth, with Cromwell as its leader. In that year, he took an expeditionary force to Ireland where Royalists and Roman Catholics were in rebellion against the Commonwealth. The sieges of the Irish towns of Drogheda and Wexford and the massacre of the inhabitants by Cromwell's men imprinted forever a hatred for Cromwell among the people of Ireland. Cromwell himself returned to London in May, 1649, leaving his son-in-law, Henry Ireton, to complete the subjugation of the land and restore the authority of the Commonwealth. Cromwell had returned to England to prepare to deal with a new threat from Scotland; the Scots had declared themselves in support of the son of the executed king, Charles I. The young king, Charles II, led the Scots into England where they were met by Cromwell at Worcester in 1650, and defeated; the Commonwealth was saved.

The latter chapters of *Cromwell* deal with the years 1653 to 1658 when the "Great Puritan" reached the heights of his career. Continuing friction between the Parliament and the army led to the expulsion of the "Rumpers" in 1653, and the formal ending of the Long Parliament. Then, with the support of the army, Cromwell called for nominations for a new Parliament of one hundred forty-four members. But this Assembly of Saints, as it came to be called, proved as discordant and unsatisfactory as the Rump; after only a few months, Cromwell told them to begone. Following that, a written constitution, the Instrument of Government, was adopted. This established an executive office, the Lord Protector, a Council of State, and an elected Parliament; and Oliver Cromwell was named Lord Protector of the Commonwealth of England, Scotland, and Ireland.

In the last five years of his life, Cromwell, as Lord Protector, sought to "bring reforms without damaging constitutional forms" and, on the whole, he failed. Two elected Parliaments were dismissed by the Lord Protector when they disagreed with him. Unrest in the counties prompted his placing of a semimilitary rule of Major Generals to reinforce the local governments, while a puritanical censorship and control was imposed over many of the arts and simple pleasures of life. And the religious quarrels did not abate despite a wide degree of toleration for the sects. Only in foreign affairs did Cromwell's regime shine; a war with Spain brought the capture of Jamaica, and the taking of Spanish treasure ships, while an alliance with France brought the port of Dunkirk into English hands.

The high point of Cromwell's life surely came just one year before his death with the offer by the Parliament that he accept a crown and be proclaimed as king. For reasons which are still not clear, he refused the great honor. Howell repeats his words of refusal: "I am ready not as a king, but as a constable . . . a good constable to keep the peace of the parish." And a year later, God's Englishman, the Lord Protector Oliver Cromwell, died in the palace of Whitehall.

The final chapter of this book is an excellent essay called "Cromwell and the Historians" which brings together in summary fashion some of the different interpretations of Cromwell's character and accomplishments as seen by historians since the seventeenth century.

Howell's *Cromwell* is confined almost entirely to the life of the man himself; very little attention is given to the times and the society in which he lived. The writing is clear, coherent, and quite undramatic. Howell attempts to be judicious in his assessments of Cromwell's actions but, on balance, he is pro-Cromwell and repeatedly offers justifications for the man's conduct. Some findings of recent historical research are included here; however, Howell concludes that Cromwell remains "enigmatic and elusive," a very private man whose innermost personality is still not fully understood.

For the reader with very little knowledge of Cromwell, this biography would be a good place to start, and it might whet his appetite to further study of the man. But for those who have already decided that Cromwell was either a pious Puritan hypocrite, or a man who "meant honestly in the main," this book will do little to change their opinions.

James W. Pringle

Sources for Further Study

Choice. XIV, November, 1977, p. 1267.
Kirkus Reviews. XLV, March 1, 1977, p. 261.
Library Journal. CII, May 1, 1977, p. 1010.
New York Review of Books. XXIV, June 9, 1977, p. 39.
Publisher's Weekly. CCXI, March 7, 1977, p. 94.
Times Literary Supplement. December 9, 1977, p. 1453.

DANIEL MARTIN

Author: John Fowles (1926–   )
Publisher: Little, Brown and Company (Boston). 629 pp. $12.95
Type of work: Novel
Time: 1930's to the present
Locale: England, chiefly Oxford and London, and California

The story of a man's renewal of a relationship with a long-lost friend and lover

> *Principal characters:*
> DANIEL MARTIN, an English playwright and Hollywood scriptwriter
> NELL RANDALL, his former wife
> CAROLINE MARTIN, their daughter
> ANDREW RANDALL, an English country squire, Nell's present husband
> ANTHONY MALLORY, an Oxford professor of philosophy and college friend of Daniel
> JANE MALLORY, Anthony's wife and Nell's sister
> BARNEY DILLON, another Oxford classmate of Daniel, now a television personality
> JENNY MCNEIL, a young English actress working in Hollywood, Daniel's current mistress

John Fowles's novels have always been splendid stories, richly written, capable of setting a mood and sustaining it over long pages of narrative. Yet there has always been something mysterious and almost surreal about them. *The Collector,* a story of human possessiveness, parallels the hobby of butterfly catching; *The Magus* describes an encounter with other-than-ordinary knowledge and power; *The French Lieutenant's Woman* is an attempt to re-create the ethos of Victorian England and to explore the labyrinths of Victorian sexuality. All these novels are at the fringes of reality, all in the twilight world where the ordinary shades into the mysterious, and the imagination seeks to create worlds of meaning and significance from the most ephemeral of evidence. *Daniel Martin* is quite a different book, a book set in the full light of day, in the full realities of our time and our world. The novel begins with the phrase, "Whole sight; or all the rest is desolation." The rest of the book is an attempt to see life, one life, whole, and thus to recover it from desolation, to retrieve it for meaning, for significance, for what it can say to others.

The life is that of Daniel Martin, Oxford graduate and serious playwright turned Hollywood scriptwriter with no illusions about the social value of his profession. He who was a husband and father is now turned casual lover and serial polygamist, and is currently having an affair with a young English actress the same age as his daughter. The son of an Anglican vicar steeped in the traditions and landscape of his native England, Martin is now an expatriate, living in the quintessential American landscape of Southern California. He is, therefore, Everyman who feels cut off from past, from origins, who is in exile from all that was, who flees into and thus is prisoner in the present, the momentary, the transitory, the ephemeral.

But the movement of this novel is a turning-back and a turning-within. Because Martin's affair is with Jenny, an English actress, he is turned back toward his origins. And in the midst of their relationship comes a transatlantic telephone call from his former wife Nell to say that an old Oxford classmate, Anthony Mallory, is dying of cancer and wants to see him before the end. So the journey backwards begins. It is a journey that will take him back to the old country, to old friends, to lost but not forgotten issues, hurts, loves, passions. In his research for a movie on the early twentieth century British hero Kitchener, it will take him back to the realities of the British past. Finally, on a trip to Egypt, it will take him back to the beginnings of human history. But the physical journey only parallels a deeper journey, a journey into self, into the origins of values and emotions and feelings, into the realities of love and death, of brokenness and forgiveness, of reality and illusion. Fowles sets out in this novel to present a man struggling to see himself whole; the result is a remarkable literary achievement, a book almost unique in our time in the richness and complexity and power of its vision.

The plot is simply told: Daniel and Anthony had been friends at Oxford, where Anthony had taken a first in philosophy, and Daniel, a fourth in literature. While there they had met two sisters, Nell and Jane. After college, Nell and Daniel married, had one daughter named Caroline, and, in the course of things, were divorced. Nell remarried another Oxford classmate named Andrew, and now lives with him in his family's country estate. Daniel went on to a string of casual and not-so-casual liaisons with a wide variety of women. Anthony and Jane married after college, had several children, and are still married when the novel opens. They are still in Oxford, where Anthony has become a professor of philosophy. But this marriage, too, has gone sour; Jane has a lover, while Anthony is dying of cancer. There is but one complication in what is an all-too-conventional and ordinary situation; once, before any of them left college, Daniel and Jane had a brief, one-day-long affair, a sign that there was more to their relationship than just friendship, more that could not be accommodated into the ordinary interaction of potential brother-in-law, sister-in-law.

This is the past that Daniel flies back to in response to Anthony's plea for a final visit, a past clouded by ill-feeling over Daniel's breakup of his marriage with Nell. And what Anthony, on his death-bed, calls Daniel to is a redemption of that past, an overcoming of estrangement, a renewal of relationships, a forgiveness of past differences. Specifically, he hopes that Daniel can do something for Jane, something to make up for what Anthony feels are failures on his part in their marriage. This task Daniel undertakes, first through spending time with her on a visit to the home of his former wife, then through inviting her to visit his English country retreat, and finally through taking her on a ten-day cruise on the Nile while he investigates potential locations for a projected movie on the English colonial experience in Northern Africa.

What Daniel discovers while getting to know Jane all over again after so many years is that in some strange way the working-out of his life, the finding of meaning in his life, is bound up in his relationship with her. She has become a profoundly withdrawn woman, defeated and hard to reach. But in the time he spends with her, he finds her introspection conducive to his own self-reflection; as he gets to know her, he discovers himself. From somewhere early in the book, we get the suspicion that in some way Daniel and Jane will discover a future together, in spite of the fact that everything seems to be against such an eventuality. Gradually, however, impediments fall away: her current lover deserts her, her own resistance to going on the trip with him dissolves, her reluctance to enter into anything other than casual conversation with him gradually melts. And yet what is finally left is the past, the past that both unites them and separates them. How all that will work out gives the book its suspense and tension, which Fowles orchestrates marvelously. He gives his novel the qualities of a mystery story, a narrative that moves at a leisurely pace, yet sustains interest and builds tension to hold and involve the reader.

Daniel Martin, therefore, is that sort of book for which one does not want to give away the ending; each reader deserves the pleasure of seeing the final working out of all the strands of the narrative, and experiencing the final splendid pages. What a reviewer *can* do without depriving potential readers of the novel of that experience is to point out a few elements that contribute to the overall impact of this major literary work. One of these is the drawing of Fowles's minor characters. Caroline, Daniel's daughter, now having an affair with Barney Dillon, yet another Oxford classmate of Daniel, is deftly presented. She is yet one more aspect of Daniel's past with which he must be reconciled, one more person who forces him to reexamine his present situation. Her relationship with a man old enough to be her father is too close to Daniel's relationship with a woman young enough to be his daughter, and so he is forced to reconcile his feelings about both relationships. As usual in this book, the resolution cuts both ways; he finds he must give up his mistress, but he must also accept what his daughter decides to do. Barney himself, a writer with pretensions to seriousness, now become little more than a television personality, forces Daniel to reevaluate his own commitment to a profession equally transitory, equally destructive to the lives of those involved in it. But the minor character most fully drawn because she is allowed to speak for herself is Jenny McNeil, the young British actress with whom Daniel has an affair. She, too, is in the process of discovering herself and the reality of her humanity. The high value which she places on Daniel is occasionally a corrective to Daniel's self-deprecation. She must lose him, finally, but our sense is that their relationship has been good for both of them and has made possible the future which must separate them.

Even as Jenny emerges in the book through letters she writes to Daniel in England, so does a major theme about the relationship between art and life. Over and over, the book draws our attention to itself as a book, as a work in the process of being written. The speaker throughout is Daniel, except for an occasional chapter written by Jenny; he, on occasion, tells us of his reactions and second thoughts about what he has just written. At the end of the book, Daniel knows that the novel he wants to write, and has thought about writing, can never be written; the speaker, describing himself as Daniel's "ill concealed ghost," says that he has made the last sentence of Daniel's never-to-be novel the first sentence of this one. What happens in this book is that the real story of Daniel's self-discovery becomes the novel we read; in other words, his story becomes real for us because it has become art. If we are to learn from the book, therefore, we are called to see the process of self-understanding, the task of creating our own lives, as in some way parallel to the novelist's task of creating the lives of his characters. Fowles and Martin are not the same, but we must suspect that the process of writing this book was one of self-discovery for Fowles as well.

For what this book is finally about is nothing other than the nature of human life. It is about learning that hardest of human lessons: that true love of another human being comes not through loving in them what we are or what we can make them into, but through knowing them as they are, and letting them be themselves. What finally happens between Daniel and Jane happens because Daniel learns who she is, and convinces her that he loves that person, and not someone else. Such is the freedom that love brings, such is the freedom that makes real loving possible. One testimony to the value of *Daniel Martin* for our age is that in the midst of a culture that values youth above all else, that finds itself progressively more and more cut off from intergenerational experience, here is a book that makes one feel good about being over thirty, that argues that knowing one's past sets one free in the present. It is a celebration of humanity, a defense of humanism. As such it is an enormously valuable book, a book to delight in because it helps us value who we are and what we can do. *Daniel Martin* is a major literary event because it affirms the value of our humanity and enriches our experience of ourselves and those we know. At the same time, it teaches us the value of art, its power to show us ourselves, to help us understand ourselves.

John N. Wall, Jr.

Sources for Further Study

Atlantic. CCXL, October, 1977, p. 104.

Harper's Magazine. CCLV, October, 1977, p. 87.

New Leader. LX, November 21, 1977, p. 16.

New Statesman. XCIV, October 7, 1977, p. 482.

New York Times Book Review. September 25, 1977, p. 1.

Saturday Review. V, October 1, 1977, p. 22.

Time. CX, September 12, 1977, p. 75.

THE DARK LADY

Author: Louis Auchincloss (1917–   )
Publisher: Houghton Mifflin Company (Boston). 246 pp. $8.95
Type of work: Novel
Time: From the 1930's to the 1950's
Locale: New York City and its suburbs

A novel of manners that explores the multifaceted consequences of one woman's self-focused drive toward the limelight, in which she gains her objective with tragic consequences for the three persons closest to her

Principal characters:
    IVY TRASK, editor of the fashion magazine *Tone*
    ELESINA DART, former actress rescued from alcoholism and obscurity
      by Ivy Trask
    IRVING STEIN, investment banker, art connoisseur, and master of
      Broadlawns
    DAVID STEIN, Irving's youngest son
    ELIOT CLARKSON, David's best friend and second cousin

A modern day novelist of manners, Louis Auchincloss is frequently compared to Anthony Trollope. As a recorder of a way of life the comparison is valid; however, he seems less inclined to show us the flair, the wit, or the good warm blood of his characters that marked Trollope's style. It is as though, because they are of his milieu, he wants to shield them from the probing and critical eyes of the non-U and the unwashed. Over a decade ago, S. K. Overbeck wrote of Auchincloss, "Aside from its inventive ironies, Auchincloss's prose is all polish and no spit. . . ." (*Newsweek,* March 27, 1967.) It is unfortunate that the same can be said of Auchincloss' later work, including this novel; he seems to be observing from a distance, not coming close enough for the reader to feel, taste, or smell the realities he intends to convey.

The outsiders seem more real than the highborn, wealthy WASPs in many of Auchincloss' novels, and this is no exception. Ivy Trask, a successful self-made woman, is one of the more memorable of Auchincloss' characters. The author often exploits the hand-in-the-velvet-glove ploy; this time there are two—both Ivy and her protégée Elesina Dart are classic examples of the strong, manipulating, singleminded woman.

Ivy is at heart a driven, insecure, unloved, and unloving woman. Auchincloss has her fill her emptiness by living vicariously through well-born, lovely Elesina, an actress she rescues from alcoholism brought on by two destructive marriages and a fading stage career. As Ivy succeeds in strengthening Elesina's position, she diminishes those around her. The ultimate irony is exemplified by the fact that Elesina fares so well under Ivy's sponsorship that eventually there is no longer room for Ivy in the world she has built for Elesina.

Early insecurity has made Ivy into a snob, and although her position as editor of *Tone* should be assurance enough, she revels in her close association with Clara and Irving Stein. Stein, a lawyer and former surrogate judge, is now an investment banker and art collector. As a member of the Stein inner circle, Ivy uses the devices at her command to make herself indispensable to Clara in much the same way that she did earlier to the relatives who took her in as an orphaned niece. Eventually she begins to sense a subtle change in the Steins, fears they are beginning to take her for granted, and may soon hold her in contempt. In a calculated attempt to prove she can produce something of value on her own, something to enhance her standing in their eyes, she proposes a visit to Broadlawns of her actress friend, Elesina Dart. Through the consequences of this act, an act which precipitates changes of lifestyles and a breakdown of family ties, friendships, and a marriage, Auchincloss becomes a moralist. He turns moralist, too, in his treatment of Irving. Elesina is maneuvered into a loveless marriage to Irving after Ivy sets about breaking up his marriage to the colorless Clara. In a departure from the traditional view that it is the woman who pays, he condemns Irving to a life of invalidism and impotency soon after he and Elesina take the vows.

Continuing to hew her path of disaster through the lives of those she touches, Ivy focuses on David, the Steins's youngest child, the one who means the most to Clara. She encourages an affair between Elesina and David—to hurt Clara as much as to gratify her grand plan for Elesina's happiness. By the time her husband dies, Elesina, who has become as pragmatic and callous as her mentor, gives up David for the material security bestowed by Irving's will. She has proven herself the woman that Ivy sees in her.

Elesina is goaded, by her own mother's contempt, into recognizing that she is becoming a harder and more self-focused individual than even Ivy has envisioned, but it does not bother her. Always the actress, she craves more and more attention and applause; indeed, she needs it for survival. She is certain that she has always been in control of her own life. She is convinced that if Ivy has exerted influence over her, it is because she, Elesina, has allowed it. In a revealing statement, she admits that " . . . If I was going to the dogs, it was because I wanted to. Because barks and bites attract me. . . . There's always been a streak of cruelty in me. . . . It's not attractive but I face it. . . ." Elesina is reaching the stage where she, like Clara, no longer needs Ivy. As she overcomes political obstacles in her ambition to stay in the limelight, Ivy realizes she is losing her influence over the strong-willed Elesina; she painfully admits that Elesina no longer needs or wants her. Elesina's rejection of her ill-advised help in a touchy political situation leads Ivy to commit suicide. Even then, Elesina seems little moved by another's pain. Both Ivy and Elesina are typical of the women in Auchincloss' work, who are frequently much stronger and far less admirable than his males.

Irving Stein is not portrayed with any complexity. He exemplifies the manifestation of the merchant prince mentality, although he is a lawyer. He was born to Orthodox Jewish parents, but his pursuit of beauty through art has led him to abandon his religious heritage. Irving as a young man fantasized his union with Clara Clarkson as more than it really was—a marriage for social advantage. Quite predictably, in his middle years he indulged in a series of extramarital affairs that had about them an aura of exploitation, since most were with the wives of impecunious artists who neeeded his help.

When Elesina arrives on the scene, he is ripe for the plucking, as Ivy is well aware. When Irving plans to make Elesina his mistress, he does so in the conventional manner; however, Ivy sees this as the time to suggest a more permanent arrangement. Through Ivy's astute scheming, Irving begins to think of Elesina not as his mistress, but as rightful mistress of Broadlawns—as his wife. He is moved by the revival of his youthful dreams of a happy master of the manor displaying a beautiful wife on his arm.

A memorable character, although not completely limned, is Eliot Clarkson. Eliot is David's second cousin, but more particularly his champion and friend. His story is another of the well-plotted ironies familiar to Auchincloss' readers. Eliot's friendship with David begins during a nasty anti-Semitic contretemps at prep school. Eliot's attraction is intense and on his part homosexual; he visualizes the two of them against the world, but knows this is an unrealistic dream. Accepting the fact that he must share David with others, he wonders "bitterly in time if his own intransigency had not done more for David's social career than all of Irving Stein's ambition." After David is rejected by Elesina, the two men enlist in World War II. David is killed and Eliot survives. Here the symbolism becomes obvious; a Jewish lamb sacrificed to the Nazi guns that others might live. Eliot, stationed in England, goes through the war physically unscathed. He becomes a politically radical, left-wing professor of law during the hazardous days of the McCarthy reign of terror. In his compulsion to keep alive David's memory, Eliot edits and publishes *The War Letters of David Stein*. To the readers of the book, David becomes a hero, and the mysterious woman who sent him off to war and to death becomes an anonymous symbol of hate. Elesina is not free of his influence, even in death.

Despite overplotting and contrivances, Auchincloss has succeeded in staying close to his theme of ambition to be realized at any cost. The book can be classified as predictable Auchincloss with two exceptions: he abandons his usual good taste when he caricatures, to the point of cruelty, the homosexual minority; and when he casts Jews into a pejorative, stereotyped mold. On the whole it exemplifies what one has come to expect of this writer: a somewhat humorless, urbane, ironic approach to the plight of the upper-middle class, a group, he leads one to feel, who are as much survivors in their milieu as are the guttersnipes of the urban ghetto. The sad thing is that while these characters interest one briefly, Auchincloss does not succeed in making one really care about them.

Mae Woods Bell

Sources for Further Study

Book World. August 14, 1977, p. F3.
Christian Science Monitor. LXIX, August 19, 1977, p. 23.
Harper's Magazine. CCLV, September, 1977, p. 92.
New Statesman. XCIV, November 11, 1977, p. 662.
New York Times Book Review. August 14, 1977, p. 14.
Newsweek. XC, August 1, 1977, p. 72.
Time. CX, July 11, 1977, p. 76.

DAY BY DAY

Author: Robert Lowell (1917–1977)
Publisher: Farrar, Straus and Giroux (New York). 137 pp. $8.95
Type of work: Poetry

A collection of sixty-six poems, Lowell's last before his death, which continue in the confessional mood of his recent volumes

In a poem called "Our Afterlife I," Robert Lowell tells his old friend, fiction writer Peter Taylor, "This year killed / Pound, Wilson, Auden . . . / promise has lost its bloom." Later, in "Our Afterlife II," he observes that "even cows seem transitory" and "The old boys drop like wasps / from windowsill and pane." This book is valedictory; intimations of mortality crowd the pages—not allusions to death in the abstract but a deep-gut sense of things passing away. Lowell will not prettify the process of aging and death. In a poem near the end of the collection, he makes "Thanks-Offering for Recovery" and considers taking with him to church a grotesque shrunken head. But he doubts any church would accept the head, and concludes the poem: "This winter, I thought / I was created to be given away."

Lowell's death in a taxicab between Kennedy Airport and Manhattan on September 12, 1977, lends poignance to *Day by Day,* in which the reader often sees the poet at airports—leaving someone, or being left, escaping his native Boston, or returning to it. In retrospect, Lowell's entire career seems predicated on almost equally strong desires to escape and deny, on the one hand, and to return and affirm, on the other.

Since 1944, Robert Lowell has published no fewer than seventeen books, including plays and translations. During that time, he has refused to be shelved, demurely, as befitted a Boston Lowell; instead, his political activism often attracted the glare of public notice. In 1943, he was sentenced to prison for violation of the Selective Service Act. In 1965, he publicly refused an invitation to the White House, because, as he said, artists "cannot enjoy public celebration without making subtle public commitments." He admitted his "dismay and distrust" of American foreign policy in 1965, and in December, 1968, the Justice Department included him with other intellectuals suspected of conspiracy against the draft. In January, 1968, Lowell had been refused a visa to attend a Cuban Cultural Conference, because, as a passport official said, "We did not believe it was in the interest of the United States. . . ."

Nevertheless, Lowell's poems rarely treat politics overtly and directly. His chief concern has seemed to be reconciling the dream with the reality of twentieth century American life, and, on occasion, his work has satisfied even the demands of patriotism. When Lowell, in *Day by Day,* asks how often his antics, his "unsupportable, trespassing tongue" have "gone astray and led me to prison . . . / to lying . . . kneeling . . . standing," he recalls his public as well as his private life. The poem quoted, called "The Downlook," celebrates the end, or at least the diminishment, of yet another of Lowell's personal relationships. That poem comes close to starting the collection's theme; "the downlook" between lovers leaves no greater happiness "than to turn back to recapture former joy."

Many of the poems in *Day by Day* turn back, but they do not recapture any great amount of joy. They confront the same doubts and uncertainties, the same monsters from within, that have haunted Lowell's verse almost from the start and have become more insistent since publication in 1959 of his famous *Life Studies*. By now, Lowell's themes are familiar, for the so-called "Confessional School of Poets," of which Lowell's was an early and compelling voice, has come close to dominating contemporary verse. Confessional poets—W. D. Snodgrass, Anne Sexton, John Berryman, Sylvia Plath, and, of course Lowell—do not always show their readers either beauty or truth. They show themselves.

It would be inaccurate to sum up the confessional poets under any single explanatory word or phrase. Alcoholism and mental disorder are as misleading as father-complex and existential despair. Still, when Lowell writes about reading an article on John Berryman, "as if recognizing my own obituary," he establishes kinship with the author of the *Dream Songs*. The article, Lowell tells us in "Unwanted," says Berryman's mother, "not mine," lacked an affectionate nature—"so he always loved what he missed."

Lowell has said that his *Life Studies* resulted from his impatience with prose methods in an autobiography. To a major extent, he has been writing his autobiography ever since but without the transitions and sequential logic prose requires. In *Day by Day,* the poet's earliest experiences find a place next to his present-day sensations. Poems about his fatherhood mingle with those about his uneasy sonhood. He addresses all three of his wives, apparently still wishing to understand the earlier relationships with fiction writer Jean Stafford and critic Elizabeth Hardwick as much as his latest marriage to Irish-born Caroline Blackwood. The book's final section, dedicated to Caroline Blackwood, provides the book's tentative sounding title. Some poems address her by name, but even those and others set in England, where he lived with her and their small children, betray the constant tug of the American scene which engrossed Lowell while it repulsed him.

Day by Day has its storyline, and doubtless Lowell's intimates follow it all. Perhaps it tells of the poet's return home, metaphorically as well as physically, or perhaps it does no more than tell of his resignation, if not acceptance, in the face of age and death. No matter what the central story, the reader is likely to feel like the *voyeur* character in Lowell's celebrated "Skunk Hour," out spying on lovers in parked cars. Those explicit accounts of "downward looks" between lovers and what they meant tell more than the reader may want to know. Two poems associated with airports ("Logan Airport, Boston" and "Morning After Dining with a Friend *(Some Weeks After Logan Airport")* hint at the problem: in the first, Lowell says he cannot "bring back youth with a snap of my belt, / I cannot touch you." In the second, "waking wifeless" has become a habit.

A poem like "Home," with its implicit complaints to a "you" who considers the speaker's illness a desertion, speaks of London and apparently alludes to Lowell's third wife. The poem's final lines mingle the religious and the secular: "The Queen of Heaven, I miss her, / we were divorced." Does Lowell, converted to Catholicism in 1940, the year of his marriage to Jean Stafford, and lapsed from the faith and divorced from Stafford, mean the Blessed Virgin—or a woman? Whoever, she had faith that the "divided, stricken soul / could call her Maria, / and rob the devil with a word." No matter whom the poem means, it cries out in pain and absence.

Lowell's personality emerges in *Day by Day* with all the engaging qualities of the familiar boyish photographs of him, and the critic tells himself in vain that liking the poet is *not* the point. Poetry as subjective as this invites the reader to take sides—to hope at the very least the poet will learn something from what is happening to him. In short, when the poem's subject is unabashedly the poet himself, its quality depends upon how rich, how varied, how intrinsically interesting the poet really is. Robert Lowell's self proves sufficient to sustain yet another book full of what an earlier time would have judged fit to be told only to one's priest or analyst.

Its classical title aside, the opening poem of the volume invites application to Lowell's life. "Ulysses and Circe" is ostensibly third-person, but the poet's voice intrudes in the fifth line to ask "Why should I renew his infamous sorrow?" When the first section ends with the hero's boast that "by force of fraud," he has done what no one else could do, one wonders if Lowell means himself. In "Unwanted," he calls his poetry a "farfetched misalliance / that made evasion a revelation." An important recurring word here is "misalliance"; in his "Epilogue," Lowell says "All's misalliance."

In Sections II–IV, Ulysses is a fugitive in Circe's "exotic palace," where "he dislikes everything / in his impoverished life of myth." The poet's, or Ulysses'? Ulysses speaks in Section V, but it is Lowell's preoccupation we hear: "Age . . . the bilge we cannot shake from the mop." In the sixth and final section of the poem, Ulysses returns to Ithaca and Penelope; or does Lowell return to America and to Elizabeth Hardwick, his wife of twenty-nine years? "Off Central Park" celebrates (one presumes) a return to Hardwick's apartment where, "The old movables keep their places; / . . . confidently out of style."

In "Ulysses and Circe," the lines "Nobody in Ithaca knows him, / and yet he is too much remarked" perfectly sum up Lowell's anonymity and fame. Early in the poem, "ten years to and ten years fro" and, at the end, "ten years fro and ten years to" document Lowell's comings and goings—tedium. The heroic subject diminishes with the image of the hero's gills—"Unnatural ventilation—vents / closed by a single lever / like cells in a jail." Ulysses—or Lowell?—is an oversized shark, "a vocational killer / in the machismo of senility."

The second poem, "Homecoming," reiterates the idea of the poet's "lost love hunting / your lost face" and retains the Homeric allusion. In a "town for the young" who break themselves against the surf, the aging speaker is homeless: "No dog knows my smell." Another poem, "Suburban Surf," associates Caroline Blackwood with surf, partly through its subtitle *("After Caroline's return"),* partly through images. "Lake Walk," set in Ireland, again speaks of disillusion. Seven years dwindle to "a diverting smile"; and "the misleading promise" appears "nomadic as yesterday's whirling snow, / all whiteness splotched."

Some, but not many, poems in *Day by Day* mark Lowell's strides toward quieting the old terrors, but mostly they reveal him continuing to "freelance on the razor's edge." Measuring his life in leavings and returnings, Lowell, still the little boy, registers surprise when things do not remain as he left them. The smarts to his ego during schooldays ("St. Mark's, 1933") remain as fresh as if administered yesterday; "To Frank Parker," a recollection of an evening with a friend forty years ago, comes out all sour. The June night in Massachusetts reminds him that grass and pollen produce "the asthma of high summer— / the inclination to drink, not eat." Age crops up again—"another species, / the nothing-voiced." Even survival seems of dubious value, "if two glasses of red wine are poison."

In poems to his parents ("To Mother" and "Robert T. S. Lowell") as well as in "Unwanted," Lowell peels additional protective layers from the "public man," until he touches his nerve—and the reader's. Regularly, Lowell's poems earn a tang of reality—at once local and particular and larger-than-life. Whatever else Lowell's autobiography-in-progress (now ended) may have done, it never hacked at the surface of life. Perhaps, though, Lowell should have recalled that he, not the critic, wrote the line in *The Dolphin* (1973) which undoes it all: "Everything is real until it's published."

That is the flaw in confessional poetry, even in a poem like "To Mother" with its apparent gain in compassion and understanding. At last, better than twenty years after his mother's death in 1954, Lowell can say that she is "as human as I am . . . / if I am." Was that final twist for the sake of the poem, or did the twist *really* arise from a felt change? In the long run, many of the poems here teeter between mere excellence of craft and genuine achievement, and too many of them smack of the child's "they'll-be-sorry-when-I'm-dead" line—said too late.

"Unwanted" ends with questions: ". . . will mother go on cleaning house / for eternity, and making it unlivable?" and "Is getting well ever an art, / or art a way to get well?" The possibility of mother's making eternity unlivable creates a fine ambiguity, but the final questions seem easy. Lowell practiced his art assiduously and well, but, from the looks of *Day by Day,* art did not provide a way to get well. Getting well is an art in itself, maybe impossible to achieve. The poem "Art of the Possible" proves that point.

Lowell knew the answer, or he discovered it in his "Epilogue," where he complains that his "blessed structures, plot and rhyme" will not help him make "something imagined, not recalled." He says that what he writes turns into snapshots, "lurid, rapid, garish"; the example of a painter like Vermeer reminds that "We are poor passing facts" and must give "each figure in the photograph / his living name."

Lowell is here, in this sometimes lurid, rapid, and garish photograph called *Day by Day.* And he has his living name by virtue of recording, in pain, much of America's collective anguish. His name and what he told, from 1944 through 1977, will stand among the glories and reproaches of America up to, and past, her bicentennial.

Leon V. Driskell

Sources for Further Study

Book World. September 25, 1977, p. H7.

Christian Century. XCIV, October 26, 1977, p. 77.

Harper's Magazine. CLV, December, 1977, p. 111.

New York Times Book Review. August 14, 1977, p. 1.

Newsweek. XC, September 5, 1977, p. 77.

Saturday Review. V, October 1, 1977, p. 26.

Time. CX, August 29, 1977, p. 70.

THE DEATH OF THE KING'S CANARY

Authors: Dylan Thomas (1914–1953) and John Davenport (1908–1966)
Publisher: The Viking Press (New York). 145 pp. $7.95
Type of work: Novel
Time: 1940
Locale: England, mostly Suffolk

A farcical murder mystery, primarily a surrealistic satire on the London literary set of the early 1940's, with witty parodies of notable poets and caricatures of major English critics and other arbiters of public taste

Principal characters:
 PRIME MINISTER OF ENGLAND
 HILARY BYRD, Poet-Laureate-elect
 OWEN TUDOR, Welsh poet and tippler, visitor at Dymmock Hall
 TOM AGARD, Tudor's friend
 JOHN LOWELL ATKINS, American-born poet
 ALBERT PONTING, a poet
 ROBERT GORDON, a poet
 CHRISTOPHER GARVIN, a poet
 SIR FRANK KNIGHT, a poet

A witty, often farcical satire on the brilliant London literary set of the early 1940's, *The Death of the King's Canary* was planned by Dylan Thomas in 1938, composed in collaboration with John Davenport in 1940, but not published for a variety of reasons until 1977, twenty-four years after Thomas' death and eleven years after Davenport's. Chief among the reasons for this long delay is the biographical problem. Thomas and Davenport not only parody the verse of eleven then-contemporary poets—most of them quite distinguished, others less prominent in their time and nearly forgotten in ours; they also caricature mercilessly the personal foibles of a number of these poets, and add for good measure pointed satirical sketches of other literary figures, well-known patrons of the arts, and some lesser lights: drawing-room types who support the literary salons and culture cults of the establishment.

Very likely, Thomas' editors were cautious about publishing a volume that might bring down upon their heads suits of character defamation; or they might have been influenced in behalf of some of the famous victims of the satire; or, from a practical viewpoint, they might have regarded the venture as unprofitable. Without question, the book would have appealed only to a limited audience of knowledgeable insiders who could identify the literary figures as real people. And the moment for publication was not at all propitious: English readers were too deeply involved in personal concerns of wartime survival to pay much attention to a literary burlesque. Now, however, these objections no longer carry weight. All of the significant writers who served as models for the satire are dead. And the parodies, some of which might have seemed savage when they were first written, can at present be judged on their artistic merit. So it is with gratitude that we receive this unexpected posthumous volume: an ebullient surrealistic satire composed in the least expected of forms—a murder mystery.

In a letter to Charles Fisher in 1938, Thomas first approached his Swansea friend to collaborate on a book then to be entitled *Murder of the King's Canary*. The novel was to be, in Thomas' words,

> . . . the detective story to end detective stories, introducing blatantly every character and situation—an inevitable Chinaman, secret passages, etc.—that no respectable writer would dare use now, drag hundreds of red herrings, false clues, withheld evidences into the story, falsify every issue, make many chapters deliberate parodies, full of clichés, of other detective writers.

Such a travesty presumably would have resembled Neil Simon's comedy *Murder by Death,* an intricate spoof on certain hackneyed conventions of detective fiction. According to Constantine FitzGibbon, whose Introduction to the volume is alternately helpful and cunningly mystifying, Fisher set to work on the project several months later and, in fact, produced a rough draft of a first chapter that "bears no relation to Chapter One of the Thomas/Davenport text." The original version, FitzGibbon notes, "assembles and describes characters, unknown to that text, as a committee to choose a new Poet Laureate: and that is all." Thereafter the joint effort was abandoned. In 1940 Thomas revived the idea, this time urging John Davenport to collaborate on the book. Davenport, a literary critic and former script writer for Hollywood, accepted the challenge that was "intended to be a good joke, and to make money." The authors set to work in a room that Davenport had fixed up, FitzGibbon writes, as "a model of an old-fashioned pub, complete with barrels of beer, while Caitlin [Thomas] danced in a distant summerhouse to the music of a portable gramophone."

Outside, the world was at war—1940 was a terrible year of massive bombings for Londoners—but snug in their boozy quarters, the authors sealed themselves from the shocks of reality. In their novel, to be sure, a bomb ticks and explodes on the lawn of the Prime Minister's house, but it "only killed a gardener"; and reports about a remote, somewhat comical war in Burma intrude intermittently upon the exuberant scene. But such interruptions merely emphasize the isolation of the action. The novel is closer in spirit to the frenetic 1920's or early 1930's than to the heroic decade of the 1940's. Like the early social satires of Aldous Huxley (*Crome Yellow, Antic Hay, Those Barren Leaves*), *The Death of the King's Canary* is frozen in time and set in a confined space, one in which characters who are caricatures of living people or of social types expose as mere shams their intellectual or artistic pretensions. Also, like the early satires of Evelyn Waugh (*Decline and Fall, Vile Bodies, A Handful of Dust*), the novel treats the theme of social decadence; frivolous, shallow characters betray their moral vacuity. Thus, the satire of *The Death of the King's Canary* has two objects: to ridicule the pretensions of specific individuals and, by extension, to ridicule the effete social class from which they emerge.

In its present version, the novel is quite different from the simple spoof on detective stories that Thomas originally intended to write. Instead, the book is a freewheeling assault on the inbred literary establishment that the poet both envied and distrusted. Among the poets whom Thomas and Davenport parodied, according to FitzGibbon, are such luminaries as T. S. Eliot, W. H. Auden, Stephen Spender, William Empson "and others who probably include Hugh MacDiarmid, John Squire, Keidrych Rhys, Vernon Watkins, and poets almost forgotten." In addition, important literary critics, at least one famous painter, and assorted influential persons are caricatured, among them Cyril Connolly, Augustus John, and Aleister Crowley. Also Thomas and Davenport appear (the former quite clearly as the bibulous Owen Tudor; the latter—probably—as Tom Agard, his companion in mischief).

In the guessing game that provides much of the malicious fun in reading the satire, the authors have been rather stingy providing clues. Assuredly, John Lowell Atkins is a dead ringer for T. S. Eliot: the sour, diffident, excessively cautious American poet. But other poets are more troublesome to identify. The early socialistic verses of Auden, MacNeice, and Spender, after all, are quite difficult to disentangle solely on the basis of content. We are probably safe in accepting FitzGibbon's advice: "A subtle scholar could devote a great deal of his time to speculation not only as to who is being parodied but also as to which of the co-authors wrote what in this curious book."

This final question is more than academic. Even in 1940 the reputations of the collaborators were disproportionate: Thomas the exciting poet and Davenport the competent writer-critic. Today the reader has even less interest in Davenport, whose name is remembered, if at all, chiefly for his connection with *The Observer;* on the other hand, Thomas' reputation as a poet, dramatist, short story writer, and novelist has continued to grow to giant stature in the twentieth century. So it would be useful to know what portions of the novel are Thomas', what lesser parts Davenport's. Unfortunately, the reader cannot easily separate on the basis either of style or ideas the different hands of the authors. Much of the writing must have been jointly—and spontaneously—dashed off. The prose style resembles that of Thomas' novel-fragment published in *Adventures in the Skin Trade* more than his more genial, relaxed style of *Portrait of the Artist as a Young Dog.* Indeed, he was thinking about *Adventures in the Skin Trade,* we learn from Vernon Watkins, in 1940, and by May, 1941, had completed ten thousand words of that work. Like the style of his uncompleted novel fragments, *The Death of the King's Canary* is written in tight, nervous, often elliptical prose; it is witty and full of comic juxtapositions; and it contrasts sharp, realistic details with symbolic imagery. A few passages of the text show another quality of Thomas' prose: startling Jungian, symbolic phrases that resemble other phrases from the Welsh stories also collected in *Adventures in the Skin Trade.* But these passages are scattered; and the religious-obsessive aspects of Thomas' work are less clearly apparent in this book than the social satire.

One would hope, at the least, that the brilliant parodies in Chapter One are Thomas'. But FitzGibbon cautions the reader that Thomas "maintained" his friend Davenport had written most of them. FitzGibbon's own judgment on this matter is not very helpful: ". . . if Dylan was not proud of them, he would have given their authorship to John." But he goes on to say that other critics believe the skill of the parodies "is far beyond what were Davenport's capabilities." Certainly the droll poem ascribed to "Albert Ponting" shows verbal pyrotechnics (and wit) of the highest order. If the object of the parody is, let us say, Vernon Watkins, it is also subtly a parody as well of Thomas' early convoluted metaphysical verse, especially the final line: "I raise to the mirror the maggots and lumps of my terror."

Far less important than the literary parodies, the plot of the novel— appropriately silly—functions as a slender cord on which to stretch the satire. It seems that the Prime Minister of England, forced to select a Poet Laureate among a group of incompetents, fortifies himself with brandy so that, fairly intoxicated, he picks the most outrageous of a bad lot. Hilary Byrd, the "King's canary"—His Majesty's private songbird—is (like Thomas and Davenport) the author of a book of poetic parodies. But the Prime Minister cannot discriminate well in his inebriated condition among samples of bad verse and parodies of bad verse. Nevertheless the choice is made, much to the consternation of the competing poets, who are further humiliated by being invited to attend the new Laureate's elevation at Dymmock Hall. In one of the most rollicking scenes of the novel, Byrd delivers his acceptance speech before an abashed assembly of literary twerps, systematically abusing in turn each of his poetical rivals. It is a harangue quite as amusing as Jim Dixon's drunken "Merrie England" lecture in Amis' *Lucky Jim,* but crueller. After comparing members of his audience with the most detestable Laureates in English literary history, such poetic dun- derheads as Thomas Shadwell, Nahum Tate, Nicolas Rowe, Laurence Eusden, Colly Cibber, and so on—a modern Dunciad—he is fair game to be murdered. And murdered he is, in the final sentence of the novel: "Crammed into the midget house, one foot through the stairs, his head lolling through the window, Hilary Byrd lay smiling with a knife through his throat." But who polished the rascal off? Thomas and Davenport never say. Probably it doesn't matter, anyway. For all we know, the whole screeching choir of poets murdered the king's canary. As FitzGibbon reminds us, Dylan Thomas' announced policy towards the world was "Bewilder 'em."

Leslie B. Mittleman

Sources for Further Study

Atlantic. CCXXXIX, June, 1977, p. 94.

Choice. XIV, July, 1977, p. 867.

Christian Science Monitor. LXIX, June 1, 1977, p. 31.

Kirkus Reviews. XLV, March 15, 1977, p. 308.

Library Journal. CII, April 15, 1977, p. 950.

New York Times Book Review. May 15, 1977, p. 12.

Publisher's Weekly. CXI, March 14, 1977, p. 91.

DECADE OF DECISIONS
American Policy Toward the Arab-Israeli Conflict, 1967-1976

Author: William B. Quandt (1941–   )
Publisher: University of California Press (Berkeley, Calif.). 313 pp. $14.95
Type of work: Current affairs
Locale: Washington, D.C., Israel, Egypt, Syria, Jordan

An explanation and narrative of United States policy regarding the Arab-Israeli conflict between 1967 and 1976, with particular attention to crisis decisions

> *Principal personages:*
> LYNDON B. JOHNSON, President of the United States, 1963–1968
> RICHARD M. NIXON, President of the United States, 1969–1974
> GERALD FORD, President of the United States, 1974–1976
> HENRY KISSINGER, national security adviser to the President, 1969–1975, and Secretary of State, 1973–1976
> WILLIAM P. ROGERS, Secretary of State, 1969–1973

Suppose that the common Israeli nightmare came true: the Arabs defeat Israel in battle, and threaten to overrun the country. Lives are at stake: thousands, perhaps hundreds of thousands or more Jews might soon perish in the second holocaust of the twentieth century. Would the United States intervene to save Israel, even at a serious risk of nuclear confrontation with the Soviet Union?

To answer such a question, or any other of the key questions about the Middle East, it would be of value to know exactly how our policymakers have acted and what they have thought during the Middle East crises of the recent past. Surprisingly, the general reader must search hard to find a comprehensive, objective account of American actions and motivations. The abundant journalistic and academic literature on the Middle East is selective, if not sensational, in coverage, and partisan in tone. To this generalization, Quandt's book offers one of the few exceptions. It ranks, indeed, as the best book now available for the general reader inquiring into recent American policy on the Arab-Israeli conflict.

The solidity of Quandt's contribution in this, his third book, will come as no surprise to those acquainted with his career. He has already established himself, at a young age, as a firstrate political analyst. Born in Los Angeles in 1941 and educated at Stanford and M.I.T., Quandt has been employed during the last decade by the RAND Corporation, and has served on the staff of the National Security Council (1972–1974; 1977–   ). His first two books explored "intra-elite divisiveness" in radical Arab political causes: a 1969 work on the Algerian revolutionary elite, and a 1973 work (co-authored) on the Palestinian movement. He published several noteworthy articles in the early 1970's on the comparative study of elites and on the domestic sources of United States Middle East policy. These books and articles have earned Quandt a reputation for excellence in both style and substance. They are not only well-written and well-organized, but also rigorous in methodology and meticulous in scholarship. All these virtues are displayed again in his current book. But the topic is one of such scope and complexity that even Quandt's talents are insufficient to provide us with a completely satisfying account.

This view holds true despite an additional advantage Quandt enjoyed in writing his current book—proximity to the centers of power during two of the most crucial years in the decade he covers. As a member of the National Security Council staff, he attended interagency meetings at which Kissinger and others discussed policy. He also was able to obtain, then and subsequently, interviews with American, Arab, and Israeli leaders who might not have been so accessible to a scholar less respected and less highly placed. Not surprisingly, his account of the 1972–1974 period is written with a conviction and force not matched elsewhere in the book. Yet, even with these additional resources, questions can be raised both about Quandt's general approach, and about his handling of many specific points.

To be sure, Quandt's approach is a popular one. He centers his attention on the top-level foreign policy "decision makers" in the executive branch of the government—on Johnson and Nixon, Kissinger and Ford. Most journalists and many political scientists also analyze foreign policy at the level of the individual. Not all of them would take Quandt's next, and narrowing, step: a focus on the "definition of the situation" held by our policymakers, and a particular concern with how crisis changes these definitions. Quandt chronicles three Middle East crises, and attempts to show that each one generated a "definition of the situation" that governed United States actions in the (usually) three years before the next crisis. Thus, the "lessons" of the June, 1967, war led to the "Rogers Plan" of 1969–1970; the September, 1970, Jordanian crisis was so interpreted as to create the "standstill diplomacy" of 1971–1973; and the October, 1973, war sparked the Sinai I (1974) and Sinai II (1975) disengagement agreements. Quandt's general plan is to devote one chapter to each crisis, followed by another chapter on the postcrisis period of diplomatic maneuvering; Sinai I and Sinai II, however, are each given a separate chapter.

One flaw in this book by a scholar noted for rigorous methodology is that he fails to define either "definition of situation" or "crisis." Perhaps these omissions were designed to make the book less formal and forbidding to the general reader; and specialists can easily supply the standard definitions. A "definition of the situation" relates to perceptions about the future behavior and basic characteristics of other nations, and to conceptions of appropriate ways for dealing with them. A "crisis" is a threatening event that comes as a surprise, and that allows only a short time for response. Thus, in the September, 1970, Jordanian crisis, the United States had to decide quickly on a response to the Syrian tank invasion of Jordan in support of the Palestinians. The situation was defined as one in which a hostile Soviet Union was using Syria as a proxy to bolster the Palestinians, and in which a sequence of Israeli and American military threats was the appropriate response.

More fundamental problems beset Quandt's endeavor to use a "decision-making" approach as the best means for explaining United States foreign policy toward the Arab-Israeli conflict. First, the evidence available is inevitably incomplete and unreliable. Quandt has had unusual opportunities to learn what really happened, and he has used these opportunities well. But interviews, public statements, government documents, and personal observations—the constituents of Quandt's "data base"—still leave gaps in our knowledge of what occurred. Only the two principals know what was said in the daily meetings between Nixon and Kissinger, or in the numerous telephone calls between them. When their memoirs come out, their accounts of these exchanges will probably conflict, and many readers will choose to believe neither. In short, a perfect reconstruction of policymakers' "definition of the situation" is impossible. How, then, can we generalize about the impact of crises on these definitions, when we cannot be sure of the definitions held either before or after the crises?

A second difficulty with Quandt's approach relates to what foreign policy specialists call the "level of analysis" problem. It is of no value to study the "perceptions and understandings" of Johnson or Nixon unless it can first be shown that these perceptions and understandings make some difference. And many specialists deny that they do. These specialists would explain United States policy in the Middle East by reference to other levels of analysis: to the influence of the bureaucracy, to the power of public opinion and domestic pressure groups, or to the strategic requirements for survival in the "global system." If changes at these other levels can adequately explain shifts in American foreign policy, then there is no need for analysis at the level of the individual. If, for example, pro-Israeli pressure in the United States is too strong for any President to resist, then it matters little who the President is, or what he thinks about the Middle East. Our policy in the Middle East will be explained by reference to the strength of the pressure group, not to the direction of presidential sentiments.

Quandt is well aware of this difficulty, and he deals with it forthrightly in his opening chapter. He concedes that his approach is incomplete, but vigorously argues its superiority over the three alternatives most in fashion with academicians and journalists (domestic politics, bureaucratic politics, and the strategic-national interest approaches). For each of the approaches, he provides a compact statement of the premises, an assessment of the strengths and weaknesses, and an application to the Middle East. The statements are fair, the critiques are incisive, and the applications are often brilliant. Indeed, his overall examination of the four approaches is one of the most cogent on record.

Yet, some curious problems remain. In much of the book, the individual receiving the most study is Henry Kissinger. Quandt's approach (which he calls the "Presidential leadership" approach) assumes that something important is to be learned by studying the perceptions and understandings of the President and his key advisers. But Kissinger, in his academic career, adhered to the "strategic-national interest" approach that Quandt downplays. Thus, when Quandt reveals what he believes to be the content of Kissinger's thought during crises, it turns out to be almost exactly what national interest analysts would have predicted: an overwhelming concern with the United States-Soviet Union rivalry as it threatens the physical survival, economic prosperity, and personal liberties of Americans. Since this content is what national interest analysts would have predicted, the additional value of the presidential leadership approach is not obvious.

Another problem is Quandt's static view of the other levels of analysis. If United States policy shifts, and if no concomitant change has occurred in other levels of analysis, then there would be more justification for the prominence Quandt accords to the views of Presidents and advisers. But this was not the case in the 1967–1976 period. Most dramatically, a major shift occurred in the global balance of military power: Russia moved from a position of clear inferiority to one of rough parity. Israel lost much of its support in Asia and Africa; at the same time, its political system showed serious signs of decay. The "front-line" Arab countries entered an unusual period of political stability. Little of this appears in Quandt's work; yet these changes surely made a difference in the policy the United States adopted.

A glance at some individual chapters will illustrate additional problems. Quandt's first case study, that of the Johnson Administration and the June, 1967, war, is also his weakest. This is not because of his factual grasp. As always, he has been diligent in pursuing the truth about what happened. Indeed, a book published in the same year as Quandt's—the autobiography of Abba Eban, Israel's Foreign Minister in 1967—provides independent corroboration of his account.

Where Quandt fails is in conveying the long-lasting emotional impact of the events of May–June 1967. Israelis underwent weeks of trauma from which they have not yet recovered, and then received a gigantic gift which they have not yet assimilated. The trauma came in late May, 1977, when all the world, including the vacillating United States, seemed about to abandon Israel after Nasser's closing of the Straits of Tiran, Israel's economic lifeline. Many Israelis have testified that these weeks reawakened their memories of the Holocaust; many thought that a similar fate would soon engulf them. This period of trauma permanently intensified the insecurity feelings of much of the population, creating a political fallout that lasts to this day. Quandt criticizes Johnson's vacillation and failure to deter a war; the longer term emotional impact seems to have been beyond his ken.

After the trauma came the gift. The territory under Jewish control qua-drupled. Most of Israel's population was intellectually and emotionally un-prepared for the new situation. As Nadav Safran puts its, previous to 1967, Israel had followed an offensive military policy, but not a political policy of expansionism. In the wake of May's trauma, though, few were ready to return all of June's conquests. Territory has a concreteness and tangibility that great power guarantees do not. From 1967 on, Washington's assurances would always be received with some doubt. Many of Kissinger's problems in Sinai I and Sinai II might thus be traced to Johnson's legacy—a point Quandt overlooks.

What this chapter may reflect is a common problem with the "palace approach" to diplomacy. Too much is said about positions on problems, too little about the roots of problems. Quandt's expertise on the former is admirable. But his weak presentation of the latter leaves his pages peopled with dim figures, actors who are labeled ("tough but emotional" Golda Meir) but whose actions are not adequately motivated.

Henry Kissinger stands forth as the one exception. Of all the figures in the book, it is Kissinger who receives the most complex and sharp delineation. Nixon, in comparison, is a figure somewhere in the background. Part of this contrast comes from Nixon's practice of letting Kissinger be the front man and the detail man for his foreign policy—the virtuoso tactician who both promoted and executed Nixon's strategy. Part comes from Kissinger's superior talent for self-dramatization. But one sometimes wonders how far Quandt has adopted the current academic habit of giving Kissinger credit for all of Nixon's sound foreign policy moves, and leaving Nixon to be judged only on the basis of the unsound ones.

The chapters in which Kissinger is in the foreground, the chapters on events from 1973 to 1975, are often electric with excitement. Quandt is an admirer, but with reservations. He has substantial doubts about Sinai II, but none about the intelligence, energy, and dedication of the man who forged it. One aspect of Sinai II escapes him. With his curious insensitivity to the regional arms race, Quandt overlooks the point that Kissinger, to secure Israeli approval, made commitments on arms that gave Israel absolute military superiority into the 1980's. Kissinger thereby bargained away much of the leverage on Israel that the United States would otherwise have had after 1977.

Quandt concludes his book with some guidelines for the future based on the lessons of the past. This is not the conclusion one might have expected from the start of the book; at the least, some systematic comparison of the crises should have been given, and their effect on "definitions of the situation." By this point, however, Quandt is more interested in the content of policy than in the process by which it is achieved. The guidelines he offers are intelligent ideas carefully formulated, but they do not follow inevitably from the case studies in the preceding chapters. Quandt here fails to face the fundamental ambiguity of historical events; his guidelines might have led to a better policy in the early 1970's, but no one will ever know for sure.

On the whole, Quandt's book can be compared to a strong but narrow band of light; it illuminates the areas that it covers, but it throws the surroundings into deep shadow. No one can read it without understanding better one set of factors in the evolution of our policy. But other aspects still need to be covered. One can only hope that those who cover them share Quandt's high order of analytical intelligence and dedication to establishing the truth.

William D. Anderson

Sources for Further Study

Publisher's Weekly. CCXII, October 31, 1977, p. 54.

DELMORE SCHWARTZ
The Life of an American Poet

Author: James Atlas (1949–   )
Publisher: Farrar, Straus and Giroux (New York). 418 pp. $15.00
Type of work: Biography
Time: 1913–1966
Locale: The East Coast of the U.S., mainly New York City

A study which compiles various documents about the life of Delmore Schwartz, a representative, contemporary American poet, and portrays vividly the flowering of the East Coast intelligentsia

> *Principal personages:*
> DELMORE SCHWARTZ, the American poet
> HARRY AND ROSE SCHWARTZ, his parents
> GERTRUDE BUCKMAN SCHWARTZ, his first wife
> ELIZABETH POLLET SCHWARTZ, his second wife
> JAMES LAUGHLIN, his friend and publisher for New Directions
> WILLIAM BARRETT, another friend

This biography of the contemporary American poet Delmore Schwartz collects an enormous amount of material from letters, journals, notebooks, poems, short stories, and anecdotes. The information follows a chronological pattern of exposition, as Atlas piles item upon item from the seemingly inexhaustible records on the bizarre personality of his subject. In this way, he achieves a degree of detachment, a questionable virtue given the nature of his subject matter. For clearly Delmore Schwartz was deeply disturbed during the last years of his life, and he managed during that time to alienate many people, including celebrities, luminaries, professors, students, admirers, and friends. Atlas discreetly modulates his tone so as not to aggravate further, to rebuke, or to embarrass those left in the wake of the poet's mad fantasies and conspiracies. Yet the question remains: would the biography of Delmore Schwartz have been more effective had Atlas investigated more thoroughly the nature of his subject's delusions? By examining these problems, Atlas would have discovered a penetrating thesis.

Schwartz was an intense intellectual, and Atlas traces the development of this distinguishing quality of his life. Schwartz read ferociously and voluminously from an early age, probably to escape the tormenting atmosphere of his household. His mother is characterized as a whining, manipulative, evil-tempered woman, and his father is described as a philandering, irresponsible playboy, who later deserted the family circle, even though he managed to amass a fortune and financially to support the family—mother, Delmore, and younger brother—from afar. But it seems as though he was as much a contributing factor to Delmore's emotional distress as the mother, with his pseudo-affectionate, then abandoning, actions toward his sons. While the younger brother seemed to have escaped the harmful effects of such a family setting by withdrawing into the mundane, Delmore dangerously withdrew into fantasy and books, and at an early age he set himself up to become the greatest poet who ever lived.

While not a distinguished student at public school—apparently his emotional problems were already too powerful an obstacle—Schwartz still managed to gain some favorable recognition among certain circles in the teeming intellectual atmosphere of New York City during the 1920's and 1930's. But his father's death, the realization that the elder man had dissipated a fortune, leaving little if anything for the support of his family, and his mother's growing hysteria all contributed to his increasing unhappiness and alienation from the real emotions of others. He was accepted by the University of Wisconsin, but his studies were soon aborted because of a lack of funds. He enrolled at the Washington Square College at New York University, where he truly began his career, among the literati of that high-powered intellectual society.

At NYU, Schwartz was determined to make a name for himself. He threw himself into campus activities, literary clubs, and social involvements with eminent writers and scholars who visited the university. But his relationships with others were already colored by that emotional detachment which so characterizes narcissistic personality disorders. He entangled himself in relationships with unnatural ardor. He demanded unqualifying allegiance from friends, turning that allegiance into a powerful manipulative weapon by which he dominated their lives. And finally, he broke off abruptly with his various sets of friends, usually by inventing some imaginary slight or grounds for contention. This syndrome sets the pattern throughout his life, from his relationships with colleagues to his involvements with different women. The tragedy is that he was aware to a large extent of the nature of his infirmity. Having studied Freud in the way that he studied and mastered a whole wealth of intellectual knowledge, he attempted to conduct psychoanalysis upon himself. Most astutely, he recognized "the cessation of love object in narcissism," as he described it, the idea that he was incapable of achieving an intimate relationship with another person. Clearly he was aware of his condition, but helpless to reverse it.

In addition to being unable to conduct a successful self-analysis, it seems as though Schwartz was unresponsive to psychiatric treatment when he sought it, and he went through a succession of different psychiatrists. One of the most pathetic incidents in the book occurs after his second wife leaves him, having been subjected to a "reign of terror" for years by her mentally unbalanced husband. She left word that she would not see him again unless he entered a hospital, and Delmore, in a panic, violently besieged the hotel room of a man he and his wife barely knew, having invented the improbable tale of an adulterous affair between them. Just as he was about to be hauled off to the police station, he informed the detective: "My psychiatrist tells me that I'm not crazy, I'm just angry." That same day, he was committed to Bellevue Psychiatric Hospital in New York City.

Before he descended to these depths, however, Delmore Schwartz made a remarkable name for himself among New York literati. With the publication of his first volume at the age of twenty-five, *In Dreams Begin Responsibilities,* he was heralded as the most promising young American poet. He received praise from luminaries such as Allen Tate, Mark Van Doren, John Crowe Ransom, and Philip Rahv. His circle of acquaintanceship was highly impressive. He was at one time associated with the most outstanding group of intellectuals, critics, poets, and novelists of the time, including Lionel Trilling, Alfred Kazin, Saul Bellow, Mary McCarthy, Robert Lowell, and John Berryman.

Schwartz's writings were mythological presentations of his own life. "His only subject was himself—quite undisguised," he recorded in his journal, and he conceived of his own experience as "fabulous at every point," celebrating his "detailed and avid memory, his endless tracking down of motives." His commitment to his writing was absolute, and understandably so, since through his work he channeled his pent-up frustrations and anxieties for as long as he was able. The autobiographical nature of his writings helped him to impose some discipline upon what must have seemed unmanageable drives and influxes of emotion. He experienced at times, even during his college years, long bouts of depression during which he was "trying to feel," and wondering if he had some deficiency of intellect or sensibility. He subjected his work to impossible standards, measuring his own poems against what he read with unsparing self-criticism. He turned out an impressive amount of writing, including poems, short stories, and excellent literary criticism. The literary criticism, in particular, put aside the self-conscious mannerisms and self-centeredness that sometimes flawed his imaginative works, in favor of confidence and restraint. He published essays on subjects ranging from the aesthetics of poetry to particular poets (Rimbaud, Thomas Hardy, Ezra Pound, T. S. Eliot, W. H. Auden, Allen Tate, John Crowe Ransom, Wallace Stevens, Theodore Roethke), fiction writers (Ring Lardner, John Dos Passos, André Gide, Ernest Hemingway, William Faulkner), and movie people (W. C. Fields and Mary Pickford). Like his conversational style, his essays and reviews were formidable and incisive, with a masterful sense of language, yet with the strident, humorous, rough edge that so typified his manner of expression.

Schwartz's poetry and short stories were published in the most respectable literary journals of the period, as were his essays. He was a distinguished contributor to the *Partisan Review,* where he later became poetry editor, holding that post for more than a decade. He also contributed with regularity to *The New Republic, The Kenyon Review, Common Sense, The Nation, The Sewanee Review,* and *The New York Times Book Review.* His most popular books, written early in his career, were published by New Directions under the auspices of James Laughlin, and included *A Season in Hell* (a translation of Rimbaud), 1939; *In Dreams Begin Responsibilities* (chiefly poetry), 1939; *Shenandoah* (a play), 1941; *Genesis, Book One* (poetry), 1943; and *The World Is a Wedding* (short stories), 1948. In addition, Schwartz filled notebooks and journals to the very end of his life, and he heavily annotated the volumes in his extensive library.

It was supposed to be part of Schwartz's charm that he was crazy, and one can easily see from Atlas' account that he was cultivated for this notoriety by that East Coast crowd of eccentric academics in the 1940's and 1950's—America's answer to the Bloomsbury circle. The alienated Jew, the bohemian, the *poète maudit*, the modern intellectual hero—Schwartz embodied any number of these desirable and therefore popular epithets. But most of all, he was celebrated during his lifetime as a professional maniac. The legend lives on most recently in Saul Bellow's *Humboldt's Gift,* whose hero closely resembles the poet in his later years when Bellow knew him.

Schwartz's religion was his art, and he used to believe that he could solve life's problems by sitting at the typewriter and working them through. Poetry animated the past and imbued it with form, discipline, and instructive insight. Art allowed him to escape from the world while promising him salvation: his aspiration was to discover in past experience the remedy for his suffering soul, and only when he could no longer write did he begin the long descent into madness that led to his premature death. Atlas somewhat rushes through these last years, describing an indiscriminate series of academic positions, women, and cheap hotel rooms: Schwartz could never hold onto anything long, and this problem worsened toward the end of his life. He was addicted to drugs and drinking, and possibly the psychotic condition of his last years was in part drug-induced.

It would have been interesting for Atlas to speculate in greater detail on the nature of his subject's psychopathological condition, since the poet was a devotee of Freud and his own work was so analytically inspired. This tendency to treat insubstantially the crucial etiological factors which destroyed Schwartz, who was himself so obsessed by them, is a flaw in Atlas' presentation. Such an exploration might have accounted for the poet's inability to achieve first-rate status as an American writer; the question is ubiquitous and perplexing, given Schwartz's apparently undaunted preparation and ambition. Had Atlas investigated this, he might have avoided leaving his reader with uneasy feelings about the writer's artistic as well as personal self-destruction. On the deeper level, Schwartz had no chance for enduring success from the start: the high-powered intellectual society in which he lived, which rather cruelly delighted in taking up the *poète maudit,* effectively camouflaged for a while the lack of enjoyment and emotional capacity, and therefore true creativity, of this pitiable man. A tribute to Delmore Schwartz is his valiant, lonely struggle to develop subliminal channels for so long in order to stay a severe constitutional impairment.

Gloria Sybil Gross

Sources for Further Study

Booklist. LXXIV, November 1, 1977, p. 451.
Kirkus Reviews. XLV, September 15, 1977, p. 1016.
Library Journal. November 15, 1977, p. 2347.

THE DESTINIES OF DARCY DANCER, GENTLEMAN

Author: J. P. Donleavy (1926–   )
Publisher: Delacorte Press (New York). 402 pp. $9.95
Type of work: Novel
Time: World War II
Locale: Ireland

A comic novel about the growing up and misadventures of Darcy Dancer

Principal characters:
DARCY DANCER, the hero of the novel, an adolescent open to
experience
MR. ARLAND, his tutor, a sensitive man in love
CROOKS AND SEXTON, two comic servants
FOXY, a rascally neighborhood lad
LOIS, an artist friend of Darcy

The Destinies of Darcy Dancer, Gentleman is J. P. Donleavy's seventh novel. Written in the comic spirit, it understands the difference between the serious and the solemn. The novel is about the joy and agony of growing up, but the joy is not elevated to spirituality and the agony is not uplifted into tragedy. Men and women suffer and die, but suffering and dying are not dwelt upon. Nothing, in fact, is allowed to interfere with the hero's zest in his encounter with life, nor the author's zest in his encounter with the reader.

This zest is interwoven in the novel's fabric, part of which is made up of Darcy's stream of consciousness:

> Darcy Dancer leaving the dining room. Chin down. Spine bent. Step back up these few carpeted steps. Treading on the wool woven roses. Go out. Not know where I'm going. Nor care. Why she adored. Walk. On these night time streets. Away through one's crashing dreams. Under lamplight. On the grey speckled blocks of granite. Leave the fence at Trinity. A pub Lincoln's Inn. Big closed back gates of the college. Light in the porter's lodge. Turkish turrets across the street. Down Westland Row. Stone pillars of a church. Iron pillars of a bridge. Train chugging over. Every part of her comes haunting. The slap she gave me in the face. The album of her castles. The ballrooms. The waltzing ladies and gentlemen. Charging at me on her rearing horse. All the way to the moored looming shadowy ships on this black river flowing through this black city.

The syntax of this passage is full of interest. Despite the fact that it represents Darcy silently speaking his inmost thoughts, it is in the third person. Having just seen the woman he is convinced he loves "adoring" another man, Darcy is fighting despair by distancing himself from himself: hence the third person. Verbs are also cunningly used, imperatives like "walk" indicating self-commands of actions ordinarily automatic, participles indicating continuously observed actions. Finally, the variation of sentence fragments and whole sentences—the syntactical rhythm—is part of the meaning. The whole passage consists of fragments except for brief imperatives, until "Every part of her comes haunting." Again the fragments trip over one another until the gloomy poetry of the final sentence.

Up to the sentence "Every part of her comes haunting," Darcy is preoccupied with getting out of the dining room, away from Miss von B's presence. His task is difficult to manage because his feelings keep breaking through—"Why she adored. . . . Away through one's crashing dreams." Finally Darcy seemingly masters himself and we see and hear only his observations on his nocturnal sojourn. But self-composure is impossible.—"Every part of her comes haunting." No more perfect image of lost love seems possible. The catalogue that follows is a mere smattering of this onrush of images, dissolving in the final dark sentence that irretrievably sums up Darcy's mood.

This paragraph certainly could not exist if it were not for Faulkner's and Joyce's experiments with stream of consciousness. But Donleavy's stream of consciousness is only one step removed from first-person narrative. Darcy, although perhaps not in full control of himself, is certainly in full control of the narrative. The keenness of his sensations give even his despair a buoyancy. So close to himself, he will never escape into real despair. He creates out of his anguish a poem that more than half comes to terms with anguish. Even in emotional pain, Darcy has not lost his zest for life.

Donleavy's brilliant adaptation of stream of consciousness technique is matched by his brilliance in the use of dialogue. In a boy's school, Darcy, who asserts himself against the tyranny of the other boys, is about to be punished by them. First, however, they must get a hold on him:

> Touch me and each of you will regret it in turn.
> Grab him.
> Let go of me.
> Hold him, for god's sake, hold him.
> Christ he's strong.
> Hold him, get his head in a lock. Get him down, down.
> Bloody hell don't let him loose, knocking over the candles.
> Get him . . .
> O christ, where the hell is everyone.
> I've got him.
> No you haven't, you've got me . . .
> A newspaper is alight.
> Put it out you sod.
> I can't while this . . . (Darcy) is loose
> I've got him.
> You've got me again, you sod.

Two points should be made about this dialogue. First, it is natural. Donleavy has a good ear for the vocabulary and speech rhythms of these adolescents. Second, the dialogue is self-sufficient; it carries along the narrative. We can see Darcy standing before his juvenile tribunal; we can see them grapple with him; we can see the candles knocked over in the struggle; the blind grappling in the dark; the resulting conflagration. True, the dialogue contains stage directions— "knocking over the candles"; "A newspaper is alight"—but they are a natural part of the dialogue and do not intrude on its elegance and economy.

Brilliant as these two passages are, they are not in themselves comic; to be seen as part of the comic spirit, they must be viewed in the context of the whole novel. Darcy's stream of consciousness despair is real, but shortlived. Two pages later he blackmails an acquaintance on an adulterous fling, meets "Ronald Ronald Ronald," a con man, and starts on a new adventure. In the case of the dialogue in the boy's school, it looks as if our hero's comeuppance is near at hand; he is about to be hurt and humiliated by a group of sadistic fellow students, boys he has come to detest after only one day in attendance. However, the struggle so feelingly described, and the conflagration so cunningly alluded to provide sufficient confusion for Darcy to effect his escape, armed only with sets of long underwear and a carton of fudge filched from a less than generous new acquaintance.

Thus comedy does not exclude seriousness, but keeps it in check. For the main characters of the novel are unabashedly serious. Mr. Arland, Darcy's tutor, Miss von B, the housekeeper who initiates Darcy into the mysteries of life, and Darcy Dancer himself. Mr. Arland is clearly intelligent and sensitive and unfortunately in love with a young woman who rejects him. Finally he finds what he thinks is happiness with a woman named Clarissa, and is transformed. In Clarissa's presence, he says to Darcy: "And now what would you like in the way of sandwiches. How about a smoked salmon, eh." Darcy observes: "Never before in my entire knowledge have I ever heard Mr. Arland utter the word eh. Something has distinctly changed. Even his crossed leg has his foot jiggling up and down. A movement he told me no gentleman ever makes." The affair ends unhappily. Clarissa seems unfaithful; he rejects her; she kills herself; he disappears.

This tale is hardly comic. Nevertheless it should be noted that Mr. Arland's first, rejecting sweetheart is a participant in a series of comic adventures that make clear her complete unsuitability as his future bride. Moreover, Darcy hears about Clarissa's death in the least solemn of circumstances: in the midst of a comic misadventure with a woman who, as it turns out, is Clarissa's sister.

Neither is Miss von B's story of violation, destitution, and bare survival in wartorn Poland the stuff of comedy. Still, her affair with Darcy is laced with the comedy of her snobbery punctuated by her not-quite-successful attempts at learning colloquial English. Finally, the last scene between Darcy and Miss von B is not their sad parting, but an accidental meeting where she has clearly overcome her sorrow for him in her adoration for another man.

But it is Darcy himself who is the hero of the tale. In some sense his story is that of the romantic hero growing into manhood. In his search for maturity he reaches after schooling, love, career. These are all serious matters, but Donleavy does not treat them seriously. Darcy's formal schooling is a matter of one day: his search for love is a series of comic misadventures, and his chosen career is that of the idle rich. Oddly, he succeeds at this last. After running up his bogus credit to monstrous proportions at the best Dublin shops, hotels, and restaurants, he attends the races, bets on a long shot on a tip from a casual acquaintance, and wins a fortune on a horse that is the progeny of the stallion Dancer. The accident and the coincidence are doubly absurd. Darcy does not earn his success, except by effrontery; he is Horatio Alger in reverse.

The novel's title refers to Darcy's destinies. One meaning of these destinies is undoubtedly Darcy's seemingly infinite possibilities stemming from his youth and his pluck. Another meaning is the number of "lives" he lives as a result of his comic journey. He starts out as a member of the gentry, becomes a lower and then an upper servant to the *nouveaux riche* class, and ends as an impecunious and finally a well-fixed gentleman. In part these changes in class are stages in Darcy's education. As a result of his adventure as a servant, "Never again shall I treat the servants of Andromeda Park in a thoughtless and uncaring manner." However, such insights are by the way. The main point of all these changes is to wring the last bit of comedy out of the novel. Darcy's insight into social conditions is followed by a comic encounter. Darcy as an ill-kempt servant delivers turf to the drawing room, picks up a current magazine and plops himself down on the sofa. Enter the lady of the house.

Donleavy's most recent comic novel makes delightful reading. Donleavy is a master of narrative, but he is more than that. His most important characters have the vividness of real people. They are firmly anchored in flesh and blood concerns of loving and living. However, they are not so firmly planted in seriousness as to make *The Destinies of Darcy Dancer* anything but a comic novel. Finally we are left with the author's sense of fun, his feeling for the absurdities of life and the ability of the comic spirit to overcome them.

Alan G. Gross

Sources for Further Study

Atlantic. CXL, December, 1977, p. 109.

Book World. August 28, 1977, p. F2.

Harper's Magazine. CCLV, December, 1977, p. 107.

Kirkus Reviews. XLV, September 15, 1977, p. 1003.

New York Times Book Review. November 6, p. 15.

Publisher's Weekly. CXII, Septem

Saturday Review. V, November 12, 1977, p. 27.

Time. CX, November 14, 1977, p. 111.

THE DIARIES OF EVELYN WAUGH

Author: Evelyn Waugh (1903–1966)
Edited by Michael Davie
Publisher: Little, Brown and Company (Boston). 814 pp. $17.50
Type of work: Diaries

A uniquely informed view of many facets of modern British life, including the public school experience, the Bright Young People, World War II, and fashionable literary society

> *Principal personages:*
> ARTHUR WAUGH, his father
> ALEC WAUGH, his older brother
> EVELYN GARDNER, his first wife
> LAURA HERBERT, his second wife

The Diaries of Evelyn Waugh is both as important and as formidable as the massiveness of the volume and the quality of its paper, printing, and binding would seem to proclaim. Scholars interested in modern British fiction and the social history of the twentieth century can only rejoice at the publication, in convenient book form, of the private journals of a lifetime by one of the greatest novelists of our age. The diaries are virtually complete in this edition by English journalist Michael Davie; except for the omission of a few tediously repetitious segments of the diarist's accounts of his youth and later travels, the editor has excised only libelous references or references that would (in his judgment) deeply distress living persons. The published diaries are multifaceted and fascinating: there are intimate depictions of English public school life and of the "Bright Young People," impressions of numerous journeys to exotic places, and a very unofficial view of World War II by a witty and perceptive observer. At the same time it must be added that the diaries do not make easy reading: the sheer length (estimated by the editor at 340,000 words) is forbidding, and it is not mitigated by the amorphousness inevitable in a running account of the random events of the day. Still, Waugh's diaries, in spite of such defects, are far livelier than the fiction of many current novelists; and their indubitable potential in the interpretation and evaluation of Waugh's own fiction gives these documents a significance beyond their not inconsiderable worth as informative entertainment in their own right.

It is important, however, to establish at the outset what the diaries cannot do: a critic cannot track down the incidents behind Waugh's plots, nor the persons behind his characterizations and expect thereby to discover the "real" meaning of his novels; nor can the value of the novels be judged by determining how closely they reproduce the actual events and persons of the diaries. A novelist is an alchemist who turns the monotonous material of everyday experience into art. The diaries are not a touchstone by which to test the authenticity of the novels; they are rather a testimony to the power of the literary imagination to transform the shapeless welter of human experience into an ordered whole that can be grasped and contemplated by the mind. Hence an acquaintance with the diaries can prepare the reader for Waugh's fiction (and many other contemporary British novels) by establishing a context which explains the specific details of the literary surface so that the unfamiliar customs and assumptions of what is already a vanishing milieu provide access to the import of the works, and not impediments.

Michael Davie has furnished a number of editorial features which aid the reader in deriving full benefit of the diaries. A brief preface explains the general nature and scope of the diaries and the editorial decisions involved in their publication. There is a chronological table of major events in Waugh's life, a glossary of proper names with thumbnail sketches of persons who figure prominently in the diaries, and an index of proper names. The diaries have been divided into seven sections with introductions by the editor, and there are frequent footnotes identifying or explaining obscure references in the text. Still, Davie is an Englishman and takes for granted many things that Americans may find puzzling: for example, the error Waugh attributes to a noblewoman in designating herself "The Hon. Mrs. Edward Kidd" in the entry for September 18, 1961. Moreover, Davie does not always identify more than once the last names of persons mentioned in the diaries by first name only. The reader who has forgotten a last name may read for pages about "Katharine" or "Basil" without being able to check the identity in the glossary or run down the original reference in the index. In a volume which indexes more than 1,000 names, it is easy to forget a few. Nevertheless, considering the enormous problems entailed by such a lengthy and complicated manuscript, Davie has generally handled his editorial tasks with skill and discretion, managing to answer most questions without being pedantic or intrusive.

Most of the disappointments in the diaries are Waugh's own doing. The whole is written with a peculiarly detached and reticent tone for a personal journal. The author seems very rarely to have laid aside the satirist's mask; even among family and friends, as we may infer from the diaries, he was continually assuming a role. Hence the accounts of his first marriage and his conversion are curiously unemotional; even in a personal diary Waugh betrays few confidences about himself. Only occasionally, in unguarded entries during the courtship and immediately after the marriage, does he reveal his deep love for his second wife, Laura Herbert (1916–1973). Certain critical periods and events are entirely omitted. Davie speculates that Waugh himself destroyed diaries covering his Oxford years and a sea voyage, during which he suffered drug-induced hallucinations which form the basis for *The Ordeal of Gilbert Pinfold* (1957). There is also no diary for the time during which Waugh's first marriage to Evelyn Gardner (b. 1903; "She-Evelyn" to their friends) broke up, ending in divorce on January 18, 1930. Perhaps the most astounding omission comes between the autumn of 1933 and July 7, 1936, when Waugh records the arrival of a telegram from Archbishop Godfrey announcing Rome's final decree of the nullity of this first marriage. During the preceding three years, the diaries contain not a single reference to the progress of the case in the marriage tribunal nor to the grounds on which the annulment was sought; but without this annulment Waugh, who had been received into the Catholic Church in September, 1930, could not have married Laura Herbert.

The evasions and omissions are perhaps more revealing than anything actually *in* the diaries. The burden of the novelist—especially when his subject is his own experience of contemporary society—is a painful self-consciousness, intensified in Waugh's case by the withering irony of a born satirist. It cannot be supposed that the possessor of an intelligence so keen in shredding the pretensions and delusions of others was any less aware of his own. The reticent tone of the diaries suggests the voice of a man fearful of surprising himself in a sentimental mood or a hollow action; and the hyperbolic posturing that characterizes so much of his life (in youth the reckless debauchee, in age the reactionary curmudgeon) betrays a reluctance to allow anyone to steal into the center of his personality and violate the privacy of his deepest loyalties and concerns.

It is, therefore, the comparative ingenuousness of the earlier diaries which gives them their greatest interest, though to be sure, the measured artifice of the budding writer is already latent. Indeed, the seven pages designated "The Boyhood Diary" are most notable for their precocity of style and tone. Apart from his lifelong inability to spell correctly, the eleven-year-old Evelyn would today be a prize pupil in a freshman composition class at most American universities. There is in his earliest diary a sophistication of syntax and diction, a flourish of wit and inventiveness, that even most college graduates would do well to envy.

"The Lancing Diary 1919-21" covers the last two of the four years Waugh spent as a pupil at Lancing College. This was not, of course, a "college" in the American sense, but rather what the British call a "public school," of which the American counterpart is a private preparatory school. Such institutions, intended to ready boys for Oxford and Cambridge, are "public" only in contrast to private instruction carried out in the boy's home or in his tutor's. Possibly the most interesting Lancing story is why Waugh ended up there at all. His father (Arthur, d. 1943) and his older brother, Alec (b. 1898), had attended Sherborne, but the latter was asked to leave in 1915 when caught in homosexual practices. This much could have been forgiven had the seventeen-year-old Alec not responded by publishing that same year *The Loom of Youth,* a patently autobiographical novel which indicated that a certain amount of homosexuality was an accepted and nearly universal feature of public school life. (The same charge has been made more recently by such diverse autobiographers as C. S. Lewis and Simon Raven.) The book enjoyed an immediate *succès de scandale,* and the school responded by removing Alec and his father from the list of Old Boys and refusing Evelyn admission. It is apparent from the diary that Lancing, which Arthur Waugh had chosen for his son in the hope that it might appeal to his youthful high church piety, was also afflicted with its share of homosexuality. Waugh is characteristically ambiguous regarding his own participation, if any, in such practices at Lancing; but in *Evelyn Waugh: A Biography* (1975), Christopher Sykes reveals, on the basis of Waugh's own testimony, that for a time at Oxford the novelist engaged exclusively and frequently in homosexuality, although he soon became disgusted with it and subsequently lost interest.

The main interest of "The Lancing Diary" itself lies in its poignant depiction of a sensitive boy, by turns shy and cocky, trying to maintain his self-esteem in the lonely, sometimes brutal world of the public school. Predictably, the schoolboy diary is often tedious, but there are moving passages which disclose the anguish of a youth too sophisticated and self-conscious to enjoy thoroughly the pleasures and achievements proper to his years, yet still too immature not to be bitter when he misses them.

The next two sections of *The Diaries*, "The Twenties Diary 1924–28" and "The Thirties Diary 1930–39," are together the least satisfactory part of the whole. "The Twenties Diary" is important because it furnishes the background for Waugh's first two novels, *Decline and Fall* (1928) and *Vile Bodies* (1930), which launched him on a successful literary career; moreover, his friendship with Alastair Graham probably provided some of the inspiration for "Sebastian Flyte," a crucial character in *Brideshead Revisited* (1945). Long stretches, however, are little more than repetitive accounts of appallingly tedious drunken parties. Waugh's descriptions of his desultory attempts at being a schoolmaster are sometimes comic, but the real import of this part of the diaries is the revelation, by way of contrast, of the transforming power of the artist's imagination: the novels of this period are sparkling, the diaries wearying. "The Thirties Diary," as the editor observes, becomes exceedingly impersonal in tone, but it is also important as literary background. It includes the travel notes which lie behind *Black Mischief* (1932), part of *A Handful of Dust* (1934), *Scoop* (1938), and several travel books. The other half of *A Handful of Dust* is based on the accounts of the fashionable aristocratic world in which Waugh now moved, with its opulence, decadence, hypocrisy, and malice.

By far the most intriguing and important part of the entire book is "The Wartime Diary 1939–45." As Davie points out, it was illegal for any soldier on active duty to keep any kind of personal journal, and the journal kept by Waugh comprises almost two hundred pages in the published version. This diary is the basis for four novels: *Put Out More Flags* (1942) and *The Sword of Honour* trilogy, possibly the finest fictional account of World War II in English, which includes *Men at Arms* (1952), *Officers and Gentlemen* (1955), and *Unconditional Surrender* (1961). But this part of Waugh's diaries is important in its own right. He renders vividly the confusion and sense of futility of the early months of the war, with its orders and counterorders and apparently meaningless maneuvers. Waugh was with the Royal Marines on the abortive Dakar expedition in 1940 and with the Commandos at the equally abortive Battle of Crete in 1941, and his eyewitness narratives of cowardice and incompetence are unforgettable. Not that Waugh himself was a good soldier: various commanding officers passed him from unit to unit because his acerbic temperament made him utterly unfit to serve as an officer in military action. His finest hour came in the winter of 1944–1945. He was posted with Randolph Churchill (son of Sir Winston) to German-occupied Yugoslavia in the British Military Mission to Tito's Partisans. Waugh tried valiantly to convince the British government that pressure should be brought to bear on Tito to insure the maintenance of religious liberty in Yugoslavia once the country was "liberated." But as a Catholic Waugh was suspected of bias, and in any case the government's policy was set: Tito was effective at "killing Germans" and nothing else mattered. Davie has generously provided Fitzroy Maclean, one of the chief architects of British policy in the Balkans, ample space for rebuttal. Maclean is not convincing. The suppression of *all* personal liberty in Yugoslavia, which continues to this day, speaks for itself. Waugh deserves credit as one of the regrettably ignored prophets who furnished early warning of the dangers of communist aggression and tyranny.

The concluding two sections of *The Diaries* are necessarily a falling off from the drama of the war diary. "The 1945–56 Diary," however, has its moments: it records the trip to Spain which provided the background to *Scott-King's Modern Europe* (1947) and that to Hollywood for a projected filming of *Brideshead Revisited*. This project fell through when, according to Waugh, he merely explained to his prospective producers what the book was about: they would accept love as a theme, even religion, but not theology. But the trip was not wasted: it provided the genesis of *The Loved One,* Waugh's macabre spoof of the Forest Lawn Cemetery. The last section, " 'Irregular Notes' 1960–65," is more personally revealing than any other since "The Lancing Diary." Much of it consists of melancholy and cynical reflections on the current state of the world: Waugh was particularly distressed by the changes in the Catholic liturgy and discipline resulting from Vatican II, and he even feared apostasy. There is also a painful and pointed explanation of his refusal to review his old friend Graham Greene's *A Burnt-Out Case* (1961), certainly not one of the latter's better books. Although Evelyn Waugh died comparatively early (at sixty-two), he was a worn-out man, weary of an increasingly vulgarized and secularized world. "All fates are 'worse than death,' " reads an entry towards the close of the volume.

The Diaries of Evelyn Waugh is an important book: it can furnish a good deal of information and pleasure to anyone interested in modern British fiction or simply in Britain, and it is indispensable to the literary scholar of the period. But it does justice neither to the man nor his work. The former, as he would have wished, has escaped us forever with his enigma intact; the novels, to which *The Diaries* is only an ancillary work, remain a treasure of the English-speaking world if it only will not neglect them.

R. V. Young, Jr.

Sources for Further Study

Atlantic. CCXL, December, 1977, p. 110.

Booklist. LXXIV, November 1, 1977, p. 453.

Kirkus Reviews. XLV, August 15, 1977, p. 918.

New York Times Book Review. October 16, 1977, p. 1.

Newsweek. XC, October 31, 1977, p. 102.

Saturday Review. V, November 12, 1977, p. 26.

Time. CX, October 17, 1977, p. 102.

THE DIARY OF VIRGINIA WOOLF
Volume I: 1915-1919

Author: Virginia Woolf (1882–1941)
Edited by Anne Olivier Bell with an Introduction and notes by Quentin Bell
Publisher: Harcourt Brace Jovanovich (New York). 356 pp. $12.95
Type of work: Diary
Time: 1915–1919
Locale: London

The first of a projected five-volume edition of the complete diary of Virginia Woolf which documents the emerging reputation of both Virginia and her husband, Leonard

For most of its length there is a peculiarly insulated quality to the first volume of Virginia Woolf's diary. We find little suggestion of her buried or imaginative life, almost no mention of the novel (her second, *Night and Day*) that she was writing through much of this period, only the briefest of critical comments on her reading, a minimum of reference to the larger social and political issues that consumed the energies of her husband, Leonard—in fact, if it were not for the occasional air raid warning and the sight of German prisoners of war, the reader would scarcely be aware of the fact that England was lost in the dark, bloody tunnel of World War I. For all of their crochets, the letters currently being published provide us with a much fuller sense of Woolf's life during the period covered by the present volume.

Indeed, the first two-thirds of the volume gives us only the barest outline of Woolf's days and ways. So reticent is the diary at this early stage that Woolf's biographer, Quentin Bell, may be correct in suggesting that the diary was initially intended for therapeutic purposes, "partly as a sedative, a way of proving to herself how normal she was." Certainly there seems to be an air of determination and self-congratulation in the keeping of the diary, an air that the diary itself scarcely seems to warrant. But, given the fuller and more complex entries in the closing pages of the volume as well as the selections already published by Leonard in *A Writer's Diary,* later volumes should prove extraordinarily interesting both to the careful critic and the gossipy reader.

Nevertheless, even through the reticence several things begin to emerge. There is, for example, the closeness of Virginia and Leonard, marked, among other things, by the frequency with which they simply went walking together: "After lunch we took the air in the Old Deer Park"; "we noticed the damaged Bridge as we walked to Kingston this afternoon. . . . We had a very good walk." However, Virginia's interest in Leonard's outside concerns could not even be termed marginal, so that they separated often enough when Leonard went to the London School of Economics, to a meeting of the Fabian executive, to groups promoting the League of Nations and the cooperative movement, to editors, to the offices of publications he himself edited, to the innumerable lectures he was called upon to give as his fame and expertise grew. She could take only a limited supply of the Sidney Webbs: "L. went to the Webbs, & I came home." Nor did she cotton much to her in-laws: "L. went to see his mother; I called on Jean." But when, in London, they went their separate ways, they met regularly for lunch or afterwards; when left at home to write, Virginia was likely to meet "L." en route so that they might walk home to Richmond together. Often enough, Leonard's moods and needs were registered in the diary along with her own: "amused me, but bored L. I'm afraid." And more than once we find the crisp comment: "We wrote all the morning." Clearly they created an atmosphere for each other in which they could work independently, possess their own souls and moods, and at the same time rest in each other.

There were differences enough, of course, and some of them, when pulled out of context, must have seemed insuperable. Virginia registered several quarrels— "We quarrelled almost all the morning!"—and no doubt there were some that she did not register. Her comments on Leonard's family and on Jews in general could, at times, be downright anti-Semitic: "I do not like the Jewish voice; I do not like the Jewish laugh," comments that Leonard must have read. There were also, of course, her recurring madness and daily fear of madness. Poignantly, the first segment of the diary lasts only six weeks, for it was interrupted by a bout of violent, screaming lunacy that, among other symptoms, took the form of a raving antipathy to Leonard himself. On February 13, 1915, she wrote: "I met L. at Spikings & we had tea, and were very happy." Two days later, the diary breaks off, not to be resumed for two and a half years.

While asserting over and over again her lack of interest in social, political, and economic matters—the very staff of life to Leonard—Virginia did accompany him now and then to some of the meetings he addressed, and she was suitably impressed by his ability as a speaker; in 1913, in fact, she had joined him on a ten-day tour of the industrial north. For four years she presided over monthly meetings of the local branch of the Women's Co-operative Guild held at Hogarth House. But, aside from Leonard's participation, she tended to find political meetings amusing at best, dreary at worst. As for the women of the Guild, "it always puzzles me to know why the women come. . . . They don't pay much attention apparently." To her, the audience at one public gathering "all looked unhealthy & singular & impotent." When Leonard spoke at Hampstead, she found the audience too "clean, decorous, uncompromising." Politics in general she saw as "an elaborate game" designed for men trained in the sport. And despite the coaching she must have had on all sides—"everyone makes the state of the country his private affair"—she insisted that she could make little sense of Labour Party politics, as immersed as Leonard and other Fabians were in the party. As for women with public missions, "their eccentricities keep me amused, when to tell the truth, I've ceased to follow their plots and denunciations"—though, conceivably, some jealousy might have been involved in the remark since Leonard, perforce, spent a good deal of time in the company of such women. Part of her feeling, perhaps, was due to the sad sense of what political and social responsibility did to one's feelings of youthful elasticity: "So we all step into the ranks of the middle aged, the responsible people, the burden bearers. It makes me a little melancholy." Despite it all, the central fact of her existence remained her relationship with Leonard.

Unmistakable, however, was her need for as many friends and acquaintances as she could muster, whether they were taken singly or in groups. The published correspondence testifies to its function in helping to spin a dense social web of those who outlined her world, and the diary takes careful note of days when no letters arrive. A party at Gordon Square was described as presenting Virginia with "2 hours of life." Another gathering, while composed of "the same party as usual," was "as usual, to my liking; so much alive, so full of information of the latest kind; real interest in every sort of art; & in people too." She assumed, in passing, that her feeling would not be shared by Leonard. Certain of her friends were particularly capable of making her vibrate in sympathy: Clive Bell, for one; Lytton Strachey, for another. If Lytton "were to walk in at this moment we should talk . . . as freely as we ever did, & with the sense, on both sides I think, of having hoarded for this precise moment a great deal peculiarly fit for the other."

There is, in fact, a fascinating entry for January 22, 1919: "How many friends have I got?" She sorts them, first, chronologically, according to their association with various stages of family history and then, over a period of a month, attempts to define the peculiar qualities of certain of them.

Indeed, we find a gallery of pungent character portraits in the diary. There is Katherine Mansfield who, on first meeting, seemed to stink "like a—well civet cat that had taken to street walking." Even at the first meeting, however, Virginia conceded that Mansfield would no doubt repay friendship, though as late as 1919 she was wondering whether she might list the author among her friends. There is Lady Ottoline Morrell, everyone's favorite comic target, spotted in the street, "brilliantly painted, as garish as a strumpet," perceived more sympathetically at times, but almost always condescendingly: "to me she always has the pathos of a creature vaguely afloat in some wide open space, without support or clear knowledge of its direction." There is Roger Fry, "in his wideawake hat," carrying a number of French books under his arm, hurrying to his editorial office at an art-history magazine, concerned with the production of a play designed by the Omega Workshops, run by Fry, and yet, in his enthusiasm, persuading Virginia into a nearby bookstore where she purchased a new French novel with money intended to pay for watch repairs. There are the many young men and women moving in and out of the Bloomsbury orbit—"cropheads" or "Bloomsbury bunnies," according to Virginia. And there are the many odd relationships and *ménages* forming the subject of delighted gossip: "Indeed I see the plots of many comedies brewing just now among our friends." And there are, of course, others: T. S. Eliot: "sharp, narrow & much of a stick"; Maynard Keynes, "a little inhuman," but "like quicksilver" in his conversation.

But, despite parties, meetings, visits; despite hours and hours of extended conversations; despite long walks and days of househunting and shopping; despite enforced periods of rest, during which her writing was carefully restricted—despite all this and much more, an enormous amount of work was produced at the Woolf household. Their famous Hogarth Press consumed great quantities of time and effort. Articles and reviews poured out of both Leonard and Virginia, the latter noting, on one occasion, that they were earning a tidy sum by their literary journalism. Virginia, at any rate, was capable of turning out an astonishing number of rapid reviews. Immediately after completing her essay, "Modern Novels," for the *Times Literary Supplement,* she submerged herself in the novels of Daniel Defoe for still another article: "I have to read one book a day in order to start on Saturday—such is the life of a hack." The next day, however, she failed to complete *Moll Flanders* because she spent the day in London, where, meeting E. M. Forster and learning that he had never read Defoe, she commanded him to do so. Nevertheless, her article, "The Novels of Defoe," appeared in less than two weeks. Of course, the most important aspect of her creative life, the production of the novel *Night and Day,* receives almost no mention in the diary, except for an occasional statement to the effect that a slight break in the flow of review books had given her time to pursue her novel. Only when it was completed could she bring herself to comment on it and, in the privacy of her diary, announce that she found it good: "I compare for originality & sincerity rather well with most of the moderns."

Max Halperen

Sources for Further Study

Atlantic. CCXL, November, 1977, p. 105.
Booklist. LXXIV, October 15, 1977, p. 349.
Christian Century. XCIV, November 23, 1977, p. 1100.
Christian Science Monitor. LXIX, October 27, 1977, p. 19.
New York Times Book Review. October 2, 1977, p. 7.
Publisher's Weekly. CCXII, August 8, 1977, p. 56.

DIRTY LINEN and NEW-FOUND-LAND

Author: Tom Stoppard (1937–   )
Publisher: Grove Press (New York). 75 pp. $6.95; paperback $2.95
Type of work: Drama
Time: The present
Locale: London

A brilliant, farcical drama about sexual scandal and political hypocrisy in the House of Parliament, coupled with a short play on English tradition and the American landscape

> *Principal characters:*
> **Dirty Linen**
> MADDIE GOTOBED, secretary of the Committee and the object of their investigation
> WITHENSHAW, M.P., Chairman of the Select Committee on Promiscuity in High Places
> COCKLEBURY-SMYTHE, M.P.,
> McTEAZLE, M.P.,
> CHAMBERLAIN, M.P.,
> MRS. EBURY, M.P., and
> FRENCH, M.P., Members of the Committee
> **New-Found-Land**
> BERNARD, a very old Home Office Official
> ARTHUR, a very young Home Office Official

Line for line, word for word—and this is a "words" play if ever there was one—*Dirty Linen* along with *New-Found-Land* may well be Tom Stoppard's liveliest and funniest work, if not one of his deepest or most ambitious. From the opening lines—five minutes of clichés in foreign tongues—the play sizzles with a continuous flood of one-liners, comic monologues, outlandish puns, extravagant metaphors, hyperbolic rhetoric, double entendres, verbal duels, sophisticated witticisms, and ludicrously corny jokes. In all, Stoppard overwhelms us with a comedic verbal dexterity, punctuated by adroit bits of physical farce, which is almost unique on today's stage, although it has many predecessors: Congreve, Sheridan, Wilde, Shaw, George S. Kaufmann, and even the Marx Brothers.

Dirty Linen and *New-Found-Land* is really a sandwich of a theatrical evening; the second shorter play, a dramatic duet actually, is inserted about three-quarters of the way through the action of the first one, prior to the working out of the main play's "problem"—although the basic conflict in *Dirty Linen* is, at best, an extremely thin one. Indeed, although the actual resolution of the play occurs offstage, during the *New-Found-Land* interlude, this indirect climax is perfectly appropriate to a play whose impressiveness derives from its wit and ideas, rather than its conflicts.

What is the play about? Political hypocrisy and pomposity, especially the British parliamentary variety, the absurdity of traditional forms and rituals, of moral double-think, of the journalistic need to make something out of nothing in order to fill space, sell papers, and "compete," the artificiality and irrelevance of both politics and journalism to real life, and, above all, the split between what is actually done and the nonsensical, cliché-ridden language we invent in order to describe and conceal the doing of it.

Dirty Linen involves the attempt of a parliamentary sub-committee (the "Select Committee on Promiscuity in High Places") to submit a report on the recent and extravagant extracurricular sexual activities of that august body:

> McTEAZLE: . . . there is no phrase as certain to make a British sub-editor lose his sense of proportion as the phrase "Mystery Woman." This Committee was set up at the time when no fewer than 21 Members of Parliament was said to have been compromised. Since then rumour has fed on rumour and we face the possibility that a sexual swathe has passed through Westminister claiming the reputations of, to put no finer point upon it, 119 Members. Someone is going through the ranks like a lawn-mower in knickers.

Their fact-finding and reporting are greatly complicated by the fact that all save one of the male committee members can be included among the fallen and that their new secretary, Maddie Gotobed (Stoppard has never been a slave to subtlety), is, indeed, the "Mystery Woman," having risen in the ranks with remarkable speed despite dubious secretarial qualifications (Q: "You do speedwriting, I suppose?" A: "Yes, if I'm given enough time," or, Q: "Do you use Gregg's or do you favour the Pitman method?" A: "I'm on the pill").

Most of the play's humor, in the best farce tradition, comes from each committee member's attempt to keep his relationship with Maddie secret from his colleagues. As McTeazle puts it:

> . . . the tragedy is, as our luck would have it, that our gemlike love which burns so true and pure and has brought such a golden light into our lives, could well become confused with a network of grubby affairs between men who should know better and some bit of fluff from the filing department—

This speech indicates, however, a degree of self-control that is quite beyond these men when they actually come in contact with her. Their public images collapse and their "private" selves break into their every speech and gesture. For her part, Maddie reacts to the mens' moral gyrations with a combination of eager helplessness and naïve disregard, as her physical actions continually contradict her verbal protests of innocence, and her "knickers" (underwear) are scattered about the stage like confetti.

The major conflict in the play comes from French, a "puritan" committee member, the only one (excepting Mrs. Ebury) who has not had previous contact with Maddie. His intervention threatens to abort the whitewash, as he demands an honest report, put together by gathering evidence, hearing witnesses, and tracking down rumors. He insists that they "name names," unaware of the fact that all of his male colleagues will be among those named. But his conversion, which occurs offstage during the *New-Found-Land* interlude, is never really in doubt. Maddie Gotobed is a power that no mere man could possibly withstand. Indeed, the author of the final committee report is Ms. Gotobed herself.

And that is altogether appropriate, since Maddie not only represents the positive virtue of honest sexuality, but Stoppard's other ideas as well. Throughout the play her common sense is constantly juxtaposed against the hypocritical clichés of the MP's. From the beginning of the drama she is openly puzzled by the committee's purpose and she becomes more heated on the topic as the drama progresses. It is she who ascribes this public over-concern with politicians' private sex-lives to an essentially frivolous journalistic establishment. Although only talked about, the press is probably a more central target of Stoppard's biting wit than the politicians.

While French is being overcome by Maddie offstage, the second play, *New-Found-Land*, takes over the stage. Two Home Office civil servants appear, ostensibly to discuss the naturalization request of an American. This American, a dubious "artistic type," is presumably the real-life theatrical director Ed Berman, whose pending British citizenship occasioned the plays in the first place. *Dirty Linen* was originally intended as a tribute to the event, but soon grew away from the topic. Thus, Stoppard wrote and inserted *New-Found-Land* in the body of the play as his personal accolade to his friend, colleague, and the play's director, both in London and on Broadway.

While even less of a "play," *New-Found-Land* is, perhaps, even funnier than its companion piece. It actually consists of two verbal arias, a lengthy paean to "old traditional England," as personified in Lloyd George, by Bernard, the ancient, doddering civil servant, followed by an even longer and funnier travelogue about America delivered by Arthur, his young companion. The former is amusing, the latter hilarious, and between them Stoppard sketches an instant portrait of America that is perceptive and biting. But it is Arthur's "Greyhound Tour" of America from coast to coast, a collage of every media cliché, motion picture vignette, travel poster, popular gossip, and comic book, that is the most brilliant comedic set piece of both plays. Arthur's ebullient tirade goes on for a good fifteen minutes of uninterrupted monologue, ending in a final, wonderful effusion.

This extravagant verbal feat, the high point of a most verbal pair of plays, well demonstrates the paradox of Stoppard's successful plays in particular and the current British theater in general. In a theatrical era where text is minimized, ignored, or used, at best, as a blueprint, where the playwright is accorded a minor role in favor of director and actor, where language is increasingly treated as simply one of many useful devices, where improvisation is employed and disciplined classical acting thought passé, where ideas are considered irrelevant, Stoppard insists on the primacy of the text, the centrality of language, and the necessity for ideas, and his plays are resounding successes, both artistically and commercially.

Language, wit, ideas—these things have brought Tom Stoppard to the forefront of contemporary British theater, a theater that has established itself, in this period of antilanguage, as one of the most literate and verbal in the history of the English stage. Stoppard, Pinter, Storey, Bond, Osborne, Beckett—all are, in their unique ways, masters of the verbal idiom at a time when the vitality of the British stage is satisfying, exciting, and provocative.

Keith Neilson

Sources for Further Study

Choice. XIV, May, 1977, p. 379.
Library Journal. CII, March 1, 1977, p. 628.

DISPATCHES

Author: Michael Herr (1940–   )
Publisher: Alfred A. Knopf (New York). 260 pp. $8.95
Type of work: Personal narrative
Time: The Vietnam War
Locale: Vietnam

A personal account of the Vietnamese war told through vignettes and personal observations

Michael Herr's *Dispatches* is a collection of reportage written when the author was special assignment correspondent for *Esquire*. His assignment was the Vietnam War; not, as he interpreted it, the military strategy, or the politics of the war, but what it is like to be in the midst of a war—how brutal the experience is and how exciting. Because it is written from this vantage point, Herr's book deserves a special place on the crowded bookshelf of volumes concerning America's most disillusioning war. The novels, the historical works, the memoirs of generals are all necessary to the avid student. But there are few books which, like Herr's, are dedicated to the feelings of the common conscripted soldiers who really fought the war, men who were unlikely to write about their feelings and experiences when they returned—if they returned.

The author is what sociologists call a "participant-observer." He is a student of military life without being a soldier; he studies that life by temporarily becoming part of military units in and out of combat, without becoming a combatant himself. In this sense Herr's book parallels William Foote Whyte's *Street Corner Society,* a study of the social structure of an Italian slum. However, although Herr's relations with American soldiers are very much like Whyte's relations with his street corner society, the aims of the two authors are entirely different. First, Whyte's aims are theoretical, while Herr's are emotional; second, Whyte is studying street corner society only, while Herr is interested as much in his own reactions as he is in the stories of the soldiers he writes about.

Thus Herr's book has no overall theoretical or narrative structure. Rather, it is a series of impressions—narrative and personal glimpses of the war. The chapter entitled "Illumination Rounds" is perhaps the purest example of Herr's method. It consists of twenty "stories," each presumably an illumination round, an anecdote designed to give special insight into the war the way a tracer bullet makes a target easier to see at night. In one story, the author is in a helicopter that takes fire and has to reland; in another, battle-fatigued soldiers have an unsatisfactory encounter with some Red Cross girls; in still another, a noncommisioned officer recalls a bizarre meeting between a soldier and a girl at Fort Bragg. All of these anecdotes are written with an immediacy and power that requires little comment:

> As the troops filed out of the helicopter, the [Red Cross] girls waved and smiled at them from behind their serving tables. "Hi, soldier! What's your name?" "Where you from, soldier?" "I'll bet some hot coffee would hit the spot about now."

Or,

And the men of the 173rd just kept walking without answering, staring straight ahead, their eyes rimmed with red from fatigue, their faces pinched and aged with all that had happened during the night. One of them dropped out of line and said something to a loud, fat girl who wore a Peanuts sweatshirt under her fatigue blouse and she started to cry.

Glad as one is to have so many accurate glimpses of a terrible war, one cannot help demurring that they are glimpses only. Each taken singly is a true snapshot of the war, for Herr has the ability to place us down in the middle of an incident; he has the talent of a true novelist. However, after not too many pages the reader may tire of the constant parade of superior anecdotage that leads nowhere. What do all these anecdotes mean, taken together? For if they have no total meaning, there is little point to a book full of them. From this point of view Herr's work seems more like a notebook—a series of individual entries in search of total structure and the added meaning that such structure would give them.

As has been said, Herr differs from the prototypal "participant observer" in that he deals with emotions, not theories. He also differs in that he is as interested in his personal reactions to the war as he is in the reactions of those he observes; in many selections there is a clear difference between the personal and the descriptive. The first anecdote from "Illumination Rounds" demonstrates this difference. Herr is talking about his trip in a helicopter transporting replacements. He is new, excited. The helicopter begins to take fire; a soldier across from him and a door gunner die; the pilot is mortally wounded. The dying pilot settles the helicopter down on its original landing zone. Herr's observations are so acute that the reader feels present at the incident. The first indications that the helicopter is taking fire are frighteningly depicted: "We were all strapped into the seats of a Chinook, fifty of us, and something, someone was hitting it from the outside with an enormous hammer." The description of the aftermath is equally deft: "One of the door gunners was heaped up on the floor like a cloth dummy. His hand had the bloody raw look of a pound of liver fresh from the butcher paper." At the same time, we get an inside look at Herr's private reactions, which reflect his inexperience:

As the chopper rose again and turned, [the boy's] weight went back hard against the webbing and a dark spot the size of a baby's hand showed in the center of his fatigue jacket. And it grew—I knew what it was, but not really—it got up his armpits and then started down his sleeves and up over his shoulders at the same time . . . and the boy was hanging forward in the straps again, he was dead, but not (I knew) really dead.

Herr has a clear view of his position as a voluntary observer of human terror and misery. He is a noncombatant in the midst of war; a volunteer—a man who does not have to be there—amidst conscripts counting their days until release. His distaste for battle is evident, as is his fascination for it. He is a man of peace, yet he makes his living from destruction and death. Herr has as his credo, "you were responsible for everything you saw as you were for everything you did." His responsibility for what he saw is clear: he must tell the truth, for "conventional journalism could no more reveal this war than conventional firepower could win it, all it could do was take the most profound event of the American decade and turn it into a communications pudding." He recognizes that the American soldiers he associates with think of him as unnerving, think of him as crazy, even hate him. But he does have his role to play and they understand it—to bear witness: " 'Okay, man, you go on, you go on out of here . . . but I mean it, you tell it! You tell it, man. If you don't tell it. . . .' "

Herr has no political position on the war; he is not for the North Vietnamese, the Viet Cong, or the Americans. He and his colleagues "all had roughly the same position on the war; we were in it, and that was a position." In *Dispatches,* Americans seem to get the most criticism. They treat prisoners brutally; they carry photograph albums with snapshots of severed Viet Cong heads; they make necklaces of severed Viet Cong ears. The American high command acts stupidly and lies endlessly. However, the impression of partiality is an illusion. Herr is merely being open about the army he is following. He by no means romanticizes the NVA: "(Another rumor of those days, the one about some 5,000 'shallow graves' outside the city, containing the bodies of NVA executions, had just now been shown to be true)."

In *Dispatches,* of course, politics is definitely a minor interest. At the forefront, along with his reactions, is Herr's portrait of the war and of the common soldier. A special horror is inherent in warfare where civilian and combatant cannot be readily differentiated. Herr brings a can of cold beer to an American surgeon. He opens the door on "a little girl . . . lying on the table. . . . Her left leg was gone, and a sharp piece of bone about six inches long extended from the exposed stump. The leg itself was on the floor, half wrapped in a piece of paper." In another vignette, the author and a colleague are running along a street under fire when they see "a house that had been collapsed by the bombing, bringing with it a young girl who lay stretched out dead on the top of some broken wood. The whole thing was burning, and the flames were moving closer and closer to her bare feet. In a few minutes they were going to reach her."

Death is an everyday occurence. The dead, civilian and military, line the streets, are scattered in the fields. They are piled up like logs, tied up in rubber body bags, covered with mud-splattered ponchos. Because death is so ever-present, because "every day people were dying because of some detail that they couldn't be bothered to observe," death comes home most powerfully in indirect ways: a paratroop ceremony in which the boots of the dead are lined up in formation; a cast-aside flak jacket on the back of which the owner had listed the months served in Vietnam: *"March, April, May . . . June, July, August, September, October, November, January, February,* the list ending right there like a clock stopped by a bullet."

In the midst of these grim scenes stand the common American soldiers—the "grunts." They are not sentimentalized; their callousness and brutality are clearly depicted:

> One of [the soldiers] was saying that Americans treated the Vietnamese like animals.
> "How's that?" someone asked.
> "Well, you know what we do to animals . . . kill'em hurt'em and beat on'em so's we can
> train'em . . . we don't treat the Dinks no different than that."
> And we knew he was telling the truth.

But the truth is more complicated. The American soldier is brutal, but to condemn unreservedly his brutality is to ignore the horrible pressures he is under. Continually in mortal danger, always in need of sleep, always exposed to the obscene horrors of war, he, as well as the Vietnamese, deserves some sympathy: "I think that those people who used to say that they only wept for the Vietnamese never really wept for anyone at all if they couldn't squeeze out at least one tear for these men and boys when they died or had their lives cracked open for them."

Michael Herr's *Dispatches* reaches its heights as a personal account of the Vietnamese war. It is not so much a memoir as a series of forays in a search for truth: What does the war mean to these soldiers, to those civilians, to me? The answer to this question is necessarily complex and involves the discarding of easy answers: that we were right, that they were. It involves the rejection of black and white moral judgments, but not the suspension of judgment. In the end, the truth cannot be summarized, but it is clear that if countries win wars, people do not; they merely suffer. Nevertheless the excitement of war is undeniable. This ineradicable voyeurism is at the bottom of Herr's attraction; this, and a need to bear witness.

Alan G. Gross

Sources for Further Study

Harper's Magazine. CCLV, December, 1977, p. 108.
Library Journal. CII, November 1, 1977, p. 2249.
New Times. IX, November 11, 1977, p. 66.
New York Times. November 25, 1977, p. C23.
Newsweek. XC, November 14, 1977, p. 102.
Time. CX, November 7, 1977, p. 119.

THE DOUBLE WITNESS
Poems: 1970-1976

Author: Ben Belitt (1911–   )
Publisher: Princeton University Press (Princeton, New Jersey). 71 pp. $7.50; paperback
$2.95
Type of work: Poetry

A fifth volume of mature poems by a master craftsman who makes no concessions in his art

The Double Witness runs against the tide of contemporary confessional poetry. Here is no self-pity, no sentimental nakedness. Ben Belitt writes handcrafted poems, both meditations and lyrics of the sort that have not been in fashion these last fifteen years or more. It is the sort of poetry that the undisciplined reader will probably dismiss as "academic": in other words, it makes considerable demands on the reader's mind. About these poems, Belitt has said:

> This volume—my fifth—extends and deepens a preoccupation I have had with the visible and invisible manifestations of people, places, and things. It offers a variety of poems of formal and textural density and, in addition, a system of doublings and solitudes whose oppositions express the drama of reality and appearance.

Any poet dealing with invisible manifestations is basically a Romantic, a visionary. But Belitt does not see angels in trees like William Blake; he is not a mystic. His visions peer into the nature of people and landscapes to get at truths not present on the surface. Like Neruda, Machado, and Keats, who are his touchstones, Belitt continually affirms the worth of the individual, continually insists that art gives meaning to our existence. As Wallace Stevens defined modern poetry, Belitt's poems are the act of the mind finding what will suffice.

Like the good translator that he is, Belitt is almost too much aware that any event or object can be seen from at least two perspectives, that every thesis contains its antithesis. Throughout these poems, it is the doubling of vision that produces the conflicts, the tensions that make the poems work: internal/external, light/dark, past/present. For example, in the fourth section of the volume, *This Scribe, My Hand,* the poet is constantly aware of his spiritual and artistic kinship with Keats:

> You are there
> on the underside of the page,
> a blue flower in my Baedeker,
>
> writing on water, I know it.
> The paper pulls under my pen. . . .

Unlike the popular confessional poets who sometimes write as if the world were not created until their birth, Belitt knows that it is the past that gives the present meaning, that it is not uniqueness that makes experience precious but its heritage. In his bleakest insights, he feels his kinship with Baudelaire, Machado, Dante, and Keats. What makes the bleakness bearable is the realization that the poet is not alone.

It is this realization that also makes great demands upon the reader in the form of allusions—classical, literary, and historical. For example, in Belitt's poem "Swan Lake," it is essential to the poet's irony that the reader be familiar with the ballet of that name. It would also help if he were vaguely familiar with Ovid's *Metamorphoses* and had seen at least a reproduction of Picasso's "Guernica." The poem contrasts, ironically, the external beauty of the swan with its brute personality. Painters, poets, musicians, and sculptors have traditionally used the swan to personify beauty and grandeur. Belitt's double vision reminds us that the swan is unsentimental, knows nothing of art, and has a deep streak of "homicidal hate" that hisses "Bastards! Bastards!" to any intruder. Out of tawdry, frequently base reality, the artist creates beauty; this beauty, in turn, transforms the way in which we perceive reality.

If the reader has not observed the testy bad humor of a male swan, he will not appreciate the poem, for it violates his sentimental view of swans. If the reader has not experienced the swan in art, he will miss the irony entirely. The poet demands that the reader, too, have lead a double life—the life of the mind and the life of experience. He makes no concessions. Belitt's demands are not new; he has been insisting upon them since his first volume of poetry, *The Five-Fold Mesh* (1938). Over the last forty years, his intensity has become more precise, but no less demanding. In *The Double Witness,* his fifth volume of poetry, he has become a word master operating at the height of his art.

As Howard Nemerov has noted, Belitt tends to write poems in sequences. In *The Double Witness,* there are five sequences, the last three of which are the most tightly formed. Section III, "Solitudes," is subtitled, "Homage to Antonio Machado," whom Belitt translated in 1963. Section IV, "This Scribe, My Hand," revolves around John Keats. Section V is called "Block Island: After *The Tempest,*" and is tightly related to Shakespeare's last play. In his earlier books of poetry, Belitt used similar sequences focused on themes, people, and places. This habit is clearly a rage for order. Like Wallace Stevens, Belitt is too much aware that the world of experience is chaos. The poet's role is to produce order, the supreme fiction. This Belitt does without ever forgetting that all orders crumble, that chaos is inevitable. In the poem "Southeast Lighthouse," Belitt clearly delineates the problem of chaos, which he says "is always there." The circling light pierces the blackness, but only in thin segments and never for long. The light is order, reason, but only a gesture against the chaos of darkness.

The antinomies of light and dark run through a number of these poems: the sun-bright beach *versus* the darkness of the sleeper's eye; the darkness of the catacombs *versus* the bright day where "we burn in the sunlight, afraid." Not infrequently the chaos that reigns just beyond the pool of light is death itself. At sixty-eight, Belitt makes his art in the face of death:

> I write, in a posthumous way,
> on the flat of a headstone
> with a quarrier's ink, like yourself:
>
> an anthologist's date and an asterisk. . . .

The measure of a man's art is its ability to sustain him to the very end. One thinks of Yeats making poems in the lap of death, of Renoir with the brush tied to his arthritic hand, of Beethoven making music in spite of his deafness. Belitt's art seems likely to sustain him in the same mode, albeit in a minor key. As he says, "The whole of our art is to double our witness, and wait."

Belitt is a Romantic, but most impressively, he is an old Romantic, the most difficult stance to sustain. Keats, Byron, and Shelley died young, and the older Wordsworth's poems do not sustain the vision of his youth. Whitman's visions essentially faded by 1866; the next quarter century of his poetry lacks the fire. The Bible tells us that young men shall see visions and old men shall dream dreams; but Belitt still sees visions. In a remarkable poem, "Kites: Ars Poetica," he gives us both a visionary experience and the heart of the Romantic poem. Kite-flying is equated with the art of writing poetry: the kite is the poem; the flyer, the poet. Alluding to Franklin's kite, Belitt reminds us that power and light, the assumption of knowledge in a blinding flash, can result. The artist can also become his art:

> I feel myself go up,
> unreeling aerial rigging out of my side
> and shedding a helix of thread,
> an invisible top in the air,
> a spider climbing the light—
> till the whole web bells, and goes tight—
> and I am flown by the kite.

The image of burning fire runs throughout this collection: the xerox illumination that burns the image on to paper; the slow oxidation of a swamp; the firehouse where his friend, Paul Feeley, painted; the burning sun. Fire is both illumination and destruction. The artist becomes a self-consuming artifact, burning himself out to create his art. It is the art that matters.

Without reprinting whole poems, it is difficult to describe fully the manner in which Belitt skillfully links poems within each sequence. Words and phrases reappear in different contexts, not only linking one poem to another but also gathering force of association in the process. Howard Nemerov has noted that the meaning of a Belitt poem "is gained . . . from listening to recurrences and obsessive preoccupations in a series of poems." This linking process is most admirably accomplished in the "Block Island" sequence, where not only are the antinomies of dark/light, land/water links between poems, but quotes from Shakespeare's *The Tempest* continually link the poet to Prospero on his final island.

Other images and events link this book with Belitt's earlier volumes. "Full

Moon: The Gorge" looks back to his Gorge sequence in *Nowhere But Light* (1970); "An Orange in Merida" looks back to poems in all of his earlier books. It is as if Belitt were insisting that there is order, there is plan, all is not chaos. In "An Orange in Merida" he says the orange is "ceremonious," using the word in much the same manner as Yeats. The orange is Egyptian, "Rameses' bounty," its peel unwinding like "the grave clothes of Pharaoh." The speaker watching illiterate natives peeling oranges is linked backward in time to the Egyptians, "And the dead reawaken."

The Double Witness contains the poetry of a memorous man remaking the world of chaos into a fictive order. These are the poems of a translator who knows he can double himself with his object, indeed double the past in himself. These are the mature poems of a craftsman.

Michael S. Reynolds

Sources for Further Study

Library Journal. CII, October 15, 1977, p. 2166.

A DUAL AUTOBIOGRAPHY

Authors: Will (1885–   ) and Ariel Durant (1898–   )
Publisher: Simon and Schuster (New York). 420 pp. $12.95
Type of work: Autobiography

The story of the Durants, individually and as a couple, in which they discuss their personal lives and opinions as well as their professional lives as writers and their writings

Will and Ariel Durant have spent their lives bringing the gifts of philosophy and history to thousands of people in the form of their books and lectures, and their dual autobiography may be the best gift of all. They have described here the joys and the sorrows of their journey across so many decades. We are treated to stronger and more personal opinions than they often have expressed in their public speeches and written words.

The book is arranged chronologically with Will and Ariel alternating in the narrative. Much of the story is devoted to their personal lives and their infatuation with each other, but a great amount of space is also devoted to the social and political events that influenced their intellectual development. The contrapuntal arrangement of their observations gives rise to something of a dialogue and is far less distracting than may be supposed. That they chose to present a dual autobiography is not surprising, for the last several volumes of *The Story of Civilization* were a joint project. It might be, in fact, very difficult for this inseparable pair to produce individual autobiographies.

Perhaps the most inviting and intriguing chapter is the first, where Ariel, without much of Will's editorial hand, describes her childhood and adolescence. Ariel comes across as part feminist/radical socialist and eventually part dutiful wife in the old style, a fascinating combination. Her political fires seem to mellow as her attention and energies have turned more and more to the "family business" of writing books. Throughout the remainder of the work, those sections written by Ariel that alternate with the sections written by Will have come under his polishing pen, and her thoughts frequently reach us through his graceful style. That Will seems to have taken on the general editorial duties is also typical of their roles in life, ever since they became acquainted as teacher and pupil at the Ferrar School in New York so long ago.

By all rights the Durant marriage never should have worked. There is a thirteen year difference in their ages. Will was well educated and well read when they met, while Ariel was just discovering books and ideas. Will had been reared in a strongly Roman Catholic family, Ariel in a less strongly Jewish one. But their love was strong enough to overcome such inauspicious circumstances, and to abide through the weeks of loneliness and separation that they endured for so many years while Will was on the lecture circuit. In our day of all too frequent divorces it is heartening to find a pair that could overcome a number of formidable obstacles and remain so devoted.

Nevertheless, this autobiography does not exclude some moments of doubt and accusation—Ariel's terrible loneliness while Will was away, for example, or a number of petty jealousies. These are all honestly, if blushingly, shown in excerpts from their correspondence. In this regard, the Durants play Everyman and Everywoman for their readers. In the end, they have come through it all, given patience and perspective, with a rock-solid marriage, and in so doing may shed a positive light on similar experiences for others.

Will's concern for his repudiated religious beliefs is a theme that is recorded throughout his life. He began firmly grounded in the Roman Catholic Church, so firmly grounded, in fact, that the natural course of his life led him into a seminary to study for the priesthood. As he read more and more theological and philosophical works, he came to value the creative wonder that is man's mind more than the dogma of his Church. He left the seminary and rebounded into the radical socialist libertarian Ferrar School as a teacher. By comparison to many others connected with this institution he discovered that his views are really fairly moderate. Thus began a lifelong reevaluation of his personal religious faith and his political preferences against a background of intellectual exercises and discoveries as well as more personal and emotional experiences. Thousands of his readers have experienced similar struggles, many while officially adhering to a particular faith or political stance.

This aspect of the autobiography is not as overburdening as it may sound. It is, rather, a great strength in the story to watch Will Durant struggle with so many doubts and conflicts and yet resolve them into a philosophy of optimistic patience and perspective. It is refreshing and almost amusing to watch as he discovers, in his summation, that his idealistic socialism has mellowed into more idealism than socialism.

Will particularly celebrates the abilities of the human mind. Many reviewers and historians have complained that Will Durant is a popularizer of history, and Durant has spent considerable effort to answer that charge. What his critics seem not to have comprehended is that such a designation should carry no negative connotations. He writes for a different audience from that envisioned by the academic historian, but his audience is no less valid. He explains it best in the preface to *The Story of Philosophy:*

> Perhaps each kind of teacher can be of aid to the other; the cautious scholar to check our enthusiasm with accuracy, and the enthusiast to pour warmth and blood into the fruits of scholarship.

And yet the question remains why so few people read the scholars, and so very many read the Durants?

What seems to have started Will Durant's success and continued it, is his ability to share with his readers his own enjoyment of historical research and his curiosity and excitement over what he discovers. He reads and distills his readings, putting them into a larger context, and then shares with a very personal pleasure his findings. It is this enthusiasm for his discoveries that engenders a like enthusiasm for history and philosophy on the part of his readers.

While enthusiasm is the key ingredient here, it would be of no consequence were he not a very good and hardworking writer. In this synthetic approach to the recordings of civilization the Durants interpret the events and movements of history, art, science, and philosophy for the reader in order to draw these various aspects into one cohesive picture, illuminated with many biographical essays. The term "synthetic" often has a negative connotation suggesting that which is not real, and to use it without a word of explanation would be a disservice to the Durants. Something that is synthetic, in the true meaning of the word, is a combination of various elements drawn together into a cogent whole. Theirs is a synthetic autobiography just as their books were synthetic, or integral, history.

Aside from its great worth as the autobiography of a fascinating pair, the book includes many short biographies of leading writers and public figures of the last several decades, since many of them were friends or correspondents of the Durants. Luckily, these persons are all represented in the index to the book, which was thoughtfully provided to make these items retrievable.

The Durants take a genuine delight in laudatory reviews of their work and share thank-you notes from the great and glorious of our time in such an innocent way that it almost seems that they are surprised to have been the objects of such attention. There are moments in the work that this emphasis on the positive becomes almost smug, even though they do quote generously from negative reviews as well. The deceivingly smooth flow of their lives from year to year is perhaps a function of Will's pen gliding over the final draft of most of the chapters. This makes the book very pleasant to read, but it might have been a little more fun if more of Ariel's pithiness had been interspersed as in the first chapter.

The Durants each wrote an ending to the book. Will once again synthesizes the more dominant elements in his life into a typically philosophical essay. Ariel, as is her wont, admits more poignancy to her summation, emphasizing again the great love that has sustained them throughout. Ariel is quite correct in closing with the observation that they have led enchanted lives. From inauspicious beginnings, through the uncertainties of social change, depression, and wars, they have stayed together in a wonderfully close and stable relationship and managed a family "business." Their life's work is something which they enjoy immensely, and they have made a great deal of money doing it. Moreover the fruits of their labors have brought understanding and pleasure to thousands of people.

Margaret S. Schoon

Sources for Further Study

Book World. November 27, 1977, p. E1.
Booklist. LXXIV, October 15, 1977, p. 352.
Kirkus Reviews. XLV, September 1, 1977, p. 564.
Library Journal. CII, October 15, 1977, p. 2154.
Publisher's Weekly. CCXII, September 19, 1977, p. 135.

EDISON
The Man Who Made the Future

Author: Ronald W. Clark
Publisher: G. P. Putnam's Sons (New York). 256 pp. $12.95
Type of work: Biography
Time: 1847–1931
Locale: The United States

A biographical study of the life of Thomas A. Edison which focuses primarily on Edison's professional career as an inventor and business entrepreneur

Principal personages:
THOMAS A. EDISON
ALEXANDER GRAHAM BELL, inventor of the telephone
HENRY FORD, organizer of the Ford Motor Company

Ronald Clark's excellent biography, *Einstein: The Life and Times,* has raised expectations far beyond the level that has been attained in Clark's study of *Edison: The Man Who Made the Future.* The latter, generously sprinkled with quotations, is a narrative account of Edison's life with little attempt at sophisticated or critical analysis of the biographical activities and events and with only brief efforts at comprehending the real man as distinguished from the legend. Clark has constantly before himself the subtitle of his book, "The Man Who Made the Future," and takes pains, often unconvincingly, to demonstrate the validity of this interpretation.

Thomas Alva Edison was born in Milan, Ohio, on February 11, 1847, to Samuel and Nancy Edison. Early in life, he exhibited considerable interest and skill in reading such works as R. G. Parker's *Natural and Experimental Philosophy,* the writings of Thomas Paine, and Newton's *Principia,* which convinced him that "I am not a mathematician." Indeed, Edison proved to have much more interest in practical experiments than in theories. Clark contends that even as a boy, Edison manifested three characteristics that were to remain with him all of his life: "They were quickness at turning chance circumstance to his own benefit, a refusal to be deterred, and a relentlessness—some would say ruthlessness—in exacting as much payment for a job as traffic would stand."

Edison's early successes came as a result of opportunities presented to telegraph operators during the American Civil War. During this period, he moved from community to community filling one telegraphic position briefly before moving to the next. By 1865, he had worked in a half dozen towns and cities and in the next few years would continue to stay in a job only until he had learned what he could from it and then seek to expand his knowledge elsewhere.

Soon after he went to Boston in 1868, Edison invented the automatic vote recorder and an improved stock ticker. He then began to work on a multiplex telegraph to send multiple messages over a single telegraph wire. In 1869 he went to New York City and, in the view of Clark, turned his full attention to becoming a professional inventor, eventually setting up Pope, Edison and Company to provide inventions and instruments for "the application of electricity to the Arts and Sciences."

Through this company Edison produced his Universal Stock Printer, brought out a new "gold printer," and rented the latter to various agencies. The sale of this service to Western Union provided him with money to undertake additional experimentation. Moreover, General Marshall Lefferts of Western Union began financing some of Edison's research. Money received from improvements to Western Union equipment permitted Edison to establish workshops and research laboratories in Newark, New Jersey, where he brought together a competent staff who became devoted to him. At this new facility Edison improved the automatic telegraph, which permitted high speed transmission, and invented the quadruplex telegraph, making possible the sending of multiple telegraph messages simultaneously over a single wire. As a consequence of the quadruplex Edison was involved in his first legal suit. He had received financial and other support from Western Union and had promised the invention to them, but instead had deviously negotiated with and sold it to Jay Gould's Atlantic and Pacific Telegraph Company. A spectator at the trial recorded in his diary the observation that Edison "has a vacuum where his conscience ought to be." Clark points out and then attempts to soften the charge of duplicity, but the case remains a blot which Edison himself recognized. Legally Edison was permitted to sell to whom he chose, but his negotiation with Gould was of questionable morality.

Also during this time in his career, Edison was hired to find ways around patents, which says much about the business practices in the mid-1870's and the 1880's. Businessmen who did not wish to pay for patents but who wished to profit from the ideas, sought out inventors such as Edison to evade patents. In his work of evading patents, Edison often provided excellent inventions and improvements, for the work required a thorough understanding of all aspects of the technologies and physical principles involved in the inventions.

In 1876 Alexander Graham Bell invented the telephone, and Edison began working on the apparatus to improve it. He undertook significant changes which revolutionized the device and made it practical as a popular means of communication. Constructing an effective carbon transmitter, Edison gave Western Union a communication system with which to challenge Bell. The fight between Western Union and Bell, in which Edison was directly involved, raged on both sides of the Atlantic, while both men provided inventions to give advantage first to one side and then to the other. Finally in England on June 8, 1880, the competing corporations merged into the United Telephone Company.

While the Edison-Bell feud was being fought, Edison was busily involved with other inventions such as the electric pen, which eventually led to the duplicating machine; he also improved the typewriter and made it into a working instrument. In 1876 Edison moved his workshops to Menlo Park, New

Jersey, where he assembled an outstanding staff of dedicated workers and inventors. The climate he generated at Menlo Park was intellectual, stimulating, and infused with a spirit of community and mutual support, and the result was a constant stream of inventions and patents in a wide variety of areas. Here Edison astonished his staff with the invention of the phonograph, and in 1878 he created the Edison Speaking Phonograph Company. The phonograph caught the public interest and soon, throughout the United States, audiences sat in rapt attention listening to recordings of all manner of sounds. Although much of Edison's fame came from this invention (he was asked to demonstrate it for President R. B. Hayes), he lost interest in it soon after its successful demonstration.

Edison had for some years believed that electricity could be employed in the service of humankind to revolutionize life and ease its burdens. He first acted in the area of the use of electricity in lighting, beginning his study of the problem in 1878. The prevailing lighting systems of the day were gas or the electric arc, with gas representing almost a monopoly of the lighting industry. As Edison approached creation of an incandescent lamp, the first problem was that of what material and shape would be most effective for a filament. The Edison Electric Light Company was established to facilitate Edison's work. Patenting a bulb with a platinum filament in 1878, Edison continued his experiments. In October, 1879, Edison succeeded in producing a bulb with a carbon filament that lasted for about forty hours. He obtained a patent and the press spread the word throughout the United States. Edison used light bulbs to illuminate his home and other buildings at Menlo Park. Since the Pennsylvania Railroad ran tracks to Menlo Park and visitors often came, the spectacle of such illumination proved very impressive and was clearly a triumph for Edison.

His success with lighting convinced Edison that he was launched on an exceedingly significant development and that he should undertake a more difficult and more significant effort—the wide distribution of electricity from a central generator. Effective lighting depended on this. Improvements in the light bulb went forward in the period, so that sales of bulbs had reached 45,000,000 by 1903. From new offices in New York City, Edison attempted both to manage his corporate empire and continue his interest in invention, particularly in a central generating station.

Part of the development of the generation system was undertaken in the early 1880's when Edison divided up a district into a number of small areas, each served by feeder wires; this avoided the need for long feeder wires. Copper was further reduced by a three-wire system. Edison and his Menlo Park staff next worked out an insulation system to prevent electricity in buried wires from seeping into the ground, and then developed a large dynamo. The problem of consumers overloading the system was solved by the invention of the fuse. Edison also produced a working electric meter to determine the amount of electricity used by customers. In order to move ahead in these and other areas, Edison created the Edison Lamp Company, the Edison Machine Works, the

Edison Shafting Company, the Thomas A. Edison Construction Department, and the Edison Electric Illuminating Company of New York. Edison's corporate empire grew as his interest expanded. His generating station proved effective enough to found the Edison Isolated Lighting Company, created to install such stations across the United States.

The organizational structure of Edison's corporate empire was leaving him little time for invention; he needed help. In 1881 Samuel Insull was hired by Edison and eventually brought order to his empire. With corporate and financial matters securely in the hands of Insull, Edison turned to the considerable problems of developing his electrical system. He achieved international success in establishing electric lighting systems in Belgium, Holland, Italy, and England. Dynamos were developed for shipboard use. Constant improvements outdated equipment rapidly but pushed electrification ahead. On September 4, 1882, at 3:00 p.m., the J. P. Morgan Company on Wall Street was, amid ceremony, lit with some four hundred electric bulbs. Soon thereafter Edison started the first hydroelectric plant. Moreover, some three hundred generating plants were operating by early 1883. Uses other than lighting were also developed for electricity, such as electric fire alarms and electric railways.

After filing a number of patents relating to an electric railway, Edison joined in 1881 with S. D. Field to form the Electric Railway Company of America. Together they installed a demonstration track at the Chicago Exposition and established the practicality of the electric railway system; but, practical or not, the public and Edison lost interest in the system for more than a decade after its invention.

Clark contends that in the decade between 1880 and 1890, Edison crossed the border between the famous and the celebrity. The decade was also important because Edison's failure rate increased. The author argues that "whatever the cause, genius began to flicker." In this period, Edison purchased a home in West Orange, New Jersey, a suburb of Newark. The laboratories of Menlo Park were left to fall into disuse and ruin while new laboratories and research facilities were constructed near Edison's new home. Affiliated companies were constructed near his West Orange home. The National Phonograph Company, the Edison Business Phonograph Company, the Edison Phonograph Works, the Edison Manufacturing Company and others were soon constructed. Also from 1885 onward Edison was involved in initiating some two hundred lawsuits at a cost of two million dollars to protect his patents. Increasingly Edison was also involved in generating publicity. The most determined of his propaganda campaigns involved his stubborn support of direct current in opposition to alternating current. The difficulty with direct current was that it could only be effective at a limited distance, and, as use of electricity grew, direct current ran into problems. Nikolas Tesla supported alternating current even though he worked for Edison. Becoming infuriated with Edison's tactics, he quit and went to work for George Westinghouse. At Westinghouse, Tesla produced a practical system of alternating current that eventually replaced Edison's direct current. The Edison propaganda campaign had failed.

By 1888 Insull's organizational efforts resulted in the formation of the Edison General Electric Company, and Edison surrendered control of much of the industrial complex he had fathered. By 1889 his name was dropped from the company and he emerged an embittered and, for a time, almost unbalanced man. Unfortunately, Clark does not go into the details of this period, which, one suspects, might have been very useful in understanding his subject's personality.

Meanwhile, Edison again returned to improvement of the phonograph. He recognized that the primary use of the phonograph would be the recording of music, but, as in his advocacy of direct current, he again backed a loser: he insisted on the cylinder over the flat record even though the cylinder had far more limited use than the record. Only in 1913 did he give in to the record—but not before it was clear that "The Man Who Made the Future" had guessed wrong again. In the late 1880's, Edison had turned to moving pictures and by 1888 had taken out a patent on the kinetoscope. Several improvements were made in the 1890's, but by 1896 he lost interest, ceased development, and turned his attention elsewhere.

The next problem with which Edison became involved was extracting iron from low grade iron ore deposits. He planned very expensive and complex industrial installations which became models for uranium extraction in the United States in the 1940's. The installations were brilliantly conceived and technically a triumph. Unfortunately, the discovery of rich deposits of iron ore in the Mesabi range of Minnesota made the installation irrelevant and Edison, after losing some two million dollars, closed his plants. Edison next turned to cement houses which he successfully developed, but which the public refused to purchase. Again guessing wrong, Edison collaborated with Henry Ford to produce an electric automobile. Although contributing significantly to the development of the battery, Edison eventually had to recognize that the gasoline and not the electric automobile represented the wave of the future.

Edison's work during World War I was involved with providing synthetic substances to aid the war effort, the most important of which used carbolic acid and benzol. He was able to develop techniques for producing these chemicals, and also to aid the Navy with torpedo detection, more efficient periscopes, and other improvements in equipment. The end of the war brought a period of real decline for Edison, and Clark has little of substance to say about the inventor until his death in 1931.

Ronald Clark has written a rather dull account that provides the details of Edison's inventions, but little insight into Edison the man. Lacking dates at critical points and jumping, regardless of chronology, from issue to issue or invention to invention, the story is difficult to follow. Finally, detailed descriptions of important events, such as Edison's loss of control of his corporate structure, are too often lacking. The interesting subject and handsome format of this book have not been matched by the writing of a biographer from whom readers have come to expect more.

Saul Lerner

Sources for Further Study

Kirkus Reviews. XLV, August 15, 1977, p. 892.
New York Times Book Review. November 13, 1977, p. 70.
Publisher's Weekly. CCXII, August 22, 1977, p. 56.
Times Literary Supplement. November 4, 1977, p. 1283.

THE EMPIRE OF REASON
How Europe Imagined and America
Realized the Enlightenment

Author: Henry Steele Commager (1902–   )
Publisher: Anchor Press/Doubleday (New York). 342 pp. $10.00
Type of work: History
Time: 1750–1800
Locale: America and Europe

A detailed description of how late eighteenth century America was the fulfillment of the ideas and beliefs of the Enlightenment

Principal personages:
GEORGE WASHINGTON, first President of the United States
JOHN ADAMS, second President of the United States
THOMAS JEFFERSON, third President of the United States
JOSEPH PRIESTLEY, scientist and discoverer of oxidation
BENJAMIN FRANKLIN, colonial agent and diplomat
THOMAS PAINE, author of *Common Sense* and *The Age of Reason*

Late in his career, Henry Steele Commager, in his bicentennial volume, *The Empire of Reason: How Europe Imagined and America Realized the Enlightenment,* has sympathetically portrayed a glorious beginning for the United States based upon the ideas of the Enlightenment. Commager contends that

> . . . it was Americans who not only embraced the body of Enlightenment principles, but wrote them into law, crystalized them into institutions, and put them to work. That, as much as the winning of independence and the creation of the nation, *was* the American Revolution.

More than any other nation at its founding the United States was the fulfillment and fruition of the Enlightenment.

This scholarly and eloquent volume pursues its thesis relentlessly as it probes the ideas both of American and of European *philosophes*—that international community of intellectuals, consisting of educators, revolutionaries, rationalists, Deists, men of letters, statesmen, and citizens of the world, who sought useful truths. The underlying principle on which they all agreed, and which was the foundation of their perceptions of nature, God, and society, was order. They were occupied with organization, classification, codification, and systematization, from Baron d'Holbach's *Système de la nature* (1770), to Montesquieu's *Spirit of the Laws,* to the *System of Nature* of Carl Linnaeus, to Adam Smith's *Wealth of Nations,* to the work of Comte de Buffon, Diderot, and others.

In the mid-eighteenth century Philadelphia was the capital of the American Enlightenment, the intellectual and cultural center of the American colonies presided over by Benjamin Franklin. America's *philosophes*—Franklin, Thomas Jefferson, Benjamin Rush, John Adams, Thomas Paine, Joel Barlow, Manasseh Cutler, Joseph Priestley, Benjamin Thompson—were an outstanding group almost unmatched in any European nation. Confident that Reason would solve all of their problems, they were also dedicated to Progress, the belief that the future would bring improvement to all aspects of life. Scrutinizing the past and analyzing and organizing the present, they were convinced that the future should and could be better. History became a reservoir out of which the *philosophes* derived support for their critique of eighteenth century society. Studies of ancient Greece and republican Rome increased in quality and quantity. Pope translated the *Iliad* and the *Odyssey* into English and Gibbon wrote his *Decline and Fall of the Roman Empire.* The ancient world became the theme of painting, music, and sculpture. Many Europeans were particularly attracted to Greece, while most North Americans admired and sought to emulate republican Rome. History provided examples around which to shape the future.

A climate of curiosity and desire to expand the limits of knowledge led to a period of exploration in the eighteenth century that eventuated in the accumulation of vast quantities of scientific information and the mapping of previously unexplored areas. Under the impact of this interest in exploration, the interiors of both Russia and North America were mapped by the Russians, Spaniards, French, Scots, and American colonists. Siam, Burma, India, and China were all rediscovered and exploration also extended to Africa and the Middle East.

As explorers penetrated North America they initiated a debate about the nature of the New World and its inhabitants. A general assumption of the Enlightenment was that human nature was everywhere uniform, except that men differed in accordance with variations in their environments. Out of this assumption, individuals of the early Enlightenment attempted to explain America and the Indians. Why had America emerged so late in history? Why had it been so unimportant in the history of the world? The European answer was most unflattering: America had a distinctly inferior environment; its inhabitants were therefore inferior, and civilization gave way to barbarism.

In reaction to this indictment emerged a formidable defense by America's *philosophes,* directed by Thomas Jefferson. His *Notes on Virginia,* an outstanding work which attracted much European attention, provided ample scientific information that there was nothing inferior about America. Jefferson also supplied Buffon and other European scientists with bones, skins, animals, and plants to demonstrate the superior flora and fauna of the New World. Jefferson, Charles Thompson and others supplied information about the American Indians that conveyed the impression of strength, intelligence, nobility, and superiority over the European. A second argument in behalf of American superiority was the spectacular population growth that continued throughout the colonial and early national periods. Such population increases could only mean, according to Jefferson, that the American environment was far superior to that of Europe. Third, it was argued that the environment in the New World was rapidly being improved by Americans through their scientific accomplishments and efforts at self-government.

The conclusive argument was the political system that Americans had established based upon freedom, equality, and self-government. Such an exemplary legal and constitutional system was inconceivable anywhere in Europe, where the dreary despotism even of states governed by so-called enlightened rulers was totally different from the New World experience. Surely here was the strongest proof of American genius and superiority. Americans had developed a tradition of writing constitutions that limited the authority of politicians and administrators, and had developed, as well, judicial review to curtail the authority both of legislators and executives. These political devices became guarantees of liberty and the means of avoiding despotism. Americans were to have a government of laws, not of men.

Not only did Americans employ good governmental principles, but, to the astonishment of Europeans, they had an impressive array of competent and skillful statesmen who assured the effective working of these principles. Moreover, Americans shared a common heritage and tradition; as a nation they agreed on fundamentals and were thoroughly familiar with the practices of democracy. The notion, for example, of popular suffrage may have seemed absurd to Europeans, but it worked naturally for Americans. So did the unheard-of notions that government should be left to the common man, and that office holders were public servants. And yet, how was it accomplished?

Commager argues that nationalism was responsible for the success of the Americans in constructing their Constitution of 1787 and in establishing government under it. Instead, however, of requiring many centuries to develop as in Europe, American nationalism had emerged with an unexpected rapidity. A sense of community, according to the author, "came from the people; it was an act of will." The rapid rise of nationalistic feeling was based on the belief that America was unique in history—a belief which was nurtured by the country's religions. Religious associations and ties were the earliest form of cement for American nationalism. While the most obvious religious development in uniting Americans was the Great Awakening, eighteenth century colonists also cooperated on political and military matters. The Revolution was a shared experience for Americans, Commager argues, and one to which they could relate as a nation. All of these factors persuaded Americans to act, think, and work in behalf of common objectives, purposes, and projects.

Coming from the people, nationalism in America produced institutions based upon democratic reason and common sense. Such institutions were not founded on the inherited jealousies and vested interests which had characterized Europe; in the New World the slate had been wiped clean of such rivalries and prejudices. Reason and practicality were given a full measure of authority along with democracy—that corrosive of pretension and arrogance among office holders.

Given these ingredients, Commager writes, "In America politics was the universal preoccupation, legislation the universal resource, and constitutions the universal panacea." Thus, most Americans were preoccupied with and involved in momentous events that brought about the political inventions of judicial supremacy and judicial review, the separation of powers, the balance of powers, "office without pageantry," "administration without bureaucracy," and the political party. Constitution-making had been a part of American colonial life from the *Mayflower Compact* on, and was so commonplace an experience that it had been institutionalized in the form of the constitutional convention. This body legalized revolution. It permitted men to undertake all manner of political and governmental change peacefully; they could revise government, unlike in the European situation in which revolution was the unfortunate but sole means of changing government.

Moreover, the Americans were to develop federalism into a system which permitted a central government strong enough to sustain itself, while allowing a full measure of local self-government and individual liberty. Such federalism enhanced democracy by supporting and encouraging wide citizen participation in governmental processes. Americans also provided an answer to colonialism, one of the most perplexing and difficult problems in Western civilization—a problem that had led to the American Revolution. Through the Ordinances of 1784, 1785, and 1787 (the Northwest Ordinance), Americans devised a system permitting colonial territories to obtain a status of equality with the original thirteen states of the Union rather than remaining forever in a status of political inferiority. The institutionalization of constitution-making, federalism, and providing an answer for colonialism were profoundly creative and unparalleled political legacies of eighteenth century America.

An even more significant legacy involved "securing the blessings of liberty." Relying on Locke, Montesquieu, and others, Americans in 1787 attempted to create a government that would prevent tyranny and thereby preserve liberty. The line of reasoning that the Founding Fathers pursued was traced in *The Federalist Papers*, and particularly in Madison's *No. 10*. The prevention of tyranny and the preservation of liberty could be accomplished by balance and separation of governmental powers. Thus political mechanisms could frustrate greed, ambition, tyranny, and the natural tendency in all men to employ government for personal benefit. To these principles of separation and balance, Americans added yet another: the guarantee of certain fundamental rights which could not be abridged. The Bill of Rights was an assurance and promise of liberty additional to the workings of the Constitution of 1787. Separation, balance, and rights were also translated into limitations on the authority and functioning of state governments. Tyranny was to be avoided and liberty secured by placing powerful restraints on the powers of governments.

The effect of the American effort to limit government was to reduce the scope of arbitrary government more thoroughly than had been done at any time in history. The American government was to be a government of law in the most comprehensive sense, with the courts interpreting the law. Such a role for the courts meant that even the will and power of the majority had been limited. Hence, the possibility of tyranny was further reduced and liberty was accordingly expanded.

Not only did Americans excel in translating the ideas of the European Enlightenment into American principles, but they were exceptional for their successes in creating working governments that fulfilled in practice these very principles. The success of American government could not be paralleled in any European nation. This is the proof for Commager that it was in America that the Enlightenment was realized and an "Empire of Reason" created.

Commager's book is an eloquent, thoughtful, imaginative, and well-written tribute to and appreciation of America, the founding of the United States, and the genius of the Founding Fathers.

Saul Lerner

Sources for Further Study

Booklist. LXXIII, April 1, 1977, p. 1137.
Library Journal. CII, April 15, 1977, p. 916.
National Review. XXIX, September 30, 1977, p. 1123.
New York Times Book Review. August 14, 1977, p. 10.
Saturday Review. IV, May 14, 1977, p. 20.

ESSAYS OF E. B. WHITE

Author: Elwyn Brooks White (1899–   )
Publisher: Harper & Row Publishers (New York). 277 pp. $12.50
Type of work: Essays

A collection of essays originally published over a span of more than forty years in which one of America's most celebrated prose stylists writes about country and city, man and nature, the remembered past and the world of tomorrow, and writers and writing

The warm reception of *Letters of E. B. White* in 1976 has led to the most welcome publication of a collection of thirty-one of White's essays, most of which appeared originally in *The New Yorker, Harper's,* and other magazines over a span of more than forty years. The essays range in length from the two-page "Riposte," answering J. B. Priestley's assertion that Americans believe hen eggs are good only if they are white, to a twenty-six-page account of a voyage, remembered many years later, by a youthful and naïve Elwyn Brooks White from Seattle to Alaska and back in 1923. The arrangement of the book, as White says in a brief Foreword, is "by subject matter or by mood or by place, not by chronology." There are seven groups of essays: "The Farm," "The Planet," "The City," "Florida," "Memories," "Diversions and Obsessions," and "Books, Men, and Writing." Several essays have not been published before in book form.

"A loose sally of the mind," wrote Dr. Johnson defining *essay* in his *Dictionary,* "an irregular indigested piece; not a regular or orderly composition." The form (or lack of form) permits quick shifts from one topic to another and, in White's practice, not only allows veering or tacking as with a whimsical wind pushing his sailboat on Penobscot Bay, but also includes many parenthetical interruptions not limited to a mere word or phrase. White likes parentheses, and his frequent use of them helps to make his essays sound like amiable talk from an intelligent, urbane man with some interesting comments to make and an often amusing way of making them. In "Coon Tree" he remarks that his doctor has ordered him to put his head in traction for ten minutes twice a day, and he parenthesizes: "Nobody can figure out what to do with my head, so now they are going to give it a good pull, like an exasperated mechanic who hauls off and gives his problem a smart jolt with the hammer."

White's parentheses usually contain no more than one sentence, if even that, but occasionally he needs more room. In enumerating and describing the changes that have "modernized" his old kitchen in Maine, he complains that there is no longer a tub to wash his dog in. Then he adds a parenthesis: "I give our current dachshund one bath a year now, in an old wash boiler, outdoors, finishing him off with a garden-hose rinse. He then rolls in the dirt to dry himself, and we are where we started."

White has often been praised for his prose style, which is so easy and flowing that it seems effortless, but the casualness is deceptive; it has been carefully attained. Literary echoes sound occasionally, yet they are natural, not pretentious. As he listens to a farm helper spading rocky earth for the burial of a pig that has died after long suffering, White says somberly to himself, "Never send to know for whom the grave is dug, it's dug for thee." One winter in Maine he recalls how a Florida beach he used to enjoy visiting has been "developed" and thus has been ruined for him, and he indulges in a rueful biblical pun, "And if the surf hath lost its savor, wherewith shall we be surfeited?"

White's occasional figures of speech reflect his experience of both rural life and city life. He looks at bundles of fir-balsam wreaths ready to be trucked from Maine to Boston or New York for the Christmas trade, and to him they are "aromatic dumplings [for] hungry dwellers in cities." Young firs are also ready for the long haul, "standing as close together as theatergoers between the acts." On another occasion he watches an old gander that has lost a fight with a young gander and has sat alone in the hot sun for two hours. "I felt deeply his sorrow and his defeat," writes White. "I had seen his likes often enough on the benches of the treeless main street of a Florida city—spent old males, motionless in the glare of the day."

When he was young, White tried writing verse and once had published in a Louisville newspaper a sonnet on a horse that won a race at Churchill Downs (beating a horse that White had bet on). In later years White occasionally returned briefly to verse, several examples of which he reprinted in *The Second Tree from the Corner* (1954), but he recognized early that his normal medium was prose. Yet the music and even the rhythm of poetry still sound in phrases and sentences of his later prose, as in "A Report in January," written from his Maine home in 1958:

> The days ahead unroll in the mind, a scroll of blessed events in garden and in barn. Wherever you look, you see something that advertises the future: in the heifer's sagging sides you see the calf, in the cock's shrill crow you hear the pipping egg, in the cache of topsoil down cellar next the furnace you see the seedling, and even on the darkest day the seed catalogue gives off a gleam from some tomato of the first magnitude.

White and his beloved wife Katharine, who, following a long illness died shortly after *Essays* was published, had a number of homes during their forty-eight-year marriage. There were several apartments in New York—the opening essay, "Good-Bye to Forty-Eighth Street," describes the leaving of one of these— but "home" in the essays usually means the white farmhouse in North Brooklin, Maine, which the Whites bought in 1933 and in which White still lives, having, as he remarks in the Foreword to *Essays,* "finally come to rest." This farm house is the scene of many of the best pieces in *Essays,* whether they were written there or not.

Readers of White's volume of letters or of most of his earlier books may remember that he finds nature's creatures—from insects all the way up the evolutionary ladder to man—by turns entertaining, amusing, or enlightening and sometimes saddening or almost maddening. Animals and birds, both wild and domesticated, often appear as characters, either major or minor, in his verse, his fiction, and his essays. He once wrote a seriocomic ode on a cow that had died from a bee sting, and the protagonists of all three of his books for children are nonhuman, although Stuart Little combines the appearance of a mouse with the speech and other characteristics of a highly intelligent and well-mannered boy.

In the early 1930's White had a Scotch terrier named Daisy ("an opinionated little bitch") who purportedly wrote several letters to Mrs. White reporting on the activities and troubles of her husband. One of Daisy's newsy letters is included in *Letters of E. B. White,* and her obituary appears in White's *Quo Vadimus?* (1939). Of the whole series of dachshunds that show up in White's writings over the years, Fred is the chief, an energetic, troublesome, and yet endearing dog (Fred's dead now, dammit, as White once wrote) who is as unforgettable to White's readers as he is to his former master. Fred furnishes the comic relief in "Death of a Pig," which is reprinted in "The Farm" section of *Essays.* The piece is a sad and ironic story of a pig which is bought to be fattened and then slaughtered for his pork but which White goes to extraordinary trouble to try to save from dying of an undetermined illness that finally destroys him. During the several days and nights of the struggle, Fred is all over the place, observing and supervising ("his stethoscope dangling") as White and two veterinarians try vainly to cure the pig; and Fred staggers along behind White and his helper Lennie as they drag the pig's body to its burial place. "The grave in the woods is unmarked," writes White in conclusion, "but Fred can direct the mourner to it unerringly and with immense good will, and I know he and I shall often revisit it, singly and together, in seasons of reflection and despair, on flagless memorial days of our own choosing."

A mother raccoon plays the principal role in "Coon Tree," a little nature comedy enacted mostly in or on the trunk of a tree in front of White's Maine home. As White meticulously describes the coon's "thorough scrub-up" before her nightly foraging and her slow and careful descent of the tree, one is reminded of the close and patient observation of animals and birds by Henry David Thoreau—one of White's favorite authors—who in the nineteenth century found in nature the same kind of pleasure that White has experienced in the present one. Another comic nature essay is "The Geese," though it ends in pathos. White ingeniously arranges to have eggs from a super-laying goose hatched by her less productive sister and then somewhat later observes sadly as the elderly gander who fathered the goslings is beaten and run away by the goslings' young and vigorous uncle on the maternal side.

White is skeptical about much of what has been and is being done by modern scientists and technologists, and he wonders about their predictions regarding the kind of world that is being projected for future generations. "I would feel more optimistic about a bright future for man," he says, "if he spent less time proving that he can outwit Nature and more time tasting her sweetness and respecting her seniority." Again, in "Sootfall and Fallout," in which a troubled, anxious, fearful tone predominates, he comments, "I hold one share in the corporate earth and am uneasy about the management." Even as early as 1939, when he wrote "The World of Tomorrow," a report on the New York World's Fair, he complained that there was too much technology and too little life in what he saw.

"Here Is New York," one of White's best-known essays, was written in the summer of 1948 and appeared first in *Holiday* in 1949 and later as a small book. Although it pictures a New York quite different from the present one, White has included the essay in his collection because he remembers the former city "with longing and with love." It is a beautiful memorial to a city that was.

White goes back to the 1920's to compose a fond memorial to the Model T Ford in "Farewell, My Lovely," which was first published in *The New Yorker* over the pseudonym Lee Strout White. Suggested by a manuscript sent in by Richard Lee Strout, the essay nevertheless draws largely upon White's own memories of the Ford, since he and a friend, Howard Cushman, traveled across the United States in 1922 in a Ford roadster that White had bought for about four hundred dollars. White comments on the many gadgets that could be bought from Sears Roebuck to equip or decorate the car, which "was born naked as a baby"; and he mentions some of "the lore and legend that governed the Ford," including what to do about the "extravagantly odd little device" called a timer. White once tried spitting on his timer to remove a possible hex. The essay will stir the memories of those who drove the old Model T, and it may pique the curiosity of jaded younger drivers bored by the modern car, which needs only a turn of the ignition key to start and which then moves forward smoothly to driving speed without even a manual changing of gears.

The three authors White recalls with affection and respect in his final group of essays are Don Marquis, Will Strunk, Jr., and Edward Howe Forbush. Marquis was the creator of Archy, a poetic cockroach who typed his poems in lower case because he couldn't manage the capital key, and Archy's racy feline friend Mehitabel, whose mottos for living were "toujours gai" and "wotthehell wotthehell." The essay was first written as an introduction to a 1950 edition of *the lives and times of archy and mehitabel.*

Will Strunk was the professor who taught White English usage and composition at Cornell, using his own little text, *The Elements of Style,* and issuing his oral imperatives in triplicate, as when he laid down Rule Thirteen: "Omit needless words! Omit needless words! Omit needless words!" White's adulatory essay on Strunk led to a publisher's request that White prepare an updated edition of *The Elements of Style,* and the book has enjoyed considerable success as a text.

Edward Howe Forbush was an ornithologist who died in 1929 just before completing his master work, *Birds of Massachusetts and Other New England States.* In "Mr. Forbush's Friends" White writes of his pleasure and profit from "reading around" in his set of *Birds of Massachusetts* over two decades. He particularly enjoys Forbush's "immense enthusiasm for anything that has feathers," the abundance of well-organized information he gives, and the use the author makes of his "large company of informers, or tipsters" who feed him such information as that furnished by a Massachusetts lady who heard a catbird sound "Taps" and who "Believes bird picked it up from hearing it played at burial services in nearby cemetery."

E. B. White will never win a Nobel Prize for Literature. As he says in his Foreword, essayists are considered second-class citizens. White has won a whole group of lesser awards, however, the earliest being several honorary degrees in the 1940's and 1950's and the latest a special Pulitzer citation in literature and the arts in April, 1978. He richly deserves every award.

Henderson Kincheloe

Sources for Further Study

Book World. August 28, 1977, p. F2.
Business Week. October 17, 1977, p. 21.
Commonweal. CIV, November 25, 1977, p. 765.
New York Review of Books. XXIV, October 27, 1977, p. 42.
New York Times. September 19, 1977, p. 33.
Newsweek. XC, October 3, 1977, p. 97.
Publisher's Weekly. CXII, July 11, 1977, p. 68.
Saturday Review. IV, August 20, 1977, p. 63.

THE FABIANS

Authors: Norman and Jeanne MacKenzie
Publisher: Simon and Schuster (New York). Illustrated. 446 pp. $12.95
Type of work: History
Time: 1884–1913
Locale: England

A study of a small socialist discussion group which grew to become a major force in British politics and government

Principal personages:
ANNIE BESANT, writer and social reformer
HUBERT BLAND, one of the founders of the Fabian Society
SYDNEY OLIVIER, civil servant; early Fabian
EDWARD PEASE, founder and long-time secretary of the Society
GEORGE BERNARD SHAW, propagandist and agitator
BEATRICE (POTTER) WEBB, social scientist and agitator
SIDNEY WEBB, leading light of the Fabians; Member of Parliament
H. G. WELLS, novelist and social critic

During the middle years of the reign of Queen Victoria, a few young men took to meeting occasionally in the lodgings of Edward Pease near Regent's Park, London. They talked of personal problems and considered how they might "help on" the improvement of British society. By January, 1884, there were nine enrolled, dues-paying members of the group. One of them thought they should have a name and suggested the Fabian Society—from the ancient Roman general Fabius Cunctator, who had withstood Hannibal by tactics of boldness and caution combined. That rather odd choice was matched by a vagueness of purpose. Frank Podmore, Edward Pease, and Hubert Bland made up the executive of the Society, but they admitted "they did not know what to do" with the group. Edith Bland, Hubert's wife, added that, while the Fabians were the "nicest set of people" she ever knew, she could not say precisely what their intentions or purposes were.

Membership in the Society increased slowly during the next several years; there were still only sixty-seven Fabians in 1886. In general the Society attracted young middle-class intellectuals inclined toward socialism. At the Fabian meetings they found a relaxed, congenial atmosphere in which to vent their opinions. The Society did not insist upon adherence to any specific theory or ideology, which was the secret of its appeal. Members could lecture, debate, and discuss almost any topic, and they did so freely.

A notable addition to the Society's roster came in May, 1884, in the person of George Bernard Shaw, a recent immigrant from Ireland. Now in his later twenties and very poor, Shaw had, unlike most of the other Fabians, not attended a university; so he had made the British Museum his university. There he imbibed the writings of Henry George, Nietszche, Marx, and the economist W. S. Jevons and became a convinced socialist. Between spells at the Museum, Shaw attended meetings of various political and social reform organizations which sprang up all over London in the 1880's; he was particularly attracted to the Marxist Social Democratic Federation. He also consorted with the bohemian crowd which gathered in cafes around the British Museum; the short-haired women and long-haired men who ran the "gamut of personal and political eccentricity." From the bohemian eccentrics, Shaw took up a number of food and dress fads along with evolutionist and free-thinking notions which he carried over to his later life and writings, and to the Fabians.

Others joined the Fabians about the same time as Shaw. Annie Besant, an intense young woman with various dreams and plans for social reform, became a member in 1885. In that year also, Sydney Olivier and Sidney Webb, both civil servants employed at the Colonial Office, found in the Fabians a forum for their reforming interests. The talents and dedication of Shaw, Besant, Olivier, and Webb were soon recognized, and they were all chosen to the Fabian executive in 1888.

Those new executives then set the Society toward a clearer purpose and a more definite program. It was decided to present a series of prepared talks on the general theme of socialism. Each executive member was assigned a specific topic: historical background of socialism, socialist economics, capitalist industry, property under socialism, morals, and social production or collectivization were the topics chosen. The lectures were delivered in 1889, the texts then were collected, edited by Sidney Webb and published by the Society as the *Fabian Essays*. These essays served as a prospectus and program for the education and propaganda work that the Society now began. Following up on the publication of the *Fabian Essays*, the Fabians launched the "Lancashire Campaign," a lecture tour in the northern provinces in which the members would attempt to persuade industrial workers of the merits of socialism.

The work went well. About twenty thousand copies of the *Fabian Essays* were sold each year. In the provinces, new branches of the Society were established and, in London, additional Fabian groups formed. By 1890, total membership reached about one hundred and fifty persons: Mrs. Emmeline Pankhurst, who later led the fight for female suffrage, James Keir Hardie, Will Crooks, and Ben Tillett, spokesmen for the newly forming unions of unskilled workers, were among the more noteworthy recruits of the Fabians.

But the most valuable addition to the membership at this time was surely Beatrice Potter. She came from a wealthy family and had received all of the privileges of an upper middle-class Victorian girl, including the opportunity to meet many of the leading figures in British life. In her twenties, Beatrice fell in love with the rising politician, Joseph Chamberlain, but he did not reciprocate her love. After six years of romantic suffering and thoughts of suicide, Beatrice came out of her personal torment and turned to other concerns. Social work, particularly gathering facts about the lives and labor of the poor of London became her great interest. During the course of that work, she came into contact with the Fabians, began to attend their meetings, which she called "a very pretty piece of intellectual communism," and was persuaded to join them.

Beatrice found more than she had anticipated at the Fabian Society when she met Sidney Webb there. He fell in love with her and after several years of pursuit, persuaded her to marry him in 1893. In later years, Beatrice characterized their married life as the "utter essence of British bourgeois morality, comfort and enlightenment." They were more than just marriage partners; for the rest of their lives, the Webbs were professional colleagues and associates sharing a common work and rejoicing in mutual successes. Sidney resigned from the Colonial Office—they could live amply on Beatrice's inherited income—and the two devoted themselves to social research, writing, and Fabian propaganda.

Some members of the Society—Annie Besant, Hubert Bland, and Shaw, among others—thought in the early 1890's that the time was ripe for the Fabians to take the lead in linking up the labor unions with reform groups such as the Social Democratic Federation to form a new British Socialist Party. But the Webbs disagreed; Fabian aims, they believed, would be better served through "permeation" of the existing major political parties than in forming a new party. At the first annual conference of the Society in London, February 1892, the majority of the members agreed with the Webbs and opted for permeation: to supply "ideas and principles of social reconstruction to each of the great political parties in turn," and thus gain piecemeal reforms. When the permeation strategy was adopted, the Society splintered; some members resigned, others drifted away. Annie Besant, for instance, turned to the mystical teachings called Theosophy. But Shaw acquiesced in the "permeation racket," and henceforth, he and the Webbs formed a kind of dominant triumvirate in the Society.

The Webbs offered the specific aims of the Society: publicly owned tramways, gas, electric and water supplies, fair wages for public employees, and measures for improved health and housing. Graham Wallas devised the Fabian slogan "Postulate, Permeate, Perorate." And Shaw recommended the strategy of voting for the better man of either major party against the worst as the means of gaining the Society's aims.

By 1894, the Society had reached ten years of age; its leading members were now in their later thirties. The Society had acquired its own offices on the Strand with Edward Pease as salaried permanent secretary. New members appeared, among them James Ramsay MacDonald, a young Scottish socialist who later became the first Labourite Prime Minister. MacDonald had been instrumental in forming the Independent Labour Party and now he hoped to bring a closer collaboration between the Fabians and the ILP. But Shaw and the Webbs rejected those MacDonald overtures. The Society would continue its work of lecturing, pamphleteering and persuasion separately, not as an appendage of the Independent Labour Party. Sidney Webb believed the Society should act primarily as educators, not as political agitators. Socialism was the ultimate goal for both Fabians and the ILP, but, to Webb, socialist collectivization must come slowly through the transformation of state and municipal enterprises.

In the provinces, however, many of the Fabians were impatient with Webb's "gradualness" strategy, and collaboration between the provincial Fabians and the Independent Labour Party developed in defiance of the Londoners.

Meanwhile, a large bequest by a sympathetic businessman to the Fabians enabled the Webbs to establish in 1896 an enterprise very close to their hearts: a school for social research called the London School of Economics, where young people would be trained in social statistics and analysis to promote socialism. The school flourished from the beginning, and remains today as an important center for economic study.

The Webbs journeyed to the United States in 1896 partly to determine whether the Americans were ready for Fabianism. They met Theodore Roosevelt and found him most remarkable. Beatrice regarded Woodrow Wilson as "an attractive-minded man." They liked Salt Lake City and thought it too bad that Mormon polygamy had not been allowed to test principles of "scientific breeding." Chicago, on the other hand, was "unspeakable . . . viler than tongue can tell." In all, as they departed, Beatrice concluded that the United States was not ready for socialism yet.

Fabian membership rose and fell over the years. When they celebrated their twentieth anniversary in 1904, the Society had less than seven hundred members, and even fewer who regularly attended meetings at Clifford's Inn. Over two-thirds of the original members had fallen away, many of them in protest when the Society had backed British imperialism against the Boers in South Africa. As the MacKenzie's put that approval, the Fabians "had begun with the idea of a civilizing mission in darkest England; which had now been extended to darkest Africa. But it was the same doctrine of an elite offering salvation to the poor."

In its third decade, the Society took a new lease on life when a wave of reform sentiment again swept over Britain in the Edwardian era. By 1907, Fabian membership reached two thousand, about one-fourth of them being women. H. G. Wells, a younger member, tried to get the Society to abandon the permeation strategy and support socialist candidates for Parliament, but Shaw and the Webbs held firm for permeation, and the Society majority rejected Wells's recommendation. That would be about the last time the "Old Gang" stood together, however. By 1908, the old friends were drifting apart. Shaw married, lived in the country, and mostly spent his time composing plays and traveling. Sidney Webb served on the London City Council for a number of years and then was elected a Member of Parliament. Beatrice became engrossed in Poor Law reform and woman suffrage.

The Society did launch one more successful endeavor, however: the founding of a weekly newspaper called *The New Statesmen and the Nation,* which, in time, became one of the leading intellectual journals in Britain.

On the eve of World War I, the old Fabian Society had about run its course. Its educational, propagandist, and permeation activities had brought a substantial degree of socialism to many aspects of British life. They had achieved much, yet not enough. Essentially, the Fabians believed they had a mission to civilize and regenerate society, and to see it governed by a disinterested intellectual elite, like themselves. That mission had not been accomplished; "I am haunted by the fear," wrote Beatrice Webb, "that all my struggles may have been in vain."

There is an Epilogue in *The Fabians* which looks at what happened to the Society and some of its members after World War I. In the 1930's, the Society was still alive, but was little more than a "constituent of the Labour Party." Permeation had finally been abandoned, and many of the essential ideas of Fabianism had been adopted as official Labour Party policy. Several younger members of the Fabian Society, who had studied at the London School of Economics—Hugh Dalton, Harold Laski, Herbert Morrison, and Clement Attlee—were prominent in the labor movement in the 1930's and after.

By the end of World War II, Fabian Society membership had a new resurgence, reaching over ten thousand. In 1945, over half of the Labourite Members of Parliament were Fabians, and ten of them, including Prime Minister Attlee, were in the Cabinet. So, in the mid-twentieth century, the Fabian Society was alive and well with greater numbers and perhaps more influence in British life than in the era of the Old Gang.

The Fabians is a long, but wholly enthralling book. The scholarship and use of original sources are judicious and intelligent; and the writing cannot be faulted. It might have been desirable to have included some of the published documents of the Society, such as the *Fabian Essays,* in an appendix so the reader would have a better perception as to exactly what the Fabian programs were. In all, the book is to be highly recommended for both the general reader and for the specialist.

James W. Pringle

Sources for Further Study

Choice. XIV, September, 1977, p. 908.

Economist. CCLXIV, July 2, 1977, p. 111.

Listener. XCVII, June 30, 1977, p. 866.

New Statesman. XCIV, August 5, 1977, p. 181.

Observer. July 3, 1977, p. 24.

Punch. CCLXXIII, July 20, 1977, p. 132.

THE FACE OF BATTLE

Author: John Keegan (1934–   )
Publisher: The Viking Press (New York). Illustrated. 354 pp. $10.95
Type of work: Military history
Time: 1415, 1815, and 1916
Locale: Agincourt, Waterloo, and the Somme

Through accounts and analyses of three battles, the author tries to understand better what the experience of battle is really like

Principal personages:
HENRY V, King of England
ARTHUR WELLESLEY, Duke of Wellington
SIR DOUGLAS HAIG, later Earl Haig

John Keegan is Senior Lecturer in War Studies at the Royal Military Academy, Sandhurst (the British equivalent of West Point). He admits in the very beginning that he has never been in battle, nor near a battle. In those two statements is an opening key to this book. *The Face of Battle* is an effort to derive from the historical sources a better understanding of what it is like to be *in* battle—not just to narrate the events, but to come closer to a realization of what the participants felt. The method is a description and analysis of three battles: Agincourt, Waterloo, and the Somme. Keegan surrounds the battle accounts with an introductory chapter and a conclusion, which provide much of the value of his work. The method is justified, for not only are the battle accounts fascinating and innovative in themselves, but they demonstrate the observations made in the more general portions, and bring the analyses to life.

Keegan's introduction is in large measure a study of military history, at once a defense and a critique, but also an effort to rescue the genre from its limitations. The authors of military history have been largely staff officers intent on "lessons," teachers in the military schools with much the same attitude, and amateur students of history, or of battle, or of both. The limitations derive from these facts, but lie deeper. The writers of military history have rarely gone beyond the fighting; they have taken what Keegan calls the "win/lose" approach, which isolates the military story from the rest of history. He likens this method to the English and American trial by jury, which he calls "accusatory," an aggressive process intended to reach a verdict. The alternative approach is the French "investigatory" proceeding, in which the judge has wide powers of interrogation and investigation to aid in arriving at truth. Whatever the merits of the two legal procedures—a matter for serious thought—the analogy is a valuable stimulus to an examination of the preconceptions behind historical writing, especially but not exclusively military historical writing. The implication is that practicing historians, military and otherwise, may not be fully conscious of the theoretical underpinnings or ramifications of their procedures.

Keegan's point, however, is especially applicable to the battle historian; if battle is not a crime, it is at least a definite event, and therefore possessed of parallels. In the "court of history," the question is always, Who was guilty of the result, if it was defeat, or responsible for the result, if it was victory? This commonest of approaches makes statements such as, "If General A had not extended his flank . . . ," or, "If General B had moved up five minutes earlier. . . ." Obviously, this is too narrow an approach. Not only is it unsafe to assume that the result of battle hinges on some single decision, but it is also true that not all battles have clear victories or defeats for which credit and blame can be distributed. Deeper and more important, if the historian looks only for guilt or innocence, blame or responsibility, he will not reach an understanding of the total event or process in all its background and complexity.

Keegan uses two examples to illustrate typical qualities of military history writing in the past; one is the English "philosopher of war," Sir Edward Creasy, the author of *The Fifteen Decisive Battles of the World,* first published in 1851 and often reprinted, extended, and imitated. Creasy, accepting the Victorian aversion to war but fascination by it, concentrated only on those battles which, as his title indicates, decided the course of history.

The second example is Julius Caesar and his *Gallic Wars,* which is illustrative, perhaps originative, of much battle writing. Not only Caesar's but most succeeding battle accounts are from the view of the general, whether or not written by him. The resulting difficulties are obvious: the tendency to self-glorification; the limits, both physical and intellectual, of the view; and, more important to Keegan's argument, the creation of a seemingly clear and simple picture out of a very complicated and confused set of happenings.

For the main body of his book, Keegan has chosen three battles, all English, and all told from that point of view: Agincourt (1415), Waterloo (1815), and the Somme (1916). The accounts are not typical battle narratives; we have little of the generals' plans and orders, though the successive movements are described. Rather the emphasis is on what actually happened, so far as it can be discovered, and that means what the men in battle did. There is attention, for instance, to the soldiers' condition before the battle. At Agincourt and Waterloo, they were tired with marching, and at Agincourt, with waiting in line; at Waterloo, many had spent the night in the rain. Keegan suggests the probability in many cases that they were sustained by liquor, perhaps actually drunk—a probability he supports from the record, but one which is rarely mentioned in conventional accounts.

The character of the troops and their relationship with their superiors at Agincourt are obvious concerns. Knights and men-at-arms, for instance, were unlikely to feel any desire for combat with mere archers; there was neither profit nor prestige in such a confrontation. Class lines distinguished officers from enlisted men at Waterloo, and usually at the Somme, but with somewhat different results. Methods of recruitment are taken into account at the Somme especially, where many outfits came from the same town and even the same civilian occupation. Keegan offers realistic appraisals of the encounters, framed in terms of the arms involved: for instance, infantry and cavalry against archers at Agincourt; infantry and cavalry against artillery at Waterloo, infantry against machine guns at the Somme. The author successfully captures the mood of confusion, noise, mud, falling comrades, enemies, and horses dead, wounded, or riderless; it is all pictured, vividly but in a low key. The rhetoric is not that of a battle piece; Keegan's treatment is basically analytical, not narrative.

Keegan asks practical questions. Why was the British square used and what was it like to be in it? What were the trenches, and complexes of trenches, and how do soldiers go about taking them? And, especially, how did men behave, and why? Why did some individuals and some groups go forward under fire, and others not? Why did men break—or more realistically, perhaps, why did more *not* break? What part did the hope of gain play—ransom for prisoners taken at Agincourt, looting at Waterloo? How much influence had the respect of fellow-soldiers, how much the leadership of officers? What effect had patriotism and self-esteem? How often was physical compulsion used—some Waterloo troops were driven forward by their officers' swords. What actions were due to fatigue? To shock?

The answers are sometimes speculations, sometimes a convergence of modern experience and theory with what is known of the contemporary conditions. The experts, each in his separate world, no doubt will have objections to Keegan's method—the battle historian to details of his accounts, the military men to his judgments of discipline or the lack of it, the psychologists and sociologists to his theories about men in groups and men under stress. What is important about Keegan's book is that, while the questions it asks are not the usual ones, they do seem to be the ones historians *ought* to ask.

In his summary, Keegan moves toward the present and the future, and discusses the ways in which mechanization, and the elaboration of modern technology, have changed battle, and the ways in which the impact of war falls on total populations, not on the military alone. There is the suggestion that the strain of battle, and the fear of it, may grow—may eventually even render it obsolete. It is an intriguing discussion, related to the historical analysis, but not necessarily validated by it.

In fact, one of the values of the book, but also one of its peculiarities, is the range of subjects treated in a comparatively brief space. The author displays considerable literary skill, particularly in his ability to include a wide and, at first glimpse, seemingly unrelated, set of interests or facts. The Somme account, for instance, includes not only some notion of trench warfare in general, and of the English society from which the "Kitchener army" came, but a note on the Russian front, and a discussion of the literary aftermath of the battle and the war.

The peculiarities and limitations of *The Face of Battle* are minor compared to the value of the book. It is cleanly and attractively written, and it rests on the solid foundation of its sources; both general reader and historian can enjoy it and profit from it. Two groups especially should have this book recommended to them: those interested in military history, whose usual version of it is the location of X division on the left flank, and the nonmilitary historians, who regard it not as unimportant, but as beneath the dignity of the intellectual and professional. Both may have their eyes opened; some may be moved to plow farther and deeper the ground which has been opened. History could be enriched; and it is possible to hope that increased and enriched understanding may eventually help toward an abolition of battle itself.

George J. Fleming

Sources for Further Study

Book World. September 18, 1977, p. E5.
Commonweal. CIV, September 2, 1977, p. 566.
New York Times Book Review. September 4, 1977, p. 23.
Publisher's Weekly. CCXII, August 8, 1977, p. 68.

FALCONER

Author: John Cheever (1912   )
Publisher: Alfred A. Knopf (New York). 211 pp. $7.95
Type of work: Novel
Time: The present
Locale: Falconer prison

A middle-class, middle-aged professor, a drug addict who has slain his brother, tries to adjust emotionally, sexually, and spiritually to life in prison

> *Principal characters:*
> ZEKE FARRAGUT, a professor, drug addict, and fratricide
> MARCIA FARRAGUT, his bisexual wife
> JODY, a prisoner, Farragut's lover
> CHICKEN NUMBER TWO,
> CUCKOLD,
> RANSOME,
> STONE,
> TENNIS, and
> BUMPO, other prisoners
> TINY and
> MARSHACK, guards
> CHISHOLM, Deputy Warden

The New Yorker goes to the jailhouse. That's not too surprising. Writing all those masterly *New Yorker* stories, as moralist in residence, in suburbia, in Ossining, near Sing Sing Prison, about upper-middle-class *angst,* Cheever must have finally felt obliged to commit one of his characters to prison, to imagine "how it would be." Fortunately, prison life itself is not finally Cheever's subject; he seems to assume his readers know all about that, as, in every sense that matters, they do.

Farragut, forty-eight, impulsively kills his brother Eben in a fit of rage suppressed since childhood. The nature of the killing, the brevity of the novel, and Farragut's "passion for blue sky," like Meursault's, may remind one of Camus' *The Stranger.* But Cheever's readers will recall more aptly his interest in relationships between brothers in "Goodbye, My Brother," one of his best stories, in "Brother," and in *The Wapshot Chronicle* and *The Wapshot Scandal.*

Cheever often delineates the special contradictions and absurdities in the character of the upper-middle-class male. Moving in an ambience of nostalgia and sentimentality, his characters often escape through dreams and prolonged waking fantasies from the monotony of routine lives and settled psyches; those escapes result in nightmare disruptions that are occasions for the stories. Disillusionment, emptiness, *ennui,* and loneliness break out in tentative or bizarre, joylessly calculated, or impulsive rebellions. Now one of those men, a man of privilege, of the professions (a teacher), a drug addict since his army days, goes to prison, leaving his son and his bisexual wife behind in suburbia.

Fiction, says Cheever, should "reflect the exaltations, the discursiveness, the spontaneity and the pratfalls one finds in a day." In *Falconer,* prison-pent feelings, routines, customs, ceremonies, and rituals become parallels that offer perspectives on everyday life in the "free world." The effect of this novel is suggested in what Auden said of Yeats: "In the prison of his days, teach the free man how to praise." Imprisonment of the self in one's own emotions—Cheever has often implied that metaphor; now he turns it around. Either way, the metaphor is trite, but Cheever's explorations make it richly suggestive. Is Falconer a regular prison, like Sing Sing, or an asylum for the criminally insane? Cheever is generally ambiguous enough to allow either possibility. Falconer sounds like another name for Farragut. What one reviewer said of a certain kind of Cheever story applies to *Falconer:* "It is as if Marquand had suddenly been crossed with Kafka."

So, from a fresh perspective, *Falconer* is another of Cheever's social satire, comedy-of-manners fables, and prison is a metaphor of the suburban human condition. But more aptly and originally, prison is a metaphor for sexual limbo. Melancholy is the predominant mood of all Cheever's stories—even when he is being cheerful. He leaves us with a sense of mortality, mutability, and pathos on the verge of collapse into bathos. His style, even in his frequent witty moments, is suffused with sadness, as if written during a hangover the morning after a cocktail party.

Two elements seldom found in a typical *New Yorker* story dominate *Falconer*—profanity and raunchy sex, almost entirely onanistic/homosexual. Prison life is an incessant see-saw of tumescence-detumescence. Just as Farragut must have his allotted drug fix every day, he must also have Jody, his young conniving lover, an addiction acquired in prison. Humiliations related to food, shelter, and sex are routine. Nude searches are frequent; the final section begins: "So they were naked again." Group masturbation in the "Valley" is another haunting metaphor of sexual pathos.

In their imaginative flights and escapes, Farragut and Jody are a sort of composite Icarus figure. Cheever's richly ambiguous style and his way of presenting characters and events prevent one from being absolutely certain that the escapes literally occur. After a long build-up, Jody escapes in a visiting bishop's helicopter, disguised as an acolyte; it is a very brief scene that takes one's breath. The point of view then abruptly shifts from third person, focus on Farragut, to focus on Jody, outside Falconer. Although he usually focuses on one character, Cheever is almost always a modified Trollope-like omniscient narrator. But this shift is disruptive, *unless* we enjoy the possibility that in the scene outside Falconer, Farragut imagines himself to be his lover Jody.

The progress of Farragut's own escape is more prolonged, more suspenseful, more imaginative, more darkly comic—he replaces his dead cellmate in a canvas sack. The possibility that both escapes are imagined justifies and gives continuity to Cheever's point of view strategy. And one feels the exultation Hermann Hesse provides in "My Life: A Conjectural Autobiography," in which

Hesse paints on his prison wall a blue train, already half inside a tunnel, and, before the eyes of his jailors, boards it and rides away.

Whether the escapes are literal or imagined, or intended as deliberate ambiguity to suggest both simultaneously, the novel's ending is not only unfashionably happy, it is ecstatic:

> Stepping from the bus onto the street, he saw that he had lost his fear of falling and all other fears of that nature. He held his head high, his back straight, and walked along nicely. Rejoice, he thought, rejoice.

Cheever trots out the usual rogue's gallery of convicts and guards, but filtered through Farragut's sensibility, they look and sound more interesting this time around. Ransome killed his father. A criminal organization pierced Stone's eardrums with an ice pick, framed him, and gave him an expensive hearing aid. Tennis claims to have won the Spartanburg doubles, twice in a row. "I'm listed in the sports encyclopedia. . . . I'm here because of a clerical error." Bumpo, "the cellblock celebrity . . . was supposed to have been the second man to hijack an airplane." Chicken Number Two was a jewel thief. "I was very charming. Everybody knew I had class. And . . . I had willingness." Cuckold, cellblock merchant of contraband, "iced" his wife by mistake the night she told him none of the three kids were his. He tells Farragut long stories about his promiscuous wife and about a brief encounter with a homosexual in a motel. Chisholm, Deputy Warden, "gets his kicks out of watching men in withdrawal" from drugs. Marshack is a guard with the instincts of a born killer. He shaved his head to enhance his image. " 'The shaved skulls,' Farragut thought, 'will always be with us.' " Tiny is an obese guard who slaughters twenty cats when one of them eats his London broil. "There were more cats in Falconer than convicts."

Leaving out details or even a sense of Farragut's life as a professor (what did he teach?) may seem to some readers less like authorial strategy than caprice. Why delay Farragut's memory of the scene in which he killed his brother? Because he couldn't face it? But that explanation isn't conveyed. "Why did you kill your brother, Zeke?" asks Chicken. Why at that point, near the end of the novel? It seems contrived. Does Cheever assume a convention of delay? The flashback exposition is interesting in itself, but Cheever deals it out in discrete blocks.

The structure of *Falconer* is justifiably anecdotal and episodic. The tonal shifts from satirical to lyrical to realistic to ironic are effective because Farragut's mind, emotions, and imagination are adrift, sometimes wilfully. Never fatal or tragic, the irony is sometimes the arbitrary irony of transient literary effect. Many of Cheever's stories—and certainly this novel—are governed by original concepts that he executes with a mingling of conventional and surprising literary elements and devices. We feel the energy of imagination in every line.

Readers may sometimes wish Cheever would express emotions and ideas in dialogue and scenes more than in commentary. It is difficult to remember what happened. Cheever is so good at the commentary technique that *what happens* is a mood, an impression, and usually that is enough. Sometimes he offers a preposterous or out-of-key line or episode the reader cannot believe but likes so much he *makes* it fit, or accepts it as *lagniappe*. For instance, Eben tells Farragut that his wife watches television so catatonically that one time, to make her see him, he went on the game show *Trial and Error;* following that rather far-fetched anecdote, Farragut kills his brother, a scene full of off-key notes, as when Eben kisses the living room rug.

Cheever's two *Wapshot* books were too long for his talent. *Bullet Park*'s 245 pages came closer. *Falconer* is the perfect length for a man who has written more than one hundred *New Yorker* stories (see his seven short story collections). *Falconer* is a long *New Yorker* story, a little longer than a novella. Cheever writes a Chekhovian kind of story, suffused with a Proustian preoccupation with the past, memory, and nostalgia. Like Faulkner, he has created his own world in his stories and novels. Some readers may compare him with two other *New Yorker* writers, Salinger and Updike, and perhaps with James Gould Cozzens and Louis Auchincloss, but such comparisons leave Cheever's special qualities untouched. He is at once the most typical of the *New Yorker* writers and the least stereotyped, the least often predictable.

Despite his three earlier novels, one thinks of this writer, whose first story appeared in 1930 when he was eighteen, as a short story writer of great variety and even, for him, an experimental venturesomeness. When we list major American writers, we do not include those who are mainly short story writers. But like Peter Taylor, Katherine Anne Porter, J. F. Powers, and Frank O'Connor, Cheever is a major writer. He is not a public figure. He has never been involved in the social and political movements or aesthetic controversies of the past five decades. Even in *Falconer* the infamous Attica prison riots and slaughter only hover over Farragut's cellblock in rumors and radio waves. Cheever has only tenuous associations with academia. He has, quite simply, been a professional writer all his adult life. As early as 1964, John Aldridge called Cheever one of our "most grievously underdiscussed important writers." Despite some popular and critical success and the *Newsweek* cover story when *Falconer* appeared, that assessment remains accurate.

A genuine product of New England upper-middle-class traditions in life and literature, whose formal education ended with his expulsion from Thayer Academy at South Braintree, the sixty-five-year-old Cheever seems to be one of the most socialized, domesticated of men, retaining the innocence of the insulated. One imagines, however, that beneath the pretense and disguise is really a Martian whose effort to remain coolly detached is often discouraged by ineffable sadness that in his many reports he tries to make effable.

Like Horace, who delighted as he instructed, Cheever is a dark moralist who creates stories in a cheerful mood of play. He tells us he was taught, in his Puritanical family, "that a moral lies beneath all human conduct and that the moral is always detrimental to man." His aim as a writer has been to "record a moderation" of the teachings of his family. Cheever delineates the nuances in the tensions between the Blakean poles of innocence and experience in each of his characters. The tension and the contrast between Cheever's superconscious omniscient voice and the characters' intermittent self-scrutiny, that result in partial insights which undermine motivations and behavior, produce ironies the reader knows only Cheever can conceive. His compassion is spiked with ridicule, his fables collapse, at moments, deliberately into farce.

Cheever tells us that he "attempts to celebrate a world that lies spread out around us like a bewildering and stupendous dream." He writes fiction to confirm his feeling "that life itself is creative process." He is a prophet of the apocalypse who reveals a sometimes disconcerting power of positive thinking. "Literature as I see it is more a giving than a diminishment." Like Bellow's, Cheever's vision is affirmative, seeing something in us that transcends our self-made limbos. He writes with one foot on the narrow, wobbly plank world of Harlequin, the other in the brooding world of Hamlet. But finally, his imagination neither profoundly disturbs nor transforms our consciousness. In describing upper-middle-class life as faithfully as Balzac, he does not seem to attempt, or presume, like Rilke, to say, "You must change your life." But one cannot ask, even of a major writer, everything.

David Madden

Sources for Further Study

Choice. XIV, September, 1977, p. 857.
Hudson Review. XXX, Summer, 1977, p. 310.
Listener. XCVIII, July 7, 1977, p. 30.
New Statesman. XCIV, July 15, 1977, p. 91.
New Times. VIII, April 1, 1977, p. 63.
Observer. July 10, 1977, p. 24.
Sewanee Review. LXXXV, October, 1977, p. 687.

A FEAST OF WORDS
The Triumph of Edith Wharton

Author: Cynthia Griffin Wolff (1936–   )
Publisher: Oxford University Press (New York). 453 pp. $15.95
Type of work: Literary criticism

An analysis of Edith Wharton's major works in the light of her psychological development which shows how her life and art interacted to enrich each other

While Edith Wharton has been recognized as one of America's outstanding novelists ever since the publication of *The House of Mirth* in 1905, interest in her life and work has increased dramatically in the last ten years as a result both of the new focus on women writers and of the opening of her private papers to scholars in 1968. R. W. B. Lewis' fine biography, published in 1975, has contributed much to a new understanding and appreciation of Wharton's achievements, and *A Feast of Words* should bring many more readers to her books. Cynthia Griffin Wolff's study is a brilliant synthesis of biography, literary criticism, and psychological analysis that provides new insights into Wharton's novels and short stories through a discussion of her emotional development, and at the same time demonstrates how her writing contributed to her transformation from an affection-starved child and neurotic young wife into a confident, creative, mature woman.

Drawing on Lewis' *Edith Wharton: A Biography,* Wharton's own autobiographical writings, and studies of her psychological development by Anna Freud, Eric Erikson, R. D. Laing, and others, Wolff shows how Wharton struggled for much of her life to compensate for the emotional deprivations of her childhood in the most privileged stratum of New York society. The villainess of the story in Wolff's view was Edith's mother, Lucretia Jones, a domineering, often cold and moody socialite whose feelings about her daughter seem to have been alternately possessive and rejecting. Young Edith turned for affection to her nurse and to her adored father, though she craved her mother's approval to an obsessive degree, setting impossibly rigid standards for her own thoughts and behavior as a child and an adolescent.

While she was repressing her anger and resentment of her mother and her passionate love of her father, the child found one way to satisfy her starved emotions—words. She spent hours "making up," sitting or walking around with a book in her hand "reading" aloud stories of her own invention about people like her parents and their friends. As she grew older, she begged for scraps of wrapping paper to write down these compositions—Wolff finds Lucretia's stinginess in this regard quite unforgivable. Edith had completed a novel, *Fast and Loose,* by the time she was fourteen, and had written enough poetry to fill the small volume her mother had privately printed when she was sixteen. Lucretia's action even in this matter is seen as damaging, for in choosing this "respectable" path to recognize her daughter's talent, she was establishing her control over what had been Edith's private world.

Wharton's literary efforts came to a temporary halt with her debut when she was seventeen, and for the next decade she tried to mold herself into what Lucretia Jones's daughter should be, a "nice" girl, a proper young matron, preoccupied with clothes and beaux, not books and ideas. After an abortive engagement and a brief romance with Walter Berry, who was later to become her closest friend, she was married in 1885 to Edward Wharton, a Bostonian of independent means, suitable social standing, a love for travel that she shared, and almost no interest in things of the mind.

The marriage was a disaster for both, though they must have had periods of pleasure during their European journeys in their first few years together. The repressions and unresolved conflicts of Edith's childhood, Wolff suggests, made it impossible for her to function effectively within her marriage either sexually or socially. She suffered frequently from asthma and nausea for twelve years, revealing in physical symptoms the feelings she could not express in any other way. Her roles as daughter (Lucretia remained a dominant force in her life until she died in 1901) and wife left her feeling caged, imprisoned. Again she turned to words as a way of asserting her own identity. She published a few poems and short stories during the early years of her marriage, but it was not until after her emotional collapse and recovery in 1898 that she chose writing as a real vocation. From this point on she was able to work out many of her internal conflicts in her fiction and at the same time gain a new sense of personal worth as her books won recognition and respect.

Wolff entitles her chapter on the works written between 1889 and 1911 "Landscapes of Desolation," an apt description of the fictional worlds Wharton created at this stage in her life. The Bunner sisters of an early short story, Duke Odo of *The Valley of Decision,* Lily Bart of *The House of Mirth,* Justine Brent of *The Fruit of the Tree,* Ethan Frome—all are denied in one way or another the fullness of life. They live, literally or metaphorically, in enclosed spaces, and their efforts to create meaningful relationships are crushed by fate or society. Women, especially, seem doomed to sterile, unfulfilled existences. The lesson to be learned, Wolff notes, is "submission to suffering, with no release save the release of death."

Wharton's growth beyond this point of view can be attributed to a number of events in her life: her mother's death, her husband's mental illness that resulted in separation and divorce in 1913, her professional success, and, perhaps most important, her three-year affair with American journalist Morton Fullerton. At the age of forty-five Wharton experienced real sexual fulfillment for the first time, and although she was aware almost from the beginning that the affair would not be a permanent one, she rejoiced in it, writing in her diary: " 'I have drunk of the wine of life at last, I have known the thing best worth knowing, I have been warmed through and through never to grow quite cold again till the end.' " The scars of Wharton's early emotional deprivation could never be entirely erased, but this relationship did much to help her see that life holds out more than pain and endurance. Out of this new, broader understanding came a number of her best works, among them *Ethan Frome,* the last of the "landscapes of desolation." Wolff suggests that it gains much of its power from Wharton's full realization of what Frome's isolation meant. By presenting his withdrawal from life as a "horror," she showed her rejection of the assumption that had bound her for so long—that repression was "an existential necessity of life."

Wharton settled permanently in France after her divorce and turned her attention as a writer away from victims resigned to their destiny toward characters who "proclaim an almost muscular need to meet the forces that would shape their lives." The works written between 1912 and 1920 are "novels about men and women who confront their fate, and the novels are suffused with the intensity of their quests." Some are inevitably more successful than others. *The Reef,* Wharton's first attempt to explore "the immensely convoluted, many-sided problem of sexuality" fails to come together fully, but she succeeded much better when she returned to the subject in her New England village tale *Summer* in 1917.

The Custom of the Country (1913), the satirical saga of the willful beauty Undine Spragg, shows the author's creative powers fully developed. At the heart of this book Wolff sees a preoccupation with "psychic energy—power, assertion, drive, ambition." Here Wharton looks at a civilization in the throes of dramatic change: the old, aristocratic, often ineffectual society of her youth under assault by the powers of money and industry. Wolff points out the skillful shifting of perspective by which Wharton is able to show the faults and the virtues of the two conflicting cultures as well as the "complexity of human nature in the actual world." In her voraciously ambitious heroine Wharton was able to exorcize the demons of her childhood, those frighteningly strong desires for comfort and affection that so terrified her that she had to bury them in her subconscious. Undine, Wolff suggests, is "initiative run amuck," but by presenting the dangers of her excess of energy, Wharton was able to accept the value of energy properly controlled and to lay aside yet another "ghost of an earlier and more primitive self."

Like *The House of Mirth, The Custom of the Country* demonstrates Wharton's frustration with a world that offered women so few outlets for their initiative. They could only mirror the world that produced them; the sole action open to them was marriage. Undine's progress up the ladder of prestige and wealth is significantly from husband to husband.

The society that limited women's horizons so severely was quickly changing, however, and Wharton was soon to find in the plight of the World War I refugees ample opportunity to exert her own formidable energies. She raised money, found homes and work for thousands, established workshops to employ displaced women, and set up day nurseries and classes for children, receiving from the French Government the title of Chevalier of the Legion of Honor in recognition of her service to her adopted country.

It was the war, ironically, that led Wharton to an appreciation of the values of the world of her youth—that world that for so long had represented repression and sterility for her. Visiting war-ravaged villages, she saw civilization, in the form of family traditions and the routines of everyday life, being crushed, and as a result she began to turn her thoughts back to the New York of her childhood to write what many consider her finest novel, *The Age of Innocence*. As her hero, Newland Archer, renounces Ellen Olenska, the woman who represents for him sensual and emotional fulfillment, and assumes his responsibilities to his family and society, Wharton asserts her own conviction that true maturity and satisfaction rest on an acceptance of the best values of one's past.

Sadly, the world Wharton had finally come to appreciate in 1920 had been essentially destroyed by the war. The resolution and balance she achieved in *The Age of Innocence* was of necessity a temporary one, for life and the onset of old age presented her with new problems. She continued to live in France, surrounding herself with friends as substitutes for the children she never had and writing until the last weeks of her life. Her fiction of this final period is distinctly uneven in quality. She responded rather stridently to the excesses of the Jazz Age, and she was too far out of touch with the United States to capture the speech patterns and mores of contemporary society as effectively as rising young writers such as Sinclair Lewis and F. Scott Fitzgerald. Yet Wolff finds much to praise in many of the later works. Some of the short stories, "Roman Fever," for example, and the novellas that make up *Old New York*, rank among her best, and at least two of the novels, *The Mother's Recompense* and *The Children*, deal sensitively with the themes that preoccupied Wharton during her later years: the relationship between the generations and the pains of aging. In both works Wharton faces the truth that life cannot be lived through others, that one cannot recapture youth either through a child, as Kate Clephane tries to do in *The Mother's Recompense*, or through a love affair with a young person, Martin Boyne's dream in *The Children*.

Although she was lonely at times and deeply distressed by the death of such close friends as Henry James and Walter Berry, Edith Wharton continued to live intensely into her seventies. The fragments remaining of *The Buccaneers*, the novel on which she was working at the time of her death, show her still concerned with questions of youth and age, love and reconciliation—and writing better than she had in years. Wolff comments near the end of her last chapter, "The buoyant optimism of *The Buccaneers* suggests the jubilation with which the old woman's intrepid spirit has succeeded in redressing the miseries of her youth."

Wolff raises two questions in her Prologue. Why did Wharton, "living in a society that did not encourage men to work and that positively discouraged women from any occupation save having babies and being a good hostess," write? And having decided to write, how did she do it so well? There is no way to determine the origin of that first impulse to "make up" but Wolff suggests throughout her study that Wharton often used her writing to come to terms with herself and her world and that at least one of the reasons she wrote well was that she was able to integrate into her works what she had learned from her experiences.

Wolff's comprehensive study of the interaction of Wharton's life and art is as fascinating as a novel itself. More important, perhaps, it should send readers back to Wharton's own work, not only to *The House of Mirth, Ethan Frome,* and *The Age of Innocence,* but also to undeservedly neglected pieces such as *The Reef, Summer, The Custom of the Country,* and the other novels and short stories illuminated by Wolff's detailed and perceptive analyses.

Elizabeth Johnston Lipscomb

Sources for Further Study

Choice. XIV, July, 1977, p. 686.
Ms. VI, November, 1977, p. 80.
National Review. XXIX, September 30, 1977, p. 1127.

THE FORK RIVER SPACE PROJECT

Author: Wright Morris (1910–   )
Publisher: Harper & Row Publishers (New York). 185 pp. $8.95
Type of work: Novel
Time: The present
Locale: The borders of Nebraska and Kansas

A witty and imaginative domestication of the science fiction genre, in a mysterious and suspenseful fable about the triumph of the imagination

> Principal characters:
> KELCEY, a writer
> ALICE, his wife
> HARRY LORBEER, a plumber, proprietor of Fork River Space Project
> DAHLBERG, a house painter and onetime author

Since publication of his first novel in 1942, Wright Morris has been moving toward consummation of his hero-witness theme by means of his ordinary but strange characters, his witty, resonant style, and his mind-expanding conceptions. *The Fork River Space Project* is as quiet and meditative as *Fire Sermon* (1971) and *A Life* (1973), his two recent novels, and as eerie and bizarre as the novella *War Games* (1972) and several stories in *Real Losses, Imaginary Gains* (1976).

Morris first gave us "The Word from Space" in 1958, delivered by a cosmic mailman. That fantasy begins: "What reassured me was how normal everything looked." A similar tone is sustained throughout *The Fork River Space Project*, which is a sort of literary UFO approaching the Science Fiction galaxy. Having explored inner and outer territories, starting from Nebraska, Morris suggested in 1967 that he might take us into orbit. *In Orbit* examined the varying effects on many different kinds of people of a twister and a kid (who resembles a space man) on a motorcycle, as these two happenings simultaneously hit a small Midwestern town.

In *The Fork River Space Project*, Dahlberg, a house painter and onetime writer of semi-science fiction, and Harry Lorbeer, a plumber and proprietor of "The Fork River Space Project," change the lives of Kelcey, an aging writer of "humorous, fantasy-type pieces," and his young second wife, Alice. This short novel is Kelcey's witty and lyrical meditation on a constellation of images that revolve around two mysterious and suspenseful questions: Did the population of Fork River, Kansas, vanish in a twister or a spaceship? Are Dahlberg and Harry planning a space trip, and will Alice go with them? Though Kelcey is more interested in mulling over the implications of these questions than in answering them, and though the story elements are filtered through Kelcey's musings, *The Fork River Space Project* may prove to be Morris' most accessible fiction since his first, *My Uncle Dudley*, and may attract the wider public he has always hoped to reach—and which he deserves.

Near the end of the novel, Kelcey finds Dahlberg meditating nude in the ghost town schoolhouse that houses the space project. "I've been giving some thought to it," Kelcey tells him. Increasingly, his life turns on "speculation." "How explain it?" he asks, rhetorically. What we have been experiencing is Kelcey's almost total articulation of his thoughts, as if the novel were a long essay by Loren Eiseley, Morris' late good friend.We have collaborated with him in fusing thought and feeling through images, body wisdom, intuitions, reasonings, moments of pure being, visions, and, above all, imagination. All those categories of perception and modes of thinking are integrated in Kelcey's sensibility, his conceptual imagination.

In different ways, Harry and Dahlberg become heroes to Kelcey and Alice, their witnesses. Alice's response is to become Dahlberg's lover. Alice is a further refinement of Morris' wisecracking, audacious woman-as-catalyst, beginning with the Greek in *Love Among the Cannibals,* continuing with Etoile in *Ceremony in Lone Tree,* Cynthia in *What a Way to Go,* and Joy in *Fire Sermon.* Kelcey discovers Alice and Dahlberg alone: "They were in orbit. They were where everybody wanted to be." Later, he thinks: "Some people are determined to get into orbit. Was it so unusual that one of them was my wife?" As he approaches the lovers, Alice says to Kelcey: " 'You look far away!' Was I wrong in thinking that she liked that better?" He keeps telling himself "it's her own life," not his. He sees "her face tilted upward, as I had often seen it, radiant with expectations"—that he knows he cannot fulfill. Kelcey is older than Alice; she was a young commercial artist when she met him on a summer cruise. Kelcey's response to Harry and Dahlberg is to transform himself through his imagination. Harry "started me thinking—or should I say seeing? On the mind's eye, or the balls of the eyes, or wherever it is we see what we imagine, or imagine what we see." Dahlberg's father, an early inventor of a space rocket, and Harry's father, a railroad magnate who opened the West and built Fork River to glorify his wife, passed on to their sons a tendency to blend fact and fiction. Dahlberg wants *"to restore awe . . .* without awe we diminish, we trivialize, everything we touch." Kelcey quips, "My heart belongs to Harry," the visionary. And Kelcey feels "a surge of warm fellow feeling for Dahlberg," under whose Buster Keaton deadpan, "I see his brain pan twinkling like a constellation." Dahlberg tells Kelcey, "This is *your* project as much as it is *my* project."

Imagination is Kelcey's state of mind, in which what he sees is less important than what he imagines. What he hears and sees "boggles the mind" and gives "cause for wonder"—two of many clichés whose original freshness Morris resurrects in lively contexts. Kelcey closes his eyes "to see more, as well as less," one of several paradoxes that aid perception and energize Kelcey's rhetoric. His overexcited imagination also produces dreams that reach back to prehistory and project into the space age. He cautions Alice not to look at anything too closely. "The jig is up as soon as" a UFO, for instance, "is identified." She takes his advice, follows the wisdom of the body, and goes into love orbit with Dahlberg, causing psychological space to expand between herself and Kelcey, to whom she begins to seem like the first visitor from space.

Kelcey achieves the state of awe, but for him "the experience of unearthly, celestial transport is a matter of imagination"; he doubts the astronauts had it, and Morris suggests the experience of Alice and Dahlberg and Harry, in space, or in love, are not as varied and intense as the ones Kelcey conjures in the sanctuary of his imagination, simply by closing his eyes.

Kelcey's hero-witness relationship with Dahlberg and Harry teaches him how to expand his imaginative powers until he can have their experiences, including Alice's, vicariously while deepening his own. Their effect on his imagination makes him feel weightless in space, buoyant, transformed. "Somewhere between where was I, and where I am, is where I am." Outwardly, Kelcey shows affection by teasing, emotion by obviously withholding it, conviction by sarcasm. But now he has new emotions, and enjoys the full bloom of his feelings. Near the end, he experiences pure being: "My sensations were so primal I lacked a word for them. A plant might feel as much, or as little, as I did. There was not a shred of consciousness in it. I was in the world like a stalk of celery." Constantly stimulated superconsciousness enables him to reach that state, wherein he is cleansed and rendered receptive to rarer sensations later.

To focus and give a comic perspective on these concepts about the workings of the imagination, Kelcey gives us, twenty pages from the end, the story of Taubler and Tuchman, which he had promised halfway through. (Morris made earlier use of this set-piece device in *Ceremony in Lone Tree* and in *One Day.*) In the summer of 1939, when he was a student in Paris soaking up culture, Kelcey met Taubler, a crazy genius who "preferred the illusion to the reality," and "who was the space trip of my life." The empty plains of Kelcey's childhood in Nebraska was the physical preparation for Taubler, and Taubler and Tuchman were the metaphysical preparation for the imaginative space flights Dahlberg and Harry inspire.

Kelcey went to Paris to be "flabbergasted," a word that burlesques Dahlberg's concept of awe. A fortune cookie told him he would make new friends and begin a new life; but that new life does not begin until decades later with Dahlberg and Harry, who parallel Taubler and Tuchman. Taubler thinks Americans are a hoax invented by movie producers; Dahlberg years later declares, "Life on this planet is a hoax." Having transformed Parisian scenes in his artistic imagination and thus made them his creations, Taubler signs his work by painting his name on walls all over Paris; Dahlberg paints Kelcey's sun deck, making it a launching pad for the imagination. When Taubler showed him the earth through a telescope, all Kelcey was capable of seeing was his own lashes. Taubler had painted on a wall the earth as seen from space; Harry offers a similar view in Fork River and teaches Kelcey to see it. Tuchman tells Kelcey that Taubler has his "own system . . . and you'd better believe it." Years later, Harry says, "You better believe it . . . or it's not going to happen." "I could believe it. Hadn't he already painted me into it?" Kelcey says of Taubler, and that's true of Harry and

Dahlberg, too. Tuchman, himself a witness to Taubler, explains to this new, young witness, "You've got to make your own world, then live in it." Having told us that story, Kelcey suggests that his own experiences tell him that it is better to imagine a space adventure than to experience it, or that only by imagining it can one experience it.

Although *The Fork River Space Project* is a short novel, it is abundantly and complexly image-laden, thought-provoking, and poetically suggestive. Through his imagination, expressed in a witty, paradoxical, punning style, Kelcey ponders the nature of human perception and experiences intuition in rarefied moments that Morris embodies in charged images. "The way to change the world was to change one's perspective." "All perception was extrasensory." He meditates on images of space and of twisters. "The view *from* space compels the awe that will enlarge man's finite nature." He feels he shares "the cosmos with the vast indifference of the prime mover." A sense of time permeates the novel. He imagines and dreams images of prehistoric man in caves at Stonehenge (he is partial to the Ice Age), of pioneer American history.

To enhance those abstract concepts and science fiction itself, our most bizarre genre, with a sense of everyday reality, Morris domesticates them with such images as these: "I . . . stood for a moment in the draft from the refrigerator, the chill, impersonal winds of space blowing into my face." A space ship will give off "a whirring sound like a musical top." In the note she leaves Kelcey before soaring off with Dahlberg, Alice asks him to get the lights and phone disconnected at the now totally abandoned Fork River.

Two major motifs that characterize the American experience throughout history are the expectations aroused by the landscape, with its prospects for spiritual and physical development, and the long waiting for those expectations to come to pass. Those two concepts, often repeated with many variations, illuminate the vision Harry and Dahlberg and Alice share, but it is Kelcey, the most imaginative witness, who has the talent for waiting, satisfied meanwhile with what those expectations stimulate in his imagination. One of the qualities Kelcey has that the others lack and that prevents him from being a true believer and from attempting to act out expectations, visions, and dreams, is his sense of humor. Dahlberg tells him that he is a very funny man. As a type, Kelcey was in the cave back in the Ice Age. "And I am there at the fringe of the circle gawking." As witness, he tells Dahlberg: "If anything should happen, somebody should be there to report on it."

A possible objection to the meditation technique may be that what the reader experiences is Kelcey's total articulation of every element in the novel; by mulling everything over himself, he may leave too little for the reader to experience and imagine, and thus undercut the mystery and awe. The meditation technique allows Morris to justify his use of the old device of stimulating suspense, then delaying the next narrative stroke by exposition or meditation.

Even for so short a novel, *The Fork River Space Project* may strike some readers as underpopulated; outside the depopulated town of Fork River (except for Harry, Dahlberg, and Lindner, who is a kind of caretaker) the world consists only of Kelcey and Alice and two minor characters, Miss Ingalls, a librarian, who provides Kelcey with information about Dahlberg, and Dr. Fred Rainey, a weather seer, who provides Kelcey with scientific explanations and further information about Harry. But this paucity of people lends an aura to the novel that enhances Morris's effects.

The Fork River Space Project is the seventh of Morris' nineteen novels to be told in the first person, a point of view perfectly suited to a book that demonstrates the power of the imagination, leavened with lucid intelligence. Unvarnished, Morris' style is grainy, textured. As Kelcey says of Dahlberg's style, "you have to let him tell it." In his own way. And Morris' way is elliptical. You have to let him meditate on people, situations, concepts, images. But the reader must collaborate. The reader's active participation is built into the dialectic of Morris' style.

In his lamentably neglected book *About Fiction: Reverent Reflections on the Nature of Fiction with Irreverent Observations on Writers, Readers, and Other Abuses* (1975), Morris talked about style, among other things. Having noted that "the facts, so called, are in: the imagination is out," Morris invokes the spirit of Yeats: "As I altered my syntax," said Yeats, "I altered my intellect." We observe that process in Morris' works, and in Kelcey's mind as he meditates. But for the reader who has not learned to read (as the writer has learned to write), the syntax may be difficult to follow. "Nothing is explained, or will be explained: what is shown must be perceived, apprehended," says Morris of Camus' *The Stranger.* "The reader's pleasure is often in proportion to what is left unsaid, or ambiguously hinted." To read such fiction well is to grasp some of the skills involved in its creation. Later, he says, "What we choose to call 'style' is the presence in the fiction of the power to choose and mold its reader."

The Fork River Space Project is Wright Morris' finest novel since *In Orbit.* Ultimately, space is "the territory ahead" that Huck Finn sets out for at the end of Twain's classic. In each of his novels Morris has been heading for that space behind the eyelids where imagination, mystery, and awe make everything possible. In Fork River, he satisfies the great expectations his earlier novels have raised, and at least for a season, and perhaps for decades, the image of the American experience Morris has captured will haunt us.

David Madden

Sources for Further Study

Best Sellers. XXXVII, November, 1977, p. 231.
Booklist. LXXIV, September 15, 1977, p. 140.
Kirkus Reviews. XLV, August 1, 1977, p. 803.
New York Times Book Review. September 25, 1977, p. 14.
Publisher's Weekly. CXII, August 22, 1977, p. 59.

FOUND, LOST, FOUND

Author: J(ohn) B(oynton) Priestley (1894–   )
Publisher: Stein and Day (New York). 135 pp. $8.95
Type of work: Novel
Time: The present
Locale: London and rural England

A light, satirical social commentary in which a civil servant, lacking in purpose and usually adrift in alcoholic fogs, is challenged by a pretty, cynical social researcher, to find her if he is interested in knowing her better

> Principal characters:
> TOM DEKKER, a young, divorced civil servant attached to the Ministry of Export Development and Promotion
> KATE RAPLEY, also divorced, who works for the Community Research Social Science Council
> MADGE LEEDS, a secretary of Tom's superior at the Ministry
> S. K. OVERTON-BRIGGS, a pompous bureaucrat

If one is to take *Found, Lost, Found* seriously it is necessary to recognize that J. B. Priestley is a writer of prodigious output, whose fiction is as much social comment as are his essays and his criticism, and that he has been producing work for more than a half century (his first novel, *Adam in Moonshine*, was published in 1927). As it happens, this latest short novel is much like his first; it is a charming, light, romantic, escapist bit of fiction; one has to dig for the symbolism, and might not bother to do so were it not that the work is by Priestley.

The title appears to tell it all: boy meets girl, boy loses girl, boy gets girl. On further consideration, however, the story does have another level when one remembers Priestley's penchant for symbolism and social criticism in his work; it then becomes a mischievous look at the civil services, psychiatry, women's liberation, the theater, and other manifestations of the embattled Englishman in the last part of the twentieth century.

The action centers around the acceptance of a challenge from his girl by a moderately alcoholic civil servant; the challenge is to prove he can generate enough initiative and self-discipline to find her, if he wants her.

The protagonist, Tom Dekker, exemplifies the plight of the middle-level civil servant in England—victim of boredom, frustration, and irritation at bureaucratic dullness, inclined to hide behind a polite facade while inwardly carping at the façades erected by others. Priestley has taken each character and exaggerated it to create a kindly caricature so that one laughs with, rather than at, the broadly sketched foibles of modern-day Englishmen.

Dekker is handled most sympathetically of all the characters. Through him, we see the condition of man as it is today, a condition of diminishing sense of purpose in the face of increasing anonymity and expanding government regulation—enough to drive anyone to drink. Dekker retains his sanity by floating through each day on a cloud of gin, one of the simplest and most accessible solutions to any problem. He is characterized as having a quick wit and ready humor; Priestley uses him as the vehicle for some clever one-liners and bits of comedy, though some of the comedy is contrived, forced, and too hearty; one gets the impression that the author padded the action to provide a substrata to support the witty passages.

Psychiatry comes in for its share of risible but irascible comment in the person of Dr. Belham, who is supposed to help Dekker, but who is patently in need of help himself. Quick-tempered and arbitrary, he admits that he went into psychiatry to try to correct his own weaknesses. This gives Priestley a chance to use one of the less subtly placed epigrams: "We are living in a garden of neuroses. . . ."

Related closely to psychiatry, sociology fares no better with Priestley's pen. Kate Rapley is limned as earnest, serious, and prone to reform—reform being the right, as God gives Community Research Social Service Council to see the right. S. K. Overton-Briggs, head of the Council, is a bureaucrat making up in self-importance for what he lacks in understanding. Briggs's pomposity leads his secretary to tell Dekker that if she did not show proper respect, "I'd be out—treading water again in the typing pool."

Priestley is a prolific playright; author of twenty-one plays, he knows his theater. His good-humored jab at amateur theatricals, through a chapter on the North Green Drama Club ("squashed between a delicatessen and a dry cleaner's"), tells a great deal about that sort of theater and the people who are drawn to it. His characterization of modern theater, less kindly done, is the best piece of satire in the book, wildly Oscar Wildelike in mood. Priestley makes evident his distaste for experimental theater and those who flaunt tradition for the sake of relevance, through a preposterous sequence in which two directors talk about their offbeat productions of *As You Like It* and *Antony and Cleopatra*.

Women's liberation activists also come in for their share of attention, as does the civil service's tendency to "play the initial game." Mrs. Dragby of Women's Social and Political Liberation Front, greets Dekker, "Do sit down, Mr. Dekker. We here at the W.S.P.L.F. don't see much of you at the M.E.D.P. We spend rather more time with the B.O.T. and the M.O.E. and of course the F.O. and the H.O. . . ." "Sounds rather as if you're just rollicking with the alphabet."

Older women are viewed in an Edwardian manner, and categorized through the medium of Kate's aunts: the lonely middle-aged divorcée trying to stay young, pathetic in her attempts to attract a man; the horse- and dog-loving hearty maiden lady; the oft-married beauty who has an eye for wealthy men, and marries then divorces them to live well on the sizable settlements extracted from each through the divorce proceedings; and the women's libber who would probably settle for submission and another man had she not become a dynamic public figure after her husband's demise.

Throughout the tale, Priestley's prejudices show themselves. He does not care for America or Americans. From his literary treatment of the American in the story, and from his sensitivity to criticism from this side of the Atlantic, it is safe to assume that he has his reservations about us. He distrusts labor unions, and disapproves of garrulousness, the motives of today's students, and the methods of today's police. There is the implied indictment of a mechanistic, bureaucratic society that dehumanizes man, consistent with statements made in earlier works. While criticizing mass media, educational systems, and lack of self-motivation, he also deplores the weaknesses of those who succumb to apathy.

This book suffers from a negative first impression. Superficially it is a bit of escapist fluff, of no substance, and of no consequence—the oversimplified drivel one reads in second-rate magazines. The work has more the aura of a light stage comedy: stylized characters, some clever dialogue, and more atmosphere than action. It has its bright moments, however—a creative solution to a problem, and evidence of wit and sophistication. It is not up to the standards one expects of a major writer who has produced such works of art as *The Good Companions, Bright Day,* and *The Image Men.* Priestley has said of himself that from time to time he likes to forsake the novel proper in order to indulge in mere tale-telling. The work under consideration falls into that category, and Priestley seems to have written it with considerable self-indulgence; it will not be listed among his major works.

Mae Woods Bell

Sources for Further Study

Booklist. LXXIII, March 1, 1977, p. 993.
Choice. XIV, June, 1977, p. 536.
Library Journal. CII, April 1, 1977, p. 835.
New York Times Book Review. August 28, 1977, p. 10.

GATES OF EDEN
American Culture in the Sixties

Author: Morris Dickstein (1940–   )
Publisher: Basic Books (New York). 300 pp. $11.95
Type of work: Literary criticism

An analysis of the culture of the 1960's based on the premise that the literature of an age reflects the culture that fostered it and can serve as representative of the total national consciousness

Morris Dickstein is a contributing editor of *Partisan Review* and has published in such journals as *New Republic, Commentary,* and *The New York Times Book Review.* He was educated at Columbia and Yale and is now Professor of English at Queens College. His forte is literary criticism, and although the subtitle of *Gates of Eden* addresses the topic of American culture in the 1960's, Dickstein uses an analysis of the literature of the decade to represent the culture of the decade.

The book can be divided into three basic parts, although it is not strictly chronological in coverage. The first section covers the events of the 1950's that laid the groundwork for the following decade; the second, the 1960's proper; and the third, an evaluation of the 1960's from the perspective of the mid-1970's. Dickstein's experience of the 1960's and consequently his record thereof, is colored by his having been a product of the 1950's, thus making him older than the most active of the radical students of the 1960's. This vantage point provides a perspective that he might not have had otherwise, but it also may be the cause of his tendency to idealize the cultural changes that he witnessed.

Dickstein first delves into the intellectual and social milieu of the 1950's, especially as reflected in the literature, to provide a backdrop against which to display the dramatic cultural upheavals of the 1960's. His primary concern in this regard is in discussing the emergence of the Jewish novel as an important force in American fiction of the time. He actually begins with the Jewish writers of the 1930's and 1940's, with their emphasis on the secular Jewish intellectual as the essential alienated modern man—alienated both from his traditional culture and from the American national culture.

Although Dickstein analyzes much of both the Jewish literature and the Jewish criticism of the 1950's, his most extensive commentary is reserved, curiously, for an analysis of one specific political event: the trial and conviction of Julius and Ethel Rosenberg. To him, the treatment that they and their case received from the intellectual community was a signal of the total loss of America's previous idealism concerning her moral innocence. Dickstein claims that this emphasis on the Jewish experience and significance in the 1950's can be paralleled with the experience and significance of blacks in the 1960's.

The author begins his discussion of culture in the 1960's with an analysis of the role played by Allen Ginsberg beginning in the late 1950's in providing a break from traditional literary forms of expression. He emphasizes that the culture which developed in the next decade was liberating, providing freedom to express sensual enjoyment. Sexual frankness was one way in which this change of emphasis was made manifest, but it can also be seen in a new visionary style of writing and the element of fantasy apparent in the literature of the time. Opposed to this and yet interwoven with it was a demand for relevance, especially for political relevance. The synthesis of these two strains, embodied in Allen Ginsberg, is what Dickstein describes at one point as Romantic Socialism. He sees in the 1960's such a deep-seated change in sensibility as to alter the entire moral climate of the culture, and he tries to show that this change to a new sensibility was permanent. The self was still the most important concept, but in combination with a concern for social justice. This Utopian goal—in both politics and personal life—was a movement toward a modern Eden.

The ideological milieu created earlier by the writings of Marcuse, Goodman, and others provided the basis for the permanent cultural revolution which expressed itself through black writers, rock music, black humor, the new journalism, and more experimental and modernist fiction. Although Marshall McLuhan claims that the novel died in the cultural revolution to be replaced by the electronic media, including, to an extent, rock music, Dickstein rejects this claim. He instead insists that while the traditional realistic novels were no longer relevant, there was a new breed of novelists who used black humor and antiheroes to make their points. Dickstein handles many of the older cultural heroes like Ginsberg and C. Wright Mills perceptively, but comes into his own in the evaluations of Mailer, Vonnegut, and Heller. He claims Heller's *Catch-22* is the best novel of the time, particularly because its black humor is in its structure rather than in oneliners or gags.

The new journalism was another of the manifestations of the 1960's new sensibility, as seen both in fairly established papers such as *The Village Voice*, and in much more underground writing. The new journalism addressed itself to topics not covered by the traditional journalists, written in styles that were also nontraditional. A new journalist might, for example, write about things political or pornographic and do so in a very personal style full of opinion, or deal with it in a fictionalized form.

While the Jewish writers of the 1950's were experiencing and writing about individual alienation, the black writers of the 1960's were expressing deeply felt frustrations of an entire social group. Many of the racial struggles of the decade were a basic reason for the politics of confrontation that were prime movers in the cultural revolution. In his section on black writers, Dickstein draws a distinction between the old (Baldwin) and new (Cheever) black writers but emphasizes that their ultimate value is in being good writers whether or not they write from the perspective of the black experience.

Dickstein most enthusiastically examines rock music as the cultural focus of the decade, the mirror of the entire revolution. To him the epitome of the new sensibility as reflected in music was Bob Dylan, who was less concerned with melody than with message. His folk music was a staple in the new moral solidarity that was a part of the politics of confrontation. The evolution of folk into rock was a move from the single voice with a simple acoustic guitar to psychedelically complex pieces by groups with wildly imaginative names. Dickstein examines Dylan's works as thoroughly as he does any of the novelists. He acknowledges the impact of both the Beatles and the Rolling Stones, but more in the degree that they reflected the culture than as primary agents of change.

Dickstein next contends that one of the true tests of a great writer is the degree to which he reflects his times. In the section entitled "Fiction at the Crossroads" he examines the works of Barthelme and Wurlitzer, which he uses as representative of the coming of age of the second modernist period in fiction. In his ironic fables, Barthelme uses fantasy and symbolism to make his point obliquely, addressing the self by playing on the reader's emotions. Conversely, Wurlitzer's narrators are nearly catatonic zombies. Wurlitzer's fantasies of self are nearly primal, concentrating on the stratum below that of individuation. In neither of these writers' works is there a heavy burden of content. The novel here is nothing beyond a collection of words to act as a catalyst for reaction. Dickstein warns that even these experimentalists have, in the 1970's, tended toward self-imitation rather than fresh new forms and that such neglect of their moral responsibility to break new ground may leave the present decade in literary and cultural limbo.

In his epilogue, Dickstein purports that one of the primary contributions of the 1960's to the national consciousness was a distrust of people or institutions that claim objectivity, a realization that people make decisions subjectively in science and the professions just as well as in art. Journalism and literary criticism, for instance, have previously been thought to be most professional when most impersonal. The new sensitivity to the self theoretically allows such previously objective writers to inject their personal ideas and reactions into their reports and yet maintain their value as journalists or critics. Dickstein obviously hopes that the reader will agree with this position since in this work of literary criticism he does exactly that. This is by no means an objective narrative of what actually happened in the 1960's, but a subjective combination of literary criticism and political history of the times in the very manner of the new sensibility that Dickstein celebrates.

Dickstein has produced a very scholarly work in many ways, but it is quite personal in tone. It is consequently not as balanced an analysis as many readers might seek. At the end of the book, Dickstein summarizes his life as a student and his subjective reactions to many of the trends of the last twenty years.

Dickstein claims to examine "what life felt like" in the 1960's, but his New York-Jewish-radical perspective and analysis confined to a small segment of writers cannot provide that sweeping view. By using this analysis to generalize the total experience of the decade, many significant experiences and events are not included. While he manages to provide a perceptive and thorough evaluation of many of the major trends of the decade, their meaning, and their permanent contribution to the national culture, his method of analysis is still very personal reflection, which may not be the ideal method that he perceives it to be.

As the 1960's were liberating and romantic, the pendulum has swung into a more structured and formal attitude in the 1970's. As André Gide says in *The Immoralist,* to free oneself is nothing, what is arduous is to know what to do with one's freedom. The national consciousness and literature will reflect this struggle for a meaningful shape for the liberated energies of the 1960's in the 1970's, at least until the pendulum swings again.

Margaret S. Schoon

Sources for Further Study

Choice. XIV, July, 1977, p. 662.
Commonweal. CIV, November 25, 1977, p. 758.
Dissent. XXIV, Summer, 1977, p. 439.
Modern Age. XXI, Summer, 1977, p. 424.
New Times. VIII, May 13, 1977, p. 70.
New York Review of Books. XXIV, August 4, 1977, p. 17.
Yale Review. LXVI, June, 1977, p. 620.

A GENIUS FOR WAR
The German Army and General Staff, 1807–1945

Author: T. N. Dupuy (1916–   )
Publisher: Prentice-Hall (New Jersey). 362 pp. $14.95
Type of work: History
Time: 1807–1945
Locale: Prussia-Germany

A study by a retired army officer and military historian of the institutionalization of excellence and the application of genius in the Prussian-German Army after the Napoleonic Wars

> *Principal personages:*
> GENERAL LUDWIG BECK
> OTTO VON BISMARCK
> GENERAL WERNER VON BLOMBERG
> FRIEDERICH EBERT
> GENERAL WERNER VON FRITSCH
> GENERAL FREDERICK FROMM
> COLONEL AUGUST VON GNEISENAU
> GENERAL WILHELM GROENER
> GENERAL FRANZ VON HALDER
> GENERAL KURT VON HAMMERSTEIN-EQUORD
> GENERAL PAUL VON HINDENBURG
> ADOLF HITLER
> GENERAL ERICH LUDENDORFF
> GENERAL HELMUTH VON MOLTKE (THE ELDER)
> GENERAL ALBRECHT VON ROON
> GENERAL GERHARD VON SCHARNHORST
> GENERAL ALFRED VON SCHLIEFFEN
> GENERAL HANS VON SEECKT

What can be said of a people as contradictory as the Germans, who gave the world Hayden and the Holocaust, Beethoven and Buchenwald? A nation of bright, industrious men who constructed great ships and grand philosophies, and also planned their wars, decades in advance, with equal care? We must analyze such people cautiously; our minds have been molded by their militarism, politics, and monumental defeats (on the heels of their great triumphs in the early stages of the same wars). We can still watch seas of German humanity goosestepping across flickering newsreels in a mindless apotheosis of Hitlerism. Films like *Triumph of the Will,* Leni Riefenstahl's brilliant documentary of the 1934 Nazi Party rally at Nuremburg, even today stir our latent fears of Germany. Strutting brigades of fancifully dressed Uhlans, self-styled Huns, and Storm Troopers emblazoned with death's head insignia parade grimly before the camera's eye, a collective personification of German military history. Crowds orgasmically chant *"Ein Reich, Ein Volk, Ein Führer"* with a joy emanating from some medieval, Teutonic oversoul. We sense that those masses of faceless people, hypnotized by the rasping voice of their charismatic leader, had found fulfillment in their willing submission to the State.

Perhaps the answer lies in Prussia, a nation founded in darker ages in the Eastern marches by Teutonic Knights. Ringed by expansionistic and warlike peoples, possessing no natural defensible boundaries of any consequence, it pursued militarism through necessity. Prussia became, as Baron von Schrötter proclaimed, "not a country with an army, but an army with a country." Mirabeau later observed that "war is the national industry of Prussia." And that nation, through decisive nineteenth century victories, became the master of Germany.

Are these thoughts exaggerated stereotypes, historical half truths, or simply legends, reinforced by our willingness to believe the worst of the Germans? Trevor Nevitt Dupuy, the author of *A Genius for War,* supports the last view and argues that the Prussian-German is—and was—a reasonable human being. Between 1815 and 1945, Germany engaged in only six "significant" wars, he notes, while France and Russia in the same period fought ten and thirteen respectively, and imperialistic Great Britain, seventeen. The "peaceloving" United States participated in seven, including lesser wars against Seminoles and Philippine Insurrectionaries. Germany, concludes Dupuy, fought less frequently than most major European powers.

Colonel Dupuy's interest in German military history began with his World War II studies, conducted in association with the Historical Evaluation and Research Organization. HERO attempted to evaluate military performance, using an objectively quantified combat model based on sixty engagements fought during the struggle for Italy. HERO began by assigning the more experienced *Wehrmacht* a ten percent battle superiority. But it found that German troops invariably defeated American infantry when they should have lost, according to the model, and concluded that a thirty percent edge was more accurate. HERO also found to its surprise that the presence or absence of superior American air power had little effect on results. German soldiers, concluded Dupuy, had delayed a predictable defeat with intelligence, skill, and dedication, a performance that he labels "genius."

The Colonel next examined "the riddle of 1944." After a successful tactical withdrawal on the Continent following D-Day, the Germans, almost incredibly, launched a major offensive (the "Battle of the Bulge") which drove eighty kilometers through Allied lines before finally grinding to a halt. Dupuy marvels at an army that recognized it had lost the war on the beaches, yet conducted a brilliant retreat, and then launched a major offensive with some likelihood of success.

Dupuy interviewed numerous allied troops after World War II who had fought Germany (he had fought against Japan) and found them uniformly impressed by their opponents, in full agreement that Germans usually fought not only aggressively but also highly intelligently. Those who had not fought Germany, buttressed by the Pentagon, which refused to support Dupuy's research, dismissed his ideas as "fudge factors." Dupuy then produced objectively demonstrable World War II casualty figures. A hundred Germans could fight one hundred and twenty American or British soldiers *as equals,* he asserted, and inflict fifty percent more casualties than taken. Students of the military arts call this a "high average score effectiveness." Interestingly, today's popular World War II combat games assign the German side a similar edge for the game's results to approximate reality.

Dupuy's search for an explanation for superior German battlefield performance has drawn him to study the military history of Prussia-Germany from the Age of the Fredericks to the debacle of Berlin in 1945. He concludes that Germany successfully institutionalized, through its General Staff, officer corps, and standing army, a system that predictably applied military genius in war. That alone explains Germany's ability to field the world's best armies for a century. There was little, Dupuy claims, in German culture that predisposed its members toward excessive order or blind obedience; they were hardly the mindless robots portrayed by Hollywood—and Berlin—filmmakers. Dupuy forcefully dismisses zeal for the fatherland or the *führerprinzip* as particular explanations of German military success.

Dupuy is convinced that Germany had developed no significant military traditions before the last century. Certainly Prussia achieved a certain respectability under the Great Elector and his son Frederick William I, and Frederick the Great used the army willingly, but aside from his inclination for uniformed giants, changed it little. Dupuy, unimpressed with the quality of German soldiers in the eighteenth century, compares them rather unfavorably with the crack Swiss mercenaries of that era.

A Genius for War insists that Germany's modern military excellence is rooted in the post-Napoleonic reform of the Prussian Army. To defend this idea, the author presents the argument that the Prussian Army was devastated by the Corsican upstart on several occasions between 1806 and 1813, beginning with Jena-Auerstadt. By 1815 the eighteenth century Prussian Army was gone, providing the perfect base for *de novum* reconstruction. Dupuy's thesis, like Mark Twain's spurious obituary, greatly exaggerates the death of the Prussian Army. Certainly its soldiers died in droves in the Napoleonic bloodbaths, but its staff, officers, and training system survived. Equally important, Napoleon's mistreatment of Prussia between 1806 and 1813 convinced that survival-minded state of the wisdom of generous future support for its army. Despite Dupuy's desire to connect Germany's military greatness to the post-1815 reform era, the all-important, close Prussian Army-state relationship is quite linear back to the early eighteenth century.

The General Staff, a concept buried in antiquity, is Dupuy's key to the success of the reorganized Prussian Army. Traditionally general staffs were collections of aides, messengers, and record keepers, a military household serving the commanding general. The new Prussian General Staff made that pattern obsolete; it assumed an independent existence as the central agency for war planning and execution. It was empowered to utilize whatever existed in the nation that it deemed of military value, not excluding the ransacking of the past for clues to future victories. Its structure was organized around the study of Prussia's major enemies, France, Russia, and Austria. In 1859 the General Staff added a section to plan civilian railroad construction routes for future army use. Clausewitz' advice that "the essence of military genius is to bring under consideration all of the tendencies of the mind and soul in combination towards the business of war" became Prussia's *obiter dictum*.

The reorganized Prussian Army formed a strange parallel to Plato's *Republic*. The General Staff was to consist of military "men of gold," the officer corps, "men of silver" and the rankers, loyal bronzemen. The General Staff called on the best and the brightest to become the ultimate battlefield talent, counterbalancing incompetent, unremovable generals and vacuous monarchs. To this end, young officers were "tagged," posted to advanced military schools, exposed to a wide variety of duties, and moved through the ranks.

The post-Napoleonic General Staff system was the creation of a group of remarkable military reformers who dominated the army for decades. Scharnhorst, who began his work well before Waterloo, advocated the modern idea that applied intelligence was militarily superior to iron discipline. He might have been the greatest of the reformers, at least in battle, but he died in 1813 of a minor, festering wound. Gneisenau and Boyen ultimately influenced the army more by supervising the birth of the General Staff after 1815. Clausewitz was a great military theorist rather than commander of troops. Director of the War School, political conservative and military radical, Clausewitz failed to impress his Prussian Junker colleagues who, though Dupuy argues to the contrary, generally found intellect a suspect quality. He resigned, turned to writing, and founded a still respected reputation as a military commentator. His contemporaries and their successors, less well-known men in uniform and in the War Ministry, brought the Prussian Army to a superb state of readiness by mid-century.

These military autocrats introduced progressive ideas at all levels. They succeeded in partially opening the senior ranks for a few of the brightest sons of the bourgeoisie. Advanced tactics and formations became as welcome as political change was deplored. The breech-loading Dreyse rifle was universal by 1860, and was used until replaced with the revolutionary bolt action Mauser, while the cautious American army used its quaint Civil War era trap-door Springfield—and black powder—as late as 1898. The German mind equally quickly appreciated the fire power of steel-barrelled artillery, machine guns, and blitzkreigs.

Clausewitz' phrase "the business of war" sticks in the mind. Exactly: the German General Staff was a board of directors for the war business, using the generals as its training leaders and battlefield managers. Formed to protect

Prussia, it evolved over the next hundred years into a cartel for expansion and aggression in a well-established, dangerous marketplace. The General Staff accepted Great Britain and France at par, discounted Austria (after 1866) and the Russians (after 1905), and traded with Danes, Poles, Czechs, and others as minor commodities. Germany, that prosperous land of cities, trade, factories, arms, and autocratic politics had created an army with the same meticulous execution that later produced the Mercedes Benz and the Porsche. Sadly, the development of democratic institutions lagged far behind.

How good was the General Staff system? Dupuy asserts again and again that it fostered or practiced *genius*. Genius is a strong word, conveying an image of a body of Einsteins in uniform, perennially grouped about a map table, conversing brilliantly in some eternal *kriegsspiel*. Or was the General Staff, to use Dupuy's other catch phrase, merely "institutionalized excellence?" Ultimately, the reader is unconvinced of either claim. The general retention of aristocrats of the old Prussian-Junker school in senior positions continued until 1945, and the bourgeois were but a few among the nobility. The near total exclusion of bright, if untitled proletarians from the top continued until after World War I. In the last analysis, the source of the General Staff's success lay in its permanent association with a supportive, war-minded nation, willing to pay generously for meticulous preparation, expensive military toys, and limitless attention to detail.

The officer corps received equally close attention from the reformers and their successors. Dupuy is convinced that the army demanded brains, but a title apparently secured quicker advancement; he cannot completely ignore Prussian anti-intellectualism. The brave Scharnhorst, for example, was a peasant with a new title, who sat ill with an army that called him a "Hanoverian bookworm." Granted the various academies and schools established by the reformers weeded out the dunces and certainly upgraded the army's general level of competence, but the result was more often competence, rather than "genius."

Chance played a small role in the officer's advancement; he underwent a highly complex, overlapping training system. His career commenced with selection, then proceeded dutifully through examinations, special training (lectures, schooling, the reading of military journals), historical study, initiative conditioning, responsibility, acceptance of perfectionist goals, and continuous objective performance analysis and regeneration. An amorphous but continuous "leavening" process constantly sifted the ranks. The icing on the cake was the *kriegsspiel*, or war game (a prototype of "Panzer!" "Breakout!" and other popular board games). Sandboxes modeled on real battlefields, with teams, umpires, rules, and dice representing the "fortunes of war," provided a chilling approximation of reality and solid mental conditioning.

This attention to detail produced the superior German army, says Dupuy, not genetics, German super-efficiency, blind obedience, or defensive desperation. He accepts the existence of a well-developed German sense of methodical behavior and organizational sense, but assigns it little significance. One of his "proofs" is the conduct of Howard's XI Corps of the Army of the Potomac, the "German Corps," in the American Civil War. This uniformed mob of recent German immigrants to the United States excelled at spit-and-polish inspections, but its battle record was so dismal that Grant eventually dissolved it, deliberately spreading the Germans and their sorry military reputation around the army. From this example we must presumably conclude that, without a proper general staff, Germans make poor soldiers.

Germany underwent a ceaseless internal political power struggle after 1815, and the army had to pick its way with care while maintaining an ostensible political neutrality. Austria and Prussia rivaled each other for mastery over Germany until the War of the Brothers in 1816 placed Germany's future securely in Prussian hands. Petty states and confederations jostled one another for various advantages. Throughout Germany liberals fought conservatives and bourgeois fought aristocrats. Meanwhile emerging business-industrial cartels came to wield enormous economic power.

The army secured its preeminence in this feuding land in the Franco-Prussian War. The ideas of the reformers were tested against those of their chief rival, and the Prussian Army achieved its supreme moment: total victory, a proclamation of Empire in the fallen enemy's capital, and juicy reparations. Germany, thanks to its army, could now assume its proper, if belated, place in the sun. Never again would such a victory occur to German arms, though the events of 1914 and 1940 seemed close. A united, Prussian-dominated Germany emerged from that war with a sense of omnipotence, secure behind an army apparently capable of executing every command, and every enemy, if necessary. Bitter lessons would be administered to the ambitious German militarists by grand coalitions in the future, but the late nineteenth century seemed a golden age for German arms.

The Army played its national role wisely. It considered Germany a partnership among three equals; itself, the state, and the people. The generals retained the royal ear, detested creeping bourgeois democracy as much as Bismarck, and tapped German prosperity to support a bigger and better army. Over the years the Army respected and obeyed the politicians as a matter of the highest principle, but it often appeared neutral against some (the Weimar Republic) and dutifully neutral for others (Bismarck and the baleful Hitler). Dupuy concludes, like a good soldier, that the German Army was nonpolitical and obedient; ultimately its failures are chargeable to the politicians.

Colonel Dupuy, a retired officer, is a noted military analyst, writer, and director of his own research organization. He has, in *A Genius for War*, produced a military textbook, written in suitably pedestrian style. His overall chronological approach is appropriate to the subject, though his chapters are short, overly subdivided, and rather choppy military reports. Events and men are too frequently introduced, then dropped without explanation. Dupuy's constant repetition of his major thesis convinces the reader less than would a less grand and more defensible argument centering on thorough preparation and organization.

Prints and photographs of prominent generals are clearly reproduced, but these pictures hardly humanize them, for we see a collection of scowling, walrus-mustached, overdecorated parodies. Certainly the photo of William I, replete with monumental mutton chops, great golden epaulets, and at least twenty medals, was obtained from central casting. In contrast, Clausewitz and Harden-burg seem almost friendly, but von Schlieffen and Ludendorff, judging from their studied sneers, spoke, like the Cabots and Lodges, only to each other and to God.

Maps, with some overly cluttered exceptions, are well drawn and informative. The bibliography is quite adequate for an expository work of this nature. The many appendices in the rear of *A Genius for War* are busy places. One contains a chronology of German history since 1806, another, a summary chart of Prussian-German military leadership since 1808. Several contain complex statistical summaries. Modern European military performance is charted by battle, time, and troop strength. Success is expressed according to casualties taken and inflicted, and a final "score effectiveness" is included. Dupuy also finds it necessary to append defenses of Schleicher and Halder.

Dupuy reveals a hawkish message for the future in an epilogue. He recognizes America's historical dislike of the general staff concept; late in the last century Secretary of War Root suggested that the U.S. Army emulate German methods. General Nelson Miles's rebuttal expressed an aversion to the presence of an alien, totalitarian militarism in a democratic society. But that was at a time when the rapacious Old World seemed far away. We must free ourselves of these antiquated ideas, advises the Colonel. Our present arms are substandard, our army directed by a "sort of" staff system modeled on a French imitation of the German original. The Soviet Union has a real German-style general staff, and we had better look out. America must learn the lessons of German history, form a New Model Army, and secure its national future, Dupuy concludes.

Does good come from war? That is hardly a fashionable question in 1978, but since 1945 the West and the East, Capitalist and Communist alike, have peacefully enjoyed a thrice-divided German people. Official crocodile tears are shed about German unification, and occasional border jostlings do occur, but the World War II Allies have done their work well. The Austrian seems contented with his culture, prosperity, and separation, and East and West Germany are two nations, nicely conditioned to believe that unity is less important than their political and economic ideologies. What a grand solution to the German problem, satisfactory to all, including the Germans.

Lance Trusty

Sources for Further Study

Kirkus Reviews. XLV, August 15, 1977, p. 894.
Library Journal. CII, October 1, 1977, p. 2060.
Publisher's Weekly. CCXII, September 5, 1977, p. 63.

THE GENTLE BARBARIAN
The Life and Work of Turgenev

Author: V. S. Pritchett (1900–   )
Publisher: Random House (New York). Illustrated. 243 pp. $10.00
Type of work: Critical biography
Time: 1818–1883
Locale: Western Russia and Europe

An account of the life and writings of the Russian novelist and short story master which ranges from his youth on the vast 5,000-serf estate ruled by his tyrannical mother to his death near Paris

Principal personages:
    IVAN TURGENEV, Russian novelist, playwright, and short story writer
    VARVARA PETROVNA, his tyrannical mother
    PAULINE VIARDOT, a Spanish-born opera star
    LOUIS VIARDOT, her French husband
    LEO TOLSTOY, Russian novelist

In its history, the novel has undergone many permutations; different authors have molded the form to suit the needs of their particular geniuses. Sometimes, in different localities, it developed in quite opposing directions, only again to be transformed by the genius of one person or of a group of writers. In England, the novel originated in the middle-class realism of Richardson and Defoe, while in Russia it can be traced back to the quite different prose and verse novels of Pushkin, with their highly romantic, vividly tapestried, Oriental qualities. These contrasting beginnings determined the later developments of the novel form in these two countries. The English novel always seemed to be rooted in the details of everyday life, while the Russian novel was inclined to fly off into explorations of the supernatural, the bizarre, the psychologically unexpected, and the politically dangerous. But there have been exceptions, the writers who sought to emulate the quiet, reasoned manner of the Western European writers, who were influenced more by the realism of the English novel and the style of the French writers; perhaps the foremost example of the "Europeanized" Russian writer is the "gentle barbarian" about whom Pritchett has written so sensitively and well: Ivan Turgenev.

The work of Turgenev seems more contemporary than ever before; a hundred years after they were written, his novels and stories speak to readers with a freshness and significance that perhaps even his contemporaries did not feel. While we admire the genius of many of his colleagues, often while reading their books we must make concessions to the passage of time from when they were written to our own era, but this is seldom required with Turgenev's works. Why does Turgenev seem to be "modern" in both subject matter and style? V. S. Pritchett addresses himself to this question, among others, in this extraordinary discussion of the man, the writer, and his times. *The Gentle Barbarian* may be the definitive study of Turgenev; seldom has there been such a perfect union of literary biographer and subject as in the case of V. S. Pritchett and Ivan Turgenev.

For decades, Turgenev seemed the least important of the four great nineteenth century Russian writers, less profound and obviously great than Dostoevski, with whom he quarreled, Tolstoy, for whom he prepared the way, and Chekhov, whom he influenced. He was the aristocratic, self-conscious artist whose gentle love stories and carefully constructed, exquisite novels drew prose pictures of the strange world of the Russian country gentry and their serfs. But if Turgenev was all of this, he was, of course, much more. He was committed as few writers ever have been to telling the truth. Apolitical, he did not avoid writing of political subjects, but when he did, he nearly always brought down upon himself the wrath of the opposing factions, each believing that he was prejudiced against them. His enemies, and often his friends, could not understand his determination to analyze all aspects of a situation and to present what he found, without holding up any side as right or wrong. You must be committed, they told him. He *was* committed, more than they knew, but to a higher principle than political dogmas. His integrity was pure in relation to his art, and his discipline was awesome.

Pritchett is fascinated by the process by which a great writer such as Turgenev is created. Certainly, Turgenev was molded to an extraordinary degree by the strange and difficult relationship he had with his terrifying, sadistic mother. Without overemphasizing the point, Pritchett makes clear the influence of Varvara Petrovna on Turgenev's later life, on his work, the fact of his bachelorhood and his love affairs, even on his psychological makeup; a case in point, for example, was the fact that Turgenev felt that he needed to be a possession, to *belong*, to any woman in his life, as he and everything else on the great estate had belonged to his mother. She was a tyrant, ruling her estate like an absolute monarch. She enjoyed punishing her serfs for mistakes, either real or imagined, and was capable of completely gratuitous cruelty. Ivan Turgenev's distaste for the system of serfdom was born in the years during which he watched his mother's cruelty. When Ivan's older brother married against her wishes, she cut him off without any money, not relenting even when he gave her three grandchildren. She remained unmoved even when the three children all died during one terrible year.

Ivan was Varvara Petrovna's favorite, but she found ways of hurting him, too, chiefly by inflicting pain on the serfs whom he tried to defend from her wrath. Everything in the miniature world of her estate belonged to her, the thousands of "souls" who worked for her, the forests and fields, the villages, the huts in which the peasants lived, everything. Even Ivan belonged to her, and although he lived many years after her death, he never married; he was unable to overcome the feeling that he still was part of her inventory.

However, he did love other women, and the relationship that meant the most to him in his life was the affair with the famous opera singer, Pauline Viardot.

Over many decades, his relationship with the temperamental Spanish singer had many fluctuations, but always he returned to her and her husband. The oddest aspect of this affair was that Turgenev was good friends with Pauline's husband. It is probable that for most of the duration of the relationship between Turgenev and Pauline Viardot, it was a platonic, romanticized affair in which he worshiped the great singer and was friend more than lover. Pauline, who was the model for the singer in George Sand's famous novel *Consuelo,* both stimulated and interfered with Turgenev's writing. He claimed that he could not write unless he was in love, but when he was with her he tended to fritter away his time on petty duties for her or her children. The most satisfactory arrangement seemed to be when they were apart, bound together only by the florid letters which he wrote to her; it was at these times that he created some of his finest works.

Pritchett chronicles with economy and shrewdness the changing fortunes of Turgenev's friendships with Tolstoy and Dostoevski. He was a good friend to the young Tolstoy, who was a decade younger, and helped the beginning writer to get started. He later devoted much time and energy to assisting Tolstoy and many other Russian writers to get translated and published in Western Europe. Almost singlehandedly, Turgenev made the nations of the West aware of Russian literature; yet his friends seldom realized how diligently he worked for them and how well he represented their works to the Western European literary world.

The literary history of Russia is filled with quarrels, with hysterical scenes and duels and tearful reconciliations. Pritchett brings some sense and tact to his recounting of the literary battles in which even such a restrained individual as Turgenev was involved. He explains the paranoia that drove Goncharov to quarrel with Turgenev and practically everybody else; more importantly, he discusses the ups and downs of Turgenev's relationship with his revolutionary-agitator friends Bakunin and Herzen. Perhaps the most famous literary quarrel dealt with in the book is the one between Turgenev and Dostoevski over the Slavophile movement and Turgenev's expatriot way of life. Beyond slogans and ideology, Dostoevski resented Turgenev's wealth, his elegance of manner and speech, his affectation (as Dostoevski called it) of European styles. He did not see how Turgenev could continue to write about Russia if he lived in Europe. Turgenev apparently was more affected by Dostoevski's remarks than he cared to let most people know.

Pritchett perhaps is at his best in discussing Turgenev's genius as a writer. He indicates the subtleties of Turgenev's style, the techniques which he employed to capture the layers of nuance for which he is famous. He labored to hold the moment between noticing and not noticing; this, he felt, was art, not just recounting what one nakedly saw. He was fascinated by the waywardness and timelessness of seeing, by the light and shadow of seeing, and by the playing over of what had been seen. In his fiction the past and present mingle in a stream.

There are two masters of seeing in Russian literature; Tolstoy and Turgenev. But, while Tolstoy sees vividly, as if he is an animal, Turgenev, who is equally exact, makes it clear that what is seen already is changing. This aspect of his writing creates a feeling of poignancy in many of his stories and novels.

When Turgenev began writing, there was no established tradition of storytelling or novel-writing in Russian literature. He was forced to be a founder and innovator; he was at the beginning of that series of great novels which paralleled the awakening of the Russian people. Behind him was only the work of Pushkin, notably *Eugene Onegin*. Turgenev was only slightly drawn to French models; he did not like Balzac and had not yet encountered Flaubert. He did admire Gogol, but his temperament would not let him write in the grotesque vein of the author of *Dead Souls*. He possessed a natural tendency to write in scenes; his novels, therefore, are structured like plays, and they influenced writers such as Chekhov. Through diligence and singlemindedness of purpose, he helped to create the Russian novel.

From his first stories, one is amazed at how much Turgenev conveys of the subterranean emotions, especially in his scenes of country house life. The watchful, timeless silence of Russia permeates his fiction. He is perhaps most famous for his love stories, for the tenderness and sadness of his descriptions of young love. The permanence of his love stories is dependent on his sense of love as a spiritual test, as a test of moral character, as well as a diagnosis of the spiritual condition of each generation.

Early in his career, the notion of the "extraordinary man" fascinated Turgenev. This subject runs through his work like a theme, culminating in his most famous novel, *Fathers and Sons*. But even when he dealt with large themes, he tended to underplay them; he shrank fastidiously from Balzac's coarse exuberance. The approach was everything, the style the necessity which guided the work. His portraits are not only of his heroes and heroines, but of particular epochs. He observes and listens, presenting characters who are many-faceted, complex, real. His work is never didactic, but is rooted in his deep commitment to truth.

V. S. Pritchett, himself a talented novelist and short story writer, as well as a shrewd critic and literary commentator and a student of Russian literature, has explored with subtlety and compassion the interplay between Turgenev's extraordinary life and his writing. This biographical essay will be read and appreciated for decades to come.

Bruce D. Reeves

Sources for Further Study

America. CXXXVII, July 2, 1977, p. 16.

Atlantic. CCXXXIX, June, 1977, p. 94.

New Leader. LX, May 23, 1977, p. 17.

New Statesman. XCIII, June 24, 1977, p. 858.

New York Times Book Review. May 22, 1977, p. 1.

New Yorker. LIII, May 30, 1977, p. 113.

Time. CIX, May 23, 1977, p. 103.

THE GIANTS
Russia and America

Author: Richard J. Barnet
Publisher: Simon and Schuster (New York). 190 pp. $8.95
Type of work: History

An account of how Russia and America emerged as the world's two superpowers after World War II, and an analysis of their present relationship to each other

Those familiar with the style and substance of Richard Barnet's other works, *Global Reach* (with Ron Müller), *The Roots of War,* the *The Economy of Death,* and *Intervention and Revolution,* may be somewhat disappointed by this latest book. *The Giants: Russia and America* possesses none of the trenchant criticism of United States foreign policy that distinguishes these other works. The dominant tone of this work can only be described as sober and subdued. Not that Richard Barnet has suddenly converted to orthodoxy and shed his role as a revisionist critic of U.S. foreign policy; the ideas expressed in *The Giants* are perfectly consistent with the author's previous positions taken over the years. It is simply that the tone of this latest book is much more moderate and balanced than one would have expected from an analysis of Barnet's other works. No doubt part of the reason for this balanced judgment is due to the fact that when it comes to parceling out blame for continuing the arms race, there is plenty of criticism to go around on both sides. The foreign policy elites of both superpowers have generally operated under the assumption of the worst possible case.

What does Barnet attempt to do in *The Giants*? First, he briefly describes the changes that have taken place over the past sixty years of peaceful coexistence with the Soviet Union. What Barnet finds unique about the present age is not that all the Cold War stereotypes have disappeared, but that both sides are getting to know their counterparts better. Representatives of the Soviet and American governments have met each other numerous times across the negotiating table. These contacts have been useful in gaining a more realistic perspective of the opposition. While there is some danger that these contacts may lead to new misconceptions of the opposition, this situation is certainly preferable to the one which prevailed during the height of the Cold War when neither side talked directly to the other.

Second, Barnet describes how *détente* came about, focusing mainly on that "correlation of forces," as Kissinger used to call it, which was responsible for the change of policy toward the U.S.S.R. Barnet leaves the impression, however, that *détente* began with the election of Richard Nixon to the White House in 1968. While the process of *détente* was certainly strengthened by the Nixon-Kissinger Administration, the roots stretch back much further. From the Soviet perspective, Malenkov's speech before the Supreme Soviet in August, 1953, can be considered a turning point in U.S.-Soviet relations. It was in this speech that

Malenkov enunciated the doctrine of peaceful coexistence with the capitalist West which forms the basis of the Soviet view of *détente.*

Barnet next attempts to define what *détente* means in the contemporary environment, and he identifies it with the series of wide-ranging agreements that have been negotiated between the United States and the U.S.S.R. The most important of these agreements include SALT, the Berlin accords, and a 1972 agreement negotiated between Nixon and Brezhnev in which the parties pledged themselves to consult with each other concerning "the development of situations capable of causing a dangerous exacerbation of their relations." As part of this agreement, the two nations recognized "a special responsibility . . . to do everything in their power so that conflicts or situations will not arise which would serve to increase international tension." As Barnet correctly points out, it is this latter agreement that has engendered so much controversy in the West. *The Giants* leaves several important questions unanswered. For example, under the rubric of *détente,* does the United States have the right to expect that the Soviet Union and her allies such as Cuba will not encourage and support revolutionary movements in Africa? What about the widespread violation of human rights in the Soviet Union directed against Jews and dissidents which threaten to make a mockery of the Helsinki accords? How should the United States react to such problems? Unfortunately, Barnet never makes it sufficiently clear whether *détente* should be conditioned by Soviet behavior in these two areas.

Fourth, Barnet sketches the image of the enemy that exists in the minds of Soviet and American decision-makers. Not surprisingly he finds these images distorted by years of misperception. Although there is nothing new in this presentation, it is nevertheless important to be reminded of the impact which false images have had on foreign policy formulation.

Surely one of the most crucial issues that exists between the United States and Soviet Union concerns the nature of the strategic military balance today. Barnet reviews in depth the main components of this balance—strategic nuclear forces, the Soviet and American navies, and conventional military forces that each side has stationed in Europe. He finds American power sufficient in every field to deter the Soviet Union from mounting an attack against the United States or her NATO allies. He agrees that the relative power of the Soviet Union has grown substantially over the past several years; the significance of this increase, however, is subject to interpretation.

Barnet, for example, does not believe that the national security of the United States has been endangered by recent increases in military spending by the U.S.S.R. He does not see the Soviet leadership trying to achieve a "theoretical war-winning capability" that would enable them to fight and win a nuclear war with the United States by striking first and holding back a retaliatory force sufficient to blackmail the United States into submission. Such alarmist fears expressed by Paul Nitze and others associated with the Committee on the

Present Danger are, he believes, not warranted.

Finally Barnet examines the role that foreign trade plays in the U.S.-Soviet relationship. He points out, for example, that American multinational corporations played a major role in helping to foster *détente* with the U.S.S.R. Economic titans such as Donald Kendall, David Rockefeller, and Armand Hammer urged closer U.S.-Soviet relations in order to create the kind of political environment in which it would be possible to promote greater trade with the Soviet Union. From the Soviet side, the stimulus for closer economic relations with the United States came from top Soviet leaders who were interested in accelerating the transfer of new technology to the U.S.S.R.

From a policy standpoint, the most crucial issue concerns the political wisdom of technology transfers to the U.S.S.R. Opinion in the United States is sharply divided over this controversial issue. Those who favor technology transfers usually argue that these links will help the United States maintain some leverage over the Soviet economy. As the Soviets become increasingly dependent upon these technologies, their behavior at home and abroad should be moderated. Skeptics of *détente*, on the other hand, maintain that the transfer of sophisticated technology to the U.S.S.R. should be resisted since this has profound security implications for the West. Barnet eschews simplistic explanations of this complicated problem. He recognizes the very real dangers of sharing our knowledge of computers and electronic equipment with the Soviets. At the same time, however, he sees the U.S.S.R. as becoming part of a more interdependent world and finding it more difficult to return to outmoded economic conditions.

The basic thesis of the book is succinctly stated when the author writes, "There will be no possibility of a lasting detente without a fundamental change in the military relationship." What troubles Barnet and other scholars is that the process of *détente* has not penetrated very far, and foreign policy elites on both sides are still prisoners of the past. How to breakdown the cycle of fear and distrust that plagues the U.S.-Soviet relationship is the crucial issue facing the two superpowers. Barnet has a more ominous fear that the "Giants" may stumble into war by miscalculation. As the Soviets attempt to flex their muscles as a world power, the danger of confrontation may grow. Unlike the past when the Soviet Union was relegated to a position of inferiority, today they have achieved parity with the West in nearly all fields. In a future crisis situation, Kremlin leaders may choose not to back down from the brink as Khrushchev did in the Cuban missile crisis. If this happens, the two superpowers may find themselves in a war that no one wants and neither side can win.

Although this book was written during the early days of the Carter Administration, Barnet strikes a prophetic note on the future of U.S.-Soviet relations when he sees the Carter Administration as downgrading the importance of *détente* with the U.S.S.R. Not even Barnet, however, could have projected how far relations between the two countries would degenerate since the heyday of *détente* in 1972. While we are in no immediate danger of going to war with the Soviet Union, our relations with the Kremlin are being increasingly strained by what we perceive to be Soviet meddling in African politics. In the latest crisis in Zaïre, President Carter has even suggested that congressional restraints on his ability to conduct foreign policy should be reviewed. If this is done, it might mean a return to the interventionist policies of the past with all the potentials for miscalculation that Barnet and others fear.

In conclusion, *The Giants* is an important book for those concerned about the present state of U.S.-Soviet relations. Barnet not only helps to demolish many of the myths that continue to plague American relations with the Soviet Union, but he also places these relations in perspective.

Richard L. Langill

Sources for Further Study

Booklist. LXXIV, October 15, 1977, p. 340.
Human Events. XXXVII, November 12, 1977, p. 12.
Kirkus Reviews. XLV, September 1, 1977, p. 959. ·
Publisher's Weekly. CXII, October 10, 1977, p. 62.

THE GINGER TREE

Author: Oswald Wynd (1913   )
Publisher: Harper & Row Publishers (New York). 294 pp. $10.00
Type of work: Novel
Time: January 9, 1903 to August 20, 1942
Locale: Aboard a ship en route between England and China; Peking and Tokyo

A recounting through letters and journal entries of the tale of a very proper young Scottish girl who goes to China just after the Boxer Rebellion to become the bride of the military attache at the British Embassy in Peking

Principal characters:
> MARY MACKENZIE, a Scotswoman living in Asia
> RICHARD COLLINGSWORTH, her husband and military attache at Peking
> COUNT KENTARO KURIHAMA, a Japanese aristocrat and Mary's lover
> MARIE AND ARMAND CHAMONPIERRE, French Embassy personnel
> ALICIA BASSETT-HILL, a spinster missionary
> AIKO SANNOTERA, a Japanese aristocrat and liberated woman
> BOB AND EMMA LOU DALE, an American couple living in Tokyo
> PETER NASSON, Mary's friend and lover

This novel narrates the tale of a young, sheltered, very proper Scottish girl who has been reared by a rigid, self-righteous, reticent widow in South Edinburgh. The girl is sensitive, compassionate, and by nature drawn to people. She finds the restrictions and repressions imposed upon her life intolerable when she moves to Peking and marries a very proper and sexually repressed man. The confinement of the life of the embassy personnel in the period following the Boxer Rebellion, plus the discomforts of the change of lifestyle, and the strangeness of the foreign land and customs, all combine to make her feel lonely and depressed. The lack of communication with her husband and her ultimate realization that there is really no love between them increases her sense of isolation, which is intensified by the spectacle of the warmth and affection so openly shared between Marie and Armand when she accompanies them on a holiday to the Western Hills near Peking while her husband is away on duty.

Mary's impulsive love affair with Count Kurihama which occurs at this point is delicately narrated, and seems, strangely enough, quite a natural thing for this lonely, frustrated, generous young woman to do. The event is decisive in determining Mary's future. She is henceforth bound to the Orient both by her affection for her lover and by her blood ties to their son, Tomo. At first she feels totally alien in Japan, where she has no friends, no relatives, no knowledge of the language, and no control over her own destiny. Later, when she takes charge of her own life and moves to make a career, a home, and a set of friends for herself, she adapts herself increasingly to Japanese ways and adopts the attitude that Japan is now her home, despite her British citizenship.

In the final section of the book, Mary sees herself as akin to the ginger tree, the alien plant which has taken root and flourished in the Japanese garden, but which the gardener dislikes, calling it a foreign thing which can never be a suitable plant for an authentic Japanese garden. She acknowledges that she will never be accepted truly by the Japanese, despite her love of Japanese culture and her attempts to conform and to preserve their traditional culture and heritage against the inroads of Western concrete, electricity, and industry. She regards her deportation from Japan as exile from her home, rather than as a return to her home. The poignant final scene is deeply moving in its warmth, tenderness, and utter finality.

The author has told the entire tale as a series of journal entries and letters from Mary to her mother and to her friend Marie. This method of narration is difficult to handle, but the author has done so very capably. The sense of immediacy and intimacy is heightened by the device of the journal-letter format. The limited point of view of the girl, her speculations, errors of judgment, and hopes and fears, all function as elements in the shaping of the point of view and in the emotional tone of the narration.

Not that Mary, the journal and letter writer, ever goes into detail in describing her own emotions or even her general emotional state very often. Her Scottish upbringing and proper Victorian reticence combine to make it impossible for her to communicate such intimate details as her private emotions and still remain true to her character. Happily, the author has conveyed such authenticity of Mary's character, that he can leave the reader to guess, or to infer, those things which Mary cannot bring herself to write. Mary's reticence is not dissemblance, though. She is honest in her thoughts, in her actions, and in her relations to others. She admires this quality in others too, although she often suspects others are not entirely honest with her. This suspicion occasionally causes her to misjudge others and to make mistakes, which she stolidly records without excuse or apology, accepting her errors and limitations of judgment just as she has accepted her "errors" in behavior.

Mary is the soul of humility, acknowledging her passiveness, her sinfulness, her helplessness, and her lack of insight into others as well as herself. But this humble, realistic appraisal of herself is leavened by a defiant, cool assertion that whatever she is, she will survive and make the best of what comes.

And indeed much does happen to Mary Mackenzie. She is embroiled in the political and social upheavals of early twentieth century Asia in a very personal and inextricable way. The Boxer Rebellion, the rule of the Empress Dowager Tsz'e Hsi, the Japanese-Russian battles, the Emperor Meiji's death, World Wars I and II, various major earthquakes, fires, *tsunamis,* and even the depression of the 1930's are all important elements affecting the life of this remarkable woman. She is at times passive, yielding, and buffeted by dynamic forces around her. But she gathers strength and determination from such episodes, and emerges with new courage, new independence, and new decisions about what to make of her life. The sheer magnificence of her survival and the unfolding of her career despite the rejection, ostracism, impediments of sex, language, culture, and society are developments fascinating to watch.

Mary begins as an occasionally defiant and willful girl, but one strongly imbued with traditional ideas of Presbyterian and Scottish Victorian morality and duty. She appears to undergo a sea change with her transport to an alien culture on the other side of the globe, and finds that she no longer fits into the tiny bastion of Victorian propriety which is the Embassy Compound in Peking. Mary's growth, her increasing development of a capacity for love, understanding, patience, and forgiveness, and her courage in the face of shocking and unpredictable events and losses make her finally emerge as an exceptional woman, but a wholly believable one.

The character of Kentaro as perceived by Mary is admittedly incomplete, but probably represents a fair depiction of Japanese character as revealed to "foreigners" who cannot truly participate in Japanese life and culture. Mary's relationships to other Japanese, such as Aiko, her employers, maids, and neighbors, give further insights into personalities shaped by so different a culture. Indeed, the entire range of characters other than Mary is that of a gallery of portraits viewed through her eyes, and reflecting therefore her limitations of vision. The characters have life, but they lack somewhat in depth and solidity. In contrast to all of them, Mary emerges as a towering figure of great strength and courage, but resigned to her small weaknesses. One such weakness is her initial suspicion of overtures of friendship. But then her enthusiastic warmth and delight in people seems all the more charming when she finally allows herself the luxury of openness and trust.

The language, the narrative style, and the tone of the book are for the most part a triumph for Wynd. It is a difficult task for a male author to try to narrate an entire novel through the personality and the language of a woman, and yet the language and the characterization ring true. One can believe that such a woman as Mary Mackenzie would have written in such a way. Occasionally there are peculiarities of syntax which may cause a momentary confusion to the reader. But these are rare, and probably reflect the bilingual background of the author.

The novel is enjoyable for the characterization and for the storyline, which moves briskly enough to assure the reader that each chapter will contain exciting, important episodes in the story. More than that, the depiction of scenes limning the cultural milieu of China and Japan in the early part of the twentieth century is fascinating, and these images come to life with a carefully detailed series of vignettes and descriptions. Such descriptive passages are concise and always smoothly employed in the amplification of the storyline. None could be deleted without diminishing the story in a real sense.

This novel charting the development of the mind and character of a young girl from innocence through much adversity, occasional joy, and great loneliness, accomplishes its task with skill and conviction. But it simultaneously charts the attitudes which the Japanese adopted toward foreigners and things foreign during the same span of time: their pride, running to arrogance; their rejections of foreigners as intimates, and adoption of Western techniques and mechanization; and their driving determination to achieve dominance in Asia and thus gain recognition as a power in the world. All these attitudes and more are revealed and brought to life as vital shaping forces in the evolution of world history, made concrete through the actions of characters in the novel. In a very real sense, the book becomes a personalized history lesson, a look at how the dynamics of the large social forces at work in the world impinge on the small private world of a woman seeking to survive in an alien land.

The world of Mary Mackenzie is a personally ascetic one. There is little description of luxuries; and architecture, clothing, food, and scenery in general are touched on rather lightly, leaving much to the imagination of the reader. Rather better, though, are the descriptions of natural scenes and phenomena. The tremor of an earthquake, the swell and surge and crash of a *tsunami*, the raging terror of Tokyo afire, are envisioned meticulously and evoke a sense of the reality and immediacy of the event which transcends the printed page.

The book is in many ways a commentary on the social and moral values of the period, both Japanese and Western. Mary was rejected, despised, and cruelly deprived of her children by both cultures. She was never able to establish herself as a socially acceptable person in either world, despite her manifest talents and successful business career. Mary's growth with respect to personal relationships is largely demonstrated in her relationships with men. Her relationships with women characteristically begin with some suspicion and reserve and move to an acceptance and lasting friendship, but she maintains a clear-eyed sense of the women's strengths and limitations. With men, there is a decided difference. Mary begins her journal with an ill-defined romantic idealization of her fiancé. She never comes to know or understand this man who becomes her husband. Her rather uncritical admiration of Armand, her impulsive and unexamined attraction to Kentaro, and her passive acceptance of the decisions men make on her behalf during her early years only gradually change as she matures and establishes herself in the business world. Here she finds that she can and must act independently, and defy the attempts of men to manipulate her and keep her in a subject position.

Her success in doing this brings a measure of anguish and social approbation which she had not anticipated, but just as she has endured the rejection she suffered by taking a lover, so she endures the scandal which results when she asserts herself in the business world. From strength and conviction gained by such experiences, she comes more and more to deal with men as equals, bargaining with the banker for a favorable arrangement in setting up a business, ignoring the advice of her lawyer to follow her own hunches about how she should invest her money, and declining to marry Peter, because, finally, respectability is less inviting than personal independence. She even declines to marry Kentaro because the marriage cannot be on her terms, with her son returned to her and acknowledged as their child.

The Ginger Tree does not have a happy ending. There is little of happiness throughout the novel, and that little is dearly bought. But adversity becomes Mary Mackenzie. She thrives on it. And she takes comfort and joy in small things, like a letter from a friend. Or like the stubborn presence of an alien ginger tree in a Japanese garden.

Betty Gawthrop

Sources for Further Study

Booklist. LXXIV, November 1, 1977, p. 464.
Kirkus Reviews. XLV, August 15, 1977, p. 880.
Library Journal. CII, August, 1977, p. 1681.
New Yorker. LIII, November 7, 1977, p. 222.
Observer. August 14, 1977, p. 23.

GOLD AND IRON

Bismarck, Bleichröder, and the Building of the German Empire

Author: Fritz Stern (1926–   )
Publisher: Alfred A. Knopf (New York). Illustrated. 620 pp. $17.95
Type of work: History and biography
Time: 1815–1945, with a concentration on the period 1859–1893
Locale: Germany

A pioneer study in which Stern analyzes the joint work of Otto von Bismarck, the Prussian statesman, and Gerson von Bleichröder, the Jewish banker, in forging German unification and in shaping the destinies of the German Empire

> *Principal personages:*
> OTTO VON BISMARCK, Minister-President of Prussia and Chancellor of the German Empire
> GERSON VON BLEICHRÖDER, Bismarck's personal banker, adviser, and confidant
> WILLIAM I OF HOHENZOLLERN, King of Prussia who was proclaimed German Emperor in 1871
> WILLIAM II OF HOHENZOLLERN, King of Prussia and German Emperor, 1888–1918
> BARON JAMES DE ROTHSCHILD, Head of the Paris Rothschild bank who corresponded frequently with Bleichröder on political and financial matters of interest to the French and Prussian governments
> ADOLF STOECKER, Court chaplain of the Hohenzollerns and outspoken anti-Semite
> HEINRICH VON TREITSCHKE, prominent historian and outspoken anti-Semite

Fritz Stern, Seth Low Professor of History at Columbia University, is a leading authority on modern German history. His earlier books in this area include *The Politics of Cultural Despair: A Study in the Rise of Germanic Ideology* and *The Failure of Illiberalism: Essays on the Political Culture of Modern Germany.* Now, to these impressive works he has added the monumental *Gold and Iron: Bismarck, Bleichröder, and the Building of the German Empire,* the first study of Gerson von Bleichröder, Otto von Bismarck's personal banker and confidant. Stern spent almost two decades in researching the book, which is based primarily on Bleichröder's voluminous correspondence with Bismarck and members of his family and with the House of Rothschild in Paris. As the title indicates, the central theme of the book is the joint work of Bismarck and Bleichröder in shaping the destiny of Germany at the moment of its great upsurge of power.

In its overall scope, the book is divided into three areas of concentration. Part One deals with the rise to prominence of Bismarck and Bleichröder and Bleichröder's role in helping the Prussian statesman bring about the unification of Germany. The second part analyzes their multifaceted collaboration in shaping the domestic, financial, and foreign policies of the new German Empire.

The concluding part deals with the Jewishness of Bleichröder in relation to the Jewish community, to German society and politics, and, above all, to German anti-Semitism. In the last third of the nineteenth century anti-Semitism in Germany and other countries was undergoing a transformation from a passive, "respectable" brand characterized by mere social prejudice toward a clannish group, to a more aggressive type whose proponents demanded curbs on the growing power of the Jews. Ironically, Bleichröder's very service on behalf of the recently unified Reich combined with his own social prominence and financial prestige contributed immensely to the emergence of this new, more intolerant anti-Semitism.

Bismarck chose Bleichröder as his personal banker in 1859, just three years before his own appointment by King William I as Minister-President of Prussia. By 1864, Bleichröder had become a member of Bismarck's inner circle of advisers, a prestigious position which he would hold for the next twenty-five years or so. During this period, in which he was often referred to as the German Rothschild, Bleichröder's responsibilities grew steadily as did his own personal wealth and power. He served Bismarck not only as his personal banker but as his political adviser as well, and all of Europe came to know him as Bismarck's secret agent. Bleichröder's numerous financial and political contacts throughout Europe comprised an intelligence network whose effectiveness was frequently superior to the official state intelligence agencies. In particular, he maintained a voluminous correspondence with Baron James de Rothschild, who was head of the Paris Rothschild bank until his death in 1867. Baron James frequently transmitted to Bleichröder valuable information on financial and political matters that touched the delicate and declining relations between France and Prussia during the 1860's. Bleichröder also used his sources of information on financial matters to build up personal fortunes for himself and Bismarck. Despite the tangle of public and private business between the two protagonists, Stern concludes that Bismarck did not formulate policy in order to advance his private interests.

According to Stern, one of Bleichröder's most important services to Bismarck was his effort to secure financial backing for the first two wars of German unification; namely, the Danish War of 1864 and the Seven Weeks' (Austro-Prussian) War of 1866. Together, these wars enabled Bismarck by 1867 to unify the German states north of the Main River under the Prussian-sponsored North German Confederation. Bismarck's desperate need for money to finance these wars—a need which Stern notes has been totally ignored by later historians—became apparent to him in 1863, when Denmark proclaimed the incorporation of the Duchy of Schleswig, thus severing that territory's traditional union with the neighboring Duchy of Holstein, itself a member state of the German Confederation. Bismarck intended to go to war if necessary to drive Denmark from Schleswig, but he was unable to secure from the Prussian Diet the necessary funds for military expenditures. Consequently, Stern writes, Bismarck turned to Bleichröder and used his connections—among them, the Rothschild banking houses throughout Europe. Bleichröder did indeed have "connections" with the Rothschilds, but no money was forthcoming from them, for, as Stern quotes Baron James de Rothschild, "it is a principle of our Houses not to advance money for any war." Stern, furthermore, is vague in describing precisely how Bleichröder went about financing the six-month Danish War while it was being waged. The author's most concrete reference to Bleichröder's activities in this regard is that he "seems to have urged that the government mortgage the bonds of a loan, already authorized by the [Prussian] Diet for railroad construction," to bankers who would supply the government with immediate funds. Otherwise, throughout the chapter on the Danish War, Stern repeatedly informs the reader that Bismarck still needed money, thus leaving some doubt as to how effective Bleichröder's quest for capital actually was during the course of the war.

Stern leaves no doubt, however, about Bleichröder's success in raising money for the Seven Weeks' War. In July, 1865, as relations between Austria and Prussia steadily worsened, the Prussian government and the Cologne-Minden Railroad signed an agreement, arranged by Bleichröder, that provided Bismarck with much of the money he needed in order to meet the military expenditures of an Austrian war. The agreement, Stern notes, was the outcome of protracted negotiations, in all of which Bleichröder was involved as both the company's banker and one of its directors. Under terms of the agreement, the Prussian government renounced its prior right to purchase the stock of the railroad, in exchange for thirteen million talers. In addition, the government was no longer obliged to maintain a large guarantee fund which had been set up to provide backing for minor lines associated with the Cologne-Minden Railroad and to cover possible interest payments on the railroad bonds. The elimination of this fund thus freed another seventeen million talers for Bismarck's use. After the successful conclusion of the Austro-Prussian war in July, 1866, Bleichröder provided further assistance to Bismarck by collecting the indemnity imposed on Saxony, an ally of Austria. In a similar fashion, Bleichröder was instrumental in arranging the transfer of the French indemnity after the Franco-Prussian War of 1870–1871.

Bleichröder, by arranging the funding of Prussia's great victory over Austria, not only contributed to German unification but also, at least indirectly, to the end of the constitutional crisis which had plagued Bismarck on money matters since the beginning of his ministry in 1862. The liberal opposition to Bismarck's foreign policy collapsed now that he had broken Austria's historic influence in Central Europe. Finally, then, on September 8, 1866, the Prussian Diet voted to accept the government's bill of indemnity, which gave retroactive assent to previous governmental expenditures that had been made without parliamentary consent.

Despite his close collaboration with Bismarck and his acquisition of great personal wealth and power, Bleichröder embodied what Stern refers to as "the ambiguity of Jewish success." For all of his public and private success, he was never quite able to obtain full respectability and acceptance from those whom he served. It is true that in 1872, at Bismarck's urging, William I ennobled Bleichröder, the first Prussian Jew to be so honored without converting to Christianity. Bismarck, however, made his recommendation orally, not in writing. The formal patent of ennoblement, moreover, was amended so as to delete the customary reference to those "who sprung from good families." Emperor William simply could not bring himself to proclaim that Bleichröder had sprung from what Prussians would call a good family. Ironically, Bleichröder had been raised to the ranks of the nobility because he had undertaken to salvage the fortunes of Prussian Junkers who had lost money in the collapse of some railroad projects in Rumania. Far from appreciating his efforts on their behalf, the Prussian aristocrats considered him little more than an embarrassing necessity.

Stern leaves the reader with a depressing portrait of Bleichröder: a man totally blind by 1880 who sought to emulate the values and lifestyle of his pseudolegal nobilitarian peers, whose acceptance of him was at best conditional. Most of the old Junker aristocracy, who would not have anything to do with Bleichröder socially, bitterly condemned members of the Bismarck family for attending the banker's lavish parties. Interestingly, their denunciation of Bismarck's relations with Bleichröder found its parallel in the new anti-Semitism that was unleashed during the 1870's.

Stern treats Bleichröder as the hostage of the new anti-Semitism which arose in Germany in the years of depression following the great financial crash of 1873. The very term "anti-Semitism," as the author points out, was first coined in Germany at this time; its adherents propagated the myth that the Jews, because they were now the true power in Germany would, if unchecked, corrupt the German character. Consequently, anti-Semitism demanded that the state should revoke or restrict the rights of Jews. Bleichröder's financial power and his recent elevation to the nobility made him the most obvious target of the new anti-Semitism. In Bleichröder, the anti-Semites found the living embodiment of all the Jewish stereotypes: the Jew as promoter and plotter, as corrupter, as one who amassed a fortune on the stock exchange instead of earning his daily bread by the sweat of his brow. There was, then, as the author demonstrates, a violent anticapitalistic sentiment in the new anti-Semitism. But this sentiment was not confined to the anti-Semites; they simply exploited the view held by many observers that the evil forces of materialism, greed, and moral decay were endangering the fabric of society in the new Empire. In time, more people were prepared to blame these manifestations of corruption on the Jews. Bismarck's enemies went so far by the mid-1870's as to insist that the chancellor was under the influence of a Jewish conspiracy to dominate the state that was masterminded by Bleichröder.

The author describes in considerable detail the difficulty which Bleichröder encountered in coping with the increasingly vicious anti-Semitic attacks on the Jews in general and on himself in particular. It was bad enough to be attacked by such anti-Semitic popularizers as Adolf Stoecker, the court chaplain of the Hohenzollerns, and Heinrich von Treitschke, the prominent historian. But what hurt Bleichröder even worse was that none of his contacts—he never had any real friends—in the ranks of the Prussian elite and Bismarck's entourage came to his defense. Rather, they maintained an embarrassed silence where he was concerned. What is more, during the 1880's, the Bismarck regime began a policy of covert discrimination against the Jews that the civil service continued under Emperor William II. Tragically, then, the very state which Bleichröder had helped create came to adopt or at least condone anti-Semitic attitudes. His detractors continued to heap insults on him to the very end of his life in 1893.

In the eighty odd years between his death and the publication of *Gold and Iron*, Bleichröder remained, in spite of his important contributions to Germany, what Stern calls an "unperson" in German historiography; he represents, in the author's words, "everything that has been left out of German history." Bismarck himself set this pattern by making only one passing reference to Bleichröder in his three volumes of memoirs. Subsequently, the editors of Bismarck's collected works did not publish so much as a single letter of the chancellor to his banker. German historians have focused exclusively on one of the two protagonists of Stern's account, writing some seven thousand volumes on the Iron Chancellor since his death in 1898.

Hence, Stern's book, though marred by a repetitive writing style, assumes great importance not only for its contribution to German history but to German historiography as well. As history, *Gold and Iron* provides the reader with an in-depth study of a critical period in the development of modern Germany. In this context, Stern's discussion of the character of late nineteenth century anti-Semitism is particularly illuminating. Historiographically, Stern weaves a biographical portrait of Bleichröder into an analysis of the social and economic life of the German Empire. This technique is something of an innovation in itself, for as Stern notes, contemporary German historians have tended to shun the importance of the individual in history, and their fascination with the structure of society often dulls their concern for the spirit that animated it. Henceforth, historians will be obliged to take into consideration the role of Bleichröder in financing the unification of the nation that chose to vilify and ultimately forget him.

Edward P. Keleher

Sources for Further Study

Central European History. X, June, 1977, p. 165.
Listener. XCVII, June 23, 1977, p. 830.
Times Literary Supplement. August 12, 1977, p. 986.
Virginia Quarterly Review. LIII, Summer, 1977, p. 99.

THE GREAT REPUBLIC
A History of the American People

Authors: Bernard Bailyn, David Brion Davis, David Herbert Donald, John L. Thomas,
  Robert H. Wiebe, and Gordon S. Wood
Publisher: Little, Brown and Company (Boston). Illustrated. 1,267 pp. $20.00
Type of work: History
Time: 1492–1976
Locale: The United States

  Six historians attempt not merely a narrative retelling but an analysis of the total history of the United States

It is sometimes observed by critics and readers of history that professional historians have carved out specialties for themselves, and those who write "popular history" usually concentrate on the dramatic event or the exciting personality. The one- and two-volume histories purporting to cover the whole story almost always turn out to be textbooks, especially college texts for the survey course. The tradition of a single scholar attempting to write a complete history of the United States intended for the general public seems to have died out in favor of specialization.

This situation makes *The Great Republic* as remarkable as its publishing history has been unusual. The "original" edition seems to have been intended as a text, and the otherwise identical hardbound edition meant for the more general market. It bears many of the marks of the better college texts: carefully defined division into parts, chapters, and sections of chapters, suitable for assignment and study; plentiful and useful maps; an abundance of illustrations, including six "color essays" which tellingly use the arts of a period to display its character, progress, and problems; chronological charts; reading suggestions after each chapter; appendices including the Declaration of Independence and the Constitution; a table of population and area growth; a table of presidential elections; a list of presidents up to and including Jimmy Carter; and an index. *The Great Republic* is a handsome and usable text; it has not a single author but six, all recognized in the profession. They include winners of the Pulitzer and Bancroft prizes, and of the National Book Award. Each has written one of the six parts, approximately equal in length, about a particular period in United States history: to 1760, Bailyn; 1760–1820, Wood; 1820–1860, Davis; 1860–1890, Donald; 1890–1920, Thomas; and 1920–1976, Wiebe.

The authors' approach may hold some surprises for the general reader. Columbus' voyage is more or less taken for granted; so is the *Mayflower*'s. But there is a considerable discussion of the administration of the Spanish colonies in the New World, and of demographic factors in early Massachusetts. Captain John Smith is covered in a paragraph, and Pocahontas does not appear; but the mechanics of the tobacco trade are detailed. *The Great Republic* is not old-fashioned history, nor is it the careful, bland mixture many accuse textbooks of being. For example, James Madison is described as "the greatest political thinker of the Revolutionary era and perhaps of all American history," while Thomas Eakins rates as "the greatest painter of the post [Civil] war period." On the other hand, there was "that bumbling incompetent, Ambrose E. Burnside, whose one redeeming feature was that he knew he was bumbling and incompetent." And the reference in the Suggested Readings summarizes the biography of A. Mitchell Palmer as "the portrait of a national villain." Such outspoken opinions may arouse controversy, but they certainly add vigor and interest to the story.

In their Introduction, the authors set forth two general themes which unify the book, and presumably the history it recounts. One is the development and testing of free political institutions; the other is the tension between majority rule and minority rights. Lest this thematic, and apparently political, approach seem simple, the authors profess their more general view of history: it is not the mere accumulation of fact, but a mode of understanding. The view, moreover, is not deterministic; economic, political, cultural, and social forces interact and influence one another "in no predetermined pattern." These themes and the viewpoints set the compass for the voyage, but they cannot convey the richness of the journey. The familiar story of colonization and growth, for instance, takes on new meaning when such factors as great demographic differences, population growth, age distribution, and imbalance of sexes, are stressed, and the enormous difficulty of maintaining a European or English culture and social system in the new environment is described.

One of the insights suggested, for example, is that the colonists were essentially conservative, and regarded their desertion or mutation of the old ways as regression rather than advance. The colonial economy is put into the context of the European and West Indian commercial world, and, later, the Colonial principles and presuppositions about the British constitution and the "rights of Englishmen" are viewed in the context of eighteenth century English thought. The "corruption" of governments like Sir Robert Walpole's, with their dependence on patronage and management, was bitterly attacked in pamphlets and treatises which circulated in the colonies; it was the threat of such royal corruption as well as more immediate grievances, which underlay the Colonial protests. What such an example demonstrates is that while the stated themes may have been political, they rested both on a web of beliefs and suppositions, and on the real and felt structures and interests of the society. The first part, Bailyn's, points to the rise of *élites*, planters in the Chesapeake region, merchants in New England, who did not have much of the character of an aristocracy, yet who held a crude economic and political power.

Similarly, Gordon Wood's analysis of the writing of the first state constitutions, which in some ways he puts ahead of the document of 1787, stresses the idea of republicanism, which was not simply a rejection of monarchy, but an ideal of an uncorrupt, free people. If Hamilton and the Federalists clung to the notions of strength and leadership as necessary to the national survival, the Jeffersonians saw themselves as the protectors of the Republican idea.

Familiar themes—national expansion, immigration, the reform movements of the 1830's and 1840's, the controversies over slavery—reflect deeper lights than ordinary treatments afford. War, even the great central crisis of the Civil War, receives attention, but a different stress from the traditional emphasis on generals and battles. Attitudes, both causative, supportive, and obstructive, are important; so are the changes the wars brought to government and society. Although acknowledging the controversy over the degree (if any) to which the Civil War accelerated or magnified the growth of American industry, Donald stresses the problems and partial solutions involved in supplying manpower, material, and especially money. He leaves little doubt of the impact of the Civil War in nationalizing not only American government, but American society.

Donald's section, entitled "Uniting the Republic," has two other noteworthy passages. The account of the Civil War points to the many ways in which the two sides were alike. Not only were the commanders of both armies schooled at West Point on Jomini in the version of Dennis Mahan; politicians on both sides were experienced in the same methods, and often could not break the old habits. Second, Donald opens his treatment of Reconstruction with what he calls "counter-factual history." There were, he suggests, a number of possibilities open in 1865: to Lee's army, to carry on guerrilla war; to the Union government, to enact a conqueror's peace, confiscating, imprisoning, even executing; to the freed slaves, to rise in revolt. The fact that none of these paths was taken throws new light on that tormented episode—tormented in its historiography as in its own reality. It is the failure to alter fundamentally the Southern system that receives the most attention. At the same time, the mainly implicit, sometimes stated, explanation is made clear: the Northern majority had other concerns than the future of the South, and was bound, furthermore, by racist feeling nearly as much as that of the Southerners. The great controversies of the last century receive a treatment not so much evenhanded in the sense of middle-of-the-road or nonjudgmental, as less controversial because they are put into larger contexts and supported by new views.

The most noteworthy characteristic of the book as a whole is the sense which is conveyed, not just announced, of the complexity and interweaving of forces, events, interests, and people. There are no statements of single or simple "causes," no tracing of every development to one conclusion. Something of the confused, mixed nature of reality as it must have appeared to the men and women who lived it comes across in the authors' accounts. Amid the complexity, however, one strand runs continuous. The authors seem convinced, and are persuasive on the point, that *ideas* are shapers of history—not merely the ideas written in books and pamphlets, but the ideas, notions, and even prejudices, however unclear and contradictory, by which people make as much sense of the world as they can. The exploration of these ideas, and the tracing of the changes they underwent under the influences, for instance, of the frontier, the city, or the process of industrialization, is one of the authors' greatest achievements.

If one wants to make the long, difficult, sometimes painful voyage of discovery through the history of the colonies and the two centuries of the great republic itself, it would be hard to find a sounder vessel than this volume, or more skilled navigators than its six authors. The voyage, of course, is not ended. One looks at the wonderful last illustration, however—the "tall ships" passing the Statue of Liberty—with the conviction that the voyage was worth pursuing, and even with an eagerness to continue.

George J. Fleming

Sources for Further Study

Choice. XIV, September, 1977, p. 932.
Library Journal. CII, May 15, 1977, p. 1182.
New York Times. May 4, 1977, p. 31.
Time. CIX, April 25, 1977, p. 87.

A GUIDE FOR THE PERPLEXED

Author: E. F. Schumacher (1911–1977)
Publisher: Harper & Row Publishers (New York). 147 pp. $8.95
Type of work: Philosophy

A short, difficult book which reveals the spiritual and metaphysical basis underlying the author's famous work Small Is Beautiful

Anyone who collects evidence to prove that great achievements can come late in life needs to consider the case of E. F. Schumacher. Born in 1911 in Bonn, Germany, Ernst Friedrich Schumacher intended to become an economics professor like his father. To that end, he studied at Bonn, Berlin, Oxford, and Columbia University in New York. He began teaching at Columbia, but the intense thirst for practical work which marked his whole career made him increasingly discontented with academic life. Repulsed by Hitler's Germany, he settled in England in 1937 and went into business. When war broke out, Schumacher—like most German-born subjects—was interned; the government required him to labor on a Northhamptonshire farm for two pounds a week. But he soon gained release and worked both as a journalist and an associate of Lord Beveridge, a principal architect of the British welfare state. Following the war, "Fritz" Schumacher returned to Germany as an economic adviser to the British Control Commission. In 1950 the Labour government named him an economics adviser to the National Coal Board, which operates Britian's nationalized coal mines; he eventually became head of planning.

Schumacher remained in this post for twenty years, all the time contributing editorials for *The Times, The Observer,* and *The Economist.* His position with the Coal Board provided him with a variety of important challenges. He found himself embroiled in a portentious debate on the future of energy resources; his unorthodox analyses led him to predict a petroleum crisis, and he thus opposed those economists who in the late 1950's were calling for the closing of the mines. Schumacher also observed the tendencies of a key large-scale nationalized organization. Accepting the NCB's right to exist, Schumacher nevertheless supported efforts to decentralize the coal industry, devolve decision-making, and strengthen viable low-level organizational forms. Some of Schumacher's inspiration here came from the British Guild Socialist tradition—especially R. H. Tawney—and Roman Catholic social thought. (Schumacher converted to Catholicism and associated himself with such left-wing Thomists as Jacques Maritain and Etienne Gilson.) The Coal Board also sent Schumacher on numerous missions to Third World nations, and he became increasingly preoccupied with the question of the relevance of Western models for economic development. In 1965 he established the Intermediate Technology Development Group, a private company which assists developing nations to create the sort of technologies appropriate to their abundant-labor, low-capital situation.

Had Schumacher singlemindedly channeled his efforts into the Intermediate Technology Group, his influence outside the narrow world of "development economics" probably would have been negligible. But in 1973 Schumacher assembled a series of his papers, lectures, and essays; these he published in England and America under the odd title *Small Is Beautiful: Economics as if People Mattered.* While the book caused some excitement in Britain, American reviewers largely shunned it. Three years later, as the nation—stunned by the Vietnam defeat, an oil pricing crisis, and a general erosion of institutional authority—began to seek new perspectives, Schumacher's book was rediscovered. Elliot Richardson, Ralph Nader, Governor Jerry Brown, and other luminaries testified to the book's brilliance. By mid-1976 some ten thousand copies a month were being sold; ultimately the book, translated into fifteen languages, became a world bestseller. Said Peter Barnes in *The New Republic,* "I had never heard of E. F. Schumacher before reading this book. After reading it I am ready to nominate him for the Nobel Prize in economics." Many noneconomists echoed similar sentiment, for the work possessed an extraordinary cross-disciplinary relevance.

What was Schumacher's message? In fact, to those who listened closely there were two quite distinct messages, one socioeconomic and the other moral-philosophic. The first of these took the form of trend-identification and analysis. Schumacher often called attention to four closely related tendencies, the first of which is the ever-increasing size of everything in industrial society: organizations, machines, transport and communication systems, cities. "We suffer," he wrote, "from an almost universal idolatry of giantism." Nearly lost is the wisdom that for every activity there is an appropriate scale, and that for psychological vitality a society needs a rich variety of small, personalistic groups. The second tendency is the victory of complexity over simplicity in most spheres of existence. Is it written, asked Schumacher, that machines and organizations *must* be sources of bewilderment for their beneficiaries? Can't some of the ingenuity expended in their making go towards rendering them intelligible? Like social theorist Ivan Illich (whose ideas resemble those of Schumacher in a number of ways), Schumacher frequently pointed to the maddeningly complex and quite uneconomic structure of modern food transportation networks to illustrate this point. A third trend is the high capital intensity of most productive undertakings. To enter any significant area of production one must control a vast amount of capital. This requirement consigns energetic persons of modest means to the role of subservient "job holders," unable to exert their creative powers. Lamentably, this trend is increasingly evident even in Third World areas, where indigenous capital is in short supply and small labor-intensive enterprises are desperately needed. And finally, Schumacher pointed out the escalating violence of man's technologies. Epitomized by long half-life pesticides, the proliferation of nuclear power plants, and the adaptation of agriculture to machine imperatives, such violence begets equally violent "ecological backlashes."

In very general terms, Schumacher's proposed solution for these problematic tendencies is a radical orientation of scientific and technical inquiry. The aim must now be to "make things small, so that small people can make themselves productive." The new slogan must read: "production by the masses, rather than mass production." Elegance, grace, proportionateness, simplicity, energy-efficiency, nature-enhancement—these qualities can be embodied in a new generation of tools, insisted Schumacher. On the organizational plane, large impersonal corporate structures (both public and private) need to experiment with devolutionary and federalistic schemes. The firm of the future might well be "a well-coordinated assembly of lively, semiautonomous units, each with its own drive and sense of achievement."

But to give technology "a human face," one must first understand what it is to be human. It is at this point that Schumacher's second message was spoken, a moral and philosophic Word which dwelt intriguingly amid all the words about economics and society. In chapters dealing with such prosaic topics as land use, intermediate technology, the role of economic theory, and nuclear energy, readers found themselves face to face with notions like "levels of being," "cardinal virtues," "the principle of subsidiarity," "the exclusion of wisdom." They heard the heretical claim that economics ought to be less concerned with the wealth of nations and more with the health of human character. For man is not the self-gratification machine that classical and contemporary economics takes him to be. Man, Schumacher boldly affirmed, is the pinnacle of creation, made for fellowship with God, suited to a calling higher than that of "consumer/profit maximizer."

Although Schumacher invoked Buddhism, Gandhi, and "the traditional wisdom of mankind" in his polemic against "economics" (which economics? one wonders), it is clear that his main inspiration is Roman Catholic moral philosophy. Those familiar with the political writings of such neo-Thomists as Maritain, Gilson, Pope Pius XI, and Heinrich Rommen will find Schumacher's writings to be less original than many have thought. Like Schumacher, the leaders of the Thomist revival in this century have accused capitalism of possessing the same materialist metaphysics that Marxism openly embraces. Like Schumacher, they too see positivism, pragmatism, the idea of natural selection, and the Freudian emphasis on unconscious motivation as belittling and cheapening the human self-image. What must be restored, they argue, is a panoramic image of man's high place in creation. Or, in Schumacher's words, "It is only when we can see the world as a ladder, and when we can see man's position on the ladder, that we can recognize a meaningful task on earth."

In *Small Is Beautiful,* Schumacher's philosophic and religious standpoint guided his analysis of concrete issues; but except for the famous chapters on "Buddhist economics" and education, it largely remained implicit and undefended. Pressed by admirers to issue a more detailed statement of his *Weltanschauung,* Schumacher completed *A Guide for the Perplexed* in 1977. He did not live to witness its reception, for a stroke ended his life on September 4 of that year. As that reception has been largely unfavorable, and as Schumacher revealed himself to be more an eclectic sage than a philosopher, some providence may perhaps be divined here.

To call Schumacher a sage rather than a philosopher is not to gainsay the value of his work. *A Guide for the Perplexed* is in many ways a striking synoptic vision of man's place in nature. Yet a vision is not the same thing as an argument; true argumentation has the immense virtue of bringing conflicting syntheses to bear critically on each other. Schumacher abhorred Cartesian dualism, positivistic science, behaviorism, all forms of materialism, pragmatism, skepticism—in short, modernity. But rather than expose the shortcomings of these positions through analysis and careful reasoning, he was content to denounce them, ascribe to them dangerous consequences, and then invoke "the ancient wisdom tradition of mankind." The latter he was more concerned to describe and praise than defend. Thus, his attack on modernity has a distinctly reactionary quality about it.

Recognizing these limitations, we may still appreciate his reconstruction of "the wisdom tradition." In Schumacher's view, the tradition rests on four principal convictions. First, nature is hierarchically structured, with each level being ontologically discontinuous with what is above and below it; further, the macrocosmic world's hierarchies correspond to a natural hierarchy of human faculties. The third conviction is that knowledge is fourfold and includes these distinct yet complementary fields: self-knowledge, knowledge of the inner life of others, knowledge of the self as an objective phenomenon, and knowledge of the world apprehended as casually determined. Fourth, determinism and freedom are two necessary modes of viewed reality, with the acknowledgment of freedom entailing a recognition of a group of insoluble existential problems.

Schumacher's hierarchic vision—he praised the venerable notion of the "Great Chain of Being"—restores to the universe *inherent* values. Empiricists begin with a world of pure fact, brute matter; they are thus forced *a priori* to distinguish facts from values and consider values to be nonmaterial, subjective phantoms. The empiricist starting point ignores the "grades of significance" displayed in the world. Creation contains meaningful progressions: from lifeless *materia,* through sentient organic life, to intelligent and then self-conscious existence; from common (natural elements, microorganisms) to rare (the fully self-conscious man); from outer to inner; from beastly to angelic; from passivity to activity; from necessity to freedom; from disintegration to unity.

Cognate progressions can organize personal development, so that anyone who would truly imitate nature moves beyond sensuousity to rational discipline, innerness, and philosophic contemplation. This right developmental pattern is self-vindicating, for the person discovers that when he exercises his higher faculties (reason, virtue), corresponding realities in the cosmos are opened to him, realities which he "needs" (in a nonphysical sense) to experience. Or, as Aristotle put it, "Contemplation is the highest form of activity, because the intellect is the highest part of our nature, and the things apprehended by it are the highest objects of knowledge. . . . Therefore the activity of contemplation will be the perfect happiness of man."

For Schumacher, as for Aristotle and St. Thomas, the cultivation of the contemplative faculty reveals to the philosophic soul the divine character of reason itself. Man is both brutal and angelic, but the inherent bias in nature is "upward" and "inward," so it is correct to say that man's true destiny is the beatific vision of God. The human task then is to become progressively freer of the domination of reason by the senses. Small wonder, then, that Schumacher was fundamentally opposed to the ideology of economic growth; for by making growth the highest goal, entire societies are consigning their citizens to arrested development. Instead of weaning them from excessive reliance on physical gratification, they transform consumption into man's highest and most "natural" art.

It is telling that for Schumacher the mystic is very nearly the model of the fully actualized human being. His book quotes from a wide variety of mystical sources, and even retells the curious story of Therese Neumann, a celebrated German mystic who, after thirty-five years of living only on the daily Eucharistic meal, died in 1962 at the age of 64. The work properly observes here that such liberation from material constraints cannot finally be attributed to any spiritual exercise. "Only when the striving for 'power' has entirely ceased and been replaced by a certain transcendental longing, often called the love of God," may such "higher powers" be acquired. The beatific vision is a divine gift, not a human production. Schumacher's intense admiration for the mystic was qualified only by his belief that the fourth field of knowledge—causal inquiry—is too often ignored by those engrossed in the Way. In general, though, when Schumacher spoke of the need for a "new model of civilization," he meant that the present model is defective because the highest human type, the mystic, is effectively banished from it.

By now the range and general character of Schumacher's ideas are clear enough. That the author never acquired the famous British distaste for grand syntheses is also plain. Complains Harvey Cox, "The trouble is that Schumacher violates his own best advice. He goes big. He pours on too much and therefore is not persuasive." There are other irritants. In his haste, Schumacher lumped together his (mostly unidentified) intellectual opponents, labeling their work with fuzzy pejorative names like "scientism" and "evolutionism." His conception of science was based on such ideologues of science as August Comte and Vilfredo Pareto; he seemed quite unaware of the revolution in the understanding of the scientific enterprise since Einstein and Heisenberg. The very opaque distinction he drew between descriptive and instructional sciences makes his other commentary on this subject seem entirely suspect. Like all those who enthuse over the perennial philosophy, Schumacher overlooked the strong internal tensions in that philosophy, such as the tensions between immanentalist and transcendentalist, Gnostic and non-Gnostic, Platonist and Aristotelian.

The perplexed shall not, therefore, gain much specific guidance from this book. But they may be stimulated by it to consult Schumacher's excellent sources or intrigued enough to turn back to *Small Is Beautiful,* where Schumacher's vision found its ideal context.

Leslie E. Gerber

Sources for Further Study

Christian Century. XCIV, October 12, 1977, p. 925.
Christian Science Monitor. LXIX, September 28, 1977, p. 23.
Economist. CCLXV, October 1, 1977, p. 129.
Kirkus Reviews. XLV, July 1, 1977, p. 717.
New Statesman. XCIV, October 7, 1977, p. 481.

THE GULAG ARCHIPELAGO: THREE
Parts V-VII

Author: Alexander I. Solzhenitsyn (1918–   )
Translated from the Russian by Harry Willetts
Publisher: Harper & Row Publishers (New York). 558 pp. $16.95
Type of work: History and autobiography
Time: 1918–1956
Locale: The Soviet Union

The continuation of the history of the Corrective Labor Camps in the Soviet Union, to which is added the story of the Special Camps, hard-labor institutions for political prisoners, and the practice of exile to desolate regions within the country

The Gulag Archipelago: Three is the conclusion of the massive work that Alexander Solzhenitsyn planned in penal servitude and wrote from 1958 to 1967. The first four parts of the work appeared in English translation as Volumes I and II in 1974 and 1975, and were chiefly concerned with the Soviet system of the Corrective Labor Camps, the means by which the Communist Party under Stalin enslaved uncounted millions of innocent people.

The person who has faithfully read through the first two volumes will nevertheless find some surprises in this conclusion to Solzhenitsyn's epic history: despite the manifold cruelties of the slave-labor camps described in the earlier parts, the Corrective Labor system was not the worst that the Soviets could devise for their own countrymen. The penal system had still more chains it could hang on its prisoners, and especially on those unfortunates convicted under Article 58 of the Criminal Code—the political prisoners. Those chains are shown to the world in Part 5, "Katorga," and Part 6, "Exile."

Although history will classify the twentieth century as the most barbaric and bloody ever recorded, those who hope for the future of the human race will find a few shreds of comfort in Solzhenitsyn's work. We find in Volume III that dictators are as fallible as democrats, and in this volume, for the first time in this epic of pain, a few beams of light break through. *Katorga*, the title of Part 5, means "hard labor," and designates yet another chain of islands in the Archipelago of punishment that stretches through the Soviet Union. In 1943, Stalin decided to segregate the politicals and certain other types of prisoners, taking them out of the Corrective Labor Camps and moving them to Special Camps, institutions of hard labor where, it was thought, they could be more effectively controlled and exploited. But rather than placing still another burden on the inmates, the hard labor camps proved a means of unintentionally lightening their load.

Stalin's plan was crushing enough in its conception: it provided for twelve hours a day of back-breaking work on an inadequate diet; it provided for locking the prisoners into their huts at night, without access to latrines; it provided for them to be held almost incommunicado from the outside world, from their friends and families; and finally, it provided as usual that their guards could shoot them down for the slightest infractions, or even for no infraction at all, without fear of punishment. In some places the plan did not work, though, with the harshness its developers desired, for two reasons.

First, the segregation of the prisoners turned out to be a great blessing. In Volumes I and II, Solzhenitsyn recounts story after story of the persecution of the political prisoners, not through the unaided efforts of the camp administrations, but through the use of prisoner informers. The administrations had a second ally in the thieves, the professional criminals in the camps, who regarded the politicals as their legitimate prey, and plundered them with the unofficial blessings of the jailors. When the politicals were removed to the hard labor camps, the numbers of the professional criminals among them were at least diminished. For the first time, the politicals could achieve something of a feeling of solidarity, a feeling of united rather than individual suffering under their oppressors.

The second reason is the more important. The katorga system began in 1943, and a different kind of political prisoner was being sent to the camps. Prior to World War II, the political prisoner was often a Communist Party member caught in one of the numerous purges, or a member of one of the several leftist, but non-Bolshevik parties. But now the camp numbers were swelled with returning military men who had been captured and imprisoned by the Germans; with whole cadres of members of nationalist movements, especially Ukrainians; with those Russians who had administered territories under the German occupation. These new convicts were frequently men with experience of resistance, or at least with experience of disciplined group behavior. For the first time there came to be organizations and lines of authority separate from those imposed by camp discipline.

Solzhenitsyn is particularly concerned in this volume to answer those critics who ask why, if life in the camps was as brutal as he depicts, no one tried to rebel. His answer is that they did try; that they rebelled singly and in groups; and that their resistance was continual, and took many forms.

He begins on the level of individuals and small groups. Thus in these pages we find the first stories of successful resistance to the ravages of the thieves; eventually this resistance, by ones and twos, leads to the forming of underground prisoner organizations who reply to the thieves in kind, visiting rough retribution as well on informers and stool pigeons. He discusses many escape attempts, some of them successful despite enormous odds against them. A prisoner contemplating escape more often than not had to plan for a trek across hundreds of miles of trackless desert, in the face of propaganda that had made him appear a savage to the civilian population. He could expect anyone he met to hand him over to the authorities without hesitation. And there is a kind of wistfulness to these tales of escape, too; despite all their experience in the system, the prisoners tried to escape not to Japan or India or Western Europe, but often simply to return to their homes. Nevertheless, there were prisoners who mounted try after try, ending only with their freedom or their death.

Solzhenitsyn proceeds to large-scale revolts, hunger strikes, and work stoppages, culminating in the armed rising at Kengir, which held the camp against the authorities for forty days. However, the result was the same in each case: first, some initial, limited success, then ultimate failure. And the author draws two conclusions from these histories: first, when challenged, the system would grind to a halt. The successes of the revolts depended on uncertainty in the administration of the MVD, which ran the camps. The rulers of the camps faltered, especially after the execution in 1953 of L. P. Beria, the head of internal security. Prior to his death, camp leaders knew they could murder the striking prisoners in safety; after it, they were not so sure for a time.

The second conclusion is more sobering; the final failure of the prisoner revolts resulted from their betrayal by high party officials. The word of the government, solemnly pledged, could not be trusted. And it could not be trusted because public opinion did not and does not exist in the Soviet Union. With complete control of all forms of communication, the government could prevent any word of the revolts themselves from ever reaching the attention of their own public or the attention of the West. An investigating committee from Moscow could promise whatever it liked to the prisoners, secure in the knowledge that no one would hold its members accountable for the fulfillment of those promises.

But these stories of battles against hopeless odds hold the same lesson as does the story of the rising of the Jews of the Warsaw Ghetto against Hitler's SS: no power can ever repress people in absolute security. And the stories have an additional, special lesson for Americans: the event that sparked hope among the prisoners of the Archipelago was the outbreak of the Korean War. They thought it meant the beginning of a third World War; readers of the book in America need to ponder how far a human being must be pushed before he will welcome an atomic war. And we need to reflect also whether some kinds of existence are not worse than the threat of atomic destruction. The politicals thought so.

Katorga is the subject of Part 5; Part 6 takes up exile, the third prong (after the Corrective Labor Camps and the hard-labor Special Camps) on Stalin's pitchfork. The system of exile, like so many of the repressions detailed in the whole work, began in the 1920's and 1930's with the deportation of anyone branded a *kulak*—not only prosperous peasants, but also unsuccessful peasants—anyone who would not join a collective farm. The sweep included millers, blacksmiths (reclassified as *petit bourgeois*), anyone that a bureaucrat held a grudge against; and the total reached fifteen million from this source alone. The exile was not a relocation to some settled rural or urban community, but often it meant that a group of people with hardly anything but the clothes on their backs would be dumped on the barren bank of some subarctic river. In circumstances like this, it is not surprising that a sentence of exile was often indistinguishable from a sentence of death; it just took a little longer to execute.

One could be exiled for several reasons: for being of the wrong nationality, for instance, or for having served a term in the camps, or even for living in the wrong place. The first of these Solzhenitsyn discusses as a reverse migration of nations, for whole peoples were moved from the west to the barren central and eastern parts of the Soviet Union. In this way the Volga Germans were deported, and Greeks who lived in the Caucasus. The list of those removed goes on and on: the Chechens, the Ingush, and Karachai, the Balkars, the Kalmyks, the Kurds, the Crimean Tartars—all names almost unheard of in the West, and all forcibly deported from their homelands. To these must be added those who simply resided where there was a partisan movement: the Ukraine, or the Baltic states of Lithuania, Latvia, or Estonia.

And to these, but later, are added those men and women who served their ten- or twenty-five-year sentences in the camps. Solzhenitsyn himself, after serving out his sentence, is not released to resume his life in freedom, but is exiled to Kok-Terek, a miserable mud-hut village of four thousand in northern Kazakhstan. The exiles who are ex-prisoners find themselves stuck in still another Catch-22; they cannot establish a legal residence in their places of exile until they have jobs, and they cannot get jobs until they have legal residences. Therefore the lot of the more "fortunate" of them is much like slavery: if they do find work, their employers realize that they can squeeze their workers as much as they like; if the ex-prisoners quit, or are fired for complaining, they will starve.

To add to all this, there is an alternative to exile—banishment. The difference is that one can be banished (and subjected to all the disgrace and hardship of exile) without even the kangaroo trials the exiles usually undergo. One can be banished by "administrative action," as many were for the crime of being Moslems or Baptists.

The concluding part, "Stalin Is No More," briefly discusses the changes in the system since 1953, especially those since the Party Congress at which Nikita Khrushchev denounced Stalin's reign as the "Cult of Personality."

Since those events, there have been changes; thousands were released from camp or exile, and rehabilitated. But rehabilitation does not mean an admission that the government was wrong, and the prisoner was innocent, but only that his crime was not so bad. Those who were responsible for all the false imprisonments and deaths were not punished, but either remained at their posts or retired on government pensions. In 1953, the secret police, the KGB, was abolished; it was replaced six months later by the MGB with the same personnel.

Solzhenitsyn has just a single point to make in the final part, and it is this: although things have changed, they have changed only in practice, not in principle. Instead of thousands of political prisoners sentenced under Article 58 there are relatively few; there are still political prisoners, although their sentences have been camouflaged under other sections of the Criminal Code—a trumped-up charge of rape is as easy to process as a trumped-up charge of treason. If their numbers are fewer, there are still plenty of political prisoners in the camp system. And, more important, there are no safeguards that the same thing will not happen again. Solzhenitsyn demands that the guilty be punished; partly, of course, his cry rises from the yearning for an abstract justice. But there is a still more practical reason: until an open and full accounting of the Gulag system is made, and until those responsible for its erection and administration admit their guilt, it can happen again. It can happen until the Communist Party admits that it is both fallible and responsible to those it governs. Had those two obvious truths been accepted in 1917, *The Gulag Archipelago* would never have had to be written.

Walter E. Meyers

Sources for Further Study

Los Angeles Times. June 22, 1978, Part IV, p. 4.
Partisan Review. XLIV, Summer, 1977, p. 637.

HARRY HOPKINS
A Biography

Author: Henry H. Adams
Publisher: G. P. Putnam's Sons (New York). Illustrated. 448 pp. $15.00
Type of work: Biography
Time: 1890–1946
Locale: Iowa, New York City, Washington, D.C., London, Moscow, Casablanca, Teheran, Yalta

Adams tells the life story of the principal relief administrator of the New Deal, and one of its most controversial figures

> *Principal personages:*
> HARRY L. HOPKINS, FERA-WPA administrator, Secretary of Commerce, presidential assistant
> FRANKLIN D. ROOSEVELT, President of the United States
> WINSTON CHURCHILL, Prime Minister of the United Kingdom
> JOSEPH STALIN, dictator of the USSR
> HAROLD L. ICKES, Secretary of the Interior, PWA administrator

Henry H. Adams, a former professor of English, has written a four-volume history of World War II, and this biography reflects the background knowledge which that task provided. The material on Hopkins comes mainly from the Hopkins papers on microfilm at the Roosevelt Library in Hyde Park, and Adams' extensive research makes it unlikely that more new information about Hopkins' life and work will be forthcoming. After the preliminaries, Averell Harriman's Foreword, and a Prologue built around Hopkins' resignation from the Cabinet in August, 1940, Adams' account is basically chronological, and divided into two sections, the shorter dealing with Hopkins' prewar career and the longer with his last crucial services. The proportions show the author's assessment of the relative importance of the two periods in his subject's life.

Authors are not responsible for publisher's blurbs, but somebody should be held to account for a wrapper which reads on the front under the title, "The life story of the man behind FDR, the New Deal, and Allied strategy in World War II." Hopkins was tremendously important, as Adams' whole account proves, but that importance is obscured, not shown, by hyperbole. Better testimony is Harriman's opening in his Foreword to Adams' biography: "If Sir Winston Churchill had been asked which two Americans, other than President Roosevelt, had done the most to defeat Hitler, he would have unhesitatingly replied, 'Among the military, General Marshall, and among the civilians, Harry Hopkins.'" What kind of man could evoke such a tribute?

Hopkins' beginnings were ordinary: an Iowa birth and for the most part youth, a father who was a harness maker and salesman, and a mother who was a former schoolteacher intent on the education of her children. He attended Grinnell College and achieved no high record of scholarship, but developed an interest in history and politics, and benefited from the influence of a professor who taught "Applied Christianity." It was apparently this professor who steered Hopkins into his first career by recommending him for a counselor's post at a New Jersey summer camp for poor boys. Adams suggests that Hopkins took the offer because it would give him a chance to see the East; he did stop on the way—it was 1912—to see the Republican Convention in Chicago and the Democratic Convention in Baltimore.

Throughout this early account, Adams is sparse with analysis and explanation; the absence of documentation is almost certainly the reason. Yet some speculation occurs: not merely one professor, but the whole "Progressive" idea, and the growing importance of social work, might well turn an Iowa boy of 1912 in that direction. At any rate, as Adams tells it, the experience of the summer camp was Hopkins' introduction to urban poverty and to urban ethnicity—the boys came from New York slums. Hopkins went from summer camp to a New York settlement house, and from there to the world of professional social work in the metropolis.

Several things are implied, though not stated, in Adams' account of Hopkins' career from 1912 to the Depression. He worked for the Association for Improving the Condition of the Poor, for the city government, for the Tuberculosis Association, for the Red Cross—a variety of mostly private agencies and organizations. He became an organizer, executive, and expediter, rather than a case worker. He developed a reputation for getting things done, but in his own way, not always by the rules. And in the "prosperity" of the 1920's he was never out of contact with those who did not share the prosperity. Not, Adams' account makes clear, that he was poor or monkish. Hopkins liked the company of the rich; he liked to live well. The point, rather, though Adams does not express it, is that Hopkins was never able to accept the prosperity as being the prerogative only of the rich.

Hopkins' second career began during the Depression, when Roosevelt, as Governor of New York, put Hopkins in charge of a temporary relief project which provided work for the poor. When Roosevelt went to Washington, in the midst of all the emergencies of the Hundred Days, he accepted a plan largely conceived by Hopkins for grants-in-aid for work relief, and made Hopkins administrator. Hopkins said he expected to last six months; he lasted almost six years. Under a variety of names and acronyms—FERA, WPA—the organization he directed spent money to relieve unemployment; it did not simply offer "relief," but jobs.

Thereupon hangs Hopkins' first great reputation. The jobs were of all sorts, for the unemployed were a varied mass of people. Streets and bridges were repaired and forests replanted, and there were also theater and art projects, and the great writers' project of collecting massive amounts of material for American history and folklore. Hopkins' job as he saw it was to keep the money flowing and the men and women working. He dealt with state and local politicians often desirous of building a machine out of WPA workers; he persuaded the budget authorities and the Congress to come up with at least some of the money; he faced a horde of critics, including most of the press, whose definition of WPA work was leaf-raking and shovel-leaning.

And he feuded with Harold Ickes, or Ickes with him. Adams' tone is generally sympathetic to Hopkins, but sober and factual. Ickes, of course, was anything but sedate, and he was in competition with Hopkins for money, prestige, and power. His Public Works Administration was supposed to undertake the larger, long-range projects, while Hopkins worked on the smaller and less expensive ones. But the lines were never clear, and Roosevelt's administrative style confused them further; Ickes was convinced Hopkins was undermining him, and put his suspicions into his diary. Adams does not take Ickes' complaints too seriously, although he does admit in some passages that Hopkins could be a ruthless and skilled adversary in bureaucratic in-fighting. Basically, however, he is portrayed as an informal, red-tape-cutting administrator who had enormous energy and drive and a full command of his responsibilities.

In other areas the author's treatment seems on the bland side. We are given the facts of Hopkins' first marriage, divorce, and second marriage, but little beyond bare facts. The picture of Hopkins the race track and party frequenter, perhaps overdone by his opponents, is barely acknowledged. Instead of personal information, Adams stresses the accomplishments of Hopkins' agencies (especially in emergencies such as the 1937 and 1938 floods), Hopkins' increasing rapport with the President, and his political ambition. The highest ambition was for the presidency in 1940; there can be no doubt of Adams' evidence that Hopkins wanted the presidency and thought he had a good chance, and no doubt that Roosevelt encouraged him, both privately (the evidence is necessarily by Hopkins' own account), and publically (by appointing him Secretary of Commerce). The question is, how deeply committed was Roosevelt, who was never one to give himself away? Also, one has to wonder whether a Democratic party which had defeated most of Roosevelt's efforts to eliminate unsympathetic senators and representatives in 1938, and which proved so reluctant to accept Henry Wallace for vice-president in 1940, would have nominated Hopkins. In any case, the ambition was never tested; Hopkins' serious illness, which led to his resignation from the Commerce position, also ended his presidential hopes. It also opened the way to his most important achievement, which is Adams' principal story.

Hopkins stayed at the White House; he was Roosevelt's manager, in fact, for the third-term nomination at Chicago; but as the war in Europe and in Asia grew more desperate with the fall of France and the air assault on Britain, it became Hopkins' preoccupation, as it became the President's. Hopkins' official title was Presidential Assistant, and he also became a powerful member of the numerous committees set up first for the defense effort and Lend-Lease to Britain, and later for the United States war effort itself. He was expediter and allocator of supplies, breaker of bottle-necks, and constant gadfly. He was also Roosevelt's personal emissary first to Churchill and then to Stalin. Again, supply was his great concern. His questions to the British and Russians were: What do you need and how much? His questions to American industry were: What can you produce and how soon?

Beginning with the trip to England in January, 1941, Hopkins flew when necessary to the British Isles and to Moscow. He accompanied Roosevelt to the wartime conferences. Adams is detailed and clear about the trips, and about Hopkins' continuing ill-health and near-exhaustion; the picture of his subject's dedication and great output of energy is one of the best he draws. Along with it is the picture of a man of very great ability. Adams several times emphasizes Hopkins' grasp of complicated processes of supply, and retention of the masses of facts and figures necessary to enable him to see to it that the job was done.

And yet, it is no contradiction of Adams' account, nor any diminution of Hopkins' dedication and ability, to suggest another context. Hopkins' success in speeding the production of ball bearings came not from any official position, and only in part from his powers of persuasion, but in considerable measure because his phone call began, "This is Harry Hopkins from the White House." Even more, his importance to Churchill and Stalin was that he represented Roosevelt. What he said represented Roosevelt's thought; what they said to him would be reported directly and accurately to the President. The service was enormously important, but it depended on the relationship of the two men, and there was never any doubt who was chief and who was subordinate. One point, however, should be made: Hopkins had the ability to reduce matters to essentials, to find the knot that untied the whole complicated issue, to strike through to the point. Particularly in wartime, this was a most valuable asset.

Adams' book clearly reflects this and other qualities. The private Hopkins is talked about, not conveyed; maybe he cannot be. The public Hopkins and his achievements we see largely as he himself saw them, but that is a necessary limitation. Hopkins was an important figure, and this book helps us to understand how and why.

George J. Fleming

Sources for Further Study

Choice. XIV, October, 1977, p. 1118.
Christian Century. XCIV, November 2, 1977, p. 1010.
New Leader. LX, July 4, 1977, p. 18.
New Republic. CLXXVII, September 24, 1977, p. 29.

HEARTS AND MINDS

The Common Journey of Simone de Beauvoir and Jean-Paul Sartre

Author: Axel Madsen (1932–   )
Publisher: William Morrow and Company (New York). 320 pp. $10.95
Type of work: Biography
Time: 1905–1977
Locale: France

A new look at the lives of one of the most important and celebrated couples in the history of French letters

> Principal personages:
> SIMONE DE BEAUVOIR, French feminist, fiction writer, and essayist
> JEAN-PAUL SARTRE, French philosopher, playwright, fiction writer, and political essayist

When Jean-Paul Sartre was asked last year if his works would have been any different had he not known Simone de Beauvoir, he answered that everything he had written before he met her contained the essentials of his thought. He added, however, that because of their fifty-year close friendship, his writings certainly bear the impact of their common experiences and struggles. Axel Madsen's *Hearts and Minds* is neither a literary promenade nor another investigation of philosophical debates. It attempts to uncover the affinities between Beauvoir and Sartre as individuals and as writers, to show how the two reacted to a particular political and intellectual milieu, and to present the reader with simple yet human facets of their longtime liaison.

Some readers may be confused, at first, by the book's title. Those who remember the 1975 documentary on Vietnam, *Hearts and Minds,* could mistake this new book for the script of the film by Peter Davis. Perhaps to avoid any ambiguity, a subtitle has been added with specific references to the author's main objective: to depict the relationship between Beauvoir and Sartre. The parallel between the film and Madsen's book cannot naturally be perceived on the level of substance but rather in the intentions of both director and author. Through a montage of interviews and newsreel footage, Davis had created a powerful visual essay whose purpose was to understand the attitudes and beliefs of a generation: the Westmorelands and the Rostows, the Ellsbergs and the Stones. By adopting a similar title, Madsen sets the tone for his book. He interviews his main subjects, Sartre and Beauvoir, looks into their writings, immerses himself in the France of the postwar era, and attempts to grasp the attitudes and feelings of that period.

Sartre and Beauvoir met in 1928 as students of the prestigious Ecole Normale Supérieure in Paris, where they studied philosophy, Greek, logic, and psychology. The following year, they took the difficult state examination for the *agrégation,* a competition in which Sartre's name was listed first. Beauvoir ranked second. Music, writing, American novelists, and cinema brought them even closer, and before he was off for his military service, Sartre proposed a two-year negotiable contract which would bind them, yet which would safeguard each one's freedom. At a time when the education of respectable bourgeois girls was geared towards motherhood and rearing a family, Beauvoir opted for a lifestyle that went against the grain. Feminism was either a taboo word or unheard of in most parts of the country, and her rejection of accepted social conventions (an attitude seen by her critics as a sign of eccentric tendencies) expressed one woman's desire for self-fulfillment and control over her own destiny. Ironically, the man who was to become her life partner was a *machismo* until the age of fifteen, as Sartre would concede later. He was surrounded for many years by a group of women composed of his mother, grandmother, and their friends; his father died when he was two years old. It was in this milieu, encouraged by a domineering grandfather, that he learned the superiority of man over the "second sex." If his liaison with Beauvoir did not turn into a battle of the sexes, it was often put to the test, and it endured in spite of their outside paramours, or as Beauvoir liked to call them, their "contingent love affairs." For those who perceived Beauvoir's dependence on Sartre as paradoxical with her outspoken stand on feminism, she would answer that the fact that she recognized and admired his superior political activity in no way downgraded her nor weakened her rapport with him. In effect, their relationship was long-lived because of their mutual respect. She was his best and most useful critic and vice versa.

One of the virtues of this book is that the biographical data does not take over the narrative completely. Madsen, the accomplished biographer of another statesman of French letters, André Malraux, relates the chronological events of Sartre's and Beauvoir's lives to other significant contemporary incidents. Thus, the reader is offered a comprehensive and dynamic picture of France, and enabled to see the two authors' main works in their context, set against the background of wars, political polemics, and intellectual currents.

Sartre dominated the Parisian intellectual scene for more than a decade in the postwar years. Almost every aspect of French letters is affected by his thought, whether it is the novel, the drama, or the philosophical essay; a score of articles and prefaces add to his already voluminous production. Except for two or three of his popular works, Sartre is not widely read in France nowadays. The diminishing interest in his writings among French scholars and students alike in his own country can be traced to various factors, one of which is the loss of actuality. Sartre's popularity was no doubt the result of his intellectual versatility, but it also resulted from his ability to fill the void created by World War II. He grasped the contemporary mood and responded to the individual's pessimism by confronting it with the notions of freedom, responsibility, and *engagement.* Beauvoir's novels and other writings often echoed Sartre's concepts of existentialism or expanded his theories. In *Hearts and Minds,* Madsen gives us a useful account of the two writers' production and is able to show with clarity the gradual progression of their thought as well as the context of some of their most important works. His study goes even further by emphasizing their individual political consciousnesses.

In about forty years, France had witnessed the occupation of its territory by the Nazis; the ineffectiveness of succeeding governments in dealing with economic matters; the debacle of its foreign policy in Indochina and its agonizing involvement in Algeria; the emergence of General De Gaulle from his retreat and the birth of the Fifth Republic; the May, 1968, events; and the downfall of the man who had solved the Algerian question. While most intellectuals espoused causes and joined political parties, Beauvoir and Sartre stood away almost suspiciously from any group that might hinder their independence. Their apparent aloofness, which brought them criticism from the left and the right alike, meant only that they were willing to engage in any worthwhile mission as long as it did not impose the dictates of either a government or a political party, or the dogmas of a religion. Indicative of this independent stand *vis-à-vis* any ideological or institutional group are Sartre's indifference for the much coveted *Légion d'Honneur,* his lack of interest in a potential professorship at the prestigious Collège de France, and his categorical refusal of the Nobel Prize.

Probably the most vociferous attacks on Sartre came from the French Communist Party (P.C.F.), which singled him out first as an *agent provocateur* during the German occupation. Sartre had managed his way out of the German camps and joined forces with a group of intellectuals in writing anti-German propaganda for a clandestine newssheet. Rumors originating with the P.C.F. soon spread that he could not be trusted, on the grounds that his means of escape from the camps was not very clear. Curiously enough, it was during his years of imprisonment at Stallag XIID at Trèves that he wrote a little-known play set in Jerusalem, *Bariona,* in which he vents his hatred for the Nazis. In spite of the ill-founded accusations, Sartre favored a *rapprochement* with the French Communists and would eventually lend them his support by working with the Comité National des ecrivains. As a Communist sympathizer, he was tempted at times to join the Party, but felt that being one of them would mean the deprivation of his individuality and free choice, which he was not ready to relinquish for the sake of belonging to a group. Sartre's existentialism came under vigorous scrutiny by the Party ideologists and intellectuals, who described it as anti-humanist or as being the product of a foreign influence: that of Heidegger's "naziism." Moreover, it was feared that his theories either discouraged or prevented people from joining the Communist Party. Surprisingly, it was in 1952 with *The Communists and Peace* that Sartre demonstrated his ardent support for the P.C.F. and world Communism. It was not that he now espoused Marxist dogma, but that he believed sincerely that the P.C.F. offered the best solution for France. On the other hand, he could not be against the proletariat, a group in which he placed much of his faith. The Russian intervention in Hungary in 1956, however, dealt a severe blow to his friendly relations with the Communists. He criticized vehemently the Soviet invasion, and called for the Soviet writers to denounce publicly their government's maneuvers. Most important, in the Revue *Les Temps Modernes,* of which he was the Director, he summarized the thirty years of the P.C.F. as years of hypocrisy, and he demanded the de-Stalinization of that Party.

Had his amicable ties with the P.C.F. not been severed in the aftermath of the Hungarian tragedy, they most certainly would have been on the Algerian question. While the Party adopted an ambiguous position in this instance, Sartre from the beginning was firm and decisive in his antiwar stand, and he made no secret of his sympathies for the National Liberation Front of Algeria (F.L.N.). For the one million *pieds-noirs* (as the French community in Algeria was designated then), the return of De Gaulle to active politics in 1958 was interpreted as the pursuit of past colonial policies and a reassurance that *Algérie française* would remain as such. An *Algérie algérienne* was the more inconceivable in many French minds, particularly for the economists in the government, since the loss of that territory would be translated into a loss of what France needed most: natural gas, agricultural products, new markets, and, of course, cheap labor. Peace with the F.L.N. would also cause a massive exodus of fearful Frenchmen: a situation France never envisaged when it sent its troops to that part of North Africa in the nineteenth century. Thus, economic factors played the larger role in constructing French foreign policy; perhaps this was De Gaulle's thinking when in Algeria, he shouted to a delirious crowd of *pieds-noirs* his famous: "I have understood you."

France was slowly entangled in its own version of Vietnam, and the war she was to confront for almost a decade carried its toll of innocent victims on both sides. Sartre wrote in that period what many consider his best drama. Set in postwar Germany, *The Condemned of Altona* alluded to contemporary political incidents in France and Algeria by discussing among other things the question of guilt as well as the demystification of military heroism. His solidarity with Algerian fighters took one more practical step when he met in Rome Frantz Fanon, a Martinican psychiatrist and member of the Algerian provisional government. Subsequent to their talks, Fanon's *The Damned* included a violent preface by Sartre in which he declared his total support for Algerians and other colonized people. Beauvoir took up the case of a young Algerian terrorist girl, Djamila Boupacha, indecently tortured by French soldiers. Besides attracting public attention, the article she submitted to *Le Monde* recounting the matter caused some embarrassment to the French government, which retaliated by having that newspaper's overseas edition suppressed in Algiers. Never before had Sartre and Beauvoir been involved so wholeheartedly in a cause as in the Algerian affair, and never had their personal lives been so much at stake. (Sartre's apartment was bombed twice.) They spoke at rallies against torture and torturers, voiced total disapproval of their government's policies, and signed the Manifesto of the 121 at the risk of a five-year imprisonment. This document, an appeal to the French left to make known their unconditional support for the

Algerian movement, denounced the war and even encouraged the draftees to disobey. It is, no doubt, this equal belief in human justice that prompted them to participate later in the Bertrand Russell International War Crimes Tribunal, to approve of the student riots in Paris in May, 1968, and, in the case of Sartre, to take in 1970 the directorship of the government-banned Maoist newspaper, *La Cause du Peuple*.

Age is putting an end to their combative temperaments. But only a few years ago, Beauvoir signed the Manifesto of the 343 and campaigned for an appropriate abortion bill, and Sartre talked to the workers of the Renault automobile installations. Both were seen on boulevards handing out banned newspapers, before being picked up by police vans.

From political indifference to commitment to radicalism, and finally, to militancy: these have been the major steps in Beauvoir's and Sartre's half-a-century "common journey" as suggested by the reading of *Hearts and Minds*. Much has been written on the two authors individually, but Madsen adopts a distinct new approach by composing a dual portrait which vividly illustrates how intensely their lives have been interrelated. *Hearts and Minds* is not a large book, unfortunately, and on occasions one has the impression of reading through condensed data. Although most of the material here is familiar, Madsen's study is nevertheless commendable for its vivid, honest, and objective portrayal of a revered couple whose liaison has almost become a legend.

Charles Elkabas

Sources for Further Study

Booklist. LXXIV, October 1, 1977, p. 262.
Books West. I, October, 1977, p. 41.
Christian Science Monitor. LXIX, November 3, 1977, p. 22.
New York Times Book Review. September 25, 1977, p. 3.
New Yorker. LIII, November 14, 1977, p. 218.
Progressive. XLI, December, 1977, p. 55.
Saturday Review. V, October 1, 1977, p. 28.

HENRY'S FATE & OTHER POEMS, 1967-1972

Author: John Berryman (1914-1972)
Publisher: Farrar, Straus and Giroux (New York). 194 pp. $7.95
Type of work: Poetry

A posthumous collection of previously unpublished poems by one of America's most reputable poets

One Minnesota morning in January, 1972, John Berryman ended his life, presumably in a fit of the depression which dogged him, by plunging himself onto the ice in the Mississippi River from a bridge in Minneapolis. At the time of his death he left a large body of unpublished work. In 1976 his publisher and friend, Robert Giroux, saw to the publication of *The Freedom of the Poet,* a collection of prose pieces, mostly literary criticism. The present volume adds to the material by Berryman now available to the reading public a number of poems which represent, according to John Haffenden, who wrote the Introduction, but a fraction of the unpublished poetry. Haffenden reports that several hundred Dream Songs and miscellaneous poems have yet to be published. In addition to the poetry he reports there is a "harvest" of essays on Shakespeare, including a critical edition of *King Lear* and a biographical study of the playwright. Also, there is a book on dream analysis, some plays, and some stories and essays not published in the 1976 volume. From any point of view, John Berryman was a successful writer, as well as a successful professor of literature (he taught for more than thirty years, off and on, at Harvard, Princeton, Wayne State, and the University of Minnesota). From his own viewpoint, the fatal weakness in any writer was a lack of seriousness, a lack of purpose, and failure to heed the artistic voice within one's self: no such weakness can be ascribed to John Berryman, for he worked hard and purposefully at his craft.

In the Introduction to *Henry's Fate & Other Poems,* John Haffenden advises the reader that many of the poems in the present volume were written while the poet was working on the poems that were published in *Love & Fame* and *Delusions, Etc. of John Berryman,* but he also warns the reader that one may not presume that the omission of certain poems from those volumes was due to, in Berryman's opinion, their poorer quality.

Part I of *Henry's Fate & Other Poems* consists of uncollected Dream Songs. Those poems which Berryman called Dream Songs have been judged consistently the greatest of the poet's achievements, despite his earlier (and rightful) fame from his long poem entitled *Homage to Mistress Bradstreet.* Two volumes of the Dream Songs appeared during the poet's life: *77 Dream Songs* in 1964 and *His Toy, His Dream, His Rest* in 1968. The Dream Songs were, according to the poet himself, finished. But Berryman continued to write them and those in the present volume were written in 1968 or later. The forty-five Dream Songs have been printed, so far as it is known, in the chronological order of their writing.

The title poem reintroduces Henry, an imaginary character who inhabits the

world of Dream Songs. Henry is a white American, middle-aged, who sometimes makes an appearance in black-face. Henry, according to his creator, is a
human being who suffered an irreversible loss, who has a friend referred to as
Mr. Bones (who seems to be Death). Henry refers to himself often, the references
being in first person, second person, and third person. Indeed, the Dream Songs
are, in Berryman's own admission, about Henry. Haffenden suggests in the
Introduction to this volume that the Dream Songs dramatize the vicissitudes of
the sense of human identity, that Henry is, at least in some sense, mid-twentieth
century man. But as a *persona* Henry has aroused dissent, particularly where his
meaning is concerned. Certainly the poet said that he did not regard Henry as an
extension or substitute for himself, and yet the careful reader of the Dream
Songs is aware that what happens to Henry also happened to the poet who
created him. The poetry of Berryman, especially the Dream Songs, has
consistently been regarded by literary critics as confessional, personal poetry of
a type common among poets of the 1950's and 1960's.

Recollecting "Henry's Confession," published in 1964, the reader is aware
that Henry speaks in that poem of his father's death by a bullet, too close to the
death of Berryman's father to be simple coincidence. And in recollecting the
same poem now, the reader will remember, too, perhaps painfully, that
someone, *persona* or poet, speaks of "joining my father" in "a modesty of
death." In the title poem of this volume we find the poet writing of Henry's fate,
referring to Henry as "he," but giving him small daughters and predicting his
fate, in 1968, as being dead, with no forwarding address. The personal,
expressionistic elements in Berryman's poetry are hauntingly inescapable. A
man exposed to professional therapy many times in his life, Berryman seems to
have applied therapeutic, confessional techniques to himself. And one recalls,
too, that, reared within Catholicism as a child, Berryman returned to that faith in
his maturity. He seems to have been able to look at himself as someone else, but
at the same time to see only himself. One can acquire the eerie feeling that even
Berryman's fine critical and biographical study of Hart Crane was motivated by
an obsession with suicide: Crane, like Berryman's father, like Berryman himself,
was a suicide. Even more closely, Hart Crane disappeared into the waters of the
Gulf of Mexico, as Berryman found his end at the hands of the mighty river
which feeds the Gulf of Mexico. As for identity, it is revealing that the poet was
born John Smith in McAlester, Oklahoma, but that he went through life with
another man's name—in a culture which emphasizes the patronymic and its
symbolic significance. No wonder, from one point of view, that "Henry's Fate"
says "Crusht him out/surprising God, at last, in a wink of time./ His soul was
forwarded./ Adressat unbekannt."

Another side to Berryman comes through occasionally. As has been noted, he
took his work as a poet seriously, believing that seriousness of purpose was of
utmost importance to every writer. In "The assault on immortality begins" in
this volume we find commentary on the awarding of Nobel Prizes, with the

observation that Ibsen and Frost never became Nobel Laureates, although ". . . Icelanders and Latin Americans have it, for the birds." And then there is the suggestion that the Swedish Academy is ignorant of both Chinese and American English. But we also note in the first line the poet's reference to his assault on immortality, not astounding in one so seriously a poet. In his own view, life treated Berryman badly, and readers have rather generally agreed with the poet. He was an intense man, given to drinking too much and to smoking too much. "Great flowing God, bend to my troubles, dear" illustrates with graceful fluidity of thought, typical of Berryman's poetry, the way in which he thought and expressed some of the problems his intensity brought home to him. In this poem he reflects on a way of life of more than two decades, which he may not be able to leave, despite the pleas of the wife who loves him. In the poem the *persona* sees that life is not himself, but a set of habits, like the ghastly habits (to use his word) that we find in tragic drama. And the final lines of the poem remind the reader of John Berryman's own career as scholar and literary critic, for these lines recall to the reader the density of his knowledge of Renaissance literature and the Shakespearean plays in particular, for the Henry of the poem, unlike a Hamlet, walks on in life, surviving his holocaust.

Perhaps like Hamlet, too, Berryman could not be sure that his achievements were such as he had dreamed, in which he could take pride. In "He sits in the dawn, if it can be called dawn," we find Henry thinking of his dreams, of the disappointment of life. It is a failed Henry, one who, though not wholly in despair, counts his losses in the dim light of dawn, with wife and child lying innocently asleep, unaware of his thoughts.

What was Berryman's view of life? Some critic-interpreters have found his view (and they may be correct) to be an ironic one. Throughout his career he appears to have hunted for a poetic expression that was, at the same time, his own expression: this is the dilemma of the confessional poet. Indeed, like Dr. Severance, the protagonist in Berryman's novel, *Recovery*, the poet seems to be reaching for something on which to rely for guidance in recovering from alcoholism and depression, from a personal chaos. In the Dream Songs, those published in this volume as well as those published earlier, Berryman appears at his best, with his utilization of Henry and Henry's Mr. Bones, even in the duality of Henry as white and, at times, as black. Language, as in all poetry, holds the key to understanding the work, if not the poet. Berryman moved through a wide range of diction, from the flat ordinariness of exchanges in everyday conversation to the more formal language commonly thought of as literary or poetic. His ability to see himself and others is extraordinary and seldom dull. He had the ability to see in an everyday occurrence, in a personal occurrence, something worth his intense attention—as in the Dream Song entitled "Hallowe'en." His little daughter, age seven, with her insistence on going with other little girls to "trick or treat," led her father on to see that the childish independence is the first step to the child's lessening need to depend on Daddy, even, indeed, the first step toward the time when Daddy will depend upon his child.

Part II of *Henry's Fate & Other Poems* contains some miscellaneous poems which illustrate the range of Berryman's later writing. For example, "Enlightening Morning" recounts thoughts about a letter from a young woman, a sad but merciless letter. Looking at what she says, the poet sees her life and his to be as disparate as their ages, as he says, "I've not been where this girl is. . . ." Noting that she thought of him as an oddity, an anachronism, a dinosaur, he remarks that she strikes him as some entirely new form, a pathetic carnivore. Other poems in this section deal with Minneapolis, where Berryman lived for many years, with Che Guevara, and with some remembered incidents from the past. Part III of the volume contains "Fragments and Unfinished Poems." Included here is another version of "Washington in Love" that Berryman published earlier in *Delusions, Etc. of John Berryman*. The earlier version contained but seven lines; the version published here, dating from January, 1970, was discovered by Haffenden in the attic of the poet's house in Minneapolis, sixteen pages clipped together. Discussing his find, Haffenden says in the Introduction, "They are reproduced here just as Berryman wrote them, complete with disjunctions and occasional lack of punctuation. I feel that they merit attention as throwing light on Berryman's methods of working, insights and style, as parts of an ambitious, if unfinished poem." Also in Part III is "Proemio," a beginning to what the poet apparently anticipated, had he lived, to become his third great work, after his earlier successes with *Homage to Mistress Bradstreet* and *The Dream Songs*. Again, according to Haffenden, the subject of this later poem was to have been the poet's quest for a subject, a quest "at once fulfilled and abandoned" resolving itself as concentration on the next generation, in Berryman's three children. The poet's own notes suggest that the unfinished work would have been wide-ranging in scope, instructing his children in everything the poet knew well or was perplexed by.

Gordon W. Clarke

Sources for Further Study

Christian Science Monitor. LXIX, July 8, 1977, p. 23.
New Leader. LX, August 15, 1977, p. 14.
New York Times. August 26, 1977, p. C19.
Virginia Quarterly Review. LIII, Summer, 1977, p. 94.
Yale Review. LXVII, October, 1977, p. 72.

THE HISTORY OF THE GERMAN RESISTANCE, 1933-1945

Author: Peter Hoffmann (1930-   )
Translated from the German by Richard Berry
Publisher: The MIT Press (Cambridge, Mass.). 847 pp. $19.95
Type of work: History
Time: 1933-1945
Locale: Nazi Germany and Nazi-occupied Europe

The most comprehensive study yet to appear on the subject of German resistance to Nazism

> *Principal personages:*
> ADOLF HITLER, Chancellor and *Führer* of Germany, 1933-1945
> CLAUS SCHENK GRAF VON STAUFFENBERG, Chief of Staff of the Replacement Army, 1944, and leading conspirator in the plot against Hitler of July 20, 1944
> CARL FRIEDRICH GOERDELER, Mayor of Leipzig to 1937, and top civilian leader of the resistance movement
> HANS OSTER, Chief of Staff of the Abwehr (Armed Forces Intelligence) to 1943 and a leading figure in the military wing of the resistance
> FRANZ HALDER, successor to Beck as Chief of the General Staff, 1938-1942
> LUDWIG BECK, Chief of the General Staff to 1938, and later a top leader of the resistance
> PAUL JOSEPH GOEBBELS, Minister for Popular Enlightenment and Propaganda
> HEINRICH HIMMLER, *Reichsführer SS* and Chief of the German Police

As in other areas of Third Reich history, the literature on the German resistance against Adolf Hitler and his National Socialist dictatorship has continued to burgeon since the end of World War II. Peter Hoffmann, who since 1970 has occupied the Chair of German History at McGill University in Montreal, has contributed numerous articles in German and English on the various attempts to assassinate Hitler. In 1969 and 1970, respectively, Hoffmann brought out the first and second German editions of *The History of the German Resistance,* the title under which the English edition appeared in Great Britain and the United States during 1977. Hoffmann has extensively revised and expanded the book in preparation for the English translation in order to incorporate the findings of his own recent research as well as those of other authorities. What emerges, then, is the most comprehensive study to date on the vast and complicated subject of German resistance against Nazi tyranny.

Hoffmann, in taking cognizance of the thousands of books and articles written by others on the subject of resistance against the Nazi regime, believes that these publications, whatever their individual merit, all share one failure, namely, an inadequate basis of source material. Such a deficiency where present in other works certainly does not apply in the case of Hoffmann's book, as its forty-one pages of bibliography—half of it consisting of unpublished source material—would readily attest. In writing what may be the definitive account on the German resistance against Nazism, Hoffmann is convinced that the plot against Hitler of July 20, 1944, and its tragic failure can only be understood if the previous history of the movement is known in detail. Accordingly, the author states that his primary concern in writing the book is "to clarify the course of events connected with those numerous attempts to overthrow the regime or assassinate its leaders which progressed beyond the stage of mere thought and discussion."

An examination of the general scope of the book does indeed reveal a thorough analysis of the numerous plans for a *coup* against the National Socialist regime and the planned or attempted assassination of Hitler and his minions. Main areas of concentration include, among others, those plans for a *coup* between 1938 and 1940, which stopped short of the assassination of Hitler; the views of key resistance leaders and groups on the political reorganization of post-Hitler Germany; the many assassination attempts against Hitler between 1933 and 1943; and the dual role which Colonel Claus Schenk Graf von Stauffenberg agreed to play in 1944 as assassin of Hitler and leader of the *coup* against the Nazi state. Hoffmann devotes more than one-third of his account to Stauffenberg, whom he describes as the real driving force, from late 1943 to July 20, 1944, in the attempt to assassinate Hitler. Throughout the book as a whole, Hoffmann pays more attention to the conspiracies of the military establishment than to those of the various political factions, which ranged from conservative to Communist. He does, however, discuss at some length the uneasy cooperation which developed during 1944 between Stauffenberg and Carl Friedrich Goerdeler, Mayor of Leipzig to 1937, who was largely recognized throughout the war as the top civilian leader of the resistance movement.

Unfortunately, the author's devotion to detail in discussing the complexity of the resistance movement is not always synonymous with his announced intention to clarify the course of events which eventuated in the plot of July 20, 1944. The book is divided into ten parts, which in turn are subdivided into a total of forty-eight frequently overlapping chapters of very uneven length, some running only two or three pages. Within this awkward framework, the chronology and descriptions of some key events are often muddled at best. Thus, for example, the author at one point seems to indicate that in the fall of 1943, Stauffenberg had a hand in drafting both a list of reliable political figures in districts throughout Germany and a comparable list of trustworthy military liaison officers. In subsequently elaborating on these lists, the author makes no mention of any contribution by Stauffenberg to the list of political conspirators. Similarly, the description of Stauffenberg's daily progress in July, 1944, is marred at points by a confusing and sometimes snarled juxtaposition of dates and events.

These defects, however, do not obscure certain trends in the history of the German resistance movement which the author seeks to convey. Aside from isolated attempts by disgruntled malcontents to kill Hitler, the assassination of the Führer generally did not figure in the plans of the military conspirators prior to the beginning of 1943. One notable exception to this general rule during the first part of the war is to be found in the plans of a small group of officers led by, among others, Hans Oster, Chief of Staff of the Abwehr (Armed Forces Intelligence) to 1943, who shortly after the outbreak of World War II in September, 1939, actively worked to assassinate Hitler. By and large, however, between 1938 and 1942, most of the military conspirators and their political counterparts, such as Goerdeler, wanted only to overthrow the regime and then force its leaders, including Hitler, propaganda minister Joseph Goebbels, and SS leader Heinrich Himmler, to face the responsibility for their crimes.

During the period 1938–1942, the organized conspiracies against Hitler were characterized by frequent and abrupt stops and starts. Hence, the threat of the outbreak of general war on the occasion of the Czech crisis in 1938 spurred the military conspirators to attempt a *coup*. Foremost among the leaders of this *coup* were General Franz Halder, newly appointed Chief of the General Staff, and his predecessor, General Ludwig Beck, who, by early 1942, was recognized as one of the top leaders of the resistance by most of its elements. Halder was prepared to give the signal for a military revolt as soon as Hitler issued the order to march into the Czech Sudetenland. When, however, at the last moment, the Western powers gave in to Hitler's demands at the Munich Conference of September 29–30, war was averted and the *coup* collapsed. A year later, Hitler's spectacular victory over Poland, although it unleashed a general war with Great Britain and France, further undercut the military conspiracy, as most generals now refused to participate in any *putsch*. But once Hitler announced his intention, shortly after the completion of the Polish campaign, to launch an offensive in the West, Halder's interest in a *coup* again quickened, only to recede when the attack was postponed until 1940. Thus, on the whole, Halder and most of the top generals refused to give any serious consideration to a *coup* during 1940 and 1941, the period of Hitler's most spectacular triumphs.

Hoffmann states that it was the opening of the Russian campaign in the summer of 1941, which finally crystallized the opposition of the generals against the Nazi regime. As the Wehrmacht rolled up great victories against the faltering Red Army, the generals expressed shock toward the SS atrocities against Soviet Jews and outrage over the widespread implementation of the Commissar Order which called for the summary execution of Communist commissars who were captured on the field of battle. Consequently, enthusiasm for the regime began to decline and at the same time the will to resistance grew in many important staffs and headquarters, particularly in Army Group Center, which was holding the battle line in front of Moscow. Hoffmann insists that the initial impetus to resistance did not come from the defeats of 1942 and later, although they certainly contributed to the diminishment of the prestige which Hitler had won through his earlier military victories. This is a debatable point, for it undoubtedly took the catastrophe at Stalingrad to effect the genuine conversion of many generals to the resistance movement. In any event, by early 1943, the serious reverses on the Eastern Front combined with the Allied demands at the Casablanca Conference for unconditional surrender produced a mood of deep despair throughout Germany and the military establishment. It was against this backdrop, as Hoffmann relates in considerable detail, that various military officers plotted to assassinate Hitler during 1943 and early 1944. By June of 1944, Colonel Graf von Stauffenberg, who up to this point had been involved in helping others to arrange attempts on Hitler's life, now decided to undertake the deed himself.

Stauffenberg's decision to be the assassin of Hitler meant that he was now going to play a dual role in the conspiracy, for in the latter part of 1943, he had assumed responsibility for developing plans for the *coup* which would take place immediately after the assassination. These plans called for the Replacement Army, consisting of reserve and training units, to seize key installations, party headquarters, and other Nazi centers of power throughout the Reich. In this scheme, Stauffenberg and his fellow conspirators cleverly made use of a military plan, known under the codeword "Valkyrie," which called for the Replacement Army to be ready to counter raids by Allied airborne troops and to put down any uprisings among the millions of foreigners who were forced to work in Germany. Stauffenberg's various military assignments enabled him to become intimately familiar with the structure of the Replacement Army and to manipulate it in preparation for its use in the *coup*. In particular, in late June, 1944, he was designated as the Chief of Staff of the Replacement Army, in which capacity he had direct access to Hitler. Because of the severe combat wounds which Stauffenberg had suffered while in North Africa, costing him his right hand, two fingers of his left hand, and an eye, no one in Hitler's entourage, including the Führer himself, would suspect that such a crippled officer could be an assassin. Thus, on July 20, 1944, Stauffenberg succeeded in placing a briefcase containing a bomb in the conference hut of Hitler's headquarters, called *"Wolfschanze"* (Wolf's Lair) in East Prussia. During a meeting held that day by the Führer, the device exploded, but Hitler miraculously sustained only minor injuries.

Hoffmann devotes the balance of his study to the failure of the *coup* and to the arrest and punishment of those involved in it. Stauffenberg, he relates, managed to return immediately by plane from *Wolfschanze* to Berlin to assume the direction of the *coup* in the capital. When it became known that Hitler had survived the attempt on his life, the *coup* in Berlin and elsewhere in Nazi-occupied Europe quickly collapsed. Stauffenberg was arrested on the evening of July 20, and summarily shot early the next morning. Propaganda Minister Goebbels directed the suppression of the *coup* in Berlin while *Reichsführer* Himmler set his Gestapo on the trail of those involved in the conspiracy elsewhere throughout the Reich. Those arrested were subject to torture, mock trials, and, in many cases, to the death penalty. Many death sentences were not carried out until April, 1945, within a month of the end of the war.

The History of the German Resistance sheds new and important light on the strengths and weaknesses of those who participated in the numerous and unsuccessful efforts to overthrow Hitler and his regime. Because of the book's deservingly high place in the vast historical literature on Nazi Germany, one wishes that the author and the translator had done a more thorough job in writing and editing the English language edition. The result would have been a more readable book, devoid of muddled chronology, unclear references to people and events, and other problems mentioned earlier; all of these shortcomings only serve to complicate needlessly a subject that is already complicated enough. Some of these flaws arise from one of the book's great strengths: its thoroughness. Thus, Hoffmann sometimes loses his reader in tracing Stauffenberg's every move through the critical days of July, 1944, and in recording the details of the abortive July 20 *putsch* which ensued after the unsuccessful attempt on Hitler's life. By contrast, the author's account of the arrest, trial, and execution of those involved in the *coup* is generally much clearer. The thoroughness of Hoffmann's study is also reflected in the almost two hundred pages of source notes and in the massive bibliography, which affords the reader the best available reference to the literature on the German resistance to Hitler.

Edward P. Keleher

Sources for Further Study

Book World. May 15, 1977, p. H9.
Booklist. LXXIII, June 1, 1977, p. 1474.
Economist. CCLXIII, May 28, 1977, p. 140.
New York Times Book Review. April 3, 1977, p. 13.
New Yorker. LIII, June 29, 1977, p. 119.

HISTORY OF THE OTTOMAN EMPIRE AND MODERN TURKEY

Volume II: Reform, Revolution, and Republic: The Rise of Modern Turkey, 1808-1975

Authors: Stanford J. Shaw and Ezel Kural Shaw
Publisher: Cambridge University Press (New York). 518 pp. $29.95
Type of work: History
Time: 1808-1975
Locale: The Ottoman Empire (Turkey, Southeast Europe, the Middle East)

A historical survey of the Ottoman Empire and the Turkish republic including its economic, social, and political development in the nineteenth and twentieth centuries

Principal personages:
MAHMUT II, Sultan of the Ottomans, 1808-1839
ABDULMECIT I, his son, Sultan of the Ottomans, 1839-1861
ABDULAZIZ, his brother, Sultan of the Ottomans, 1861-1876
ABDULHAMIT II, son of Abdulmecit, Sultan of the Ottomans, 1876-1909
MUHAMMAD ALI PAŞA, Prince of Egypt, a progressive-minded rival of the Sultans
KOCA MUSTAFA REŞIT PAŞA, leader of the Tanzimat (reform) in the nineteenth century
KEÇECIZADE MEHMET FUAT PAŞA, his protégé, a leading Ottoman reformer
MEHMET EMIN ALI PAŞA, protégé of Reşit Paşa, a leading spokesman for reform
AHMET ŞEFIK MIDHAT PAŞA, a capable Ottoman administrator, a spokesman for Turkish nationalism and constitutional government
MEHMET KÜÇÜK SAIT PAŞA, Abdulhamit's most important adviser
AHMET CEMAL PAŞA, a leader of the Young Turks, one of the dictatorial triumvirs during World War I
ENVER PAŞA, another Young Turk triumvir
MEHMET TALAT PAŞA, the third triumvir
MUSTAFA KEMAL ATAÜRK, modern Turkey's greatest statesman, the father of the republic
ISMET INÖNÜ, Ataürks's most important associate, President of Turkey after his death

With this book the Shaws complete their two-volume history of the Ottoman Empire and modern Turkey. In it they describe the attempts to regenerate the empire in the nineteenth century, its ultimate collapse, and the birth and growth of the twentieth century republic. Since books in English on the history of Turkey are rare, this is a valuable addition to the literature, especially as it gives an excellent account of the economic and social changes that have occurred in the last two centuries. Furthermore, since the authors write from an unashamedly Turkish point of view, it presents an interpretation almost never seen in scholarly literature.

The major emphasis of the history is on the process of reform and modernization within the Ottoman Empire and modern Turkey. The authors take us from the initial efforts of Mahmut II—especially the "Auspicious Event," that is, the destruction of the corrupt conservative and outmoded Janissary military corps—through the Tanzimat (reforms) of the nineteenth century; the constitutional projects of Midhat Paşa and the Young Ottomans; the Young Turk movement of the early 1900's under the direction of the Committee of Union and Progress (CUP); ending with the truly revolutionary transformation of Turkish society carried out under Mustafa Kemal Atatürk.

Previous accounts of Turkish reforms almost universally explained them as reactions to external pressure from the Great Powers of Christian Europe and dwelt on the failures and inadequacies of the attempts. The Shaws pay almost no heed to the external factors and explain the reforms as genuine native Turkish programs to modernize Ottoman society. Furthermore, while admitting insufficiencies and lack of hoped-for achievement in a number of areas, the authors consistently stress the successes.

Although the Shaws clearly sympathize with the efforts of Ottoman reformers, they also are apologetic for the various governments and rulers, whether the Sultans, Young Turk triumvirs, or republican presidents—at times even to the detriment of dissident reformers. Thus even though Abdulhamit abrogated Midhat's constitution and probably had its author assassinated, the Shaws are loathe to condemn the autocrat; rather, they emphasize the progress of his reign to counteract his reputation among Europeans as a tyrant. Most of all, the Shaws admire the Young Turk leaders of the CUP. This logically follows their opinions not only because in many ways the CUP represents the epitome of all they admire in Turkey, but also because the group has been the target of unjust attacks from the Christian West. In Western eyes the CUP triumvirs were the pro-German tyrants of the World War I era, those who had promised so much by bringing down Abdulhamit but in the end fulfilled so little of that promise. To the Shaws, however, the CUP were reformers who did not find it necessary to tear down Ottoman institutions *à la* Atatürk. (The Shaws to be sure also admire Atatürk as a Turkish hero, a great patriot, and of course the legitimate successor of the Sultans; but they still leave the clear impression that they have more sympathy for the kind of reform within the old institutions that the men of Tanzimat and Young Turks like Talat, Cemal, and Enver hoped to accomplish. Furthermore, Atatürk is treated much more sympathetically as a ruler than as a rebel.) With some justice they try to salvage the reputations of the Young Turk leaders by demonstrating the effects of their legacy on republican Turkey. As they do with the other imperial and republican rulers, the Shaws minimize the CUP's faults as resulting from circumstances beyond their control.

In a further example of excusing government excesses, the Shaws distort the effects of the prejudicial Capital Levy Tax of World War II. This tax discriminated against non-Turkish minorities in the republic and was a blemish on the record of the usual egalitarian rights extended to all citizens by Atatürk and generally continued by his successors. (Bernard Lewis in his superb *The Emergence of Modern Turkey,* which gives a scholarly yet sympathetic history of the modern state, has an excellent analysis of the tax and its effects.) The Shaws, however, imply that the tax affected all citizens equally and explain away its injustices as bureaucratic misunderstandings.

There can be no disagreement with the Shaws that past Christian accounts of Turkey have been unfairly negative and that the prejudices against the Turks in Western opinion need to be rectified by more balanced approaches. However, instead of writing a balanced account of Turkish history, the Shaws have taken a defiantly pro-Ottoman and pro-Turkish position, minimizing all faults of the governments and society and, even more unfortunately, portraying the non-Turkish minorities within the empire and the European powers without in the same unrelentingly hostile manner that they accuse Christian authors of using in their writing about the Turks.

Moreover, the authors show an unprofessional ignorance of non-Turkish history. For example, twice they refer to the discarded theory that Russian foreign policy was based on a desire for warm water ports including even the Persian Gulf—a geographical absurdity. We must assume the sincerity of the authors, but the descriptions of non-Turkish affairs in comparison to the well-researched excellence of the noncontroversial sections of the Ottoman narration have the appearance of a contemptuous parody on the treatment of Moslem society by popular European authors. This is especially ironic, as one of the chief criticisms of Ottoman society by Christian scholars has been the charge of Turkish contempt for all that was not Islamic.

In their treatment of the non-Turkish national movements within the Ottoman Empire, the authors are sure to rouse the ire of these nations. (Indeed, Professor Stanford Shaw has, unfortuantely, been the subject of threats and harassment by Armenian students at UCLA for his pro-Turkish lectures.) Not only do the Shaws minimize Moslem atrocities against Christian minorities to the point of almost, though not quite, denying their existence, they also claim that many more atrocities were committed against the Moslems by Christians within and without the empire. The Bulgarian and Armenian patriots of national liberation become small bands of terrorist criminals influenced by outside agents and agitators from Christian Europe. Of course, there is no doubt that in all societies with a minority problem, one group's patriots are the other's villains. Furthermore, there were indeed atrocities committed on both sides in the turmoil which attended the decline of the Ottoman Empire. However, instead of taking the opportunity to examine these events in an impartial and scholarly light, the Shaws join in the polemical fracas. While it is true, for example, that the Armenian holocaust of World War I cannot be strictly compared to the Nazi actions against the Jews in World War II as some have claimed (there was no systematic bureaucratic plan to eradicate the Armenian nation by the Turkish government, and the massacres were a response to Armenian uprisings), the tragedy of the Armenian nation in Turkey did not have the insignificance that the authors assign to it. In another passage while confronting the Greek assertion that Atatürk's forces burned Smyrna (Izmir) to the ground in 1922, the Shaws characteristically and aggressively counter: "Perhaps the last atrocity of the war was the suggestion, quickly taken up by the Western press, that the victorious Turkish army was responsible for burning the conquered second city of the old empire. Actual culpability has never been proved."

There was indeed a concept of order in Ottoman society, and religious and national minorities had their places in the empire beside the Turks and Moslems. However, we cannot deny the fact that the non-Moslem millets were in an inferior position; nor can we ignore the history of the empire, particularly the overriding factor that the Ottomans had captured Christian lands and that the non-Moslem people of those lands both in their own view and that of their conquerors were a vanquished people.

The Shaws' view of the national movements leads to their serious misinterpretation of the causes of imperial decline and the possible alternatives for the Ottoman fate. The authors consider the minorities' quest for national independence a superfluous result of Christian fanaticism. If the Christians had shown a little patience, they contend, the self-initiated reform program of the government and the natural development of the Ottoman society would have created an egalitarian state based on an Ottoman nationalism. In reality, however, under the circumstances Ottoman nationalism could never have been a viable force. The differences between Moslems and Christians were too great to be reconciled. Furthermore, the reform movement was developing toward Turkish nationalism rather than Ottoman stability. Midhat Paşa—perhaps the greatest Ottoman administrator of the nineteenth century, and certainly one of the greatest reformers, the author of the constitution of 1876—opposed any territorial curtailment of the empire, and stressed the need for protection of minorities, but as minorities, not as conationalists of the Turks. Midhat's contemporary Young Ottomans, as well as the subsequent Young Turks, continued this movement toward Turkish rather than Ottoman nationalism. Conservative Turks, on the other hand, continued to seek imperial salvation neither in Turkish nor Ottoman nationalism, but rather in the Şeriat (religious law) of Islam. They opposed all modernization and reform. In the end the culmination of reform accomplished by the greatest of all modern Turkish innovators, Atatürk, resulted in a purely Turkish nationalist secular state—the Ottoman institutions, the non-Turkish lands, the Islamic law were all voluntarily given up. Furthermore, by this time even the non-Turkish Moslems, such as the Arabs, had developed their own national movements.

Pointing out individual "foreign agents" or small groups of "extremists" as the perpetrators of nationalism is beside the point. The nationalist ideology traveled rapidly from country to country in the early nineteenth century. Regardless of whether foreign or native preachers introduced it, or whether friends or enemies provided the example, the nationalist ideology was readily accepted by the rising generations of all nations. The Christian peoples of the Balkans learned it from France, Germany, and Russia as well as one another. The Turks learned it from the Christians. The Arabs, Persians, and Kurds learned it as well. Moreover, it was this nationalist ideology which brought the empire tumbling down, and reforms, whether initiated by the Sultans and their advisers on their own accord as the Shaws contend, or forced on the empire by the European powers as the traditional Christian interpretation states, could not prevent it. In conclusion, as a useful survey of Turkish history the Shaws' study succeeds, but as a counterinterpretation of the traditional views it offers only the Turkish side without a convincing destruction of the old arguments.

Frederick B. Chary

Sources for Further Study

American Historical Review. LXXXII, October, 1977, p. 1029.
Choice. XIV, March, 1977, p. 115.
History: Reviews of New Books. V, May, 1977, p. 151.
Virginia Quarterly Review. LIII, Summer, 1977, p. 99.

HITLER'S WAR

Author: David Irving (1938–   )
Publisher: The Viking Press (New York). 926 pp. $17.50
Type of work: History
Time: September 3, 1939, to April 30, 1945
Locale: Europe

This analysis views Hitler as a man of great military ability who was nevertheless surprisingly weak in imposing his will on his subordinates

Principal personages:
ADOLF HITLER, the Führer
MARTIN BORMANN, his powerful secretary
JOSEPH GOEBBELS, Gauleiter of Berlin and Reich Propaganda Minister
HERMANN GÖRING, Commander in Chief of the Luftwaffe and head of the Four-Year Plan Office
HEINZ GUDERIAN, famous German tank commander
WALTHER HEWEL, liaison officer at Hitler's headquarters
REINHARD HEYDRICH, SS General who was the brain behind the extermination camps
HEINRICH HIMMLER, SS Reichsführer
ALFRED JODL, Chief of the OKW operations staff and Hitler's closest military adviser
WILHELM KEITEL, Field Marshall and Chief of OKW
ERICH VON MANSTEIN, Field Marshal, Hitler's favorite offensive general
THEO MORELL, Hitler's doctor
ERICH RAEDER, Grand Admiral and Commander in Chief, Navy
ERWIN ROMMEL, Field Marshal and charismatic general
ALBERT SPEER, Hitler's scheming Munitions Minister

During 1942, Adolf Hitler praised a biography of William II written by an Englishman and expressed the opinion that foreigners sometimes made very objective historians. He went on to remark that he was having transcripts made of all his important conferences and that some day perhaps an "objective Englishman" would write his story. As David Irving relates this incident, it is clear that he wants to be the objective Englishman Hitler prophesied. The result is a controversial and sometimes vexing book.

In Irving's approach to his subject, pride of place goes to the eleven years he spent going through the primary sources. Great emphasis is placed on sources he located which no one else has utilized; in fact, this sometimes seems to be his main criterion in judging the importance of a source. He writes history as scoop. Irving wants to escape from the incestuous relation between historians who trade the same stories back and forth, and so he has spurned published works on Hitler. Irving's object is to reconstruct the war as Hitler viewed it. He does this with a careful, almost day by day, analysis of Hitler's orders, the intelligence reports he was receiving, the transcripts of his war conferences, and diaries of people closely associated with him, some of them used here for the first time.

Irving empathetically rethinks the war from Hitler's perspective, a bold approach from which most historians have been deterred by the repugnance of the subject. Irving is able to accomplish this because his Hitler is completely sane and turns out to be not so bad as we had imagined.

Irving's method imposes a very narrow focus on his book. It begins abruptly with the invasion of Poland and the reader flounders for many pages before he gains his bearings. The book ends without conclusion 823 pages later with the suicide of Hitler. Irving is totally preoccupied with Hitler's day by day military and political decisions, so there is no room in his long book for such crucial factors as the role of ideology or a systematic analysis of Hitler's personality. Naturally, an account based entirely on the "nuts and bolts" decisions Hitler had to make once he had started his war places him in his most pragmatic light, yet this narrow focus also distorts the image of Hitler and is the most serious weakness of Irving's book.

The author's most controversial conclusion is that Hitler did not order the extermination of the Jews and indeed did not even know about it until at least October, 1943, and may not have learned about it until SS General Ernst Kaltenbrunner told him one year later, in October, 1944. Irving's argument is partly one of silence. No document has ever been discovered in which Hitler ordered the massacre of the Jews and Irving has been unable to find any mention in any of the diaries he has read that anyone ever discussed the matter with Hitler. Irving buttresses his argument of silence with circumstantial evidence. On several occasions Heinrich Himmler stated that he had taken on himself the responsibility for the final solution, statements which Irving interprets to mean that Himmler made the decision himself. Hitler himself said late in the war that the whole matter was Himmler's business. Moreover, all of Hitler's explicit references to the Jewish problem referred only to the deportation of the Jews to the east. On November 30, 1941, Himmler telephoned SS General Reinhard Heydrich from Hitler's headquarters and ordered him to stop liquidating the Jews. Irving believes this proves that Hitler was actually insisting the Jews not be exterminated, and he attaches such importance to the episode that he includes a facsimile of Himmler's telephone note recording this call. That the extermination of Jews was suspended after Kaltenbrunner conferred with Hitler in October, 1944, confirms to Irving that Hitler never wanted the final solution during the war.

For Irving, then, the final solution was partly the initiative of a crackpot, Heinrich Himmler, and partly an *ad hoc* solution adopted by local authorities to the near insuperable problem of what to do with the millions of Jews dumped on them from all over Europe. Irving argues that only about seventy people knew what was happening and Hitler, who was completely absorbed in the war and had abdicated his authority in other areas, was not one of them.

Throughout the book, Irving scrupulously sticks very close to his evidence, so much so that the reader yearns for a perspective in which to place and evaluate the evidence. It is only in the matter of the final solution that Irving endeavors to extract an interpretation from the evidence that many readers will find remarkable. His reason for this is that this argument is the keystone to two of his main conclusions—that Hitler was sane and that his authority during the war was surprisingly limited.

Himmler was a crackpot; Hitler was not. Irving is convinced Hitler was a pragmatic man who would never have wasted scarce resources for such an irrational purpose as killing Jews. Hitler's idea was to make use of the Jews as forced laborers and as hostages; killing them defeated both purposes. Irving acknowledges that Hitler was indeed ruthless and brutal. Deporting the Jews was bad enough, and his violent anti-Semitism, which Irving labels pathological, created the atmosphere in which the extermination of the Jews could take place. Hitler ordered the liquidation of Communist political commissars and pitiless reprisals against the partisans. But these atrocities had some purpose to them and were not different in kind from the terror bombing tactics of the British air force sanctioned by Winston Churchill. Irving's contention that Hitler was a normal wartime leader is an effort to deal a knock-out punch to the psycho-historians.

What kind of wartime leader was Hitler? Irving finds him quite ineffective. He was unable to assert his authority, and as he became increasingly enmeshed in the minutiae of tactical military decisions, his authority in other matters slipped away. His orders to develop a fighter-bomber jet plane which would be effective in thwarting an amphibious landing on the Atlantic coast were ignored and it was too late when he discovered the jet propulsion program had constructed only a fighter plane. He was consistently misled by Albert Speer and the Peenemünde rocket scientists about both the progress and the potential of the A-4 program so that he committed resources to that program which could have been more useful elsewhere. Even in military affairs, his generals frequently ignored his orders. This erosion of his authority was a pity, since Irving believes he was usually right and his subordinates wrong. Many of Hitler's plans bogged down in personal rivalries between Albert Speer, Hermann Göring, Martin Bormann, Joseph Goebbels, and Heinrich Himmler. Irving views Hitler's inability to get a grip on the machinery of state and party in Nazi Germany and the resulting slackness of effort and inefficiencies as his greatest failure.

Irving believes that Hitler as a military leader tended to lose his nerve and never mastered the ability to deploy effectively large armies; but despite these reservations, his admiration of Hitler's military gifts shines through. He believes that Hitler had gained great technical mastery through an impressive systematic reading program and that he knew by heart the great works of military strategy by Frederick II, Moltke, Schlieffen, and Clausewitz. His instincts were almost always right and his generals were by no means as perspicacious as they claimed after the war.

Time and again the author confounds the conventional wisdom about Hitler's military mistakes. He shows that Hitler was receiving intelligence reports of ominous military preparations in the Soviet Union, and presents Hitler's attack in June, 1941, as a preventive war instead of a gratuitous military blunder brought about by an irrational obsession for *Lebensraum*. Given the fatal underestimation by German intelligence of Soviet military capacity, Hitler's decision to attack was perfectly reasonable and his optimism was shared by the entire army. Only Göring and Admiral Erich Raeder had misgivings.

Irving believes that Hitler's plan to encircle Moscow was much sounder than the direct assault favored by General Brauchitsch and the army. If Hitler had not been ill at the crucial moment, the generals might not have been able to subvert his plans and Moscow might have fallen. That winter, during the crisis of the Soviet offensive before Moscow, it was Hitler who saved the day by his determination and courage, which prevented his dispirited generals from retreating. In the summer offensive of 1942, General Bock repeatedly resisted Hitler's orders to move his armored divisions south, and a chance to encircle the Russian army was lost. Hitler was frequently betrayed by German intelligence, which grievously underestimated Russian reserves and which completely failed to predict the Soviet summer offensive of 1942, despite Hitler's gravest misgivings and explicit requests by him to be alert for an offensive.

Irving argues that the monumental catastrophe at Stalingrad was a shared responsibility, but, as in so many things, after the war it was blamed on Hitler through fudged memoirs, fake diaries, and tampered OKW diaries. Hitler's mistake was to brag prematurely and publicly about the fall of Stalingrad, and this made him loathe to abandon the effort. Once the Soviets had encircled the city, Hitler, contrary to postwar reports, was surrounded by optimistic generals who believed that the Soviet encirclement was temporary. By December 18, breakout had become a logistical impossibility and so all the talk about Hitler's blind refusal to allow it lacks substance. Moreover, the Sixth Army was tying down seventy Soviet divisions which could have jeopardized the entire southern front if released.

Irving shows that it is a myth that Hitler never allowed strategical retreats. It was not until 1944, after Russian troops had entered German territory, that he issued a no retreat order. He repeatedly urged on his generals his prediction that the Allied invasion would be in Normandy or Brittany, but they ignored him in favor of their expectation of a direct cross channel invasion. Then German intelligence vastly overestimated Allied reserve strength, causing Hitler to hesitate to commit his reserves because of his fear of a second invasion in another place. The collapse of the eastern front in the summer of 1944 was abetted by defeatist generals who advised their men to surrender. Only Hitler prevented a complete collapse; without him, Irving believes the Russians would have been on the Rhine within a month.

Irving does not believe that Hitler's hope of reversing the course of the war during the last year was mere fantasy. He had ordered the Luftwaffe to build up a secret reserve of fighter planes which would enable him to throw two thousand planes into the struggle for France at one stroke. One hundred and fifty new Mark XXI submarines were to be ready by the end of 1944. The disagreement over Poland between the Allies lent substance to the hope that the Soviet-Anglo-American alliance would split if Germany could gain time. Irving believes Hitler could have reaped the cold war benefits that fell to Konrad Adenauer if he could have prolonged the war another year or so.

This notion that the Allies might have come to some sort of accommodation with Hitler, despite all that he had done, is a remarkable one to say the least. It is reflected in perhaps its most vexing form in Irving's idea that Churchill's policies were unfortunate for Britain. Irving continually emphasizes that Hitler had no designs on the British empire. He seems to agree with Hitler that it would seem more natural for Germany and England to be fighting Bolsheviks and the Yellow Peril together instead of Germany and Japan fighting Great Britain and Soviet Russia, to the mutual ruin of European supremacy. Without ever quite saying so, he leaves the impression that the Duke of Windsor, with his pro-Fascist leanings and his hopes to mediate between Great Britain and Germany, understood British interests better than Churchill.

Such eccentric judgments only detract from the real value of Irving's book. His meticulous analysis of the decision-making process in Germany during the war is an indispensible antidote to the self-serving memoirs of Speer, General Heinz Guderian, and Field Marshal Erich von Manstein. No other book provides a closer examination of Hitler as a war leader. Irving's persuasive demonstration of the limitations of Hitler's authority should lay to rest once and for all the Hitler-as-scapegoat school of history. His portrayal of Hitler as a man whose decisions were always rational and usually right but who failed because he was an ineffective leader who was unable to impose his will on his subordinates is an important revision of the conventional view and deserves consideration. But Irving's narrow focus prevents a definitive portrait of Hitler, and his curious lack of understanding about the meaning of the war will leave some with the impression that he goes beyond revision to exoneration, and this fault may prevent the book from receiving a serious hearing.

Paul B. Kern

Sources for Further Study

Books and Bookmen. XXII, July, 1977, p. 6.
Commentary. LXIV, September, 1977, p. 76.
Economist. CCLXIII, June 18, 1977, p. 131.
Listener. XXVIII, July 7, 1977, p. 27.
National Review. XXIX, August 19, 1977, p. 946.
New Statesman. XCIV, July 1, 1977, p. 18.
New Yorker. LIII, August 29, 1977, p. 82.

HOLY THE FIRM

Author: Annie Dillard (1945–   )
Publisher: Harper & Row Publishers (New York). 76 pp. $6.50
Type of work: Mystical theology

A visionary prose poem of extraordinary compactness which searches the natural world for manifestations of God and Christ

Holy the Firm is a work whose leading allusion is to a concept drawn from esoteric Christianity. Holy the Firm, according to Dillard's medieval sources, is a created substance which occurs within planets—below earth, minerals, salts; it serves as a bridge between the material and the spiritual worlds, for it is "in touch with the Absolute at base." Looking backwards to Christianity's great medieval flourishing, Dillard finds a concept which is utterly contemporary and even futuristic. For the idea of "Holy the Firm" explains, she believes, the infinity of time and the curve of space.

Allusions to the Middle Ages abound in all of Dillard's work, and it is as a medieval religious pilgrim that her stance as narrator and artist should be understood. Here we must distinguish between the tourist and the pilgrim. For the tourist, places are ends in themselves, scenes to be consumed by the ravishing eye. For the pilgrim, places are means—of refreshment, of soul-building, of education about the Way. To the pilgrim, allegory dissolves mere scenery, the picture forces its way through the picturesque. Dillard's writings beautifully depict earthly places, but she is no tourist. Nor, as some would have it, is she a sort of roving regionalist, though this is a plausible notion. Reared in the city, she adopted the Blue Ridge creeks, valleys, and hills around Roanoke, Virginia, during and after her days at Hollins College. She married poet-novelist Richard Henry Wilde Dillard in 1965; she now is scholar-in-residence at Western Washington State College and lives alone on northern Puget Sound. But these settings and situations are ancillary, accidental: for Dillard is a pilgrim, comprehensible only in terms of her *telos.*

Dillard startled the critical world with *Pilgrim at Tinker Creek,* which won the Pulitzer Prize in 1974. Viewed by many as a naturalist who brilliantly revealed the intricacies, fecundity, and violence of nature, Dillard has been compared to writers as disparate as Thoreau and Melville. Nature is not her real focus, however. She says about her work, "Art is my interest, mysticism my message, Christian mysticism." That mystical Christianity—and its revelations in the natural world—resonates most strongly in *Holy the Firm.* In fact, the ultimate meaning of all her work is missed if Dillard is interpreted as a Thoreauvian transcendentalist. The faults many critics find in her—her extreme allusiveness and the density of the imagery, her failure to consider what humans have done in and to nature, her "escapism"—can all be accounted for if the reader under-stands from the outset that Dillard's main subject is not *Creation* (Nature), but *Creator.* The categories with which to comprehend Dillard's achievement are those of religion—spiritual autobiography, meditation, mysticism, theology. Thus, the appearance of *Holy the Firm* forces one to reconsider all of Dillard's previous efforts.

With this critical perspective in mind, Dillard's statement that *Pilgrim at Tinker Creek* is "really a book of theology" becomes extremely important. Ostensibly the book records the changing patterns of nature over a year, as Dillard peers closely at a few acres on Tinker Creek, in the Blue Ridge Mountains. But since the year is liturgical as well as natural, this "journal" is a mystic meditation on the terror and glory of God's creation. The terror is captured in such detailed episodes as the giant water bug sucking out the frog's life blood, the mindless tracking of the pine caterpillars which leads them to starvation, or the praying mantis consuming her mate as he couples with her. Also revealed is creation's glory, experienced only in unselfconscious instants, selfless epiphanies of complete understanding. Dillard's mission is to *see* fully. She asks for toothpicks for her eyes, as she searches for the vision of the "tree with lights in it" that the newly sighted child glimpsed when its bandages are first removed. Though they can be sought for, such moments are grace, given in fleeting instants, recalled only by the mind and changed when verbalized.

Dillard expresses this idea—so like that of Joyce or Proust—in recounting her vision of the light changing on the mountains. She is waiting on the hot pavement of a gas station, petting a puppy: "The air cools; the puppy's skin is hot. I am more alive than all the world." Then,

> I look at the mountain, which is still doing its tricks, as you look at a still-beautiful face belonging to a person who was once your lover in another country years ago: with fond nostalgia, and recognition, but no real feeling save a secret astonishment that you are now strangers.

Her pilgrimage is enlightened by numerous fellow pilgrims: she borrows eclectically from Heraclitus, Thomas Merton, Edwin Way Teale, Heisenberg, Isak Dinesen, Blake, Julian of Norwich, Jakob Böhme, Pascal—from anthropology, physics, biology, philosophy, theology. About her studies she says, "I bloom indoors in the winter like a forced forsythia; I come in to come out. At night I read and write, and things I have never understood become clear."

Her first book of poems, *Tickets for a Prayer Wheel* (1974), reprinted many of her contributions to such publications as *The American Scholar, The Atlantic,* and *Southern Poetry Review;* there are new poems as well. While some poems are visionary and difficult, using private, religious symbolism, others are more accessible. Dillard does very well with topical or occasional poems which refer to an epigraphic opening quotation. "The Man Who Wishes to Feed on Mahogany" is one of the best of these. A poem about poetry and the creative process, its imagery and form are tightly controlled. The central image comes from a comment by Chesterton (as quoted by Borges) to the effect that poetry cannot be made about someone who wants to eat mahogany because this feeling is not "commonplace." Dillard's poem characterizes that uncommon person and extends the idea; nature has its being because humans love and desire: "Crosses grow as trees and grasses everywhere,/ writing in wood and leaf and flower and spore,/ marking the map,—Some man loved here;/ and one loved something here; and here; and here." The title poem of the volume prefigures the ideas and images of *Holy the Firm*. The prayer wheel "tickets" are various prayers, as the narrator begins, "Our family is looking/ for someone who knows how to pray."

A parable of Creation and the Incarnation, a revelation of grace in the face of the suffering and evil of the world, *Holy the Firm* is concentrated, spare, deep, intensely poetic. The emphasis is still on the narrator's relationship with the Infinite and his Creation. The unifying symbol is fire, and the book gathers its meaning from two burnings—of the moth in the candle flame and the face of seven-year-old Julie Norwich in a terrifying freak accident. The female moth, drawn to the candle, burns crisply in a second, but then the body shell becomes a wick and feeds a flame: "She burned for two hours without changing, without bending or leaning—only glowing within, like a building fire glimpsed through silhouetted walls, like a hollow saint, like a flame-faced virgin gone to God." Alluding to the great medieval mystic Julian (Juliana) of Norwich (1343-ca. 1413), Dillard shows us little Julie Norwich, whose burnt lipless face dissolves in soundless pain: "That skinlessness, that black shroud of flesh in strips on your skull, is your veil," she says to Julie. Burnt moth and child both become metaphors for grace, for emanations of the Divine, for the life of the nun, and finally for Dillard herself—who equates her vocation as a writer with the glowing moth and finally with Julie Norwich: "I'll be the nun for you. I am now." Julie and Dillard become one (they had looked alike from the first). Divine love is revealed—*literally*—to be the answer to the question of evil and suffering in the world. Medieval anchoress Julian's answer was the same in her *Revelations of Divine Love* (ca. 1396). Her striking image of creation as "a little thing, the quantity of an hazelnut," is appropriated in Dillard's vision of the golden-haired smouldering god brought in by the cat, his hot skull "the size of a hazel nut."

Dillard's compact poetic style bristles with images, brims with sound: "There is not a chink. The sky is gagging on trees." Her playfulness with religious and secular conceits reminds one of both the metaphysical poets and of Gerard Manley Hopkins' extreme visual and aural imagery of nature. Like them, she must be read aloud:

> The god of today is a tree. He is a forest of trees or a desert, or a wedge from wideness down to a scatter of stars, stars like salt low and dumb and abiding. Today's god said: shed. He peels from eternity always, spread; he winds into time like a rind.

She rings the changes on such words as fire, holy, nun, spirit, salt, god—repeating images, adding more meaning each time. Inflated poetic language is often interfaced with homely metaphors from everyday speech, clichés taken apart and supercharged with new meaning: "Welcome again to the land of the living, to time, this hill of beans."

Dillard's visions—of the tiny god, of uncharted islands in the Sound, of the Christ in the bottle of communion wine, of the transmogrification of Julie Norwich into a seraph burning for God—culminate in the vision of Christ's baptism, as she loses her self in the whole. Reminiscent of other mystic visions, her description defies description; finally words and analysis are useless:

> It is the one glare of holiness; it is bare and unspeakable. There is no speech nor language; there is nothing, no one thing, nor motion, nor time. There is only this everything. There is only this, and its bright and multiple noise.

But Dillard, as artist, cannot leave it at that. The artist—who combines matter and spirit, who is both thinker and nun—is the wick for the flame of the holy: "What can any artist set on fire but his world? . . . What can he light but the short string of his gut . . .?" The artist, both holy and firm, is able to reconcile two traditional views of the world—disclosed in the doctrines of immanence and emanation. Immanence, or pantheism, holds that Nature is one with Creator; Christ is unnecessary. For the emanentalist, Nature is wholly other, linked to Creator through Christ. The artist provides the link, "in flawed imitation of Christ on the cross stretched both ways unbroken and thorned," between spirit and matter. Thus, like many Christian mystics, Dillard combines heart and intellect in her answer to the paradox:

> And the universe is real and not a dream, not a manufacture of the senses; subject may know object, knowledge may proceed, and Holy the Firm is in short the philosopher's stone.

Margaret McFadden-Gerber

Sources for Further Study

America. CXXXVII, October 8, 1977, p. 219.
Atlantic. CCXL, December, 1977, p. 106.
Book World. October 16, 1977, p. E6.
New York Times Book Review. September 25, 1977, p. 12.
Time. CX, October 10, 1977, p. 113.

HOUSEBOAT DAYS

Author: John Ashbery (1927–   )
Publisher: The Viking Press (New York). 88 pp. $7.95
Type of work: Poetry

A major collection of verse by the distinguished contemporary American poet

With the publication of his twelfth volume of poetry, John Ashbery moves to the forefront of a select group of contemporary American poets. To be sure, his reputation as an artist of considerable technical resources, intelligence, and vigor has long been established. Nevertheless, among even his dedicated readers Ashbery has certainly been a puzzling master to classify. Sometimes critics have placed him with the so-called "New York School"—which is neither a school nor movement of poets as such, but more accurately a geographical grouping of selected writers with similar superficial characteristics. Among the characteristics which Ashbery shares with a number of these poets is his dazzling virtuosity; his calculated witty effects; his imitation in verse of certain modes of modern art, such as abstract-expressionism; and his attraction to "psychological" subjects. On the other hand, Ashbery is quite different from the New York poets in several significant ways: he is deeply in earnest, whereas the representative New York poets are conspicuously frivolous, often to the point of self-parody; and he is disturbing—a poet who cuts deeply to moral issues and wounds—rather than, like most of the New York group, genially entertaining.

What has confused some critics in their proper estimate of John Ashbery's achievement is the artist's seeming inconsistency. His work ranges from long, technically exacting verse of great distinction to minor experiments, clever pieces of self-indulgence. For example, his *Three Poems* (1972) is a volume of extended prose-poems that resemble personal essays. Similarly, *The Vermont Notebook* (1975) is, at least on the surface, a scrapbook of poetic trivia: catalogues of names and objects and pieces of satiric observation, with only brief passages of poetic intensity. Yet even these volumes, outwardly contrasting with a "serious" collection like the powerful *Self-Portrait in a Convex Mirror* (1975), hint at the poet's serious purposes. He appears to be working out a design, refining a language with which he can express his true voice as a poet.

With *Houseboat Days*, that voice is distinctly articulated. Ashbery no longer is experimenting to achieve effects; this method is sure, his communication direct—at least as direct as we are likely to expect from so complex and fertile an intelligence. The collection mostly of short or medium-length lyrics but including one long masterly dialogue, "Fantasia on 'The Nut-Brown Maid,' " demonstrates Ashbery's maturity as an artist. Not a single poem lacks significance; and at least a dozen are permanent contributions to American poetry.

This is not to say that Ashbery is a poet easily accessible to the multitudes. A tragedian, he is aware of human limitations, especially the limits of romantic dreams. The sharpest tension in his verse is the paradox between complete receptivity to emotion and the failure, ultimately, to be moved. Like Wordsworth of the "Intimations Ode" or Coleridge of "Dejection: An Ode"—both poignant expressions of the loss of sensitivity—Ashbery treats as his major subject the similar theme of passive perception that cannot flame into joy.

Among contemporary writers, Ashbery most nearly resembles Philip Larkin. Like that poet, he believes that stoic resignation is the best policy for an individual who senses his own limitations. If the modern world forbids him romantic joy, a sensible poet will not, to be sure, gnash his teeth in romantic agony. But Larkin is considerably more cheerful than Ashbery. Indeed, the English poet seems somewhat relieved to understand, in view of the fact that he lives in an unheroic age, that he has no obligations to carry the burdens of world-sorrow. Ashbery, on the other hand, is disheartened. His stoicism masks an agony of despair. "I don't set much stock in things," he writes in "Houseboat Days,"

> Beyond the weather and the certainties of living and dying:
> The rest is optional. To praise this, blame that,
> Leads one subtly away from the beginning, where
> We must stay, in motion.

The "beginning" he speaks about is existential: self-involvement. No matter how temptingly beautiful the external world may be for others, it is a sham for him. Like the disconsolate Prufrock, Ashbery's speaker reflects that

> The surge creates its own edge
> And you must proceed this way: mornings of assent,
> Indifferent noons leading to the ripple of the question
> Of late afternoon projected into evening.

But T. S. Eliot's speaker is suicidal—that is to say, purposeful, though toward destruction. Ashbery's speaker lacks the conviction even to advance in a purposeful fashion.

The ineluctable awareness that life is richly various—perhaps exciting—for other people, but is only an empty misery to the speaker is the center of Ashbery's tragic vision.

> To flash light
> Into the house within, its many chambers,
> Its memories and associations, upon its inscribed
> And pictured walls, argues enough that life is various.
> Life is beautiful.

Or so life may be to the fortunate. To Ashbery the cliché that "life is beautiful" is an unspeakable irony. In "The Wrong Kind of Insurance," his speaker, a high school teacher, comments wryly:

> All of our lives is a rebus
> Of little wooden animals painted shy,
> Terrific colors, magnificent and horrible,
> Close together.

Ashbery's vision of disaster overtakes him most terribly when he is most sensitively aware that others are, or ought to be, happy. Perception, therefore, colors circumstance. In "Daffy Duck in Hollywood" he writes:

> Not what we see but how we see it matters; all's
> Alike, the same, and we greet him who announces
> The change as we would greet the change itself.

Because "All life is but a figment," he believes that we must choose what really matters to us. In "The Lament upon the Waters," he says that "The problem isn't how to proceed/ But is one of being. . . ." Yet "being" is not the same as living. In the "Fantasia," a dialogue reminiscent of the manner (and intensity) of Yeats's final poetry, "He" says that

> Something has to be
> Living, not everyone can afford the luxury of
> Just being, not alive but being, at the center,
> The perfumed, patterned center.

To a poet who perceives but cannot fully feel joy, the distinction between "living" and "being" is a crucial one. In *Three Poems* he had earlier stated (in his usual elliptical fashion) the autobiographical problem. "All right. Then this new problem is the same one, and that is the problem: that our apathy always renews itself, drawing energy from the circumstances that fill our lives, but emotional happiness blooms only once, like an annual, leaving not even roots or foliage behind when its flower withers and dies." Similarly, in *The Vermont Notebook* he had expressed the "problem": "Nevertheless, there are a lot of people here who are sincerely in love with life and think they are on to something, and they may well be right. Even the dogs seem to know about it—." But the poet, with a soul dead to feeling, can only witness the joys that others—dogs, "old ladies," even the "horny grocer boy" who may be Pan in disguise—may feel.

Little wonder, therefore, that Ashbery's *persona* is tragic, self-involved, ironical. The "I" of the poems is curiously impersonal. Although the poems seem to be written for the conventional reader, they are actually expressions of self. The reader, an intruder, listens to an intense inner debate. Ashbery's verse is not really written for us; it is written for Ashbery. What appears at times to be self-indulgence on the part of the poet can be explained from the reader's quite natural misinterpretation of the customary poet-audience relationship. The reader expects the poet to reach out to him: whereas Ashbery has merely "sold" the poem as a public performance. The poem belongs to the poet.

Without understanding this special quality of self-involvement, a reader cannot fully appreciate *Houseboat Days*—nor, for that matter, the other volumes of poetry. The landscape of Ashbery's poetry is his mind. Although individual poems relate occasionally to time and place, he rarely focuses upon specifics that define either. One could scarcely learn from *Houseboat Days* what was happening in New York, in America, or the world in 1977. The world consists of

Ashbery's perceptions. As a result of this orientation, he is the least "public" of modern poets. He spares his readers the usual literary name-dropping and self-congratulation common in the work of other poets. Also he spares the reader autobiographical maunderings. For this reason, his poetry is remarkably impersonal (one might almost say sexless). Although individual poems may, in fact, be written for friends or in response to specific circumstances, the verses appear to be quite as dissociated from personalities as from matters of specific time and place. Instead, they concern the metaphysics of time and place. In the "Fantasia" he meditates:

> But if each act
> Is reflexive, concerned with itself on another level
> As well as with us, the strangers who live here,
> Can one advance one step further without sinking equally
> Far back into the past?

He has no answer, only more questions, doubts. "And who am I," he asks, "to speak this way, into a shoe? I know that evening is busy with lights, cars. . . . That the curve will include me if I must stand here." For the present, that thought is enough for Ashbery.

Yet the nagging question persists: Will the poet passively "stand here," content that the curve of meaningless existence includes him in its ambiance? In what direction will his poetry flow? One must be cautious in predicting the course of Ashbery's career. Certainly, *Houseboat Days* continues the reflective mood of *Self-Portrait in a Convex Mirror*. Even more meditative and philosophical, his recent volume explores the limits of perception, the dry reaches of sensation. With his extraordinary technical powers, Ashbery can write with seemingly effortless fluency, refining hard ideas until they gleam with a lustrous finish. Not since John Berryman has an American poet attempted on so bold a scale to think in song, to turn life into lyric. Like Berryman, Ashbery writes with spontaneous grace, an impressionist of despair; unlike Berryman, he avoids self-pity, self-laceration. Instead of composing elegies for his generation of poets, he graves modest elegies for his dying self. With each volume, the tragic tone intensifies:

> And we may be led, then, upward through more
> Powerful forms of poetry, past columns
> With peeling posters on them, to the country of indifference.
> Meanwhile if the swell diapasons, blooms
> Unhappily and too soon, the little people are nonetheless real.

Leslie B. Mittleman

Sources for Further Study

Book World. October 30, 1977, p. E1.
Booklist. LXXIV, October 15, 1977, p. 349.
Christian Science Monitor. LXIX, October 12, 1977, p. 22.
New York Times Book Review. November 13, 1977, p. 12.
Publisher's Weekly. CCXII, August 15, 1977, p. 57.

HOW TO SAVE YOUR OWN LIFE

Author: Erica Jong (1942–   )
Publisher: Holt, Rinehart and Winston (New York). 310 pp. $8.95
Type of work: Novel
Time: The 1970's
Locale: New York, Hollywood

A sequel to Fear of Flying *which traces the protagonist, Isadora Wing, as she flies west to Hollywood, migrates back to New York to leave her husband, and then soars westward again to a new lover*

> Principal characters:
> ISADORA WING, the heroine
> BENNETT WING, her husband
> JOSH ACE, her lover

In *Fear of Flying* Erica Jong created a female protagonist who tried to rid herself of the trappings of home, husband, and security when she ran off on a journey through Europe with Adrian Goodlove, a British, nonchalant, often physically impotent psychiatrist. Although Adrian and Bennett Wing, Isadora's husband, shared the same profession, Adrian was more exotic than her Chinese spouse because he was so unpredictable. After Adrian left her in Paris, however, Isadora returned to Bennett's hotel room to take a bath. *How to Save Your Own Life* begins three years after the events of this first novel. It is obvious that Isadora needed more than a physical cleansing, and, unfortunately, the prose and ideas offered in Erica Jong's new novel are tepid, like bathwater that has been sitting for too long.

As *A Chorus Line* is a Broadway musical about the problems that dancers face when trying out for such a production, so *How to Save Your Own Life* is a novel about the personal and professional difficulties that a famous novelist encounters when she achieves fame. In the middle of this novel she announces to her readers that her next book will be entitled *How to Save Your Own Life;* this is the book we are reading. Who has created these pages—Isadora Wing, Erica Jong, or the fictitious Candida Wong of the equally fictitious *Candida Confesses* that is related somehow to Isadora Wing of *Fear of Flying?* The identification crisis that Isadora Wing grapples with in the text when she tries to disassociate herself from Candida Wong presents serious difficulties for the reader who tries to discern who is the "amanuensis to the Zeitgeist?" Perhaps, Ms. Wong-Wing-Jong has revived the mixture of autobiography and fiction that was so popular during the 1920's in American literature. After all, F. Scott Fitzgerald purportedly lifted passages from Zelda's diary as well as excerpts from their lives when writing his short stories and novels; certainly, the same literary license should be available to a female writer of the 1970's. Besides, now someone might write a sympathetic biography of Mr. Jong's life.

In the novel, the problem of merging autobiography and fiction is one with which Isadora and Bennett must deal, but which they never really resolve. From a female writer's point of view, Bennett is exposed as a husband who can come to terms with his wife's spiritual and sexual undressing, but forbids her and threatens to leave her if she uses his past experiences in her new novel. Isadora resents and refuses to tolerate this attitude. She writes, "It is one thing to demythicize women, to expose one's self—but it is quite another to demythicize men, to expose one's husband. A man's hypocrisy is his castle." It is this hypocrisy and the hypocrisy of others that greatly disturb Isadora. Bennett is constantly being praised for putting up with a wife who has written a book that confirms that not only do heroines actually have sexual fantasies, but that they also confess them. The thought that he is now telling her what to write and what not to write about infuriates her artistic sensibilities. She is tired of the patient, humorless husband role that Bennett has chosen to play, and she desires to become the wife who threatens to embarrass him professionally.

Although Candida confessed openly, Bennett has waited several years to reveal his longterm love affair with Penny Prather. Isadora is personally hurt when she discovers that he could feel passion for another woman; however, when she realizes that Penny and Bennett had been using her study—where she wrote her first poems and stories—for their assignations, she is professionally outraged. Her anger is intensified by the realization that they had been reading her unpublished manuscripts after coitus. Such castles of hypocrisy must be torn down with waves of prose. And so she writes, and often writes well, even though Bennett warns her at the end of the novel as she leaves him that she can never do so again without him.

Personal and professional hostilities mesh and embitter Isadora, too, as she remembers Bennett insisted that she use his name at the end of her poems and on the cover of her novel. Isadora, before overcoming her fear of flying, was troubled by what name to use. At first, she signed her poems with her maiden name, "Isadora White," but Bennett was disturbed and disappointed and characteristically reacted as a Freudian psychiatrist would—such a choice obviously pointed to a preference of father over husband. Isadora, too, responded in a characteristic manner by feeling guilty. Now, though, with newly discovered fame and hostility, she resents his having his name emblazoned upon jacket covers and gilded editions, and being listed in *Who's Who*. Her name has been lost, while his has been made famous by her efforts.

Isadora's successful efforts and notoriety, however, are often troublesome to her. At a writing conference in Chicago, she dislikes being committed to obligatory publishing parties where she receives distasteful sexual propositions and tiresome requests to read manuscripts written by some stranger's nephew. Although she can remember when she thought of editors and publishers as demigods, she is not ready for this kind of acceptance. Alone in her hotel room, she is physically, mentally, and emotionally frustrated. Isadora masturbates and relieves one of her anxieties, but two others remain. While she lies in bed, she imagines that a series of critics, like a chorus in a Greek play, enter her room and pronounce her work "dead." However, it is her heart, not her mind, that seeks flight. She feels as if she is dying, and, after some hesitation, places a call to Bennett. This interruption of his sleep annoys him, and he cryptically tells her to write a poem.

The professional psychiatrist gives the advice of a professional writer, while Isadora, the professional writer, acts as a psychiatrist to the authors of fan letters that resemble those of a "Miss Lonelyhearts" column. One such letter is included in the novel, complete with mental and written replies. What Isadora thinks, in this case, is not what she writes. The interchanging of roles between Isadora and Bennett is like the streamers of a mismanaged Maypole: they keep passing one another while weaving a web of misunderstanding in the rite of marriage.

Like Johann and Marianne in Bergman's *Scenes from a Marriage,* Isadora and Bennett have stopped speaking the same language. Their conversations are filled with deception and lies. Since the reader is allowed to see what Isadora is actually thinking and can with some imagination assume what Bennett is thinking, an end to this relationship is welcomed, but it is very slow in coming. First, the female protagonist feels drawn to recount the details and circumstances surrounding Bennett's affair with Penny. The living conditions in an Army camp in Germany during the late 1960's, the disastrous skiing trip that resulted in Isadora's breaking her leg, and her frequent conversations with a male friend all help Isadora to put together the pieces of a past that make her present seem less fragmented, yet neither complete nor solidified.

Before she plunges herself into the past, she attempts to formulate a picture of herself through the network of her friends. To avoid seeing Bennett, she visits with all seven of them. Through these characters, the reader is given some glimpses into Isadora's past self and present personal problems. Gretchen Kendall, a feminist lawyer, tells her that she's heard this "I'm leaving Bennett" routine before and encourages her this time to do so; Hope Lowell, her fairy godmother and muse, says the same thing—only more poetically (what else would you expect from a muse?)—and reaffirms the beauty of love; Abigail Schwartz, her shrink, helps Isadora to uncover past repressions; Jeffrey Rudner, a doctor and her lover, offers her sexual gratification; Jeffrey Roberts, a writer for cosmetic advertisements, offers the same on a permanent basis; Holly, an artist and cultivator of ferns, tells her to live and love because she is a mammal, not a fern; and, Michael Cosman, a general practitioner from Great Neck, helps her to become hysterical and then advises her to return after she is more rational. Isadora states that writing takes an enormous amount of energy. How can she have any left after all these conversations, all of which belabor the issue of her leaving Bennett?

Sprinkled throughout the pages that explore Isadora's hesitation about leaving Bennett are explicit passages of their sexual encounters; however, none are as detailed nor as sensual as the excerpts which describe her lesbian affair with Rosanna Howard before her trip to Hollywood or her participation in an orgy at Rosanna's home after her journey to the Coast. To Isadora, lesbianism is exciting, sexually fulfilling, but distasteful. The orgy helps her to link up with anyone—except Bennett. Both provide her with brand new experiences in her life that now excludes Bennett.

Sandwiched in between these encounters is a *bona fide* love affair. In Hollywood, Isadora meets and loves Josh Ace, a twenty-six-year-old bearded screenwriter. Isadora and Josh speak the same language, and often they stay up all night doing so. He loves her writing and does not want to become a mere character in her next novel. Josh desires her life and gets it.

Something peculiar happens to Isadora's observations in this celluloid area of Hollywood. The castles of hypocrisy are now real ones, but she does not desire to destroy any of them. She becomes extremely visual and studies outward appearances like the eye of a camera. Colors, textures, sizes, and shapes assume an unaccustomed importance. Palm trees, pink hotels, big cars, parties, drugs, Jacuzzis, posh apartments, mansions, and Olympic-size swimming pools are the accoutrements that accompany this change about people and things. Feminism is metamorphosed into femininity, as even the act of coitus has lost its former significance. In addition, she is duped by a slick female producer who wants to make a film of *Candida Confesses.* Beliefs and artistic sensibilities, which were once of supreme importance, become in California quite meaningless. So, when she returns to New York on business she writes to Josh and ultimately leaves Bennett.

How to Save Your Own Life, then, is anything but a novel about how to do so. Jeannie Morton, Isadora's friend who commits suicide the summer before the protagonist's journey to California, advises her to live. Yet, Isadora relies more on other people's advice, security, and chance meetings than she does upon herself in her how-to-do-it-yourself manual. She does not leave Bennett until she is reassured of Josh's love, and in this new affair, she succumbs to the power of the male-dominated relationship. She moves to Hollywood to join her lover and previously mailed poems, which are included in this text. Although passages from this novel are as powerful as those found in her first, it seems that Isadora Wing has conquered her fear of flying, but is now afraid to tread alone on the ground.

Kathryn Flaris

Sources for Further Study

Atlantic. CCXXXIX, April, 1977, p. 92.

Best Sellers. XXXVII, June, 1977, p. 70.

Listener. XCVII, May 12, 1977, p. 634.

National Review. XXIX, April 29, 1977, p. 498.

New Republic. CLXXVI, March 19, 1977, p. 34.

New York Review of Books. XXIV, April 28, 1977, p. 6.

Newsweek. LIII, April 4, 1977, p. 140.

Saturday Review. IV, April 30, 1977, p. 27.

Times Literary Supplement. May 6, 1977, p. 545.

HUGO BLACK AND THE JUDICIAL REVOLUTION

Author: Gerald T. Dunne
Publisher: Simon and Schuster (New York). Illustrated. 492 pp. $12.50
Type of work: Biography
Time: 1886–1971
Locale: Clay County and Birmingham, Alabama; Washington, D.C.

A biography which illuminates Hugo L. Black's influential personality while it stresses his part in altering the role of the Supreme Court and the doctrines of constitutional law

Principal personages:
> HUGO LA FAYETTE BLACK, United States Senator from Alabama and
> Justice of the Supreme Court of the United States
> FRANKLIN D. ROOSEVELT, President of the United States
> WILLIAM O. DOUGLAS,
> FELIX FRANKFURTER, and
> ROBERT H. JACKSON, Justices of the Supreme Court
> EARL WARREN, Chief Justice of the Supreme Court

Justice Oliver Wendell Holmes is reported to have attributed much of John Marshall's greatness to the fact that he was *there*—present in the early shaping years. It is also true of Marshall, Holmes himself, and a number of other notable justices that they were there for a long time. The serious-minded ought not assess such statements too lightly, but they are justified in noting other characteristic qualities of great justices, such as intellectual power and clarity; the courage of conviction; an instinct for essentials; and persuasiveness with brethren of the Court, the bar, and the public.

By such criteria, Hugo Black belongs in the category of influential judges, and high on the list. Gerald Dunne's account uses still another basis to judge Black's importance: Black as Justice was participant, protagonist, and sometimes driving force in great changes in the thinking of the Supreme Court.

One of the virtues of Dunne's account is his emphasis on the complexity of and the contradictions in Black's character. In so much writing about the Court, its work, and its divisions, justices are forced into categories—liberal or conservative, activist or defender of the status quo—and it is a matter of relief, even rejoicing, to find a biographer who understands that paradoxical, shifting human qualities cannot be thus constricted. Black the man, not just Black the Justice, is Dunne's subject, and the paradoxes and contradictions abound.

By inference rather than explicit statement, Dunne links Black's character to his background and development. Born in the hill country of Clay County to a storekeeping father and given a strict Baptist upbringing by a family very concerned about education, Black earned a law degree at twenty, and built a career in Birmingham as a lawyer for unions and the poor, a prosecutor, and a police-court judge. Ambition, intelligence, and combativeness were notable traits in his personality; so was a strain of thought and behavior most easily classed as Populist. Ambition and demagoguery, Dunne suggests, were not absent, but they were not the whole story.

The climax of Black's early career was election to the United States Senate, after a campaign marked by energy, skill with publicity, and appeal to the poor and unprivileged. His newspaper advertisements, in an obvious thrust at the lists of notables sponsoring opponents, read "Paid for by himself." Black's election was also important for an episode that was later to create great difficulty and controversy in his career. The Ku Klux Klan was a power in Alabama politics, and Hugo Black, for whatever reasons, joined; he resigned in time for the Senate campaign, but the resignation (accusers could say) reads like a formality, and he unquestioningly had Klan support.

The new Senator made something of a reputation as a radical, and began a course of self-education. He also faced, in 1928, a severe test for a politician in officially dry, Protestant, Klannish Alabama: the nomination of Alfred E. Smith of New York, an urban Catholic. Black's Senate colleague, J. Thomas Heflin, probably the most notorious of anti-Catholic prominent politicians, left the party. Black formally endorsed Smith; but he had not attended the convention that nominated him, and he remained quiet through the whole campaign, as Dunne emphasizes.

The significant Senate career of Hugo Black began with the Depression and with the election of Franklin Roosevelt and a Democratic Senate and House. Black's reelection in Alabama gave him a new position in the Senate; his main attention was on the recovery and reform of the crippled economy. He sponsored labor bills and he joined with George Norris in the battle for the Tennessee Valley Authority—a continuation of an old feud with Alabama Power. But his notable success, according to Dunne, was not legislative, but investigatory.

In fact, Black's conduct of Senate inquiries is, with the Klan episode, a major thread in Dunne's outline of his subject's career. Certainly, it gave Black his first national reputation. Chairing a committee investigation of public utilities, he displayed all the prosecutor's skill in finding the weaknesses in the testimony of hostile or reluctant witnesses, and revealing their confusions and contradictions. Witnesses and their friends complained of browbeating, and many people questioned the legality of Black's methods in acquiring private papers, and subpoenaing whole categories of telegrams from Western Union.

Dunne also points out that, if the ostensible purpose of the inquiries was legislative—writing laws to prevent repetition of the abuses of the 1920's—its main result, and quite possibly Black's objective, was to focus public attention on the abuses, and direct public anger against the utility magnates, lobbyists, and their political servants whom he accused of perpetrating them. For this, not the judicial or the legislative but, rather, the prosecutor's role was required. Even more, says Dunne, what it required was skill in reaching public opinion—in other words, using the media, which in the 1930's meant to some extent radio and motion pictures, but mainly the newspaper and magazine press. This skill, Dunne argues, Black had in a high degree—in fact, next to the master himself, Roosevelt. A certain cynicism goes with this—Dunne more than once quotes

Chairman Black to the press outside the hearing room, "Come on, boys; the show's going to start."

The conduct of the utility hearings made Black known and, in the expected circles, hated. It also made him one of the most reliable and outspoken New Dealers. Dunne even speculates on his chances for the 1940 Democratic nomination, at least for the vice-presidency. In Roosevelt's word, that one is "iffy," but it suggests something of Black's record and repute, and helps explain the shock-effect among the opponents of the New Deal when Roosevelt gave his first Supreme Court appointment to Black, and in circumstances embittered by the recent ill-fated proposal to "pack" or "reform" the Court. However, the tremors were nothing compared to the revelation, after Senate confirmation, and after Black had privately taken the oath, of his past membership in the Ku Klux Klan. Dunne tells the story early, out of chronological order, but effectively, and again stresses Black's talent for using the media, in his account of the radio address in which Black defended himself, and, apparently, closed his side of the controversy.

The real story of Hugo Black, and the meat of Dunne's book, begins here. Justice Black left much more of a mark on the nation than Senator Black, and his judicial career was even more subject to controversy than his senatorial one. There were arguments over constitutional law, and over the policies the law inhibits or permits; there were (at least in the gossip columns) personal antipathies and conflicting ambitions among the "brethren" (as the justices call one another); there was the sometimes underlying and frequently dominating issue of the stance and function of the Court itself. In other words, Black was at the center of what Dunne rightly calls a judicial revolution. Its exact nature, and its intertwining with the forces suggested above, and still others, is examined. And the author is too careful, too aware of the complexity of his subject, to oversimplify or generalize.

In the 1920's and 1930's, the Supreme Court had been accused of substituting its judgment of policy for that of elected legislatures. This was especially the case in the use of the Fourteenth Amendment to limit the states' power to regulate business and industry, and to protect both property and contract. The dissents of Holmes and Stone, particularly, accused the majority of reading their social and economic preconceptions into the Constitution. The "Roosevelt Court," whose reconstitution began with the Black appointment, reversed that trend. Though some decisions of the term preceding began the reversal, no longer was New Deal legislation constantly running the risk of unconstitutionality. Many of the same commentators and justices, however, who had condemned the use (or abuse) of the Fourteenth Amendment in economic matters, and who had called for self-restraint by the Court, had also wanted a more active Court in defense of individual rights and liberties.

Here were great problems for the Roosevelt Court, which were to be inherited by the Warren Court of the 1950's as well. The legal problem, which Dunne explicates by cases rather than abstract exposition, is twofold. First, to what extent can the Court make the Bill of Rights bind the national government? The issues are not only of First Amendment freedoms of speech and religion, but of procedural rights, and protection from self-incrimination, search and seizure, and the like. Here Black's position was emphatic, and many thought extreme: he read the Constitution literally. The second issue concerns the states. Traditional doctrine held that the Bill of Rights bound the Congress, not the states, and that the Fourteenth Amendment had not fundamentally changed the rule. Black and others began to hold the "incorporation" theory—that the Fourteenth Amendment made the other amendments binding also on the states.

In addition to a full examination of Black's judicial record, Dunne relates the clashes of principle and of personality on the bench and in chambers that Black had with other justices, notably Robert Jackson and Felix Frankfurter. The charges leveled against Black and the majority of the Court were similar to those brought by earlier critics of the "conservative" Court: the justices were making law and policy, not judging; they were writing sociological, not constitutional, opinions; they were usurping the place of the legislatures; they were moving into a political thicket. Throughout the public issues, however, Dunne's focus is always on Black. The picture he paints is of a man aggressive in the Senate and in judicial argument, as well as on the tennis court, yet noted for charm and kindliness; acclaimed by the liberals, yet old-fashioned in his patriotism and even more in his unsophisticated, literal view of the Constitution.

Hugo Black and the Judicial Revolution is not a book only for scholars; Dunne's remarkable achievement is that his interpretation, for all its insistence on complexity, is clear. Any layman with a reasonable knowledge of recent history and constitutional government will benefit from this lucid and intelligent account.

George J. Fleming

Sources for Further Study

Choice. XIV, November, 1977, p. 1277.
Commonweal. CIV, August 19, 1977, p. 537.
Harvard Law Review. XC, June, 1977, p. 1733.
New Leader. LX, August 1, 1977, p. 17.

THE HUMAN SITUATION
Lectures at Santa Barbara, 1959

Author: Aldous Huxley (1894–1963)
Edited by Piero Ferrucci
Publisher: Harper & Row Publishers (New York). 261 pp. $10.00
Type of work: Essays
Time: The twentieth century

A series of lectures which examines the planet on which we live and our place in the ecology as well as man's relationship to his society

Aldous Huxley was one of the great minds and writers of the twentieth century. A Britisher educated at Eton and Oxford, he turned to literature in his twenties, becoming internationally known as a novelist. Although his work as a novelist still tends to overshadow his other writings, he was also the author of essays, biography, drama, poetry, and short stories. Prior to World War II he migrated to the United States, where he lived until his death. According to his editor, Piero Ferrucci, Huxley delivered the present series of lectures, or ones very like them, at a number of institutions, including the Massachusetts Institute of Technology and the Menninger Foundation. The editor reports that he chose the series delivered at Santa Barbara for the University of California because that series was the most comprehensive.

This series of essays includes sixteen of the original seventeen; the editor omitted the eighth lecture, entitled "The Future Is in Our Hands," because it was but a summary of the preceding ones. Of these lectures Huxley wrote, early in January, 1959, to Matthew Huxley, that he intended beginning with the biological foundations of the human situation, such as the state of our planet, population problems, and the relationship of heredity to environment. He said he would then proceed to treat of techniques in every field of human endeavor and how such activity affected the social and political order. Finally, as he put it, he would discuss the individual human being and his potentialities. Of the task he had undertaken Huxley commented, "It is an impossibly large project—but worth undertaking even inadequately, as an antidote to academic specialization and fragmentation." Few persons living in the twentieth century could do what Huxley did in these essays, for he called upon a wide-ranging experience and knowledge to help his readers better understand the problems human beings share with one another. Although eighteen years elapsed from the delivery of the lectures by Aldous Huxley to their publication in 1977, they remain surprisingly adequate and up-to-date; pieces of information contained within them have become outdated, but the essays themselves remain remarkably pertinent for their readers. Huxley set out to build bridges between art and science, between objectively observed facts and immediate experience, and between morals and scientific appraisals; he styled himself, indeed, *pontifex,* or bridge-builder. He believed that the man of letters can perform a valuable function by bringing together a great many subjects, showing the relationships among them. Our educations, as much now as when he spoke, lead us to keep separate what we learn from our immediate experience.

Before such interests were as popular as they are today, Aldous Huxley began his series of lectures by looking at the relationships between mankind and our native planet. In "Man and His Planet," Huxley ranges through some of the effects man has had on our environment, some of them good, but many of them destructive. He notes that we have deforested huge areas of the world in the interests of agriculture, only to have faulty agricultural practices ruin the soil over the centuries. He reminds us that the forests of Europe, which once covered most of the continent, were also devoured for such reasons as building houses, heating buildings, constructing ships, making glass, and smelting metal ores. What we do and have been doing, he rightly tells us, makes a gloomy picture. We need, he suggests, to see the use of the environment in more than a purely practical way, to look at it from a moral and aesthetic stance—as he puts it, "with a philosophical trend in our mind." In "More Nature in Art," the next essay in the series, he states that we have the necessary information and knowledge to prevent further ecological damage, even to repair much past damage, but that there is a gap between what can be done and the likelihood of its being done, for changes in our treatment of our world involve hundreds of millions of people. New ideas must be communicated to those people and, even more difficult, they must be persuaded to adopt ideas and methods which, if imposing temporary hardship, insure long-term benefits. Committed as we are in Western civilization to education, persuasion, and democratic methods, we nevertheless find the task of changing people's ways more difficult than if we adopt coercion. Huxley makes the interesting and unusual point that our art could help, if artists working in all media returned to representational modes from their present use of abstract forms. Such a realistic art, combined with a good ethic and a good philosophy, would, he suggests, greatly enhance our chances of salvaging, even improving, our planet.

Of all the essays in this present collection, perhaps "The Population Explosion" will seem most relevant two decades after it was written, if for no other reason than that its topic has been one which has had considerable public attention. But the chief interest in this essay ought to be on what Huxley says about the relation of population to human well-being and human values in general. Population figures are for most persons difficult to understand fully; the meaning of some of Huxley's examples may escape both our understandings and our imaginations—such examples as that in early Paleolithic times the total human population on earth was probably less than twenty million, or that in the fifteenth century there were fewer than a million Indians in North America east of the Rocky Mountains. Even such a recent change as the more-than-fifty-percent increase of the population of the United States since 1940 is a difficult concept to understand, even among people old enough to have experienced and observed the change. But the real thrust of Huxley's essay is not statistical: he asks first of all what the practical alternatives are. He suggests that one choice is to let nature solve the problem, through starvation, disease, and warfare. Another choice is to increase industrial and agricultural production, but it appears already that we must collectively work harder to stay where we are. His third alternative is to increase production while at the same time trying to reestablish the balance between birth and death rates by intelligent and humane methods. Huxley understands the difficulties, which he terms colossal, in limiting population, for controlling the birth rate is a problem involving medicine, chemistry, biochemistry, physiology, sociology, psychology, theology, and education. One specific problem, he tells us, is that some worldwide, or at least regional, agreements on birth control will be necessary for success, but that political leaders do not think in biological terms. Furthermore, the rapid population increase makes educating people and raising the material standard of life almost impossible.

When Huxley moves to looking at the individual human being, he becomes most interesting, for he espouses causes which he knows have not found favor in many quarters. His positions sometimes run counter to ideas which have become institutionalized, so that his positions threaten vested interests. For example, Huxley takes to task the behavioral psychologists, including J. B. Watson and B. F. Skinner, pointing out that they have clearly tended to eliminate hereditary factors as influences on human behavior, without regard for what geneticists have proved to be true. Huxley also suggests that modern psychiatry has neglected the genetic influence on mankind because its practitioners and theorists have simply paid no attention to the human body. Huxley's conclusion is that to make the most of the genetic variability which exists in humankind we must improve the environment, but that we can disregard genetics only if we are willing to imperil our values. He develops a monistic view which insists on bringing mind and body together, not separating them, as philosophers and theologians through the ages often have done.

The lectures contained in *The Human Situation* were given in two groups. In the group delivered in the spring of 1959, Huxley tried to look at the future of the world, suggesting that the most prominent view of the world is one of tempered optimism, but that nuclear weapons, especially the hydrogen bomb, have reintroduced the old idea that the world could end abruptly and catastrophically. Following the lead of Bertrand Russell, Huxley looks at three short-term possibilities. One is nuclear war which eliminates mankind; the second, nuclear war leading to a return to barbarism because of the breakdown of the complicated industrial and communications systems; the third, the creation of a single world state. While Huxley sees the third as the only desirable alternative, he recognizes that there are many vested interests which militate against its happening by any democratic means. But for the short-term in our future Huxley says he hopes for more attention to basic scientific research, for he stoutly believes that we stand on the threshold of profound discoveries about our human nature and external nature.

In the lectures delivered later, in the autumn of 1959, Huxley turned from the world as a whole to looking at individual human potentialities. He believed it important that we recognize the profound difference between the generalizations we can make about societies and the generalizations we can make about individuals. In "The Individual Life of Man," Huxley tries to prove that the single human being's life lies quite largely outside the history of a given time, outside the activities which historians later see as significant. Huxley cites Vasili Rozanov's view of private life: "picking one's nose and looking at the sunset." Huxley calls this a beautiful definition, given the interpretation that private life consists in enjoying one's own physiological reactions and one's own aesthetic and inspirational reactions. One result of our focus on private life, he insists, is that we do not experience progress subjectively, although we may observe it, either at firsthand or through our reading. A second result of the focus on private life is that we interpret the world in terms of the individual's life, which is nonprogressive; old people going down find it at least difficult to see the world around them as going up.

In the latter lectures of the series which deal with the individual human being it is a different Huxley speaking from the one in the earlier lectures, or at least a different Huxley from the one known to readers of his novels and other earlier work. In the latter lectures he turns, in part, from science to mysticism, from observation to vision. Over and over, the reader sees him trying to unite the realm of common sense with the realm of vision. In the essay entitled "The Ego," the author reviews conceptions of mankind from Homer to the present, and proposes that our physical constitution equals our unconscious, that we are the kinds of individuals we are because of our very organisms. For the most part, he bases this view on his understanding of William H. Sheldon's work in describing human beings psychologically, as well as physiologically, in terms of their being combinations of three physical types: the endomorph, the mesomorph, and the ectomorph.

So, too, in "The Unconscious," Huxley takes an uncommon view. He deplores the refusal of openminded scientific people to consider such phenomena as telepathy, clairvoyance, and precognition. He insists that we must learn to think in terms of parapsychology, even though, as he puts it, in academic circles parapsychology is regarded as a kind of intellectual pornography. Huxley also espouses a positive view of visions in the "Natural History of Visions." He examines the induction of visions by isolation, hunger, and drugs, and speaks with great sympathy of inducing visions by changes in body chemistry through the use of drugs. Rather than seeing such use of drugs, whether natural or synthetic, as distortions of the human organism, he praises the distortions as mind-expanding and transcendent. Further, in his final lecture he speaks glowingly about using drugs to enable persons to achieve their potentialities in the material world as well as in a world of visions. He hopes that pharmacological means can be found to increase human efficiency and endurance, to give psychic energy, and to enable us to endure sustained tension. It was this interest in consciousness-expanding techniques which gave Huxley a new career and new fame late in life, as an exponent of psychosynthesis.

Gordon W. Clarke

Sources for Further Study

Booklist. LXXIV, September 15, 1977, p. 114.

Christian Science Monitor. LXIX, November 30, 1977, p. 29.

Kirkus Reviews. XLV, July 1, 1977, p. 708.

Library Journal. CII, August, 1977, p. 1648.

National Review. XXIX, September 2, 1977, p. 1000.

Publisher's Weekly. CXII, July 25, 1977, p. 61.

I HEARD MY SISTER SPEAK MY NAME

Author: Thomas Savage (1915–   )
Publisher: Little, Brown and Company (Boston). 242 pp. $8.95
Type of work: Novel
Time: The present, with flashbacks
Locale: Crow Point, Maine; Seattle, Washington

A genealogical tracing of a family through four generations, culminating in the reunion of brother and sister

> *Principal characters:*
> TOM BURTON, a successful novelist
> AMY McKINNEY NOFZINGER, his sister adopted at birth by the McKinneys
> ELIZABETH (BETH) SWERINGEN BURTON, his mother
> EMMA SWERINGEN, THE SHEEP QUEEN, his grandmother

Tom Burton, the central character of Thomas Savage's tenth novel, is patterned very closely on the author. They are the same age, and both are novelists with the same publisher; their immediate families are also similar. Whether the rest of the novel is factual is not relevant, for Savage writes convincingly of the forebears of the fictional Tom Burton. In a novel whose title gives away its punch line as this one does, it is difficult to maintain suspense, but the intricate weaving of the many strands of the story keeps the reader wondering how the various parts will ultimately fit together. The book achieves its intrigue through the author's juggling of several storylines, switching from one time and locale to another, without supplying the necessary connections until the pieces begin falling into place by themselves. Gradually all coalesces at the end.

The book opens with a description of Tom Burton and his family in their home at Crow Point, on the Maine coast. We learn of Tom's career as a novelist and of his novelist wife and grown children. We also get a hint of his family heritage from his comments that his aunts could not understand why he would leave the Rocky Mountains, and that he wanted to get as far as he could from the Montana ranch of his youth where his "beautiful, angel mother" was so unhappy. This idyllic introduction is abruptly dropped as the next chapter begins the apparently unrelated episode of a young twenty-two-year-old mother giving up her newborn child in the year 1912. This child turns out to be Amy McKinney.

Amy McKinney's life is then related in detail. She is adopted by the McKinneys to replace their own son who had been killed by being thrown from a horse. The McKinneys were good, ordinary, uninspired people. Amy's life is only briefly disturbed when a malicious child acquaintance mentions that she is an adopted child. But Amy quickly recovers from the shock and accepts her foster mother's reassurances. After the death of her adoptive parents she goes through a rather loveless and sterile marriage with Philip Nofzinger, followed by a very amicable divorce.

Throughout his description of Amy's life, Savage's keen sense of family ties is evident. That is, Amy's whole existence, though not marred by any overt tragedy, comes across as a very dull, uninspiring, almost emotionless affair. She feels no real sense of belonging to a family, and since she has no siblings, the death of her parents ends any sense of belonging. Her cousins feel that the family's prized silverware should go to real family rather than to the adopted outsider. Savage is guilty of stacking the cards against Amy. The McKinneys are not consciously comparing Amy to their own lost child and thus depriving her of a normal childhood; they are giving her the best of which they are capable. They are simply a stodgy couple who keep to themselves and would rear any child to be dull and emotionally deprived.

It is only after her divorce that Amy seriously thinks of the note her father had left in his safe deposit box for her. Mr. McKinney had believed in the right of an adopted child to learn of her real parents despite the laws to the contrary, and being a lawyer he had had the wherewithal to procure the name her mother had signed on the release papers. With the help of a lawyer Amy discovers the real names of her mother and father, and after a fruitless search for her father (she was directed to a deceased derelict with a similar name), she is apparently reconciled to never discovering who her real parents are. With this the story of Amy gives way to a new set of characters.

The second section of the book is set in the small, dying mining town of Jeff Davis Gulch where one of the last remaining prospectors, George Sweringen, discovers gold. George and his family are dropped while the narration picks up Emma Russell, who "quite a long time ago" left Illinois for Idaho Territory to teach school. In Idaho, the plain but highly intelligent Emma marries Thomas Sweringen, the son of George, who had invested his gold in property and had begun a dynasty. The major portion of the book deals with Emma, whose shrewdness and luck in business results in her increasing the family's holdings and becoming known as the Sheep Queen. All through the relation of these events the reader is kept guessing what each segment of the story has to do with the others; and unless he is keeping track of the names and the confusing chronology of events, he will not see the connection. It is part of Savage's technique to give clues by reference to historical events such as the inaugural date of Benjamin Harrison and the date on which Idaho became a territory; and the reader must keep track of the complex time sequence.

The Sheep Queen and her family, especially her daughter, Elizabeth, are lovingly and minutely described. Elizabeth is much more attractive than her mother; she is her father's favorite child and is given the best education possible. When the story is picked up, she is promised to a young man of good family whom she does not love. Here, family ties are strained. Her father sympathizes with her lack of love for her fiancé, but her mother is more concerned with amassing new family ties as if they were another piece of property. This is the only lapse the family suffers. In years to come the family's members go through many divorces, possibly because they find their own company so much better than that of anyone else. Through all, the family sticks together. Their clannishness extends to a kind of ancestor veneration because "We felt our ancestors were worth worshipping."

In this case Elizabeth disappoints her mother by forsaking her fiancé for the traveling salesman, Ben Burton. At this point, the names and events start falling into place. These are the names Amy learned of as being her parents. Yet, there is the improbability of a married couple giving up a firstborn child for adoption and keeping even the existence of such a child a closely held secret within a family that is so close.

Back in the present time, Amy's interest in her ancestors is reawakened and she gets in contact with Tom Burton's aunt expressing her belief that she is the daughter of Beth Sweringen Burton. Knowing as much as he does about his ancestry, Tom Burton of course denies the possibility. How could his mother have had a child and no one of the close-knit family known of it? Then, like a detective story gradually revealing one clue, one hazy memory of the past after another, the pieces start to fit together.

Tom's mother, Beth, who had been resigned to marry the young man of her mother's choice, decided instead to run off with the traveling salesman whom she married. Tom discovers that his mother and father, Ben Burton, were married at the time Amy was born, adding to the improbability of Amy's being an abandoned sister of his. It is impossible for him to accept that his mother could have given up a legitimate child. Illegitimacy is the only reason he can think of for a mother to give up her child, and he could not imagine his own mother could have been guilty of such a transgression. Savage cleverly depicts Tom's gradual acceptance of the fact that Amy may be the daughter of his "no good" father and another woman; he 'has come to believe his family's description of his father who had divorced his mother when he was two years old. His one meeting with his real father had convinced him of Ben's unreliability and phoniness. So, he is ready to accept that Amy may be his half-sister, but nothing yet can convince him they have the same mother, for Beth had signed a fictitious name to the release.

In a long, rambling letter to Amy after he has pieced things together, Tom Burton recounts the death of his mother ten years earlier. He relates that his grandfather had outlived the Sheep Queen as well as Beth, and then he states, "But there was an earlier death that accounted for the sadness that never left my mother's face even at the end." That death was of the Sheep Queen's favorite, her son Tom-Dick, who was her hope for the future of the Sweringen family. He died while his sister Beth was pregnant, and a few weeks later Beth gave birth to her first child, a girl. And because that child was a girl, Tom Burton says, his mother gave her up "to show her mother a woman could survive a loss greater than her own, greater because it was voluntary." Although this solution is highly improbable, it is due to Savage's skill as a writer that he manages to bring it off. He never even brings up the question of how Ben Burton would have taken to his wife's sacrifice; it is unlikely that a father would stand idly by and allow his flesh and blood to be given up. That the birth could have been kept secret from him as it was from Beth's sisters is more unreasonable for the reader to accept.

This highly improbable sequence of events is explained by the family's closeness. But, the point of the sacrifice seems lost if no one in the family was aware of it. (Beth's sister vaguely recalls a letter referring to a miscarriage.) If the family is so close that one member would sacrifice so much, it is small wonder that the Sweringen family is so riddled by divorce. Besides, the child itself is part of that family, and Savage does not explain how such a callous act can be reconciled in a family of such strong instincts.

Another improbability is the way Savage handles the last section of the book. When all the pieces to the puzzle have fallen into place for him, Tom Burton does not telephone as the average person would; instead he writes a letter to Amy. And this twenty-six-page letter reads more like a novel than a letter, holding off the crucial revelation until the very end, making it unlikely that the recipient would very easily follow all the details since she has not been privy to all that has gone before in the book. Yet, in spite of these minor lapses, the book succeeds in keeping the reader entertained and interested until the very end. The most serious drawback of the novel is the tremendous demand it places at times on our credulity.

Roger A. Geimer

Sources for Further Study

Book World. October 30, 1977, p. E8.

Kirkus Reviews. XLV, August 1, 1977, p. 805.

Library Journal. CII, November 15, 1977, p. 2364.

New York Times Book Review. November 13, 1977, p. 26.

Publisher's Weekly. CXII, August 8, 1977, p. 64.

West Coast Review of Books. III, November, 1977, p. 30.

THE ICE AGE

Author: Margaret Drabble (1930–   )
Publisher: Alfred A. Knopf (New York). 295 pp. $8.95
Type of work: Novel
Time: The present
Locale: England and Wallacia (a fictional Balkan country)

A novel whose characters lead lives disrupted by catastrophes common to our time, and thus display the problems of an iced-over England

> *Principal characters:*
> ANTHONY KEATING, a property developer
> ALISON MURRAY, his mistress
> MOLLY, Alison's ten-year-old, brain-damaged daughter
> JANE, Alison's nineteen-year-old daughter
> LEN WINCOBANK, a former property developer, now in jail
> MAUREEN KIRBY, his mistress
> GILES PETERS, Keating's partner
> KITTY FRIEDMANN, a friend of Anthony and Alison

Events associated with the characters of Margaret Drabble's latest novel when listed off seem bizarre: a mother has borne one brain-damaged child and another, now a teen-ager, who has been imprisoned in a Balkan country behind the Iron Curtain; a woman has had her foot blown off by an I.R.A. bomb in a London restaurant; a property developer has been imprisoned on fraud charges; a fairly young television executive turned property speculator has both lost his fortune and suffered a heart attack. But as the novel develops, one sees that their stories are meant to appear not freakish but representative—representative, that is, of the troubles that are afflicting British citizens and, in fact, Britain itself. Most of the exciting events have happened just before the novel begins, moreover, so that it is mainly concerned with a time of passivity and waiting; the characters are, one might say, iced in.

Like her last novel, *Realms of Gold,* Margaret Drabble's book focuses chiefly on two lovers in midlife but intertwines their story with a number of others. It is much more obvious in this novel than in the previous one, however, that the characters are types chosen to illustrate contemporary English life and the vicissitudes peculiar to it. Fortunately, Drabble's ability to develop believable and sympathetic characters and to write well in a lowkey, finely ironic style prevents the book from being boringly schematic. Moreover, her inveterate cheerfulness keeps *The Ice Age* from becoming a gloomy catalog of disasters.

Yet such a catalog may be inferred from the characterizations, events, and commentary of the novel. London is a "sinking ship," spilling over with people, garbage, and motor vehicles. Masses of concrete buildings stand empty, having proved not to be what anyone wanted to live in or rent for offices; in fact, belief in growth as an ideal to strive for has also been a casualty of the slump. No ideal or vision has replaced this belief; there is instead fear and despondency, disgust with corruption, and lack of confidence. Economically there is a slump, yet inflation accompanies recession. There is random terrorism: death can strike anywhere at any harmless, goodhearted person. Accidents, it seems, are becoming more frequent and more intense. Of course there are physical ills characteristic of our time: the heart attack that strikes a young businessman; cerebral palsy; breast cancer. Also, cracks and decay appear in domestic as well as public life: children reject old traditions, taking to drugs and easy sex; wives are dissatisfied, and both husbands and wives are unfaithful; divorces are common, so common that some people have several. Homosexuality surfaces. God is out of date, and mysterious influences from outer space are in. Intellectually there is a change, too: a classicist, committed to preserving the tradition of scholarship, finds that students are no longer interested and that in the end he has lost interest himself both in classics and in composing poetry; like a dryad in a myth he seems to have been changed into a tree.

As the list shows, Drabble has attempted to be impressive but not comprehensive. Cold War difficulties and political prisons are introduced through the scenes set in Wallacia, but international problems are otherwise omitted, as are the dangers of pollution, the evils of political corruption, the problems of dealing with labor unions, racial problems, energy problems and many others. She is suggesting a variety of typical problems of life in England today; however, she is most interested in stressing the emptiness, the lack of social values and ideals, the boredom, the selfishness, the depression, the insecurity of individuals.

As *The Ice Age* begins, its characters and England itself are sunk in depression, bogged down in problems they do not know whom to blame for and don't know what to do about: "A huge icy fist, with large cold fingers, was squeezing and chilling the people of Britain, that great and puissant nation, slowing down their blood, locking them into immobility, fixing them in a solid stasis, like fish in a frozen river." But as the novel moves along, things appear to be improving somewhat, although perhaps at glacial speed; and the end of the book is positively hopeful in a qualified way. Two-thirds through, a nightclub entertainer who specializes in insults and black comedy is introduced so that his point of view may be rejected. The English have lost their feeling of innate superiority, and they no longer deserve to be insulted and knocked about. At this point England is portrayed as not frustrated, not stuck fast, but "passing through some strange metamorphosis, through the intense creative lethargy of profound self-contemplation." Finally, the last sentence of the book assures us that "Britain will recover."

Anthony Keating is the character from whose experiences a reader can most readily discern Britain's problems and anticipate her recovery. At the beginning of the novel, Keating is on ice at his country home, High Rook House, recovering from a heart attack. He has been forbidden excitement, whiskey, cigarettes, and sex; he is quite alone and very bored. He is worried about his mistress and his business, now near bankruptcy, and his problem of how to pay for High Rook, which was bought as a refuge for simple living and loving. But, he tells himself, it appears to have been purchased too late. Perhaps Drabble is suggesting that we cannot accept the modern world, and that when we have got what we want, we retire to the life characteristic of some earlier age.

Anthony, who is thirty-eight, comes from solid, middle-class Yorkshire stock and was provided with a public school and university education. But he broke away from the tradition when he rejected the Church, rejected the idea of a profession, and went into an industry peculiar to our time, television. Eventually he found himself bored and directionless. He had no political or religious creed and nothing either calling him or driving him. At this point he rebelled even further by casting aside his career and pension and entering the risky business of buying and developing tracts of property. Drabble, who deals heavily in symbols, uses two to suggest Anthony's attitudes and problems; one is the Imperial Delight Company, and the other is his heart attack.

The name of Anthony's firm, the Imperial Delight Company (named after a candy company whose site he took over), gives a sense of the power and pleasure he felt in his new enterprise. In this novel adults love developing property as children love to eat candy. Property speculation is a romantic and exciting game to be played for personal, not social, reasons. On one piece of property is an old gas storage tank; Anthony's heart soars like a bird at the sight of his derelict gasometer. But there is no solidity either to his existence or to his business interests. In good times he felt himself to be "a modern man, an operator, at one with the spirit of the age"; when the balloon burst, the general emptiness left behind affected him as well as the age itself. An abandoned, empty gas storage tank, stripped of its romance, is emblematic of what is left.

The heart attack that lays him up is, of course, real, but it is also symbolic of the uneasiness that has attacked Anthony. He finds himself not really suited to the sharp dealings and gambles of his business and perhaps not entirely suited to Alison, his mistress. (For, like other modern men, Anthony has divorced his wife Babs, easygoing mother of his four children, and taken up with someone else.) His period of enforced physical idleness is succeeded by a protracted alcoholic debauch before the final action of the novel which leaves Anthony physically but not spiritually imprisoned. He is still iced-in, but his heart has recovered.

Len Wincobank (note the significant name) is another property developer who is now on ice in Scratby Open Prison. He and Giles Peters, one of Anthony's partners, serve as foils for each other and for Anthony. Len has made his way up from a background of mean poverty. Giles, on the other hand, is very wealthy and in fact something of a rebel in that he is refusing to be a third-generation dilettante. One has a sense of viewing a British television documentary in which persons interviewed have been carefully selected to represent the upper class, middle class, and the lower class. Both Len and Giles love risky deals. Giles is a floater who cannot sink; he grabs at anything. Though he has known Anthony since university days, he has no compunction about cheating his old friend. Len, a more attractive character, is the new businessman of the 1960's. Although he has been convicted of fraud, he is still a person of more scruples than Giles and is, furthermore, a man of greater vision. The vision, however, is not of human happiness and comfort in an enormous expanse of buildings but simply of the buildings. He lost out because lazy, complacent, stick-in-the-mud Porcaster (yes, Pork City) rejected his vision of its rebuilding and renewal. Len's mistress, Maureen Kirby, also came from a poor family; she made her way up through hairstyling, shorthand, and sex to a fine life with Len. There was a Rolls-Royce, plenty of money, luxurious travel, lots of good times. Though delighting in this childish carnival existence, Len and Maureen could hardly believe in it—luckily, because they both lost it. Though Giles, Len, and Maureen are all temporarily down, they are all resilient and at the end of the book they are all about to bounce back. Their values are selfish and their standard of conduct not high, but all have energy and intelligence, and Len and Maureen are goodhearted and exceedingly sympathetic.

"These are terrible times we live in," Kitty Friedmann, wrote to Anthony. She, too, is laid up; she lost a foot and her husband was killed when an I.R.A. bomb went off in a restaurant in London. The fearful injustice of such terrorist attacks is emphasized by Kitty's simple, generous, and friendly nature. But, like most of the other characters, she, too, is recovering.

An unhappy situation from which there is no release, however, is that of Alison Murray, a woman who has not managed to define herself or her role properly or to find emotional satisfaction. Once an established actress, she willingly renounced her career in order to be a good wife; that is, she refused to be more successful than her husband, from whom she is now divorced. When her second child, a cerebral palsy victim, was born, Alison concentrated her love on this deprived child. Her older child, in her turn deprived, grew up hostile, resentful, and self-pitying. As the novel begins, this daughter, Jane, is in prison in the Iron Curtain country of Wallacia, charged with drug possession and with killing two men in an automobile accident. This little family is thus representative of several of the disruptive ills of modern domestic life. Jane at the end of the novel will emerge from prison and show signs of abandoning her stance of determined alienation. But Molly will be forever locked in the prison of her jerky, retarded self. Finally, Alison, who has lost Anthony, appears to have invested her intelligence, her energy, her love without any emotional return. Drabble seems to suggest that Alison, like Molly, is permanently iced-in. Her suffering is simply painful; it will not open up any new life for her.

Drabble's broad canvas, her well-developed and sympathetic characters, and her technique of occasionally addressing her readers directly give the book some of the comfortableness of a nineteenth century novel. Her unobtrusively witty style, realistic detail, and ear for conversation make the book a pleasure to read. Unfortunately, the representative nature of the characters and the heavy symbolism are at times too obvious. Conversely, the basis for the author's optimism about Britain is too vague. Her faith appears to be placed in British courage and fortitude and in a Puritanical belief that suffering can sometimes be useful. Through Anthony she suggests a spiritual change; predictably this is expressed partly through symbols. The book begins as a pheasant falls; like Anthony, it has been struck by a heart attack. At the end of the novel a rare bird, a tree creeper, rises up toward the snowy mountain heights. Through disappointment and suffering, Anthony's heart has been renewed. This suggestion is nebulous but reassuring. Britain, too, one may hope, will not only survive the ice age but emerge regenerate.

Mary C. Williams

Sources for Further Study

Atlantic. CCXL, December, 1977, p. 108.

Book World. October 23, 1977, p. E1.

Harper's Magazine. CCLV, October, 1977, p. 87.

Illustrated London News. CCLXV, November, 1977, p. 103.

New Republic. CLXXVII, October 22, 1977, p. 28.

New Statesman. XCIV, September 9, 1977, p. 343.

New York Review of Books. XXIV, November 10, 1977, p. 28.

New York Times Book Review. October 9, 1977, p. 7.

Newsweek. XC, October 17, 1977, p. 114.

Progressive. XLI, November, 1977, p. 55.

Saturday Review. IV, August 20, 1977, p. 63.

THE IMPERIAL EXPERIENCE IN SUB-SAHARAN AFRICA
SINCE 1870

Author: Henry S. Wilson
Publisher: University of Minnesota Press (Minneapolis). 415 pp. $18.50
Type of work: History
Time: The nineteenth and twentieth centuries
Locale: Africa south of the Sahara

A study which investigates the history of sub-Saharan Africa from 1870 to the 1970's and analyzes the British, French, German, Belgian, and Portuguese presence in the area and the African responses to these colonial regimes

Henry S. Wilson is an accomplished scholar and a specialist in the history of Africa south of the Sahara. In *The Imperial Experience in Sub-Saharan Africa Since 1870* he tackles a subject rendered difficult by its scope and diversity. The resulting book is the eighth volume in the important new series, *Europe and the World in the Age of Expansion.* Wilson makes a significant contribution to this series, which is designed to incorporate new questions and interpretations unearthed by modern historical scholarship on Europe's expansion in the modern era.

This volume provides a focus on both African and imperial history. Wilson claims that only when the two "are drawn together as mutually complementary factors can a satisfactory historiography of the imperial experience in Africa develop." In this volume, the compelling and important reinterpretation of the imperial experience that Ronald Robinson, John Gallagher, and Alice Denny set forth in their well-known study *Africa and the Victorians,* which among other things accentuated the non-European or African factors in the partitioning of that continent, is placed in a wider perspective. Wilson acknowledges and uses the products of recent research on the African factor in the imperial equation, but he doubts that the imperial factor in that same equation can be reduced to a subsidiary element, a type of imperial response to a local situation. Although Wilson places his principal emphasis on the imperial episode, for the sake of setting and continuity he also includes material on the prelude to the partition of Africa as well as on its twentieth century aftermath.

No single volume on so vast a subject could be comprehensive. Recognizing this fact, Wilson elected to structure his book around chapter-length topics essentially placed in chronological order. Wherever possible within each of these selected topics, he illustrates specific dimensions of the subject by utilizing examples drawn from recent case studies. Such a method allows the author to illustrate various practices, attitudes, and assumptions that characterized both Africans and Europeans at specific times and places of their imperial experience.

The Imperial Experience in Sub-Saharan Africa Since 1870 is filled with revisionist arguments that in turn enhance the significance of the work. The idea, for instance, that African societies existed in "static equilibrium" before the so-called "scramble" for colonies and position in Africa began is now challenged by the contention that during the century before the European partition, the inhabitants of the continent underwent an "African partition of Africa." In fact, the European presence in Africa intruded into existing diplomatic and military patterns of competition. In a similar manner, traditional historical accounts have failed to consider African religious ideas as a subject comparable to Christianity or Islam. In the past the belief was commonly held that African religions lacked the necessary spiritual resources to adapt to the challenges the Africans encountered as they engaged a wider world than the highly localized one of their ancestors. However, recent studies reveal that indigenous African religions were undergoing a revolution of their own when Western Christian ideas began to spread in Africa, and that the indigenous religious revolution has been the forgotten factor in explaining how Christianity was able to penetrate so deeply into Africa. This emphasis on "African creativity rather than passivity" has occasioned the need for contemporary scholars to reexamine the entire mission-ary experience in Africa. Wilson consistently incorporates such new interpreta-tions into his study with the result that his work is widely suggestive.

Several themes are given special emphasis in this book. First, throughout the volume Wilson repeatedly explains how the subject at hand can be com-prehended by grasping the constant interaction of the imperial and African factors. For example, when he discusses the political consolidation of West Africa and the Congo, he stresses how imperial policies interacted with the "local ecological and cultural situation" present in the small and medium-sized African communities of that area. Accordingly, imperial policies such as assimilation, association, and indirect rule are placed in a more realistic perspective than that provided by many earlier studies. Another case in point is provided by the author's interesting treatment of the theory and practice of colonial education. After examining the French, Belgian, and British ap-proaches to colonial education, he concludes that in actuality the process cannot be explained simply in terms of the Europeans acting as "donors and the Africans as recipients." The Africans had more initiative in matters of education than previously supposed.

The second major theme of the book relates to the end of empire. In this case Wilson explores two basic topics: the growth of African nationalism and the impact that European circumstances had on the rapid decolonization of Africa. Of course, one would expect the relationship between the two world wars of this century and the condition of Africa to receive thorough attention, and it does. In fact, Wilson claims that the years encompassed by World War II represent a watershed in the development of modern Africa. The most interesting aspect of his handling of this subject, however, is his treatment of the interwar years in Africa. His account of the changes that occurred during those years is illuminat-ing, perceptive, and convincing.

Aside from such major themes, the book contains numerous subsidiary topics that are developed at length. The influence of geography on historical development, the nature of African frontiers and boundaries, various strategies of imperial policy, cultural dimensions of the contact between Europeans and Africans, patterns of urbanization, and economic subjects such as development, underdevelopment, and welfare are all explored by Wilson. The result is a volume rich in examples of the political, economic, and social ramifications of the imperial presence in Africa.

The book, however, does have flaws. Wilson's approach to his material is selective rather than comprehensive, and, although he alerts us to this approach in his Preface, there are some historiographical items omitted that one would wish to see included. Nevertheless, personal preferences regarding his selection of material should be restrained, for the contents of the book are not only consistently vital but also based on important new scholarly probings. Yet there remain several basic difficulties occasioned by the scope of the book and the number of particular subjects it embraces. In any undertaking of this type there is a problem of the integration of material to face, and in this volume it remains a problem encountered but not fully conquered. A more bothersome aspect of the volume is the author's style. One finds an unevenness of narrative flow, a tendency towards fragmentation, and sometimes a frustrating abruptness of presentation. Considering the format of the book and the way in which the chapters are divided, well-developed concluding paragraphs at the end of each chapter would have improved the clarity of argument and would have mitigated some of the stylistic difficulties mentioned above. Wilson provides excellent introductory sections for each chapter, but, with few exceptions, he fails to give equivalent care to summary statements.

Notwithstanding these few critical imperfections, *The Imperial Experience in Sub-Saharan Africa Since 1870* is a major book. It provides valuable historiographical commentary as well as broad and fundamentally clear interpretations of many of the tangled aspects of the African labyrinth. The analytical contents of the book are complemented by extensive notes that constitute nothing less than a summation of recent literature of the field. Wilson wrote this book mainly for serious students of history; they will find it a fascinating and invaluable scholarly tool.

James D. Startt

Sources for Further Study

Choice. XIV, December, 1977, p. 1413.

IN MEDITERRANEAN AIR

Author: Ann Stanford
Publisher: The Viking Press (New York). 88 pp. $5.95
Type of work: Poetry

Poems in six thematic divisions which are lyric without tight structure, dramatic without direct conflict, and narrative without complex plot

"One Swallow does not make a Winter" was a witticism of the 1940's inspired when Ivor Winters' disciple Alan Swallow devoted his small press to an exclusive group of poets; Ann Stanford was one of the poets who studied under Yvor Winters at Stanford, and she published her first volumes with the Swallow Press. She has since won many prizes, appeared in the Borestone "Best Poems," been included in anthologies and a variety of magazines from fugitive to slick, received fellowships, and published critical articles and books on, among many other things, women poets such as Ann Bradstreet and May Swenson.

The first poem, "Glimmerglass," sets the tone in a timeless place, the center from which the circular plot with its portraits and landscapes emanate, the ring of house, lake, and shore, outside of which is the "unbroken forest" where "the enemy waits." The last verse, "Listening to Color," reveals "My message keeps/ turning to yellow where few leaves/set up first fires over branches/tips of flames only, nothing here finished yet." The *personae* throughout are the central and informing intelligence of the poet, as spy, as observer in many guises. Stanford's method is classical in its restraint, using varied tempo, cadenced rather than stressed stanzas, and modulated rhythms. Imagist with played down metaphors, the poems are distinguished by their original idiom.

"Our Town" and "On Music" furnish echoes of Robinson and Dryden with remarkable variations in modern instances which give the reader pause. They are celebrations of technical excellence almost as abstract as music, the latter poem translating the idea of "Song for St. Cecilia's Day" through Purcell into Benjamin Britten. The same feeling persists in what might almost be called a transliteration of Euripides into "The Burning of Ilium" with a riposte as current as news from Israel, Cambodia, Ireland: the streaming refugees, "the dust of cities falling," a dead child in a mother's arms. The theme is extended in "Libraries" to include the greater vandalism in almost Pindarian terms of ideas and intellect destroyed yet nurtured still.

Quite opposite in feeling is a group of portraits, especially of owls. Old Owl appears in a verse as prelude to a section of bestiary pieces, in which all the creeping, flying, scampering creatures rejoice in his disappearance, while the *persona* wishes or calls for his return as muse: "Come soon, sweel Owl./I miss your velvet note/ and the soft slip of your wing." "The Owl Inside" follows as in a nightmare exploding into color and sound, then recalled in "The Message": ". . . Not to wake/ while owls rummage the trees/search runnels of grass, not seen,/heard, heard into dream." Other birds appear in other poems, always exactly described but extended to symbol not exact, the unresolved mysteries celebrated yet not understood. The key to this dilemma appears in "Language" as it does in a previously published "The noun/is what is feared . . ." that is, how to make the naming intelligible beyond language. More explicit portraits leave no doubt; "Prophet" is John the Baptist, Cellini imprisoned seeks light as artists' only tool, all the women in the Perseus series speak exactly. Perseus, after his conquests, wonders if he is a hero in a poem of existential inauthenticity and anguish.

There is no title poem, but the sequence under that heading, the eleven verses whose *I* is the abstracted pursuer, the *We* either those spied upon or the power behind the chase, has all the elements of a Delamare landscape and a Robbe-Grillet plot, with their sharp focus on unresolved terror. The locale shifts from a mysterious, apparently Italian villa, to the forest, a train, a city largely seen through the eyes of a counterespionage agent, blundering, fearful, lonely, astute, alienated—anything but the stereotypical spy, since he has no idea of his mission, has lost contact with his leader, and longs to join and embrace those he is terrorizing. They in turn fumble with fake maps, act out their roles as if coconspirators. The mood is dominated by the Sirocco, the heat penetrating and undermining both statuary and morale. The plot takes a Kafkaesque turn to irresolution which carries over to the next section of poems, especially "Exiles," in which the actors in the drama cannot go home again:

> We sort out noises at night
> watch where we walk by day.
> But the sky lurks like a spy. Our words
> turn against us, what we keep is a threat.
> They're bound to be after us.

This is a chilling scenario where nothing happens, where terror is the final moment, where the cast is galvanized into inaction.

Dream and memory alternate to create a dual point of view in the reassuring poems of other sections. The most striking example of twin focus is in "Mr. D.," where death takes a brief holiday, seen through the rattling eyes of the collaborator as a comforter, a nurse in tweed, who "told me how to dream without dreaming/like roots under the snow in winter./Dark, and knowing that darkness, warm/and held like a comfort around me." There is no autobiography, no hint of the confessional poet's stance, either here or in "After Exile" where dream and memory reach a resolution of faith:

> It was not the dream that did it.
> It only reflected
> the serpent of power rising
> from the roots of earth
> into the head where the hair
> flew out like sprays of a flowering tree.
> Blossoms falling wherever the feet
> half-touched the ground
> the girl with new-risen breasts

running through doorways
into the green garden
where trees grew overnight
placing themselves in trim rows
and the blooms of azaleas, acacia,
and pomegranate split the air with color,
whole skies of blooms covered the ground
but it was the fountain that rose like a serpent
ricocheted over every tendril of the green garden.

The remembered roots, the dream of life prevailing in a kind of epiphany make of this cadenced poem of stress and unstress an epitome as well. The same sense of mystery is apparent in another dreamed remembrance of things that are not past or present but eternal: "There was a man unseen/before, shone on the porch of dream/the light behind him bright/ his face seen and never seen/ before" suggests the ineffable. Yet the settings of the poems are often specific, such as a ranch in California, where the reality is so strong that she believes things will never change if she revisits the past: "Whatever I do, my uncle is going to be here/smoking his cigarette, talking of shorthorn cattle. . . . If I come back, things will start again." This poetic affirmation, a license never to be revoked, is the celebration of life while being lived, the affirmation which Ann Stanford proclaims.

The Stanford seasons have, however, some discontent. Heat is often insufferable; cold is too often numbing. "The trouble is we are always reminded of something/beside the point" which kills "that old child's morning game of resurrection." The doubt is not enough to make the sun and moon go out, as Blake said it might, but it gives a slight edge to the mood of the poems.

William Tillson

Sources for Further Study

Choice. XIV, November, 1977, p. 1217.
Hudson Review. XXX, Winter, 1977–1978, p. 585.

IN THE NAME OF THE PEOPLE
Prophets and Conspirators in Prerevolutionary Russia

Author: Adam B. Ulam (1922–   )
Publisher: The Viking Press (New York). 418 pp. $15.00
Type of work: History
Time: 1866–1881
Locale: Russia, England, Switzerland

A description of the left-wing anarchist and populist terrorist groups that appeared in Russia during the reign of Alexander II

> *Principal personages:*
> NICHOLAS I, Tsar of Russia, 1825–1855
> ALEXANDER II, his son, Tsar of Russia, 1855–1881
> ALEXANDER III, his son, Tsar of Russia, 1881–1894
> JOSEPH V. DZUGASHVILI (STALIN), leader of the Soviet Union, 1929–1953
> KARL MARX, founder of scientific socialism
> DMITRI KARAKOZOV, Russian terrorist whose attempt to assassinate Alexander II in 1866 began the era of terrorist ideology
> ALEXANDER HERZEN, well-known and respected dean of Russian anti-government ideologists, editor of *The Bell*
> NICHOLAS CHERNYSHEVSKY, radical anti-government ideologist, regarded as the philosophical godfather of the terrorists
> MICHAEL BAKUNIN, father of Russian and international anarchism
> MICHAEL KATKOV, a reactionary journalist, spokesman of the pro-government Russian nationalists
> VERA FIGNER, a woman populist and terrorist
> SERGE NECHAYEV, an insane anarchist
> VERA ZASULICH, a romantic woman populist tried for the attempted assassination of the governor of St. Petersburg, later a founder of Russian Marxism

Adam Ulam is a highly respected professor of political science at Harvard University. His numerous books on the government and leaders of the Soviet Union have had wide circulation and brought him a justly deserved reputation for impeccable scholarship, and, rarer still, the reputation of a professor who writes readable books. As a member of the prestigious Harvard Russian Research Center, he also has established himself as a leading Kremlinologist, a foremost intellectual general for the American side in the Cold War. With *In the Name of the People* Ulam ventures once again into the topic of Russian intellectual history. (He has done so previously with *Ideologies and Illusions: Revolutionary Thought from Herzen to Solzhenitsyn* [Harvard, 1976].) Furthermore, he once again demonstrates his erudition, wit, style, and scholarship as well as his continuing moral indignation at Russian (and Soviet) political behavior and practice.

In the Name of the People recounts the development of Russian anti-government movements during the reign of Alexander II, from the abortive attempt of the terrorist Dmitri Karakozov on the life of the Tsar in 1866 to the successful assassination of Alexander by members of the People's Will in 1881 This was the age of the Nihilists and the Populists who broke with the Russian tradition of purely intellectual literary dissent and introduced into imperial politics social activism, including the use of terror. The previous generation of dissenters was epitomized by Alexander Herzen, who became the seminal force for anti-government activity for all of Russia in the future—not only the anarchists and socialists, but the liberals and moderate constitutionalists as well. Herzen spent long years in exile in London (he died in 1870) where he edited his political journal *The Bell,* and where his home became a mecca abroad for Russian dissidents. Ulam emphasizes his reputation as the leader of Russia's so-called "second government," that is, the anti-government. The author compares Herzen as the leader of the second government with Nicholas I, the leader of the first, showing that they did not so much represent polar extremes in Russian political life but, rather, formed mirror images, products of the same society playing different but intertwined roles.

Throughout much of Herzen's period of activity, the primary issue of Russian politics was serfdom or, more precisely, how should serfdom be abolished, for by mid-century both government supporters and dissidents agreed that this oppressive economic system must cease if Russia was to survive in the modern age. When Alexander brought serfdom to an end in 1861, Herzen wrote in exaggerated, but genuine, respect reflecting the sentiment of his generation "Thou hast conquered, O Galilean." Ironically, the liberation unleashed a wave of uprisings in the Russian empire among both peasants dissatisfied with the economic settlement of the act and minority nationalities—particularly the Poles—waiting for their national "liberation." It was in this atmosphere that Karakozov, a Russian of gentry origins, tried to kill the Tsar while in his customary fashion he strolled in a St. Petersburg park among the public without much security. When asked why he did it, or more precisely what he wanted, the would-be assassin responded merely, "Nothing."

For Ulam, Karakozov represents the new dissidents, the men and women who, while they still regarded Herzen with respect as an intellectual guide, sought their models among the heroes of the writings of the political novelist Nicholas Chernyshevsky, the first spokesman for social action. Unlike Herzen, Chernyshevsky remained in Russia and spent much of his life under detention or in prison—a martyr of the tsarist autocracy. The first and the second government had moved further apart.

It is the ideas and activity of these new men that makes them for Ulam the prophets of revolution. His account of them, however, is not merely a description of their ideas and actions, but also of their personal lives and romantic (in all senses of the word) entanglements. These personal biographies give the book much of its charm. Although at times the accounts become something akin to gossip, Ulam's stylistic ability allows him to carry off the narration. Their practice of free love, their communes, and their civic marriages (equivalent to Anglo-Saxon common-law relationships, but often bigamous and not always consummated) revealed the young Russian rebels to be anti-Victorian social as well as political revolutionaries; while many of their characteristics give substance to Ulam's veiled comparison of the Russian radicals to their American counterparts of the 1960's. In one unforgettable scene Ulam describes the wife of the governor of Moscow entering her niece's bedroom and finding the Populist Nicholas Morozov undressing. When the aunt inquired into this shocking behavior, her niece bullied her into retreat with threats to move out. "Of course it was nothing so innocent as trysting," Ulam writes, "Morozov was using a casual acquaintance's house to change to appropriate clothes prior to going to propagandize in the workers' quarter." Trysting between the radicals, however, also occurred quite often more as an act of social defiance than as an appeasement of sexual appetites or romantic desires.

Obviously, young Russian women as well as men were deeply involved in the new social action. Given the small size of Russia's intellectual class, it was inevitable that the daughters of the gentry as well as their sons entered into the universities and professions after the initial barriers were lifted, and from there into the world of social protest. Compared to the liberal and bourgeois societies of the West, nineteenth century Russia showed remarkably advanced notions of women's emancipation. Among the many women who became prominent in radical circles, two, Vera Figner and Vera Zasulich, made exceptional impact in the movement. Figner was the leader of the People's Will, the terrorist organization which assassinated Alexander; and Zasulich, who had attempted to shoot General Fyodor Trepov, the governor of St. Petersburg, who had publicly beaten a radical student, was the defendant at a controversial trial (for the attempt) and "beat the rap" by playing on the sympathy of Russia's liberal public opinion. After the trial she fled from Russia and became a founder of Russian Marxism, a collaborator of Plekhanov, Lenin, Martov, and Trotsky. As a young girl she had been a friend and admirer of Serge Nechayev—the prototype of irrational and extreme anarchism; hence, her political career spanned the alpha and omega of Russian revolutionary history. (Ulam also brings into his narrative some of the activities of Sophia Perovskaya, perhaps the most famous Russian woman revolutionary of the age, but he discusses her exploits and importance to a lesser extent than those of the two Veras.)

In general, Ulam sees the terrorist associations of nineteenth century Russia and their activities as forerunners of the Bolsheviks who completed the revolution in 1917. Yet at the same time and not necessarily contradictorily (compare the case of Herzen and Nicholas and see below) the tsarist government foretold the Soviet regime as well. Throughout the book the author sprinkles references to Stalin, always in an unfavorable light, comparing his actions to some activity of the government or the terrorists. The leniency of the tsarist justice system is compared to the severity of the Soviet system. The revolutionary eccentricities and ideologies of the Populists are shown to be models for the Marxists of the twentieth century.

These conclusions are greatly overdrawn. To Ulam's credit, he does not go to the distorted lengths of other Western commentators of Soviet society, in equating the Bolsheviks with the most insane of the terrorist cells, depicting the Marxists as an unstable band of conspirators reflecting neither Russian nor Western traditions. Nevertheless, although Ulam appears to stress the unity of Russian history as well as the integrated whole of Russian politics in the nineteenth century, both dissident and sovereign, he is unwilling to assert the definitive conclusion that the Soviet regime is indeed the product of Russia's traditional society and history, not an aleatory happening resulting from the fancies which insane children conceived in the seedy quarters of the anarchists and terrorists.

It is true that Russia's socialist movement had its roots in the Nihilist and Populist movements in the 1860's and 1870's, but the effect of Marxism was to moderate and stabilize the progressive dissidents rather than the reverse. The early Nihilist and Anarchist philosophers, like Chernyshevsky and Herzen, were hostile to Marx; they viewed his materialist conception of society and glorification of the proletariat as alien to the spiritualism of the Russian "soul" and the condition of Russian society. Furthermore, the terrorist movements in the nineteenth century appeared as a by-product of the collapse of tsarist society. Marx himself viewed this collapse as the beginning of Russia's entry into the bourgeois stage of history. (This is a judgment, incidentally, in which Russia's socialist Mensheviks—whom of course Ulam and his colleagues in general treat more favorably than the Bolsheviks—concurred.) The Anarchists and Populists saw the salvation of Russia in the physical elimination of the governmental superstructure starting with the Tsar himself. Then the Russian peasant bound in his village commune—already a form of Communism—and bolstered by his spiritual anarchism would rule himself in a blissful anarcho-communist state. That this latter was a naïve and unrealistic view cannot be denied, but the Marxist view of a bourgeois Russia as it turned out was also unrealistic. There simply was not a Russian bourgeoisie sufficiently large to carry out the required capitalist revolution of Communist theory. Furthermore, both views neglected what was perhaps the major force then destroying the empire—the rising national expectations of Russia's non-Russian minorities, which comprised more than half the empire.

Karakozov made his assassination attempt in the wake of a Polish revolution. Ulam does not disregard the national factor entirely, but he does put it aside. In one sense this is legitimate, because he is interested in the Russian terrorist response to tsarism, not the minority response, but without the minority aspect the major success of the Bolsheviks, indeed their legitimate right to rule in Russia, cannot be fully understood. Thus the emphasis which Ulam implicitly and explicitly places on the Nihilist-Populist-Bolshevik connection becomes overstated.

Poles, Jews, and other non-Russian minorities joined all the dissident groups and participated in their activities, but the basic thrust of the dissident ideologies was Russian; indeed, these radicals demonstrated outright hostility toward the minorities and their national liberation movements. The attempt by the People's Will to use anti-Semitism to arouse the peasants against the Tsar was quite scurrilous. On the other side, Michael Katkov's Great Russian national movement was the major progovernment antiradical ideology of the period. The Tsar's son, Alexander III, who despised his father's partial liberalism as a sign of weakness and yielding to the terrorists, was a Great Russian chauvinist and a sympathizer of Russian-dominated Pan-Slavism. Moreover, we can further underscore the nationalist importance by noting that in the perspective of later history, Russia's fate could well have been the imperial dissolution which awaited Austria-Hungary and Ottoman Turkey.

In the light of these facts, the major importance of the Russian revolution of 1917 was that Russia survived. The Bolsheviks oversaw this survival, not because they adopted the programs of the anarcho-terrorists of the 1870's or the tsarist repression of the previous age, but because they oversaw Russia's survival by molding the concepts of Marxism for Russia's needs (unlike the Mensheviks). They retained what was indispensable to state survival from the previous regimes, and they borrowed what was necessary for mass support from the Populists in ways in which even the more legitimate heir of the Populists, the Social Revolutionary Party, did not. Both tsarist institutions and radical ideologies were in the Russian tradition, and it is this single overriding fact which Ulam in the final analysis does not completely admit.

Frederick B. Chary

Sources for Further Study

Choice. XIV, September, 1977, p. 930.
Christian Science Monitor. LXIX, August 11, 1977, p. 22.
Current History. LXXIII, October, 1977, p. 128.
New York Times. July 6, 1977, p. 24.
Political Science Quarterly. XCII, Summer, 1977, p. 358.

INFANTS OF THE SPRING

Author: Anthony Powell (1905–   )
Publisher: Holt, Rinehart and Winston (New York). 214 pp. $10.00
Type of work: Memoirs
Time: 1905–1926
Locale: England

Vastly informative about the sorts of young Britons who attended Eton and Oxford in the early 1920's, this first volume of Anthony Powell's memoirs is rather less revealing about Powell himself

Principal personages:
ANTHONY POWELL
HUGH LYGON and
ROGER SPENCE, his schoolmates at Eton
HENRY GREEN, his closest friend at Oxford
MAURICE BOWRA, an influential teacher at Oxford
EVELYN WAUGH,
GEORGE ORWELL,
CYRIL CONNOLLY, and
ALFRED DUGGAN, Powell's classmates at Oxford

Devotees of Anthony Powell's witty and astringent prose style will enjoy *Infants of the Spring,* the first volume of his autobiography. It begins in the dim past of the twelfth century, with tales of an eccentric forebear named Rhys ap Gruffydd, and ends with Powell at age twenty, having come down from Oxford, "enveloped in a fog of naïvety" and about to "dive headfirst into the opaque waters of London life." Much of course is chronicled in between, as Powell, taking his guiding epigraph from Joseph Conrad's *Chance,* manages both charmingly and informatively "to keep the ball rolling," as does Conrad's narrator with the nonchalant Marlow. This idea of casually, entertainingly maintaining the conversation, keeping the air filled with inquiry, with analysis of as much as possible of what happened—in an attempt to discover the remarkable—is Powell's purpose. Thus, the overall title for the volumes of his autobiography will be *To Keep the Ball Rolling.*

Readers not devoted to Powell (or unless avid genealogists) will not get much beyond his first twenty or thirty pages. Anyone seeking Powell's usual immediacy of drama, wit, and quirky character will have to wade at first through some stretched points and anecdotes which Powell finds of high interest. But to fans of his novels, his research into the dim past of his family will be heavy going. Only a Powell admirer or an Anglophile can justify it perhaps as being a lambently appropriate approach to the roots of one who would later create the magnificent twelve-volume fiction, *A Dance to the Music of Time.*

Powell was the only child of a professional soldier and an aristocratic beauty who played the banjo for charity benefits. Frequent changes of military station moved the family around a great deal. On his father's side, young Powell's roots grew out of the country of the Welsh Border; on his mother's side they were of the wolds and fens of Lincolnshire. This mix of bloods and traditions produced an array of stories on both family sides about eccentric and dissipated forebears. Powell grew up hearing the stories and participating in them with strange uncles, aunts, and countless cousins. Powell tells of one old gentleman who loved to take visitors on long walking talks, occasionally accenting his tales by thrusting his cane between his listener's striding shins. As the person fell, the old man would calmly catch him, laugh, and continue with his discourse. Certainly, this battiness of background contributed much to the creative imagination which went into *A Dance to the Music of Time.*

There are brilliant examples of Powell's uncanny exactness of rendering an event or a character here. In Chapter I, "From Whence Clear Memory," he mentions that his first recollection at age two was of snow descending in small flakes outside a hotel window. Then he mentions how, at age six, he was stimulated by a long beam of sunlight filled with dust particles slanting through an upper window on a staircase in his home. With a precision impressive because it defies both time and the ineffability of the moment, he writes that he had been conscious of ". . . approaching the brink of some discovery; an awareness that nearly became manifest, then suddenly withdrew. Now the truth came flooding in with the dust infested sunlight. The revelation of self-identity was inescapable. There was no doubt about it. I was me." For those who would get to know Powell better in *Infants of the Spring,* that is unfortunately one of the very few genuine insights to himself Powell provides. Most often he is the narrator-observer, overshadowed by persons around him, realizing himself only through the light they reflect around themselves and him. Because of this "Nick Jenkins" sort of reticence, one learns a great deal about Powell's contemporaries, and very little, actually, about him and his immediate family. Possibly such discretion, such self-effacement, is natural and even fruitful in a writer whose major role has been to chronicle faithfully and wrily his age, to report the glory and twilight of a unique kingdom and era. One has the feeling that Powell indeed feels Conrad's Marlow correct when he says of that other "Powell" that he was not exactly remarkable. Powell does not seem to be intentionally holding back—he is too honest a writer for that. Rather, he seems to feel uninteresting by himself. What fascinates him is England, the time, the other people. What interests Powell most, then, in keeping this particular ball rolling, is observing and reporting with stunning accuracy the doings and ideas of others who were around him. They, he reveals to us and to himself, *are* remarkable people.

Powell's judgment is apt. He knew an astonishing number of movers and shakers, and early spotted greatness in many of them. Though this volume ends with his youthful leavetaking of Oxford, Powell has not limited himself, along the way, from moving ahead in time to share with us stories about the careers and ends, brilliant and otherwise, of many of his school chums. Typical is the quietly unathletic boy with spectacles he remembers as having been the butt of cruel jokes, who is recalled as having become a major general in what Powell calls "the Hitler war." There are friends who are brilliant in youth only to become lost in lassitude as adults. There are scandals and heroisms. Through it all, Powell's craftsmanship depicts his time in terms definitively, essentially upper-crust British. Sociologists and historians will find here a rich lode of ore for their particular smelters. Powell is depicting richly, from the inside, a rare world, superbly conscious of itself as important but fleeting. He describes it as a world most beautiful, perhaps, in its stiff-upper-lip resistance to the inevitable crumbling of its idols. Sheer fatigue of blood and brain would do many of Powell's old-family-scion friends in; two great world wars would get many; loss of empire would throw many into irreversible spins; ennui, the dissolution of class structure, and the post-World War II utter absence of grandeur would betray nearly all. Through it all, history, the very music of time, would dance them all to its own increasingly depressing tune.

In Powell's memoirs of his school friends, and of their various lives and productivities, there is always a stringently contained but nevertheless affecting sense of the beautiful, tragic, or tragicomic futility of it all. It is all very sophisticated, even wise, but very Britanically elevated and brittle, or aloof, even superior in tone. Very likely, it is the sense of futility, the consistent assurances of the twentieth century that fate has her way despite our best efforts, which causes this defensive intellectuality. In Powell's hands the device is natural; it is a stance which works. What else can a man of intellect, breeding, taste do? He will not grovel; he will not condescend; he cannot descend; he wishes not to withdraw, for therein lies illness. The creative alternative is to see the world and life as an interesting adventure, if melancholy. There resides part of Powell's artistic salvation: his sophisticated sense of adventure, his cerebral curiosity as to what will next come along. Joined impressively to this is his sense of discipline and his extreme devotion to craft. His tone seems to suggest that though the times may be more tragic than comic, more reprehensible than admirable, with more of the crass than class, it is what we have. It is happening, and there is the treasure of honor to be grasped in reporting it all inordinately well. How deeply he cares and consequently how superbly he controls the expression of that caring is the source of his power.

Having laid his foundation of history and family in the first third of his book, Powell's account grows more lively when he gets to his days at Eton. Eton was life. The customs, studies, and personalities there were more real for Powell than all the melancholy boredom, the childhood inactivity which had come before. Eton became metaphoric nation, family, and religion. There at last, it seemed to him, the results made the reasons for actions and thoughts appropriate and apparent to him. Life took on meaning. He began to exercise discernment, to allocate his energies to causes—mostly aesthetic ones.

Academically, at Eton he seemed most involved in the study of art. Significantly, his interest in art seems never to have flagged. A recurrent device of his in *Infants of the Spring* is to characterize someone by revealing their taste in art, by mentioning representative and illustrative works owned in their collections. Obviously, Powell feels that a man is known by the artistic company he keeps hanging about his walls. He tells us, for instance, that his father's taste ran to Beardsley, Conder, Ricketts, and to illustrators such as Rackham, Dulac, and Thomson. Powell knew these enthusiasms revealed his father's nonmilitary facet, his protected inner life, and perhaps for that reason, he seems particularly gentle in his treatment of his father's excitement over artists apparently not high on his own list. At Eton, too, he came to know acquaintances by their artistic tastes. In a story cogently revealing the laughably pretentious style of his fellow student Brian Howard, he quotes him as responding to a questioner, " 'I can always sell my Gris.' 'But what will you do then?' 'Oh, write—paint—don't fluster me.' " Powell also mentions, with admiration for his having made the discovery first, his friend William Acton's possessing an early collection of Picasso reproductions.

Aside from his interest in art, Powell's main devotions at Eton seemed to be the study of human character. He was precocious in his ability to select friends who would prove substantial persons. In the chapter called "The Game and the Candle," he employs the device of reprinting a 1922 list of contributors' names found in the initial copy of *The Eton Candle,* a publication of the Eton Society of Arts. The list, like all such lists, appears at first stark and dull. In contrast, Powell's systematic, leisurely, yet sprightly telling of his acquaintanceship with each of these boys is riveting. He sees each of them as fascinating, significant, and finally as being revealing segments of the large picture of Britain and the period. It is impressive to Powell—and he makes it so to us—that this narrowly selected group of young Britons revealed in their failures, their excesses, their triumphs, and their beauties a cross-section of the traits of a nation. Told in Powell's gracefully terse style, each of their lives is a drama of high interest. Typical of his affectionate yet objective blend of observations about even the wastrels in his peer group is the story of Hugh Lygon, son of Lord Beauchamp, leader of the liberal party in the House of Lords. Lygon, Powell writes, was "amiably unintellectual"; and after leaving Oxford, later, he suffered bad health, tried various occupations—most having to do with gambling—including being a stable hand, and later while traveling in Germany he fell and died in his thirties. In contrast, one of the successful friends Powell recalls was Roger Spence, who served with quiet distinction in both the diplomatic service and all through World War II. Spence became a brigadier general, and was so devoted to duty that he died of overwork. Powell notes with obvious approval that "doing his duty, behaving well, being quietly agreeable," seem to have comprised Spence's stoic and productive code.

Between the extremes represented by his fellow students Lygon and Spence are other equally illustrative stories. Powell recalls their lives with mingled relish and regret. These were his friends, his fellow actors. This was a stage on which life was lived to its fullest. Their drama has been played—both brilliantly and badly—to mixed reviews. Sadly, too, the curtain is drawing closed.

The next major and less pleasant influence on his life was Powell's going up to Balliol College at Oxford. Sardonically, he recalls the reasons for his selection of that college as being the usual "syndrome of Dreaming Spires, Lost Causes, Zuleika Dobson, Sinister Street . . . Balliol's effortless superiority sounded as good as anything else." Though it was to be instructive, Powell's Oxford experience was never to give him the pleasure Eton had. By his last year there he was eager to get away from its cloying atmosphere and its precious cliques.

At Oxford, Powell found his generation to be singular as the first in a decade to attend a university not tinged by ex-soldiers and war. Students older than he who had been in the war were altogether set apart; younger people there never caught up with them. One senses Powell's longing to participate more fully in their strangely aloof maturity and movement toward still undefined forms of existence. This sense of being cut off from those older than he contributed to Powell's strong sense of identity, of the specialness he attributes to himself and his contemporaries.

In this new context, Powell continues to dwell on the personalities of his friends, giving only occasional glimpses of himself. Among the illustrious and memorable names Powell mentions in this section, "The Close and the Quad," are those of Evelyn Waugh, Henry Green, Denys Buckley, George Orwell, Cyril Connolly, Maurice Bowra (who kidded Powell about his heterosexuality), and Alfred Duggan. Of each of these men he tells entertaining and informative stories. Along the way, there are scores of others about lesser personalities. Out of it all emerges a sense of the tone and texture of what it must have meant to be at Oxford in the 1920's. It was a time of change, yet of unique and peculiar adherances to traditions long since beyond meaning. Most of all, what Powell renders here are the attitudes of various people whom he knew. Some of the attitudes are traditional, some radical, all of them vehement; all taking place amid scenes of unmitigated minglings of dissipation, effetism, homosexuality, scholarly excellence, literary productivity, and political flux. All this was more serious than the participants knew. A new war already was brewing, and it would sweep them all up in its exciting, exacting embrace. Powell suggests that the balance of silliness and seriousness he experienced at Oxford was not unlike the later demands made by the world on his generation. In the midst of all this change and challenge at Oxford, he provides a charming specific about university life which reveals his own conservative, down-to-earth side. Mentioning that he had a basic (and sparse) three hundred pounds to pay his school bills, he goes on to note justifyingly that "apart from paying college bills one was stockpiling all sorts of necessities in the way of clothes that had to be only gradually renewed." Powell also makes a note of mentioning that he, untypically of his generation, left Oxford without debts.

Two representative personalities of the many most memorable and illustrative to Powell of the Oxford years were his friend Henry Green and his teacher

Maurice Bowra. Green wrote his own account of this period in his book *Pack My Bag*. With Green, Powell realized and articulated his discomfiture with Oxford. Beyond that, he seems to have genuinely liked Green for his energy, for his devotion to writing, and, most of all, for his extremely individualistic mode of conduct. Typical of Green, he notes, is his unabashed unwillingness to play rugger for "the glory of the team." He also notes that Green was a legendary drinker; that he saw a film a day; that he ate fried fish and steak every night; that he shaved with ordinary washing soap. Ultimately, Green was to impress Powell with his decision to leave without a degree and go to work in the family plumbing fixtures business. As a businessman, Green continued to write capable but modestly recognized novels.

Another factor which brought Green and Powell together was their mutual admiration of their teacher, Maurice Bowra. Both saw his shortcomings but overlooked them because he was obviously, uncaringly brilliant. He listened to them, kidded them, and calmly, self-assuredly encouraged them—made them believe in themselves.

Bowra, openly homosexual, was a scholarly and powerfully opinionated young don whose *forte* was his ability to stay abreast of the *avant garde* in all things intellectual. He could be exhilaratingly entertaining and sardonic in his attitudes towards all things. Powell notes that Bowra's approaches to life, jocular yet practical, provoking both laughter and trepidation, were singular to the moment, hard to reproduce. Bowra was personality-in-residence, and, as such, influenced Powell and his peers by consistently shaking them loose from their too-easily-gotten moorings. Intellectually, he bullied his students into being unconventional thinkers. Powell noted that it was best to know Bowra for a time, then get away, returning later to appreciate what he had to offer. True to his idea, Powell closes *Infants of the Spring* with a memory of a 1960's visit which he, his wife, and his son paid to Bowra, and of a Hellenic cruise they all took with him. The scene, forty years later, ends in the same tone. Bowra is still out front, still scandalously, provokingly different and charmingly influential. It is typical of Powell's approach as a writer that his objective insights into both Green and Bowra do not erode his affection for them nor his ability to show them clearly and memorably. It is impossible to escape the feeling that one has seen characters very much like both Green and Bowra depicted in any number of American and British spy films and novels. They are Britannic types. It is due to Powell's sensitivity and ability that they are more than mere types in his depiction of them.

Infants of the Spring will surely be sniped at by some readers for its apparent name-dropping. Its seeming consciousness of status makes it open to such criticism, too. Indeed, fault-finders will point to the multitude of parentheticals, such as "(later to become lord so-and-so)"; they will label it as being too traditional, even formulaic, in structure, and they will not like its being so unrevealing about Powell himself. Admirers of Powell's craft, however, will see that this master of observation and rendering has been totally true to his aesthetic convictions here. To him, the memoirist, as the novelist, was put here to observe, experience, and report faithfully and accurately. *Infants of the Spring* does that admirably. Let us hope that Powell keeps the ball rolling. It has a fascinating path yet to journey.

Thomas N. Walters

Sources for Further Study

Book World. October 9, 1977, p. E3.

Booklist. LXXIII, July 15, 1977, p. 1694.

Christian Science Monitor. LXIX, November 4, 1977, p. 35.

New York Times Book Review. September 4, 1977, p. 6.

New Yorker. LIII, October 17, 1977, p. 195.

Saturday Review. IV, August 20, 1977, p. 63.

JACK

A Biography of Jack London

Author: Andrew Sinclair (1935–   )
Publisher: Harper & Row Publishers (New York). Illustrated. 297 pp. $12.95
Type of work: Biography
Time: 1876–1916
Locale: The United States (including Alaska and Hawaii), London, Japan, Korea, the South Pacific, Australia, Mexico

A major new biography which tells the absorbing story of a self-made author and political radical whose rise to fame and wealth was followed by long suffering and apparent suicide

> *Principal personages:*
> JACK (JOHN GRIFFITH) LONDON, journalist, novelist, short story writer, essayist
> FLORA WELLMAN LONDON, his mother
> BESS MADDERN LONDON, his first wife
> CHARMIAN KITTREDGE LONDON, his second wife
> JOAN LONDON, his older daughter
> ELIZA LONDON SHEPARD, his half-sister
> GEORGE STERLING, a poet, bohemian, and friend of Jack
> ANNA STRUNSKY, friend and lover of Jack

In histories of American literature and studies of American fiction Jack London is usually considered a minor figure in the development of literary realism and naturalism in the early years of the twentieth century. Arthur Hobson Quinn in 1936 dismissed him quickly with the comment that he was a journalist who wrote "too hastily and too often" and whose vogue was passing, "for there is something impermanent in the very nature of the literature of violence." A decade later, Robert E. Spiller remarked that London was a "vigorous, naïve, and prolific" writer who personified the romantic impulses of the new century and who left "a small body of writing which, for sincerity and vitality, deserves to be rescued from the oblivion to which his artistic faults threaten to condemn it." George F. Whicher was less favorably impressed and wrote in 1951 that London had "little sense of the artistic sincerity of his work and was never unwilling to combine his poetic memories of the great open spaces with popular and highly profitable sentimentality." Edward Wagenknecht, in *Cavalcade of the American Novel* (1952), called London "a hack writer of genius" whose writing "was never more than a means to an end, and the end was material advancement." The general public in America perhaps remembers London now only as the author of *The Call of the Wild* and *The Sea Wolf* and of several Alaskan stories such as "To Build a Fire" and "Love of Life," which have been reprinted in many high school and college textbooks and collections of short stories. By contrast, he is reportedly the most popular of all American writers in Russia, and in France a publisher has recently been reissuing his complete works.

Andrew Sinclair's major new biography of Jack London tells the life story of an amazing young man who fought his way upward from illegitimacy as an infant, through rough and dangerous experiences in a great variety of occupations, to an immensely popular success as a novelist and considerable notoriety as a political radical, and who died, an apparent suicide, at the age of forty. Sinclair also attempts to correct some false impressions about London that can be traced back either to Jack's myths about himself or to earlier biographers who lacked access to many materials that were made available to Sinclair.

London was born in San Francisco in 1876, the son of Flora Wellman, a spiritualist, and John Chaney, a vagabond and astrologer, who had deserted Miss Wellman after she refused to have an abortion. When the baby was only a few months old his mother married a widower, John London, who gave his name to the child. The boy was always called Jack to distinguish him from his adoptive father. Jack did not learn the identity of his real father until he was almost a man. He wrote to Chaney then and felt intensely the sting of rejection when Chaney denied the paternity and refused to see him. Jack achieved a minor sublimated revenge in an early story entitled "A Thousand Deaths," in which a son kills his probable father who has cruelly tortured him. The stigma of Jack's origin was not exorcised, however, and it contributed to his later mythmaking about his family background. Jack's sense of rejection had earlier been instilled by his mother's having neglected him for other interests, one of which was lavishing on the young son of her stepdaughter Ida the affection she had denied her own son.

The poverty of his family led Jack to drop out of school at thirteen and take a series of jobs requiring long hours of often hard physical labor and scant pay. He became an oyster pirate in San Francisco Bay, joined a gang of delinquents in the city, sailed as a seaman on a sealer bound for Japan, nearly died of shingles on the way back, hoboed across the United States, was arrested as a vagrant in Niagara Falls and jailed for a month, and then decided at nineteen that he would return to school and get the education which would enable him to escape the hard and perhaps derelict life that must otherwise almost certainly be his fate.

Jack became interested in books in his early schooling but later had had little time for them until his return made him determine that through both intensive and extensive reading and study—up to nineteen hours a day—he could make up six years of school in two. After a year in high school and five weeks in a cram school, he studied independently with furious application and was admitted to Berkeley as a special student; but he left after his second semester and thus ended his formal education. His continued voracious reading for the rest of his life, however, influenced his thinking and his writing.

Among authors Sinclair cites as exerting a literary influence on London are Kipling, Stevenson, Twain, Milton, Dante, Poe, and Wells. As early as 1900 Jack admitted to a friend, "I would never possibly have written anywhere near the way I did had Kipling never been." Three years later he published an essay, "The

Terrible and Tragic in Fiction," in which he praised Poe's use of terror in his writing, terror such as Poe himself had known. Jack had experienced similar fears in troubled dreams and frightening nightmares, and he felt a psychological kinship with Poe. In a footnote to his *The Iron Heel* London wrote that H. G. Wells was "a sociological seer, sane and normal as well as [a] warm human." Sinclair sees the novel as possibly deriving from London's reading of Wells's "When the Sleeper Wakes" and "A Story of the Days to Come." The Wellsian influence is also present, thinks Sinclair, in London's *Before Adam.*

Other writers who helped to direct or develop Jack's views and his philosophy of life were Karl Marx, Charles Darwin, Thomas Huxley, and Herbert Spencer. Through them and through friends he met during what he later called his "frantic pursuit of knowledge," London became a socialist but, as Sinclair puts it, "of his own special persuasion." He believed in a socialism that was both evolutionary and revolutionary, and he believed also that it would be established by the white race, which he considered superior to others. Because he wrote so rapidly and because he churned out so much of his fiction and so many of his essays to meet the continuing demand for money to pay for his extravagant style of living, he was often inconsistent. It did not disturb him that he wrote for a capitalist like William Randolph Hearst while he remained a Socialist Party member. Nor did it bother him that he so often championed individualism whereas orthodox socialism taught that the individual should be submerged into the group. Some of London's later views derived from Friedrich Nietzsche, Sigmund Freud, and Carl Jung, all of whom, London believed, helped him to understand himself as well as other people better.

After Jack left Berkeley he planned to write for a living, and he began to produce a stream of essays, stories, and poems that in turn brought a horde of rejections from editors. In desperation he worked briefly in a laundry for thirty dollars a month and then, with his stepsister Eliza's elderly husband, James Shepard, he joined the Klondike gold rush in 1897. Shepard turned back because of ill health, but Jack continued the journey, suffered physical hardships, contracted scurvy, was frustrated in his search for gold, kept a log of the whole trip, and finally returned to San Francisco a year after he had left, bringing only $4.50 worth of gold dust and, though he did not know it at the time, enough memories and observations to provide him much of the wealth he was later to gain from writing about Alaska.

Jack turned to hack writing to escape starvation, was encouraged by a publisher's offer to bring out a volume of his stories, fell in love with Anna Strunsky, a young Russian Jewish girl whom he had not money enough to marry, and then married a poorer girl, Bess Maddern, whose fiancé had just died. For a while the companionate marriage seemed happy enough but, though Bess gave him two daughters, she could not offer the emotional and intellectual stimulus he needed. For such stimulus and for entertainment as well he soon turned to a young poet, George Sterling, and a bohemian group called the Crowd, which included Charmian Kittredge, who would become first Jack's lover and later his wife.

The Crowd for a while provided an outlet for some of London's boundless energy. In childhood he had scarcely known what it was to play with other children. He and the Crowd now indulged in physical sports, practical jokes, and picnics. But he soon realized that he must escape from such play; it amused but it led nowhere. He disciplined himself to write a thousand words a day. There were constant demands for money for both his own household and his mother's, and selling his writing was his only means of getting the cash.

Jack also rebelled increasingly against his loveless marriage to Bess. He began a love affair with Anna Strunsky, accepted an offer to report post-Boer War conditions in South Africa, got only as far as London when the offer was withdrawn, and stayed to investigate slum conditions in London in order to write *The People of the Abyss.* He then returned to try to patch up his marriage, drove himself to write two novels, escaped again on a sloop voyage with a friend, and then began an affair which would culminate in his marriage to Charmian Kittredge the day after his divorce from Bess.

Before marrying Charmian, however, he had traveled to Japan and Korea to report the Russo-Japanese War in 1904, published his tremendously popular *The Sea Wolf,* had another brief love affair, begun to write *White Fang,* and bought a California ranch.

Though now a famous writer and capitalist landowner of sorts, Jack still retained his socialist views; he preached his socialist doctrine in numerous lecture halls, announcing the future takeover of governmental power by his socialist "comrades." He published in 1907 *The Iron Heel,* a sensational futuristic novel predicting the domination of North America by a Fascist-type dictatorship in the United States and a similar domination of the Far East by Japan.

Finally tiring of the notoriety he had gained and the pressures of his life, Jack planned for himself and Charmian a seven-year round-the-world voyage which would provide education, adventure, and new sources of writing material. Temporarily interrupted by the San Francisco earthquake, the uncompleted voyage on his expensive boat, the *Snark,* finally proved a disaster. The *Snark* was sold for a fraction of its cost, and Jack returned home suffering from various maladies including yaws, the treatment of which was to give him permanent arsenic poisoning from salvarsan. To allay the pain from his decaying body, of which he had earlier been so proud and even boastful, he managed to endure the few remaining years of his life only because of the massive amounts of drugs he consumed.

Despite his sufferings he continued his writing, publishing *Martin Eden,* a largely autobiographical novel which ends in suicide for its protagonist, and *John Barleycorn,* another autobiographical account, which pictures his struggles with alcoholism. To pay off his many debts he also turned out a mass of inferior writing. He brought on more debts through additional land purchases, lavish entertaining, and attempts at scientific and technologically progressive farming. Though money poured in, it also drained out rapidly while London fought, through constant medication, to stave off the final loss of mind and body. He died November 22, 1916, apparently from an overdose of morphine and atropine. Whether the overdose was intentional or not has been argued since by biographers and others. Sinclair believes that if it was intentional, Jack did not plan his death, but instead either decided impulsively to end his long torture, or possibly tried merely to deaden his pain with no terminal result intended.

In chapter-by-chapter notes at the end of *Jack*, Sinclair has well documented his absorbing biography of London, and he has supplied an excellent index for students and other readers seeking information on particular aspects of London's life and work. Interest in the biography may well lead to a revival of interest in London's best writings as well as some of his less-known works.

Henderson Kincheloe

Sources for Further Study

Booklist. LXXIV, September 15, 1977, p. 129.

Chronicle of Higher Education. XV, November 21, 1977, p. 13.

New Republic. CLXXVII, October 8, 1977, p. 34.

New Yorker. LIII, October 17, 1977, p. 194.

Saturday Review. V, October 1, 1977, p. 29.

Time. CX, October 10, 1977, p. 112.